## WOOD'S THEATRE. B. MACAULEY, Manager.

Engagement for one week only of the talented emotional actress,
MISS LUCILLE WESTERN.
Tuesday and Wednesday Evenings the great character drama the—CHILD STEALER.
Thursday and Saturday Evenings—OLIVER TWIST.
Friday Evening and Matinee Miss Western's new play—"THOU SHALT NOT."
Monday, May 1.—The charming and gifted actress—
MISS MARY ANDERSON. 1t

## Pike's Music Hall---To-Night.

LAST APPEARANCE.
This Tuesday Evening, April 25, 1876,
THE BOSTON
**PHILHARMONIC CLUB**
GRAND CONCERT,
With MISS LAURA SCHIRMER, Soprano.
Admission, $1; gallery, 50c. Seats secured without extra charge at Dobmeyer & Newhall's music store.
ap24-2t

## Cincinnati Ball Park.

GRAND OPENING GAME.
**ST. LOUIS**
VS.
**CINCINNATI**
TUESDAY, APRIL 25.
Game called at 3 p. m.
Tickets for sale at Hawley's, Perry & Morton's book stores, Davis', Kramer's, and Donovan's cigar stores.
Trains leave Plum Street Depot 2, 2:30, and 3:30 p. m., railroad time. Cars reserved for ladies. 1t

## Robinson's Opera-House.

THURSDAY AND FRIDAY EVENINGS, April 27 and 28,
**UNDINE.**
Grand Romantic Fairy Opera in 4 acts, by A. Lortzing. Full Chorus and Orchestra under the direction of Prof. Carl Barus.
Admission—Parquet, Dress Circle, and Balcony, $1; Gallery, 50 cents. Seats can be reserved without extra charge on Wednesday and Thursday, April 26 and 27 at Dobmeyer & Newhall's Music Store, Fourth street, near Walnut. Overture will begin at ½ of 8 o'clock. Curtain rises at 8 p. m. precisely. ap24-5t

*Advertisements, Cincinnati Commercial, April 24, 1876, on the eve of the first Opening Day in Cincinnati*

*Opening Day, 1953 Crosley Field*

# Opening Day

## Celebrating Cincinnati's Baseball Holiday

Copyright © 2004 by John Erardi and Greg Rhodes

Published by Road West Publishing

All rights reserved.
No part of this book may be reproduced or utilized in any form or by any means,
electronic or mechanical, including photocopying, recording,
or by an information and retrieval system,
without written permission from the publisher.

ISBN: 09641402-6-8

Road West Publishing
1908 Dexter Avenue
Cincinnati, OH 45206
1-513-861-6151

Phone orders: 1-800-431-1579

Printed in the USA by C.J. Krehbiel Company, Cincinnati, OH
Cover design by Elaine Olund

The Bob Littlejohn oral history (pages 35-36) originally appeared in the book, *Hornsby Hit One Over My Head: A Fan's Oral History of Baseball*. Excerpts from *Hornsby Hit One Over My Head: A Fan's Oral History of Baseball*, copyright © 1997 by David Cataneo, reprinted by permission Harcourt, Inc.

Cover photographs and credits:

Front (clockwise from top):
Ernie Lombardi congratulates Frank McCormick, Opening Day, 1941, Crosley Field (Road West Publishing)
Fans in right-field bleachers at Palace of the Fans, Opening Day, 1905 (Road West Publishing)
Opening Day Parade, Riverfront Stadium (Cincinnati Reds)
Frank Bancroft (Jon Boss)

Back (clockwise from top):
Opening Day, 2003, Great American Ball Park (Road West Publishing)
Johnny Bench, Vice President Gerald Ford, Hank Aaron, Pete Rose, Opening Day, 1974, Riverfront Stadium (The Cincinnati Enquirer)
Sparky Anderson and friends, Opening Day, 1996, Riverfront Stadium (Cincinnati Reds)

# OPENING DAY

## Celebrating Cincinnati's Baseball Holiday

by
John Erardi
&
Greg Rhodes

ROAD WEST PUBLISHING · CINCINNATI, OHIO

*Opening Day, 2003, Great American Ball Park*

# Table of Contents

**Introduction by Jim O'Toole** ... 10

**Frank Bancroft: Father of Opening Day** ... 13

## 1 Opening Day Stories ... 25

| | |
|---|---|
| John Murdough | 25 |
| Billy Werber | 31 |
| Bob Littlejohn | 35 |
| Tom Turner | 36 |
| Bob Boehmker | 37 |
| Betty Heskamp | 38 |
| Bill Giles | 39 |
| Joe Nuxhall | 40 |
| Don Zimmer | 45 |
| Bernie Stowe | 46 |
| Mrs. Bernie (Priscilla) Stowe | 50 |
| Mrs. Ted (Eleanor) Kluszewski | 50 |
| Mrs. Roy (Jody) McMillan | 51 |
| Gene Bennett | 52 |
| Russ Nixon | 53 |
| Jim Greengrass | 54 |
| Chuck Harmon | 55 |
| Frank Robinson | 57 |
| Buddy Bell | 62 |
| Dave Parker | 64 |
| Pete Rose | 66 |
| Randy Marsh | 68 |
| Ed Brinkman | 71 |
| Jim Maloney | 72 |
| Bob Uecker | 73 |
| Leo Cardenas | 74 |
| Tony Perez | 76 |
| Lee May | 78 |
| Tommy Helms | 80 |
| Joe Torre | 81 |
| Johnny Bench | 81 |
| Don Gullett | 82 |
| Sparky Anderson | 83 |
| Dave Concepcion | 85 |
| Dusty Baker | 86 |
| Steve Garvey | 86 |
| Jack Billingham | 87 |
| Joe Morgan | 89 |
| Ken Griffey, Sr. | 90 |
| George Foster | 90 |
| Will McEnaney | 91 |
| Don Sutton | 92 |
| Pedro Borbon | 92 |
| Hal McCoy | 94 |
| Ray Knight | 98 |
| Ron Oester | 99 |
| Marty Brennaman | 100 |
| Dave Collins | 105 |
| Nick Esasky | 106 |
| Mario Soto | 106 |
| Ted Power | 107 |
| Dwight Gooden | 107 |
| Tom Browning | 108 |
| Eric Davis | 110 |
| Kal Daniels | 111 |
| Chris Welsh | 111 |
| Tracy Jones | 112 |
| Lloyd McClendon | 112 |
| Paul O'Neill | 113 |
| Lenny Harris | 113 |
| Marge Schott | 114 |
| Todd Benzinger | 114 |
| Danny Jackson | 116 |
| Rob Dibble | 117 |
| Norm Charlton | 117 |
| Lou Piniella | 119 |
| Jose Rijo | 119 |
| Joe Oliver | 122 |
| Hal Morris | 124 |
| Barry Larkin | 124 |
| Billy Doran | 125 |
| Jeff Reed | 126 |
| Craig Biggio | 127 |
| Jeff Bagwell | 127 |
| Fred McGriff | 127 |
| Mark Grace | 128 |
| George Grande | 128 |
| Jim Tarbell | 129 |
| Pokey Reese | 130 |
| Sean Casey | 130 |
| Ken Griffey, Jr. | 130 |
| Todd Walker | 131 |
| Aaron Boone | 131 |
| Adam Dunn | 132 |
| Austin Kearns | 132 |
| Rick Stowe | 132 |
| Remembering John McSherry | 136 |

## 2 History Of Opening Day ... 141

## 3 Findlay Market Parade ... 156

Jeff Gibbs ... 158

## 4 Year by Year at Opening Day ... 165

**Opening Day Scrapbook** ... 295
Timeline ... 295
Records and Milestones ... 308
Opening Day Log ... 313

**Photograph and Illustration Credits** ... 317

**Sources and Acknowledgments** ... 318

*To Christopher, my indispensable tech man;*
*to Gina, for whom every day is Opening Day,*
*and to Violet, who once was lost but now is found.*
JGE


*To Ben, who loves a holiday*
GLR


*And, to our readers:*

This book is our attempt to divine the mystical connection between a city and its baseball team through the story of the annual rite known as Opening Day.

Nowhere else would such a book be conceivable. For no other city has an Opening Day tradition like Cincinnati's. Due to a unique combination of factors, the Reds are the only team that opens each season at home, and for many years Cincinnati had the day to itself: The first professional team played the first game of the season.

Over the decades, the tradition has grown into a city-wide celebration of the national pastime and the glorious role the Queen City had in its founding. History spawned civic pride, which begat parades, proclamations and parties, and perhaps inevitably, pachyderms on a baseball field.

If all this makes sense, you probably grew up a fan of the Reds, and will find this book a keepsake of Opening Day memories.

If this doesn't make sense, well, let us introduce you to this peculiar tradition known as Opening Day in Cincinnati.

As Sparky Anderson put it, "It's a holiday, a baseball holiday! Ain't no other place in America got that!"

"If you're an out-of-towner on Opening Day, you'd think it was a national holiday. The whole town goes nuts."

*Jeff Gibbs, Findlay Market*

"I hated the day when they did away with the tradition about Cincinnati being first. Now, anybody can start off the season, and they lost a great thing. We were special—this is where professional baseball started—and baseball should have stayed with the tradition. History is important, and they turned their back on it."

*Tony Perez*

"If you don't try to get out of school on Opening Day, there's something wrong with you! It's right up there with Christmas."

*Buddy Bell*

*Opening Day, 1963, left to right: Johnny Edwards, Vada Pinson, Gordy Coleman, Tommy Harper, Pete Rose, Frank Robinson, and Gene Freese*

# Introduction
# Jim O'Toole
## My Opening Day Memories

I always liked getting things started. The game can't start until the pitcher throws the ball. No inning, no at-bat, nothing can start until the pitcher throws it. There was a time—and most of us can remember it—when the whole major league season didn't begin until the Reds starting pitcher threw the ball. I wish it were that way today. But Cincinnati's Opening Day is still the best.

Authors John Erardi and Greg Rhodes asked me to give my oral history of Opening Day in Cincinnati, just as they did everybody else in the book. They liked mine so much they made it the introduction, so I am still getting things started!

Opening Day means the world to me. I have great memories of it as a player. And every year we still build a family reunion around it. Back when I was playing, we were starting the family "reunion." We had five kids before I left Cincinnati in 1966. My wife would come over from Mt. Washington with all the kids in tow. Ultimately, we had 11 in all. People talk about the Findlay Market Opening Day Parade, but, hey, we had our own "parade!" And we're still having our own parade. We get the whole family together for Opening Day—Cincinnati, Boston, Jasper, Wyoming and my old hometown, Chicago. Twenty-two mothers and fathers, 25 grandchildren. Now you know why I need 50 tickets! It's not easy getting 50 together, but we manage to do it.

At Crosley Field, Opening Day was always our biggest crowd of the year. It was the only time we'd fill the ballpark, except, occasionally, when the Dodgers or Giants would come in for a weekend series. There was nothing like Opening Day morning, either. In spring training, we got measured for our new uniforms. Then, we'd get north and everybody would be switching pants in the clubhouse before the game because nobody's fit. There was an Irish guy—Crowley—who was with MacGregor. They made the uniforms. Crowley was their rep. We'd give him all kinds of garbage! *Hey, Crowley, what did you do with those measurements you took in spring training?*

Every time I went to spring training until the day I retired in 1968 I strove to be the Opening Day pitcher. To me, it was the greatest honor

*Jim O'Toole (second from right) posed with part of the O'Toole clan gathered at Great American Ball Park for the 2003 opener. From left are brother-in-law Terry Wall, Wall's wife, Wees, O'Toole's daughter Josie Karwisch (center), and son Bill O'Toole (right). All told, the O'Tooles filled 50 seats.*

for any player to pitch the first game of the season. It was like the World Series. You got totally focused. Opening Day in Cincinnati made me play above myself. I knew everybody in all the lower rows of the grandstand at Crosley—we had to walk through the stands at the old park—and I was pitching for them, too. It was a neat thing to get to pitch Opening Day in Cincinnati. To me, it means hey, you're number one!

My first Opening Day memory was in 1959—my first year in the big leagues—and it wasn't even our opener. We were in Philadelphia for their Opening Day. We'd already had our opener. I don't remember who started the game for us in Philly. I was in the bullpen, even though I'd won 20 games in the minors in 1958 with 23 complete games, and was the "Minor League Player of the Year." I came up at the end of that season and threw a two-hitter against the Milwaukee Braves in September. Then, the day before we opened in 1959, I pitched a one-hitter and struck out 10 against the Chicago White Sox in Indianapolis. That doesn't sound like "bullpen" to you, does it? Not to mention, the Reds had just gone through 1956, 1957 and 1958 when, if they'd had a little more starting pitching, they'd have won it every year. But Mayo Smith, our manager, was old school. *You'll get your turn, but you've got to wait.*

Anyway, here we were in Philly and our starter was having some trouble. Mayo said: "Get O'Toole and Mike Cuellar up!" I'm thinking, "What's he doing getting two left-handers up?" You always get up one lefty and one righty! Well, Mayo walks to the mound and signals for the lefty. Miguel—that was Cuellar's first name; he's from Cuba—says to me, "Jeemy, what deed he say?" I said, "He wants you!"

The bases were loaded and Gene Freese was up. Back then, Freese

*The O'Tooles posed with their five children (with one more on the way) on family day at Crosley Field in 1966. Jim holds Peggy. In front of Betty are (from left) Jimmy, Holly, Johnny and Lucy. The clan eventually grew to 11, the unofficial record for offspring of a Reds player.*

was a Phillie. He didn't become a Red until 1961. Miguel threw one pitch, and bam! Grand slam! Cuellar was in Havana a week later.

In the 1960 opener at Crosley Field, I did something that wound up changing the rules of baseball to this day. I pitched six innings of relief, gave up two hits, struck out four and shut 'em out. Brooks Lawrence had come in one inning earlier and thrown one pitch. Our center fielder, Vada Pinson, made a leaping catch at the wall. He saved a triple or a home run. We took the lead in the bottom of the inning. I pitched well for the next six innings, so the official scorer gave me the win and cited the clause in the rule book about "a reliever who is judged by the scorer to have been the most effective pitcher" could be given the win, even if he wasn't the pitcher of record.

Four months later, National League President Warren Giles said, "Wait a minute! Brooks Lawrence was the pitcher of record when his team went ahead. He gets the win." And that's been the rule ever since. The same thing happened in the American League that year. Hey, I could have used that win. I was 12-12 that year, even though in my book I was 13-12!

In 1961, I got my first Opening Day start. I still felt like a rookie. Joe Nuxhall was gone that year—he'd been traded to Kansas City, the first and only year since 1944 that he wasn't with the Reds—and we had Bob Purkey, who'd been around longer than me, and Joey Jay, who we'd just acquired in a trade with Milwaukee. A lot of time the brass wants to make a trade look good—they'd just gotten rid of a great player and a fan favorite in shortstop Roy McMillan—and I figured Jay might start. But I got to spring training early that year, determined to get into the best shape possible.

We were opening with the Chicago Cubs, and I knew it was a big opportunity for me. My whole family would be coming down from Chicago. "Hutch"—that was our manager, Fred Hutchinson—told me just as we were breaking camp, "You're going to be my starter. I'm going to pitch you one time on the way north, and then it's yours." I always looked forward to pitching in front of the big crowd, because the fans here were so great. It was a great thrill to be picked. As it turned out, I wound up striking out Ernie Banks a couple of times and I got two hits. What a day that was! We went on to win the pennant, and that makes it even more special looking back on it. I see where Frank Robinson says that Opening Day 1961 was a lot more than one of 154 games. He's right. We felt we had a good club, even though nobody knew it but us. Like Frank says, sometimes the first game can really set a tone.

I was supposed to open in 1962. We'd just arrived at the ballpark the night before. We bused over from Indy. My wife was a little late picking me up—my mom and dad had just come in from Chicago and she couldn't get them going—so I figured, what the heck, I'll shave. I reached in my duffel bag to get my razor, and it sliced the index finger on my left hand. So much for starting that opener. In 1963, I opened again. That was Pete Rose's first game. He went 0-for-4, and I got a hit. Heck, he could've had an RBI if he could've gotten a hit! I was on base for him.

In 1964, Jim Maloney opened. In 1965, I opened for the last time. I lost, 3-2, to Milwaukee, my first opening day loss. I was 2-1 for my career on Opening Day; I would've been 3-1, if they hadn't taken that win away from me in 1960. And, who knows, maybe I would've been 4-1 if I hadn't cut my finger in 1962. Even at that, two Opening Day wins for the Reds puts me up among the leaders. I think the only two Reds pitchers who have won two or more since then are Mario Soto and Tom Browning. I mean, think about it. Some pretty good pitchers never won two openers: Maloney, Gary Nolan, Don Gullett, Jose Rijo. Soto is the champ; he won four in a row in the 1980s, and you'll read his story here, too. In 1966, I was traded to Chicago. I was making "too much money"— $30,000! My last year in the big leagues was 1967. I retired before the 1968 season started, and I've been going to Opening Day as a fan ever since—36 in a row, 44 of the last 45 since my first one in 1959. That's a lot of Opening Days, but a lot of fans have got me beat. You'll read their stories here, too.

People have always told me, "Jim, you could write a book." Well, I never did. But I'm proud to be a part of this one. I hope you enjoy it as much as I did.

*O'Toole spent just three months in the minor leagues before being called up to the Reds in 1958. He won 94 games for the Reds, 20th in club history. He was elected to the Reds Hall of Fame in 1970.*

*Flashing the form familiar to Reds fans from the 1960s, O'Toole fires a ceremonial first pitch prior to a Chicago Cubs game in 1999. O'Toole was honored as the "Father of the Bride." His daughter, Mary, was to be married that evening to the nephew of the CEO of the Cubs.*

# Frank Bancroft

## The Father of Opening Day Recalls the Start of the Opening Day Tradition

### by Frank Bancroft as told to (and imagined by) John Erardi

*"Yesterday's big crowd was handled without a hitch of the slightest kind. Business manager Bancroft had everything in prime condition. He had a place for everything, and everything in its place. Banny is the king of them all when it comes to handling the business end of a baseball club."*—**The Cincinnati Enquirer, April 19, 1895.**

*"He may be down, but never out.
I'll tell you now, he's a good ol' scout.
He's Johnny on the Spot.
What it takes to please, he sure has got."*
—**Cincinnati-born blues singer Mamie Smith, in "You Can't Keep A Good Man Down," Okeh Records, Feb. 14, 1921.**

Frank Bancroft is the "Father of Cincinnati's Opening Day."

The former hotel operator, theater-troupe promoter and baseball-team barnstormer saw to it that everything was just right for a celebration.

How well did Bancroft achieve the creation of this circus-like air in 1895? It still permeates Opening Day in Cincinnati to this day.

Bancroft—aka "Banny" or "Bannie"—was the Reds business manager from 1892 through 1920. But he was also a pioneer: He scheduled the all-black Page Fence Giants for a two-game exhibition vs. the Reds at the Reds ballpark a week before Opening Day, 1895; in a 1908 barnstorming trip to Cuba, he scouted (and later signed) Armando Marsans and Rafael Almeida, the first Cuban natives to play in the American major leagues, and he initiated the leasing of Redland Field for the entire season of 1921 to the Cuban Stars, the first Negro League team to have such an arrangement. This was bold, unprecedented behavior for a baseball executive of that era.

Banny was renowned for his abilities as a raconteur and revenue-generator. It is believed he squeezed in more exhibition games for his teams than any man in history…and had a good time doing it. Every story about him in his later years contains references to his remarkable vigor.

He died on March 30, 1921, at age 74, two weeks before Opening Day.

In the following memoir, drawn from newspaper articles, periodicals, Civil War letters and conversations with Bancroft's descendants and researchers, we put words into Banny's "voice" as the Ol' Scout himself could have spoken them in early March 1921.

Whenever possible, we quote Bancroft exactly as he was quoted in the relatively few stories about him during his lifetime.

He truly was one-of-a-kind.

Call me Banny. Everybody else does.

Everybody, that is, except Jack Ryder, the baseball scribe at *The Cincinnati Enquirer*. He calls me "The Father of Opening Day."

I prefer what the Cubans call me: *"El Lobo de Plata."* The Silver Wolf. For my silver locks and my lean and hungry look. At numerous banquets they have also called me *"El Padre de Beisbol"*—The Father of Baseball in Cuba—usually after too much rum.

*Frank "Banny" Bancroft, business manager of the Reds from 1892–1920 and the Father of Cincinnati's Opening Day.*

But after Jack pinned that "Father of Opening Day" title on me, my compadres here in the Queen City have been asking me questions. "Who are you, Banny? Where did you come from? How did you make Opening Day what it is? Why did you go to all that trouble? And where is it all headed?"

What follows is the straight goods.

Tellin' it and sellin' it has always been my philosophy.

How do you think opening day got started in Cincinnati, anyway? We'd "tell it"—here comes your team barnstorming north for opening day—and then we'd "sell it" at the ticket office. The steady drumbeat of news would start up during the off-season, and it would grow louder in spring training and build toward a crescendo as the team played its way north. And that was my job—to travel with the team as its business manager, promote it to the writers and the fans at every opportunity, and do all that I could to get the players' names in the big type by opening day.

As I write this, Opening Day is only five weeks away. Normally at this time of year, I would be down south with the team, "the boys" as I call them. We've taken our spring training in such places as Louisiana, Texas, Florida, Alabama, Georgia. As I write this, the boys are in Cisco, Texas. I wish I were there.

It has always been one of my favorite things to spread the national game. Hot Springs…Havana…Honolulu. I've been all those places with the boys. But now, the barnstorming is over. It is time, finally, to spin out my story. What follows is everything of consequence that happened in my life that had an impact on the way I—as a master promoter—treated Opening Day in Cincinnati. From the very start, because of my experience in running hotels and operating ice rinks and managing minstrel troupes, I knew it was all about promotion. And nowhere was I tested the way I was tested in my first trip to Cuba. We were the first American professional team to play there.

Nineteen years before T.R. led the charge up San Juan Hill, I made my first trip to Havana. It was 1879. It was my first year in pro ball, operating the Worchester, Massachusetts team. We added some eager souls from Boston and headed for the Keys, and then Havana. Our ferry creaked and quaked across the Straits like a drunk lurching for the can. It got so ghastly, we thought we were going the way of the *Pequod*. Our traveling party's expenses were being paid by the Hop Bitters Company of Rochester, New York, but I noticed those alcohol-soaked cough lozenges weren't settling anybody's bellies. One by one,

## "Where Ya' From?"

Have you ever noticed that the first question people ask when they meet you for the first time is: "Where ya' from?" I'm from Lancaster, Massachusetts, 35 miles west of Boston. The terrain in Lancaster is rolling and heavily wooded. You can't see everything from everywhere. In what is now Clinton, where I was born, you can see the mountains to the north from only a few vantage points.

I was always in search of those vantage points—and would be, my whole life. It helped me in all the businesses I was in; I never was satisfied with the way things appeared to be. I always wondered what they looked like from a different angle. That helped me on Opening Day, too. I was always on the lookout for new ways of doing things. Always looking for a new vantage point.

I understand now, as I look back on it, why I was always on the move. My mother died when she was 24 years old. She died four days after giving birth to Francis C.—"C" as in Carter—Francis C., as in me. You could say I killed my mother. It's a morbid thing to say, I know. But it's a fact. I don't know what my mother would have thought of the life I have lived. Hopefully, she would have been proud of it. After all, I used my legs and my lamps to see what the girl, Ann Carter, could have only imagined.

From Lancaster, she saw the pink sunrises to the east…but she never got to see the whaling island of Nantucket.

She saw the various shades of green and blue of the mountains to the north, each layer rising higher than the one that came before it, until it seemed the entire landscape was but a staircase to the heavens. Mother's feet never touched them.

She saw the glorious purple sunsets to the west…but she had no physical sense of what lay out there.

I would see the world for myself. Not until years later did I understand I was also seeing it for her.

Maybe I played base ball for her, too. I couldn't get enough of it. Base ball. That's how we spelled it back then. Two words. Town ball, some people called it. Town ball, base ball, baseball. The kind that gets thrown, like the World Series. We played it at Kilburn's Academy in Lancaster, where my daddy sent me to school. I was a pitcher and catcher. Back then, it was all crack-of-the-bat stuff for me, because I was playing the game, not watching it. There wasn't anybody *to* watch, no stars to follow, no professional game.

the players beseeched me: "If I don't make it, tell my wife I love her." Or, "Tell my beloved my last thoughts were of her." I guess they figured since I'd been around since baseball was invented that the good Lord wouldn't let me drown. So, finally, I said to them, one and all: "What be I, a fish?" They managed sick grins, as good as could be expected under the circumstances, and later quoted me as though I were the Bard Himself. When we finally got ashore in Havana Harbor, we would have kissed the very ground we walked on—if only we could have puckered up. Too much heaving had left our lips too numb to form a kiss.

It was on this trip that I met a senorita. Name of Lolita. *Vaya munecita!* She taught me to rumba. *Ay Caramba!* The brown skin, the olive eyes, the perfume in her hair…*Ay Ay Ay*, I was spoony. When I told Lolita why I was in Cuba—promoting the game and raising jack—she answered: *"Hago cualquier cosa para el arte y el dinero."* "Anything for art and a few bucks." Oh, did Lolita ever hit the nail on the noggin. To this day, that little saying remains my personal credo.

We packed even their bull rings for our ball games against the locals, but the government officials demanded that we pay a hefty tax on our paid admissions. So, in the dead of night, we left on a tramp steamer bound for Florida, and barnstormed our way to New Orleans. We played Saturday and Sunday games the rest of the winter and each of the boys cleared $800. Some of that they left behind in the parlor houses. But I'll leave that story to somebody else.

I vowed that I would always come back to New Orleans and one day to Cuba—the dinero being numero uno. (Well, *tied* for numero uno: Mr. Dinero and I were in a dead heat-a for Senorita Lolita.)

After the major league season in 1908, I led a group of Reds back into Havana Harbor. How taken were we with Cuba after that four-week stay? We came back to the States tanned and fit, puffing Partagas cigars and looking positively resplendent in our *guayaberas*, the pleated cream-colored shirts worn outside the pants. We were the first major league team to play in Cuba. And this time I was savoring memories not of Lolita, but of Jose Mendez, who had shut us out for 25 consecutive innings. I was no more likely to bring Mendez home with me in 1908 than I was Lolita 30 years earlier. Who would he have pitched for in Cincinnati—the Excelsiors? Mendez was too dark for the league. Eventually, we did get two players from Mendez's

*Frank Bancroft, with Cuban friends and ballplayers, posed at a dinner party on his 1908 barnstorming trip to Havana. Bancroft is seventh from right, beneath the statue.*

Almendares team: Armando Marsans and Rafael Almeida. "Two of the purest bars of Castilian soap ever floated to these shores," the press described them. Light-skinned, of course. Still, they added color to our red, white and blue. They debuted with us on the Fourth of July, 1911, in Chicago. When we christened our new ballpark, Redland Field, at Findlay and Western, on Opening Day, 1912, Marsans was our right fielder.

How did I come to hang my hat in Cincinnati, anyway? After managing six major league clubs in 11 years, I came to the Queen City in 1891 at the invitation of King Kelly, manager of Kelly's Killers, of the American Association. I was 44 years old and full of vinegar. We drew more fans for our opening-game parade in 1891 than we did for most of our games! Our ballpark was on the flood plain in a place called Pendleton, not too far from Coney Island.

After I left Kelly's Killers for the Reds following the '91 season, another upriver phenomenon—Miss Mary Seifried of Portsmouth, Ohio—sparked my lamps. I tied the knot in Portsmouth on November 1, 1893. So much for my footloose past, flitting from pillar to post like a flim-flam man.

From the beginning, it was in my nut to get the turnstiles singing for the opening game. I knew we had a built-in advantage because we were going to open every season at home. The schedulers always made sure of it. It had everything to do with the fact that we were the southernmost club in the league: We had the best chance to have the best weather. In '94, we had a new park and I thought it would be our first banner opening day. Instead of a gala, we got gales—*rain*, the way Noah knew it.

Which brings us to 1895. That was the opening game where everything came together: the hiring of one of our own from Cincinnati, the great Buck Ewing, to captain the club and play first base…the steady drumbeat in the Cincinnati press as we barnstormed our way north from Mobile, Alabama….the competition for the right-field job between a veteran and a greenhorn…the resurrection of the streetcar parade—electric ones, for the first time!—with Weber's Band out front… the exhibition games at home, especially with the Negro team, the Page Fence Giants, and Charlie Comiskey's crack Minneapolis squad. All of it climaxed to a veritable crescendo by Opening Day. For me, it was a blueprint for the inaugural game; it was always in my noodle at the holiday's helm. Basically, it's been a corker ever since '95. After that, we made a few refinements, but we never had to fix it.

In '95, we had a cracking good club. We barnstormed our way north from Mobile, arriving in Cincinnati on March 30, two and a half weeks before opening day. We played exhibition games almost every day against all the best local amateur teams, and began to pick up steam with a week to go. That is when the Page Fence Giants "rolled" into town. They were the Negro team based in Adair, Michigan, led by Bud Fowler and Grant Johnson.

They traveled in a fancy Pullman car, made just for them. It is where they took their meals and hung their hats. They sidetracked their car Thursday morning and came zipping down the ramps in their brand-new Monarch Bicycles and weaved their way through Little Bucktown, singing and chanting and calling out to all the pretty girls to come out to see them play the Reds that day and the next. Little Bucktown, that is where the colored folks lived. In the lower West End, at the corner of George and Freeman Streets, just across the railroad tracks. The Giants advertised the game, their two-wheelers and their manufactory sponsor that made woven-wire fences. That was back when the manufacture of a good bicycle—and a good woven-wire fence—could make you a millionaire.

The Page Fence Giants played us in two exhibition games during that week before Opening Day, and damn near beat us in one of them. Oh, did their fans ever hoot and holler when the Giants jumped out to a 2–0 lead. We came back to trim them, 11–7—imagine that, seven come eleven!—and Fowler made two singles.

By Godfrey, it was good to see Bud again! He was a "back-East" fellow as well—born in Ft. Plain, New York, and raised in Cooperstown—and he played on some white teams in Massachusetts in the late '70s, when I was just getting started managing in pro ball myself. Now here he was, 49 years old, and fresh as a daisy! He was still a smasher as a second sacker. Fowler, William Malone and Grant Johnson were all major league timber. I'd have beaten the greedy John McGraw to all of them—and to the dark-skinned Cubans, too—if I'd had the chance. Neither one of us had the chance. Lord knows we both tried.

It was good to see what the *Enquirer* man wrote: "Both teams played harmoniously and the game may properly be described as a symphony in white and black." Our boys were a classy bunch. No team led by Buck Ewing and Bid McPhee would be any other way. They were gentlemen of the first order.

Our last exhibition game was the Tuesday before Opening Day, which fell—as it always did back then—on a Thursday. There were years, though, when the schedule-makers wanted us to start the season on Friday, but I wouldn't do it. *"Hangman's Day!"* Can you imagine? Friday may be all right for some purposes, but it goes for Sweeney, as far as I'm concerned! Luck is a big factor in baseball, and I never heard of any one having good fortune on Friday. No siree, we'll not start the season on Friday, so long as my noodle is in good working order.

After Tuesday morning's practice, but before that afternoon's exhibition, the clubhouse was a beehive. Fans and the front office are always excited about Opening Day, but the best word I can use to describe the players is anxious. For

*Frank Bancroft brought in the African-American team, the Page Fence Giants, from Adrian, Michigan, to play the Reds in two exhibition games prior to the 1895 opener.*

# How My Civil War Service Affected Me

I walked away from school at noon recess at Kilburn's Academy in 1861 when I was 15. There was glory to be got, and by God, I aimed to get my share. I was "war crazy." I figured it would be easier to lie about my age and my identity across the border in New Hampshire, and so I walked and hitched rides all the way to Nashua. It was 30 miles, as the crow flies or the boy's bunions scream, depending on who's doing the traveling. I took the alias of "Henry F. Coulter"—there were many Coulters in Lancaster, too many for the authorities to trace me. I wanted to join the Navy. They told me I'd be able to do that when I got to Boston. It was the first in a litany of lies. They gave me a drum and put me in Company A, 8th New Hampshire Volunteers. When I marched out of Nashua bound for the train station, I had that blue cap pulled down over my eyes, so nobody could make me out.

We rode to Boston and then shipped out for the Gulf of Mexico. First stop, Ship Island, just off the coast of Mississippi, then up through the delta into New Orleans. I spent the first three months in a hospital in New Orleans fighting dysentery. When I finally escaped the sawbone's clutches, I decided I wasn't going back for all the cotton in Calahoula County.

One day, during the early days of the war, I saw a large buzzard in the sky. Everybody was standing around looking at it, wondering if it had come for them. I said, "S-s-say boys, th-th-there g-g-goes one of J-J-Jeff Davis' e-e-eagles." Everybody roared. At the time I said it, I didn't think it was all that funny, but the men sure did.

You see, back then I stuttered a little bit. And it got worse when I was nervous. And there was plenty to be nervous about on the Red River in Louisiana in 1864.

I found I could make groups of grown men laugh—not just one teacher at a time the way I did at Kilburn's. Being such a skinny runt, I looked funny to them, I guess. "Brutus" is what the men of the Eighth called me. *Animal stupid.* The boys thought the joke was on me.

But nobody was laughing when the man riding next to me took a bullet in the head; his brains splattered all over me. Nobody was laughing when I took a bullet at Hog's Bend, Louisiana. Reb sniper got me in the left thigh. I'd been running messages for Col. Davis.

I was 17 years old.

In camp, they dug the bullet out of me, then shipped me back to New Orleans to recuperate. I wanted no part of it. I disappeared, then rejoined Company A. I was glad when the war finally ended. I departed it the way I went into it: banging on a drum. Only this time, the tune was different: "When Johnny Comes Marching Home."

I always did like a parade.

I learned a lot in Louisiana. I was a boy of 15 when I arrived, a man of 19 when I left. I was there four long years, no furloughs.

Here is what I took from Port Hudson, Louisiana, in 1863: The freedmen—the black men—had never before been in combat as a unit. The question on everybody's mind was, "Will they fight?"

No one need have worried. Sergeant Anselmas Planciancois of the 1st Louisiana Native Guards spoke for an entire race when he told his Colonel after he was presented with the Stars and Stripes before going into battle, "Colonel, I will bring back these colors in honor or report to God the reason why."

Sgt. Planciancois never knew what hit him. A Rebel shell blew off the top of his head and splattered his brains over the flag he had pledged to defend. I remember hearing the report that day: in fierce fighting, the 1st and the 3rd had 37 men killed, 155 wounded and 116 missing. Of all the Union troops in battle that day, only one lost more men than the 1st. Years later, I learned of the letters home from white soldiers: "The Negroes fought like devils, they made five charges on a battery that there was not the slightest chance of their taking, just to show our boys they could and would fight." And: "A race of serfs stepped up to the respect of the world, and commenced a national existence."

I feel just the way that conniving son of a female dog John McGraw does: I'd have had Negroes playing for us a long time ago, if there wasn't an unwritten rule against it. There were great colored players to be had, and at a good price. But there was no changing the "rule." The owners would have ganged up on us.

I would have signed every one of those great Cuban players, too. Muggsy McGraw knew that! He was sure I would have picked him clean. And he was right, because I'd made the inroads with all my barnstorming trips to Cuba. I knew the players. But, do you remember the time I signed two light-skinned Cubans to play for the Reds? Armando Marsans and Rafael Almeida played for us in 1911, but I caught holy hell. The league magnates did not like the notion at all.

Well, I did what I could. Every chance I got, I scheduled exhibition games against colored teams. The competition was good and both teams made a buck. The times just weren't right for anything more.

them, it is the beginning of the bean harvest. Soon, everything will count—hits and half-eagles, foozles and five-spots. No player likes to be heckled, but it's a little easier to stomach when it comes with a shekel.

A new shipment of bats had just arrived and I never saw such a scraping and oiling of the lumber. Some of the boys put in hours honing those bats with glass. Others held them in the fire until the ends were burnished a brownish-black. "Flame-tempered," said Tacky Tom Parrott, as though he knew the tree trade back home in Portland, Oregon. Whether this process was for appearance, or for toughening the wood I do not know, but the "look" was pleasing to the eye. Some of the boys even sent their new sticks across the street to the barber-chair factory to have them turned down just right to suit their personal fancies.

"Give me the bat, the one that feels good to me, and I will make the other fellows extend their grounds," said McPhee. Biddy was a whale of a second sacker—the best I ever saw—and a regular third-rail fellow to boot.

Our groundkeeper, John Schwab, gave the 20-ton steamroller an especially vigorous workout that Tuesday, but not without a price. It broke through an old well in deep left field. All the hands at the ball yard, with three or four outsiders, took an hour to pry it out. It went in to the hubs. Anybody but a Schwab, I'd have been concerned about the field being ready for opening day. Superintendent Schwab never blinked. He was, and is, our miracle man.

John Weber, the musical director of Weber's band, announced in the *Enquirer* on the morning before the opening game that he had composed a new march and was dedicating it to Captain Ewing, our new manager and first baseman who was raised on the East End. John said he would spring it on the fans at the concert before the game. All of this helped sell tickets, of course, and I was all for that. After all, that was my job, wasn't it? Anything for art and a few bucks, remember?

Even though there was no exhibition game the day before the opening game, we had a light practice that day. The boys spent part of their time adjusting sliding pads to their new white pants. They knew they would be bounding about like Baskervilles this year. With the arrival of Captain Ewing, our training camp had seemed to ooze pepper and ginger. From what I could see, there was plenty of horseradish to go around. Buck had a terrific team for his taste: not an ice wagon among them.

Latham, feigning an Irish brogue, joked that he wished he had such a cushion for his caboose when he was growing up in Lebanon, New Hampshire.

"These would have saved me arse from me mither's spankings," said Latham, holding aloft the sliding pads with his left hand and simultaneously signing the words with his right to our deaf mute outfielder Dummy Hoy. "Of course she might have thought I was eating too many praties, given the softness of me behind."

Latham was a humdinger. The fans loved him, because he was such a showman. Loud, but never profane, he was a regular vaudevillian out there on the coaching lines. By '95, he was almost used up as a third baseman; some days he was a dead wall which nothing could pass, the next he wobbled on every hit that came to him, like a boxcar on a coal railroad. But he pulled in the fans like George M. Cohan.

Another crate of bats arrived—these were Louisville sluggers from Logansport, Indiana—and the boys descended upon them like wood mites.

That night, there was a lively tilt at the Gibson House when Captain Patsy Tebeau arrived with

*The 1895 Reds were featured in this Cincinnati newspaper promotion on the eve of Opening Day. Business manager Frank Bancroft is included (far right, center) along with manager Buck Ewing (left, center).*

his Cleveland Spiders. Of course I was there to greet the competition. "Patsy Bolivar," we called him. When he started to tell me how easy it would be for his boys to down the Reds, that's when I flashed my winter winnings from betting on the bang tails. I told him that I'd wager any kind of money that the Reds would win two out of the three. He squirmed and fish-tailed around it. Finally, he asserted: "I have no money to squander." *Ha!* Nothing harpoons the hot air out of a huckster like the holding up of hard money! What I wanted to buy, Patsy Bolivar no longer wanted to sell. I enjoyed shutting him up. I'd have enjoyed it even more separating him from his shinplasters because I knew we could take all three games in that opening series.

Ol' Sol, bless his fiery heart, rose and shone for the opener, and pulled out the people like a celestial pied piper. Back then, we needed the weather to be with us. The aerial sponge squeezer could easily keep the fair-weather fan and his long green at home. Storm clouds carried not only rain, they carried a price. Yes, indeed-y, when "Ol' Jupe"—bad skies—threatened, it cost us at least $2,000. Two grand! Why, that was a full season's salary for most of our players. But, on Opening Day '95, I had no worries. With the sun out, the streets were full of fans, and their ladies followed. They were as bright-eyed and as rosy as a field full of June flowers. What a welcome relief it was to have their touches of color here and there!

It was as though Edison had electrically wired not only the street cars, but the cranks as well. Everything was in apple-pie order. A new Seventh Street electric line that would transport the fans to and from the grounds was unveiled that opening day. That, along with the John Street Line, made seven different lines of cars to the yard. Nobody in balldom had streetcar accommodations in as fine as fettle as ours. It was to the streetcar company's benefit, of course, because a first-rate ball team meant more nickels in the kitty.

We had the players report to the clubhouse by 8:30 on opening day morning to get dressed. Their spangles were made of a creamy white flannel, much superior in quality than I had ever seen or felt in a baseball uniform. It was the stuff you would find in the finest suits at John J. Shillito's at Seventh and Race. An odd thing, though: you'd have thought we had never taken the boys' measurements, given the way they were exchanging tops and bottoms in the clubhouse, searching for just the right fit.

The streetcar company had a car waiting to take the team into town. A little before 10 o'clock, we wormed our way through the crush of people lined up out front of the Gibson House. It was a huge throng of well-wishers, hundreds of them, but somehow the boys managed to squeeze through without getting their spangles too rumpled. When it came time for us to head for Fountain Square, where three electric carriages awaited, the street was so crowded with people

*The 1895 opener featured a three-car streetcar parade through downtown Cincinnati. Included in this illustration are Frank Bancroft (left), Reds owner John Brush (top) and new manager and Cincinnati native, Buck Ewing (right).*

—thousands of them, shoulder to shoulder!—that a policeman was needed to clear the way.

Walnut Street was a congested mass of humanity from Fourth Streets to Fifth Streets. Fountain Square swarmed and surged like an ant hill on a strike. "All aboard!" shouted Arlie Latham. Somehow, we were able to wiggle our way out of Fountain Square without running over somebody. The band struck up a spirited popular air, and from every side came exclamations of joy, congratulations blended together with encouraging encomiums. Through most of them ran the name of Captain Ewing: "Hello, Buck!" "Land 'em to-day, Ewing!" "Knock 'em out, Buck!" "Hooray for Buck Ewing!" Gangs of boys ran the breath out of their bodies trying to keep up.

It was a notorious knockdown for the players right from the start, and in return for such a demonstration they all bowed and tipped their flannel caps until the white beaks turned gray. Right fielder Charles Miller barked at dogs along the line and got many a smile from the folks hanging out of the upper casements. The journey through the East End was like a general alarm. It brought out all the inhabitants who gave the boys good cheer and many a loud "Hooray."

Did Weber's band have the people singing and swaying and sashaying? You know what they say. If you can please a professional athlete, you can please anybody. I would know. Back home in New Bedford and Springfield, I had managed center-stagers, prima donnas and bright-lighters—and none of them had anything on a star ballist.

Well, the boys loved the airs of Weber's Band. They were especially moved by the music of the hula hula dance, swaying to its beat. Tom Parrott whistled every number that the band played. Morgan Murphy induced Dummy Hoy, our clever little left fielder who is deaf and cannot hear a note, to keep time to the music. Hoy, who also cannot speak, was soon engaging in a finger conversation with Murphy. Hoy held his nose, as though he'd just come upon a pile of cow dung back home in Houckstown. Everybody laughed. The mute was the only man who didn't like the music of Weber's Band.

The residents of West Fourth Street shouted welcomes from front doors and windows. On Elm Street near Ninth, all heads turned toward a doll on a two-wheeler. Oh, what a looker! Long gams and a face to launch a thousand three-baggers. Her light-colored bloomers—with matching bow in her curly brown hair—were fetched up just below the knee to reveal dark stockings. Her blouse was fetched up at the elbow to reveal matching dark sleeves.

To our delight, she fetched up beside our team's car. Our left fielder, Bug Holliday, complimented her on her elegant turnout, but all she wanted to know was the whereabouts of "Zimmer," the Cleveland backstop. We called for him, but the handsome catcher had not made the trip. Maybe it was for the better. The girl was a pulse-quickener. Her kind has ruined many a ballplayer. She faded away to Court.

## The Pied Piper of Porkopolis

This is the story of how I gave opening day its beat. I learned soon after arriving in Cincinnati in 1891 that the Reds had first held a two-horsecar parade in 1890. It was led by a marching band and it included the home and visiting team. In 1891, Kelly's Killers and the Reds both had parades.

The parades had begun as a way to drum up interest in the opening game. We weren't the only city in which there were opening day parades in the 1890s. In fact, Louisville had a lulu of a parade; so did St. Louis and Pittsburgh and New York.

In 1892, I joined the Reds as business manager, but we didn't do the parade. We didn't do one in 1893, either, and in 1894 we had to cancel it because of bad weather.

What got me interested in resurrecting the parade was something I heard at the fair—the Chicago World's Fair—in 1893. I was always one for music. I had managed theater troupes and minstrel shows in New Bedford and ran the Gaiety Theatre in Springfield, Massachusetts. I always had my lamps lit for a promising act, musical or otherwise.

At the Fair, I saw the Midway with its newfangled giant Ferris Wheel. I saw "White City," which was the giant plaza all lit up by the electric lights invented by Thomas Edison. But what I *heard* was the music. The Negroes had written it and they were playing it and white Americans were tapping their toes, swaying their bodies and moving their lips to it. That was it! I must turn Opening Day into a street party complete with music! I noticed that the bandwagon in the circus parades is always the last car. I wanted to return Weber's band to the front, the way it was in 1891.

After the baseball season was over in '94, I directed the Reds on a barnstorming trip to New Orleans. I had taken teams to the Crescent City many times in the past. And I had fallen in love with the airs of the marching brass bands. Why, they were everywhere! Negro bands including dark Creoles, white bands including light Creoles, and sometimes all-African bands. There was something about the Negro brass bands that especially appealed to me: the strut in their steps, the smile on their faces, the sun glistening off the brass bells of their horns and the buttons of their uniforms, not to mention their ebony hands and countenances. They marched and played in a golden-brown glow. Oh, how the notes from their trumpets danced upon the air!

And that is when I *knew*: I must put Weber's Band out front. The music of the band is the call to the party, the invitation to the ball. "John C. Weber," I told the veteran maestro, "I hereby proclaim you, 'The Pied Piper of Porkopolis!' Now, go out there and electrify us!" And that is what he did.

A few years later, when the magnates felt the need had passed, they simply discontinued the parades. The last one I ran with the Reds was in 1902. But a wonderful thing happened. In a couple of years, the parade was back! But it wasn't the Reds who continued the opening day parade in Cincinnati—it was the people! The people started doing their own parades to the grounds, forming up in their tallyhos, and—years later—in their smoke wagons.

Many of the fans were dressed in the different costumes of their social groups. Some of them would have done a Halloween-er proud. I hear that last year, there was a group from the Findlay Street Market house with a loud air so raucous that it almost made one wonder if they'd gotten into the home-brew. I think they could be around for awhile.

*Frank Bancroft, ever the promoter of the national pastime, posed (back row, in suit) with an All-Star team he took to Hawaii in 1914 on a barnstorming tour.*

What a hubbub the streetcar parade created! When I saw the way Weber's band drew the people out of the chairs in their rooms on the upper casements, I knew: By thunder, we've got it!

If I needed any more proof, I just had to read the *Enquirer* the next day: "The idea of the club's making a car circuit of the city, headed by Weber's great band, showed that somebody in the management had a head on him! This event was an amazing, even a paralyzing, success. Nothing could have been planned to better sound the feelings of the town in general on the baseball questions, and the result of that experiment was a surprise to the most sanguine expectations. Why, the very electric wires thrilled with their duties and flashed the news ahead."

The Queen City had caught the fever. Early in the afternoon, City Hall was deserted, and the boys from the railroad offices, stores and factories all helped to swell the mighty throng that was headed for the grounds. As early as 12 o'clock the electric cars bound for the western part of the city were loaded down. By 1 o'clock, we had a small-sized mob at the main gate. When the gates opened, there was a rush like a thousand buffalo stampeding.

Every base ball enthusiast in the city that was out of work, could lay off, or had a convenient relative to die, was at the game, and the result was that the four quarters of the park were packed with a crowd the likes of which I'd never seen before.

The grandstand was filled to overflowing. The old pavilion was taxed to its utmost, and the terrace seats and bleachers were packed and jammed with fellows whose limit is "two bits" to see a game of ball. All the seats filled up and we had to stretch the ropes in the outfield for the hundreds who rooted from the outfield embankments.

The peanut vendor was on hand, the sandwich man did a land-office business and the lemonade man was equally happy. It filled the heart of a promoter to see all of that cash business being transacted, and it filled the soul of a fan to gaze upon John Schwab's verdant grounds. There is not a stage in all of baseball as smooth and as green as Superintendent Schwab's. To the sporting men in the crowd, it looked like a billiard table. To me, it looked like an emerald island in a sea of gray in the west-end neighborhood.

I didn't see much of the game that day because I was busy counting the receipts, but I did poke my head out to watch our boys come onto the field. While the Clevelanders were busy twirling the ball over the greensward, a clapping of hands down near the entrance caused every face to be turned in that direction. This applause deepened into a thunderous demonstration, through which came the Cincinnati Reds, like the conquering heroes they were—the famous Buck Ewing in the van. Oh, the ovation they received! They were clad in their immaculate white suits, accented with red sweaters, stockings and the name of the Queen City written as though in the blood of the Cleveland victims across each lusty breast.

Two magnificent floral pieces appeared on the field. One was a huge ambuscade of roses and smilax of horseshoe design, a tribute to the popularity of Captain Ewing from the tobacco merchants. The other one went to our catcher, Farmer Vaughn, from Clermont County.

The momentum was suspended briefly when the two teams lined up at the home plate facing the grandstand. They were on dress parade to hear what his honor, the Mayor, had to say about the opening of the League season. If only the Mayor were there! The private box, with our gorgeous decorations of flags and bunting, was empty! Fortunately, the delay was brief. Mayor Caldwell was ushered through the crowd and the roar resumed. He did not embarrass himself too greatly, although Captain Ewing smiled upon being addressed as "Colonel." It could have been worse. A few years later, there was a good mayor of Cincinnati who made a speech at the opening game, and when he wound up his oration, he shouted valiantly, "And now, gentlemen, I hope you both win!" Speeches by the mayor have been at a discount around this part of the state ever since.

But Mayor Caldwell was the first to soliloquize at the opening game. He paid homage to the old Red Stockings and threw out a ceremonial first pitch to the umpire. It was the first time that had ever been done, too. His honor hit it dead on the doornail when he said that people in this town are extraordinarily proud of their ball team.

# What I Learned Managing Six Base Ball Clubs and a Three-Piece Band

After the war—knowing that I'd like to get into the bed-and-board business and, by extension, the show business—I started as a desk clerk at a hotel in New Bedford, Massachusetts, and worked my way up to running the place. You may have heard of it: the Bancroft House.

When the chance came to manage the New Bedford team in the New England League in 1877, I jumped at it. Halfway through the season I could see how cracking we were, and I said, "The blue blazes with this, let's go barnstorming and make some real dough," and that is what we did.

In 1879, I took over the team in Worchester, Massachusetts, then took them into the National League in 1880. In between, I took some of the boys on a junket to Cuba.

After Worcester, I managed Detroit, Cleveland, Philadelphia and Indianapolis before settling in Cincinnati as the business manager.

Why did I keep moving around so much? The owners! They wanted to make all the big decisions, but I knew better than they what it took to keep the purse full. If you layered the baseball knowledge in their noodles atop one another, it would be thinner than the ham in the sandwiches in the Philadelphia ballpark. Why do you think I still hold the record for most clubs managed? That's right. Seven of them! I even had the Reds for a spell in 1902. I came down from the front office after a 10-year layoff, and still had the Midas touch. We went 9-7, but who's counting? (Me, I guess.) It didn't hurt my lifetime winning percentage any—375-333, .530—a far sight better than Mr. Cornelius Mack is going to end up with, at the rate he's going.

I also tried my hand at the entertainment business. In Massachusetts, I operated a theater, two ice-skating rinks and a music house. I had Liberty Hall, The Opera House, the Adelphi rink and the Bijou rink. I had Saturday night soirees and a Siberian carnival. I had so many acts I was in competition with myself. Why, I was a veritable individual amusement trust!

Through it all, I developed quite a reputation as a promoter. I soon learned you couldn't sell a sack of bricks as a trunk of gold. The newspaper boys would see right through you. Sometimes it paid to undersell an event rather than oversell it. If I had an act I wasn't sure of, I would say, "Boys, this show is the worst I ever saw; be as easy as you can with me."

I suspect that is why they would sometimes look the other way, as when I advertised "an orchestra of three pieces." Well, it did have a piano, a piano stool and a piano player! It was all great fun, and I even made some green. I lost some, too. One winter, I managed an act of trained seals. I figured I couldn't possibly lose money on that act, based upon what I was paying the professor who trained them. Then I received the bill for their ice and fish. I lost my shirt! I still like animal acts, but to this day, when there are trained seals on the program, I can't bear to watch. I get up and go out, moaning as I go. By the time I arrived in the Queen City, I had the combined knowledge of Barnum, Bailey, the Ringling Brothers and ol' John Robinson out in Terrace Park with his giraffes and elephants and chimpanzees all rolled into one. Promoting Opening Day was just another show. But it turned out to be the longest running show I ever had!

And why shouldn't they be? Cincinnati had the first professional team, and it was the 1869 Red Stockings who were the roots of the national tree.

Captain Ewing gathered the players around him and said, "Now, boys, let's go in and play ball for all we are worth. If we win to-day's game I will buy every man in the team a new hat." Bug Holliday gladly took up the gauntlet: "Well, we'll come pretty near sporting new dices. I feel like we are going to come under the wire first to-day."

What a day it was for the batsmen! Runs were sprouting like hay seeds in Harrison. We trimmed the Spiders 10–9. Captain Ewing's foot was still a bit sore from where he had been hit by a batted ball a few days earlier, but he caught Patsy Tebeau between second and third base with two out in the ninth. Ed McKean was scoring from third as Buck ran Patsy back toward Bid. "Throw home! Throw home!" Patsy yelled. "No, it's you that I'm after!" Buck answered. And it was Patsy that Buck bagged. A one-legged man with a noodle is better than a bonehead.

The next two games—before swelling crowds—we kicked them in the slats again. *Three straight!* Captain Ewing surely had the boys playing a sugar-brand of ball. As I look back on it, that was as sweet as an opening day could be. We had many glorious ones, mind you, but none were ever better than that one with Buck, back in '95.

# BANNY'S 10 TIPS FOR OPENING DAY

Here, boiled down to their essence, and free of charge to you future Reds magnates—or those of you who fancy yourselves to be future magnates—are "Banny's Ten Tips for a Successful Opening Day." Read them now, or read them later, but don't ever forget them. They are my Bouquet To The Future. I venture to say these "Ten Tips" will work in any era. I compiled them after the magnificent opening game of 1895, and I have never had to deviate far from them.

 Try to have at least one really good local player on your team, every year. We had two that year, Harry "Farmer" Vaughn and Buck Ewing, the best catcher who ever wore the spangles. Have some players on your team the fans can build an *affection* for. Besides Ewing and Vaughn, we had veterans Bid McPhee and Arlie Latham—chest in, and chest out, respectively!—but the fans adored them both. Not to mention Dummy Hoy, the deaf mute from Houckstown, as fast a player as I ever saw and a cracking outfielder. His play was of the high-grade kind that glistens with quality and comes only in five-pound boxes.

**2** Pump in some new blood. There is nothing like it. Give the fans someone novel to root for. If this greenhorn delivers in the opening game as some do, the fans will adopt him as their own. In '95, Charles Miller, our 26-year-old right fielder, wore the hero's garland. Oh how the Cincinnati fans and the scribes love the Red who plows up the West End with his proboscis! Do you recall what a clatter Dusty Miller created? The Toledo youngster strewed buttons all along the base line, and wore holes in his brand new shirt sliding to the bases. Nothing like his baserunning has been seen since the days of old King Kelly, of tender memory. Miller scored three runs and drove in four with spanking hits at critical moments. He was clear grit to the bottom. And do you remember that voice? It was a cross between a steam whistle and a buzz saw that he used to great advantage on the lines. "It is long since a young player has begun his career with brighter prospects than Charles Byron Miller," proclaimed the *Commercial Gazette*. I love to see a young man get his name in the big type!

*In gaily decorated wagons, the Cincinnati Reds enter League Park, the home of the Reds from 1894 to 1900. This is one of the 28 Opening Days orchestrated by Frank Bancroft. Bancroft believed in giving the Opening Day crowd pomp and ceremony. And he loved a parade.*

Introduce new spangles every year. Prominently display these uniforms before the season starts. Players are proud of their getups, and so are the fans. We showed them off in the big window at Grandpa Hawley's.

 Give the fans—and the news fellows—something new to ponder on the grounds every year. For example, in 1895 Superintendent Schwab put the voodoo on Bug Holliday's hoodoo. Bug claimed his lamps couldn't pick up the pitcher's slants on a sunny day with that Woodsdale Island advertising board in right-center field. It was a jonah for him. John Schwab erected a center-field fence 20 feet high and 100 feet long and painted it blacker than Bug's disposition after being struck out by Ol' Sol. We also added a separate entrance to each of the three sections of the park—amphitheater, pavilion and bleachers—to make it easier to handle the crowds on Opening Day and the Fourth of July.

 Invite some dignitaries, and some special guests, and notify the crowd of the latter. In '95, we had Aaron Champion, Charlie Gould and J. William Johnson from the original Red Stockings and we sat them in their own box, to be admired.

 Suffer the children. They are your future. In the fourth or fifth inning of every game, including Opening Day, I would walk to the gate where the urchins had gathered. Absentmindedly, I would swing it open, turn my back, look up in the air, whistle a tune. I was oblivious to the onrush. *Gate-crashers? What gate-crashers?* We were all children once, weren't we?

 Design a special program for the opening game, as a keepsake. Not that Porkopolitans need reminding, but it's a way of making sure you take nothing for granted. In '95, we produced a scorecard with the help of John Reilly, our old first baseman, now a lithographer of the first order. On the cover, he depicted the 12 stages of baseball life. Long John would know. He's lived every one of them.

 Schedule some crackerjack exhibitions right there in the home park for the days leading up to opening day. Why, in '95, we played two weeks worth of games! My favorite was the Page Fence Giants, the Negro aggregation from Adrian, Michigan. You will never have a ballpark big enough to house every fan who wants to come to the opening day game.

 Schedule a big parade, and pull in the players. In the early years, we put the boys in their spangles and in streetcars to tour the city the morning of the game. And music! The more music, the better! We put Weber's Band out front of the parade in '95, and had them, as always, play an open-air concert on the field while the boys warmed up.

 Always remember: Opening Day is "The People's Day." I regret allowing the magnates to discontinue the parade in 1903. The magnates believed we didn't need to have a parade to promote Opening Day anymore. That was a mistake. Fortunately, the people saved it. Whatever the club can do to enhance the fans' connection with the parade will serve the club well. Is not the man who cleans up after the elephants as much as part of the circus as the man on the flying trapeze? Of course he is! Don't hide your light under a bushel basket! Show off the parade! The fans in the pavilion enjoy seeing the paraders come onto the field. The parade is Cincinnati. It is all colors, all walks of life, all gathering behind one single notion, in ever-lovin' motion. It is the circus come to town, same time, every year!

CHAPTER 1

# Opening Day Stories

*These stories were collected in 2002 and 2003, and cover a span of more than 70 years. Players, front office personnel, broadcasters and fans offered their memories of Opening Days dating back to the 1930s.*

*You will soon discover that these interviews cover far more than recollections of Opening Day. In most of the interviews, people springboarded from the Opening Day subject to other episodes prompted by the conversation. Opening Days often evoked memories of spring training, major league debuts, and teammates and opponents. Soon the conversation was off in a new direction. Originally, we considered saving these tangents for a later project, but we decided to include the vast majority of each interview in this book. Opening Day does not occur in a vacuum; it is a part of the vast mosaic of experiences that our subjects recalled.*

*Most of these interviews were recorded and then transcribed for the book. While we made every effort to reproduce each interview word for word, we did find it necessary to correct some minor factual mistakes. Not every Opening Day hit remembered, as it turned out, was a home run. We suspect some of the respondents may also notice that they are not quite as profane in print as they are in person.*

## John Murdough

*Murdough worked in the Reds front office from the early 1940s until 1967, serving as ticket manager, traveling secretary and business manager. He first attended Opening Day in the 1930s.*

My Dad was ticket manager for the Reds. He was an accountant, and he and another fellow had an accounting business. But my dad always went out to Crosley on Saturday and Sunday and sold tickets. When the Depression came along, the accounting business went to hell, and he was made ticket manager for the Reds.

I played some baseball as kid. I was going to play in the old Buckeye League when I got out of high school, but then I got a job working with the Reds all the games, including Sundays, and I couldn't play ball. My dad saw me play a couple of games, and he said you'd better take the job.

He died in 1941, and they hired me in the ticket office. I came out of the war and went back into the ticket office and a couple of years later, I was made ticket manager. I was ticket manger until 1952, then became traveling secretary.

*My first opening day I remember I was in the sixth grade. It would have been about 1931.* I got out of school to go. The teacher was a baseball fan and she knew where I was going. She didn't say anything. Montgomery Grade school. Mrs McDermott. My dad was there. I would come home with him.

Why did I start going to openers when I did? I guess I figured it was about time to start going. I figure I've been to 70 opening games. The only years I missed I was in the service.

What comes to mind when I think about those early openers is the bad weather. Findlay Market would come in and march around the field. Impressed me. Impressed the kids, that's for sure. They came in an entrance in right field, between the bleachers and the grandstand.

Opening Day was always a great thrill. Everybody would dress up. They dressed up. Wore a tie. An overcoat. A social event. I'd go dressed up as a kid. Shirt and tie. Later I'd wear a sport coat, a suit even.

As a kid, I'd take a streetcar to Peebles Corner in Walnut Hills. Then over to Spring Grove Avenue, and then I'd take a bus from there, or walk a couple of miles to the park.

After the game streetcars lined up on Dalton Street. People jumped on them, like they do the streetcars in San Francisco now. People'd run along them and jump on.

The first ballplayers I really remember were Curt Walker, Red Lucas, George Grantham. Walker was probably the first player I knew personally. The Reds office was near home plate at Crosley Field, and my Dad would be in the office. They had a seat right out at the corner of the office up behind home plate, and anybody that needed something from the dugout, I was the messenger. I had to take things down to Curt Walker and couple of times and he was so nice.

In those days you didn't have phones in the dugouts, and the wives would call with a message, and they would bring them out to me and I would take them down to the dugout. Walker seemed to get more than any of them. He'd be out on the field during practice and see me and wave. I'd point to the message I had in my hand, and he'd come in the dugout and get it.

Opening Day was always a full house. They put people on the field out on the terrace. When I was ticket manager, I was supervising the sale of those seats. I think we put 10-12 rows out there.

*Those temporary seats took away from the game. Routine fly balls became hits, doubles.* It was awful. There were no rest rooms, concessions couldn't get out there. Seats were crowded so close together. Hell, if it rained you were finished. You got wet. If you had to go to the bathroom, forget it. Women raised hell. A ball hit close to the seats out there, if a Red hit it, the fans just stood there, they wouldn't budge, wouldn't give an inch to the other outfielder. But if the other guys hit it, there'd be a path for our outfielder to try to catch it.

We stopped the seating out there because it got to be too much trouble. We had the "goat run" about that time, out in deep right field, and we could put the overflow out there, it was standing room.

The night before Opening Day you went crazy, thinking of all the things you hope were working. Was the scoreboard ready? Was the PA working? You tried to check all that out. I'd be out there at 5 o'clock in the morning on Opening Day. Made sure the visiting clubhouse was ready. Usually you needed heat and made sure the heat was working. There weren't major items, but they were going to become major items if they weren't handled.

We read everything we could get a hold of about baseball when I was growing up. My dad got the *Sporting News* and I read it. But he wasn't too much of a fan. His interest was more the ticket office. The game those days started at 3 o'clock and we would get out of school and run home to listen to the games on radio.

Harry Hartman was one of the early announcers I remember. A cigar company—Black Ibold cigars was one of his sponsors—and he'd say, "Put a 'Black Pete' in your mouth and enjoy the game!"

Chick Hafey was here about that time in the early 1930s. He was pretty well done by the time he got to the Reds. That was when Sid Weil, the owner of the Reds, went out and he had Hafey, Babe Herman and Taylor Douthit playing the outfield. I think we finished last even though he had a hell of a payroll in those three guys. The Cardinals dropped a lot of ballplayers that were all done on Sid Weil. I knew Weil later on in life. He was a great fan. He tried like hell as an owner.

*Ernie Lombardi, he was great. He was a favorite on Ladies Days. The women loved him.* We had to restrict the number of reduced tickets, because they would all come out to see him. The dressing room was right up above the offices at the end of Findlay, and Lom would be the last guy dressed. He didn't want to leave on Ladies Day because they waited for him. Kids would wait for him, too He would keep three or four old balls up in the dressing room and would throw them out the windows of the dressing room up on the third floor. The kids knew that and they would wait out there. One day, some guy drove up just as Ernie was tossing out ball and it went right through the guy's windshield.

Lom would be catching in a game that didn't mean anything. Maybe the Reds were getting beat six or seven runs or were way ahead, and he had these little white beans in his pocket and he would drop them in the batter's shoes. They'd take off running for first base and all at once they'd pull up and wonder what was wrong!

He hit the ball as hard as anybody who ever lived. Third baseman played him 10 to 12 feet deeper than normal, all the way back in the grass. Lom could throw, too. Bucky Walters would always say, "Why

*Johnny Vander Meer (left) and Ewell Blackwell (right), leaders of the Reds pitching staff in the 1940s, met with John Murdough at the Reds spring training facility in Tampa, Florida.*

don't they put Lom in the Hall of Fame?" Lom would sit there behind home plate and a guy would steal, and Lom would throw him out side-arm without standing up.

I got so damn mad at the sportswriters later on, out in San Francisco. Lom was working at the lunch counter in the press box. I don't think he needed a job, but he was working there because he liked being around the ballpark. And these writers would sit there and yell, "Hey Lom, bring me a beer." "Make me a sandwich." I finally told those writers they ought to be ashamed of themselves. Here was one of the greatest players and you are treating him like a bartender. It burnt me up.

*Ewell Blackwell was an easygoing guy, but players sure hated hitting off him.* Especially right-handers. Sid Gordon, with the Giants, he came up in the ticket office one night to call his wife, and I heard him say, "I'm playing tonight, but I don't really want to. Blackwell's pitching. I'd rather take the night off."

In Brooklyn, to get to the field, you had to go through the Dodger dugout, and we'd be coming out and Blackwell would be going through the dugout, and Roy Campanella would be there. Campy was a funny fellow, and he would holler out, to Blackwell, "Hey Big Guy, when are you working?" Blackie would say, "Thursday." Campy would holler down to the second-string catcher, "You is catching Thursday."

I first saw Blackie pitch in Nuremberg, Germany. He was pitching for an Army team. I saw a game there and he pitched a couple of innings. I didn't know who he was then. Just a guy pitching for an Army team. I was stationed near Nuremberg and just happened to see the game. I was overseas 2 ½ years. Missed openers in '43, '44 and '45.

One of the guys who worked for the Reds back then was Lee Allen, who handled PR for a short while and then wrote all those baseball books. Lee was a character. One story they always tell about him involved some guy who just came in the office. Looked like he was about 35–40 years old. From Tennessee or somewhere. He's carrying a bat and a glove. He says I read in the paper you guys need a hitter.

So Lee comes out to meet with him. And he's sizing the guy up and decides to have a little fun with him. He's gonna work him out right in the office. "So, show me how you lean over to field a ground ball?" The guy's got his glove on and he's showing Lee. "OK, so how do you swing the bat?" Now he's swinging the bat, both ways. Right-handed and left-handed.

*So now Lee says, "Can you slide?" The guy says, "Sure." Lee sends him down to one end of the hall and he comes barrellin' ass down the hall and Lee yells, "Slide!"* The guy slides and breaks his ankle. Fortunately, Warren Giles or Gabe Paul wasn't around to see this. Lee gets the guy in his car, took him up to the hospital, called the club physician. So they set the ankle, put a walking cast on him. Lee to took him down to the bus station and got him a ticket out of town. Lee, out of his pocket, gave him some money. He was worried. But that was the end of that guy. Nobody ever heard of him again. Only time Lee Allen every conducted a try out.

Lee and Frank Grayson, who was a Cincinnati sportswriter, used to take their vacations together, and they would go down to different areas around Kentucky, Tennessee, Ohio, Indiana, look at old gravestones of old ballplayers. That was Lee out doing his research. *[Allen's years of research produced several books and became the basis of the library at the National Hall of Fame, where he worked in the 1960s.]*

Then there were some of the visiting players that would come in, create a little commotion. One time we had a kid working the scoreboard, and he would ride Ducky Medwick of the Cardinals. Always riding him. We didn't know it. So one time, Ducky went over there just when the game ended and there was a padlock on a door leading inside the scoreboard, and Medwick locked it from the outside and left. So this kid who's working the scoreboard has to stay around to take down all the numbers and by the time he finished, there wasn't anybody around. And he couldn't get out. His mother called. Anybody seen him? Finally we got the night watchman to go out, and he found the kid in there. But he didn't have a key that would fit. We finally had to get another guy out of bed to come and let the kid out. Ducky really fixed that kid. Next day, Ducky was apologizing. He didn't mean to cause that much trouble.

*In the late 1940s, in Jackie Robinson's early days, black people would come in from Atlanta, Knoxville, all the southern cities to see Brooklyn when they played here.* For Saturday and Sunday games when the Dodgers came in, they ran special trains all over the south, and from Dayton and Indianapolis, a lot of busses coming in. You thought the Dodgers were the home team. The fans loved him. Of course, most of the fans watching him play then were black. They were coming to watch Jackie play. The white fans were outnumbered.

I don't recall any bad treatment Robinson received, or that it was too much out of the ordinary. You heard some stuff from the white fans about not coming out, but we didn't see it at the gate. Our crowds were always big when Brooklyn was here. Robinson was such a gentleman, very gracious and very cooperative in any way he could be. Our players didn't say much, never heard any of our players say anything. Except Rogers Hornsby when he was managing the Reds in 1952 and part of 1953. He hated the black players. He was terrible.

There was a trade with Milwaukee in 1953; we gave them Joe Adcock. It was for Rocky Bridges and Jim Pendleton, a black outfielder. Hornsby nixed the deal. He said he wouldn't have Pendleton. So they threw in some cash.

One year in spring training—must have been about 1958—we went over to Havana to play. We had a working agreement with the Havana Sugar Kings. We were supposed to go the following year, too. We had three games scheduled with Baltimore. But those got wiped out. Geez, the first year the government was so gracious, what a great thing we had come, great things for international relations. But the next year, the government told us we'd better not come. Castro came and that was that.

We would break camp in Florida a couple of weeks before Opening Day and play exhibition games on the way back. They always sent me home a couple of days during spring training to make sure everything was getting ready for the opener.

We would try to sleep on the train as much as possible on those trips north, because that way the team could stay together. The black guys could stay with us. But if we had to stay in hotels, we would have to make other arrangements for the black players, like Frank Robinson and Bob Thurman.

*They were good guys. It was terrible on those guys. I mean these were big money guys—at least then—and it wasn't right.* But in those southern towns the only places they could stay were with black families, and they stayed with doctors or funeral home directors. Often, they were the leading professional black families in these little towns, the leading black citizens.

We had a family in Tampa that looked forward to the black players coming every year. She cooked for them, did the whole job, they paid her well, and I always gave her extra money. She took in Pinson, Robinson all those guys with us in late 1950s and early 1960s. We were the first club in Florida to finally get into a motel with all our guys. Causeway Inn in Tampa.

That was in 1962, the year after we won the pennant, the first year we were there. I was making the normal rounds looking for a place and the owner was from New York and he said, "It's OK, we'll take them in." I told him everything had to be right. The waiters and waitresses, the bartenders have to be nice, the swimming pool has to be OK.

But then somebody went to get a haircut, and the barber said, "We don't cut colored hair." It looked like the whole thing was going to blow up.

It was tough all around. We couldn't always find doctors for the players if they got sick or hurt. Tough to get them into to see a dentist. We were lucky in that we had a doctor in Tampa who would take care of our black players. It was a shame, it was a dirty shame. When I first started going to Tampa, they had colored drinking fountains, colored rest rooms. They couldn't take a drink of water if they wanted it.

Bob Thurman, who had played in the Negro Leagues for years, could hit like hell. Here's a funny story about Thurman. When we traveled on the train, we ate on the train. Thurman would say to Waite Hoyt and me, or Alex Grammas, whoever I was sitting with at the time, Thurman would say, "You guys sit with me and I'll show you a great steak." He'd tell the black waiter, "Hey, these honkies are OK, now take care of them." Geez, we'd get a steak that would look like a big Sunday roast!

We usually came north with the Senators and played exhibitions. Jacksonville, Columbia, South Carolina, Charleston. We'd play our farm clubs and each other. One year we were in Hazelhurst, Georgia. We had more people at that game—about 6,000—than lived in the town.

As we got up north farther, we might play Baltimore, Detroit. The clubs were pretty well cut down, but there might be another five or six guys who might be cut on the way north.

*In 1963, Pete Rose made the team before we left Tampa. After every exhibition game, Chesty Evans, the clubhouse guy, would come in and say, "That damn Rose kid is still out there hittin'."* He'd get a couple of players, maybe some young kids hanging around to play outfield, and he'd hit both ways. Hands were bleeding, blistered from holding the bat. He'd do the same thing on road games. Come back to Tampa and hit some more, if he could find somebody to throw to him.

Every day they played an exhibition game. The press would come in to see Hutch—Fred Hutchinson our manager. Somebody would always ask, "How long you gonna play the kid at second base?" Hutch would say, "What the hell am I going to do with him? He's doing everything I ask of him. What am I going to do, tell him he can't play ball?" Nobody ever worked harder. You asked him to pitch, he would have pitched. He was the third-string catcher.

Pete and I got along fine. One time—after the 1963 season— Pete was in Ft. Knox in the service, and this girl came into my office. She introduced herself as Karolyn Engelhardt, and said, "Pete and I want to get married. Will you tell Pete's father?" "What do you mean, me tell him? Pete's gotta tell him." She says, "Pete's father doesn't like me. Pete doesn't want to do anything to make his father unhappy. Pete wants you to." Well, I didn't do it.

That was the first time I met Karolyn. I really came to like her. We'd have giveaway days, hand out glasses or things to the fans, and I would call Karolyn and she would get the wives together to help out giving out the glasses.

Joe Nuxhall was another great guy. After the 1961 season, Kansas

City announced it released Nux and the Reds called him and told him to report to our farm club in San Diego, and we would give him every chance to come back to Cincinnati. He came back to Cincinnati in the middle of the 1962 season.

When he came back from San Diego, he would run in the afternoon. Way before the game, he would run clear out to center field to the terrace. We started to noticed a path out there, and wondered, what the hell is causing that? Groundskeeper was raising hell. Maybe we had a broken water line or something. Here Nux was running in the same place every day.

*Pete Rose broke in with the Reds in 1963, during John Murdough's tenure as club business manager.*

I did some of the player signings. Bill DeWitt, the general manager, did some, and the farm director did some. I had signed Nux one afternoon just before spring training started in 1961. I went in to tell DeWitt he was signed, but DeWitt was gone for the day. Now, Frank Lane—the GM at Kansas City—and DeWitt were close and they would get together on trades. Mr. Crosley had told DeWitt that with Joe having such a bad year in 1960, you ought to try to move him because the fans are on him and for his own sake he should be moved. Lane calls DeWitt the next morning wanting to make a deal. So DeWitt traded Nux. He called me and told me, and I thought, "Oh geez." Here I signed Nux and DeWitt, not aware of it, had traded him!

I had to call Nux tell him he was traded. He jumped all over me. Madder than hell.

I was also the one that had to call Klu in 1958 to tell him he was traded. Mr. Crosley wanted to trade him. Gabe Paul called me and told me he had traded Klu to Pittsburgh, and told me to call the press, told me to call Klu. Gabe didn't want to tell Klu.

*So I called Klu. "Klu, I don't have good news for you. You've been traded to Pittsburgh." He said, "For who?" And I said, "Dee Fondy." He said, "Oh no. No, no. John, quit your damn kiddin'." "Klu, I'm not kidding you." He couldn't believe he'd been traded, and for Dee Fondy!*

Right after the trade was announced, Crosley asked me about the deal. "What can this Fondy do?" he asked me. "Boy, can he run," I said. Crosley said, "That's good, because Klu can't." Crosley seemed happy with that. Of course, I didn't tell him that Fondy couldn't hit.

The Robinson trade happened a little differently. DeWitt called a lot of us in the front office together right when he was considering the Robinson trade and asked us to vote on it. It was unanimous. Everybody realized that we needed a pitcher. The year before—1965—we hadn't won. But Deron Johnson drove in 130 runs and we figured he would get better. But we had to have pitching. Baltimore offered Milt Pappas and Jack Baldschun. I talked to Harvey Haddix, one of our pitchers, about the Pappas and Baldschun, and he said, "Pappas will win 18 for you. And Baldschun's a good relief pitcher."

So we thought we had a good trade, a starting pitcher, a good reliever. But then Deron fell flat on his face. Pappas just lasted a couple of years. He didn't have a chance here. The fans hated the deal. Pappas was like a stepchild. Plus, he was a prickly guy; he didn't win any friends.

All-Star Games, I remember the 1953 game in Cincinnati. Ted Williams was coming in for the game; he was just back from Korea. It was going to be a real big deal. We checked everything out the night before, the morning of the game. Then all of a sudden, the PA wouldn't work. Just before the game we found out. Our PR guy, Hank Zurieck came over and said, "PA's not working. Good luck." We had a guy in the control room trying to figure out what the hell had happened. Everything was all fouled up. We're on the field fiddling with it, and all at once over the PA you hear, "That damned thing isn't workin'." So now all at once it worked.

I have this picture, all the guys that made the All-Star team back in 1956, all dressed up ready to get on the train for the game in Washington. There was Klu, Wally Post, Johnny Temple, Roy McMillan, Gus Bell. Geez, all those guys are gone now.

In 1956, when we were going for the home run record, the last day of the season we had been eliminated from the pennant race. Birdie Tebbetts was considering putting in all his hitters, his home run hitters at every position. That was going to put Roy McMillan on the bench, and McMillan told him, "You do that, and I'm taking my three home runs away from the team total."

In 1956 was when they charged the Reds fans with stuffing the ballot box. And they did it again in 1957. Waite Hoyt, the Reds radio announcer, could sell anything. He started out pushing Kluszewski and then expanded it to include other players. Hoyt talked it up on the radio; Ruth Lyons did it on TV and radio on her show. I mean she got women who had never heard of baseball to vote for the Reds.

So the club never really did do that much. We printed up 50,000 ballots to send out to our ticket sellers around the region. They started calling back the next few days. All their ballots were gone. They wanted more. I thought then this was going to get out of control.

As far as the votes were concerned, WKRC helped sponsor the thing and a lot of the votes wound up over there to be counted. They had a little office area and they had ballots all over the place, stacked up against the wall. Places like P&G and big companies were printing out the ballots on mimeograph machines!

I remember NL president Warren Giles sent Dave Grote, his assistant, over to count them, and Grote walked into that room. He says, "How many you say are there? Well, then, that's it." He wasn't going to try to count all those things.

And what was funny, all this talk about stuffing the ballot box and the Reds players shouldn't be there, well our guys played a big part in it and we won the game [Cincinnati players had six of the NL's 11 hits in 1956; the next year, the NL lost, but again the Reds players fared well, combining for three hits and two RBIs in a 6-5 loss to the AL.]

*The 1961 World Series was the hardest event we had to do. We worked day and night on tickets.* We had so many requests for tickets. Normal procedures in the World Series was to sell your three or four games in a strip, together. Well, DeWitt says we got to take care of more people. So we broke them up. We sold single games. Limit of two. We had mail you couldn't believe.

A postmaster in Dayton had put a box out on the street just for the ticket applications, and at 9 o'clock the station closed down, and they sent a truck down to Cincinnati. They must have carried eight or ten mailbags full of letters into our office. Hell, we were sold out by then. We had to turn around and send all those checks back.

*The traveling party of the Cincinnati Reds heading to the 1956 All-Star Game included (from left), Mr. and Mrs. Brooks Lawrence, Mr. and Mrs. Ed Bailey, Mr. and Mrs. Johnny Temple, Mr. and Mrs. Ted Kluszewski, Mr. and Mrs. Birdie Tebbetts, Mr. and Mrs. Gus Bell, Mr. and Mrs. Roy McMillan, Mr and Mrs. John Murdough, and Frank Robinson.*

Most of the years I worked with the club, Powel Crosley owned the team. He would come down to the ballpark to see the games, but other than that, we wouldn't see much of him. He didn't get involved in the day-to-day business of the club. He let the general manager have at it. He had that little car, and he was a big man, About 6'6". He drove in the parking lot outside of Crosley Field one day in his little car, and one of the rookies said, "Where in the hell did you get that car?" He didn't know who Crosley was. Crosley said, "Well, I built it. And, I own the club." I guess that about summed it up. What else was there? "How soon can you be ready to leave, Rookie?"

*Crosley was a good guy. He always had ideas. He owned an island off Georgia, and he raised these Sardinian donkeys. They're no bigger than a good-size dog. Sardinian donkeys, geez. He sent them up here for us to give them away. At the games. We had Sardinian Donkey giveaway days. These damn Sardinian donkeys running around. We'd give them away, draw somebody's name out of a hat.* Guys bring their kids up and find out they won a Sardinian donkey. Some of them weren't too thrilled. We had to buy some of them back. They're cute as hell, you could ride them. Crosley would ship them up here. He thought it was a great idea. Groundskeepers would let them out during the day, roam around. We had to get a vet to come out and give them their shots. We were not always thrilled to see these things show up.

Another of his ideas—Crosley heard about this guy, a former boxer, who had this program to make you better coordinated, using BB guns. He threw up a disc and you shot at it with the gun. Crosley loved this idea, and he had it set up at spring training. Clyde King, who was a Reds coach in 1959, he had one eye going this way and one going that way, and *he* was shooting it and hitting them. You didn't put the gun up on your shoulder, you just held it against you, concentrated on the object and you could do it. I did it. I could shoot houseflies. You went through a training session, and it was a lot of fun. The players liked it.

Crosley was a great believer in physical condition. He came into spring training once, wanted to see guys take their calisthenics. The regular trainer was late that day, and Mayo Smith was the manager and he said, "Somebody lead calisthenics." Hal Jeffcoat, one of the pitchers, said he'd do it. Jeffcoat was going to take full advantage of this situation. Jeffcoat is ripping their tails off. Nobody could complain. Crosley thought it was just great.

Crosley was a great owner. He didn't bother anybody. Gabe Paul did all that for him, he ran the club, and he was pretty relentless on managers. He was gung ho. "We gotta win. We gotta win." You would be on the road and Gabe would be back in Cincinnati, and you'd get a call at two in the morning. "What's goin' on? How come we lost that game? Where's the manager? I wanna talk to him." "I don't know, Gabe. It's two in the morning." "Well, go find him." He was a great guy, though. He knew his baseball. When DeWitt took over, it was a little more relaxed.

Why is Opening Day so special? It's such a big buildup to the thing. Findlay Market used to buy lots of tickets and sell them. We had an opening game list for a lot of people who would come only to that one game all year, and people would get the same seats every year. We had people on that list for years who had died, but their sons or daughters or somebody would send in the order and use the tickets. Every seat other than the bleachers was reserved for Opening Day. All sold in the off-season.

That game was a big money-maker for the team. We could charge a dollar extra on the tickets for Opening Day. Then it became a half-holiday. Offices closed up downtown. Schools would close sometimes. State government people came down, all the city officials.

*I remember how you would get up in the morning and go to the ballpark, just hoping the sun was out.* Parking was always a disaster. And we would have a hell of a time with the kids climbing up the center-field wall. Those damn kids could go up that wall like they had a ladder out there. Like cats going up a tree. We had one who would taunt us. He'd climb up there, get thrown out and he'd be right back in the ballpark. I don't know how he did it.

I had an idea to sell Opening Day tickets with two vouchers with it to two other games. You would have to buy three tickets and you could turn the vouchers in for any other game during the year. There was such a demand for the tickets. Hell, you figure if a guy was coming out to Opening Day, he would want to see two other games. But the owners never wanted to.

I loved Opening Day. We'd work like hell. We could never get everybody tickets who wanted one.

# Bill Werber

*Werber broke into baseball in 1930, and played 11 seasons. He was the Reds' starting third baseman from 1939 through 1941. Werber, who was elected to the Reds Hall of Fame in 1961, turned 95 on June 20, 2003.*

I remember Opening Day, 1939, pretty darn well. There was water coming into our dugout! *[The Ohio River crested at 58 feet, and a low spot in the ramp leading to the Reds dugout was covered by water.]* I knew all about the floods in Cincinnati, because I'd seen that photo of Reds pitcher Lee Grissom in a rowboat in center field when they had the flood of '37.

When I first arrived in Cincinnati—April 1939—it didn't take me long to realize how big the Reds were in everybody's daily life. We were like the weather—always there. Reds fans hadn't had a pennant-winner since 1919, so they were very hungry for a winner. But, even with that, there was an intensity I'd never seen before. It amazed me.

*It was as though the players in Cincinnati were a part of everybody's daily lives, like the sun coming up in the morning, and everybody always knew how we'd done the day before. People identified with us.*

One day in the summer of '39—it was nip and tuck between us and the St. Louis Cardinals that whole summer—I was driving to Crosley Field for the ball game. I was low on gas, so I stopped at a filling station on the West Side. I lived on Neeb Road, just off the 12th green at

*(From left) Bill Werber, Billy Myers, Lonny Frey and Frank McCormick shared stories at a 1960 reunion of the 1940 championship Reds.*

Western Hills Country Club. I didn't play golf, but my wife and son did; I liked having dinner at the club, and I got to meet a lot of nice people. The fellow at the filling station recognized me, sitting behind the wheel. He fell on his knees, clasped my hands, and looked up to the sky and said, "Please, God, let him win today!"

And that was the general feeling in Cincinnati, everywhere you went. Everybody could talk Reds baseball, and would do so at the drop of a hat.

I remember the very first visitor I had in Cincinnati. It was Frank Glade, the personnel director for Kroger grocery stores. He pushed the doorbell, and was carrying this great big fruit basket.

Dave Willey was another one. He owned a big lumber company. He didn't want to come by—I later heard he told his wife, "Damn dumb ballplayers!" and we had a laugh about that—but she told him it was their "Christian duty" and she led him over. Well, I never did have a bigger fan than Dave! He'd come to a lot of games, sit in their company's box and watch my swing through his binoculars, and after dinner that night he'd come by and tell me what he saw! He was a good batting coach, and I liked listening to him, because he was usually right! And when I'd hit a home run, he'd make a big tub of peach ice cream and bring it by.

Jack Schiff was another one. He was the head honcho at Cincinnati Financial. He stopped by one day with a big box of chocolates and said, "I just wanted to welcome you and your family to the neighborhood." We were good friends until the day he died, and now his son, Jack Jr., runs the corporation.

It wasn't as though we snuck up on anybody that season in 1939. I knew as soon as I came over to the Reds on the last day of spring training that we were going to be good. I'd been in a holdout situation with in Philadelphia because Mr. Mack, the owner and manager of the Athletics, wouldn't give me a $1,500 raise. The Reds had finished only six or seven back in '38, and we had the makings of a terrific pitching staff with Paul Derringer and Bucky Walters, and of course, Johnny Vander Meer, who had those back-to-back no-hitters.

I grew up in Berwyn, Maryland, little country town with a post office, feed store, barber shop and grocery store, and not a paved road to be found. Berwyn was located only about 10 miles outside of Washington, D.C. It was later absorbed into College Park. So, Berwyn doesn't exist, anymore—just in my mind, I guess.

I was born on June 20, 1908, in my grandparents' house. Berwyn was a great place to grow up, because there were two streams running on either side of Berwyn. My brother, Fritz and I—Fritz was four years older—spent a lot of time in those creeks. We swam and hunted water moccasins there. Fritz would run trap lines in the winter; he was after muskrat and mink. We'd get up at four in the morning and set out to check those trap lines. We'd skin the muskrat and mink, turn it inside out, trim off the fat and hang it up to dry in the woodshed. Then we'd clean up, eat breakfast and catch a streetcar into D.C., for school. After the skins had dried out, we'd send them off to Topeka, Kansas. We'd get $8 or $10 a bunch. To a couple of young boys, that was a king's ransom.

We had a big garden in the backyard, and we planted corn, beans, tomatoes, potatoes and rabbit food: lettuce, cucumbers, radishes. There were a lot of bugs on the leaves of the potato vines and it was our job, mine and Fritz's, to pick them off and put them in a Mason jar, to show we'd done our job. We always ate well. If we wanted fried chicken, why we'd just chop off the head of a chicken with a hatchet and our mother would fry it up.

We played all the sports. I can't say that we ever wanted for anything. My father had his own insurance agency, and that's the line of work I later went into. I played basketball and baseball at Duke, and signed with the New York Yankees after my freshman year, effective after I graduated.

*I broke in with the Yankees in 1930, five days after my 22nd birthday. Yes, Babe Ruth was there. He led the league in home runs and walks just as he always did. In my first at bat, I drew a walk, then Babe hit a long home run. I wanted to show my speed, so I tore around the bases. I think I crossed home before Babe reached first. I sat down in the dugout, and after Babe crossed home plate, he came in and sat down next to me. He said, "Son, you don't have to run when the Babe hits one!"*

I remember this great prank Babe pulled. He was a big practical joker. We had played a day game in Detroit, and Babe wanted Ed Wells, a left-handed pitcher, to go out on a double-date with him. Ed was going to get married at the end of that season, and was a man of impeccable habits. He didn't want to go out—he had pitched that day and said he was tired—but he didn't want to get on Babe's bad side. Babe assured him the girls were all right, so Ed went along. Babe told him the girls liked to drink, so he would bring a fifth of gin, and Ed should bring a bag of oranges as a mixer.

They took a taxi a little way out of town, and when they got to the house where the girls were supposed to be, Babe opened the screen door and rang the doorbell. This big guy, bigger even than Babe, comes to the door and says, "It's you! The bum who's been after my wife! I'm gonna kill ya!" He pulled out a pistol and shot Babe right in the gut. Babe yelled out, "I'm hit Ed! Run for your life!"

Well, Ed goes tearing out of there, oranges flying everywhere! He's scared out of his mind, and runs all the way back to the hotel where the Yankees are staying. Tony Lazzeri is one of the first guys Ed sees in the hotel lobby. Lazzeri tells Ed, "Babe's been shot. And it don't look good. He's asking for you." Well, Lazzeri and a couple other Yankees walk Ed up to Babe's room. It's all dark in there, and Babe is laid out in bed. He has talcum powder on his face—giving him this deathly appearance—and a big ketchup stain on the front of his shirt. But Ed doesn't know any of this. He thinks Babe really has been shot! Earle Combs is weepin'. "He's dying, he's dying."

Babe was going to say something to Ed, have him lean down so he could whisper in his ear. But Ed was so taken in by the whole scene—*the great Babe Ruth is in a hotel room in Detroit, dying of a gunshot wound from a jealous husband, and Ed's the guy Babe was out with*—that Ed passes out cold, right on the spot. When he comes to, everybody's just roaring! But Ed's so shook up he can't even laugh. And we never did get him to laugh about it. I guess if you were him, maybe it wasn't too funny. But, oh gee, we all thought it was hilarious, and nobody laughed harder than Babe.

I made the big leagues for good in 1933, and played 10 more seasons. I learned a valuable lesson in 1934. By then I was with the Red Sox. I kicked a water bucket full of ice in the dugout, and broke my big toe. It required surgery, and from that point forward, I played in pain, eight more seasons. But what I learned was this: your career can end at any time. After that, I worked hard every winter selling insurance from my father's office. I was taking care of my family, and after I retired from baseball, I went to work full-time selling insurance, and it paid off handsomely.

During spring training in 1939, the last one before we headed north, our shortstop Billy Myers came up to me and asked: "How are you on pop flies?" I told him I was fine, and he said, "Well, then, go ahead and take all of 'em you can get to. I'm bothered by the sun."

The sun in Tampa didn't seem all that difficult to me, so later I asked around and I learned that Billy had messed up a pop fly or two the year before in Cincinnati, and people had gotten on him pretty good. After a while, I spoke with the writers—Tom Swope, Lou Smith—and asked them to lay off Billy a little bit. I told them, "A good write-up might help him and the team." Billy really was a hell of a player and a nice guy. They took it from there.

On his first at bat on Opening Day, Billy received a real nice round of applause, and that kind of set the tone for the rest of the season. Billy was a key man on our club. Everybody liked him, and he had a good, sharp needle. He'd jab anybody, even the big boys—Lombardi, McCormick, Derringer—and he'd keep them in line, in a good-natured way. He wasn't big physically but he was very valuable.

Coming up north from spring training, we traveled on the train with the Boston Red Sox. They had the three cars in front of us. We had played a lot during spring training—the Red Sox trained in Sarasota—and Ted Williams had just joined the Red Sox that spring. We had a real fine pitching staff. Bucky won 27 that year, and Paul 25, plus we had guys like Vander Meer, Jim Turner, and Junior Thompson. But Williams was murdering them! We played all the way up through Alabama, South and North Carolina and West Virginia. Our last game with them was in Charleston. Well, by now, Paul's just plumb tuckered out by not being able to get *anything* past this skinny kid from San Diego.

*Paul throws this high-arcing pitch, kind of like that eephus pitch Ted later hit for a home run in*

*The Reds raised the 1940 championship flag at Crosley Field on Opening Day, 1941.*

*an All-Star Game, and Paul hollers, "Hit that, you son of a bitch!" Well, Ted hitches his bat a couple of times and, wham! He hits a towering fly over the right-center field wall.* And Derringer jaws at him all the way around the bases. It was pretty funny. Paul was just frustrated, that's all. Williams would do that to you.

I have nothing but good things to say for the people I played with and for in Cincinnati. Bill McKechnie was a patient and kindly man, who wasn't critical of us. If he had something critical to say, he said it in the clubhouse outside the earshot of the writers. I remember in spring training, 1940, some of the players wanted me to say something to him, suggesting that a couple of our guys were should be replaced, if we were going to shore up our weaknesses and win the World Championship. Bill's response to me was, "Maybe so, Bill. Maybe so. But these fellas have gotten us this far, and I'm sticking with them."

*I remember in 1940 that we played the whole season as though we had something to prove. We were embarrassed about being swept by the New York Yankees in the World Series.* We vowed that 1940 would be different. We felt we had a better ball club than that.

Frank McCormick was a prince of a guy, a terrific hitter, and a pretty easy mark. I loved to kid him, like the time he wanted to be admitted to our "jungle club," a group of us infielders. He wanted it after only a week of hustle, and we told him it would take a *month* of hustle. Then just when he thought he was in, we told him his nickname was "The Hippopotamus"—he was slow afoot—and he said, "If that's my nickname, I don't want in!", and we said, "OK, OK, you're in. You're 'The Wild Cat.' That's the name you want; that's the name you got."

Paul Derringer is the right-hander I'd send out there if I had a game I just had to win. He's my all-time righty, and Lefty Grove, who I played with in Boston is my all-time lefty. Derringer had lots of guts, lots of savvy, and good control. He'd also mix in a spitball every now and then. He enjoyed himself. On the night he pitched, he'd go out and have a good time—a *real* good time—but he'd be out there running the next day, "getting the poison out." I remember going to his funeral in 1987 in Osprey, Florida, and sitting next to Gabe Paul, and after the preacher got done eulogizing Paul—"philanthropist," "family man," "doer of good deeds"—Gabe turned to me and said, "Is he talking about *Paul?*" We had a good laugh about that! I hadn't seen Paul since we'd last played together, so I'm sure he'd changed in a lot of ways.

Bucky Walters was a better all-around player than Paul—Bucky had come up as a third baseman—and was a good hitter and fielder, and Paul was envious of that. They were different in personalities—Bucky was quiet—but they were both fierce competitors. Bucky was the NL MVP in '39, and how dominant do you have to be to win the MVP as a pitcher? Well, Bucky was that dominant.

*Did you know the average time of our games in 1939 and 1940 was an hour and 40 minutes? It's true! That's how good Paul and Bucky were, plus we had a great defense.*

Ernie Lombardi was one of the nicest fellows you'd ever want to meet. Very easygoing, and a damn good catcher, none better. He had the best throwing arm I'd ever seen. Better than Gabby Hartnett, better than Bill Dickey. He threw a nice light ball—it came in like a feather, and it was always right on the money.

Lonny Frey was my closest friend on the Reds and I gravitated to him immediately. Before coming to Cincinnati, he played shortstop for Brooklyn for five years and played a year for the Cubs and the Reds purchased his contract to plug their hole at second base, and oh did he fill it! I call Lonny a "character" player, best when the chips are down. He was a big reason we won the pennant in '39 and the World Series in '40. He lives in Hayden, Idaho. I call him, and he writes to me.

I'll never forget the play Ival Goodman made in a crucial, late September game against the St. Louis Cardinals, in '39. We were battling them for the pennant. They were right on our heels. The game was tied, 3-3, in the seventh inning and Ducky Medwick led off with a screaming liner over the head of Harry Craft, our center fielder, and one of the best in the game. Harry was off and running as soon as the ball left the bat, but the ball went over his glove and hit off the center-field wall. Medwick was thinking triple all the way, but Ival, anticipating the ball was going to be over Harry's head and that Harry wasn't going to be in position to play the carom, played it himself and threw a strike to me at third base. We got Medwick by a mile! And there went the Cardinal rally. We won the game and the pennant on that play, and, boy, were the fans happy! That was the city's first pennant since 1919.

I liked Mr. Crosley. I remember him taking a bunch of us deep-sea fishing, and we got seasick. And, one spring, I came down with hives in Havana and Mr. Crosley flew me from Havana to Miami on his private plane. They tested me for something I might be allergic to. He didn't know much about baseball, but he was a very tolerant owner.

I'll tell you a funny story about our general manager, Mr. Giles. I liked him enormously. During spring training in '39 when I had come over in the trade from the Phillies, he paid me a $1,500 raise that

Connie Mack wouldn't agree to, so that I'd report to the Reds. Then, at the end of that season, he asked me, "What do you want to play for next year?" I said, "Mr. Giles, you know my value. Go ahead and make me an offer." Well, Mr. Giles made me an offer for $1,500 more than I planned to get out of him. And I said, "Mr. Giles, back in the spring, you didn't have to give me the $1,500 raise I was asking for. So I'm going to give you the $1,500 back now." And he took it!

# Bob Littlejohn

*Littlejohn grew up in Cincinnati and worked as a Reds usher when he was in high school. He attended more than 60 openers. He passed away in 1999. His recollections were first published in the book,* Hornsby Hit One Over My Head, *by David Cataneo, and excerpts are reprinted here with permission.*

Opening Day here in town was always something special. The first opening game I saw was in 1932. Somebody gave my dad a couple of seats. We ended up sitting in these cold steel chairs. I can remember how chilly it was. Dad picked me up at school at noontime and it was a driving snow coming down, and I can remember in the afternoon editions of the papers, they both had a picture of Crosley Field—it was Redland Field then—and they showed the snow coming down.

If everyone who was excused from school went to Opening Day, there'd have been about fifty thousand people there. You'd get on a bus going to school, and all the girls were writing excuses to go to opening game for all the kids. The school got wise to them, so they sent postcards out. So the kids had to hurry home to waylay the postcard. Then they found out that was being abused, so they started school at 7:30 Opening Day so everybody got out at one o'clock. It was always a festive time. Everybody was excited to see the season get started. There were all kinds of parties around town.

*In 1936, I went all by myself. I was in the eighth grade. I got the ticket for Christmas. I couldn't wait for Opening Day.* This one little biddy eighth-grade teacher, she couldn't wait to get ahold of my mother. "Did you know he went to the ball game on Opening Day?" I went to the school in the morning and then hopped on the streetcar and went to the ball game. My mother said, "Is that so? That was his Christmas present."

In 1934, Larry MacPhail came in here, and they started the Knothole Club. I was in the sixth grade, I guess, and everybody in school got a Knothole card and you got to see the games 100 percent free….It got to the point where you could go any days except Ladies' Days, night games, which were seven games a year at that point, and Sundays. So we could go down as many as four or five times a week.

We'd get a streetcar and go down by ourselves, show our card, and go in, and we felt we were late if we didn't get there an hour before game time to watch everything that was going on. Then, after the game was over, we'd get our autograph books and wait for the players to change clothes. I got all kinds of autographs and never paid a dime for them.

The Reds had a clubhouse over the main entrance. They were up on the third floor of this building. One time I was standing down below, standing all by myself, I'm looking up the window, I see some commotion, and here's Babe Herman leaning out the window. He dropped the ball down at my feet. All I had to do was pick it up. It wasn't a brand-new ball. It was kind of scuffed up, so I just used that to play with.

I saw the first night game. Sat in the bleachers. It wasn't a sellout. This was in '35. I had to be in on it. It was history. At that time, the night games didn't start until 8:30. But they didn't last more than two hours. You could set your watch by it.

When I got to high school, in the paper they said they were putting on ushers at the park. I ushered down there during some of the best years for the Reds. I started ushering there in '37 and ushered through '38, '39 and '40.

Nineteen forty was the only time in Reds history when they won the last game of the World Series at home. I was working that game. Our whole family was there. My folks, they were tickled to death to get seats in the bleachers.

I've seen all the home World Series games in Cincinnati except

*Bob Littlejohn (right front) ushered at the final game of the 1940 World Series and was on the field as the Reds celebrated after the final out. Littlejohn attended more than 60 Opening Days.*

1919, and that's before my time. I've seen every opener since 1936, with the exception of the two years I was overseas in the service. I've got tickets for the next Opening Day already.

# Tom Turner

*Turner was raised in the Cincinnati suburb of Glendale and played in the Mexican League and the Negro Leagues. Turner is one of about 20 men from Cincinnati who played in the Negro Leagues from 1920 to 1950. We have included his oral history here as a tribute to those men who couldn't play in the white major leagues, but nonetheless had Opening Days memories worthy of posterity.*

The Negro Leagues had Opening Days all across America, including right here in Cincinnati. There were the Tigers back in 1936–37, the Buckeyes in 1940 and 1942, the Cincinnati-Indianapolis Clowns during World War II, and the Cincinnati Crescents who played here in 1946.

I don't recall specifically getting to any of those openers, but I probably did. The Tigers and Clowns played their games at Crosley Field when the Reds were out of town. The Negro League teams always played doubleheaders on Sunday. The Tigers even wore hand-me-down uniforms from the Reds, and probably could have beaten the Reds. The Tigers had a great pitching staff—Lou Dula, Porter Moss and Jesse Houston. The manager was Ted "Double Duty" Radcliffe and one of the outfielders was Neil Robinson, who everybody says would have been in the Hall of Fame if he had played in the major leagues.

I don't recall exactly the first Reds game I went to, but I guess it would have been some time in the late 1920s. My family moved here in 1927. My father got work with the New York Central Railroad in Sharonville as a fire-knocker.

The first game I recall, I think the Reds were playing the Cardinals. *They had this infielder, and when they warmed up, he'd be doing everything with the ball, jumping up, picking up the ball with his heels*—that's where I got that stuff, watching him do that—yeah, he could pick it up with his heels, flip it up and catch it!

I played for the Dayton Monarchs of the Indiana-Ohio League in the late 1930s. Those teams were farm clubs of the Negro Leagues. I'd play ball on weekends. During the week, I was working for families in Glendale doing whatever needed to be done. I worked as a cook and gardener, even as a butler! I'd get paid seven or eight dollars a week. Then, on weekends, I'd play a game on Saturday, and two on Sundays, and I'd make $36 a week for those games. That was good money.

When I joined the Army in World War II, I was stationed at Ft. Huachuca, Arizona in special services. Our baseball team played in Mexico, and so, when the war ended, there was interest in me playing ball in Hermosillo, so that's what I did. The money was good there, too. Bob Lemon, who was the New York Yankee manager at one time, was our manager.

*Opening Day in Hermosillo—in all of Mexico—was a festival.* Everybody would be there. The game was on a Saturday. Mexico was baseball-crazy. You'd see a mother pushing a stroller, and there'd be a baseball cap hanging down from it!

There was a lot of anticipation of Opening Day. The players did our own field, picked up whatever stones might be on the infield, lined it off with lime, and guys with automobiles would come down and take a wooden drag and drag the infield, to smooth it out. Everybody was involved! All the while the townsfolks were barbecuing a whole hog on an open pit and they'd sell the barbecue pork sandwiches during the game.

Mexicans played their national anthem, and they played ours, too. They'd have a lot of music and singing, all during game time. It wasn't that big of a stadium, but they'd fill it with 18 to 20,000. They'd have their festivities all day long. It was like the Super Bowl. They had all kinds of entertainers: magicians, musicians, dancers, singers, some of the most beautiful singing you ever did hear. I've always loved the ceremonies on Opening Day.

*Tom Turner played in Opening Day games both in the Negro Leagues and the Mexican League in the 1930s and 1940s.*

After the Saturday opener in Hermosillo, we'd go out to eat. We'd have this whole room to eat, owners and everybody. And the first thing they would do, is they would bring out this great big, hot pepper, and great big onion. And they would pass that around. And everybody would take a bite off of that pepper. And when it got to me, I didn't know what I was going to do—I don't like hot peppers or hot onions—but I had to take it. That was my first one. It felt like it just growed in my mouth! I made an excuse to get up and go to the rest room, and I spit it out. That thing tore me up!

They'd have a dance after a doubleheader on Sunday, but the dance wouldn't start until about five minutes after 12 in the evening. You see, they wouldn't dance on Sunday. I'll never forget the night Bob Lemon and I walked into the dance hall after a Sunday doubleheader and the band stopped playing the song they were playing, and started playing the national anthem. That always set me off, that national anthem. I always—always!—have a feeling when I hear the national anthem, especially if somebody can really sing it.

In the Negro Leagues, I played with the Chicago American Giants. We had spring training in Jackson, Mississippi, and then we barnstormed north with the Kansas City Monarchs. We played games in Meridian, Mississippi; Selma, Alabama; Little Rock and Pine Bluff, Arkansas; and Omaha, Nebraska. We played in front of big crowds, but it was the Jim Crow era, different drinking fountains, one for "whites," one for "coloreds." I remember ordering hamburgers through the pigeon holes in the back of restaurants. We couldn't take showers at the ballparks. We'd just have to roll up on our uniforms and jump back on the bus. You wouldn't get a bath until you got to a black home or a black hotel that had tubs working.

*Oh, was it ever good to make it to Chicago! There were 47,000 people in the stands for Opening Day!* We were playing the Kansas City Monarchs. What I remember best was all the beautiful women in so many of the seats. You never saw such a conglomeration of women, dressed to kill. Hats and everything, really beautiful. And photographers were everywhere! See, Chicago is a big town, and it's a black town, too. There's a lot of black people in Chicago, still is.

Opening Day in Chicago, 1947, that was the day of my first home run. I can still feel the bat hitting the ball. I hit it so good, I could feel the bat bend in my hands. I never had that happen again. Just that one day. It was a third-decker, left field. It was up there, man! Off Chet Brewer. He was my meat, all the time. He pitched for Kansas City. And I had 5-for-5 off him in Pine Bluff, Arkansas, in a night game. I could just hit Chet. I don't know what it was. I used a 36-inch, 35-ounce bat. Not real heavy. But I liked the long bat. Louisville Slugger. Jackie Robinson model. Guy at a sporting goods store on Fourth Street would order them for me every year. Cost me three and a quarter.

*What was it like being a Negro Leaguer in 1947 in Chicago? You really want to know? To me, it was just about like heaven.* Because I always wanted to play ball. You see, I was aware of the Negro Leagues from a young age. My uncle, Tom Wilson, was responsible for starting the Nashville Elite Giants. Later on, they moved to Baltimore, and became the Baltimore Elite Giants. I was named after him. He was the one who nicknamed me "Pigtail," man! Anyway, I finally made it into the Negro Leagues, and I was in the clouds!

I always got hits. Wasn't a day went by I didn't get hits. I'm not lying to you. Nobody shut me out, but one time. That was in Nashville, Tennessee. We played the Newark Eagles, Roy Campanella's team. I was up four times, and down four times. A little ol' left-handed guy got me.

Opening Day was a great day for me, but it was also a trying day. It's a funny thing, but after it was all over, you felt kind of flat. You were so anxious about the day coming, and it was such a great day, all those ceremonies and music and pageantry, and you were so up, so into playing that game, there was no way you were going to avoid feeling a letdown when it was all over.

Sunday, though, you were right back at it. You'd play doubleheaders at Comiskey Park, and you'd be right back on the road, barnstorming. Twelve o'clock at night, you'd leave Chicago on that bus, and you'd be gone.

# BOB BOEHMKER

*Boehmker attended his first Opening Day in 1933, courtesy of "Opening Day" attendance rules at St. Aloysius School in Covington.*

I was in the sixth grade at St. Aloysius on Seventh and Main Streets in Covington. The teachers were Franciscan nuns, from Oldenberg, Indiana. I was living on Philadelphia Street, a block-and-a-half from the school. I was 11 years old, a couple months shy of 12.

My teacher was Sister Pius, a great, big, chunky lady. I had to promise her I'd find her two big boxes, and if I did that, she'd let me out at 1 o'clock. I'm sure she knew I was going to the ball game. The Opening Day game was about 2:15 or 2:30 p.m. in those days. It was just the idea of "going to the ball game for Opening Day" that motivated me to ask Sister Pius to let me out of school early that day. I couldn't have pulled that off any other day. Different rules applied for Opening Day.

I picked up the street car from Seventh and Main to the Dixie Terminal—the old Green Line, end of the line—and then I walked up one block to Fifth and Walnut and rode to Court Street. In those days, they ran all those specials, and they used to come up Findlay, and let you get out and walk a half of a block to the ballpark, not much more than that. It was still "Redland Field" back then.

*The streetcars were always jammed, people standing all over them.* There weren't many people with cars. Nobody could afford them. The Green Line was a nickel. And the other one, the one in Cincinnati, was something like three tokens for a quarter, or a dime, straight. So, that'd be 15 cents goin' and 15 cents comin'. Mother would've had to find that 30 cents someplace. She probably took in wash that day. We didn't have any money in those days. It was the Depression. I didn't eat or drink anything at the ballpark. I didn't have any money for it. I was just glad to be there.

I didn't have a ticket for Opening Day, but that didn't concern me too much because on the streetcar on the way to the ballpark, I'd try to start up a conversation with a fellow. Then when we got to the ballpark, I'd just walk on in with him. Most people were nice enough to say, "Sure, stand here with me and we'll go right on through." I don't think too many kids knew about that—walking in with an adult like that—they didn't know you could do it. But I was 12 years old, and somehow I found out. It was probably because I'd done it before during the summertime and I had learned the ropes.

*I'd sit up in the upper deck, in the last seven rows. They always had a big crowd at the opener, even during the Depression.* The Reds played the Pirates. The Pirates had a heck of a club in '33. Pie Traynor, Arky Vaughn, the Waner brothers—Paul and Lloyd, Big Poison and Little Poison. They were favored to win the pennant, but I don't think they did.

Jim Bottomley was there—left-hander, first baseman. I remember he hit a triple that day, most exciting play in baseball. I think he scored the Reds only run.

Lombardi was there. He'd come over the year before from Brooklyn. I think Si Johnson pitched that opener and did pretty well. Besides Johnson, the Reds pitchers were Eppa Rixey, Red Lucas, Ray Kolp, Larry Benton and Benny Frey. Rixey might have been the only left-hander.

The Reds weren't very good in the early '30s, but they always drew well for Opening Day. The Findlay Market Parade was the big thing.

After sixth grade, we moved to Sanfordtown because my father died, and Grandpa took us all in. It was a while before I got to an Opening Day again—not until the mid-1950s. But I'll never forget the day Sister Pius let me out at 1 o'clock to go to Opening Day when I was in the sixth grade.

# BETTY HESKAMP

*Heskamp has attended Opening Days since the 1930s.*

I started going to Reds games in the 1930s, with my dad. That was back when they had Ladies Days!

Dad was a traveling salesman, and when he was in town, in the summertime, we'd go to Reds games. I'd meet him up at Fifth and Walnut—we lived in Bellevue, Kentucky—and we'd ride the trolley car to the game.

*The biggest difference between going to Opening Day back in the 1940s, 1950s and 1960s compared to now is that a lot more people wear red now.* It seems like it wearing red really took off when the Reds moved into Riverfront Stadium.

Opening Day is such a big, big day in Cincinnati—not just for the individual fans, but for companies who entertain their customers that day at the ballpark. My husband's dad started the family business—Heskamp Printing—back in 1922, and entertaining customers on Opening Day is something we've always done. We'd meet up with other people and go to the game, and then we'd go out to dinner after the game, you know, make an entire day of it. A lot of people did that.

Opening Day has such a party atmosphere to it—it's like going to a big, big party is the best way I can describe it. It's the whole thing of "going to the game," and you get caught up in it. It's what you do if you're in Cincinnati and you can get tickets to the game. It's all part of it. Everybody's in a good mood. It's a great day. It's Opening Day in Cincinnati!

*No day says "Cincinnati" like Opening Day, because Opening Day is Cincinnati.* I can't imagine

Bob Boehmker, who saw his first Opening Day game in 1933, took in his first game at Great American Ball Park with his grandchildren, 70 years later.

Cincinnati without Opening Day, and I can't imagine Opening Day without Cincinnati. It's something that gets passed on down through the generations. My last Opening Day with my late husband, Harry, was 2001 and, then, in 2003 I didn't go to Opening Day, but my son and *his* son, who is my grandson, Matt, went to Opening Day. And that was Matt's first Opening Day. So, you see, that's already the fourth generation, and it just keeps going and going and going.

# Bill Giles

*Bill Giles' father, Warren Giles, was general manager of the Reds from 1936 to 1951. His club won the National League pennant in 1939 and the World Series in 1940. Warren Giles later became the 12th president of the National League, from 1951 to 1969. Bill is the owner of the Philadelphia Phillies.*

I remember Frank McCormick—I was pretty young when he was socking the ball around Crosley—and he would always give me boxes of Wheaties, because back then, whenever they hit a home run, they got a case of Wheaties.

McCormick, of course, was part of that great 1940 team. When we won it all in 1940, I remember tugging on my mother's dress and saying, "Why is Daddy crying? We won, didn't we?"

I remember Hank Sauer; he was one of my favorites. He taught me how to chew tobacco by wrapping it in Doublemint chewing gum—it kept you from swallowing it. That would've been in the late '40s.

When I was growing up in Cincinnati, going to Opening Day usually got you out of going to school, and when it didn't, I just cut! But I never missed the entire day of school. I'd take the streetcar from school to the ballpark, even on Opening Day. It was the most exciting day of the year in my family—the beginning of the season, the beginning of spring, the first real chance to be outdoors, no matter how cold it was.

By 1947, I was working in the ticket office, sorting mail-order requests. I was 13 years old. I remember the trainloads of black fans coming in from Birmingham when Jackie Robinson broke in. The stands were always full on the weekends when the Dodgers came to town; the stands were about 80 percent black.

I remember Smitty's Band in their black-and-orange uniforms. And I remember shortstop Eddie Miller, who when the Reds were coming to bat would sit out on the field, near the stands, if it wasn't his turn.

Everybody's heard the stories about how the infielders played Ernie Lombardi 20 feet back in the outfield grass and how he hit a lot of singles off the walls—but what I remember is when he was catching and a foul ball was hit into the stands, he never even looked at it. He had a sixth sense about which balls were playable, and which ones weren't. He would just keep staring at the pitcher, and hold out his hand for a new ball.

My dad sat in the stands, about 20 rows back. Later, he built a box behind home plate that could seat eight people. I'd sit with him the entire game on Opening Day. Before the game, I would go in the dugout. I wanted to be a batboy, but Dad didn't want the players to think I was spying on them, so I was never the batboy.

Dad was big on cleanliness, *especially* on Opening Day, because the ballpark was going to be full and that was your chance to make that great first impression. On Opening Day he'd go around and check all the rest rooms personally, including the ladies' rooms. One woman saw my dad inspecting the bathroom, and she ran out looking for security, yelling *"There's a man in there smelling the toilet seats!"*

During the week, I would go to day games and take the streetcar after school and see the last half of the game. I kind of had the run of the place after the games. My dad would get together with the coaches, and manager, writers and broadcasters, after the game, for a few beers and sandwiches. After a while, that'd get kind of boring. There was a night watchman with a little billy club, and I would go with him and close the gates, close up the ballpark. Sometimes, my buddies and I would get our hands on the wicker wheelchairs at the ballpark and have races up and down the ramps.

When they made dad NL president, he said he would take the job if he could keep the office in Cincinnati. I was a sophomore or junior in high school, and he didn't want to uproot me.

Years later, when I went to Philadelphia as the owner, I said, "What do we do on Opening Day?" They said, "Well, we have the Salvation Army band, about 15 people, come out and play, and some council-

*Bill Giles' father, Warren Giles (left) and owner Powel Crosley watched a Reds game in the early 1950s. Warren Giles, who was general manager of the club from 1936 to 1951, left the Reds to become president of the National League.*

man throws out the first pitch."

*I said, "No, no, no. We have to create something special." You know, because I grew up in Cincinnati, thinking Opening Day was like Christmas.*

The first year—would have been 1971—I had the ball dropped from a helicopter. The helicopter got a lot of attention, so the second year I went after this guy, let's call him the "kite guy." I'd seen a story about him in *Sports Illustrated*. He would jump off of cliffs with this kite on his back and soar down to the ground. So, I'm thinking he could do this right out of our upper deck!

So we built him a ramp, 12 feet wide, in the upper deck, a hundred feet long, built out over the seats in right field. He was supposed to water-ski down this ramp and float onto the field.

But a players' strike delayed the start of the season, and the kite guy had to cancel out on us. But we had advertised it, and I was committed to it. I looked in the Yellow Pages. No kite men. I had a friend who knew a guy from Cypress Gardens in Florida who did this sort of soaring, and I brought him up here and offered him $1,000 to do it.

He looks the situation over and said, "I can't do it."

"I'll give you $1,500."

"OK, I'll do it."

"Well, aren't you going to practice?"

*And he said, "Mr. Giles, if I'm going to kill myself, I want somebody besides you to see it."*

That day—Opening Day, '72—I'm up in the booth next to the PA. The organist started to play the buildup to the jump. The PA announcer says, "Here's the kite man!"

The guy didn't move. Nothing. So I said to the announcer, "Maybe the kite guy didn't hear you."

So the announcer says again, "HERE'S THE KITE MAN!" And again, the guy doesn't move. I got a walkie-talkie with me and I call out to one of our promotion guys who's out there with him.

"What's wrong, can't he hear the PA guy?"

The promotion guy radios back: "He hears the PA guy fine. He's just scared; he doesn't want to go."

Well, God, I can't blame the guy. I mean, it's a windy day and he's at the top of this 100-foot-long, 12-foot wide ramp and it's a pretty good dropoff to the field. But the show's got to go on, right?

*So, I say, "Well, there's 46,000 people waiting on him. Can't you just give him a push or something?"*

So, they gave him push, and he went about 10 feet, veered off the ramp, and crashed into the stands. He got up and kind of threw the ball into the bullpen. People are booing and cheering and laughing. It was so bad, it was good.

The next year we tried it again. This time, the price was $5,000. We moved the ramp to center field, doubled the width of it and beveled the edges so he couldn't fall off. He made it down the ramp, but didn't sail off it like he was supposed to. The wind caught him and sucked him down. He just sort of *whomped* down in center field. It was sort of funny. People seemed to like it. It was just hoaky enough.

Two or three years later, we did it again, different guy this time, and he made it to the mound just fine.

One year we had this guy named "Benny the Bomb." This guy was nuts. He put himself in a wooden box and the box blows up. He pops out with the ball. It was another one of those, "it's so bad, it's good."

Every year, we do *something*—whether it's kites or parachutes or people shooting themselves out of cannons. It's the Cincinnati in me. It's all with the goal of making Opening Day something special.

In 2003, I was supposed to drop a ball out of a helicopter above the stadium and Tug McGraw, down on the field, was going to catch it. We practiced it in Florida and Tug actually caught it—but because of the war, they wouldn't let any aircraft above the stadium. The year before that, we had a person on a high wire on a motorcycle hanging upside down over the right-field line, and he threw out the first ball. That one actually went well. Maybe we're finally getting the hang of it!

# JOE NUXHALL

*Nuxhall first attended an Opening Day game in 1944, the same year he became the youngest player to appear in a major league game in the modern era. After several seasons in the minors Nuxhall returned to the big leagues in 1952. He started the 1956 opener, and the rain-delayed home opener in 1966. After 15 big-league seasons, he moved to the radio booth for Opening Day, 1967, and has been paired with partner Marty Brennaman since 1974.*

The first Opening Day I saw, I was in a Reds uniform—in 1944. I hadn't been to an Opening Day before that. I'd been to two, maybe three, regular-season games, but never an opener. On Saturdays back then, they had something called the Knothole Gang, run by the YMCA. We got a card for a quarter or something. We'd take the bus down to Cincinnati, and sit in the upper deck in left field. I can recall only two games for sure I went to when I was a kid. One was the Boston Bees, and the other was the Pirates.

For the '44 opener, the Reds said "C'mon down, we'll give you a uniform, you can watch the game from the bench." I was playing junior high baseball at the time. I was getting a lot of guys out up in Hamilton, so the Reds brought me in because they were so short of

*Joe Nuxhall, at the age of 15, saw his first Opening Day game from a seat in the Reds dugout in 1944. Less than two months later, he pitched against Stan Musial and the St. Louis Cardinals.*

players because of the war. Most of the regular Reds players were in the armed services. There was no thought of putting me in that game. I was strictly a spectator.

I don't think they thought I was going to get in that other one, either, in June! They didn't promote it or advertise it. It just sort of happened. We were playing the St. Louis Cardinals who'd been in the World Series the year before. I had come down to a few games and sat on the bench—like I had at the opener—but there was never any hint I was going to actually get in a game.

So, anyway, on this day, I had my usual best seat in the house—in the Reds dugout. The Cardinals were way ahead, and were hitting line drives all over the place. I was admiring the way they could hit. Just then, the manager, Bill McKechnie, yelled for me to warm up. But I didn't hear him. The second time he yelled, I looked down at him, and he said, "Yeah, *you*. Go warm up." All of a sudden, things weren't so interesting. I wasn't sitting back admiring anything. I was wild warming up, but when I got in there I retired two of the first three batters I faced, and then all of sudden, it hit me. I realized where I was. I was scared to death! Two or three weeks earlier, I'd been pitching against 13 and 14-year-olds in junior high school. *Now here I was pitching against Stan Musial and the St. Louis Cardinals. And the wheels came off. I gave up two hits, five walks and a wild pitch. Wow!*

I came back up for good in '52, when I was 23 years old, after seven seasons in the minors. Here's where I was: Lima, Ohio; Birmingham, Alabama; Muncie, Indiana; Charleston, West Virginia; Columbia, South Carolina, and Tulsa, Oklahoma.

So my next Opening Day would have been 1952, but I don't remember much about it. My role was mop-up, period, and as it was, I didn't get into a game until May. It was almost a month. It was in Brooklyn. The Dodgers scored 15 runs in the first inning, 12 of them after two out! I wasn't involved in that inning, but Luke Sewell—he was our manager then—told me to warm up and he put me in in the sixth.

I was nervous, more nervous than I was in '44, but it was kind of a "controlled" nervous. Here I was walking out there to face Jackie Robinson, Duke Snider, Carl Furillo, Gil Hodges, Roy Campanella and Pee Wee Reese! My attitude was, "throw strikes and see what happens." Sewell was just glad I was able to get somebody out. I pitched three shutout innings. Our general manager Gabe Paul told me after the game that if I hadn't gotten in and done well, I was headed back to Tulsa after the game. Back then, you could carry 30 players a month into the season, but then you had to cut down to 25. I was on the bubble.

The first opener I was in was in '54, in relief in the third inning against the Braves. That's the game I hit Andy Pafko late in the eighth inning. It's the one thing I recall clearly about that day—they carried him off on a stretcher. I was scared to death. That was the last thing I wanted to do. It was a fastball in; it took off. It hit him just above the temple. He wasn't moving at all. I was afraid I'd really hurt him. It was quiet as could be in the ballpark. Total hush. *[Pafko was saved by the protective lining inside his cap. He never lost consciousness. He was taken to Christ Hospital, and was diagnosed with a mild concussion.]*

*In '56, I got the Opening Day start—the only one of my career—and that was a high honor.* Back then, our opener was the first game of major league baseball for the season, and that was part of the honor.

The Cardinals' starter was Vinegar Bend Mizell. We faced each other a lot in our careers. It seemed like every time I faced the Cardinals it was him. He had a crazy delivery. He was *way* back in his motion, and from the batter's box you couldn't see his head at all. And, boy, then he'd come down at you, and, oh! On top of that, he was just a little wild, so he had guys at the plate wondering right from the get-go.

I don't remember a lot about the night before, just that I was nervous and had trouble sleeping. I was up at my house in Hamilton. I couldn't wait for the game to get started. I was champin' at the bit. It was like pitching the second game of a doubleheader. I used to hate that! You know, having to wait it out. And Opening Day, of course, takes a while to get going. After we got done hitting, the visitors had to hit—back then, they hit an hour—and then there were the ceremonies. It seemed like 18 hours before we finally got started. If it had been up to me, I'd have been warming up an hour before the game started, because I was about to jump out of my skin.

I was going along pretty good—it was 2–2 in the ninth with two outs when Red Schoendienst hit a little bouncer back to me. I messed it up and I knew right then I was in trouble. There he was, "Stan the Man," comin' up to bat. Tie game, ninth inning, and here I just let a guy on that would've got me out of the inning. I still recall the pitch to Musial; I can still see it today. A hanging slider that was *right there.* He knocked the s— out of it. He hit it about halfway up the Sun Deck. That was an "oh-no" pitch. When you let loose of it, you say, "Oh no!" You know where it's goin'.

I'd gotten him out the first four times—all on sliders—and, of course, I'm going to go back to that pitch, because I'd had success with it. The difference is that those four sliders I'd gotten him out on, weren't in the same place I threw him the slider in the ninth. It was a no-doubter. Musial was the first guy who'd gotten a hit off me when I came into that game in '44.

*Joe Nuxhall's family (including wife Donzetta, and sons Phil and Kim) posed for the 1957 Reds yearbook.*

*You talk about Opening Day, one of the best fights I ever saw happened Opening Day.* It was probably about 1954. In left field. I was out there in the outfield, shagging balls during batting practice. I couldn't even tell you what started it. There were three guys in the portable seats in left field—you know, the seats the Reds put in front of the wall on Opening Day and then roped it off—and these two guys from a butcher shop, from somewhere in the neighborhood, came over. I guess they knew the usher, who let 'em in for batting practice. The butchers still had their aprons on, bloodstains from cutting up the meat. Well, all of a sudden, the two butchers start arguin' with the three guys in the seats. There wasn't but, oh, say, five feet between the two butchers and the guys they were arguin' with.

And, then, all of a sudden, boom! Hammer city. These two butchers like to kill those three bastards. They knocked over the fence—there were seats tipped over, seats up against the fence, seats over the fence—I mean, they knocked the goddamn hell out of three guys. And those three guys were big guys! And those two butchers like to kill 'em. *You'd hear a whack! And there goes one of the three guys rollin' across a row of chairs, and the other butcher'd pick him up and bam! And down the guy would go again. It looked like a bleepin' bowling alley out there!*

Back then, a lot of the fans used to go to the breweries before the games. There was Hudepohl, Burger and Red Top. They were all within walking distance of the ballpark. A bus load of fans, say from Hamilton, would come in, and the breweries, say Burger, would empty the garage where they kept all the trucks, and they'd put a buffet in there—you know, baked beans, potato salad, ham and all the beer you could drink. And then they'd all go to the ball game. By the time they got to the ball game, half the stadium was hammered.

We had a helluva club in '56. If we'd just had a little more pitching, we could've won it. We almost did. We finished two games back of Brooklyn. Early in September, we beat the Braves three of four in Milwaukee, to pull within a couple of games of them. Then we lost a tough one, 1-0, in St. Louis and that hurt. Yeah, we sure had a helluva club.

Wally Post was underrated. I always said, he and Gus Bell were both underrated, particularly Gus, because of Willie Mays being a center fielder, too. Wally had as good a power as anyone. He'd hit the goddanged ball, and it was *tagged.* Hell, he used to get his wardrobe every year hitting that damned Siebler Suit sign at Crosley Field. Of all the guys playing today, the guy who reminds me of him because they are built similarly, is Bobby Abreu, even though Abreu is a switch hitter. But they're put together the same way. Wally was a strong man. He'd look bad on one pitch and the pitcher'd say, "Oh, I got him now!" and the pitcher'd throw that son of a bitch again and Wally'd hit it 440 feet. He'd hit it out, straightaway center at Crosley, no problem.

And he was a great guy, too. Nicest guy you'd ever want to meet. We hung around together a lot. In spring training, we all lived in the same neighborhood. Johnny Klippstein was another one. There was a place in Tampa, off West Shore, just a little ol' family-type bar, they always had hard-boiled eggs and pickled eggs. After we worked out, we'd always stop there and have a couple of beers and some hard-boiled eggs. I'll never forget—hell, this was almost 50 years ago—this guy who came into the bar almost every afternoon wanted us to invest in this new restaurant, Burger Chef. He was in the meat business, sold meat to the restaurant. He tried like hell to get us to invest us in Burger Chef. It was Wally, Gus, Johnny Klippstein and myself, the four of us, sitting at the table. The guy told us fast-food burgers would be a thing of the future, and here was our chance. Hindsight is wonderful, ain't it?

Wally worked for his father-in-law who owned a canning company up in Minster, Ohio, canned tomatoes and I forget what else. Wally did a lot of public relations for him when we were on the road during the season—Philadelphia, Pittsburgh, Chicago, St. Louis. Wally's father-in-law would say, "Wally, this fellow, a Mister Joe Jones in Philadelphia or wherever, buys some of our product. When you get there, would you give him a call for us?" And Wally would take the guy to lunch and leave him tickets for the ball game.

Yeah, it sure was a shame when Wally died. He was only 52.

Oh, I'll tell you one more Opening Day story. Happened in 1960. One of the celebrities around town would always sing the national anthem on Opening Day, and on this particular day it was Bonnie Lou. It was colder than hell that day. I walked into the dugout before the game and Bonnie Lou was sitting right there next to the water cooler. I knew her. We exchanged pleasantries. *Then I looked at the water cooler and said, "Well, I might as well get this thing loosened up!" You got to remember I was pretty well known for having a temper back then. But I was only kiddin'. All I did was I shake it a little bit—it didn't move but an inch—but I broke the damn water line! Needless to say, the "leak" was directly on Bonnie Lou—and I do mean leak! I drowned her! Aw, I mean I was so damned embarrassed! She was the only one that got wet. And she was there just to sing the national anthem!* They got her dried out best they could—she didn't have time to change, and besides she wouldn't have had a second set of clothes. I think she had a coat on, so that helped a little bit. Boy, was that embarrassing.

People always wonder how I got involved in announcing. It started before I went to the booth in 1967. About 1962, I bought a Gulf Service Station in Hamilton, and my brother worked there. A fella from WMOH came down to sell us some advertising. It was Lee Moore, Hunk Moore we called him, and *he said, "Would you be interested in doing Miami basketball?" I said, "I dunno. Whaddaya want me to do?" He said, "Play-by-play." I said, "Play-by-play! You gotta be kiddin' me!" He said, "No, I'm not kidding you." And I said, "Hell, I'll try anything once."*

I think the reason they were interested in me is that I was pretty well-known up there, and I was coming off a good year, a good come-back after being gone for a year. WMOH needed somebody, so I said, "OK." And they said, "We've got to go sell it." We went to Kahn's meats, Coca-Cola and Wayne Dairy in Richmond, Indiana, and sold it, and that's how it all started. It turned out to be a helluva break for me. I hadn't had any thought whatsoever of being a broadcaster.

I had played basketball and I loved it. It was my favorite sport. So, I knew something about the game, but I had no idea what doing play-by-play entailed. I knew there were 10 players on each team—and

*Drenched in champagne, Joe Nuxhall interviewed Pete Rose and Johnny Bench. Some of Nuxhall's most memorable broadcasting moments have come during player interviews.*

learning Miami's players wasn't bad—but you had to look at the opposition and be able to identify each one of them, and a lot of times you couldn't see the numbers during game action so you'd be sort of fumbling around. It was a chore. I don't think I did so good the first 15 games, until I got an idea of how to prepare for it. Funny thing is, after I got the hang of it, I really enjoyed it. I think basketball play-by-play is a lot easier than doing baseball. I think basketball is the easiest sport there is, because it's all action. There isn't any dead time, no sittin' around and bulls—in'. Marty might say something else, but that's my opinion.

My color guys were Hunk Moore and Ray Motley, who was the station manager. He did Hamilton and Miami football and basketball for ages. We had plenty of guys to talk about for Miami—Charlie Coles, Skip Snow from Sabina, Charlie Denkins, from Cincinnati, Jeff Gehring from Toledo, some pretty doggone good players.

Oxford was a tough place to do games back then—it was at ol' Withrow Court, before they built Millett Hall—because all the stands were on one side. There were like three rows of bleachers and you were right against the wall. And it was rockin' and rollin' at all times. The sound would come back there and hit that wall, and you couldn't hear yourself think, let alone hear yourself talk!

*I never thought of broadcasting as a career, not even when I was doing those Miami games. I just enjoyed it.* I had watched Miami play as a kid, so it was fun for me to do their games. They didn't pay a whole helluva lot, but I did it for three years—during the off-seasons, when I wasn't pitching for the Reds.

Then in the summer of 1966, the advertising manager for Weidemann Beer approached me about doing the Reds. Ray Warner was the big shot at Weidemann Brewing Company at the time, and he was behind it. I was 37, and at the most I was looking at another two or three years pitching. I was interested, but I didn't think of it as a possible career.

The whole thing was: "Would you be interested in working with Claude Sullivan and Jim McIntyre in the radio booth?" The only reason they would have even asked me is that I had the experience doing Miami basketball. I knew I couldn't pitch forever—I wasn't making a lot of money pitching; my last contract with the Reds in 1966 was for $24,000, and that's the most I ever made—so, yes, I was very interested when they started talking about it.

I knew I was going to retire soon, and after I thought about it, I was leaning toward maybe doing the broadcasts in '67. But a few weeks before we broke camp, Ted Davidson's ol' lady—his estranged wife—shot his ass in a bar in Tampa. He was the only left-hander we had. I told the front office, "Hell, I'd be glad to call this broadcasting thing off." But then I got wind they were going to trade me, and that was enough for me. I retired April 1, and went right to the booth.

The first game that spring training was against the Cardinals at Al Lopez Field. I went up there and sat between McIntyre and Sullivan. *After every pitch I would open my mouth: "Blah-blah-blah." I was a motormouth! I wore the boys out! I was nervous as hell. At least Claude and Jim knew, "Well, at least Nuxhall can talk. That won't be a problem."* It took a while to get acclimated.

Now, I've kind of gone the other way. It's so quiet, listeners say, "Is Joe in the booth?" But, you can be too talkative and be talking about things that aren't all that important.

I did "Star of the Game" during that first season, mid-season I think. Either Sullivan or McIntyre had been doing it and I took it over from them. Back then, you had to take the players over to the visitors' dugout at Crosley Field, and the microphone was right there by the public address announcer, Paul Sommerkamp, next to the dugout, home-plate side. The first guy I did was Jim Coker. I think Jimmy had hit a home run, or some damn thing.

I've had some memorable interviews. Remember Alex Johnson? That sumbitch was like talking to that refrigerator over there. I'll never forget that time he'd hit his seventh home run of the season and he'd hit only two the previous year. I said, "What's the difference between this year and last year, Alex?" I'm waiting for him to say, "I'm seein' the ball better," or whatever, and all he said, was: "Five." I coulda s— right there. Talk about having to fill dead air. He did that to me more than once!

Another "Star of the Game" was Pascual Perez of the Atlanta Braves. Latin player. Right-hander, shut us out on one or two hits at Riverfront. Skip Caray—the Braves broadcaster—always used to like to screw around with me. I went over to their booth before "Star of the Game," and I said, "Skip, how is Pascual Perez's English?" Skip gave me the A-OK sign and said, "Great. Superb. Real good." So I get Pascual on, and I congratulate him, and he says, "Thank you, thank you." I asked him a couple other questions and he said, "Yes," and "No." And finally I asked him, "You had a lot of stuff working tonight. What was your best pitch?" The sumbitch says, "I kept going around and around." He was talking about getting lost going to the ballpark down in Atlanta, and I'd asked him what his best pitch was! The next time I saw Caray, I said, "You rotten SOB!" He just roared. He loved screwing with me.

Then there was Tony Perez, early in his career. He'd hit a big home run, and I said, "Tony, where was that pitch?" Without missing a beat, he said, "Right down de cock." You know, that's ballplayer talk and Tony's English wasn't that good and he didn't think about it; he just said it. I about swallowed the microphone on that one.

*There were a lot of them—Danny Driessen, Rick Sutcliffe—but the all-time classic was probably Phil Gagliano. That one was all my fault.* It was the pre-game show, not "Star of the Game." It was before an exhibition game in Indy, and I there were a couple of guys in the dugout listening. I was interviewing Joel Youngblood. I had just started it. You know, "This is Turfside, Monday night, and my guests tonight will be…" and Phil Gagliano goosed me right there. I said, "You c—sucker!" I turned the tape machine off, and now I got the ass. So I start in again, "This is Turfside, Monday night, and our guests are…" There was pea gravel all around the warning track, and now they're throwing pea gravel and it's hitting the tape recorder.

So, I finally get the interview done and I'm just glad to get it done and over with. I give it to the clubhouse kid, and I say, "Would you take this to up to the booth upstairs? I got to throw batting practice." So, I put on my uniform and throw BP, come in and shower and go up to the booth, and I open my scorebook, and the engineer says, "Oh no, it went over the air!" I said, "What went over the air?" He said, "Somebody said, 'c—sucker,' but it wasn't you." I said, "Oh yes it was!" What had happened was that our engineer heard the opening, "This is Turfside…" and he just cued it up. And I had forgotten to warn him.

I bet it wasn't 30 seconds after that went over the air, the phone rang! It was Jack Moran, the sports anchor of Channel 9. He said, "Was that you?" I said, pretty sheepishly, "Yeah, it was me." I thought, "Oh s—, I better go look for a job in A ball."

After I hung up with Jack, the phone rings again. *Dlingggg! Dlingggg!* It was Dick Wagner who was in charge of broadcasting for the club. He was good about it, though. He just told me to apologize on the air, and that's what I did. Gagliano was just screwing with me. I was working! I almost worked myself into a new job. That would've been 1973, because Al Michaels was there. The next year is when Marty came in.

Funny thing is, after all those years pitching for the Reds, and doing games on the radio, nowadays I might be shopping in a Wal-Mart or some place else back home, and some parent will recognize me, and they'll have a little kid with them, and the parent will say hello to me and the kid will say, *"Hey, it's the Kroger guy!"* (Nuxhall roars at the recollection.) They don't know a thing about the Reds and baseball—the only place they've seen me is doing TV commercials. *Hey, look, it's the Kroger guy!* Boy, that cracks me up.

## DON ZIMMER

*Zimmer was born in Cincinnati in 1931. He began his career with the Brooklyn Dodgers in 1954. He retired as a player in 1965, but remained active in baseball as a manager and coach.*

Growing up in Cincinnati, I was not a kid that ever skipped school, but whenever Ewell Blackwell was pitching, I went to school half a day, and then I'd sneak out after lunch and go to Crosley Field with a quarter or a half a dollar to get into the right-field bleachers. I *loved* watching Blackwell pitch.

I distinctly remember going to an Opening Day when Bobby Adams—the second baseman who came after Lonny Frey—hit a home run. Later, when I was playing with the Cubs, I wound up with Bobby Adams for a while 'cause he was a coach there.

The Reds had some great teams when I was about eight years old. I'm talking '39-'40-'41. I can name most of the players then, better than I can name the players I managed eight years ago. Billy Werber at third, Lonny Frey at second, Billy Meyers at shortstop, Frank McCormick at first, Ival Goodman in right, Harry Craft in center field, Wally Berger in left, Ernie Lombardi and Willie Hershberger behind the plate…

See, what we had back then was a Knothole card. You might have a yellow card, or a green card. And a certain day, say Saturday, was your day to go to Knothole Day at Crosley Field. So, the team would go on that day. That card didn't work on Opening Day.

*I loved Crosley Field. I wish some of these young guys could see places like Crosley Field and the Polo Grounds—because they were so unique. Crosley because of the terrace, and Polo because it*

"Hey, it's the Kroger guy!" Nuxhall has become well-known among younger Reds fans for his popular food store commercials.

*Don Zimmer (center) posed with his longtime friends and Reds personnel, clubhouse manager Bernie Stowe (left) and official scorekeeper Glenn Sample, during the Reds-Yankees series at Great American Ball Park in the 2003 season.*

### *had that unique configuration—260 down the lines and a cab ride to center field.*

Probably my favorite Opening Day was when I was a player, in 1955 with the Brooklyn Dodgers. Pee Wee Reese was the shortstop. And the day before we were going to open up in the Polo Grounds, Pee Wee called me up to his room. Pee Wee and I were staying at the big hotel in Brooklyn—that's it! The St. George Hotel— and, anyway, Pee Wee had a bad back. When it would go out on him, it would go out for like two weeks. Well, it went out on him in an exhibition game we were playing the day before. I had to help Pee Wee get in bed, because he was laying on the floor. We had to call a doctor. Which automatically meant he wasn't going to play for two weeks. So, I went from thinking, "I'm gonna go watch the Dodgers open up," to being the Opening Day shortstop for the Brooklyn Dodgers!

And we won our first 10 games! At that time, it was a a record. It's been re-broke since. We won 10, lost one, and won about seven or eight more, and opened up a big lead. And, of course, the minute Pee Wee's back got better, he was the shortstop. I couldn't even tell how I did Opening Day. All I know is we won 10 straight, and the 11th game we got beat. Whitey Lockman got a base hit down the left field line. I went out to get the relay. They had a couple men on base and I threw a bullet into Campanella. But it hit the grass and skidded, hit his shin guards and went in the dugout and they all scored. And I got the error.

I think every Opening Day is special, no matter where you're at.

That's the way I look at it. I hear some ballplayers say, "Opening Day? It's just another game." If you want to believe that, you believe it. But it is very definitely something different.

# Bernie Stowe

*Bernie Stowe is a living legend in the Reds clubhouse. Bernie has served as batboy, equipment manager and clubhouse manager since the 1940s. His sons, Mark and Rick, began working for him in the clubhouse in the 1970s. Rick's story is also included in this book.*

I grew up in the West End, about four blocks away from Crosley Field, on Army Avenue. I remember the 1940 World Series with all the people being parked way up where we lived. I didn't go to any of the World Series games, but my brother, who was 10 years older than me, used to take me to games on the weekend. We'd sit in the bleachers. I was six or seven years old.

The Reds player who stood out for me was Frank McCormick. Oh, what a hitter he was—and a great guy, too.

The way I got started working for the club is that a friend of mine—Ralph Tate—got sick one day, and he worked as a visiting team batboy, and he called me and asked if I could go down there and take his place. I was 12 years old. Bucky Walters was the manager. The Board of Education got on my ass about being outside the ballpark at one in the morning, waiting for a bus to come home. You know, after the game, we had to clean the shoes and all that. Gabe Paul—the general manager—took me to the Board of Education and said, "Would you rather have this kid running around, or workin'?" That ended it.

Nineteen forty-seven is when Jackie Robinson came up. And, like I say, I was working the visitors' clubhouse. I was 12 years old, had real blonde hair. I can remember Robinson, and later Roy Campanella, saying to me, "C'mere! Let me feel that blonde hair!" They were great guys. And they were great tippers. They'd give me $5 a game—each. That was big money back then. Carl Furillo, he'd give me $20 for three games. Pee Wee Reese was a good tipper, too. You got to remember now, this is when the Brooklyn Dodgers were always finishing in the money. They had class.

It was only a few years later that we gave Sandy Koufax a tryout. Koufax was on a basketball scholarship at UC. The manager of the UC baseball team was also a bird-dog scout for the Reds and he told the scouting director, Bill McKechnie, Jr. "This sumbitch can throw it through a wall." So McKechnie had him brought over. I got Koufax a uniform to work out in. It was his first big-league uniform. Can you imagine if we had signed him? We'd have had Jim Maloney and Sandy Koufax, back to back. Oh, man! But Koufax couldn't *find* home plate, and we didn't sign him. We should've signed him, anyway, hard as he threw.

Back then, there'd be a different team in town Sunday than there was Saturday. You know, St. Louis would play their final game of the series on Saturday, and Sunday, we'd play the Cubs. That way, people got to see two different teams on the weekends, and that'd help attendance.

Dumbest thing I ever did as a visiting team batboy was the time the manager pinch-hit for the pitcher, and I didn't notice that. After the guy reached base, I go out there with the pitcher's jacket, you know, to keep his arm warm. And the guy says to me, "What the hell are ya' doin'? I ain't the pitcher!"

I did three years in the visitors' clubhouse, four years in the Reds, beginning in '50. In the visitors' clubhouse, I was the assistant to Chesty Evans. When he moved to the Reds clubhouse, he said, "You wanna stay here, or go with me?" I said, "I'll go with you." The Reds didn't tip as well. They weren't finishing in the money, like the Dodgers.

*Later, you read and heard about how Cincinnati was one of the toughest places for Jackie Robinson to play. And it was, from what I saw and heard.*
Especially after the game. As soon as he showed his head, the fans just crucified him with boos. But Pee Wee would always come up to him, give him the big hearty pat on the back, let them know he was there, and that that was what mattered, not what these folks were saying. At first, everybody thought Jackie was going to hang it up. But Pee Wee was his guy. I remember an off day the Dodgers had in Cincinnati, and Pee Wee drove Jackie down to Louisville to stay with him overnight.

Cincinnati was a tough town for that. I've heard some guys say, "Aw, it wasn't so bad." But that's not the way I remember it. Chuck Harmon—the Reds' first African-American player in 1954—caught it some, but not real bad like Jackie got. They'd get on Chuck if he struck out or something. You'd hear the "N"-word coming out of the stands. If he got a base hit, they wouldn't say nothing. When we came up through Tennessee on our way north from spring training, I can remember Chuck and Nino Escalera—he was very dark-skinned from Puerto Rico—having to go to the movies, because the local citizens wouldn't let them play in the game.

The '48 opener, I remember a little about that. Ewell Blackwell pitched. "The Whip." That's when they had the temporary seats in the outfield. *A lot of the players—the hitters, anyway—liked the temporary seats out there. And some of the players would even go out and shake hands with the people in the seats.*

Blackwell got the win that day in '48. He was a big, ol' country boy, even though he was born in Fresno, California He wasn't rushed, I'll tell you that. All the time I've been here, I've seen only one guy taller and skinnier than Blackwell—Bill Scherrer!

You remember back when the players used to leave their gloves on the field, behind their positions? Well, they wouldn't do that on Opening Day! At least not in the outfield. Anybody could've run out of the temporary seats and grabbed the gloves. That's back when the guys only had two gloves. Now, they got eight or nine gloves.

Nineteen forty-eight was the year the Reds wore satin uniforms—for night games. And the Reds' batboy, who was Dickie Ratterman, wore an all-red, satin uniform. Oh, God, they'd sweat to death in them! Four or five games at the most, and they had to get rid of them.

I was there when Klu cut off his sleeves, which was probably in 1955. At first he cut off only about the bottom two inches of the sleeves. He's wasn't a complainer, so it wasn't like I was always hearing him bitch about it. A short time later, we cut off the entire sleeve for him. We got the biggest uniform top we could find, and we cut from there. His arms were as big as my legs! It was Chesty Evans who did it. That's when it was really obvious and the commissioner's office stepped in: "You all gotta look alike. Everybody, including batboys and ballboys."

We'd always have brand-new uniforms for Opening Day. *Every* Opening Day. That's why, back in the '40s and '50s and '60s, when you see the spring-training photos, the guys are wearing *last* year's uniforms. MacGregor made the uniforms back then. Right here in town. That made it a lot easier on Chesty and me, because all we had to do was go up the road and get them. We'd call and tell them what we needed, and we'd ride up and get them.

*Guys want to look good, especially on Opening Day. When we moved into Riverfront Stadium, we bought a full-length mirror to hang up, just for that reason.*

We had some great dressers. Vada Pinson—he was the sharpest in

Bernie Stowe replaced Ray "Chesty" Evans as the Reds' equipment manager in 1968. Stowe served as the NL batboy in the 1953 All-Star Game at Crosley Field.

the uniform. It had to be just perfect. And you know how the clubhouse kids clean the shoes after the game? Vada said, "I'll clean my own shoes." He'd polish 'em before he left that night, and he'd polish them again before he put 'em on the next day. Boy, them babies, you could see yourself in them!

Opening Day morning was something. Still is. The guys'd be switching pants. They still do that nowadays! Back then, we had some guys bitchin' and moanin' even *before* they tried on their pants. Back then, there was a wider disparity from what the guys'd been measured for in spring training. MacGregor sent Botts Crowley down to spring training from Cincinnati to measure the players every year. You know the Crowleys. His brother's got the bar in Mount Adams.

I remember Reds pitcher Kenny Raffensberger. I'd say to him before a road trip, "Kenny, you want this other set of uniform tops?" You know, because he was scheduled for a start on that road trip, and the pitchers would want that second shirt because it's gonna be so hot, and they're gonna want to switch into that second shirt. But Kenny'd say (*Bernie imitates Raffensberger's deep, gruff voice*): "Son of a bitch, I might not even be here that long! Just give me *one* of them bastards."

Back then, the uniforms were 100% wool. We'd send them out to the cleaners, maybe twice, if we had a a six-game homestand. We'd send them to New Look Cleaners. Been doing that since before I got here. Rest of the time we'd just get them with a brush, dust them off and put them back in the locker. *Pee-eeu!* Damnedest thing you'd ever seen. Unbelievable. There was a little more odor to the clubhouse back in them days.

When we switched over to the double-knits in 1971, it made our lives a lot easier—just throw them in a washer and hang them up. Did it right here. After every game. Still do. The players liked them, too, liked them a lot better'n the wool ones. Everybody gets a clean uniform each day.

But then there's other things that haven't changed much at all. Like guys wearing cabbage leaves soaked in ammonia water inside their caps on real hot days for day games. Barry Larkin still does that. He likes that. Most all of them still do it.

There's better stuff inside the dugouts nowadays depending on the weather. Handwarmers if it's cold; misters if it's hot. I remember having three our four Hibachi grills in the dugout on some cold Opening Days, and for some cold World Series games. After that Opening Day when we had them and we beat the Dodgers, Dick Wagner wanted us to take them on the road, so we did.

Nowadays, everybody wears batting gloves. Used to be just on cold days. Rusty Staub started it, wearing them all the time. Back then, I can remember running up to Western Hills Country Club, buying golf gloves, just for him. He liked the real thin ones. He'd want to feel that bat. And he'd only wear them one time. One time at bat, and he'd pitch them. Unless he got a hit, then he'd wear them again.

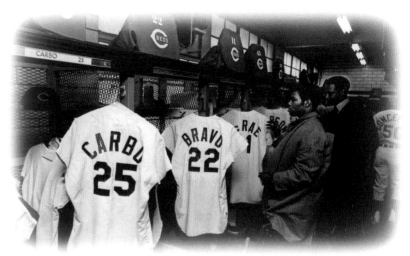

*Bernie Stowe had the Crosley Field clubhouse in order on the morning of the final opener (1970) at the hallowed Western Avenue grounds. Hal McRae (left) and Wayne Simpson check out their new "unis."*

***My big job on Opening Day back when I first started was to get the basket of fruit from the manager and carry it to the clubhouse.*** The Findlay Market people would give it to our manager. You couldn't have the manager just standing there holding a fruit basket! So, I'd take it back to the clubhouse. The manager'd say, "Here, put this out for the boys; take what you want." There weren't any pre-game spreads for the players back then. On a normal day, you'd be lucky to get an orange or something. So all that different kind of fruit, that was good stuff back then. It went pretty quick. Guys'd take a piece or two with them as they walked out the door to go home, if there was any left.

Bucky Walters was the manager when I first started. Luke Sewell was the manager when I worked the Reds clubhouse beginning in '50.

Rogers Hornsby came in '52. Oh, how the players hated him! I remember Rocky Bridges walking from the Netherland Plaza over to Crosley Field—Hornsby on one side of the street, and Bridges on the other, 10 paces behind him. Wouldn't walk with him.

I wasn't too fond of Hornsby, either. He wanted me to pitch him batting practice. Every day, early in the day, about one in the afternoon. He asked me to throw to him. Hell, I couldn't throw worth a damn, but I tried. He made me pitch off the mound, not from 50 feet away like they do today. "You throw like a girl!" he'd yell at me. Man, he could hit that ball.

My favorite player was Jim Maloney. He was a fun guy. He lived off Colerain Avenue. In the wintertime, we'd go out to his house and eat steaks. They had a butcher-friend—"Shafe" Schaefer—he owned this butcher shop, Schaefer Meats, and he'd age these steaks. Wow! Maloney was a bundle of laughs. And he was good to the rookies.

I got along well with George Foster, liked him a lot. He wanted me to come up to the dugout, and talk to his bat, "Black Beauty." So, I'd do that. (*Bernie adjusts the pitch of his voice to a high-toned squeal*): "C'mon, baby! Now don't let him down!" Foster gave me a trip to Hawaii after he hit those 52 home runs in 1977.

*Kevin Mitchell was a character. Ol' Mitch wanted to buy my T-Bird. He said, "Oooooo, that sumbitch is cleaner than the Board of Health!" He wanted me to sell it to him right now.*

When Mitchell first joined us, the first season, he heard one of the players got a Mercedes. So Mitch calls up the dealer: "Bring two of them up here—let me see which one I want." And he looks at them and says, "Yeah, I'll take both of them." That's when you know you're making too much money.

Craziest, toughest, player I ever saw wasn't Billy Martin; it was Pete Whisenant, one of our outfielders in the late '50s. He'd fight at the drop of a hat. I remember one time when he'd been out of baseball for a couple of years. He got in a fight with seven guys, and knocked out three of them. Tommy Helms said, "I ain't even gonna turn around. I know who it is." Crazy Pete.

Birdie Tebbetts was a great guy. I was the batboy. He'd tell me every year, "Go get a suit made for yourself and give me the bill." Every year! I decided one year, I ain't gonna do that. I'm just gonna get a sport coat, and save Birdie some money. When he saw the bill, he said, "I told you, "Get a suit! I want you to look good." So I went to Ramundo Tailors. I got a suit for $85. Birdie sees the bill and say, "I thought I told you, 'Get a goddamn suit!'" I said, "I did!" He said, "Well, you got a bargain then!" And he'd write out the check.

"Bernie, get yourself a suit!" Manager Birdie Tebbetts gave his young clubhouse boy, Bernie Stowe, new duds every year.

He took losing hard, though. They all do. Birdie'd lock himself in his office sometimes with a bottle of hooch. And you'd hear him screaming in there.

Fred Hutchinson, he liked the scotch. There used to be a saloon right across from the hotel in Tampa. The White Rose Bar. Whitey Wietelmann, and Reggie Otero and Hutch'd be in there, and they'd start arguing about something, like stealing bases. They'd get the bartender to give them a towel, and they'd lay it on the floor, and they'd be slidin' into each other *in the bar!* The next day, you'd seen the four of them, Hutch and the three coaches, walk in the clubhouse, and man were they hung over!

*I was there the night Hutch got so mad he threw baseballs through the window of the clubhouse at Crosley Field.* Broke the window. He told the players, "I'm coming back in here in 10 minutes, and you'd better be gone!" The players never showered or anything. Chesty Evans and I said to each other, "Oh, man, do that more often!" We got out of there two hours early that night!

Dick Wagner was somethin'. One Opening Day at Riverfront, in the '70s, we had a ballboy down each line, just like we always do. There was a smash down the line. Oh boy! The kid made a *hell* of a play. Only one problem: it was a fair ball! The umpire had to rule it a ground-rule double. Wagner calls me up: "After the game, bring those kids up here—all of them that's gonna be on the field." Wagner tells the kid, "Son, you're lucky you're still gonna be with us. But from this day on, if anybody does it, they're outta here."

Well, the very next game, oh baby. Another great catch. This time by the other kid, down the other line. *Fair ball!* Wagner says to me, "I ain't gonna talk to them sumbitches no more!" Two days in a row!

After that second one, the kid says to me, "I won't see you no more, Mr. Stowe. But thanks for everything. I don't know what I was thinking." The kid took his stuff home, and the next day, Wagner says to me, "Where in the hell's the ballboy at?" I said, "He heard what you said: 'One more of these and you're gone.'" Dick said, "Oh, no. Go call that kid. Have him come back." And I did.

Funny thing about Dick. He could be tough, but he knew how to operate a ballpark. Six months after he was fired, the people under him wished he was back. They said what a prick he was, all the while he was here, but he was gone a half a year and guys were screaming, "Bring him back!" He used to raise hell about keeping things clean. He used to go around the concession stands before they opened up the gates. And he'd check the hot dogs, and see if they were from the night before. Ice cream, whatever. You name it, he checked it. He knew how to run the field. But, when he got the GM job, well that was too much.

Lou Piniella was a character, too. We had turkey in the clubhouse one night. I had it catered. Had the guy in there carving it. We were ahead. Then we wind up blowing the son-of-a-bitchin' game. *Lou takes the bleeping turkey off the carving board and throws it off the wall. It hit and bounced right back to where it'd been sitting! And Lou—he's all worked up and agitated—he just stops and looks at that thing. He says, "I'll be a son of a bitch! I couldn't do that again in a million years!"*

I tell you, there's a million stories from all those years.

You know, there might be a tendency to think Opening Day has changed for the players. But that's not what I see. There are high fives and hugs in the clubhouse, and then they'll come out and do it again on the bench. Opening Day has always been special—from back in the '40s, all the way up to today. There's electricity. You see tears coming to players' eyes. Mostly, it's with a kid, a rookie, who didn't expect to make it. National anthem, he's standing out there on the line and you can see it.

You know, on Opening Day, there's a lot of applause for the players who were born and raised here. But then when they start playin', and they screw up a little bit, the boobirds are after them. Herm Wehmeier, that almost made me cry. The way people used to treat him. Oh, gawd, it was terrible. It'd be a 110 degrees in the shade, and he'd wear a plain jacket on the field to cover up his number. He'd even wear sunglasses, even just going from the bench to the bullpen. Oh, geesh. They'd still be booing him. That's the difference: they love you on Opening Day, especially if you're from here. But, man, if you screw up, you're gonna pay. When the bell sounds, you'd better perform.

## Mrs. Bernie (Priscilla) Stowe

I was in high school when I went to my first Opening Day. That would have been in the early '50s. I was a teenager, and I used to get seats in the bleachers. Oh my gosh! I would never let my teenager go there! It was a very cold day, and there were guys who were drunk and people set fires in the aisles to keep warm!

I didn't miss an Opening Day until I began having kids. From the time Rick was three or four years old, I used to take them all with me to the game. But I had one child, Jeff, who was born April 2nd. And I suppose you're wondering if Bernie might have missed that opener?

Are you kidding me? Bernie doesn't miss Opening Day—he never missed anything! Anyway, Jeff was born on Easter Sunday that year. That made three kids under age three, so *I* didn't make it to Opening Day that year.

## Mrs. Ted (Eleanor) Kluszewski

*Eleanor Kluszewski, the wife of the late slugger Ted Kluszewski, moved to Cincinnati in the late 1940s when her husband became a member of the Reds. She still makes her home in Greater Cincinnati and saw her husband's statue dedicated at Great American Ball Park on Opening Day, 2003.*

Opening Day in Cincinnati in the 1950s felt like Easter Sunday. The wives would call one another and ask, "What are you going to wear?" We'd dress up special and make sure everything was in order. It wasn't just us wives—*everybody* got dressed up for Opening Day. You always wanted to put your best foot forward. My favorite part of the day was just the feel of it, the start of the new season, *Opening* Day.

It was always a special day for Ted and all of the players—"All right! Let's get the season started!"— and everybody felt the same way about it. We couldn't wait.

*On Opening Day at Crosley especially, it was like the ballpark pulled the whole city into it. There were people everywhere—in the windows of the factory buildings, inside the fences, wherever they could squeeze them.*

Crosley Field got all dressed up for Opening Day. I don't remember if it ever rained on Opening Day—you know, rained hard enough for a rain delay—but many a time I remember the water being up over my shoes. There weren't all these fancy rooms for the players' families like there are today. We'd just stand under the stands until it stopped raining.

After the game, we'd go to Olsner's in Ft. Wright—their specialty was fried chicken—or Mecklenburg's where they had great hamburgers. We'd go there with Roy and Jo McMillan and sometimes Herm and Sue Wehmeier, and whoever else wanted to go. On special occasions, we'd go to the Lookout House or Beverly Hills. We always had a lot of fun. I still stay in touch with Jo and Sue. We try to take a trip together every year—they're both in Texas; Jo is in Bonham, Sue is in Plano.

*Ted and Eleanor Kluszewski in 1955, the year Klu debuted his cut-off sleeve look.*

I think people treated Opening Day really special. They still do, but it's different. Back then, the game itself was more of the focus. When we were first—when we had the first game of the major league season to ourselves here in Cincinnati—it was going to have a special quality to it. Now that we're not the first, now that we're not the only game in the country that day, I think it's made a dent in the flavor of the day. And that's all because of TV and the money. Now, it's Opening Day and it's a social thing. Now it's Opening Day and "I must get tickets." It's not about seeing the game—it's about *being* there.

The ball club has done a good job of incorporating the history and tradition of the team into the new park, what with the statues and the murals and the Machine Room and the museum that will be. But one thing I'd like to see them bring back is a float or two and a wagon from the Findlay Market parade. Let them on the field for Opening Day before the game like they used to. Not having that, takes away from the pageantry of the day. I'm sure some of that relates to security, but maybe as time goes on they will be able to restore some of that. That was always a big part of Opening Day—it was the people's holiday.

## Mrs. Roy (Jody) McMillan

*Jody McMillan's husband, Roy, played shortstop for the Reds from 1951 to 1960 and was a two-time All Star. The McMillans married in 1952, and Jody's first Cincinnati Opening Day was in 1953. Roy McMillan passed away in 1997.*

Opening Day was very exciting. There were a lot of great things about it. The players wives and families wanted to get there early for pre-game activities. We'd get all dressed up, get on over to Crosley Field. No shorts, or anything like they're wearing—or should I say *not* wearing—today!

Eleanor Kluszewski had told me what a big deal Opening Day was. She was the nicest thing to me—a real welcoming committee! She made me feel right at home. I wore high heels and this wonderful, springtime-type dress, black with shortsleeves, and I thought I looked like a real chick! I wore a long coat, too, but I was still cold. Eleanor would pick me up in their red T-Bird convertible! But we could never put that top down on Opening Day. It was too cold!

I don't think I missed an Opening Day in the eight years I was there. They used to have a little band, a strolling band, that would play jazz and Dixieland music, and they always had a band on the field before the game.

*The opener was always a very meaningful event to me, and to Roy. He was always very conscientious about how he presented himself, so, of course, nothing was out of place on Opening Day.*

*Jo and Roy McMillan attended the same high school in Bonham, Texas and were married in 1952, a year after Roy joined the Reds.*

He always shined his shoes himself, and made sure his uniform was just right. He was that way all the time, so Opening Day was just the first day of it. He got excited about Opening Day; he might even get a little nervous. He wanted to impress the fans. He wanted to do the best he could. You know, the Reds didn't win every game in those days! The players were all happy to be there, because they were all on one-year contracts. Opening Day meant they were in the big leagues for another season, making a living playing baseball.

Opening Day, 1953 would have been Roy's first Opening Day. He was 22 years old. That was my first Opening Day, too. The previous summer, my girlfriend and I drove to Cincinnati for the All-Star break. We drove Roy's car—a '51 Pontiac, dark green—all the way from Bonham, Texas, to Cincinnati, Ohio, on a two-lane road! A day or two later, my parents and my brother came in, and we went to some games. That was my first time seeing a major league park!

Opening Day and the major league life was unreal to me. I hadn't really known what baseball was until after Roy came along. I didn't even know where he was on the field! I didn't know where the shortstop played! There wasn't a baseball team at the high school in Bonham. Roy played football, and ran track and played tennis. He played softball in the summertime.

He was two years ahead of me in high school. He had a girlfriend. I thought they were the cutest things there ever was! I didn't dream Roy would ever wind up having anything to do with me. I was pudgy, and wore these old, big, thick glasses, and you know how kids put a stigma on things like that. After Roy's second minor-league season, he came home from playing baseball and he came up to the drugstore on Halloween night. We walked around the town square. Nobody had cars. And after that, we started seeing each other. He found out that a girl wearing glasses wasn't so bad!

As an athlete, he was very scrappy and not very big. He was a competitor. He wanted to win no matter what. During his senior year in high school, he attended a Reds tryout camp in McKinney, about 35 miles from Bonham. I believe it was Reds scout Jack Knott who ran the camp. Roy heard one of the scouts say, "I think he looks like a natural athlete." So, they signed him. After he graduated from high school, they started him off in Class D.

Here's a Western Union telegram from Toots Shor, the famous New York restaurateur. It's dated April 15, 1958—that would have been Opening Day. It's addressed to Cincinnati Redlegs, Crosley Field. "To Roy McMillan—Good luck, Roy. I hope this will be your best year." And its from Toots Shor. I didn't even know who Toots Shor was until I got to Cincinnati. I remember that it was very impressive to me that Roy knew Toots Shor.

Our last Opening Day in Cincinnati would have been 1960. Roy was traded to the Braves before the '61 season. After Roy was traded I stayed in Texas. So, I never did get to see an Opening Day in Milwaukee.

# Gene Bennett

*Bennett, who has been in professional baseball since 1952 when he signed with the Reds as an outfielder, began scouting for Cincinnati in 1959.*

I came up as a scout under scouting director Bill McKechnie, Jr., and then Jim McLaughlin and then Joe Bowen. I usually don't get to see Opening Day. Scouts are on the road, scouting for new talent or scouting the team your team is going to play next. I've seen a lot of *other* teams' openers, doing advance scouting, but I've only seen a handful of our own.

I believe Opening Day is like the title of that book, *Great Expectations*. Great expectations for the team and for the individual players, especially for the new guys. Fans read the articles in the newspaper throughout the wintertime—the hot stove league—and then spring training starts. Fans see the first photos from spring training on the covers of their newspaper—the first day of workouts in Florida—and then they see the early spring flowers popping out of the ground and that is when people know that Opening Day is right around the corner, even if they aren't baseball fans.

*Everybody likes springtime! Everything starts greening up, getting ready to bloom, and baseball's getting ready to bloom, too, getting ready for another season.*

When it gets around to Opening Day, I think everybody gets all wound up—we're ready to go, we're ready to do our thing now, today's the day. Everybody's wondering how the "new guys" are going to do. And as a scout, of course, that's your job, finding the new guys.

I remember when Frank Robinson first came to the big leagues with the Reds. In the eyes of the fans, the new kid is the kid who just came from no place. And the fans can't wait to be there, to see him play his first game. Of course, the scout has seen him play a *lot* of games. The scout goes way back with the kid.

And Gary Nolan, when he was young, people couldn't wait to see him get on that mound. They've heard about him, and they've read about him, and now's their chance to go there and *see* him do his thing. And, then, forever and ever, as long as people live, they'll say, "You know what? I saw that guy play his first game. I saw the first game he ever played in the big leagues."

How often do you get to see somebody get their first chance—in *any* walk of life? People want to be there to see it. The kid's getting a chance to fulfill a life-long dream: to play in the big leagues. Fans can identify with that. It's called "opportunity." There's nothing purer than that. *Here's your chance kid, no strings attached. No politics, no nothin'; what can you do with it?* People pay to see that; they love that.

*People want to know, they want to see: "Can he run? Can he throw? Can he play the Crosley Field terrace?" That's what Opening Day is.*

You know, in 1970, we had Don Gullett, right out of high school. I signed Gullett. Cliff Alexander and I did. Gullett lived just across the Ohio River from me. I lived in Portsmouth and Don was from Lynn, Kentucky. I had Don in tryout camp when he was in the eighth grade. I saw him pitch all the way through high school. He's from down in the mountains, and nobody knew him at first. And those are all the things that go into Opening Day.

I know Don's dad. I took him along to the airport in Huntington, West Virginia, that day in the spring of 1969 after we signed Don. Don was headed for the Northern League and his dad watched that plane go as far as you could see it go. The kid had probably never been away from home his whole life, and after that thing got out of sight, his dad asked me, "How quick do you think he can pitch at Crosley Field?" And I said, "Right now. *Tonight.*"

He's the one kid, in all my years, that I really believe could've gone right out of high school and pitched in the big leagues. He could throw hard. You didn't have radar guns then, but if you did, he probably threw right at a hundred. I'd go see him play in high school and his coach would say, "He's only going to pitch five innings today." He'd pitch five innings. He'd have 15 strikeouts; they wouldn't so much as foul off a pitch. He could throw hard, he could throw strikes, and every now and then he'd throw you a curveball that was just out of this world.

He spent 60 days in the minors, and that was it. When he came home that fall, the Reds brass had a meeting and they decided to bring him to spring training, because you always need extra players. And I told our guys, "I know you're inviting him there as an extra player, but you might get surprised. He might make the team." And he did! And he never went back down.

The scouts that sign a kid don't usually get to see him break in. But you know they're there, because the organization calls and tells you. I didn't get to see Paul O'Neill break in; I didn't see Chris Sabo, or Dave Tomlin. I saw Jeff Russell's first game. We called him up about the middle of the summer. And I think he went into the seventh with a no-hitter. Afternoon game. And he was only 20.

You've got a pretty good idea when you sign them, if they're going to make it. "Gully" was a can't miss. Larkin was a can't miss. If Barry would've signed out of high school, he'd have been in the big leagues before he was 21 years old. O'Neill was a can't miss guy, even though he was a pitcher. When I signed him, I said, "We think you can hit." So, we signed him as an outfielder and he was up about the time he was 21.

Opening Day! There's nothing like it. Cincinnati has the parade that is really special. It's a special thing. And they line up forever and ever to get through there. It's a big history thing. Man, I'm ready for Opening Day *now*! Let's go get 'em!

# Russ Nixon

*Russ Nixon, a native of Elizabethtown in western Hamilton County, played 12 years in the major leagues as a catcher (1957–68), all in the American League (Cleveland, Boston and Minnesota). In 1976, Sparky Anderson brought him in as a coach with the Big Red Machine, and in 1982 and 1983, Nixon managed the Reds. As a Pirates coach, he christened new ballparks on Opening Day in Pittsburgh against the Reds in 2001 and in Cincinnati in 2003. Nixon didn't get to his first Reds game until he was in the eighth grade. It wasn't an Opening Day game, but he still associates it with Opening Day.*

My grandfather, William Nixon, was the one who was a player. He probably could've played pro ball, but his father had work for him to do on the farm. He was one of the best athletes in the area at 18 years old. He was a catcher, one of the best semipro players around. He could do everything: run, throw, hit. He'd play on weekends. That was back when every town had a team. New Haven, and all those towns in eastern Indiana—Lawrenceburg, Aurora, Dillsboro—all had some pretty good athletes. And that's the way, we grew up, too: on a farm, playing ball whenever we got the chance.

In order to have a team out in that area, we had to consolidate four schools. It was just me and my twin brother, Roy, from Elizabethtown, and even by combining the four schools, we only had a total of nine players—just enough for a team.

We went up to Bridgetown to play a game when we were 13 years old. We were in the eighth grade. *The Bridgetown team had uniforms; we didn't. We just wore jeans with belts. I never liked them, so I wore bib overalls.*

They got to looking at us like we were something from another planet, but after the third inning they thought we were pretty good, because we had them down about 10 to nothing. And that's where Joe Hauck first saw us—he was the manager for Bentley Post. After our freshman year at Harrison High School, we transferred to Western Hills High so we could play Bentley Post American Legion baseball.

Other than Paul Nohr, who was the coach at Western Hills forever, Bentley Post was really special in our baseball foundation. We were in the national finals in '51, and won it in '52, and that put us in the picture to be scouted, and Roy and I signed with Cleveland in '53, when

*Two of the youngsters Gene Bennett watched move through the organization in the mid-1960s were Johnny Bench (left) and Gary Nolan.*

we graduated.

Our dad took us to our first Reds game in '48 or '49, when we were still going to school in E'town. Kluszewski was playing back then. They had all those big guys, including Hank Sauer, and it was very exciting for us, it being our first time ever in Crosley Field.

I can't remember this one player's name, but he had to be a bench player, because he came in to pinch-hit. And he had a new pair of shoes on—we were sitting close enough where we could see them. *We'd never seen spikes before! And I remember saying, "Some day I'd like to have a pair of shoes like that!"* That might be a corny thing, but I sure do remember it well. And it's something I've always associated with Opening Day, because everything is always so new that day.

The other thing I always associate with Opening Day is new uniforms. When I was with Cleveland, we didn't have fitted uniforms, and nobody else did either, except Boston. You had to make do with what you got. Despite that, the major league uniform sure felt awful good to you. I have to laugh, because I didn't know I didn't have it so good until got traded from Cleveland to Boston in 1960. Boston had their own uniform-maker—Tim McAuliffe. He actually tailored the uniforms. I went from wearing a uniform about that thick *(Nixon holds his index finger and thumb about a quarter-inch apart)* to about this thick *(holding his fingers a sixteenth-inch apart)*. I mean, my gosh, it was like going from a 1947 Chevrolet to a 1995 Cadillac!

Those are two things I'll always associate with Opening Day: new uniforms and great shoes.

# Jim Greengrass

*Greengrass played four seasons with the Reds, from 1952 to 1955. On Opening Day, 1954, Greengrass tied a major league record with four doubles, all landing in the temporary seats in the outfield.*

I loved Crosley Field. It was the most spectacular place I've ever played or ever seen. The fans were everywhere. On Opening Day, they roped off the terrace from the left-field corner all the way to right-center.

There were chairs behind the ropes all along the outfield wall except in left field, because the terrace was really steep there. People would just sit on the embankment out there, and the seats would start in left-center, in front of the scoreboard. There were also fans on top of the center-field fence, and in the windows of the buildings out on the street beyond the outfield walls. There were fans *everywhere.*

It was a great ballpark, very friendly, and Gus Bell and I would have the best time with the fans, because we'd warm up out there along the left-field line in front of the box seats, and we knew everybody out there and we'd talk with them and ask about their cousins and their aunts and uncles—seemed like we knew most all of them by their first names.

*I was the left fielder and I will tell you, Opening Day was the easiest day of the year for me because I didn't have to climb up and down that terrace!* With it being roped off behind you, anything hit over your head was probably going in there, and it was a ground-rule double. I was lucky, because I never had a play on Opening Day where I crashed into the seats and ended up with my head in some pretty lady's lap.

The rest of the time it was pretty rough. Our manager—Rogers Hornsby—would run me up and down that hill 100 times every morning to get used to it. He'd say "There's only one way to learn to play it," and he'd get his fungo bat and a bucket of balls and off we'd go. I got to where I was pretty good going up and down the terrace, and knowing which balls to chase and which to let carom off those solid brick walls.

One time—not Opening Day—Hank Sauer of the Cubs hit a ball to the left-center field wall. I went to the bottom of the terrace, caught the ricochet off the wall, and all in one motion wheeled and threw a strike to Johnny Temple at second base. Hank, who thought for sure he was going to have a double, didn't watch the ball come off the wall and just sort of strolled toward second base. Before Sauer even got there, Johnny held out the ball and said, "Hey, Hank, look what I got!" The umpire almost wound up having to throw Hank out of the game, Hank was so mad. He swore that Johnny had pulled a ball out of his pocket. That Hank was somethin'. Not fast afoot, but man he could hit. He was one of those big, raw-boned fellas, all arms and legs. I swear, if he'd grown a beard, he'd looked just like ol' Abe Lincoln.

*Every home game—including Opening Day—I'd walk to the ballpark with Roy McMillan or Rocky Bridges from the Piedmont Hotel on Fountain Square, about a couple miles.* We made that walk every day we lived there, unless it was raining. If the weather was bad, we'd call a cab or have one of the other guys who had a car pick us up.

First, though, we went down and ate breakfast at Stouffer's Cafeteria, downtown. We'd go back to the hotel, answer what mail we could, and walk out to the ballpark.

At times, I'd just walk out on the square. I don't recall a harsh word ever being said. I met a lot of people. There was a lot of activity on the square on Opening Day. I'd sit on the bench and talk to people. There'd always be people there on Opening Day. There was really a buzz in the air that day. You knew something was going on. People'd say hello, ask us how we were doing. *Go get them today. Good luck today.* Things like that. A lot of people didn't recognize me at first as much as they did later on.

We'd head for the ballpark, walk through the West End, and people'd talk and holler, and we'd stop and talk. There was no racial tension of any kind. We saw Ezzard Charles several times—you know, the fighter, the heavyweight champion—sitting out on the steps, and we'd say, "Hey, Champ! How's it going?" He'd ask us about the game the night before, or that day's game. He was a nice fellow, and pretty knowledgeable about baseball. He knew all sports. He was a heck of an athlete, and probably could have played anything.

In '54 Chuck Harmon and Nino Escalera made the club. Nino was Puerto Rican, Chuck was African-American. Nino got in the game first. Escalera was the first guy of color to play for the Reds; Harmon was the first African-American. Which of those two broke the Reds' color line? Escalera. That's the way we felt about it.

*Perhaps Jim Greengrass (left) was sharing some of his Opening Day secrets with Gus Bell in this 1955 spring training photo. Greengrass set a Reds Opening Day record—and tied a major league record—with his four doubles in the '54 opener.*

We'd get to the ballpark at 10 in the morning, and Hornsby would already be there, sitting in the dugout, waiting for us. He'd work with Roy McMillan and Rocky Bridges, the infielders, because Hornsby had been a second baseman and he would work with them on the double-play, things like that.

*Everybody remembers those four doubles I hit in the '54 opener. I hit all four of those balls good— three of them line drives off the left-center field wall that would have been doubles whether the area in front had been roped off or not.* They were legitimate doubles, and the outfielders would have had a tough time stopping me from jogging into second base after they had played the carom. The ball I hit to left, down the line, was a fly ball, and if a guy knew how to play the terrace, he might have caught it. But I don't think it would have been caught even if there weren't fans in there, because it hit just in front of the wall and dropped into the fans. The left fielder would have had to climb up the terrace and catch it, and that wasn't likely.

I didn't realize at the time those four doubles tied a a major league record. Those kinds of things just weren't brought up much back then. Just like I never knew I was the first rookie to have 20 HR and 100 RBI, or that Gus Bell and I were the first Cincinnati Redlegs outfielders to drive in 100 runs in the same year in '53. I never knew about the 100 RBIs in a rookie season until Mike Piazza broke my record a few years ago. My record lasted 40 years and I never even knew I had it!

I was watching the Braves opener against Cincinnati on TV from Atlanta a few years ago and Javy Lopez had two doubles and was going for a third and the Braves announcer, Skip Caray said, "Hey, we got a buddy, Jim Greengrass, in Marietta, Georgia, and he's got four!"

Opening Day in Cincinnati was a wonderful, friendly day. And baseball was about all the talk you heard that day. I was very nervous before the game, but I was that way a lot before big games. The greatest thing for me, of all the activities around Opening Day in Cincinnati, was going out with the ball team to visit the Mason's Burn Center on Sunday, the day before the game. We'd bring bats and balls and gloves and spend half a day out there. That was a real thrill for all of us. It made us realize how lucky we were, healthy and fortunate to be playing a boy's game. And here these kids were. We cheered them up, and they were happy to see us. It made us pretty humble. It made you want to get out on the field and rip and tear.

# Chuck Harmon

*Harmon was the Reds' first African-American player. He made his major league debut in Milwaukee on April 17, 1954—four days after Opening Day.*

I have an Opening Day story for you. But it didn't happen in

Cincinnati. It happened in Tulsa, back in '53. I was coming up through the minors. Back then, Tulsa was the Reds' top farm club.

I had a big hit on Opening Day—drove in the winning run, won the game—so I was pretty popular with the fans, because they were like any fans, they wanted to win and I was helping the club win ball games, and it started with Opening Day.

May comes around and school's out, and my wife and daughter joined me in Tulsa. I left tickets at the ballpark for them. When my wife came in, she told the ticket clerk, "Mrs. Harmon," and they handed her the tickets. Nobody gave it any thought. My wife is light-skinned, blonde and about four different nationalities—white and black and French and Indian. My daughter is not dark-skinned; she's about my skin color. They went to sit with the other players' families. They walked in and the ticket-taker didn't blink, just ripped their tickets and gave half back to them. *But then another usher saw my daughter and said she can't come in to the white section, she's black.*

And the other one says, "No, she isn't—look at her skin color." So, anyway, the usher didn't know what to do, so he let them in to sit with the other players' families. Anyway, there's a little bit of a holdup getting them seated, and meanwhile, everybody's wondering: "What in the world is going on?"

After the game was over is when I found out about it. The GM at Tulsa called me in. I got upstairs and saw my wife and daughter. The GM asked me a lot of questions, and he finally said, "I don't know what we're going to do." My wife was caught in the middle, because if she were to sit in the black section, the other blacks would say, "What's that white person doing in here?" And, obviously, the club didn't feel they could just let my wife and daughter sit with the white players' families, so something had to be done, but they didn't know what.

Well, the next day he gets Reds GM Gabe Paul on the phone. Gabe knows my wife from having visited the different ballparks when he was coming in to see the minor-leaguers play. There's some talk about shipping me out to another minor-league club, but Gabe says, "No, no, no. He's going to play *there*; he's not going anywhere."

Besides, the Tulsa GM doesn't dare send me out, anyway, because I got the big hit on Opening Day in front of a big crowd, and the fans like me because I'm helping the club win ball games. And my wife says to the Tulsa GM, "Look, I don't have to come to these games. It's my *husband's* job, not my job." She's thinking, and I'm thinking, "Let's just get to the major leagues." After all, that's the goal, isn't it? And that's pretty much the way we left it.

One day, they did come back out, and they didn't want to let them in the white section, so my wife and daughter sat in the black section down the third-base line. My wife told me the conditions weren't good, that there was an outhouse under the stands and it was dirty. She asked one of the concessionaires for some water, and he stuck his hand into the big metal tub of ice where they kept the pop and he scooped up a handful of ice and put it in a cup and handed it to her, and she said, "I'm not going to drink that!"

And, so mostly, she stayed home; she'd go just every once in a while.

I made the big club the following season. Tulsa wasn't any problem for me. That was just the way it was, you wanted to get to the big club, because you knew it'd be better.

When I got to Cincinnati, I knew some of the Reds players, I had come up with some of them through the minors. There were about five to six guys at Tulsa that year who came up in '54, including Nino Escalera. That always brings up a question I get because Escalera was a dark-skinned Puerto Rican, and he made his first appearance just before I did up in Milwaukee. [*Pinch hitter Escalera batted in the seventh inning on April 17, 1954; Harmon pinch-hit right after him.*]

So who was first? Me or Escalera? Whenever people ask me about it, the way I distinguish it is: "I was the first African-American; Nino was the first black." People ask, "Well, who was *first*? Who broke the color line?" I say, "Nino." "Who was the first African-

*Chuck Harmon and his family endured racial harassment in the minors and in the majors in the mid-1950s. Harmon was the first African-American to play for the Reds.*

American?" "Me." I don't know what difference it makes; but for history's sake, they might as well get it right.

I was in the Negro Leagues with the Indianapolis Clowns under an assumed name for a few days in 1947. I can't even remember if I ever got into a game. But I remember Goose Tatum—later he became famous playing with the Harlem Globetrotters—because I rode the bus with him. He took me under his wing. He liked me, because he knew I played basketball. Goose gave me the alias, "Charlie Fine." He didn't want me to lose my college eligibility.

Harmon was honored prior to the 1992 opener at Riverfront Stadium.

Anyway, I got along great with the Reds players. Guys are guys. They'll ask another guy about you. "Hey, you know this guy, don't you?" and the guy'll say, "Yeah!" "Well, what's he like?" You know, not because you're black, but just because they want to get acquainted. "Oh, he's a good guy." And they see how well the other guys treat you and then they seek you out, and they talk to you, talk to you about this and that, and now you've got another friend.

And that's how it went with the new guys I hadn't met, guys like Gus Bell and Wally Post and Ted Kluszewski.

Bell and Post and I, since were were outfielders, we played catch together and fooled around on the field. And Ed Bailey and Bell and Post and Matt Batts and Roy McMillan, we'd play cards. We'd play on the train all the time. Kluszewski would do that, too.

These guys like talking sports, and they know I played basketball on a national championship runner-up team at Toledo, was an All-American, and that becomes a topic of conversation. Back then, most baseball players were being signed at 16, 17 and 18, so they were intrigued to hear I went to college and they wanted to know more about it.

*I didn't have any problems with fans at Crosley Field. If I was being called any names, I didn't hear them. But I received a death threat when I played in a game in New York at the Polo Grounds in 1955.*

I pinch-hit in the 7th or 8th inning—that was a pretty rare thing with the lineup we had; usually, *I* was being pinch-hit for—and I broke up Jim Hearns' no-hitter with a broken-bat single. I got a threatening letter a week later from a Giants fan in New York. He said he was going to shoot me when the Reds came back to New York, because I broke up Hearns' no-hitter. The letter sort of tickled me, because I wasn't one of our big sluggers, and yet I'd been singled out.

I gave the letter to the trainer, and he gave it to Gabe Paul. When we went back to New York, two or three weeks later, I went to check in and was told, "Those guys over there, they want to know, 'Who's Chuck Harmon?'" Well, they were with the FBI. They just wanted to keep an eye out for me. When I got to the ballpark, they were at the ballpark, too. In the clubhouse, Bell and Post said to me, "You wanna go out now and play some catch?" I said, "Yeah!"

So we walked down the steps of the clubhouse at the Polo Grounds which was way out there in center field, beyond the fence, about 500 feet from home plate. We walked onto the field. And then Gus says, *"Jesus Christ, Wally, what are we doing out here? Chuck is supposed to get shot today!"* And they took off running for the dugout. But they came back and they were laughing. *Gotcha!*

Anyway, the death threat was reported in the New York papers. I was asked about it, and I said, "The Giants fans are really going to be mad if this guy shoots me, because then we'd have to put in somebody who can *really* hit the ball!" This is back when we had that lineup full of sluggers.

I've heard and read what Jackie Robinson said about Cincinnati and St. Louis being the roughest towns for black players, that there wasn't very much for them to do here. I didn't go downtown much. I lived in Avondale—on Goss Road, on a little street off Victory Parkway, near Xavier University. I invited Jackie up to the neighborhood on a Saturday after the game in '54 or '55. Some close friends came by to meet him. I didn't want to turn it into an open house and overwhelm him, but it was a good opportunity and Jackie got to enjoy a home-cooked meal. We had a great time.

## Frank Robinson

*Hall of Famer Robinson has been a player, manager, coach and administrator with Major League Baseball since he broke in with the Reds in 1956. He started in 10 openers in Cincinnati. His eight Opening Day home runs, including three with the Reds, are a major league record. He was elected to the Hall of Fame in 1982, and his statue was unveiled on the Crosley Terrace in front of Great American Ball Park in 2003.*

I was signed by the Cincinnati Reds almost by mistake. What I mean by that is that Bobby Mattick—the scout who scouted me and eventually signed me for the Reds—was working for the Chicago White Sox well into my senior year in high school in Oakland.

For some reason, the White Sox let him go and he started scouting for Cincinnati just before I graduated. Mattick had been so important in a short period of time ñ in my life and treated my family so well. He treated me not as a future ballplayer but as a human being and he looked at me that way. Because of all that, there was no doubt in my mind that once he signed with the Reds, I was going to sign with the Reds, too, even though for the longest time I had envisioned myself being a Chicago White Sox.

The money was pretty good, too: $3,500. I was loyal to him, and he was loyal to me, and I became a Cincinnati Red. And I'm happy that I did.

That was in '53 when I signed. I didn't make the majors until '56; I was 20. I don't remember much about the trip north from spring training and Tampa in '56, but I do remember stopping in Chattanooga, where we played an exhibition game. I think it was on a Sunday. Gabe Paul called me off the field. He was sitting up in the stands, before batting practice. He said, "I just want to congratulate you, Frank. You've made the team, and you can sign your contract." Not until then did I know I had made the ball club.

The year before, I didn't know if I had a chance to make it, even though I kept hearing that I did. It was my first invite to spring training. But I couldn't throw. I started to feel it at the end of the '54 season, in Columbia, South Carolina. Every time I would throw, I felt like someone was sticking a pin in my shoulder. I mentioned it to the manager down there, and he say, "Nah, there's probably nothing wrong with you." In those days, the mentality was to "throw it out," to throw the soreness out of the arm.

I went to winter ball that year in Puerto Rico, and on a cold, rainy night in San Juan, I made a throw from right field and my arm felt like it does when it falls asleep, you know, those little pins-and-needles in there. Gabe Paul was at the ballpark, and I went to him and said, "I can't throw. My arm's hurting." That was the end of winter ball for me, and it carried over into the spring.

I went to 12 different doctors over the winter, and every one of them had a different opinion. *"There's nothing wrong; it's all in your head,"* to *"You have a bone spur in there and you won't be able to throw again until you have an operation."* In those days, cutting on your arm was usually the end of your career. Operations on your arm if you were a baseball player were taboo. I battled it just about all of '55, and finally it started to come back a little better at the end of '55.

When I came to spring training in '56, I had to work it out. I hurt it a couple times throwing. Birdie Tebbetts—he was the manager—got mad at me one time. I was in the lineup, and he says, "Just go out there and get your hits—and don't throw!" I said, "Birdie, if a ball comes out there, I *got* to throw!" And sure enough, here comes a ball, and I picked it up at the wall and fired it back in. I had to come out of the game.

Birdie got all over me: "I *told* you not to throw!" "Yeah, but Birdie, that's just *instinct*. I'm not gonna just pick it up and *roll* it in!" My arm bothered me off and on that whole spring and two months into the season. It never was the same. I had a pretty good arm before I hurt it, but I compensated by charging the ball harder, and getting rid of it quicker to the cutoff man. If I did that, my job was over. I'd throw it to the base if I had to. I used what I had.

The morning of that first opener—Opening Day '56—would have been like any other morning, except I wouldn't have been able to sleep in as late. I would have gotten up about 9 o'clock. I was staying at the Manse Hotel on Chapel Street in Walnut Hills. That's where the young, single black players stayed. I was the only young black player on the Reds, so I was pretty much on my own. That's why it was so nice when Vada Pinson came along in '58, because there was somebody my own age to pal around with.

My teammates were OK to me at the ballpark. It was hard for them to get to know me. In spring training, I had to stay at a home in what was called the black section of town with the other black players, and we couldn't go downtown; we couldn't go to the movies, which I liked so much. And I wasn't an outgoing person, as it was. The only time I saw my teammates was when I was at the ballpark. It wasn't that anybody treated me badly; they just didn't treat me warmly. On the field, they were fine. But, they didn't *embrace* me—let's put it that way—the way teammates do today. I think it was a combination of both skin color and that the fact I was a rookie. I didn't experience any racism in Oakland, where I

*Frank Robinson celebrated with Birdie Tebbetts following the 1956 season when Tebbetts was named "NL Manager of the Year." Robinson credited his early success in the major leagues to Birdie Tebbetts, his manager in 1956 and '57.*

grew up, but I experienced it when I got into pro ball, in the minor leagues, first in Ogden, Utah. It was quite a shock.

*The setup in spring training with the whites at the team hotel and blacks at a private home, you accepted, because that's the way it was at the time.* The setup the black guys had was probably better than what the guys had at the hotel. We lived in a private home with this lady; her last name was Felder, we called her "Ma Felder."

We each had our own room, and she cooked for us. We had three or four meats on the table, all these dishes, vegetables and all that, and we also had the run of her refrigerator. All for 35 bucks a week! Plus, we didn't have a curfew, because nobody came over there to check on us. So, yeah, we had it pretty good! Chuck Harmon was there, Marshall Bridges, Pat Scantlebury.

I remember that when things changed, and we could live at the Causeway Inn with the rest of the team, we were a little upset that the living wasn't as good as at Ma Felder's!

When we were living at Ma's, though, it was tough in a way. You really didn't get a flavor and a feel for the rest of your teammates. You were just seeing them at the ballpark, and working out with them, and then all of a sudden you've got to go back to this different area of town. You never got to have dinner with them or chat with them.

When Vada joined the club, we were all still staying with Ma Felder, and Vada joined us out there, too. By the time we moved into the Causeway Inn with the rest of the team, Vada and I were still together all the time, so even then I really didn't get to associate with my white teammates that much, anyway. It's just the way it worked out. Probably the guys that treated me the best on the club were Hal Jeffcoat and Gus Bell, and a couple of other guys. I don't want to paint a bad picture. They were all OK. There was never anything negative that I heard said. Nothing in their actions toward me was negative. It was just different back then.

On Opening Day morning, I would have walked across the street—the Manse Hotel was in two parts, one the regular hotel and the other across the street for permanent guests—and got my breakfast. Bacon and eggs, toast, orange juice. I wasn't a big eater. And then I'd go back to my room and get ready. I drove my Ford Fairlane to the ballpark. It was two-tone, green and white. I had it until '61. That's when I bought a Delta 88.

*Opening Day was very exciting for me. When the press asked me before the game how I felt, I said it was "just another game." Deep down, I knew it wasn't. It was just a defense to keep my nerves and feelings in check.*

It was very special putting that uniform on for the first time. You take your time putting it on. It felt great. I didn't get overexcited—*Oh, boy, I'm putting this uniform on for the first time!*—but it definitely hit me. All the hard work, all the dreams, all the guesswork and wondering. *I finally made it. The moment is here!* Looking back on it, I can now say that first day is the most special day in your career, no matter what else you accomplish. Because it's the start of something—you don't know what—but it's a start, and you say, "I've made it; this is it." I think every major leaguer remembers that first game. It doesn't get any better than that. *This is where I want to be.* You know you're among the best, too; that's the other thing.

And I was excited, too, because it was a full house. You looked out there in the outfield, and there were people sitting in chairs behind a rope in the outfield on the terrace and I thought, "Whoa! What's going on here?" But that's the way it was until 1960 when the Reds quit putting the chairs up. I had never experienced that sort of thing before—Opening Day in the big leagues with all the people in the stands.

*Even before I got out there, the fans were yelling, "C'mon, Frank! It's your day, Frank!" It made me feel at home.*

Except for having to learn how to play the terrace, I was comfortable right from the beginning at Crosley. It reminded me of the ballpark in Columbia, South Carolina, where I had played two minor-league seasons. In those days, minor-league parks were huge. Seeing how cozy Crosley was allowed me to feel at home. The deepest part of the ballpark was at the corner of right-center where the walls came together—the right-field bleachers and the center field wall. I think that was 390-something. Nothing in the park was 400. It was a perfect park for me. I didn't have to pull the ball. I wasn't a pull hitter when I first came up. I'd hit balls from right-center to left-center. My first six or seven years, I'd hit about eight home runs a year to right field.

*The only thing distracting for the right-handed hitter was that scoreboard that came along in '57. I liked the older, shorter scoreboard, that was still there in '56.* That new scoreboard was about 55 feet high! When I first saw it, I remember thinking, "Holy smokes!" The 10 years I played at Crosley, you had to hit it *over* the scoreboard for it to be a home run. And on top of the scoreboard was the clock, and you had to clear that, too. I remember thinking, they don't like right-handed hitters here!

A few years after I left, they drew a line from the top of fence right through the scoreboard and anything over that line was a home run. As soon as I heard that, I said, "Where was that line when I was playing?" I hit maybe 10 to 15 off that scoreboard every year. Man, that would've been nice to have that line. But that's just the way it was.

On Opening Day, in the early years, when people were sitting in front of the left-field fence, the terrace didn't come into play because anything hit in the seats was a ground-rule double. It was already a short poke to left, even without the people sitting in there—328 down the line—and I'd play just in front of the people. I felt like I was practically behind the shortstop. I knew that if anything was hit over my head, it was gone. I remember two or three balls were hit over my head that first day. Ground-rule doubles. You couldn't go in there and get them. If it was *just* over your head, you'd just stand there and sort of reach with the rope up against you, and try to make the catch. The fans would get out of your way the best they could. It was kind of fun, and it was only on Opening Day. After that, it was gone. The pitchers didn't like the overflow out there, but every hitter liked it.

The real Crosley Field didn't emerge until after Opening Day in those early years. The wall above the terrace was concrete. You had to *climb* up the terrace, and you had to *climb* down it. When you got up to the top—you know, chasing a fly ball—and you didn't get there in time or it was over your head, man, you better duck. Because that ball was coming off the concrete like a missile. The shortstop better be there, because you didn't have much of a chance to climb down the terrace and retrieve the ball.

Hal Jeffcoat, who was a pitcher and a former outfielder, helped me to with the terrace. He'd come out and hit me balls for 15 minutes a day. He took it up on his own to work with me. I had problems going up it *and* coming down it. It's hard to describe for people who didn't see it. It was steep in left field, all the way to left-center field. And where the fence came out at the left-center field corner, that's where it started to taper off a little bit. Then it ran across to right field, where it was almost nonexistent. You couldn't just back-pedal up the terrace. You had to go up it sort of sideways, picking up your feet as you went. If you didn't, that's when it would get you. And coming down, it was almost like going down a hill. You had to be careful coming down. I fell going up, and coming down. Another thing is that when you were starting up the hill, the ball was over your head, but when you got up there, some of them were at your shoetops. You very rarely would have a chance to jump at the wall to catch a ball. There were some funny plays out there.

Besides the terrace, the most distinctive thing about Crosley Field from a visual standpoint—the thing that made you know you were in Cincinnati—was the laundry just beyond the left-field wall and the Siebler Suit sign on top of the roof of the laundry. Hit the sign and win a suit. I got a few suits, not a lot. I wasn't a long-drive type guy, I was more of a line-drive type guy. Wally Post got the most suits. He hit those majestic fly balls. Those suits came in handy back then, I'll tell you.

*Frank Robinson (left) and Vada Pinson were the Reds' first two African-American stars. During spring training, they and the other black players stayed in separate housing until the club found an integrated hotel.*

### My first opener was a good one, except for the ending. It was a good game. But Stan Musial hit a ball into the Sun Deck to win it for the Cardinals.

Ray Jablonski hit a home run that day, too, just before I hit my double in the first inning off Vinegar Bend Mizell. I thought I hit a home run. It just missed; it hit the center-field wall, near the top.

That lineup was a great lineup to hide in. I was a no-name youngster. Nobody paid any attention to me. They paid attention to all these other heavy hitters—Post, Kluszewski, Bell. It was a great lineup for a kid to break in with. I batted in the seventh spot on Opening Day—Roy McMillan was eighth, then the pitcher. I got an intentional walk that day, to go with a double and a single, 2-for-3. Eventually I worked my way up to the sixth spot.

In '57, I even hit leadoff a few games. Nobody wanted to lead off. We were struggling— everybody was struggling a little bit— and Birdie said, "I can't find a leadoff hitter!" And I said, "I'll lead off!" And I led off about two weeks. I did a pretty good job!

Birdie made it easier for me than it otherwise would have been. He made it easier for me with the press. They asked him, "What do you expect from Robinson this year?" He said, "You guys shouldn't expect this kid to be a superman. I'll be satisfied if he hits 15 home runs, hits .260 and drives in 50 or 60 runs." That helped take the pressure off. Based on what Birdie said, they couldn't say this guy should do this, or he's projected to do that. It was just a fun season for me. Birdie was a great psychologist. He knew how to manage, and he knew how to handle people.

*Frank Robinson homered in the 1963 opener, off Earl Francis of the Pirates. Gordy Coleman waited in the on-deck circle, next to batboy Bernie Stowe. Rookie Pete Rose was on frst base.*

*Whenever I start thinking or talking about Birdie, I light up. He was the manager for me. I was in the right place at the right time. He made my career.* If Birdie hadn't been there, if someone else had been there, I know my career wouldn't have gotten off the way it did. I think I would have been back in the minor leagues pretty quickly, because after going 2-for-3 Opening Day and doing OK in the series at home, we went on the road and I went 0-for-23! We came home, and Birdie set me down and said, "Look, we're playing the Dodgers. I'm not going to play you tonight. I want you to just sit here and watch Don Newcombe. You'll be back in there tomorrow night. I've seen too many young players come up here and get in over their heads, and never recover." That made me feel better, knowing that I wasn't out of the lineup for good. I didn't have to wonder when I might get back in there. I sat there and enjoyed the game, and watched Newcombe pitch for the Dodgers. I said, "Whoo, this guy would've been tough to face." The next day, I was back in there and I got going.

Birdie never said a harsh word to me before any of the games. He kept me relaxed, didn't let me get uptight. He was always talking to me on the bench, comfortable and easy, never intimidating. Sometimes he'd walk over and say: "How many outs? Don't look, just tell me. What's the count?" You know, keeping me on my toes.

Other days, he would whisper to me, "I want you to beat this whole team off the field next inning." I was in left, and our dugout was on the third-base side, so going into the third out, I'd cheat a little bit. Say there'd be a fly ball to right field and everybody's kind of holding up. I'd start creeping in, creeping in, and when the right fielder caught the ball, *boom*, I'd just take off, and I'd beat them all in, even the third baseman! I'd already be on the bench, and Birdie would get on the guys as they were coming off the field: *"Look at this kid! He's got a lot of hustle! You guys, you're dragging!"*

And that's just what I needed. I wasn't very outgoing as a young person. And I never went and asked the manager a question. I would let the manager initiate contact.

Nobody expected us to do anything in '61. They called us "ragamuffins." The Ragamuffin Reds. That inspired us, because we knew we were better than that. We really pulled together as a team, played together, and we had good years from guys who were coming off bad years. A lot of the guys coming in were guys coming from other ball clubs.

Fred Hutchinson was our manager. By '61, I'd gotten a little more used to him. At the beginning when he took over in '59, I didn't like him. He was tough, and I wasn't used to that. I was used to Birdie. I wasn't used to a rough, tough guy, saying what was on his mind, and saying it to the press, and not talking to me, like I'd gotten used to. It took me a while to adjust. We went at it a little, back and forth in the papers, a few times.

*We got off to a good start in '61, with that Opening Day win. We got a well-pitched game from Jim O'Toole and I hit a home run that day, and even though it was only one game, it can mean more than "one game." It gave us a little momentum.* It's kind of special to win the first one. We weren't ragamuffins that day. It was a carry-over thing. After the game we said, "Hey, we can do it." That's the attitude you get. The more success you have, the better off you are. And what better way to start the season than with an opening day win before the home fans? It was a great feeling.

Opening Day was different here than anywhere else. It was a holiday. It was kind of like a holiday in Baltimore where I went in '66, but it was almost twice the holiday here. In '66, the Orioles opened in Boston, and we came home undefeated. It was a good feeling to get your feet on the ground before you opened up at home. Opening on the road—something we never got to do as Reds—let you kind of get the bugs out, get the jitters out. You get a chance to settle down a little bit because you're not playing in front of the hometown fans, your friends and relatives.

I still get nervous before the first game of the season, though. I think the one time you don't get a little nervous, don't get the butterflies, there's something wrong. Opening Day is just a very special day, until that first at bat, or the first play, or if you're the manager, the first pitch. Until then, you've got a little anxiety, a little jumpiness.

*I've always felt there was something special in Cincinnati, and there always will be.* Coming back here, year after year, the fans have always been great. People are always very warm to me here. Having my statue at the main entrance to the new ballpark probably means more to me than my number being retired. There was a time span with the number. Now, all of sudden, here's a new ballpark and a statue. How many people—I don't care *what* they've done for a ball club—have a statue in their honor at the ballpark? That is very special, very warm, and I surely do appreciate it. Not that I didn't appreciate the number being retired, because I did. But this is just very special, a very warm thing.

## BUDDY BELL

*Third baseman Bell played for the Reds from 1985 to 1988. He occupies a unique position in Reds lore. He grew up in Cincinnati in the 1950s, watching his father, Gus, play center field for the Reds at Crosley Field. Then he returned to Riverfront Stadium in the twilight of his career in the 1980s to be watched by his sons, future big-leaguers David and Mike. Buddy Bell started in the 1986 and 1987 openers.*

I was involved in 18 Opening Days as a major league player, and a couple as a minor-league player and quite a few as a manager and a coach. But I *never* had the same feeling on Opening Day as I did when I was a kid. It was magic back then.

*As a player, I was psyched—Opening Day was a great day, something I looked forward to—but it wasn't the feeling I had growing up in Cincinnati and going to Opening Day games at Crosley Field. Back then, Opening Day was the most important day of the year.*

I was born in Pittsburgh in 1951, where my dad played. He was traded to the Reds in 1953. In 1962 he went to the Mets when I was only 10, but I remember him in a Reds uniform more than in any other uniform.

Back then, players weren't allowed to bring their kids to the ballpark like they do today. But the thing I remember best is the time Dad had a blood clot in his leg, and was out of the lineup for a month-and-a-half or two months. I couldn't even tell you what season it was. But I'd come down with him to the Crosley Field during that stretch, because he wasn't playing. Dad was getting rehab. We still have pictures of me running around the ballpark with him, and I'm in uniform. It was probably the neatest summer I ever had. My best time would've been his worst time. And it was just the opposite when he was released by Milwaukee at the end of his career. It was probably the happiest day of his life because he could spend some time with the family, but it was the saddest day of my life because I couldn't see him play baseball anymore. I would have been in the seventh grade.

In all the other cities I've played, nobody treats baseball like Cincinnati. Detroit comes close, but

*Buddy Bell watched his father, outfielder Gus Bell, play in Cincinnati openers in the 1950s.*

there's nothing like Opening Day in Cincinnati. *If you don't try to get out of school on Opening Day, there's something wrong with you! It's right up there with Christmas.*

The last Opening Day I remember as a kid in Cincinnati was 1961, because that would have been the last time my dad played for the Reds. The Reds won, and I think O'Toole pitched. After 1961—even though my dad was gone from the Reds, and I was a little bit bitter toward the Reds for letting him go—deep down I still wanted the Reds to win, and Opening Day was still a big part of my life.

I used to sneak into games at Crosley Field—not the Opening Day game, but the other games. The players' parking lot was in right field, actually kind of down the first-base line, and if the gate was open, we could get the guard's attention and we could climb over the fence. It was pretty easy, actually. Most of the guards knew me, and they just figured I had a ticket, even though I didn't. There were four or five of us who used to go down to Crosley Field on the bus. It was kind of nice to be just a normal kid, and do things like that. It was all part of being a Reds fan.

There was a unique smell to Crosley Field—a real, sharp "coal" smell. I don't even know what coal smells like, but I haven't smelled it since. I don't even know what it was. I can even remember asking, "What's that smell?" It wasn't hot dogs. It was an industrial type of smell—a sharp smell, and you couldn't get away from it. A lot of it was when there weren't a whole lot of people around. I'd smell it on mornings we used to hang out down there. It was right near the post office, next to Crosley Field, and it was inside the ballpark, too. It was everywhere. I guarantee you, if I smelled it today, I'd know that smell. No doubt about it. And, actually I still can "smell" it; that's how well I know it. It's weird, but I can be walking down the street, without a ballpark in sight, and smell something, and it reminds me of a ballpark.

There was no place like Crosley Field. I know Riverfront Stadium has a lot of memories, but Great American Ball Park is more like what Cincinnati is all about. I don't think enough pride was taken in Riverfront Stadium, and it wasn't kept up.

I've never played in a World Series—I coached in one—and played in All-Star games and big games, but nothing compares to Opening Day. There's a lot of things involved. A lot of it's just being anxious. *Are you ready*? You want to get off to a good start.

One of the biggest highlights of my career was when I got traded over here in mid-summer 1985. Paul Sommerkamp, who was the public address announcer and who I remembered from all the way back to the Crosley Field called out my name in the starting lineup. You know what I mean? *That's* the kind of thing—well, to be a Red is just special. I just hope that one day it will mean as much as it used to mean back when the Reds were one of the classiest clubs in the game.

When I played for the Reds, I still remember getting up on Opening Day and driving to the ballpark and seeing the people mingling around in the street and all the banners and all the excitement. It reminded me of how I felt on Opening Day back when I was going to Crosley Field as a kid. Seeing all of the people so fired up about Opening Day reminded me of just how lucky I was.

I remember thinking: "I know how the fans feel. I know how excited you are." And, as a Reds player, I knew I was a part of the reason they felt that way. They were fired up about coming out and seeing the Reds, and it was great for me to see that and to feel it. And that is a feeling I'll never forget.

### *I usually don't remember the games themselves real well. But I do remember Opening Day, '87.*

Terry Francona was at spring training—Francona had come over as a non-roster player—and he was having a great spring. He came over to me every day and say, "What do you think? Think I'll make the club?" I said, "I don't know."

Every day he's asking me, "What do you think?"

I said, "Terry, you're have having a great spring. But I don't know. I don't know the numbers." He wanted me to talk to Pete, but I told him, "Just keep playing."

Anyway, it's a couple of days before we break camp and Francona still doesn't know if he's made the team. Nick Esasky, who was our starting first baseman gets hit in the hand and breaks his wrist that day. Terry's thinking "Geez, I kind of like my chances now." Well, you know how sensitive ballplayers are! And that's when Nick is still on the ground, and they're still working on him!

Anyway, Terry makes the club and now it's Opening Day. He always came to the park early, and I always came late, and stayed late. So I walk into the clubhouse on Opening Day, and Terry's already in full

*Terry Francona, before his first and only Cincinnati opener in 1987, was a nervous wreck, according to Buddy Bell. Despite his anxiety, Francona was 2-for-4 with a home run and two RBIs.*

"uni," and he's holding onto his bat.

He says: "I gotta talk to you."

"Well, go ahead."

"I can't talk to you here."

So, we walk off in the corner.

He says, "Did you see the lineup?"

"No. Why do I need to look at the lineup? I just figured I was playing."

"Well, you are playin'. But *I'm* playin'."

"That's good, Terry. That's good."

"No, it isn't *good*. *I said I wanted to make the team; I didn't say I wanted to start Opening Day. I can't play. It's Opening Day in Cincinnati!*"

I'm thinking, "Oh, great, we're supposed to win the Western Division, and we got a first baseman who doesn't want to play."

He says, "I've done this in Montreal, but I don't know if I want to play Opening Day here."

Well, he goes out and goes 2-for-4 off Dennis Martinez! A two-run homer off Martinez—in the first inning! I go 0-for-5. And I say to him, "Listen, from now on, don't talk to me about Opening Day, OK?"

We both laughed. It was a great day, but some of us were a little too bit too nervous, I think.

My grandfather—my dad's father—was a big baseball fan. And I think that's one of the differences now. Back then, our grandfathers, and our uncles, were all into it. Now, this guy has this interest, and that guy has another interest, and it's not quite the same. But, even so, we still have a lot of players come out of the city of Cincinnati. I hope it continues. Cincinnati is a neat place, a special place, and it's an honor to have been a Red.

I think the new ballpark will help get things fired up again. I rode by it and saw the *"Rounding Third and Heading for Home"*. Wow! It hit me by surprise. I didn't know that was going up there. Joe Nuxhall was my dad's roommate, and they were best of friends for a long time. Marty and Joe are so great, and Marty's in the Hall of Fame, and I know it's a little bit different but I was kind of hoping that Joe might make it. But, hey, *"Rounding Third and Heading for Home,"* that's *better* than the Hall of Fame! It doesn't get any better than that, does it?

People probably think I'm kind of corny because I've been with the Indians, the Rockies, the Tigers, the Rangers, but the Reds are still "the team." It wasn't so much because of my dad but because I grew up like any other kid in Cincinnati. The Reds were "it." That's what we all wanted to do. There's just so much more to do now—there are so many more entertainment options now for kids, for everybody—but when we were growing up it was listening to the Reds—Waite Hoyt, Jack Moran, Ed Kennedy, Frank McCormick. The broadcasters were actually more a part of the Reds than maybe even some of the players.

Marty and Joe are like that today, aren't they? I turn on the radio wherever I'm at, and I can almost always get WLW no matter where I am in the country, and when I hear Marty and Joe, I get my energy back. It might sound silly, but it's just kind of the way it is for somebody who grew up in Cincinnati.

# DAVE PARKER

*Parker grew up in Cincinnati and was signed by the Pittsburgh Pirates out of high school in 1970. He played 19 years in the major leagues, including four seasons with his hometown Reds (1984–87). He started in all four openers here.*

Growing up in the West End—having a major league ballpark right in the neighborhood—had a big impact on my life. I grew up on Poplar Street, just down the street from Crosley Field. I played stickball against the Crosley Field wall.

*I was eight years old, and I'd come home and tell my mother, "I'm going to be a baseball star." And my mother would pat me on the head and say, "That's so sweet."*

Frank Robinson and Vada Pinson would arrive at the ballpark in their white Thunderbirds with red interior and portholes on the side. They must've lived in the same neighborhood, because they always arrived at the ballpark at the same time.

The clubhouse at Crosley was away from the stadium. A lot of the other kids would ask for autographs, but not me. Being from the West End, and not having a glove, I wanted a glove. So, I'd say, "Give me something to play ball with." And one day, Frank opened the trunk of his car and pulled out a glove and flipped it to me. That sealed him as my idol, right there. Later, when I made it to the big leagues, I tried to get him to remember that, but he couldn't. Vada remembered me, though. He said, "You were that little green-eyed butt always asking for stuff!"

In the seventh inning of every game at Crosley, the security people would open that big door—that big gate down the right-field line that they pulled up by a chain—and let us in. That was a big thrill to get in there to see the end of ball games.

Up until the seventh inning, we spent our time chasing down foul balls and home runs that left the park. We'd position ourselves outside the ballpark with the radio on. Then, after the game, we'd sell the balls for whatever we could get: a dollar, five dollars, depending on what kind of ball it was—a home run or a foul ball, and depending on who hit it. We'd been listening to the game on the radio, and we were able to say, "This is the ball Wally Post hit over the left-field wall in the fifth inning." Or, "This is the ball Frank Robinson hit foul out of the park on the first base side in the sixth inning." We were always hanging around the park, out there with Peanut Jim in his big top hat, selling those peanuts. Later, I sold concessions at Crosley Field—

lemonade and peanuts.

When I was in high school, I'd go to games and sit in right field in the sun deck with my girlfriend, Valerie Johnson. I remember one day in particular when we were in the first or second row and Pete Rose was playing right field, doing his thing, and I said to Valerie, "I can do that!" And I *did* do that.

My true idol, though, was my father, Richard. He worked two or three jobs to support the family. One night I needed my allowance so I could go out. When my father got off the bus after working his factory job at Lunkenheimer, I was there to meet him, and I asked for my allowance. He said, "I'll race you for it. Here to the house. If you can beat me, you get the $5."

I looked at him and laughed. I figured it was a piece of cake. He had a lunch box in one hand, a pack of cigarettes in his breast pocket and foundry boots on his feet. He was in his mid-30's. It was about 90 yards to our house, and I could run a 100-yard dash in the mid-9's.

And he beat me! But he gave me the five bucks, anyway. And he said, *"Let that be a lesson to you. You can't beat your old man in a foot race.* If I hadn't grown up in the South, I coulda been somethin', too, you know." Later, my mother told me, "Your daddy used to run everywhere."

I was drafted by the Pirates in the 14th round. I'd torn up my knee playing football my senior season at Courter Tech, tried to resume things too quickly during basketball season and missed my entire senior year of baseball. Two-hundred and some players were drafted before me. That next spring, before a spring training game against the Cubs, I hit balls out of the ballpark to all fields in batting practice and had shown my arm in fielding practice and Cubs manager Leo Durocher came up to home plate to exchange lineups before the game. He looked at our manager Danny Murtaugh and the umpires and pointed out to me in center field and said, "You mean to me that all the scouts in this country decided there were 200 sumbitches better than him?"

Anyway, that same spring I was in center field for a game, and Roberto Clemente was in right. I had just come out of high school the year before and I was sticking out like a sore thumb. I'd just met Robbie and Willie Stargell that spring. I walked around that whole spring with my mouth open—and nothing coming out of it.

Anyway, I'm in the game in center field and Willie's in left and Robbie's in right. And I'm thinkin', "What if I run into the gap and run one of them over?"

Well, don't you know there was a fly ball to the right-center field gap? There was a high sky and I couldn't see the ball, and just then a flash went by me. It was Robbie making a little basket catch right in front of me. He took care of me.

I had signed as a catcher, and I had a quick, short throw, the way a catcher throws. I was choking off the power in my arm. One day in the outfield, Robbie showed me how to reach back and get the best out of my arm. I saw that my throws were carrying another 30 to 40 yards, and it was like, *Wow*. He really helped me in my outfield play.

I used to watch baseball highlights in high school and the minor leagues. If I wasn't playing, I was watching. I'll never forget that throw Robbie made in the '71 World Series—tracking that ball down in the right-field corner, making that spin move and throwing a seed to third base to nail Merv Rettenmund. That World Series showed what Robbie was, not only to the Pirates organization, but to all of baseball. By the way, I stole that spin move from Robbie.

He was a tremendous guy, a guy you wanted to pattern yourself after. Stargell was a great hitter, too, but Clemente had that hustle and speed—his style was more conducive to my style. He never dogged it on a ground ball; he always played at 100 percent. When you saw one of the greatest players of all-time running out a ground ball, it showed you what it mean to be a true professional. Having guys like Stargell and Robbie was the best of two worlds. Willie was more subtle. He'd strike out three times in a game, and he'd never throw a helmet or a bat. Always under control, always kept his composure.

Clemente was a fiery guy. He could get pissed off; he'd get highly upset. But Robbie took time to play with the rookies and the younger players and joke and kid with the older players. And if you had a crick in the neck, he'd straighten you out better than any chiropractor. He'd take the head of a baseball bat and straighten you right out. He was the clubhouse doctor *and* lawyer—and the best player on the ball

*Dave Parker (second from left) joined Marge Schott, Schottzie and three other Cincinnati natives on the Reds in 1985: Ron Oester, Buddy Bell and Pete Rose.*

club.

It was such a loss when Robbie was killed in the plane crash after the '72 season. It was a loss to the world. There would never be another Roberto. We were a close team; that "We are Family" feeling started way before '79.

July of '73 is when I made my major league debut. I remember the day I got called up to the big leagues. I flew from Charleston, West Virginia to San Diego. Gene Clines had gotten hurt. I got there in the sixth inning. They told me,"You don't have to get dressed. You're not going to get in there now. Just watch." I went ahead and put my uniform on anyway! And I went to sit in the dugout. The next day I started. My first 10 at bats, I hit 10 seeds and didn't have a base hit to show for it! And, I'm saying to myself, "Oh, great. I'm goin' back. 0-for-10." That's when Bill Virdon stopped me in the runway and said, "Relax, just relax. We're not sending you anywhere."

I didn't start on opening day '74, but I did in '75, and that is when I really felt, "Finally, I'm a big-leaguer." It was my first full year of being in the big leagues.

Now that I had a claim on the right field job, everybody wanted to ask me if I was going to be the next Roberto Clemente. It was Willie who told me, "You're going to be a great player, but Robbie would want you to go out there and be yourself. He'd want you to be the first Dave Parker, not try to be the second Roberto Clemente."

So, '75 was my first Opening Day as a starting player. It was exciting to be on the team, to be the starting right fielder. Oh yeah, I had some butterflies that day! Had them till the first ball was hit to me, had them till the first swing of the bat. I don't remember if I got a hit that day. Sure don't. But I remember having snow in my beard. It snowed in Pittsburgh that day. But you didn't feel the cold on Opening Day.

*I think back to when I was a kid playing Knothole baseball. Your first game was almost better as a kid. I remembered what it was to get a new uniform. I was so excited didn't want to let my pants touch the floor. So when I tried on my uniform, I'd stand on top of the bed!*

And I remember the disappointment back then of having your first game rained out. Standing there at the window watching the rain drops fall. Heartbreaking.

If there's second life, I want to come back again playing baseball, because that's how much I loved it, and that's the way I played it. Education is the best way out of the ghetto, but the sports and entertainment are two other ways. For me, sports was the way of bettering my life, and bettering life for my family.

*It was exhilarating to come back home to Cincinnati as a player for Opening Day in '84. I was as nervous as a rookie.* It gave me butterflies to be a Red. Getting tickets was sort of nerve-wracking, but I had dreamed of playing with this team one day.

My most productive Opening Day game and one of my favorites—after that first one in '75, of course—was '86 in Cincinnati against the Phillies and Steve Carlton. I hit a double in the gap to knock in a run—a *hustling* double. Milt Thompson was in center field and went to his left to field the ball, and I beat the throw into second. Later, with two men on, I swung through a slider. Then he threw me another slider and I hit it out to straightaway center. The stadium was packed. And I remember after the game, we had the radio on and they were reviewing the game, and Nuxhall said, *"There's nobody on the streets up in Hamilton—they're all at the ballpark for Opening Day in Cincinnati!"*

I like that. I can still hear that.

# PETE ROSE

*Cincinnati native Pete Rose was signed by the Reds in 1960 and began his major league career on Opening Day, 1963. He played 18 of his 24 seasons with the Reds (1963–1978; 1984–1986) and was manager of the Reds from 1984 to 1989 when he was suspended by Major League Baseball. Rose appeared in a record 17 Cincinnati openers (tied with Bid McPhee). He is baseball's all-time hit leader with 4,256.*

A big moment for me in spring training in 1963 when I made the club was a game when the extra men could have gone home, but one of our coaches, Mike Ryba—he died several years later; he fell out of a tree, believe it or not—yelled at me, "Where ya' goin'? You're trying to make the club! Sit on the bench."

I pinch-ran in the 10th inning or so. And I scored on a long single and tied the game, and I think I scored the winning run in another inning. We won 2-to-1, I think it was. And I ended up hitting a double. From that time on, I was in the lineup.

I remember the train trip north that year from Tampa. I remember it because I really didn't get a contract until about four hours before Opening Day. See, when I was in spring training, I was on a Class A roster. In those days, you had Class D, C, B, A, 2-A, 3-A. Today, you got Triple-A, Double-A and A. I was on an A roster, so I was in the middle of the pack. I had two classifications to go yet. Although we didn't have a Double-A team. Our Triple-A team was San Diego.

So, to go to spring training as a 21-year-old kid, on an A roster and make the big-league team was very hard to do. You had to have somebody in your corner. The somebody that was in my corner was Fred Hutchinson.

The day before Opening Day we played in Indianapolis. We had barnstormed north. I think we did Birmingham and Macon, then Indy, then onto Cincinnati.

I remember my first Opening Day like it was yesterday. I remember it because I wasn't nervous, until right before game time. A photographer at the *Enquirer* wanted to take my picture with my mom and dad and brother at the dugout and *(smack! Rose slaps himself in the face like he's applying after-shave)* it was like waking me up. "I'm starting for the Reds!" Everybody I grew up with, everyone I came up with, wanted to play for the Reds. My whole life, I wanted to play for the Reds. And now, here I was doing it.

I can remember my first at bat, too. The count was 2-and-0 and I'm taking a pitch and I'm like this *(Rose assumes his left-handed hitter's crouch, hands gripping an imaginary bat and eyes looking back over his left shoulder, peering at the catcher's glove to see where the ball was caught.)* Umpire Jocko Conlan said to me, "What the hell you lookin' back here for?" I said, "Sir, I'm just looking at the ball." He said, "I don't need no help!"

I've got that photo of me lookin' back. I went 0-for-3 Opening Day, and I went 0-for-4 the next day, and 0-for-4 the day after that. I think I went 0-for-12 before I got my first hit.

On the eve of Opening Day, 1963, Pete Rose met with his dad, Harry (left) and Reds manager Fred Hutchinson. Rose made his major league debut the next day.

*Even though I went 0-for-3 that first Opening Day, it's still my favorite Opening Day memory. Just the fact that you made the big leagues.*
I walked my first time up, and then Frank Robinson homered. I'll never forget waiting there for Frank. It was like being a bit player in the greatest movie ever made.

I always liked Opening Day. The parade and all that—the fact that it went way back in history. That's what makes the Reds the Reds. It wasn't a hassle for me. I wouldn't get tickets for everybody I know. I'd just get them for my immediate family. I kept it manageable.

*I went to quite a few openers at Crosley Field when I was in school. That used to be one of my favorite things. If you got a ticket, you got out of school. And (laughing) I hated school.* My dad worked at Fifth Third Bank, and there were always tickets laying around up there, although the Opening Day tickets were always more in demand. But he usually got them.

You say I hit a home run on Opening Day in 1969? See, if you had asked me, "Did you ever hit a home run on Opening Day?" I'd have probably said no. I don't remember. But I do remember I started at six different Opening Day positions: second base, third base, left field, right field, center field. And I started at first base in the first opener after I came back, in 1985. We played Montreal at Riverfront, and we had every season that day. We had sunshine, we had rain, we had snow. I remember another Opening Day—1977—I woke up at 9 o'clock and there was six inches of snow on the ground! Opening Day was at 2:30 and we played the game! It was at Riverfront, not at Crosley. We'd have had problems with that at Crosley.

Opening Day in Philadelphia and Montreal was nothing compared to here. Although, the only Opening Day I had in Montreal which was in '84 was a good one. I was going for my 4,000th hit, and they had 50,000 people at the game, which is a big crowd for Montreal. I got my 4,000th that day, off Jerry Koosman. I could have gotten my 4,000th in Cincinnati, because we started that year on the road. The Expos started in Houston, played a couple games there, and then we came to Cincinnati and played a Businessman's Special, and that's the morning I got married. Sittin' on 3,999 hits. But it was the only time in my career I walked four times in a game. The next day was an off day and the next day was Opening Day in Montreal. I got my 4,000th hit on April 13th, and my very first hit on April the 13th—21 years apart—'63 to '84. How 'bout that? Both were April 13th. That's somethin'.

# Randy Marsh

*Greater Cincinnati has produced several major leaguers, but only two major league umpires: Larry Goetz, who umpired from 1936 to 1957, and Randy Marsh, from Covington, Kentucky. Marsh has umpired five Opening Day games in Cincinnati, including the festive inaugural at Great American Ball Park in 2003.*

I played Knothole ball for Cottage A.C., on Ninth Street in Covington. Second base, mainly. Johnny Temple was my man.

When I was in grade school, I lived on Pleasant Street in Covington. A block behind us lived my friend, Mike Andrews, who I played ball with. His mother owned a beauty shop. Mike's parents were divorced, but his mother was just a great mom. She worked and did everything she could to be a mom and a dad. On Opening Days, she'd plan ahead and get us all tickets for out in the Sun Deck. I went to Fourth District School, at 15th and Scott, and we took our letters to the principal to be excused from school. No problem. Everything was legit.

She'd meet us at school, at 11 o'clock, and we'd walk two blocks up to 15th and Madison, and get the bus to Third and Court, and then hop on the Green Line Bus. It was an Opening Day shuttle for a dollar, and they'd let you out at Findlay and Western— right there at the entrance to the Sun Deck. And that's where the buses parked. We'd reverse the process going home. We did that probably three years in a row. Man, that is something special, especially when you're 10, 11 years old.

*She was a wonderful lady. She's taking the day off of work, which means no income that day, and she's taking Mike and me and a couple of other kids to Opening Day.* We had a ball. And those were good teams we were watching. It was the late '50s: Frank Robinson, Vada Pinson, Gus Bell, Wally Post, Johnny Temple, Roy McMillan. I was 12 years old when the Reds won the pennant in '61, and got their clocks cleaned by the Yankees in the World Series.

And, of course, the other thing back then was Knothole cards. You could take your Knothole card and go to games on certain Saturdays. My cousins lived on the West Side, and I'd go over to their house and go down to Ludlow, and run across the railroad trestle—it'd bring you out right at Union Terminal. The only thing you'd be worried about is a railroad detective catching up with you. But, hell, you'd get across there and you get off real quick and you're four blocks from Crosley Field.

I was very fortunate as a kid to have the managers and coaches I did. Three of the coaches I had at Cottage A.C. when I was seven, eight years old, I still know today—Len Quinn, Don Whittle, Don Schneider. I still see them around town; if I speak at different things, some of them are usually there. When I went to Holmes High School, the baseball coaches there—Jon Draud and Ron Bertsch—are still friends of mine to this day.

I umpired my first game when I was 15, and it happened because my dad was supervisor of District 28, which is Northern Kentucky Knothole Baseball. His umpires for the Knothole games were either showing late on Saturday mornings, or were hung over, or didn't show up at all. So my dad and two other guys advertised and got a bunch of high school and college guys to come down. So I signed up and went to some clinics at the YMCA in Covington, then went out on the field a couple of times, and then they basically threw us to the wolves, umpiring the Knothole games.

*Northern Kentucky native Randy Marsh attended Cincinnati's opener as a boy, and attended the 2003 opener as the home-plate umpire.*

I umpired a ton of them. As soon I was too old to play, I started umpiring games. Then, I got my first car, and I was allowed to keep the car as long as I paid the insurance on it. It was a '55 Chevy Bel-Air, off-white, with a light blue interior, automatic. It wasn't a hot rod by any stretch, but it was *wheels*. So for that insurance money, *I umpired a couple hundred Knothole games in the summer—the cheapest ones paid three bucks a game; the most expensive was seven.*

I'd watch umpires on TV or go over to Crosley Field to watch. Then, out of the blue, I got to meet Harry Wendelstedt, an umpire back in the 1960s. You know where Walt's Hitching Post is, down on the 3L Highway? My aunt used to work at the Hitching Post part-time. Some of the umpires used to like to go there to eat—still do. So, my uncle called me on the phone one night and said, "Why don't you come over tonight?" So, I went out there after a game, and met Harry, and some other guys he was with, and he sent me a brochure for umpires' school. When I graduated from Holmes in '68, I took classes at UK in the summer and the fall, but then in January I said, "Umpires' school is starting up. I want to find out what it's like."

So there I was in umpires' school in Daytona Beach when I was 18 years old. And I got a job in the Appalachian League, but it didn't start until the first of June—it's a rookie league—so I came back home to work some high school and college games. The Reds were going to host Cleveland in a Kid Glove game, and there were going to be two major league umpires assigned with two local guys. Dan Romanello, assigning secretary for Queen City Umpires, said: "You wanna work that game?" I said, "Yeah!"

*So, my very first professional game was a major league game. There was Rose and Bench and Perez, and, yes, Chico Ruiz. I had just turned 19 years old. The batboys were older than me! John Kibler was the plate umpire, Shag Crawford was at second, I was at first and a guy by name of Tip Biddle was at third base. Seven years earlier I was going to games at Crosley Field with Mike Andrews' mom!*

When I got called up to the major leagues in May of '81, I was in Portland, Oregon. The league president called and said, "You're going to the big leagues in 10 days." That night, we got rained out, and I celebrated like I never celebrated before. The next morning—Thursday morning—it's about 10 o'clock, and I'm moving very slow. It's Blake Cullen, the supervisor of umpires, and he says: "Randy, there's been a change of plans." I said, "Don't tell me I'm not going to the big leagues." He said, "No, you're going. But I want you to open up in your hometown. You're going to Cincinnati." He knew I'd appreciate that, and that my family would appreciate that.

I had to get my equipment at the ballpark, and fly to San Francisco that night, where I met up with Eddie Montague, one of the umpires on the crew I was joining. We flew all night to Cincinnati. I got home, the uniforms arrived—naturally, they didn't fit—so I had to get those done, and some guys from the newspaper called because the league had put out a press release. I worked the game that night and realized, "Hey, I haven't been to sleep yet!"

But, I was lucky: 13 years earlier, I had worked my first game at Crosley Field, and now here I was working my first major league, regular-season game on the staff in Cincinnati against the Dodgers at Riverfront Stadium—and that's when the Reds-Dodgers rivalry was still going strong.

My cousin, Judy, bought a bunch of tickets—about 30 of them—and everybody was all out in left field. The other two guys on the crew were Lee Weyer and Dutch Rennert. The only advice they gave me was, "Do what got you here. Obviously, you did something right to get here."

In the first or second inning, Dusty Baker hit a ball down the left-field line—*my* line—that curled around the pole. Fair ball, home run. And I made the call. Later, Judy had a plaque made that I still have: the date, first game, first call.

*Of the 100 guys I went to umpire school with, four of us made it to the big leagues. There are some classes where nobody makes it.* The other guys who made it were Frank Pulli, Jim Quick and Joe Brinkman.

And do you know whose crew I worked on for 15 years in the big leagues? Yup. Harry Wendelstedt, who I'd met at the trailer park behind Walt's Hitching Post in the summer of '68. He put in 33 years in the big leagues. And when he retired, I became the crew chief of that crew. And his son came up and worked with me the year before last.

One of my best Opening Day experiences didn't even happen in the USA. I umpired the first game of 2000 in Tokyo. It was the first Opening Day ever off the North American continent and it was the "Opening Day of the New Millennium".

The stadium was *huge* and it was brand-new. It was so high-tech, they could shrink that thing down and hold a conference for

*Home-plate umpire Randy Marsh called the first pitch at Great American Ball Park on Opening Day, 2003. The pitcher was Jimmy Haynes and the batter was Kenny Lofton. The call was "strike one."*

only 300 people. *Everything* moved.

*The whole lead-up to that Opening Day was very weird. The umpires didn't even have a contract as of Opening Day.* I worked spring training my usual way that year; I like to go down early, work 15 games and come home for eight or nine days. It was a Monday, and my wife, Roxanne, says to me: "Don't they need umpires for Japan?" I said, "Yes. The teams are leaving for Japan this Friday, and the umpires are supposed to leave Friday, too, but we don't have a contract." There were going to be two exhibition games against Japanese teams, and then two regular-season games, Cubs vs. Mets. And she said, "Well, would you want to go with this little notice?" I said, "No!" See, I'd been over there two years before to umpire some Japanese spring-training games as part of an exchange program. It was a great trip, but I knew what was involved.

At 3 o'clock that afternoon, I received a phone call: "Randy, we have reached a temporary contract agreement with the union, and we have to get umpires there, and we'd like to know if you can leave on Friday." I said, "Yeah." I mean, what could I say? I called my one partner, Angel Hernandez, and said, "Angel, you're going to Japan on Friday," and he said "You got to be kidding me!" The other two guys were still at spring training and had to rush home. That crew was thrown together that very day. We all met in Chicago and flew together to Japan.

That was a real year in transition. It was the year that the umpires began working for Major League Baseball—no more National League or American League. So all the new uniforms had to have "MLB" on them, not NL or AL, and we didn't get them till we got over there.

What was unusual about the Opening Day game in Tokyo is we got to the ninth inning, and the Cubs were up, 3-2. The Cubs had put in a pinch hitter earlier, and the Mets manager Bobby Valentine comes up to me and says, "Randy, on the lineup card, they've got 26 guys, and they're only supposed to have 25." I said, "Look, Bobby, that's between your general manager and the league. It's got nothing to do with the umpires." So, he walks away, but then he comes back with one out to go in the game. And Bobby says, "Randy, my general manager is on my ass. I have to protest this game." *So there we are, first game of the new millennium, we're in Tokyo, bottom of the ninth, two outs, and the game's being played under protest.* Meanwhile, Sandy Alderson and Ralph Nelson are back in the MLB offices in New York, wondering, "What in the hell is going on?" And, then, as it turned out, all that had happened was that the Cubs had listed one guy's name twice!

The whole experience of opening in Japan was unique. They have screens, 15 feet high, going all the way down the lines in front of the seats, which isn't a bad idea, the way these line drives are coming off these bats these days. There's a screen above the dugouts, too. And over there they play it like a puck off the glass in hockey. On an overthrow, a ball off the screen, even above the dugout, is in play, so you got to be on your toes. After playing the two exhibition games, though, we changed it. And it's funny to see what happens when a foul ball goes into the stands: an usher comes down, blows a whistle to let you know where he is, and the fans just wait for the ball to stop rolling around, and they hand it to the usher, because the ball is "property of the team."

Anyway, we worked those four games, and got back the Friday before the Opening Day in the States, and I opened up in Cincinnati—and we got rained out after five innings! That was the year of the Griffey homecoming. I mean, we had a helluva game going—tie game—and we barely got past the fifth inning. I was trying to get it in. We waited a couple of hours. Ordinarily, you don't want to wait that long—you don't want to make the fans wait that long—but it's Opening Day and it's a full house and you're trying to get it in.

Opening Day is special in Cincinnati. It's also special in St. Louis, where they crank it up big-time because they love baseball, and now it's special in San Francisco with the new ballpark.

I umpired openers in Cincinnati in '86, '87, '98, 2000 and 2003. The last three of those were behind the plate. My first opener here in '86 was a lot of fun, working with Kibler and Bruce Froemming.

*People ask me about the feeling of yelling out, "Play Ball!" on Opening Day. But you know what? I don't think I've ever said it! I just say, "Let's go." Or maybe, "Play." But I've never said, "Play ball."*

I remember working an instructional-league game back in the early days, and hearing future American League umpire Teddy Henry say, "Play Ball!" at the start of every inning.

We said, "No Teddy, no. You just get to say that one time."

What's wonderful about Opening Day is everything's starting fresh and everybody's equal. Even the umpires. You usually have one guy you definitely want, and then the league assigns the other two guys. I try and get together with them the night before, or go in real early that day. There are some things I want to go over, to make sure everything's covered properly on the field. We chop up our responsibilities as far as making reservations, making sure equipment is shipped properly, rental cars, all that. It's like anything else that starts brand-new each year. You've got to get prepared for each new year.

The best way I can explain Opening Day behind the plate is by describing something that happened before a game in the National League Championship Series between the Giants and St. Louis in

2002. There was a young umpire—Jeff Nelson—working his first plate game in a Championship Series game. So, he was all fired up. We were up at home plate for the start, and one of the coaches who was giving the lineups to Jeff, said, "Jeff, you nervous?" Jeff said, "Hell yeah, I'm nervous!"

Well, I didn't want the coach to think Nelson wasn't going to be able to do his job. I knew it wasn't like that, so I said, "You know what though? His kind of nervous is good." The coach said, "What do you mean?" I said, "He's not nervous in a way that is debilitating. His senses are going to be so keen, he's going to be on top of *everything*." The coach said, "Hey, that's a good analogy." A little while later, Jeff looked at me and said, "Hey, thanks. You don't know how much that meant to me."

I learned that way of thinking about it in a book by Rick Pitino. He said a first-timer who's nervous and into it, is doing everything he possibly can—to the max. That's because your senses, your reactions, are going to be at their best. That's the best way I can describe being behind the plate on Opening Day. And that's what it was like for me behind the plate in Cincinnati, especially in a new ballpark on Opening Day. *That's new on top of new!* You know how a new car feels? Well, a new ballpark is a new car times 43,000—because that's how many people are in the stands and on the field and behind the scenes.

## EDDIE BRINKMAN

*While the Reds were hosting the first game in the National League in the 1960s, the Washington Senators had the honors in the American League. Their starting shortstop from 1963 to 1970 was a young Cincinnati native, Ed Brinkman. He was another in the long line of graduates of Western Hills High School—and the Bentley Post American Legion team—to make it to the big leagues.*

Every year we had what was known as "the presidential opener." The president would come by and throw out the first pitch. The first of those I would have seen was 1963, so, let's see, that would have been John F. Kennedy. Then would have come LBJ and Richard Nixon. *Security was always extremely tight on Opening Day in Washington. We had a problem even going to play catch before the game. We had to get away from the dugouts, because that is the area where the president sat.* We'd go down the lines, out in the outfield.

I wasn't political back in those days. I was 19 years old when I first came up in late '61. I had tunnel vision. I remember the clubhouse manager, the "clubby," in old Griffiths Stadium telling stories about Babe Ruth, Lou Gehrig and Walter Johnson And there I was, a wide-eyed 19-year-old, and I'm thinkin', "What in the hell am I doing here?" Talk about being over-matched! Anyway, I wasn't thinking about the president. I was there to play ball, and I struggled a lot, coming up so young. *I was more worried about the curveball, than I was the president.*

It was our biggest day of the year. The ballpark was filled, forty-five or fifty thousand. It was the only time they filled it. You remember that saying, "First in war, first in peace and last in the American League?" Well, that was *us*, the Washington Senators.

There was a lot of pomp and circumstance on Opening Day. It was the biggest sporting day of the year. *It doesn't get any bigger than the president being at the ballpark and the Marine Corps band playing "Hail to the Chief."*

You always see the photos of the president throwing out the first pitch, but you don't often see who he's throwing it to. Well, it wasn't just one guy—the catcher—or anybody like that. They sent *all* the players onto the field. We would gather in a crowd out there and the president would throw the ball into that crowd. You know, like the bridegroom throwing the bride's garter belt or the bride throwing her flowers. I never caught the ball—I probably would have dropped it, anyway. Being a young guy, I was just glad to be there. I was worried about being spiked going for the ball, so I just sort of hung back.

*Cincinnati native Eddie Brinkman (left, with Washington Senators manager Mickey Vernon), debuted in 1961 at the age of 20. From 1963 to 1970, he experienced the Opening Day pomp and ceremony in Washington, D.C.*

I don't remember anything particular about any of those games except for the pomp and circumstance. The only opener I remember as a big-league player was 1971, my first year in Detroit. I hit a home run that day and made four or five plays on my butt. I think that was my only home run of the year! I had a big day. I wanted to win the fans over. As a Senator, I'd been booed for eight years in Washington, and I wanted to try to change that in Detroit.

Opening Day in Washington was different than Opening Day in Cincinnati. I went to one or two Opening Days in Cincinnati as a kid—it would have been in the early 1950s, when I was really starting to pay attention to the Reds, being about 10 years old. I remember Johnny Temple, Roy McMillan, Jim Greengrass, Chuck Harmon. We sat up in the bleachers.

It was a friend of my parents, a dad, who came up with the tickets for those Opening Days. *I don't even remember if my parents had to give us a note to be excused from school. Back in those days, if you weren't in school on Opening Day, everybody just assumed where you were. It was a holiday.*

My brother Chuck and I didn't go to a lot of games. Our father couldn't afford to take us to Reds games. Besides, he was more into playing than watching, although he always had the radio on. He was a catcher, played until he was 45. He was still strapping on the tools over at Riverside and Sayler Park. He played with Pete Rose's dad.

Opening Day was a great day in Washington, but it didn't have the holiday spirit of Opening Day in Cincinnati.

Of course, I was looking at things from a different angle. As a kid at Crosley Field, I was one of 29,000 people in the ballpark for Opening Day. In Washington, I was *on the field* in front of 45,000 or 50,000 people. I'd never *seen* that many people before, let alone be looking up at them. It was a pretty awesome feeling.

# Jim Maloney

*Maloney pitched for the Reds from 1960 to 1970. He pitched three no-hitters, two of them at Crosley Field. Despite being the dominant Reds pitcher of the 1960s, Maloney's lone Opening Day start was in 1964.*

I got beat, 6–3, in 1964. Jimmy Wynn, another guy from Cincinnati, hit a home run off me. He hit one in the screen, down the left-field line, at Crosley.

In those days, we had the Findlay Market Parade and we were always the first team to open up. It's a little bit different now. It was a great honor to pitch Opening Day, especially here in Cincinnati, because it was the oldest team, the first team, and we had the big production down at the ballpark, even though it always was a little chilly. I remember all those flags at Crosley Field—the bands marching.

I always liked Opening Day, even when I wasn't pitching. It was a big day. All the ballplayers looked forward to it. Being first made it prestigious. The Washington Senators were always first in the American League, and we were always first in the National League. The other NL teams played the next day.

I'd been up with the Reds for about four years when I pitched that opener. Bobby Mattick, the scout who had signed Frank Robinson and Vada Pinson, and several other players out there in Oakland, signed me out of Fresno, California. Bobby was the West Coast guy for Gabe Paul, the Reds general manager. I didn't sign right of high school. I could've signed with any of the 16 teams, but the money wasn't right. We had another player on our high school team, Dick Ellsworth, who signed with the Cubs, right out of high school. There were lots of scouts at our high school games in those days. Junior year in high school is when scouts started looking at me.

*Jim Maloney (left) played with the Reds for 10 years, including five seasons with Tony Perez.*

*I don't know how hard I was throwing. They didn't have any clocks or radar guns back then. They just knew I had a lot of strikeouts.* You know you're throwing the ball pretty good when guys are swinging and missing, or swinging late and fouling them off. Ever since I was a small kid playing ball, I had a better arm than kids who were five and six years older than me. I always was blessed with a good arm. I played shortstop—I was a fairly decent hitter; I could've signed as a hitter or a pitcher—but the Reds wanted me as a pitcher.

I would've signed out of high school, but the Reds didn't offer me enough money. Nobody did. Baltimore offered me a bunch of money, and my dad said, "No, it's not enough." Back in the late 1950s, there wasn't a draft system. We were open game for anybody. In those days, scouts would come around and say, "We can do this for you," or "We can do that for you." So the player had a wedge, a little bit, anyway.

*The best offer I got out of high school was for $55,000. But I didn't take it.* The Reds stayed interested. George Bryson was a friend of my mom and dad's. He was doing Reds TV with Frank McCormick. So that gave the Reds a little "in." John Murdough was involved, too. The Reds invited me out to Seals Stadium—it was the first year the Giants played in San Francisco; you know, before Candlestick Park opened—and I worked out with the Reds.

George Bryson was good friends with Ted Kluszewski and his wife, Eleanor, and Roy McMillan and Jody McMillan. So, I met Roy and Ted and they were real nice. They said they were looking for pitchers—they had the hitters, but a lack of pitching had kept them from winning the pennant in the mid-to-late '50s—and the feeling was that if I signed with the Reds, I could get to the big leagues pretty quickly if I produced. So, all of that had an impact on it.

But, first, I went to Cal' for one semester on a baseball scholarship, and then, in the middle of the year since I was having trouble making my grades, I went back to Fresno City College. And that's when Bobby Mattick came in and upped the ante. It was a package close to a hundred thousand dollars. I wanted to play ball; that was the bottom line.

I spent a year in Topeka, Kansas. Johnny Vander Meer was my first manager. I had a wild arm, and I was green behind the ears, scared to death. This was the first year I was away from home and Johnny was like a father figure to me. He was a nice man.

I went 6-7 at Topeka, and the next year they sent me to Double A Nashville, in the Southern Association. I had just turned 20 years old.

*You ever see the old ballpark in Nashville? Sulphur Dell! Had a terrace, but it wasn't like the Crosley terrace. Sulphur Dell's was higher. As a pitcher, you'd turn around and look at the right fielder, and he'd be up on a hill out there, 50 feet above you, standing right next to the wall!*

The other difference is the Crosley terrace was all the way around. Sulphur Dell's was just in right field. Crosley Field was a small park, but at least you had to hit it pretty good. But Sulphur Dell, geesh! That was a pop fly out of there to right field. Of course, line drives out there were good because they'd hit the fence and you'd hold them to a single. So, it worked both ways.

Jim Turner, who was later our pitching coach in Cincinnati, was the manager in Nashville. "The Milk Man." I'm not sure how he got that nickname. I learned a lot from Jim. That's when things started to take off for me. I won 14 games in Nashville. I got called up in the first part of August 1960. I had spent a year and a half in the minors. The Reds probably rushed me. I wasn't quite ready. I think I won two and lost six. I was scared to death, a little bit out of my element, but Hutch told me, "Just go ahead and pitch; you're gonna be here."

In 1961, the year we won the pennant, I pitched a lot out of the bullpen, and I spot-started. I won six and lost seven. I got to pitch in the World Series—a little bit, not much—but that was some year for a 21-year-old. We had quite a staff. Jimmy O'Toole had a big year in '61. Joey Jay had a big year. Bob Purkey, too, who used to throw a knuckleball and sinker. We had Bill Henry and Jim Brosnan, "The Professor," the guy who wrote the books. He was terrific out of the bullpen. Brosnan was from Cincinnati. Elder High.

In '62, I won nine and lost seven, and then I started to really get going. In '63, I was 23-7. I had about five or six years where I won 15 more games.

I'm retired now. I live in Fresno. I remarried my high school sweetheart a couple of years ago. Before that, I was a drug and alcohol counselor. Did that for about 15 years. Then, I did it part-time in a church, at one of the largest churches in Fresno. I turned 62, so now I can go down and get my Social Security and see you later! I play a little golf, and I am still involved a little bit in helping people with alcohol and drug problems.

I love the Reds' new ballpark. You can hear the crack of the bat all the way around, no matter where you're sitting. I'd have loved to pitch here. It's a hitters' park, but not as much as Crosley was.

# Bob Uecker

*Uecker is the radio voice of the Milwaukee Brewers. Known for his humorous outlook on baseball, Uecker was a catcher for six seasons in the majors, from 1962 to 1967. He received the Ford C. Frick Award for excellence in broadcasting in 2003.*

I think I made one Opening Day start. It was in Chicago in '64 or '65. Our starting catcher, Tim McCarver, got injured in spring training. So, I caught the opener in Chicago, and I was chasing a pop fly, and I ran and hit the concrete wall next to the dugout. I got my leg caught in the drainage ditch and I had to go to the hospital. It was probably the best thing that could've happened to me. I always figured, the longer I played, the closer I was to going back to the minor leagues.

I think I got to hit one time that day, because I remember drawing a walk to force in a run. It was one of the big days of my life.

*I can tell you my memory of Opening Day. It was the same one every year. The players would be introduced, and then it was: "And in the bullpen, warming up the starting pitcher…"*

You know what I think the best thing about Opening Day is? Opening Day itself! Especially up here, where we are—Milwaukee, Chicago, wherever. After a long winter, it doesn't even have to be a good day. It can be a horses—t day, colder than crap and everything else, but it's Opening Day.

I always get a kick out of watching people come to the ballpark. On Opening Day, there just seems to be an extra urgency to get in there, you know? Because people are afraid they're going to miss something. And they're not. The game is going to start at 1:05 or whatever, so until then, nothing's going on. I don't know if it's the ballpark pulling them in, or what. But in our parking lot in Milwaukee, it's almost like the Chicago Fire, with all those grills going. The best tailgating is on Opening Day. It's a sea of smoke out there.

We opened our new ballpark with the Reds in 2001. It was an emotional day, because it had been delayed a year because of the workers having been killed there. Statues were erected and dedicated to all the workers. There are a lot of memories from that day. The president was there; he threw out the first pitch.

I like all of the patriotism on Opening Day, all of the pomp and circumstance. I like the way it fits in so well with baseball being the national pastime. But now that the war in Iraq is winding down, now that 9/11 is over, people don't want to sing anymore. For such a time, you'd look around and see all the red, white and blue, and people holding hands, and Kate Smith and all this stuff we used to do when I was a kid. *Kate Smith singing "God Bless America" is as big a part of baseball as anything else. But all of a sudden, we don't do that anymore. I like "God Bless America" being sung in the seventh inning. Now, they only do it on weekends. Why don't we do it every day?*

Having the eagle on Opening Day is something else, too. That eagle, when he comes in from way the hell out there and lands on the mound—big and beautiful, our national symbol—if you don't like that, well, you're screwed.

He's a big thing. They brought him up in the booth, and I took a picture of him. He looks you right in the eye. *"I'm gonna peck your head off."* I asked his handler, "What's he weigh? Ten, twelve pounds?" He said, "Naw, he only weighs six pounds." It's all those feathers, I guess. They make him look bigger. But that's the leanest and meanest six pounds I've ever seen. He's a mean-looking sonofabitch!

# Leo Cardenas

*Cardenas was the Reds shortstop from 1960 to 1968. He was in the final wave of players to make it out of Cuba before the Castro Revolution of 1959. He was a starter in six Cincinnati openers.*

I was in Cincinnati for the 1961 opener, but I wasn't in the lineup on Opening Day. But I was happy, because I was in the big leagues to start the season. Eddie Kasko was in there at shortstop. He was very versatile. He could play second, third and shortstop. I was the backup. Quite a a few games, I'd go in at short in the later innings and Eddie would move to another position. I hit .308, had five or six home runs. I also switched up some with Elia Chacon depending on who was hot.

Eddie was the one who gave me the nickname, "Mr. Automatic." He said I came of nowhere to make plays. Hitters didn't know where I came from. They said I had a .30-.30 arm. My arm was good back in those days.

I got into a couple of World Series games in '61. I faced Whitey Ford. He struck me out. At Crosley Field, man on second base, I hit the ball off the scoreboard. If that ball goes out, we win that game. I hit that ball off Louis Arroyo. He was Puerto Rican. He threw a lot of screwballs. We played together on the Cuba Sugar Kings in '59. That's who Mike Cuellar got his screwball from.

In '62, I was the Opening Day shortstop. Crosley Field. I don't remember what I did that day. I batted in the eighth spot. In the eighth spot, you get nothing to hit, because the pitcher comes up next. You got to chase it! But I hit .294 that season. I walked a lot batting in the eighth spot—50 to 60 times.

When I came out of Cuba, it was 1956. There were a lot of scouts from the U.S. in Cuba, looking for players. There was a scout from the Reds who they sent in every winter.

I'll never forget a Sunday when we were playing a doubleheader in Camaguey. You know Camaguey—that is where Tony Perez is from. We had a semipro league down there. A couple of scouts were watching. I had a beautiful day. *One of the scouts, the Reds' Paul Florence, liked me, but he said, "You're too skinny." I weighed 135 pounds. But at least I knew somebody was watching.*

The Reds had a lot of connections in Cuba back then, because they had a working agreement with the Cuba Sugar Kings, a Triple-A team in Havana. The Reds sent me to Havana to a tryout, and I did pretty good. They mentioned my weight again. I didn't have much fat in my diet: I ate a lot of rice and beans and vegetables. Not much milk. I ate eggs, though.

We were country people from Matanzas, about 40 miles from

Havana. Matanzas is known for its sugar-cane fields and factories. It is also known for its baseball players and boxers. For a while there, Matanzas was the Wild, Wild, West. There was no law. Baseball was going to be my way out. We had a nice ballpark, *Estadio Palmar del Junco*. Matanzas is where they played the first baseball game in Cuba in 1874.

The general manager for the Cuba Sugar Kings—Paul Miller—said he was going to pay for my flight to Douglas, Georgia, in May 1956, to attend a big Reds camp there. I didn't even have a contract. He paid my way. It was me and nine other Cubans, and they all had contracts.

*I did everything a human being can do. I was desperate to make it. I had to make it.* It was the only prospect of a job that I had. It was the only job I knew. I was from a big family—six brothers and eight sisters. The Reds thought I was 17 years old, but I was really only 16, because I added a year to my birth certificate. Back in those days, you had to be 17 to sign professionally.

One of Matanzas' best ballplayers was Sandy Amoros. He was eight years older than me. I was 10 when Sandy first made it to the big leagues with Brooklyn in 1950. Sandy gave me my first glove. It was too big for my hand—the glove had real long fingers—but it meant the world to me. I had a glove, and I had an idol.

I forged notes with one of my parent's signatures so I could leave school early on certain days and go to *Estadio Palmar del Junco* to play baseball. I got quite a spanking from my daddy one day when he found out.

To show you how connected the Reds were in Cuba, think about this. Three other young Cubans the Reds had at that camp were Tony Gonzalez, Mike Cuellar and Cookie Rojas. Not just players, but future stars! All of them except me wound up with other teams. The Reds traded them away to get other players. But they *had* them. The Reds were getting the best players in Cuba!

The only thing that could stop the Reds in Cuba was political unrest. And that's what happened. Fidel Castro came out of the mountains. When Castro came down, the Reds were doomed. *If not for Castro, who knows how good the Reds might have gotten off*

Leo Cardenas (left) congratulated Jim Maloney after a Reds victory. Cardenas and Maloney were teammates from 1960 to 1968.

*Cuban players? As it was, they got Tony Perez, and he was the last of the Cuban ballplayers for a long, long time. How many other stars would the Reds have gotten out of Cuba if it wasn't for Castro?*

Anyway, Tony Pacheco—he was a Cuban scout who later signed Perez—was our interpreter in Georgia. The Cuban players didn't know any English. Phil Seghi, the Reds scouting director, had Tony Pacheco in the office with him, and all the coaches. They were having a meeting about us. When Tony came out of the meeting, he acted like something bad had happened. He was shaking his head. He said to me, in Spanish, "Leo, you did everything you could do. They like everything you do. But they don't have no room for you."

*No room for me?* It was like the whole building came down around me. When Tony saw the look on my face, he started laughing. He said, "No, no, no. I'm joking, Leo. They are going to send you to Tucson, Arizona to C ball."

*I got $500 to sign. That might not sound like a lot now, but that was good money back in those days. I was so happy!* I started jumping up and down. Tony pointed out the phone to me and I called home and said, "I ain't coming back. I'm staying in the United States for six months."

We were only allowed to have three black guys on the team in Tucson and 22 white guys. It was me, Carlos Castilla from Venezuela, who was our second baseman, and a pitcher from the States who'd been around awhile. We rode the train all the way to Tucson. We got there two days before the season started. I played every game, didn't miss one. I hit .316, had 73 RBI and 23 home runs. After the season, I went home to Cuba.

The next season, the Reds sent me to A ball in Savannah in the Sally League. That was a pretty good jump, C ball to A ball. It was a great league. A lot of good players came out of there, including Henry Aaron. My first year in Savannah, I hit about .257 with 10 to 12 home runs. Yes, that was a tough league!

*I kept the black-white thing*

*out of it. I ignored it. The only I knew was: Play ball!* I started learning English pretty good about my third year in the minors—my wife was American, from Savannah—and that's when I began to pay more attention to the situation. I couldn't eat with the white players, but I understood. When we rode the bus from Savannah to Charlotte, North Carolina—that's a 12-to 15-hour trip—the bus would stop at a restaurant to take the guys in to get something to eat. The white guys would ask me, "Leo, do you want us to bring you something to eat?" And they'd bring it out to me. But I wasn't complaining. I was playing ball, doing what I love, getting paid for it, and with a chance to keep moving up, to get to the big leagues. I had it better than I had it in Cuba.

So, in '57 and '58 both, I played for Savannah. I played winter ball in Havana. Sat on the bench. We had a lot of great players in winter ball in Cuba, a lot of American major-leaguers. The next year, I played with the Cuba Sugar Kings. Triple-A. Next step, the major leagues. I had jumped from A ball to Triple-A. I hit .254, won the Gold Glove, and I didn't miss a game. Played all 154 games. It was great playing for the Sugar Kings. The people, they are fanatic. Like here, in Cincinnati. You give a good show, people show up. We had a nice ballpark. Big-league. We drew 18,000, 20,000. Right in the middle of Havana. Lights and everything. First-class. Still there. Even better now.

*But we had trouble in '59. Castro came out of the mountains; Batista left. Everything changed. Castro said: "The ballplayers can't make more money than the president."*

I could tell it would never be the same again. If you wanted to play in the States, you were eventually going to have to get out, and soon. That winter, our winter ball team went to Panama and won the Little World Series. It was the last one of those for Cuba.

I was in Tampa, Florida, for spring training in 1960. The Reds had Roy McMillan; I wasn't going to take his place, not that early, not at 20 years old. The Reds sent me back to Triple-A in Havana and said, "Be patient, Leo. It's just a matter of time." I was satisfied. I said, "I'll be back."

By the middle of 1960, we had to relocate the Sugar Kings to Jersey City, because of the revolution. In July 1960, after playing a doubleheader in New Jersey, our manager, Napoleon Herredia, came to my locker and said, "Listen. I've got a telegram from Fred Hutchinson. They want you up there tomorrow. They are flying from Cincinnati to Chicago, and they want you to meet them in Chicago. McMillan broke his finger. Pack your stuff."

I flew that night to Chicago. And guess who was my roommate that night? Don Newcombe. He pitched the next day. He broke Ernie Banks' kneecap. I went 2-for-4. We won. The second game, I was 0-for-2, I think. Then, we flew from Chicago to San Francisco. And who do you think was the Giants' pitcher? Sad Sam Jones. Yes, *that* Sad Sam Jones, the one who had the toothpick in his mouth and took about an hour to walk to the pitcher's mound. He struck me out four times. Next day, I was sitting the bench. Eddie Kasko was in there.

The Reds traded Roy to Milwaukee for Joey Jay after the 1960 season. Roy is the one who taught me everything. He gave me all the tips in the world. He didn't have to, but he did. He showed me a lot of secrets about this game. A lot about double-plays. How to get rid of the ball. I appreciate everything he did for me.

I loved playing shortstop in Cincinnati. Opening Day was exciting. Always exciting. You can't fool Cincinnati about baseball. They know about this game. And Opening Day was when they were the most fanatic.

# TONY PEREZ

*Perez joined the Reds in 1964 and played third base and first base through the 1976 season. After stints in Montreal, Boston and Philadelphia, he returned to the Reds in 1984. He had 10 starts and one pinch-hitting appearance on Opening Day as a Reds player. He managed the Reds briefly in 1993. Perez was elected to the Hall of Fame in 2000.*

I always liked Opening Day. I enjoyed it so much. Baseball is starting again! I didn't have it so easy the first three years. I would have appreciated Opening Day, anyway, but because it took me so long to get in the starting lineup, I think I appreciated it even more.

I came up in 1964, but I got sent back down. I was with the team on Opening Day, 1965, but I didn't start that game. I was in a platoon with Gordy Coleman. He played against right-handers, me against left-handers. I played the second game. I didn't start in 1966 either. My first opening day as a full-time starter was 1967.

As a young player, I always looked at the veteran players to see how they acted and reacted on Opening Day, and I acted the same way. What did Frank Robinson, Vada Pinson and Deron Johnson do? That way, I would know when it came my time, how to act. I didn't play a lot in 1965, but I watched a lot of games from the bench. *I learned more from Frank about how to play the game than anybody. I was one of the guys who hated to see him go. I believe I could have learned a lot more from him, by the way he played the game. He was a team player. He was the guy everybody looked up to for the way he played.*

Tony Perez battled Lee May for the first-base job when Perez first came up. Tony eventually moved to third base until May was traded to Houston after the 1971 season.

Frank was good to me; he was good to everybody. He roomed with Vada Pinson. The younger players used to go to their room when we wanted to talk baseball, you know, when we were struggling. I'd talk to them, because they'd been here the longest, and they really looked after us.

Opening Day was good for me—Opening Day was good for everybody—not because you might get two or three hits, but because you know you are in the big leagues, and because you are still playing. That goes all the way back to my first Opening Day on the team in 1965. I had a great spring training. Our manager, Dick Sisler, called me into his office on the last day and said, "We're going to take you north," like he was doing me a favor. I was thinking, "What, I didn't do enough down here?" I hit better than anybody, and I thought I was automatic. In 1964, I led the Pacific Coast League in everything. I was the MVP. So now, here I was thinking, "If I barely made this club after the year I had last year, and the spring I had this year, I might wind up being sent down again."

And here's a story about the 1967 opener. I got to spring training and I didn't have a job. Lee May was coming up—he had another terrific year in 1966 in the minors—and I was hearing I might be traded to Philadelphia or Houston. But I led the winter league in hitting and RBI, and they didn't trade me, but I still had to fight for a job with Lee May. We both had great springs, but we had to wait until just before the game started to see who was going to be in the lineup.

Dave Bristol didn't know who to choose—he had managed both of us in the minors—and here we were, the best of friends, fighting for a first-base job that was left open after they released Gordy Coleman. Deron Johnson was the third baseman.

*It was a half hour before the game, and we didn't know who was on first! Finally, Dave Bristol posted the lineup in the dugout. I was on first, and Lee May was on the bench.* Later that year, Deron Johnson pulled a muscle; they moved me to third base and Lee May to first base, and once the two of us started hitting, Deron got traded to Atlanta. It took me forever to get a starting job.

Did you know I was signed as a shortstop? People talk about Pete Rose "taking my job" at second base in Geneva in the New York Penn League in rookie ball in 1959, but the only reason I was at second base is because I was skinny and I could play a little bit. They didn't have any room for me at shortstop. They had another prospect at short, so they asked me if I could play second. Then when Pete came in, they moved me to third. I played third all the way through my minor-league career. I didn't learn to play first until 1965, but once Lee May earned a starting spot, that moved me back to third from 1965 to 1971. I moved back to first after Lee May got traded to Houston in the Joe Morgan deal.

*Opening Day means a new uniform. You know why the new uniform felt so good on Opening Day? In spring training, you traveled all around Florida, played a couple of innings here and there, and some days you didn't play at all. Then, on Opening Day, the bell rings and everything is settled. Every thing counts, especially the wins.* That's what I was after. I can't even tell you about any certain hits or home runs or RBI on Opening Day. I don't remember.

But, let me tell you—and I'm not saying this because I got traded after the 1976 season—but Opening Day in Canada, when we opened Olympic Stadium, and there were 57,000 people—57,000 people in Montreal for a *baseball game*!—and here I was in another country and they gave me *two* standing ovations. That made it special. New team, new stadium, and the fans don't know you; they only know you used to play against their team. So, for those people to recognize what I did in Cincinnati, that gave me chills. That is one of the Opening Days I recall best of all.

One of the things people might not remember is that in 1983, when Joe Morgan and Pete Rose and I were back together again, with the Phillies, I was at first base, Joe was at second and Pete was in right field on Opening Day. It felt great being in the starting lineup that day. Von Hayes was hurt. I had a good spring training, and Pete said, "I want Doggie to play first base. I'll play right field until Von Hayes comes back." I got hot—I was hitting .400 the first month —and I carried the team for awhile. Pat Corrales was the manager, and he never gave me a rest. I guess he forgot I was 40 years old! He played me every day. He asked me a couple of times, "Do you want a rest, Doggie?" I said, "No, I'll play until I cool off." I didn't cool off for a long time! I just kept hitting. Eventually, I ran out of gas.

But that was a good year—we made it to the World Series. That was the last year I was in the starting lineup for Opening Day. You never know which one is going to be your last, because you don't know about injuries and all that. But I never took openers for granted. To me, they were always special.

*I hated the day when they did away with the tradition about Cincinnati being first. Now, anybody can start off the season, and they lost a great thing. To play that first game of the year here in Cincinnati was an honor. We were special—this is where professional baseball started—and baseball should have stayed with the tradition. History is important, and they turned their back on it.*

What I remember so well about Opening Day in Cincinnati was the the guys sitting around the clubhouse before the game, trying to stretch our low-cut stirrup socks, to get a little more white showing.

Those new socks were so stiff. That's when you knew it was Opening Day.

Another funny thing I remember about an Opening Day—although it wasn't the first game of the season—was when we moved from Crosley Field to Riverfront. Pete and I, we had the same thing in mind, but we didn't talk about it before it happened. It just happened. That day, I got to the clubhouse real early; I wanted to be the first one there. I took off my dress clothes and headed for the rest room. I didn't see anybody else in there. I went into one of the stalls and sat down. I heard a voice in the next stall: "Hey, Doggie, is that you? I beat you again. I'm the first one to take a s—t at Riverfront." Is that Pete or what? He always wanted to be first—in everything.

## LEE MAY

*May played 18 seasons in the big leagues. He broke in with the Reds in 1965 and played first base. He was traded to Houston after the 1971 season, and later played for Baltimore and Kansas City.*

I'm from Birmingham. Willie Mays is from Birmingham, too—well, actually, Fairfield, a suburb. It's a beautiful area. Pine trees, rolling hills. Most of the Alabama guys come out of the south—Montgomery, Mobile. Henry Aaron, Cleon Jones, Tommy Agee came out of Mobile. Billy Williams is from around Montgomery.

*The first big-league game I saw, I played in. I never saw one as a kid. I don't even think I saw one on TV.* I was always playing. I went from football to basketball to baseball. And in the summer, I played in two or three leagues. I'd play in the morning and the afternoon and I always had a night game.

I went to watch the Birmingham Black Barons play in the Negro League. Willie played for them, but Willie was in the majors by then. I saw them play in '52, '53.

I wasn't what you'd call a good Opening Day player. When I had to turn it on, I turned it on. When I didn't, I didn't. Like in 1967, when I was trying to make the Reds, I turned it on. And then, when I was traded from the National League to the American League in 1975, I wanted to get off to a good start because it was a new environment, new ball club, new league. I didn't want to wait around. *The first American League game I played—which would have been with Baltimore on Opening Day, 1975—I hit a home run, a three-run home run off Joe Coleman to win the ballgame.* Now, that one stuck

Tony Perez, the new manager of the Reds, accepted congratlations from the Findlay Market parade organizers on Opening Day, 1993. Perez is the club leader in RBIs on Opening Day with 14.

out. Probably a breaking ball, that's all he threw.

I remember that day, too, because it was cold. It snowed, freezing rain. But it was Opening Day, and I knew we were going to play. Sellout crowd. I needed to do something. I had an awful spring; I was terrible. I knew if I got off to a slow start what was going to happen. That home run got me started. It took me a while to get in good with the Baltimore fans. Boog Powell had been their first baseman. Although I didn't have anything to do with the trade, people still hold it against you. I had to win them over. Hit enough home runs, and you'll win them over.

When you're trying to make a ball club, when you're new with a ball club, the first thing you want to do is win the respect of the other players. You do that by showing them you can help them win ballgames. They still had some pretty good ballplayers there—Paul Blair, Brooks Robinson, Mark Belanger. We had Reggie Jackson in '78, the same year Eddie Murray came up, and we won our division in '79. And we should have won the Series. We had the Pirates down, three games to one. I think we got a little complacent.

I'd say the openers in Cincinnati and Baltimore were similar. Baltimore's a baseball town, too. They'd won a lot of championships there by then. The atmosphere's still there the year after you win a championship. The electricity's still in the air. They had Boog Powell and Frank Robinson and Brooks Robinson. They had some players to bring the fans in. They didn't need a mascot. They knew how to do Opening Day.

In '67 on the last day of Reds spring training, I didn't know whether to pack my bag to go to the minor leagues or pack my bags and go north. Nobody gave me any hints. So I figured I'd just bring my bag to the ballpark, and if I wasn't going north, I could always take my bags back to the hotel. We had to play a game that morning, and after the game, they told me I made the club.

Nobody told us who was going to start at first base, Tony Perez or me. Tony may have thought it was a tossup—but only because I had a better spring. But really, it was a no-brainer, because Tony had more experience. Back then, the manager would always go with experience. Tony had faced those guys; I hadn't. He had a year and a half on me.

I wasn't one of these guys who worried about how my uniform fit. I had so many problems with the big-league pitchers, I didn't worry

*Lee May (23) was one of the members of the original Big Red Machine, when the club first earned the nickname in 1969. Sharing the stage with May were teammates (from left) Tommy Helms, Johnny Bench, Tony Perez, Pete Rose, Bobby Tolan and Darrel Chaney.*

about nothing else. I didn't think about the uniform, the shoes, I didn't think about *anything*. Because I knew if I didn't get off to a good start, if I didn't hit, I was going to be back in Triple-A.

And the guy who made that clear to me wasn't one of the brass; it was Chesty Evans, the clubhouse guy. *The first time I put a major league uniform on, I said, "Hey, this uniform don't fit." He said, "Son, just be glad you got one."*

It's true that a lot of guys exchange pants on Opening Day until they get a pair that comes close to fitting. But before 1970, it wasn't about having them tapered, it was about keeping them on. And even when you got the waist to fit, they were baggy. They were 100 percent wool. When I came up, I wore a 32 waist and they gave me a 38. Hell, I was a 32 for quite awhile. I had to gather them in and tuck them. My first four years in the big leagues, I never seen a tailor come around. A guy'd walk up and ask you your size, and you'd give it to them. Frank Robinson and Vada Pinson used to take their uniforms to a dry cleaner, which had tailor service. They'd get the uniform tapered. But from day one, after Chesty told me what he did, I never worried about how my uniform fit. Even when the nylon uniforms came in in '70, and they wanted to measure us, I said, "Look. I want a 36 waist and a 32 inseam. That's it."

People talk about my batting style at the plate, pumping that bat back and forth, but I didn't even know I did it until one night in '67 I happened to get home early and I watched it on TV—*I hit a home run, and they played it back on TV—and I said, "Damn! You look like a spastic at home plate!"* But I didn't change it. You're wrapped up in trying to think along with the pitcher, trying to get your timing, and things like that. You do that, and you'll be automatic. But if you go to home plate, thinking about mechanics, about your feet, arms and legs, you can't hit. Tony was a "quiet" hitter. He didn't have as much movement as I did. He was a better breaking ball hitter; he waited. I didn't wait. I was a fastball hitter; I was geared all the time to the fastball. Tony could wait for a breaking ball, and hit a fastball off a breaking ball. I didn't have the ability to do that.

I first met Tony the year he couldn't go back to Cuba. He could've gone back, but he wouldn't have been able to get back out. So, we played together in winter ball in the instructional league in Tampa. I guess I helped Tony some with his English; I don't know, I never thought much about that. I was just trying to know enough Spanish to communicate with him, and he was trying to know enough English to communicate with me. We didn't have a problem. He fell in love with barbecued chicken. And on weekends, I'd have to go find a place that sold barbecued chicken. It reminded him of *pollo asado*—roasted chicken—and he couldn't get enough of it.

Tony didn't go back to Cuba for a long time after that. I called Jim Bunning and a lot of people I knew in politics to try to get him a visa to go back to Cuba, and he and his wife Pituka did eventually go back. Preston Gomez had a lot of connections in Cuba, and that helped. Tony and Pituka have been back quite a bit. They took their youngest son with them, the first time some people back there had seen Eduardo.

In '91 or '92, Tony's mom and his sisters—he has four of them—came over and we had a big party at my house. And four years ago, when Tony made it to the Hall of Fame, they gave a big celebration for Tony in Miami, a big banquet, and Pituka flew his sisters in from Cuba. She surprised Tony. She hid them out at one of their friends' houses for a week—how she pulled that off, I don't know—and here comes the banquet and they announced all his achievements and then they said, "We have a surprise for you that we really think you'll like"—and they brought Tony's sisters out and Tony cried. Tony had the opportunity to bring his mom over here to live, but she told Tony, "I was born in Cuba, and I will die there." She came here twice to visit, though. His family members didn't want to live here. If you get accustomed to a way of life, and it don't bother you how other people live, it don't bother you. You don't miss it, because you never had it.

Funny thing is, in 1967, when we were fighting for a job—well, *I* was fighting for a job; Tony *had* the job—the writers tried to make a rivalry between us. I got to where I wouldn't talk about it. I think that's where I got a bad rap with the writers. There wasn't a controversy. I wasn't trying to take Tony's job; I was trying to win a spot, trying to make the ball club. All the talk didn't bother Tony any because he didn't know what the hell they were saying, no way!

# Tommy Helms

*Second baseman Helms, who earned Rookie of the Year honors in 1966, and Gold Gloves in 1970 and 1971, played for Cincinnati from 1964 through 1971. He managed the Reds in the final weeks of the 1989 season after Pete Rose was suspended.*

*My first Opening Day was 1965. What I remember best about that day was the pre-game introductions, because they'd call you out in numerical order. I was "19" and Frank Robinson was "20," so we stood side-by-side on the foul line.* That was Frank's last year in Cincinnati.

I remember 1966, because we kept getting rained out. And it wasn't like today, with all the workout rooms and batting cages inside the ballpark. Back then, you just sat around and waited for it to stop raining, and if it didn't—which it didn't—you went home. And we went home, three days in a row. I was really champin' at the bit, because I was starting at third base. We never did open at home. We opened in Philadelphia that year.

In '67, I moved from third base to second base, because Pete moved to the outfield and Tony moved to third to make room for Lee May at first base. I had to learn to play second base—just like I had to learn to play third—because I was a shortstop coming up. But a shortstop can pretty much play any infield position. I wound up winning a couple of Gold Gloves at second base, so I'm proud of that.

The craziest opener I ever had was as a Texas Rangers coach. Don Zimmer was the manager. It was the night before the opener at Yankee Stadium, and me and "Zim" and two other coaches went to the race track at the Meadowlands to relax and get some dinner, just something to do the night before the game to kill some time. It was a nice night, 60-something degrees. And I remember the usher coming down and saying, "The game's been called off." We're thinking,

*Lee May twitched the bat rapidly back and forth as the pitcher moved into his windup, a look May admitted made him look "spastic."*

*Tommy Helms had two hits in the 1971 opener against Phil Niekro and the Braves.*

"What's this? Some kind of a joke?" But it was no joke. The forecast for the next day was 12 inches of snow, and they got every bit of it. We didn't play for three days in a row! It reminded me of '66, only this time, it was snow, not rain!

We had an opener at Riverfront Stadium in '71 when it rained, snowed, sleeted and hailed on Opening Day. Woody Woodward had three errors, and we had six as a team. The wind was really blowing all over the place that day. Woody wore contacts, and he was just having a tough time of it.

*Opening Day never got old to me, not even as a coach. We always got a big crowd, always a day game, always the first game. You could count on it. It was our game. It was Opening Day and school was out. It's nothing like that now. How could you not miss it the way it was?*

## JOE TORRE

*The New York Yankees manager began his playing career in 1960 with Milwaukee. Torre loved hitting at Crosley Field, and had a great opener there in 1965 with two home runs. He has been a manager and coach since 1977.*

Do I remember Opening Day, 1965? Yes. I hit two home runs at Crosley Field as a Milwaukee Brave. I hit both of those homers off Jim O'Toole.

I did it three years in a row—hit two home runs on Opening Day, that is. Two of them were actual Opening Days, and the third one was a home opener. I guess I was ready to play when we started.

I have a lot of good memories of Crosley Field. I hit my first big-league home run at Crosley Field. May '61, off Joey Jay. First game of a doubleheader in May. It was a Sunday and that morning I went to Mass at St. Louis Church. I'll never forget that. What's ironic about that is that years later my daughter was baptized at St. Louis Church. But I had nothing to do with that. I left *that* decision to my wife on where to have our daughter baptized.

The funny part about that home run in 1961 is they had the net above the fence in left at Crosley Field. When I hit that ball, I thought it had to go over the net to be a home run. And I stumbled over first base, watching the ball, to see if it was going over the net. Luckily, it went over. I don't know what the hell I would've done if it went into the net—probably slid into second base.

Yes, I have good memories of Crosley Field. Plus, I married a Cincinnati girl. And I have four seats from Crosley Field in my backyard.

## JOHNNY BENCH

*Bench debuted with the Reds in 1967. He played 17 seasons in Cincinnati, and appeared in 14 openers. His number "5" was retired by the Reds in 1984, and Bench was elected to the Hall of Fame in 1989.*

I didn't play Opening Day my first full season in 1968. Over the winter, Dave Bristol, the manager, said, "Bench is going to have to earn the right to be the starting catcher." Don Pavletich had the best spring training you could have—he was playing the outfield, first base, catching and hitting .400—so I wasn't the Opening Day catcher. I didn't play the first four games, and then we went to Chicago and Pavletich pulled a hamstring. That was the last he caught. I caught 154 games—all but two or three that year. I caught 54 days in a row through one stretch without a day off. They didn't have the rule they have now that as a team you can only play 20 days in a row.

*I played three seasons at Crosley, but I preferred Riverfront Stadium. I liked the luxury of it.* The fact that we parked inside, the clubhouse had space, you could walk through the tunnel onto the field, and you always felt you were at arm's length. I liked the arm's length, a little bit of room between the fans and the players. They talk about the intimacy of Crosley Field, and all that stuff, but to me that was totally overrated. At Crosley, you could never run back to the clubhouse for something you needed, because you just didn't want to take that tunnel one more time down that walkway.

But I'll never forget those 20 scoreless innings that we played at Crosley Field. And we lost the game, 1–0, in the 21st inning when Bob Lee walked in a run with the bases loaded. Lee was out warming up in the 19th inning, and he flung a pitch that got past the warm-up catcher, and hit one of the security guys who used to sit on the field in those little boxes. The ball hit one of them right up side of the head, and he's sitting there, and all of a sudden, *Timberrrrr!* He just toppled.

It was like something out of a *Laugh-In* skit.

And that same game, I remember Gaylord Perry running out to the mound for the 15th inning. He'd already lost probably 15 pounds. He had pitched 14 scoreless innings, and now here he was running out for the 15th, and he shut us out that inning, too. Things like that are what you remember best about the ballparks—the stuff you saw happen there. There was some amazing stuff.

*Opening Day was always for the fans. It still is. The players don't do the parade; we didn't do the elephants; we didn't do anything like that. Basically, the players wanted to get Opening Day out of the way, so that we could relax and play baseball.*

Think about it: here you are, you've come out of spring training and you're not sure you've seen every pitcher from the standpoint of having warmed them up, to know what they've got. You've got to get 30 tickets for family and friends, and you've got to get the tickets *to* everybody and you've only been here a day, because you just came in the night before and "Where's everybody stayin'?" You're supposed to get their hotels *and* their apartments.

Everybody talked about the greatness of Opening Day, but we never knew it. We were trying to get to the park.

*The other thing I always wondered was, how can you have 50,000 people for the first game, and then all of a sudden you've got 12,000 for the next game? What happened to all those people who "love the game?"* The media always talk about, "Hey, we're great baseball fans here in Cincinnati!" But how can you have 55,000 one day, and then 40,000 of those don't care the next? If we had sold out all three games, I'd have said, "Yeah, now *this* is a great sports town!" It's all pomp and circumstance, but in a good sort of way for the fans.

I remember we had hail one game, snow another, and I had hemorrhoids so bad one game. *Aww!* Just like George Brett, but he was just a third baseman. Catchers play through it.

And I'll never forget 1979, when John McNamara took over for Sparky Anderson. John made a visit to the mound, and the fans really let him have it. I said, "Well, Skip, how are you enjoying your Opening Day so far?" He deadpanned right back, "Time flies when you're having fun."

Johnny Bench was on the receiving end of many Opening Day ceremonial pitches. In 1971, he took the toss from Medal of Honor winner Gordon Roberts of Lebanon, Ohio.

# Don Gullett

*Gullett, a native of Lynn, Kentucky, pitched nine seasons, seven with Cincinnati. His first Reds opener was at age 19 in 1970. He was the Opening Day starter in 1973 and 1975. He rejoined the Reds in 1993 as pitching coach.*

There's no opener like your first opener—especially if it's your first day in the big leagues. And 1970 was that for me. It's special, because you're getting the opportunity to do what you've always dreamed of, and that's playing for your hometown team. T*ony Perez, Johnny Bench, Pete Rose.* These weren't just names to me. As a kid, I had listened t them play on the radio.

*For me, it was a dream come true. Maybe that's a cliché to some people, but it wasn't to me.* At first, it doesn't seem real, because you've been dreaming it, and now it's *Here I am! I'm here!* It's just unbelievable. You've been listening to all the Reds games, keeping up with them, and now, lo and behold, you're with that ball club! It's a tremendous feeling. I was 19 years old.

And not only was I walking among these guys, but I've got a chance to play in the post-season. I've got a chance to be a World Champion!

And you've got all the festivities that come along with Opening Day. You've got the parade, all the media buildup, all the hoopla. It's a big deal. And you've got the hometown people there to see you. It's a tremendous feeling.

Right after I signed a pro contract in 1969, I played three months in the minor leagues, in the Northern League. I got a notice that winter to go to major league spring training. I was like a fish out of water in the sense that here I was among my idols. I'm down there running around like it's some kind of fantasy camp, but I had to be on my toes because I knew the reason I was there was to show what I could do. It was a big pump-up for me, because I was getting the opportunity to show Sparky Anderson and all of his staff and all the people there what I could do.

I was staying outside the club's designated hotel, which was the International Inn. I was over there with some minor-league kids and I remember a couple of them asked me a couple weeks into spring training: "Do you really think you have a chance to make the major league club?" I said, "Absolutely. They wouldn't have invited me here if they didn't want to take a look at me. And I want to show them what I can do." And they were kind of in awe of that scenario. I don't know if they thought I was being a little proud or a little cocky, but that was my feeling.

About a week or 10 days before the club was ready to break, pitching coach Larry Shepard told me out on the field, "Look, kid, you had a great spring, but I don't think you're gonna make it." It was kind of a downer, but I still never gave up hope. I still knew that I had some more outings to go.

Don Gullett joined the Reds in 1970. He was 0-1 in two Opening Day starts in Cincinnati.

**It came down to the last three or four days of spring training, and Sparky comes in—and I say to myself, "Here we go, I'm gonna get cut"—and he says, "Congratulations!" I'll never forget that, and what a feeling that was.**

Going north with the big club was a great feeling, and seeing Crosley Field as a player was great. I'd been there only one time, back in high school, and I'd really forgotten what it was all about. But now I had a different perspective. It was very exciting, unbelievable.

That was the year I met Sandy Koufax. He had been retired a few years. It was at Crosley Field, at a workout prior to Opening Day. He came over and sat down beside me, in the locker next to mine. We talked a few minutes. One of the things I remember is he held up these big, meat-hook hands of his—long fingers and everything—and he said, "Hold your hand up." I held my hand inside his, and his hand just dwarfed mine. He had much longer fingers than I had. He had great velocity, but those long fingers really helped him produce that great curveball of his. You talk to most of the old-time hitters, and they'll tell you Koufax's curveball is what set him apart: it just kept digging. We talked about pitching and he wished me luck.

Everything was happening so fast back then. I don't think it really hit me where I was until I got the opportunity to compete. For me, that was a few days later in San Francisco. But what I remember best was when we got back to Cincinnati—it is still in April—and Jim Maloney popped his Achilles tendon, and I relieved him. My first time up, I hit a triple off the old scoreboard, off the Longines clock in left-center field. And I stole second base that night. That is when I really felt that I belonged. I was out there competing, having fun, contributing.

As I think back on Opening Day and what it means, I think that yes, it's one game of 162, but it has an excitement that is all its own. You want to set the stage for what could possibly happen later. Everybody puts forth that effort in trying to show the people, the fans, the baseball people in Cincinnati that, hey, this is what we're about.

*It's funny how when you look back on it, you can't always remember the specifics of the Opening Day game, but the weather sort of stands out. I remember in '75—when we beat the Dodgers, 2-1, in 14 innings—the Hibachi grills were in the dugout and the charcoal was nice and glowing.* Now we have salamander-type, long heaters and hot-water bottles and big parkas and different ways of keeping warm. But it's still Opening Day, and nothing can change that.

# Sparky Anderson

*Anderson played one year in the majors, with Philadelphia in 1959. He became manager of the Reds in 1970 at the age of 36, and managed for 26 seasons in Cincinnati and Detroit. Anderson was elected to the Hall of Fame in 2000.*

Opening Day was always so important to me because it meant there was going to be baseball every day for the next eight months somewhere in America. And I still feel that way.

To me, Opening Day is kind of like taking the lock off the tomb: *We're ready now to enjoy life.* And I think for anybody who ever plays, Opening Day gives you the chills. It gave me the chills even the last five or six years in Detroit when I knew I had ball clubs that were going to have problems competing. There's still something special about Opening Day. Like I said, it's like taking the lock off the tomb. You sit there all winter, and you're totally out of your element. I think everybody has an element, and when you're out of it, you're a little bit off kilter. You're waiting for that element to come around again. And when it does, man you're ready. This is what you've been waiting for. That's the one day it always hits you—Opening Day.

*It's a funny thing, but if a guy was truthful, he would always say to himself on Opening Day: "How did this ever happen to me?" With all the people who wanted to play this game; with all the people who wanted to manage this game, how did it happen to me?* And I don't believe there's an answer to it. I'd just say some people are very fortunate. They're no better than the other person, just more fortunate.

The first major league game I saw was in 1951, when I was 17 years old. We were in Detroit for the American Legion Championship. I don't remember who Detroit played that day, but I remember being awed by it all.

The first major league opener I saw, I played in for the Phillies. We played in Philadelphia; it was our home opener. I was so nervous. Don Newcombe was pitching for the Reds. I remember, the first time up, I was just shaking. I hit a little ball off the end of the bat, right back to him. And I was so happy that I was out! I was so happy that it was over with!

In the eighth inning, it was a 1–1 game, and I singled between short and third, and knocked in the winning run, and we beat Newcombe 2–1. That's the last time I ever seen a sportswriter. After that, I didn't even know we had sportswriters, because nobody ever come around to talk to *me* no more!

Funny, isn't it, how you remember your first major league game so clearly? You know why? It's because that is the dream they all have, whether they like to admit it or not. Some of them want to forget it, now that they have so much. But their first dream was that first time. I just heard Barry Larkin talking about his first game, and he recited everything that happened. When you get to the big leagues, you have now accomplished everything you set out to do, to *get* there. You just don't know yet that you're going to have to be a lot better to stay. But you don't know that yet. It will all come to you later.

The one kid I remember so well, telling him he was going north for Opening Day, was Don Gullett. He was a hometown boy, even though he come from Lynn, Kentucky. The Reds were the team, down where he come from. Don was 19.

That was 1970, my first year managing. David Concepcion made his debut that Opening Day; Bernie Carbo, too. That was also the first year for Hal McRae, Wayne Simpson. We had eight rookies. That was Bob Howsam's whole thing—bring some young blood north, if it can help you. We wanted to plug in Griffey and Driessen one year, but we just had to wait. We would have had to have an injury or something for it to happen. Bob didn't want the young talent to sit; if you weren't going to play, you couldn't come. The only one he let me do that with was David. I did my best job convincing him that David would learn so much being here, and he did. I knew Alex Grammas—one of our coaches—could teach him so much. David named his first son after Alex.

I remember Opening Day, 1970, when we played Gene Mauch's Montreal Expos. It was the last opener at Crosley. It was a dark day, cold, some rain, not overly heavy, more of a mist rain. *Lee May hit a ball so hard it was like somebody shooting off a gun; it went over that scoreboard, and I said to myself, "Oh-oh, have I got something here."*

Closing a ballpark is memorable, too, just like opening one, because of all the memories. Crosley Field was like that. Everybody talks about the back-to-back home runs by Lee May and Bench off Marichal to win it, but what I remember is Don Gullett striking out Willie McCovey. See? There it is again, the young guy making his debut among all those established stars. When Don struck out McCovey, I knew he was ready. We had crossed over to the big leagues with him.

*Sparky Anderson surveyed Crosley Field on the eve of his first opener in 1970. Anderson's Reds won six openers and lost three, including a five-game winning streak from 1974 to 1978.*

In many ways, it's what Opening Day is all about—the season opening, a career beginning. That's why Opening Day is so special here. Cincinnati has always been first. They were always the club that opened first. Nobody else could open before them. It all started here. Yes, I love how specially it is treated here. People know what they have here. I say it all the time: "If you've never played in Cincinnati, you've never played."

And when I say "Cincinnati," we're actually saying all the way down to Louisville, and over to Portsmouth, and up to Columbus. Reds country. It's Opening Day in all those places—Reds' Opening Day—whether the people are able to come in for the game or not. It's why the Reds have always drawn well. *It's Opening Day, school's out—it's a holiday, a baseball holiday! Ain't no other place in America got that.*

# Dave Concepcion

*Concepcion's first year in the major leagues was 1970, when the Reds new manager, Sparky Anderson, put him on the Reds roster. He remained with the Reds for 18 seasons, and was elected to the Reds Hall of Fame in 2000. He started in 16 Cincinnati openers.*

*Dave Concepcion (13) teamed with Tommy Helms in the Reds infield during Concepcion's first two years with the Reds. Concepcion failed to hit safely in his first two openers, but then hit safely in his next 14. His 14-game Opening Day hitting streak is the club record.*

I was invited to spring training in 1970 because I had a good year in 1969 at Double-A Asheville, North Carolina and Triple-A at Indianapolis. They called me up to Triple-A to replace a player who had gone off for a stint in the Army. When he came back, they were supposed to send me back down to Double-A, but I didn't want to go back down, because I had a hard time down there in Asheville. Just getting into the ballpark and leaving after the games, things like that. It was a tough town for blacks. Remember, it was just a year after Martin Luther King was shot dead in Memphis.

I told my manager at Indianapolis, Vern Rapp, "I don't want to go back to Double-A ball." He said, "Well, can you play any other positions besides shortstop?" I said, "Sure, I can play anywhere you want me to play, as long as you keep me in Triple-A." I don't know what he told the organization, but I played left field and second base and third base and some shortstop. I finished the season there and I hit .341. Then I had a manager in winter ball in Venezuela, after the 1969 season, who coached with Sparky Anderson in San Diego in '69, and he told Sparky, "This kid is ready to play in the big leagues."

Sparky told the organization to invite me to spring training. I played every day in spring training. But when Sparky told the organization, "I want to take David to the big leagues," they said he was crazy, because if he took me, he'd be taking four shortstops! That had never happened before with the Reds. *Then came the biggest surprise of all—I opened the season at shortstop! Opening Day at Crosley Field and Davey Concepcion was the shortstop. I said, "Oh my God!"*

I was only 21, skinny as could be, 6-foot-2, 155 pounds. It was a blur to me, so young, not expecting to be there and certainly not expecting to be the starting shortstop, but I do remember striking out twice and made one or two errors. And I remember it was cold! But I opened the season!

Every day that season, I had to go to Sparky's office before I went to the clubhouse. It was, how do you say, obligatory. Sparky talked to me every single day. He said, "Hey, you're going to be my shortstop. Don't worry about your hitting."

So, I worked on my fielding—but I worked on my hitting, too. Sparky was saying not to worry about my hitting, but Pete Rose was getting on my ass. Johnny Bench used to get on me, too. We had a bunch of good hitters, and I was the punch-and-Judy guy, and I knew I had to work on my hitting, which I did with Ted Kluszewski. I wound up hitting .260. Not too bad. And I learned a lot talking to Tony Perez. I roomed with him for six years.

Then, in September of that year when we had the big lead, Sparky said, "No way I can let this young kid open the World Series, so I'm going to put Woody Woodward in there." He played the whole month, plus the playoffs against Pittsburgh. But, in the World Series we were having trouble scoring runs, so he put me in there to play. I played three games, got three hits, drove in three runs and hit .333. I felt pretty good about that.

The next year, I broke my hand in spring training, and I couldn't open the season. I stayed in Florida for spring training, and that broke my heart, because *I loved Opening Day in Cincinnati, loved being the starting shortstop, loved being a part of it all. All those openers, and that feeling never left me. It is the best Opening Day in the world.* New day, new year, everything you did last year you leave behind.

I loved the new "unis", new everything on Opening Day. Other teams would say to us, "You guys still got those low stirrups and no moustaches?" We said back, "Don't worry about our socks and our moustaches. We'll just go out there and beat you guys." And that's what we did!

## Dusty Baker

*Baker made his major league debut in 1968. His first Opening Day came in 1971 in Cincinnati. After retiring as a player in 1986, he continued his career as a coach and manager.*

My very first Opening Day as a big-leaguer was right here in Cincinnati, 1971. It was the first Opening Day at Riverfront Stadium. I was with the Atlanta Braves, and I was 21 years old. I didn't play, but I remember we won, there was a full house, and it was cold. It was an excellent Reds team.

I'd been in the big leagues with the Braves the previous two Septembers, but it was a really big deal to be with them on Opening Day. I remember standing around, thankful and in awe of being here. It's a dream come true, really. I remember thinking, *"How long am I gonna be here in the big leagues? What kind of a career am I gonna have?"* You wonder all kinds of things, like what it will be like like to go to all the different cities you haven't been to.

I stayed for about two weeks, before they sent me back to Triple A to play, and then I stuck the next year for good, '72. That was the first Opening Day I played in. It was the year of the strike. We started a few days late, in San Diego. I hadn't been working out during the strike, because I just figured I was the last guy on the team. But Orlando Cepeda hurt his knee, and they told me to grab my glove and go to center field, and I did. They moved Aaron to first base. I got a hit. But you know what? I remember more about Cincinnati, because it was my first.

## Steve Garvey

*Garvey starred in the big leagues for 19 years with LA and San Diego. He appeared in the 1972 and 1975 openers in Cincinnati.*

I grew up in Tampa, so I knew all about the Reds. I remember driving with my parents down Dale Mabry Boulevard—this was back in the early '60s; I was in high school—and here comes this guy hustling across the street with his duffel bag and bat. And Dale Mabry was six lanes back then! The Reds were staying at the motel across the street. I said to my dad, *"Hey, that's a ballplayer, isn't it?" My dad said, "Yeah, that's Pete Rose. He's got a great future. The Reds are hoping he'll be their second baseman this year." I mentioned it to Pete the other day and he not only remembered the hotel, he told me the number of his hotel room.*

My first home opener was 1970 against the Reds at Dodger Stadium. I had won the third-base job in spring training. About two days before we broke camp, Red Patterson—the great publicist of the Dodgers—said: "Do want to do a TV commercial?" I said, "Yeah!" He said, "OK. The part's for a rookie, which is you, and Pete Rose and Maury Wills will also be in it."

So, the day before the home opener, we shoot the commercial. I slide into second base. Pete's there, makes the tag, my hat comes off, and the umpire—Harry Wendelstedt—says, "Kid, you're out of there!" and I walk in the dugout and here's Maury Wills on the steps, and he says, "Kid, if you're gonna make it in the big leagues, you better use the greaseless formula."

Anyway, on Opening Day, we got shut out on a two-hitter. I remember more about the commercial!

In '72, we opened with the Reds, at Riverfront Stadium. I remember it being a rainy day. I wasn't starting. I think that's the game where Walt Alston sent me in for one inning, to play third base.

By the middle of the '73 season, I was starting at first base, and the rest is history. I feel like the rivalry with the Dodgers really got started in '73—because that's the year the Reds caught us from 11 games back—and it lasted for about 10 years.

*In 1975, I remember starting the season in Cincinnati, Opening Day. It was a great way to start the season, because we felt these would be the two teams that'd be battling all the way for the championship, and we had about 11 All-Stars between us.* Don Sutton started, it went into extra innings. I remember we got Mike Marshall in there, and he held them down, although the Reds won it in the 14th. I very rarely wore sleeves, but I remember about the 12th inning, I put the sleeves on because the sun was going down, and it was a freezing April day in Cincinnati.

As my career went on, Pete and I developed a connection. He and I were two guys who wanted to play every inning of every game. And we might be the only guys who set our goals at 200 hits every year. He knew every day what I was doing and I knew every day what he was doing. Our teams would play each other, and Pete'd say: "You're only two hits ahead of me, but I'll pass you in the second game of the series." And I'd say, "No you're not! And you know what? You're a switch-hitter, and I'm hitting only from the right side. This is easier for you." And he'd say, "No, it's not. You played defensive back and you've got more speed than I've got."

So, anyway, we had the same approach, the same goals, and we developed a bond. I was playing first base for the Padres the night he broke Cobb's record. It was the longest, sustained ovation I ever heard, and I heard Henry Aaron No. 715, and Reggie Jackson's after the three home runs in a World Series game at Yankee Stadium.

*For me, always being an historian of the game, opening here in Cincinnati—which was always, perennially, the first game of the year—was an honor, a tribute, and I kind of savored that.* There was the parade, and I always felt the fans had a deep appreciation for the sense of history here. I was against it when ESPN changed the opener from traditionally going to Cincinnati on Monday, and instead moving it to a Sunday night. It's OK to have a wild card every once in a while, but c'mon, keep tradition! It's too hard of a thing to establish, just to give it up at the drop of a hat.

# Jack Billingham

*Billingham's first Opening Day in Cincinnati was 1972. Billingham, Joe Morgan, Denis Menke, Cesar Geronimo and Ed Armbrister came to the Reds in a trade with Houston (for Lee May, Tommy Helms and Jimmy Stewart) in December 1971. Billingham also started the 1974 opener and gave up Hank Aaron's 714th home run, which tied Aaron with Babe Ruth on the all-time home run list.*

I'm not sure why Sparky picked me to be the Opening Day starter in '72, other than maybe he wanted to try to make the trade look good. It was April '72, the season hadn't yet begun, but everybody in town was mad about the trade

We had just come north to Cincinnati after spring training and sat around here on strike for a couple of weeks and the fans, who already weren't in a good mood because of the trade, had to deal with the strike on top of it.

I got booed a lot that Opening Day. The fans wanted Lee May at first base, not Jack Billingham on the mound. They wanted Tommy Helms at second base, not Joe Morgan.

I pitched so-so against the Dodgers. That was the day I learned about Sparky, because after the game, Bob Hertzel—the *Enquirer's* baseball writer—wrote an article that ran the day after I started that said, "Billingham wasn't very happy when Sparky came out to get him, and showed it by walking off the mound." The next day, Sparky called me in said, "Don't walk off the mound when I come out to get you. Stand on the mound and hand me the baseball. Next time, it will cost you." I told him, "I wasn't trying to show you up. I didn't pitch well."

I wasn't mad at Sparky for coming out. That was his job. I was mad at Sparky plenty of other times, when "Captain Hook" got me early, but on that day I deserved to be taken out. Sparky's rule was, "If I'm walkin', you're out of the game. If I'm runnin', I'm comin' to tell you somethin'. And if I'm walkin', you wait till I get there and hand me the ball. You can go to the clubhouse and can call me a son of a bitch, do whatever you want to do, but let's just try not to show each other up on the field."

Anyway, when Sparky came out to get me and I walked off the

Steve Garvey signed autographs at Riverfront in 1985. Garvey had three hits for the Dodgers in the 1975 Opening Day loss to the Reds.

mound, there weren't any good words said to me when I left. That kind of stands out, and not in a bad way; it just stands out in a baseball way.

We struggled at the beginning of that year—I think I started out 0 and 5—and until we turned it around, the fans weren't very happy. But we went on to win the pennant and play in the World Series.

*At the time I was playing, I thought being named the Opening Day pitcher was an honor, but I didn't realize how much of an honor.* As I got older and looked back on it and saw what it all meant, I understood that the Opening Day pitcher is usually a guy that had a real good year the previous season, a veteran that the manager thinks can handle the pressure of Opening Day—because there's a little more pressure Opening Day—the season's starting, the crowd is big, the team wants to start off with a win. I see what an honor it really was. I never competed with Don Gullett for the honor—Don and I are friends—but, yes, it always felt good to be the Opening Day pitcher.

The other Opening Day I remember is Hank Aaron's 714. There were tornadoes in the area the day before. I spent the night on the floor in the basement. I lived in Delhi, in the western part of town, and being from Florida, I'm used to hurricanes but not tornadoes. The kids were scared, and I was scared. And, actually, it was the first tornado I ever saw in my life. I don't know if it's the one that hit Sayler Park that day, but I saw it coming from the airport. There was hail the size of golf balls hitting in the mud in my yard. You could just hear it go *shewp*. And when it hit the street, it sounded like somebody was dropping a light bulb. My father and my brother had just gotten into town—they drove my car up from spring training—and they'd never seen anything like it, either. We were not real comfortable all night long. I did get plenty of sleep, though. That's one good thing. When my eyes do close, nothing happens, my mind goes blank. And the tornado had nothing to do with giving up 714.

That day, Opening Day, it was almost like when we were in the World Series in 1972. There was media all over the place, cameras all over the place. I recall being interviewed before the season and being asked: "If you were up nine to nothing, would you groove one?" I said, "No way! I have enough trouble with Aaron, why should I groove one?" He got Don Drysdale a lot; he got some good pitchers a lot. He was a great hitter.

I had a couple of hitters—and Al Oliver was one of them—who I couldn't get out. And I finally would stand out on the mound and say, "Here you go—hit the son of a bitch." And I'd throw it right down the middle, with no thought of getting him out. *Just hit the son of a bitch and get out of the way, so I can go on to the next hitter.* Well, it's amazing how many times you get those guys out when you just hand them one. They're only going to get three hits out of every 10 times up.

But, no, I didn't do that with Aaron. I had to pitch to him. You know, though, I was one of the few guys to be interviewed who said, "No, I wouldn't do that!" Why would you want to do that? He's going to hit home runs. If I face him enough, he's going to hit home runs off me.

Vice President Ford was there for the opener. He came down and shook hands and walked through the clubhouse before the game. And I proceeded to go out there and give up 714 in the first inning. I think I was out of the game in the fourth inning. It wasn't one of my most enjoyable starts. But, we came back and won the ballgame; that was the important thing. The Big Red Machine. I remember Joe Morgan coming up to me after the home run and predicted we would come back and win. He was right.

I remember the interviews afterward. It was kind of weird. Normally, the writers would talk to you at your locker, but this time we went up to the press room. *I was asked, "How do you feel about giving up No. 714?" Well, I didn't feel very good. It's Opening Day and I'm trying to start the season off good, and here it is the first inning and it's the first pitch he swung at.* I started him off with three balls, and there's 55,000 people booing at me. At home! They want to see Hank swing. I got a called strike and then I threw an outside fastball, which was my bread-and-butter. As a pitcher, you call it the obvious pitch. I was 3-1; I

*Jack Billingham appeared serene on the eve of the 1972 opener, his first Opening Day start for the Reds. He had more worries on the eve of the 1974 opener, including a tornado and facing Hank Aaron.*

wasn't going to try to walk him, pitch around him. His hands and his wrists came through and he hit the line drive over the left-field wall.

And that was the kind of home-run hitter he was: a line-drive home-run hitter. I feel I'm qualified to distinguish between the types of home-run hitters, because I gave up a *lot* of home runs. Some guys hit the high flies that just carry out, but his went out like a shot. In retrospect, it was like the one Mark McGwire hit to tie Roger Maris' record of 61 home runs. The only thought I had when Aaron connected was: "Get down! Get down!" But it just *swwweeew*—shot over the fence."

*The home run was upsetting, but one of the worse parts about it was that after he tagged home plate, all the awards started coming. It felt like I stood out there for 25 minutes! The vice president came down and made a little talk, and all this other stuff. And I'm going, "C'mon, let's go! So he hit a home run, let's go!" I mean, I knew there was history there—Babe Ruth, 714—that was impressive. But if I'd known I was going to be out there for 25 minutes, I'd have gone to the dugout and sat and been pissed off, but I had to stand out on the mound in front of 55,000 people!*

I'm with the Houston Astros in the minor leagues and I coach a lot of young kids. They keep showing the home run on the TV highlights—Hank Aaron, 714—and every once in a while a kid will say, "Hey, I saw you on TV coach! You gave up 714!" They tease me about it. And I say, "Yup, I was there. I had a good view of it." But it doesn't bother me.

I think I gave up eight or nine home runs to Aaron over my 10-year career in the NL. Back when I was with Houston before coming to the Reds, I came on in relief in the 10th inning—we were in Atlanta—and the first guy I faced was Hank Aaron. After three pitches, I was walking off the mound a loser. That's probably the one I remember the most because it's the one that was a decision-maker in the game. Shortly after that, the Astros decided that they better make me a starter. I'd come as a reliever through the Dodgers system—more of a setup guy than a stopper—but because I was going two or three innings at a time, Houston turned me into a starter by late 1970 or early 1971.

Apart from Opening Day—you know, just over the course of the seasons I spent here—we had a good staff, a lot of different personalities. Don Gullett, quiet, just went out and did the job; Gary Nolan was a character, a comedian off the field, but on it he was all business; Ross Grimsley with the big Afro, pitched well; Freddie Norman, the little guy, would go out and compete. Our job was to keep our team in it. You could tell by the fifth or sixth inning, if the other team was leading us by one or two runs, they were waiting for us to beat them. You could just see it.

I feel like pitching coach Larry Shepard kept us together. I personally don't feel he gets the credit he deserves. He was like a father to us. He'd pat us on the back; kick us in the butt. I needed that. He brought out the best in me, and in a lot of people.

He pounded it into our heads: *"Y'all got the hardest job in the world. When you walk out on that mound with the Big Red Machine, you're expected to win."* If we gave up a few runs and we lost, it was because the pitchers were bad. The hitters *never* lost a game. When we won 2–1, it was no big deal. *Jack pitched a good ballgame.* But if I went out and gave up six runs, *Billingham was hit hard; the Big Red Machine couldn't dig out of the hole the pitchers put them in.* I remember a newspaper article when we went down to Atlanta and I faced Phil Niekro. We must have scored something like 20 runs! *[It was 17 runs on August 2, 1973.]* I was sitting in the dugout for 45 minutes for one stretch while we were scoring all those runs, and I had trouble staying sharp because of it. The story read, *"The Reds Score 20; Billingham Struggles To Go Five."* That's just the way it was.

## JOE MORGAN

*Morgan arrived in Cincinnati in 1972 after the trade with the Houston Astros. He won the NL MVP award in 1975 and 1976, and was elected to the Hall of Fame in 1990. His number 8 was retired by the Reds in 1998. He hit .393 in his eight Cincinnati openers.*

Jack Billingham is probably right when he talks about getting booed in the 1972 opener. I probably got booed, too—I know how popular Lee May, Tommy Helms and Jimmy Stewart were in this town before they got traded to Houston. I don't *specifically* remember being booed, probably because that's just the way I was. I'd block things out when I had a job to do. But I do remember I made an error in my first game. You know what, though? I can't even tell you if we won the game or not. *[The Reds lost, 3–1.]*

*But I always felt very special about Opening Day. There are two days that are very special to me, and still are. Opening Day, and the first day of the World Series.* Even now, those are the times that I miss the game the most. Those are the reasons I played. To get to the World Series—it's what the game is all about—and the first day was the start of that. Those are the days I wish I was still playing. Those are the two days I want to *hit*. Even when I'm standing up in the booth, I still feel that way.

But I think the "feel" of those two days are different. The buzz of Opening Day is from having been off for five months, and you miss the game so much that you just want to get back to it. The World Series is a reward for the success that you, as a team, have had together. You and all of your teammates have really accomplished something. On the first day of the season, there's great anticipation, but getting to the World Series is more a sense of fulfillment that you've made it to where you set out for when the year started.

*I truly loved Opening Day. I liked being part of the whole team being introduced and coming out the foul lines.* That was always special to me. The journey was beginning. And it's special, because you always have some new guys coming to the big leagues for the first time. That was always special for me, as a veteran player, to remember my first day in the big leagues and to know what these new guys are going through.

My first opening day was the opening of the Astrodome. Chris Short was the pitcher for the Phillies, and I went 3-for-4. I don't think you ever forget your first opener. It was just a privilege to be in the big leagues. Back then, everybody was on one-year contracts, so you definitely counted your blessings. A lot of guys didn't know if they were going to be there the next year or not. I don't know if it's the same now. I don't know if the players look at it the same way.

My last Opening Day was in 1985. Every year I was in the big leagues, I was the starting second baseman for Opening Day. I never missed an Opening Day, from the first day I played with Houston, until I retired. I was very fortunate in that regard.

## KEN GRIFFEY, SR.

*Griffey, Sr. was a rookie in 1974, and started in his first Opening Day. He played 12 seasons with the Reds and was the starting right fielder in the glory days of the Big Red Machine.*

My first Opening Day as a Red was in 1974, and my biggest memory of it—my only memory of it, really, because it overwhelmed everything else, and rightly so—was Henry Aaron hitting No. 714.

You don't forget something like that when you're 23 years old and you're in the big leagues and the great Henry Aaron is going for the record. That Opening Day will always stand out for me.

I was in the starting lineup, playing right field. I can't tell you how I did that Opening Day—what I did at bat or how I did in the field. But I do remember Aaron's 714th like it was yesterday. The other thing I remember about it is I got sent back to Triple-A on the 14th of May. I can tell you exactly what I was hitting at the time I was sent down: .158. I wasn't brought back up until July 2.

The next year, on Opening Day, 1975, I wasn't thinking "I hope I'm here to stay this year," because I knew I was going to stay, that nobody was going to take that from me. I wasn't going to let anybody take that from me. I wasn't going to hit .158 this time. I don't remember how I did that Opening Day, either, but *I remember thinking, "This is the place to be. In the starting lineup, Opening Day, Cincinnati."*

Joe Morgan put on one of the best offensive performances ever on Opening Day with three hits (including two doubles and a home run) and five RBIs in 1978.

## GEORGE FOSTER

*Foster came to the Reds in 1971 and became the regular left fielder in 1975. He won the MVP award in 1977, and was inducted into the Reds Hall of Fame in 2003. He hit .407 in his seven Cincinnati openers.*

Coming over to the Reds from the Giants, I really started to relax and play the game. With the Giants, there were certain players who wouldn't speak to you. But, when I came over here, there were guys like Pete Rose and Johnny Bench—the stars of the team—and once Pete talked to me, I felt like I belonged. And he talked to me right away, welcomed me over. He was the first star player to talk to me here. When you have guys on your own team who won't talk to you, you feel a little more nervous about it.

I came over here in May 1971, Memorial Day. I can't say that I remember the 1972 opener. I wasn't starting. It's harder to remember the individual openers when you weren't starting. But the weather, you always remember the weather when it's bad.

In 1977 it snowed. Randy Jones pitched. They had to plow the snow off the field that morning. I hit a a triple and had a couple of RBIs. It was a great opener, because number one, I didn't think we were going to play, and number two, it was a great to have a soft-tosser like Jones out there, because it wouldn't hurt your hands when you hit the ball. No *bees* in the hands.

*Opening Day was special here—a lot more special—until Baseball started playing more than one game that day, or let other teams start first, like Sunday night on ESPN, or in Japan or Puerto Rico or wherever.* It's not as special now. It's not set aside anymore as being this special event. Sure, it's still special in Cincinnati—people here know where baseball started; they know what they've got—but it'd be even more special, if it was the only game, or the first game, like it used to be.

I looked at Opening Day as the beginning. There's always going to be a start, just like a new day. It was great to get everything going. You want to get off to a good start on Opening Day. Sometimes that sets the tone. You get a hit or two and you find that relaxes you a little bit more. But if you go 0-for-3 or 0-for-4, you're saying, "Uh-oh, the next game I got to get two hits." It's like you're playing catch-up, and it's only the second game of the season!

## WILL MCENANEY

*McEnaney debuted with the Reds in July 1974 at the age of 22 and shared the closer's role with Rawly Eastwick in the World Championship years of 1975 and 1976. McEnaney recorded the final out of both the 1975 and 1976 World Series.*

I grew up in Springfield, Ohio, 70 miles north of here, so I knew all about Opening Day in Cincinnati. But I never saw an Opening Day game until I came north with the Reds in 1975, my first full season.

Opening Day in Cincinnati was *the* official opening of Major League Baseball. And to be here on Opening Day 1975, and to see people from Springfield here, that was pretty neat.

The way I made the club in '75 for Opening Day was pretty cool, too. The last game that spring was against the Boston Red Sox, and the game went 16 innings. I was the extra pitcher just in case the game went extra innings, because all the other pitchers had been sent home. And it went extra innings all right—seven of them!

I pitched seven innings of shutout ball! Come to think of it, they could've used a guy like me in the 2002 All-Star Game in Milwaukee and it wouldn't have ended in a tie. I could've finished it off.

Those seven innings of one-hit ball are why I made the ball club that year. I just kept going back out there. Finally, the umpire said, "We're going to play one more inning and if nobody scores, that's it." Well, we did score and we won. And that was the best stuff I ever had. And I don't recall even having any strikeouts! I knew I had to shut them down, not let them score, if I was going to make the ball club, and that's what I did.

Sparky Anderson said to me two or three times that spring, "You ain't made this ball club." He said that to me *and* Rawly Eastwick. And, as it turned out, Rawly didn't make the team that year out of camp; he didn't get called up until May.

I had only two openers in Cincinnati, but we won them both, so that was pretty cool. And then to be on the mound at the end when we beat the Red Sox in Game Seven, that was the coolest thing of all. Especially knowing that we'd just won our first World Championship in 35 years. That was a long time coming—and we acted like it!

*(From left) George Foster, Dave Concepcion, Ken Griffey, Sr. and Dave Collins clowned along the foul line during the introductions for the 1981 opener.*

## Don Sutton

*Sutton of the Los Angeles Dodgers, started two Opening Day games in Cincinnati, in 1972 and 1975. He was elected to the Hall of Fame in 1998.*

Having grown up in the country, rural areas in south Alabama and northwest Florida, we all got fired up in March for the opening of spring training and then for Opening Day. Even then we knew it started in Cincinnati. *We all knew where Opening Day was going to be; it's a tradition! It's got to be there! So when I came to Cincinnati for Opening Day, I remember thinking, "Yeah, this is the way America is supposed to go about baseball!"*

Don Sutton started two openers in Cincinnati, winning one. He had a 1.29 ERA in his two appearances allowing only two earned runs in 14 innings.

I'd love to see the return of the tradition of the Reds opening the baseball season first. And it would have to be a day game. Because that's the memory I have. The powers-that-be are telling us that we're old-fashioned. I don't care. Baseball's an old-fashioned game.

You just can't duplicate anywhere else the atmosphere that exists here for Opening Day. And you certainly can't duplicate it with a night game. I remember walking in an ocean of red downtown! Everybody had their banners and their favorite players. Everybody on the street seemed like they were there for one reason. You thought the attendance was going to be 200,000, because there were 200,000 people who had Reds stuff, and they were fired up about the opening of the baseball season.

*I loved opening the baseball season in Cincinnati. My vivid recollection of Opening Day here is that it was a sea of red. You couldn't walk around any place in this city without seeing Reds paraphernalia and Reds fans. To me, it was like the State Fair of Baseball.*

It's an environment I haven't seen duplicated anywhere else. Opening Day here was not only the opening day of the "State Fair", it was the opening day of whatever you love. It was a huge event here. And although it didn't always turn out right for the Dodgers, it was fun to be in that atmosphere.

You know another thing—and I know I'm getting older; my memory's going—but I don't ever remember anything but a sunny, crisp day in Cincinnati for Opening Day. Cold, maybe, but sunny and crisp. Maybe that's not always the case. But that's the way I remember it.

## Pedro Borbon

*Borbon joined the Reds in 1970 and played 10 seasons in Cincinnati. Along with Clay Carroll, Borbon helped anchor the bullpen in the Big Red Machine era. He appeared in relief in every opener from 1973 to 1978, allowing one run in 12 innings.*

The Opening Day I remember more than any other is 1979—and it's because it's the only one I wasn't at. I played nine seasons for Sparky Anderson, but now here comes John McNamara in '79 and he had a problem with me. He suspended me for one day—and it was Opening Day! Opening Day in Cincinnati!

I had a little trouble in spring training—I was a little sick—and the pitching coach, Bill Fischer, tells McNamara, "Pete no wants to pitch." That wasn't true. I never said I no want to pitch. When I played for Sparky Anderson I never turned down the ball. I pitched for Sparky on Opening Day 1975 against the Los Angeles Dodgers and it was 26 degrees. I always took the ball. But *John McNamara suspended me on Opening Day in Cincinnati! He had me report to the stadium that morning, and then he suspended me!*

I was not happy. I said, "Bill, you and John McNamara go over to the store and buy a baseball history book and you can find out my name and learn a little bit about me." That's what got really got me suspended. They didn't like me smarting off to them. I went over to the office, and Dick Wagner said, "Pete, I can't believe it. Is this report true?" I said, "What's it say?" He said, "It says you no want to pitch."

I said, "Mr. McNamara and Bill Fischer are big liars. I have no pain." I pitched a lot that winter in the Dominican. I said I'm sick, I did not say I couldn't pitch. I said I did not want to pitch every day in spring training. I told them, "You know what I've got. I don't have to pitch every day in spring training." They took that the wrong way, and they suspended me.

I enjoyed my years with Sparky. There were some tough moments, like losing the last game of the 1972 World Series to the Oakland A's, when Sal Bando hit a fly ball in the sixth inning to Bobby Tolan, and he went down chasing it, and they scored their third run and we got beat, 3-2. It was my first time in the World Series, and I pitched in six of the seven games.

Many years later, after I was traded to the Giants after the 1979 season, I was asked by a reporter why Cincinnati never wins anymore. They said, "Did you put some sort of curse on them?" I said, just sort of joking, "Maybe." In 1988, the All-Star game was going to be played in Cincinnati; Pete Rose was the manager of the Reds. I was living in Texas, just like I am now, and I was asked on a radio show, "Pedro, are you ready to take the curse off the Cincinnati team?" "I said, 'Who said I put a curse on the Cincinnati team?" And they said, "That's what they're saying in Cincinnati." I said, "OK, it's off." Two years later, they won the World Championship.

Now, they've gone 12 or 13 years without winning, and people think I put the curse back on them. People see me and they say, "Pedro, do you still have that voodoo curse on Cincinnati?" I said, "You think I have that power? If I had that power, would I be raising parrots and canaries in Texas? If I had that power, I'd be the Superman of the World!" Instead of looking at my voodoo, maybe they should be looking at their manager or their general manager! Maybe they need a new one.

People ask me where I got the nickname "Dracula." Well, there was this brawl against the Pirates in Pittsburgh. The bullpen is the last group to get to the fight. It's a long way to the field. Somebody hit me in the back, and this big tall guy, a pitcher, had me wrapped up, and I didn't want to hit him, but he was holding me tight, had his hands around my hands so I couldn't move. The only way I could get loose was to bite him. I bit his hand, took a little piece of meat out of it. The next day, I see in the paper, that he had to take a rabies shot, because I bit him.

*After that fight, every time I went to Pittsburgh, the people, they called me Dracula.* The way I heard about that was I had a friend listening to the radio. He said, "Pedro, when you are warming up in the bullpen or when you come in the game, the radio announcers say, "The Dominican Dracula is now warming up in the bullpen," or "The Dominican Dracula is now on the mound."

I saw the radio broadcaster near the batting cage one day. I said, "Are you the one who broadcasts the game every day?" He said, "Yes." I said, "You know my name. B-o-r-b-o-n. My name is not Dracula. Any time you call me Dracula, there is going to be trouble." The guy ran back into the dugout. He thought I was going to hit him. But after that, he never called me Dracula any more. He would say, "Now getting loose in the bullpen, Borbon, from the Dominican."

*I would hear that nickname Dracula even when I would go back home to the Dominican. The people would say, "Borbon, are you eating people in the United States?" I'd say, "No!" and I would tell them the story.*

I love the fans of Cincinnati. I never had a problem with the fans of Cincinnati. I was a gentleman to the fans, signing autographs. And I'd throw the balls into the stands. One time Sparky Anderson came up to me and said, "Pete, it's going to cost you some money. You're giving away too many balls." I said, "Go ahead and fine me then." Fans are number one. They pay your salary. They're the ones who make you a star.

I live in Texas. I relax at home. I raise parrots and canaries, different kinds of birds. I raise them and I sell them. Sometimes business is good, sometimes not so good. I got into the business after I visited Mexico. I saw the beautiful birds, and I came back to the States and read a lot about raising birds and how they learn, and I bought some. I made some money, and I said,

*Pedro Borbon, the mainstay of the Reds bullpen in the 1970s, accepted congratulations from Big Red Machine stars Johnny Bench, Tony Perez and Pete Rose. Borbon appeared in six straight openers from 1973 to 1978.*

"This looks like a good business." I love animals. And I can do it at home. You do not have to be out running around. I like to work on my own.

I'm 57 years old, but I still throw every once in a while. I'm 85–88 on the gun. I'm losing my hair, but not my fastball. I never had trouble with my arm. I think I quit too early. I see many relief pitchers only throw to one hitter now. I say, "If I only had to pitch to one hitter, I'd still be pitching!"

# Hal McCoy

*McCoy has covered the Reds for the* Dayton Daily News *since 1973. In 2003, he received the J.G. Taylor Spink award for "meritorious baseball writing," and as a result, he is now "reunited" with his two mentors—the late Si Burick of the* Daily News *and Earl Lawson of the* Cincinnati Post—*who also received the honor.*

A lot has changed since I started in the business, and not just the kind of stories there are to cover. The technology's a lot different, too. When I started, we used portable typewriters; we typed our stories on copy paper and handed it to the Western Union guy, who would send it to the newspaper to be typeset. I learned a trick early on from Si Burick, my sports editor at the *Dayton Daily News*. The Western Union guys—especially at big events like Opening Day—would transmit the stories in the order they received them. That was a little tough on the writers back in those days, because you had to allow a little more time on deadline. You had to type your story, then give it to Western Union, and they had to retype it to get it to your paper. But Si told me if you slipped the Western Union guy five bucks, you'd go right to the top.

Si taught me a lot of things like like how to do an expense account. Si was my mentor as a journalist. My real mentor—as a baseball writer—was Earl Lawson. He took me aside, and for the first year or so, he said, "Just watch me." He introduced me to everybody, and I'm forever grateful. I try to do the same for young people on the beat. It all goes back to Earl. On the road, Earl took me under his wing, too, but that wasn't real good because Earl was a wild guy! Earl got me in a lot of trouble on the road.

The big thing Earl taught me was you have to approach each guy on the team differently. You have to learn each personality. You learn who to approach with a joke, who to approach seriously. You learn what not to ask, what to lead into gradually, what to come right out and say. From there, everything else falls into place.

Here's what happens if you don't learn that lesson. It was my first Opening Day. Sparky was the manager. The Reds had a sore-armed pitcher and the guy threw that day on the sideline before the game. After the game, the opener, here I am, the rookie reporter and I'm going to be the first guy to ask a question of the manager.

I say to Sparky, "How did so-and-so throw before the game?"

*Sparky said, "Son, we just won a big ballgame on Opening Day and you're asking me about a sore-armed pitcher?!"* That was a wakeup call for me. I didn't ask Sparky another question for about three weeks.

Another Opening Day I was sitting in his office before the game, and here comes the first wave of media. Sparky answers the questions and they leave. Another wave comes in. Somebody asks the exact same question that was asked in the first wave, and Sparky gives a totally different answer! I said, "Sparky! You told the first guy one thing, and you told the other guy the exact opposite!" And he said, "Well, you've got to give everybody a story!" Sparky was something else.

Each year, spring training is when it all starts for me, because it's when I start writing baseball every day again. Then comes Opening Day with all the pomp and circumstance. There's more of a media presence on Opening Day in Cincinnati than there is any other day of the year. Nothing else during the regular season comes even close.

*It's the one day of the year I wear a coat and tie, and I can't tell you why. I just feel like it's appropriate, even though I catch a lot of grief from the players. I tell them, "I dress up once a year—whether I need it or not. And this is the day."*

There's a lot more commotion around Opening Day. And I sense it right away with the players. I think they're more nervous that day. I don't know if it's nervous energy or they're excited about getting the season started or what it is. But they're *different* that day, different than any other day of the season.

Some guys rise to the occasion, some don't. I've seen some weird things, some amazing things, happen on Opening Day.

*Although McCoy prefers a cowboy hat, he dons a suit and tie for Opening Day.*

I'll never forget 1983. Dick Wagner was the general manager. John McNamara was the manager. They had a kid named Jeff Jones who played in Class A the year before. Right fielder. Had a pretty good year in Class A. He was invited to big-league camp in Tampa. He tore it up, hit like .429. Wagner not only wanted him on the big-league club, he wanted him in the starting lineup. Mac didn't believe Jones was ready for the major leagues, let alone for the Opening Day lineup, but Wagner told Mac, "You *will* do it."

I always make a habit of going up to each of the players before the Opening Day game and shaking their hand and wishing them good luck. I did that to Jeff Jones, and he looked at me kind of funny and said, "Hal, what am I doing here?" It turned out to be a pretty good question. The experiment turned out to be a disaster. Jones went on to hit about .120 for a month or so, and they sent him down to the minors and he was never heard from again.

Another guy I remember on Opening Day was Clint Hurdle. Many years earlier, he was a bonus baby—one of those guys who was supposed to develop into a super-super-superstar—and he bounced around quite a bit before the Reds got him. He started in left field for them on Opening Day in '82. The rap on him was that he was a terrible fielder. Well, early in the game, runner on second, base hit to left field, Hurdle throws the guy out at home with a *great* throw.

He gives it one of these jobs where he pulls the imaginary gun out of the holster and shoots the guy and blows the barrel. It was so funny, but it was the highlight of his season. I don't think he played in 20 games.

Kevin Mitchell was a beauty, too. He wasn't much of a fielder, either, but what does he do on Opening Day in his first game as a Red? He throws out a guy at home plate in a one-run game! Some guys just have a knack for doing things on Opening Day they never do again. It's probably the great atmosphere that gets them all jacked up.

*I've been in the business 30 years, and the biggest character I've ever met is Kevin Mitchell.* He was so funny that every day I ended my notes column with something funny he said, and I called it, "Kevin's Korner." He got to where he knew I was doing it, and he'd come looking for me. Every day. He didn't call it "Kevin's Korner." He'd say "I got one for you for 'Mitch's Corner.'" And he'd tell some story about his life on the street that'd just crack you up. Stories about his buddies, "Japanese Tony," and "Big Fat Stinky Mike," and a whole menagerie of characters.

*My friend Big Fat Stinky Mike was so fat that he took out the front seat of his Cadillac and drove it from the back seat!* He just cracked me up.

I haven't seen Mitch in a long while. I miss him. He was playing independent league ball in California. He played softball for a while, too. He made a lot of money, but he passed out a lot of it to his street buddies. Every time we went out to San Diego, there'd be 15 entourage people waiting for him outside the clubhouse. He'd come out and pass out $50 bills to them.

*Pete Rose had a Big Fat Stinky Mike in his entourage, too. Fat Mike Bertolini. He was one of those guys who were hanging around Pete in the late 1980s. Those weight-lifter guys who hung around the clubhouse were scary. Fat Mike would sit around in the manager's office and sign Pete's autograph on baseballs.* Pete always denied that Bertolini ever signed his autograph for him, but I walked into Pete's office one day, thinking Pete was in there. Bertolini was sitting behind Pete's desk and he had one of those big white waste baskets full of baseballs, and he was signing "Pete Rose" to them and he throwing them into another waste basket.

I didn't put two and two together on Pete until I read the Dowd Report. Dowd talked about the little red notebook Pete had in his desk, and I saw that. Dowd talked about him calling other managers and asking how their pitchers were. I was sitting there one day when he called Sparky in Detroit and asked him, "Sparky, how's your pitcher tonight? Think he'll win?" He chatted with Sparky for a while and then hung up the phone. I said, "Pete, Detroit's in the American

*Hal McCoy presented Jack Billingham the 1973 Johnny Vander Meer Award as the Reds outstanding pitcher of the year. McCoy has long been active in the Cincinnati chapter of the Baseball Writers' Association of America, which votes on the Reds' annual awards.*

League. Why do you care how they're going go do?" Pete said, "You know me. I'm just a huge baseball fan. I want to know everything that's going on."

*One day he pulled out the notebook when I was in there, and he got on the phone. He called somebody and said, "So-and-so, this is Pete." He's looking at his red notebook and he's saying, "Yes, no, no, yes, yes." I didn't know it at the time, but the questions on other end of the line would have been, "Do you want the Tigers?" "Yes." "Do you want Houston?" "No." And right on down the line. "Yes, no, yes, no."* And he'd shut it, put it back in his desk. That's all in the Dowd Report, and that's how it happened.

Marge? I saw my grandmother in Marge Schott. My grandmother talked the same way. The difference is my grandmother didn't run a major league team in the public eye.

*Marge did a lot of things wrong, but she had it right when it came to Opening Day. The Findlay Market Parade was her baby, and rightly so.* That, and letting the elephants go on the field. Which reminds me of Pokey Reese, who had the worst Opening Day I ever saw. He made his Opening Day debut at shortstop in '98. He made four errors—three of them in one inning—and afterward he said, "I felt like what was coming out of those elephants before the game." At least he got a good line out of it.

Marge didn't like the writers making fun of her St. Bernard crapping on the field. Jerry Crasnick—he was with the *Cincinnati Post*—got banned from the Reds' dining room for writing about it. I got banned from the dining room five years in a row for writing something she didn't like. Once, it was in spring training, before the season even started. Back when we used to have dining-room cards and Jon Braude was the Reds p.r. guy, he'd come up to me after I'd written something that Marge didn't like, and he'd say, "You know what I want!" And we'd both laugh.

What's that Babe Ruth curse they have in Boston? "The Curse of the Bambino." Well, here, we've got the Pete Rose Curse. Until 1989, most everything with the Reds was baseball, baseball, baseball. Then came the Pete Rose gambling scandal in '89, and it's been something every year since. It's unbelievable, it really is! Marge had some problems before '89, but she really got bizarre after that. She was the savior in '84 for buying the club, just a kindly old lady and the St. Bernard, and everybody loved her and all that. Then, *wow*.

It's been something every year ever since! It never stops. And, usually, it's just when you think everything's quiet, and you've got all your features stories and notes and columns all done, and *boom*! The s—t hits the fan!

Every writer around the country, whenever they see me, they shake their heads and say, "Man, we don't envy you. Do you ever get to write about baseball?" There's always something going on in Cincinnati.

There are guys with other franchises who *never* have anything happen like that. Here, we've got Pete, we've got Marge, we've got Jim Bowden, we've got who knows what? *Hell, even Robin Williams knows the Reds' beat is crazy. I was introduced to him in October 2003, before an ALCS game at Yankee Stadium as "the guy who covers the Reds." He didn't even hesitate. He placed his hand on my head and said, "God bless you, my son, do you still have your nuts?"*

Lou Piniella was my favorite. It'd be hard for me to say Lou was any more wired Opening Day than he was another day, because Lou was *always* wired. Whether the Reds were winning or losing, he was wired. When they were winning, it was "Can we keep winning?" When they were losing, it was "Are we ever gonna stop losing?" He was always running his hands through his hair, and pacing behind his desk.

After the Reds got off to that great start in '90, they barely played over .500 the rest of the year, and Lou was constantly being asked: "Are you backing into the pennant?" I heard him asked that two or three times. He managed to keep his cool.

But then, just before the playoffs started, I was sitting in his office at Riverfront, and a young fella came in carrying one of those big oversized tape recorders. He introduced himself to Lou: "I'm so-and-so from the Christian radio station." Lou nods. The young man holds the mike right in front of Lou's face and says, "Lou, there's a lot of talk that your team may be backing into the championship, because of that fast start and slow finish."

*Lou starts his answer with, "My good man"—well, you always knew you were in trouble when Lou addresses you as "My good man."* "My good man, have you ever (expletive deleted) a (expletive deleted) from behind?" The young man just stood there, frozen, holding the mike on Lou. And Lou said, "Well, (expletive deleted) is still (expletive deleted)!" All the fella could say in response was, "Thank you, Mr. Piniella" and turned around and walked out! Interview over.

After the fella left, I said: "Lou, didn't you hear him say he is with the *Christian* radio station?" Lou said, "I don't give a damn who he's with! He ought to know better than to ask a question like that!" That was pure Lou.

Another one of my Lou's stories is the day we were in San Diego toward the end of the '92 season and I was at DelMar Race Track with him one afternoon. There had been some speculation that Lou might not be back for the '93 season, but there had been no official announcement. Well, Lou hit a hot streak at DelMar. He won five of the first six races. So it's getting a little late, and I look at my watch and I say, "Lou, we'd better be going. Batting practice starts in an hour." He said, "Ah, screw it! I'm not coming back, anyway."

McCoy congratulated Jack McKeon in an award presentation in 1998. Five years later both could congratulate one another again. McCoy received the J.G. Taylor Spink Award at the National Baseball Hall of Fame in Cooperstown, and McKeon's Florida Marlins won the World Series.

And that's when I knew he wasn't going to be back with the Reds, and that's how I wrote it.

In 30 years covering the club, it's usually been a great clubhouse. I've always wondered where that comes from. Right now, I think it's Barry Larkin. Evidently, there's always been *somebody* in the clubhouse who has told the players how to act. There have been very few bad guys.

There's only one guy in the clubhouse I was ever afraid of, and that was John Denny. He's the one guy I thought was going to wind up in a Texas tower shooting people. He had those steel gray eyes that would bore right through you. I never went close to him unless I absolutely had to. He was scary.

Otherwise, the few bad guys there have been are some of the guys who I got along with best. Guys like Bo Diaz. He would talk to me, as long as nobody else was around.

*Believe it or not, I had trouble with Joe Morgan. Joe Morgan and I haven't spoken since 1979.* I probably wrote 500 complimentary stories and columns about him, and then one day in 1979 I wrote something like, "It's probably time for Joe Morgan to move on." I came in the next day and went up to him and he looked at me and said, "Don't *ever* try to speak with me again."

And we haven't spoken since. We've been on elevators together by ourselves, and we're both childish about it. We just stand there and look straight ahead. We've even played tennis a couple times in doubles, against each other on the same court, and never spoke!

I had my problems with Johnny Bench, too. He and I got into it five or six times. What I liked about Bench is he let me know the next day that he didn't like what I wrote, and then he forgot about it; he was fine. I'd rather have somebody like that.

*My number one guy for filling a notebook is everybody's number one: Pete Rose.* All you had to do was walk up to Pete and open your notebook and ask one question and he'd fill it up. Morgan was a good talker, too, if you liked hearing somebody talk about themselves in the third person.

There were a lot of good talkers in that clubhouse. Bench was a good talker. The one thing I learned in covering those two was never to approach Rose first if Bench was in the clubhouse. If Bench saw you talk to Rose first, and then you went to Bench, you weren't going to get anything. If you talked to Bench first, he'd give you good stuff. And then you could go talk to Rose, because he didn't care. He'd talk, anyway.

And, later, Dave Collins was always one of my favorites. He was excellent. He would tell me anything I wanted to know. Dick Wagner—another guy I haven't spoken with since 1979—traded Collins to the Yankees. After Dick made the trade, he walked up to me and said, "I just traded your bobo in the clubhouse."

That was the one downside of breaking in with the Big Red Machine in '73. I had no idea how good I had it. I had no idea what I was covering, what I was watching, what I was seeing. I just thought, "Hey, this is the way it is all the time!" And it hasn't been anything close since.

Opening Day in Cincinnati hasn't lost anything for me personally. I still get goosebumps. It's still a different, different day. I wish it was still the first game of the entire major league season. Cincinnati deserves that, because it's the first pro baseball team. But ESPN stepped in with those Sunday night games. That's money talking, and there's no going back now. But Cincinnati's opener is still the best of them all, anyway.

Nobody has the pomp and circumstance of Cincinnati. Not even when the Reds opened new ballparks in Pittsburgh and Milwaukee in 2001, it still didn't match what Cincinnati does on Opening Day.

No matter how good the Reds are projected to be in a given year—or how bad—Opening Day has always been the same to me. It's always special.

# Ray Knight

*Knight came up through the Reds organization and made his major league debut in 1974. He became a starter in 1979, taking over for Pete Rose at third base. He played for the Reds for four seasons, and managed the Reds in 1996 and 1997.*

I thought the world of Pete Rose. I was so privileged to get to watch him play in 1977 and 1978. Even in '73, when I went to my first big-league spring training, he treated me well. Coming up in the organization in the '70s there was always talk. *Here's a kid who plays like Pete Rose—not great ability, but tremendous heart.* When Pete saw me play in '73—and him being "No. 14" and liking horse racing—he started calling me "14A."

I was called up at the end of the '74 season. In '75 and '76, I was back in Indianapolis. In '77 spring training, we were one player over the roster limit, and it came down to Joel Youngblood or me. They already had Doug Flynn as a utility guy. But I hit about .390 in the spring, and two days before camp ended, they traded Joel for Doug Capilla, and it looked like I was going to make the club. So I was waitin' to hear something, but Sparky never actually told me, "You've made the club." Bernie Stowe never told me either. He had broken the news to me the years before that I *didn't* make the club. I asked Jim Ferguson, who was our traveling secretary, and he's the person who actually told me I'd made the club. *Yeah, kid, you've got a seat on the plane.*

*Opening Day? Heck. I got to the ballpark about 9 o'clock in the morning, I was so excited.* I couldn't believe I'd finally made it to the big leagues. I just set there and I was in awe. Sparky called me into the office that morning and said, "Congratulations." He said, "Pete's getting a little bit older, and you're going to play every second game of doubleheaders and every day game following a night game." Well, I started 11 games that year, and all of them were at second base for Joe Morgan! I had only a hundred at bats in '77 and 65 in '78—and I was up here all year long! All I did was go in defensively for Pete after his fifth at bat every night—after Pete was sure he wasn't going to get to hit again!

One thing that worked to my advantage is that when I played winter ball—I think it was in '77—John McNamara managed the Licey club in the Dominican, and I played with Estrella. In the All-Star game, I was the third baseman, and we had a couple of guys get hurt and McNamara asked me if I minded playing second, and I said, "I'll play anywhere you want me to, Skip." I didn't know John McNamara from a hole in the ground. But he liked the way I swung the bat in the league that winter, and, ironically, two years later he replaced Sparky as manager.

*I first knew something was up with Pete in the summer of '78, because I heard from guys in Triple-A that Mr. Howsam was down there looking at guys. I'd never known Mr. Howsam to be down there looking, so I just knew something was going to happen with Pete.* But I didn't know if I was going to be their guy or not.

After the '78 season, the Reds went over to Japan for the goodwill tour, and Mr. Howsam and Mr. Wagner called me up to their suite at the hotel in Tokyo and told me they had made their last offer to Pete, and that if he didn't accept it, I'd be the third baseman. They liked the way I played defense, and they felt I was getting better as a hitter. And that's how I found out—four months before it became public knowledge.

Every day that spring in '79, there were writers around me. Every day that spring, I had to make a comment about Pete. I kept saying, "Look, *somebody* has to replace him. If what I've got is enough, it'll be me. If it isn't, somebody else is going to be there."

You're always going to feel pressure, but I *knew* I could catch a ground ball. They told me, "We don't care what you hit." Of course, I knew then—like I know now—that that was kind of B.S. Because if you don't hit, you're not going to be in there—not at third base, anyway!

*I broke camp with a sprained ankle, so I wasn't in the Opening Day lineup. But, man, the boos! Fans were so mad about losing Pete and Sparky.* When the lineups were announced McNamara was booed! Rick Auerbach was at third and he made a couple of bad plays. Bunt play, runners at first and second, Tom Seaver comes up with the ball, and Auerbach's got his back turned—he was a natural shorstop—and Seaver throws the ball and almost hits him in the back and the ball goes down to the bullpen. *Booooo!* By the time McNamara comes out to get Seaver in the fifth inning, we're down, 5-1, and the fans *really* let McNamara have it. *They're on their feet booing, both hands cupped around their mouth booing, just all over Mac, and Johnny Bench, who's out at the mound with Mac, said, "Hey, Skip, how are you enjoying your Opening Day so far?"*

It crossed my mind that hey, if I was out there, at least half those boos would be for me. I could've taken a little bit of heat off Skip.

I didn't get into the lineup until the third game, and they gave it to me good. Even my first at bat, hitting seventh—you'd have thought I'd be able to hide there, at least a little bit—but when Paul Sommerkamp announced my name—"Now batting, No. 25, third baseman Ray Knight!"—here it came: *"Boooo!"*

One of the writers who'd been around a while wrote, "Give the kid a chance." I agreed with that. There were a couple guys behind the third-base dugout who hammered

Ray Knight faced an almost impossible situation in 1979, trying to replace Pete Rose in the Reds lineup. But he won the fans over by mid-summer.

me every day. *Every day.* For a month, the fans behind the third-base dugout had a chant going: "We want Pete!" They booed me until July. Up until then, I'd dive for a ground ball and somebody'd yell, "Rose woulda had it!"

But I had fought so hard to get there— six years in the minors, and two more years of sitting on the bench—and I wasn't going to let anybody take it away from me.

But then, about halfway into the season, I finally felt they believed in me. And when the fans in Cincinnati believe in you, they *love* you.

My first opener was 1980. Being on that first-base line and hearing the cheers, that was almost an overwhelming feeling. Goosebumps, chills, you name it. *As we were taking warm-ups while the Braves were coming to bat, Danny Driessen was tossing me balls and I'm throwing rockets back to him. I was so filled with adrenaline! And Danny was yelling, "Easy, man, easy!"*

The only thing that's similar to the feeling of Opening Day is All-Star Games and the World Series. Opening Day takes you to an emotional awareness to where, well, I can't even explain it. There is an excitement. I don't even know if it happens anymore—but there's an excitement about being in the big leagues on Opening Day.

The whole season is starting all over again—you've busted your butt, wintertime all the way through spring training, and it is your *life.* There isn't anything else that matters. And now we're getting the chance to go out there and play the game we love. It erases everything, no matter what you did in the past, no matter what's bad, it's a new day. It's a glorious day, and I'm a part of this. Look at all the people that *can't* be in this dugout. Look at all the people that *can't* be in this clubhouse. But *today,* I made this ball club, and I'm going out here, and they're here to see us. And I get chills now just thinking about it.

Opening Day is special anywhere. Cincinnati is a big deal because such a big deal is made that it's the Opening Day of Opening Day. But Opening Day is special *everywhere.* *It's like life beginning again. How often are you blessed with something that magnificent?* The only thing I can compare it to is the birth of a child. I get goosebumps just thinking it about.

I don't know if that's been lost over time. I just know that when we came along, there were no guarantees. You fought and fought and fought, dug through the minors, fought through spring training two or three years, broke spring training and you're finally on the roster and *whew!* But you can't say *whew!* because you're flying on the plane north, and it finally hits you when you land, but even then you can't say *whew!* because I've heard of guys flying north and suddenly being sent to Triple-A.

I don't think you really know you've made it until you walk out onto that field. And that's when you know it. And that's when you feel it. And that's why Opening Day is so special.

# Ron Oester

*Oester was born and raised in Cincinnati and graduated from Withrow High School in 1974. He played 13 seasons, all with the Reds, from 1978 to 1990 and started eight openers. But his first Opening Day memories date back to his grade-school days in the 1960s.*

I never got to an Opening Day game as a kid—it was hard to get tickets, and besides, we got to watch it on TV at school! *I remember going to grade school—Mt. Washington*

*Elementary—and watching Opening Day on TV. There were TVs in every room, and every one of them was tuned to the game. I especially remember it in fifth grade. Mrs. Peabody—she was a great teacher, and everybody liked her—had the game on.* Our principal, Mrs. Solidean, was a big baseball fan. All those TVs tuned to the game couldn't have happened without her. She had the right attitude! It seems like everybody was a big baseball fan back then. And this was a baseball town.

My first opener with the Reds was '81. I don't remember anything specific about the game, just that I was in a daze for the first inning or two. I was always that way on Opening Day. The nerves just sort of take over you. It just sort of overwhelms you, because you know how big a deal it is to people in Cincinnati. I knew only a few years before, I was on the other side of it, watching the game on TV in grade school.

It seems like we always won on Opening Day in the '80s. A lot of it had to do with Mario Soto. He won four straight openers. Mario was incredible, a two-pitch pitcher, a tremendous fastball, 95-plus, and an unbelievable changeup—it was almost like it *stopped* on the way to the plate. I'd be watching from second base as the catcher gave the signs, and if the catcher called for a changeup, I'd cheat a little bit to the pull side of the hitter. But sometimes Mario would just ignore the sign and throw a fastball. I'd say to him, "Mario, you can't be doing that—I'm trying to help you out there!" But he'd do it, anyway, you know, not shake off the catcher and cross everybody up. He didn't want the hitter to be thinking along with him. If the hitter is sitting on a changeup and then *POW!*, here comes the fastball, just *exploding* on him, he's in trouble.

*If you weren't nervous on Opening Day, you were lying!* The most nervous I ever saw a guy was Terry Francona in '87. I don't remember what I did at the plate in any of my Opening Days, but I remember Francona. I remember him stretching in front of his locker before the game that day. We *never* did our stretching in the clubhouse, but there he was doing his stretching. He was hyper. I remember Buddy Bell asking him, "You a little nervous, Terry?" And Terry says, "Yeah, I'm nervous! I said I wanted to *make* the team, not *start* on Opening Day!" We cracked up.

And then he went out and hit a two-run home run off Dennis Martinez of the Expos. It was a big home run; it put us up. And we won the game. And his wife had a baby that night or the next day. I know she was in the hospital one of those two days. That was some opener for Terry. But he didn't get all giddy about hitting that two-run homer. He was a modest guy, very modest. And he was also one of the funniest guys I ever played with.

*Ron Oester (16) and Dan Driessen greeted Tom Hume after the Reds reliever closed out the victory in the 1983 opener.*

*It was really odd opening on the road in '90, down in Houston. That was the year of the lockout, and the season was delayed three weeks. It felt weird; it just wasn't the same. It wasn't near as big a deal. I mean, what you rather play in front of? Fifty-five thousand fans or thirty thousand? They didn't have a parade; no hoopla, no floats. I would have rather opened at home.* The first game should always be in Cincinnati—the oldest franchise in baseball. They should have rearranged the schedule. But maybe not opening at home did help us that year. We won our first nine games.

# Marty Brennaman

*Brennaman began his Reds' broadcasting career on Opening Day, 1974, the day Hank Aaron tied Babe Ruth's career home run mark of 714. He has broadcast over 4,500 games with his partner in the booth, Joe Nuxhall. In 2000, Brennaman received the Ford C. Frick Award for excellence in broadcasting in ceremonies at the Baseball Hall of Fame in Cooperstown, New York.*

No sooner did I arrive here in February '74, than I began hearing about Opening Day.

People said, "This is an Opening Day unlike any other Opening Day in the country." I dismissed it, "*Fine. That's great.*" I had nothing to compare it with, so I thought, "Well, I assume they say the same thing in Los Angeles, New York, Philadelphia, St. Louis, and every other city in the country that has major league baseball." So, no, I never gave it any more thought. It just never made much of an impact on me.

But something Dick Wagner said within my first two days in Cincinnati was pretty closely aligned with what I was hearing, now that I look back on it. I was sitting in Wags' office and somebody brought in a big cardboard box and put it on his desk.

Understand now, Wagner was the guy I reported to. Bob Howsam, the general manager, didn't want any part of the radio broadcasts. Bob was a baseball guy; Roger Ruhl handled all the promotions and Dick handled everything else.

So, anyway, here comes this big cardboard box. Dick asked me if I knew what was in it.

"I have no idea."

"There are Reds yearbooks going back 20 years, plus a history of the Cincinnati Reds written by Lee Allen."

"What's this all about?"

"The people who tune to your game broadcasts are going to know more about this franchise—and more about the people you talk about —than *you're* going to know. But you know what?"

"What?"

"You're going to know *something* by Opening Day."

Dick pointed to the box; I got the message. See, at that point in time, anything Dick said was fine with me. Of course, after a few years, when I was confident in my job, everything he said *wasn't* fine. And he and I were in each other's face all the time. But he was right about the fans. He gave me an opportunity to sound somewhat knowledgeable, and I took advantage of it. I read the Lee Allen book. I read the media guides. Some of them I even took on the road with me. I had them available to me in my briefcase in the booth.

I was concentrating more on what I needed to do, than I was on Opening Day. I gave no thought to "Opening Day, Cincinnati," until about 48 hours before the fact. I was totally taken up with the routine of being the Reds' radio play-by-play man and I wasn't thinking about Henry Aaron and Babe Ruth and Opening Day. When Aaron stepped into the batter's box in the first inning, yes I thought about the possibility of him tying the record. But the *probability* of him doing it? No way. I'd never seen Henry Aaron play before in my life. I did hope that if I had the call everything could come out OK. I didn't rehearse it. I think when you rehearse it, it's going to come out contrived and people are going to pick up on it right away.

*I remember it like it was yesterday: 3-1 pitch from Billingham, line drive, home run to left. First pitch he swung at. The call was fine and it was a helluva game.* The Reds were down, 6–2, going into the eighth, and Tony Perez hit a three-run homer off Phil Niekro to pull within one. The Reds tied it in the ninth on a double by Pete Rose and won it in the 10th inning when Rose scored from second base on a wild pitch by Buzz Capra that got over toward the third-base dugout and the catcher couldn't find the ball. I've always been of the opinion that if you're a play-by-play guy, great games make you better than you are. And that was a great game.

I've done a lot of Opening Day games, but the only ones I can remember are 1974, 1996—when John McSherry died—and 1990, the only time the Reds opened on the road since I've been here. They opened in Houston because of the lockout. Barry Larkin won the game with a bases-loaded triple in the 11th inning.

And, oh yeah, I remember one Opening Day in the late 1970s when it did everything conceivable weatherwise: snow, rain, freezing rain, sunshine, you name it.

So, yes, having a game like the '74 opener helped me, but it still took me a while to be accepted here.

It wasn't that I didn't know *anything* about the Reds. As a kid growing up in the 1950s in Virginia, I collected baseball cards. I mean, I *knew* who these people were. *The first time that Joe Nuxhall and I ever met, the first thing out of my mouth within five minutes of*

Marty Brennaman is the second Ford C. Frick Award winner to make his broadcasting debut on Opening Day in Cincinnati. He joined Red Barber who debuted 40 years earlier, in 1934.

*meeting him was: "I've got your baseball card!"*
And I did. And I had more than one of them. I knew who he was, his background, his claim to fame—all from his baseball cards. I knew about Wally Post, Gus Bell, George Crowe, Stan Palys and I knew about Tommy Carroll, who was a bonus baby shortstop out of Notre Dame but wasn't worth a damn. I knew about these players, because I had their cards.

But what blew me away was how smart the people in this town were about baseball. Later, I joked about it when we went to Dodger Stadium and some Dodger would get a hit and people'd go crazy. I said, shoot, a single and people are going nuts? I said, you've gotta *really* do something in Cincinnati to get people worked up. And, at times, that's been a rap on

*Part of the success of the Brennaman-Nuxhall broadcast team is the admiration they have for one another, as well as the ability to enjoy a joke, sometimes at the other's expense.*

them. But you've got to do something to *impress* them. I don't think that's all bad. Their standards for the way the game should be played are higher than the standards in most other cities.

I felt I was qualified to do play-by-play when I got the job here, but I had to learn the *game* on the job. My introduction to baseball play-by-play was being part of a very good American Legion baseball program in North Carolina. That would have been '66, '67, '68 and '69. That Legion team played between 60 and 70 games in the summer, almost every night. I did them all, including road trips. It was a county of 25,000 people, and a 250-watt radio station. They played in a small college ballpark, and they filled it up. They won the state championship one year.

I did three years of play-by-play by myself in Triple-A in Tidewater. And then I was headed to Cincinnati, where I was going to do seven innings of play-by-play, and I had a guy—Joe—who was going to do two for me. But, however much I *thought* I knew about the game, I knew *nothing*.

*The month I was in Cincinnati before going to spring training, all I heard was how great Al Michaels was, what big shoes I had to fill. If I ever doubted my ability in a general sort of way, that was the time.* I was a big fish in a little pond in Virginia, and now here I was in Cincinnati, replacing a guy who was very popular.

Joe says that Al was blessed to have grown up in Brooklyn and to have attended a lot of Dodgers game, and to have total recall of so many great anecdotes from those days. And he was right. I had nothing like that to fall back on. I've told young people that one of the toughest things for me was to just get to the point where I was around long enough that if something occurred on the field, I'd have something to compare it to on the air.

That's why it was so great to have Joe around, especially early on. I think Joe intuitively knew that I didn't have any frame of reference to fall back on. He'd fill in the gaps. He'd tell his anecdotes, give a little history. He was a godsend in that way. He did it because he knew I couldn't, and he did it to make the broadcast better. I told him—and I've told every color guy I've ever worked with, no matter the sport—"you can't talk too much for me." I don't have an ego when it comes to that. There are certain guys in this business who basically could do the game by themselves. Vin Scully does it by himself. George Grande basically does it by himself. They don't need color guys.

I think we'd all agree that, these days, Joe doesn't have a helluva lot to say when he ain't working play-by-play. But when he does have something to say, I shut up. Because, no matter how long I've been around, Joe still knows more about what's happening than I do. So, even though I feel as though I've come to know the technical part of the game as well as anyone, I'll always defer to Joe. But, boy, did I ever give Joe some material to work with early that first spring training.

*Here we were, at the first spring training game in 1974, and I'm nervous as hell, because now all the bullshit is over with. Now, I've gotta put my act together. Now, it's gotta happen.* We went to McKechnie Field in Bradenton to play the Pirates. Back then, Joe and I used to ride the bus with the team. Game ends, I get on the bus, we're going back to Tampa, I feel pretty good. I got through the broadcast and I felt like it was OK.

The next day, we're playing our home opener in Tampa, at Al Lopez Field against the White Sox. And as tight as I was the day before, that's how loose I was the second day. Back then, we did the broadcast from the top of the stands. There was no radio booth. So, we're lined up three in a row: engineer Ken Kimball, me in the middle and Joe on my other side. Ken cues me to go on the air, and I say, "Good afternoon everyone, welcome to Reds baseball from Al *Michaels* Field in Tampa, Florida."

As soon as I said it, I knew what I said! Al *Michaels* Field. And that son of a bitch Joe, he shows me no mercy. He's *rolling*. I thought he was going to fall out of his chair. So I go to the obligatory commercial break before we came back to do the lineups, and the first thing out of Joe's mouth during the break is: *"I'll be damned! We haven't even gotten to the regular season yet and I've got material for the banquet circuit next fall!"*

Embarrassed? I was mortified! Bob Hertzel was covering the club for the *Enquirer* back then—he and Al were really tight—and I guarantee you he was on the phone calling Michaels before the first inning was over. That whole season, every time we saw the Giants and I saw Michaels, Hertzel would make a big deal of it. That's all I heard! And that's the reason that in my Hall of Fame speech the first person I thanked was Al Michaels. People don't believe that story, but you want to talk about the subconscious? That's the best example of it in the world! It's the most humbling thing that's ever happened to me.

*It took me about a half of a season to be accepted in Cincinnati. But today? As far as the baseball public in Cincinnati is concerned, I wasn't born and raised in Virginia; I didn't go to school at North Carolina. I'm a Cincinnati guy, and goddammit, you'd better not say anything about me!* That's the way people are in this town. Once they accept you, you're in like Flint, boy.

And the night I started feeling like I was finally being accepted here was in late July that first summer. The Reds trailed the Giants, 13–9, going into the ninth inning, got it to 13–12 and then Tony Perez hit a two-out, two-strike, two-run home run off Randy Moffitt to win it. I went nuts on that call; I went crazy! The station was inundated with phone calls that night and the next morning from fans who wanted to hear the call again. And when the feedback started rolling in, that's the day I said, "I've arrived!"

That was a wild game. The Reds' half of the ninth was extended because Bench hit a ground ball to first base and Dave Kingman fielded the ball. Moffitt never left the mound. If he does what he's supposed to do, the game's over. That's the third out of the ninth inning. But by not getting off the mound, Moffitt opened the door for Perez. Big mistake. Tony stepped up and went straightaway center field.

I was truly blessed when I was chosen to succeed Al, because I came to the best place I've ever lived. And since then, I've had chances to go to every major city in the country to broadcast big-league baseball, and every time it came time to pull the trigger, I couldn't do it. It had nothing to do with money. It had everything to do with lifestyle and liking this town.

*The other reason I like Cincinnati so much is because it always has been—is now, and forever will be—a radio town first, and a television town second.* As opposed, say, to the Cubs and the White Sox, where television is number one. Radio is *it* here. For all the years I've been here, and before I came here and after I'm gone, radio will always be number one. People say, "well, that's because of you and Joe." No it isn't. It wouldn't make any difference *who* it was. It's a *radio town*.

One of the things that has always jumped out at me is when people say, "I can walk downtown on game day, store after store after store, or walk through any neighborhood in the city, and not miss a pitch, because the radios are always tuned to the game." That might be over-exaggerating the point, but in many cases it's true. And it really has nothing to do with the people that do the games. Because, for one thing, the Reds are always going to have good play-by-play people here. They are going to make a point of it. People will demand it. I hope the club is smart enough to realize that radio is king with this team. But no, I take no credit for that. I do take credit for the fact that Joe and I have been together for going on 30 years. And that counts for something. I mean, we get mail addressed to "Marty and Joe, Cincinnati, Ohio," and the post office delivers it! They deliver it! I'd like to know where else that's done.

*For all of Joe's so-called "worldliness," he's the most naïve guy I've ever been around.* We were playing in San Francisco—'78, '79, something like that—and we had an engineer out there named Mike Marquard, who is now a radio executive in the Bay area. He was a great practical joker. In Joe, he saw an easy touch. Mike just *preyed* on Joe.

The best one Mike set up was during that Saturday afternoon game at Candlestick Park. It was a very small radio booth at Candlestick. We had a TV monitor to watch the replays. Well, Mike brings in his videotape machine a Panasonic VCR. There was just enough room in the booth for me, Joe, Mike and Mike's equipment. So Mike puts his VCR on the floor under his feet.

Well, the game starts and I *know* what's going to happen. I'm a part of this deal. And in the early innings, I would just start laughing, for no apparent reason. After about the second inning, during the commercial break, Joe says to me, "What in the hell is wrong with you, Marty?" I said, "It's just one of those days, Joe. Everything's funny to me." And then Hertzel shows up in the back of the booth, and Joe can't understand why Hertzel's there.

So now, we get to the seventh inning, and I come out of the commercial break and I say, "Back to Candlestick Park, the Reds leading the Giants 5-to-2, and we go to the top of the seventh. Here with the play-by-play is Joe Nuxhall."

Well, Morgan gets on first base and steals second. It's a close play at second. Morgan's safe, they show the replay. Joe's waiting for the replay, and right then, up on the screen pops Linda Lovelace in the movie, "Deep Throat," doing her thing, and I am literally crying!

Joe just flat-out stopped talking. He's pointing at the TV screen, and he literally could not talk! Joe thinks there's been some kind of electronic glitch and that the people back in Cincinnati are seeing the same thing we're seeing. I mean, the tears are *rolling* down my face I'm crying so hard!

Finally, we went to the commercial break, and Mike showed him the videotape machine. That was hilarious, too, because now Joe knew he'd been had, and everybody was just roaring.

Mike did some other stuff to Joe, too. On another one of our trips to San Francisco, Mike took a cassette recorder and went down to the P.A. announcer and had him record on the cassette, "Joe Nuxhall, long distance phone call for Joe Nuxhall in the main press box." Mike goes to the trouble of rigging this thing up to the speaker from the official scorer's booth.

First inning, I'm doing the play-by-play, and here it comes through the speaker, "Joe Nuxhall, long distance phone call for Joe Nuxhall in the main pressbox." Joe gets up and goes down to the main pressbox, then comes back upstairs and says, "I went in there and asked about the phone call for me, and they looked at me like I was stupid."

Second inning, same thing: "Joe Nuxhall, long distance phone call for Joe Nuxhall in the main pressbox." Joe gets up, goes downstairs, and again they look at him like he's stupid. Back upstairs he comes, shaking his head. *He went down there five times!* And the fifth time he went down there,

*Marty Brennaman happily endured a milk and champagne shower, courtesy of Barry Larkin (left) and Eric Davis after the 1990 World Series sweep. Brennaman considered the 1990 season his most fulfilling as a broadcaster.*

he was going down there to kick somebody's ass!

*There's just something about Joe. It's always a little bit funnier when it's happening to Joe. I think that's why people do it.*

I know the '90 World Championship meant a lot to Joe, and it certainly meant a lot to me. 1990 was probably the most fulfilling year I've ever had here, because of that championship. In '75 and '76, I didn't realize how special those World Championships were. I didn't realize how special they were until the mid-1980s, after suffering through some rough seasons. So, by the time 1990 came along, I could really appreciate it. And it meant so much to Joe because it was the only one he broadcast. In '75 and '76, there were no club broadcasts once you got to the World Series. Each club designated a representative off their team as the "club announcer" with the network.

I was involved in '75 and '76 with NBC, and Joe was not. In '90, he got to make that great call in Game 2 of the World Series when Joe Oliver had the game-winning double off Dennis Eckersley.

The '75–'76 team is the greatest team I've ever been around, but the '90 team is the most special team I've ever been around, because nobody picked them to win a damn thing. If I'm never involved with another World Championship team, my feeling is that I've had three of them, and two of the three were with arguably one of the top two or three teams in the history of baseball, and the other one was with a team that nobody gave a chance to do anything. And the '90 team was managed by a guy who to me is one of the truly great managers in the history of this franchise. And I don't know that people give Lou enough credit for that. If '90 is the last World Championship I'm associated with, it's a great one. I'll never forget how truly special that season was.

*I think the franchise has to be sure to protect the Opening Day tradition here at all costs. It has to be treated as sacrosanct.*

If there are policies that

now exist in the game that preclude certain things from happening, then this city should be cut some slack. I was disappointed years ago when the Reds' Opening Day was no longer the first game played of the major league season, and I still am. That's bowing to network money. All of us in this town took a tremendous source of pride in the fact that because the first professional team was here, that this should be—and was forever—the first game of the major league season.

I think anything that sets this game apart—"Opening Day in Cincinnati"—from all other major league openers, should remain that way. Whatever it takes, that effort should be expended. If that means treating the people at Findlay Market better—if for whatever reason they haven't been treated well—then that's what should happen.

And everything else that goes along with Opening Day in Cincinnati should be treated equally well. This is a different day from Milwaukee's or Pittsburgh's or wherever else you want to talk about. There isn't another Opening Day like this in America. Other towns say they have good opening days, and they do, but not like this one. I don't know of another city with an Opening Day parade, and if they do, it isn't the magnitude of the Findlay Market Opening Day Parade.

The uniqueness of Opening Day in Cincinnati is something that the powers-that-be should take note of, and do everything in their power to keep it that way. For the longest time, I really didn't have much to compare Cincinnati to. Wherever we went, after the Reds opened the season here, more often than not it was not the opening day for the team that we were playing. But in the last few years, I've seen other cities' openers, and I know. There's a huge difference. It's not even open to conversation.

## DAVE COLLINS

*Collins played 16 seasons in the majors, including seven with Cincinnati. Collins appeared in six openers and started two, 1980 and 1981. He stole 79 bases in '80, two short of the club record. He also served as a coach for the Reds in 1999 and 2000.*

Opening Day in '80 here was very special to me. That was my first opportunity to be in the Opening Day lineup. The year before when we made the playoffs is the year I became an everyday player, but it wasn't right away, and that's why Opening Day, '80 was special. I opened in the outfield. And, now, when I look back on my career, that was a great feeling, just to know I was in there. I was on a great team with a great tradition.

I went from being a role player to an everyday player. I overcame some challenges to do it; I worked at it; I was determined; I had to prove to people I was better than what they thought. And I think there's great personal satisfaction that comes with doing that.

*The one person who helped me more than anybody with that was Pete Rose—just watching him go about his business, always getting the most out of his ability, never giving up an an-bat or a base, never giving in.*

Pete was the guy who was the most instrumental in my career. It wasn't until 1978 that I came over here, so I only had that one year getting to see him play every day. The next year, Pete went to Philadelphia as a free agent. Pete made everybody around him a better player. And I think that's a sign of a great player. Pete did that with everybody, because of his enthusiasm and his ability to give 100 percent everyday. I think he raised the level of effort for everybody, by the way he went about his business.

Joe Morgan was the guy I learned the most from when it came to one specific area of the game: base-stealing and base-running. When I first came over here, I relied on just my speed. Joe's the first guy that made me aware of the science of base-stealing and how to apply it to help your team win—the art of reading pitchers, when to run and how to run. He was a great mentor.

Johnny Bench was good to me. He had a knack for picking up things during the course of the game. He'd pick up something on the opposing pitcher, and he'd mention it to me.

*Dave Collins had three hits and scored two runs in the 1981 opener.*

I pinch-hit in the '78 opener. I'd never experienced the electricity, the excitement, that was in the ballpark that day. *We opened against Houston—Tom Seaver vs. J.R. Richard, a great matchup, a big-time matchup.* Although it turned out to be a high-scoring game. I started the winning rally—in the fifth inning. I pinch-hit, beat out an infield single and scored. We wound up scoring five runs.

Playing in that Opening Day atmosphere, with that team, gave me the confidence to start believing in myself. There were so many great players on that team, and when you're not an everyday player, and you're struggling to try to make your mark on the game, and all of a sudden you're on a team like that, you have to find something to hang your hat on. For me it was, "Hey, if a team this good wants me with them, that says something about what they think of me." And the other thing is: "If I'm on a team like this, I've got to believe in myself, because I don't want to let these guys down." The accountability factor was high. And when I started to have success, especially success with these guys, it turned my whole game around.

I have fond memories of Opening Day here. When people refer to baseball as the "national pastime," Opening Day is what solidifies it for me. *Opening Day—that's the day that still makes it the national pastime. No other sport has a day like it. And no other city has an Opening Day like Cincinnati. You can feel it, smell it, touch it, hear it—you can see the electricity.* It's amazing, just to be a part of it.

And, when you're a player, you know that you are not so much *watching* the parade; you're in it. It doesn't get any better than that.

There's nothing like the introductions of Opening Day, and going out to the first-base line, knowing that hey, this is where it all started—in Cincinnati—and you're carrying on that tradition. It's a tremendous feeling. Even the pre-game ceremonies got to me—the Findlay Market parade coming into ballpark. When you watch that, you know the city is charged up, I mean, super-charged up.

All of that came together for me in 1980, being in the starting lineup. That's when I felt it the most, because I really felt a part of it. I had a much better day in 1981 when I went 3-for-5, but that '80 opener still means the most to me.

One thing that's funny about 1980. We faced Phil Niekro and I *didn't* get any hits. I think when I ended my career—there weren't many thing I ended up leading any category in—I had the highest batting average against knuckleball pitchers. I don't know what it was. For some reason, I could hit knuckleballs. It even got to the point where Phil quit throwing them to me. Crazy, isn't it?

## Nick Esasky

*Esasky played for the Reds from 1983 to 1988. He started in four Cincinnati openers.*

The Opening Day memory for me would be 1984, because that was my first Opening Day. I was called up in '83, in the middle of the year. We beat the Mets in the '84 opener. I got a hit and an RBI, but I can't remember much about the game.

*What I remember is standing there on the foul line and being nervous, but there was a comfort feeling in being out there with guys I had come up with or played with in spring training.* It wasn't like you were the only one out there for the beginning of the season. Even the veterans had butterflies, and they admitted it. Knowing that made it a lot easier to go out there and play the game.

But you always were anxious for that first pitch of the game to be thrown, that first ball to be hit to you, that first pitch to be thrown to you, so you could get it underway. Once the game starts, then it all goes back to what you do—just playing the game.

I was with the Atlanta Braves in '90, and my last game in a big-league uniform on a major league field was right here in Cincinnati. I came down with vertigo after that, and never set foot back on a big-league field until I came back for the final Reds game at Cinergy Field. I came up here with Russ Nixon as my manager in '83, and Russ was my manager in Atlanta in '90. So, Cincinnati was my start and my finish.

The further away I've gotten from the game, it starts to mean a lot more than when I was there. You don't think about the game being over for you. You're working so hard to achieve that and stay there. And then, it's taken from you, and before you know it, 10 to 12 years go by. Sometimes it takes a while before you really realize how important moments like Opening Day really are.

## Mario Soto

*Soto holds the three modern club records: most Opening Day starts (6); most Opening Day wins (4); and most consecutive Opening Day wins (4). Soto began his career with Cincinnati in 1977 and pitched for the Reds for 12 seasons.*

The thing I liked most about Opening Day in Cincinnati back when I was pitching is that nobody played before the Reds. The fans—everybody—was ready for Opening Day in Cincinnati. That is something that always sticks with you.

Of course, being from the Dominican, I loved to pitch in hot weather, but in Cincinnati in early April you can get any kind of weather, usually on the cold side. One year—1985—we got snow that day. That was probably the opener that I remember the most. *We swept up the snow off the Astroturf, and started again. That's not something you get to do in the Dominican.*

When you play for the Reds, and they tell you down in Florida, "You've got the Opening Day start," that's a big honor. To be able to pitch in six of them, that's something that is always going to stick with you, too.

I'm not even sure how many of those games I won. You're telling me I won four in a row?! That's news to me! I'm sure I knew about it at the time—it's something people would remind you of—but that makes my day to hear that again. I know how important Opening Day is in Cincinnati, and it certainly was important to me.

*The main thing was that I was prepared to pitch a complete game on Opening Day. Not too many guys want to do that anymore any time, let alone Opening Day—but that's how I prepared myself. I loved to pitch Opening Day.*

After my second Opening Day start, I came to expect that I'd be named the Opening Day starter, and I took great pride in that. I'd get to the stadium early. I loved the ovation we always got from the fans, welcoming us back—welcoming *me* back, for another year. It cheered you up.

Mario Soto struggled in his sixth and final Opening Day start in 1988. Pitching coach Scott Breeden (right) joined Soto and Bo Diaz, Barry Larkin and Dave Concepcion for a discussion.

# Ted Power

*Power spent 13 years in the big leagues, including six seasons in Cincinnati. He pitched out of the bullpen during most of his Cincinnati years, and never appeared in an Opening Day game.*

My first Opening Day here was 1983 after I got traded from Los Angeles. I don't have a story about Opening Day that year—I didn't get in the game

But I remember learning just before leaving spring training that year that I was not going to be a starter, that I was going to the bullpen. I thought I was going to be a fifth starter. But they flip-flopped Joe Price and me and put him in the rotation. I had wanted to start.

Then on our flight north, Soto and I almost missed the flight because we were hanging out in the airport, not at the gate. Our flight was delayed, and they didn't announce it—at least, we didn't *hear* it—until the flight had started taxiing out.

Well, they called it back and we walked on the plane and Russ Nixon grabbed me by the shirt, and snarled, "Don't you ever be f—ing late for a plane again!" And right away I knew I liked that guy.

I almost got in the '86 opener—I thought I was going to. I'd had a good year in '85, had quite a few saves, and on Opening Day '86 we had a lead with a save situation in the ninth inning, and Pete left Carl Willis in the game and he got the save.

# Dwight Gooden

*Gooden made the New York Mets as a rookie in 1984 and witnessed his first major league game on Opening Day in Cincinnati.*

The very first big-league game I saw was Opening Day, 1984, at Riverfront Stadium when I broke in with the Mets. It was Mike Torrez vs. Mario Soto. I knew about the whole tradition thing with the Reds. Back then, they always played the first game, so it was very cool to be here for that.

I remember how impressed I was with Soto, him being a right-hander like me. How often do you see a right-hander with a just a fastball and changeup? Soto developed a slider later in his career, but basically he was just fastball-changeup in his prime. And he got lefties out with it, as well as righties. Now, *that's* pitching!

*Believe it or not, the first thing that impressed me was that I remember coming out to the field early that day and seeing Dave Parker. I hadn't seen him at all during spring training. And I*

*remember thinking, "Wow, that's a big guy!"* It was all a big thrill for me, seeing the whole ballpark, because I grew up in Tampa as a Reds fan, and now here I was in Riverfront Stadium. And even though I wasn't pitching, I was still nervous, just being here.

I made my debut in the next series, against Houston. We left Cincinnati and went to Houston. I only went five innings, but got the win, 3-2.

Later that year, I remember coming out to the cage for batting practice and Pete Rose came up and said, "Doc, I've heard a lot about you. I'm glad to see you up here in the big leagues. Have a great career."

And I remember thinking, "Wow, that was Pete Rose. And I don't have anything to say!"

The first opener that I pitched was the following year, '85, in New York. Gary Carter—who I'd pitched to in '84 in the All-Star Game—had come over to us in the off-season. He was my catcher in '85. I remember him really getting me pumped for that opener. He was definitely the best. I got a no-decision that day. The game went 10 or 11 innings, and Gary Carter hit a home run off Neil Allen to win it.

And you know what else I remember about that game like it was yesterday? Facing Jack Clark. In '84, I remember him being hurt for the Giants. And during my rookie year Mookie Wilson and Rusty Staub told me, "You think you have a great fastball, right? See that guy over there?"—pointing to Jack Clark—"you're lucky he ain't playing!" I said, "Why?" They said, "Because he'll turn around anybody's fastball!" That conversation came up in my head on Opening Day, '85, when Jack came up to lead off the second inning for the Cardinals. And somehow I had him down 0-2. And I remember what Mookie and Rusty had said, and I said to myself, "I'm gonna show them. I'm gonna blow this one by him."

*Boom!*—0-2 fastball, gone! That sticks with me like it happened yesterday. And afterward, Mookie said to me, "That's the Jack Clark we were talking about."

## Tom Browning

*Browning was drafted by the Reds in 1982, and joined the club in 1984. He pitched 11 seasons in Cincinnati, highlighted by his perfect game in 1988. Browning started openers in 1987 and 1991, and started both of the Reds "openers" in 1990. The first was the official opener in Houston and the second was the "unofficial" opener in Cincinnati, eight days later.*

My first big-league camp in spring training Vern Rapp was the manager, and I wasn't going to be put on the roster to be protected that year. I hadn't been to Triple-A yet, but I went to the big league camp in 1984 and he wanted to take me north as a relief pitcher, but Bob Howsam wouldn't let him. Howsam thought I was a starter. He wanted me to go down to the minors and keep starting.

So I got called up at the end of that year, after Pete took over in August. I came up in September of '84. That in itself was a dream come true for me.

*We were in LA and the first guy to greet me in the clubhouse was Pete Rose. He put his hand out and said, "Welcome, Tom." So I paused, because what do I say? "Thank you, Mr. Rose, or whatever? I didn't know what to call him. But finally, I just said, "Thanks, Pete."*

My first start was in Dodger Stadium, wearing number 54. Struck the first batter out, Dave Anderson, 3-2 change up. Had a shutout until the ninth. Greg Brock broke it up with a base hit to right field. I grew up being a Reds fan, so I was a natural Dodger-hater. It was like a perfect beginning to a fairy tale for me. Pitching for the Cincinnati Reds. Pete Rose, Dave Concepcion, Tony Perez, against the Dodgers, against Orel Hershisher. Got my first major league hit off Orel Hershisher. I'm sure I was terribly nervous, but I really don't remember any of that. I pitched three starts in September. I was 1–0; I pitched pretty decent.

So I knew I had an inside track at the next year of making the club. Plus, Jim Kaat was our pitching coach, and he loved me, and I loved him. So that winter I busted my ass. I was running 40 minutes-plus every day; I worked out in a health spa. Everything I could. I knew this was my chance.

In the spring of 1985, I don't recall Pete ever saying, "You made the team," but I know he did. I was one of four guys. We had a four-man rotation that year right out of the gate because of Jim Kaat. I started 18 games in '85 on three day's rest.

Mario Soto started that opener in 1985. We saw all four seasons of weather that day. It started out sunny, then it was raining, then it snowed, then it rained, then the sun came out. *Soto was awesome, but all I wanted was to have his job. I wanted to be the ace. I wanted an Opening Day start.* I didn't have "ace" stuff, but I had enough moxie, and enough heart that I could fill that role. In 1987, I finally got the ball for the opener.

I had not heard anything about Opening Day in Cincinnati as a kid. I had no idea what it was about until I quit playing. Then I could see what happening all around town, what it means to people. But when you play, you go to the clubhouse while the parade is going on and people are going bonkers. You don't see any of that as a player. *First time I saw the parade was a couple of years after I retired. I came down to check out all the hoopla. They go schizo here. It's awesome.*

But in '87, I'm just getting ready for the game. I was nervous enough because it was my first Opening Day start. I figured if I got out there, I'd be OK, and you make that first pitch, get the first out. You think you can handle just about everything, because after the first pitch you just get into the game. But that was really my first experience with a full house and it's loud. I wasn't ready for the ovation. From the dugout, you hear it, you get pumped up, but you're not nervous, you're not part of it yet.

*I remember I struck the first batter out. People started cheering, and then my legs just disappeared. I couldn't feel them. I don't think I made it to the fourth inning.* My legs just went

Tom Browning earned "Star of the Game" honors in 1991, pitching five-hit ball and winning his second Cincinnati Opening Day game.

numb. I never got back on my game after that. I was fighting it the whole time.

I pitched two more openers after that and I was better. But that first one was overwhelming. I was totally unprepared for it. My legs went away in the perfect game, but that wasn't until the ninth inning.

When I came up, Pete was at first base, and it was awesome. He was the manager, don't forget. So he could talk to you and not be charged with a visit. He would always say things to pump you up. I was in Houston, ninth inning, got a shutout going. I had the bases loaded with one out, Pete came over, bounced the ball off the turf, and said, "Come on, get me a ground ball here. We'll get out of this." Jose Cruz hits a ground ball, we get a double play. Pete gets the ball at first, and throws an absolute BB at me after the last out. He could make you play. He expected everybody to play that way. I didn't mind. I loved it.

*Kurt Stillwell was trying to make the club, and Pete called him in and told him he was going to take him north. Now Stillwell was such a good guy. He couldn't swear. So Pete says, "You're going north, but I gotta hear you say, "F—!" Stillwell says, "F—!" Pete says, "Now you're going north."*

I remember one time, Pete was managing, we are playing the Padres at home. Chris Brown was playing third base. I hit a rocket between short and third. I take one step and look, and Chris Brown dives and catches the ball. So I run hard until about 10 feet from the bag, I never did watch him. But he was having trouble getting the ball out of his glove. I'm taking the last step to the bag and here comes the ball. Oh, man I got back to the dugout, and Pete chewed my ass out. "Don't you ever stop running!" That was the only time I ever did that, "big-leagued it." Pete, Davey, Tony, all those guys got in my face. And they were right.

The organization always made a big deal of the Opening Day tradition. We're the first team. We have the first game. One year there was a big flap made over Detroit starting their game before us. Marge was hot. We were 2:15 start, and Detroit was going off earlier.

Opening Day was always a little different, because you had the hoopla, the parade on the field, lining up the starters on the foul lines. Guys were always a little giddy. It's the opener, they're positive about their outlook. Being a major leaguer on Opening Day, new season, new uniforms, new spikes, all the stuff. Just the anticipation of this is the year. You're thinking, "I'd love to get me a ring." All the teams think that way on Opening Day. And it's true. You take a bad team and win the first 15 games, now you've got a confident team and they are going to be tough. That's what happened to us in 1990. We weren't a bad team, but win nine in a row out of the gate, and you think you're going to win.

*In 1990, Lou Piniella came in with this no-bullshit attitude. Lou was straightforward about the way he managed. "I don't care if you're making $100 or $100 million, if I need to get on your ass, I'll get on your ass." And he did.* We had such good chemistry that year. Everybody contributed in some way throughout the season.

I got all the milestones that year. I started the opener at Houston, and I started the first home game against the Padres. We won nine in a row. And then I got the first loss of the year. Dale Murphy hit a three-run homer off me. It was weird opening on the road that year. It was always great playing for Cincinnati, knowing you were going to start every season at home.

I always worked quick. Didn't want to waste any time. The guys loved it. I grew up in an era of fast-pitch softball. My dad played fast-pitch. I think they had a time limit to their games, so they got the ball and they threw it. So I did that in Little League. Get the ball, throw it.

*Tom Browning is one of only nine Reds pitchers who have two or more Opening Day wins.*

It worked out for me, too. I didn't have much time to think. Not that I did a lot of thinking. When you're pitching in a game, you're always thinking ahead. If I'm facing Pedro Guerrero, that third pitch, I want to get in on his hands, jam him. I knew three pitches out what I wanted to do; it would probably change from one pitch to the next, but I thought I had an idea of where I was going and what I wanted to do. Like Andres Galarraga, I could throw him 25 balls up and away and he would pretty much swing and miss every one of them. But I would have to come inside every now and then to keep him honest. I knew him and I knew what I had to do.

People always ask me about the perfect game in '88. But not many people know I almost pitched one in college—at Le Moyne College, in Syracuse, New York. I had a perfect game going into the seventh inning of a second game of a doubleheader against Siena. You only played seven innings in college ball in the second game, so this was the final inning. Our coach, Dick Rockwell, absolutely hated Siena. But a Siena guy hit one into the gap, and two runs scored, and we got beat. After the game, Coach Rockwell said to me, "How could you lose a no-hitter in the last inning?" But I got my revenge in '88 with the perfect game for the Reds. So I pitched one, anyway—although it isn't the one Coach Rockwell wanted.

It's kind of interesting how I wound up at Le Moyne, and ultimately, in pro ball. I was born and raised in Casper, Wyoming. My stepdad helped design power lines. So when the New York State Power Authority called on his services, we moved to Utica for my freshman and sophomore years in high school. The power line started in Utica and went to Montreal, Canada. My last two years of high school, I lived in Malone, New York, about eight miles from the Canadian border. While I was in Malone, one of our rivals was Massena, and their star pitcher was Jimmy DeShaies who later pitched for the Houston Astros. One particular game that Jimmy pitched against us, Coach Rockwell came up to watch Jimmy. And Jimmy beat me one to nothing and he hit a home run off me Coach Rockwell asked me if I'd consider going to Le Moyne as well, and he ended up getting both of us.

Because of the late winter and rainy spring in Syracuse, if we played 40 games a season, 20 of them were doubleheaders. I was something like 6-2 or 8-2 a couple of those years. I went to Le Moyne three years and they wanted me to go to summer school so I could play my senior year, but I said, "No, I'm gonna finish up down south." That year, 1981, I tried to get signed professionally, but that was the year of the players strike and the teams weren't signing too many people. So I went to Tennessee Wesleyan in Athens, Tennessee, and I beat the University of Tennessee and the University of Kentucky. Kentucky came down there and threw some freshman pitcher, and I stuck it up their ass. I struck out about 15 guys, and the Wesleyan coach got hold of a Red scout and he came down and asked me to come to a tryout camp and that's how it all got started.

Oh, one more thing. Major league clubhouses always had the best coffee. You get that dirt in there and that's big-league coffee to me.

# Eric Davis

*Davis had a 16-year career which began in Cincinnati in 1984. He played nine seasons with the Reds and started in seven Cincinnati openers.*

I came up in '84, and my first opener in Cincinnati was in '85. It snowed, it rained, the sun came out, everything. We won a close game against Montreal. In 1987, we beat Montreal again in our opener in

Cincinnati, and I hit a home run. But the opener I remember best was at the Vet in Philadelphia—the Phillies home opener in '85. I hit a home run off Steve Carlton. That was huge, and I still remember how excited I was.

Those are all big, but for me, the day itself—getting to put on the new white uniform and everything getting started—was the best part of Opening Day.

*I always loved the sight of those new white uniforms hanging up in the lockers at Riverfront Stadium on Opening Day.* It touched a nerve with me when I was a minor-leaguer in spring training. The major leaguers would come over to our complex. To see those bright white uniforms with the names "Bench" and "Concepcion" and "Driessen" on the back, that's when the dream started for me. Then, to be here and wearing that bright white uniform with "Davis" on the back, that was just an overwhelming feeling. It feels good even now, just thinking about it.

One reason that has stuck with me so much, I think, is that when I first came up in '84, the Reds didn't have a uniform with my name on it. The equipment managers weren't expecting me to be called up, I guess. I went in the game as a pinch hitter wearing a jersey that didn't have a name or a number on it.

We were playing the Cardinals. I hit a ball into the hole at short, and Ozzie Smith dove, caught it backhand, jumped up and threw me out. It was a bang-bang play. I thought, "Whoa, that's a hit in Triple-A." As I was running back to the dugout, Ozzie said, "Welcome to the big leagues, son."

I never got to see a Dodger opener when I was growing up in LA. My first opener was right here, in Cincinnati, in '85. And that was a great feeling. I knew what meant to be a Red. I was 13 and 14 years old when the Reds won those back-to-back World Championships in 1975-76, and I was 15 and 16 when the Dodgers lost to the Yankees in the World Series in 1977 and 1978. Those were the three great franchises back then.

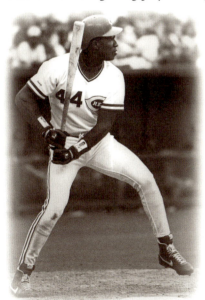
*Eric Davis led the Reds big offensive show in the 1987 opener with a home run, two RBIs and two stolen bases.*

*The Dodgers, the Reds and the Yankees were the epitome of how baseball was supposed to be. Everybody patterned their organizations after those three franchises.* To know what this franchise meant, to not only Cincinnati but to all of baseball, was tremendous. That feeling always came out on Opening Day.

## KAL DANIELS

*Daniels played for the Reds from 1986 to 1989. He started in three openers.*

My first Opening Day was '86. And even though I didn't start the game, I remember it. That's because when I was a kid, playing in front of a packed house is something I always dreamed of. *That day, it felt like every swing that was made, I was the one takin' it; every ball that was hit, I was fieldin' it, every throw that was made, I was makin' it.*

On Opening Day, '88, I had the game-winning base hit—a single in the 12th inning. The fireworks went off. That was very cool.

My feeling on Opening Day was that a new world was opening up. New life. You've just come out of spring training, your body's kind of worn down from the hot weather in spring training, then you see the people, the excitement as you go around the city. People are ready to get going. All of a sudden, you hear that first crack of the bat, and man, the race is on. There's nothing like it.

## CHRIS WELSH

*Welsh, a graduate of St. Xavier High School in Cincinnati, and a member of the Reds broadcast team since 1993, pitched five years in the big leagues, including 1986 for the Reds. However, he missed the opener.*

I went to some Opening Days as a kid, but I can't tell you what years they were. I was like every other kid who turned in his excuse and went to the game. Opening Day was huge. It was the official start of the season, and we liked that because we knew the opening of our Knothole season was just around the corner, even if the Reds opener was in cold weather.

There was one Opening Day here when I was in high school and we skipped school and came down for the game. Those are best kind, the ones where you skip school. It was totally unsanctioned. That's what makes it the best kind.

*My Opening Days in the big leagues? I was one*

of the guys who emerged from the dugout when the P.A. guy said, "And now, the rest of your team!"

But I didn't even get *that* introduction in '86. My stuff was on the truck to go north out of spring training—we were getting ready to the airport—and Pete Rose pulls me aside and says, "We're going to send you out. We decided not to put Mario Soto on the DL after all."

That would've been my only Opening Day in Cincinnati, and I wound up going down to Denver! That's when they had Paul O'Neill, Chris Sabo, Kal Daniels, Jeff Montgomery—we had a good team down there.

## TRACY JONES

*Jones played for the Reds from 1985 to 1987 and made two Opening Day starts.*

Here's the story. Opening Day, 1986. I wasn't even supposed to play. I barely made the club out of spring training. I should have been the last cut. I asked Pete, "Did I make the ball club?" He said, "I didn't say ya' didn't, did I? Get on the bus!" So, that's how I found I made the ball club.

So I go north with the club, and now I'm in Cincinnati, sitting in my locker in the clubhouse on Opening Day. Tony Perez had pulled a groin, so Pete has to juggle the lineup. He walks by on his way to go to the lounge to get a cup of coffee and he says, "You're starting in left."

I almost fainted. I had been figuring, "This is going to be a great day. I'm just going to sit in the dugout and watch a big-league baseball game." I figure no way are they going to push to play me.

*I swear, as soon as Pete told me I was starting in left, I started shaking. When he came back, I said, "Boy, am I nervous." He said, "You're nervous? I couldn't sleep all night, thinking about putting you in."*

So where do you think the first batter of the game for the Phillies—Gary Redus—hits the ball? It's a bright sunny day, there are a bunch of bright, white shirts in the background, he hits it off the end of the bat; I go back, I come charging in, misplay it, the ball pops over my head, he gets a triple and people started booing! And I thought to myself—as I'm looking in the stands—well, at least I made it to the big leagues. I'm going back down, probably right after the game. They wound up scoring three runs that inning. And Mario Soto is not too happy about it as I'm coming off the field.

Then, I get up to bat against Steve Carlton—I remember getting into the box, and my back leg is just quivering—and I hit a ball to right-center to the warning track, and it was caught.

*Well, I wind up getting a couple of hits, a stolen base, and we end up winning the game. And now I'm thinking, "Hey, maybe I can play up here!" And I'm also thinking, "Geez, is that all Carlton has?"* I mean, I know he had been a great pitcher, but I'm thinking, "Geez, this guy's got nothin'!"

So, yeah, that was quite a turnaround. What a day!

## LLOYD McCLENDON

*McClendon broke into the major leagues with the Reds in 1987. He played eight seasons and entered the coaching ranks in 1997. He is currently manager of the Pittsburgh Pirates.*

I made my big-league debut here as a player on Opening Day '87, and I made my debut as a manager here, too. It was like coming back home. I remember how nervous I was that first Opening Day as a player. *I didn't start that game. But I got into the game, and grounded out. It was a packed house. Pete Rose was the manager, Tony Perez a coach.*

At the Reds spring training site in Plant City, Florida, teammates Paul O'Neill, Tracy Jones and Tony Perez prepared for the 1988 opener.

*All these Cincinnati Reds greats, and here I was a rookie, taking it all in.*

Opening Day in Cincinnati was so unique back then—we always had the first game of the season. It was a great tradition for Cincinnati to open things up. Opening Day is so special. It's a fresh start for all of the fans and all of the players. As they say, "hope springs eternal." Everybody thinks they have a chance Opening Day.

No other sport has Opening Day like baseball. The magnitude of this game! Baseball always has been, and always will be, America's pastime. From time to time, we've tried to mess it up, but it's a wonderful sport that everybody can relate to. You can go out and catch a football, shoot a basket, but there's just something about baseball. I think a lot of people cherish it, and they love seeing it get started again. There's a sense of renewal to it. It's springtime.

## PAUL O'NEILL

*O'Neill broke in with the Reds in September of 1985. He appeared in five Opening Day games.*

Statistically, the best Opening Day I had was in Cincinnati in 1989. Somebody told me before the game, "Your name is misspelled on your jersey." I thought they were messing with me. I had put my jersey on, and didn't even look at it. But there it was: "O'Neil." One "L." After that game—I went 4-for-4 with a home run—I was going to tell them to just leave it there.

The first Opening Day I had after I was traded to the Yankees, I had four or five hits off David Cone. That was my first game at Yankee Stadium.

*But your first game as a major leaguer is hard to beat. Your heart—you can't stop it from just about beating out of your chest.* I was lucky. I pinch-hit and got a hit on the first pitch. I didn't even get to think about it. I just swung and got out of there.

I always got nervous on Opening Day. Even though I'd been in the major leagues for seven or eight years when I got traded to New York, it was a funny feeling when I went there. I remember thinking on Opening Day in Yankee Stadium, "Here we go again." It takes you back again. Opening Day is like that. Baseball is like that.

## LENNY HARRIS

*Lenny Harris had two stints with the Reds (1988–89; 1994–98) and appeared in six openers as a pinch hitter.*

I remember my very first game. It wasn't an opener, but that was *my* Opening Day. It was 1988. I got in against Fernando Valenzuela after Ronnie Oester got hurt. I was as nervous as I could be. Fernando started that game. And I was playing right next to Barry Larkin. All I could remember was that Davey Concepcion said we'd never be able to play in the infield in the big leagues as long as were with the Reds!

He said it about both of us, in spring training one time. And we didn't forget, neither! I said to Barry after I got in the game, "Look, Barry, we're in the big leagues!" And we both started laughing. I was 23 years old.

In '89, I had a good spring training. Chris Sabo had a better one and Luis Quinones had a great spring, too. *I remember Pete Rose saying to me, "You're still here? We didn't send you down yet?" I said, "Nope." He said, "Well, go ahead and call your parents—I'm taking you north with me."* I will never forget that as long as I live. We were in Plant City, Florida. That was a big feeling for me. I was a Pete Rose fan after that, man. Still is!

What a great Opening Day that was in '89. All those great Reds players who'd come up through the farm system: Tom Browning, Eric Davis, Kal Daniels, Barry Larkin, Chris Sabo. It was…baseball! You've been in the minor leagues for six years, and you come in for Opening Day, and the red carpet is out! All these people just watching you. You can't get more hyped than that. Opening Day is like a World Series. I know, because I been there. Everybody's there, everybody's welcoming you. Everybody's congratulating you. Everybody's putting on new uniforms. You're smelling a new rug in the clubhouse. There's a whole big atmosphere of that.

That's what it's all about. Red and white all over. You know, when you first sign with the Reds, they give you brochures. They show you the Big Red Machine. And they show you a high camera shot into the stadium, and it's just *full* of red and white, and you just know that's Opening Day. And you're thinking, "Man, that looks like the Rose Bowl!"

I'll never forget it, because when Reds super scout George Zuraw signed me, he said, "Remember, you've got to learn how to sign a baseball!" Because I didn't know how to write on a baseball. And that's one thing he told me, and I never forgot it. He always said, "You're gonna be a big-leaguer one day, but it's up to you!" I always kept that in the back of my mind.

*There are a lot of good Opening Days in baseball. But it's tough to top those elephants in Cincinnati.* It was different in Colorado, and in New York—

Lenny Harris posed with his wife, Carnettia, and daughter, Chanel, on Family Day in 1995.

singing the Frank Sinatra songs, and *"New York, New York,"* but it's *really* different in Cincinnati. It's like a big ol' parade. It's like a heavyweight bout getting ready to happen. You gotta tip your hat to Marge. She really knew how to open up. She knew how to party on the first day!

# Marge Schott

*Schott was president and CEO of the Reds from 1985 to 1999. Her tenure was marked by controversy and suspensions by Major League Baseball, but Schott never failed to be a tireless promoter of Opening Day.*

Because of the fans, honey. I made Opening Day a priority—because of the fans. It means a lot to the fans to see the first game. You felt it, and you could see it. Opening Day is history, honey. And you've got to keep history going.

I didn't go to Opening Day as a kid. We were all a family of girls, so there weren't many sports people, you know what I mean? We weren't playing baseball at Sacred Heart; we played field hockey. My first Opening Day game would have been when I was a limited partner in the Reds in the early 1980s.

I knew what separated us from everybody else. We had the first team, and we have the parade. *We are the only one with a parade. The Findlay Market Opening Day Parade. That is history in Cincinnati. It was my favorite day of the year.*

The players were like my family. I said to them, "How many owners can kiss you guys?"

When there was talk about shutting down the Findlay Market Parade, and they wouldn't let them in the stadium when the switch was made from Astroturf to grass at Cinergy Field, I had all the top guys of the Findlay Market Parade in my owner's box. That was ridiculous that they wouldn't let them in the stadium! The *Findlay Market Opening Day Parade* and they wouldn't let them in! The Findlay Market Parade *is* Opening Day, honey!

The guys came to my box and they said, "Mrs. Schott, this is so sweet of you." I said, "Hey, guys, without the Findlay Market Parade, we wouldn't even *have* Opening Day!"

*You know those bands that win the prize in the Findlay Market Parade? Those bands come from all over, sweetie, you know what I mean? And they should march on the field. What's that going to do to the field? Nothing! That's what thrills people, honey!*

I think Opening Day and the Findlay Market Parade are the two big things in Cincinnati. They go together!

Remember the the year when ESPN wanted us to open our season on Sunday night, and so we did that—but that wasn't our Opening Day! And so, we didn't treat it like Opening Day—and neither did anybody else in Cincinnati, either. The parade was Monday, the ushers in tuxedos were Monday, the big crowd was Monday. That's when Opening Day is, honey! Monday afternoon!

# Todd Benzinger

*Benzinger grew up in New Richmond, Ohio, 15 miles east of Cincinnati. He played nine years in the majors, including three years in Cincinnati (1989–1991). He started the 1989 and 1990 openers.*

My memories of Opening Day go all the way back to going to school in New Richmond. I actually looked forward to going to school that day because I knew that at 1:30 or 2 o'clock, we'd get to watch the game on TV.

In '89, I played for the Reds. It was the first time I was part of the Opening Day hoopla. I don't want to say the game itself is anticlimactic, but in a way, it almost is.

I can remember going to Columbus the day before to play the Indians, and my mind wasn't on that game at all. It was 35 or 40 degrees, and then, the next day, Opening Day, it was though it was on cue—sunny and 50 degrees. I can remember putting on the Reds uniform for the first time officially, and walking up the steps into the dugout. There was no bigger fan of the Reds than I was.

So, in '89, I'm walking through that long tunnel from the clubhouse to the dugout, getting ready to go up the steps, and what's going through my mind is these pictures I remember seeing in newspapers and books of these great Reds from the Big Red Machine going through this tunnel. And you know where you make that turn in the tunnel and get ready to go up the steps? Well, Marge Schott is right there—I'd only seen her a few times in spring training—and she's giving us hugs and saying in that gruff voice, "How ya' doing, honey?" And I knew she had absolutely no idea who I was. *I'm sure of that! That made me smile.*

I never got to go to an Opening Day game, but I did go to about a dozen regular season Reds games each year and I'd sit up in the red seats with my dad.

He would come home from River Downs and on a whim, he'd say, "Let's go to the Reds game." I can remember Paul Sommerkamp announcing the starting lineups as we were running across the concrete to the ticket window to get our Top Six tickets, always Top Six. So there we'd be, way up there, and my dad would really be into the game, really emotional, and he'd want to wring Tony Perez's neck if he didn't drive in the run. So, it was a great place for us to sit, for *him* to sit, because he was away from people.

On Opening Day, 1989, I looked up to the Top Six where I'd sit with my dad. *I hate to be overly dramatic about it, but I remember thinking, "Hey, I'm on the field!" It was this little movie moment, and it lasted just a split second.* Then, I had to get to work. It was one of those few times when you're a young kid, you're a major league baseball player, and you realize, "I've made it." It's one of those things you never forget— the call-up you get from the Triple-A manager who tells you you're going to the big leagues, and your first at bat in the big leagues, and, for me, my first Opening Day. And my dad actually got to sit in the blue seats! At least he was supposed to. When I got in the on-deck circle—listen, players are really aware of where their family is sitting— and I'm lookin' around, I give a glance up there to my cheering section, and there's no dad to be seen! And I wasn't the least bit surprised. I knew he was up there watching me from somewhere. I'm sure he was up in the red seats somewhere. I knew he was nervous.

You know hard it is when you're watching somebody close to you, somebody close to you in the family, and you're way more nervous than they are because you can't do anything about it. At least when you're playing, you have some control over what's going to happen.

*I can remember going to breakfast with my dad that morning. I lived out in Anderson, and we met at Bob Evans, right off 275 in Beechmont. It was 8:30 or 9 o'clock in the morning. We've got the paper, the Opening Day section, the front page, and I'm looking at all this stuff and I'm thinking, "I'm gonna play in this game!"* And that's when you start thinking, "What if I become like a Fred Merkle and make some huge, bone-headed play?" You never know!

When you're a young player, you hope you're going to play in a World Series, but there are only so many, big, big moments. If you play for the Reds, though, you get one extra big moment every year, even if your team is terrible, and that is Opening Day.

The only other time I remember having a feeling like that was before Game 3 in the World Series in Oakland in '90. We had batting practice, and I was starting at first base; Hal Morris was going to DH. I didn't play in the first two games; I just pinch-hit. There was a half hour between infield practice and the game, so I had a chance to watch TV. I'm sitting there on the couch with my shoes off, and I'm watching Jack Buck and Tim McCarver and they say, "We'll be back to Oakland-Alameda Coliseum after this message." And they show a

*Todd Benzinger, who grew up in nearby New Richmond, Ohio, and recalled watching Opening Day games on TV at school, appeared in two openers and collected hits in both games.*

blimp shot of the stadium, with 50,000 people in it. When I saw that, I started *quaking*, just for a few seconds. It was like, "Whoa, I'm going to play in this game?"

I played for the Boston Red Sox in '88, and we finished in first place, and I was the starting first baseman. I played in the playoffs; in big games, on national TV, but it wasn't like Opening Day 1989, and I'm not making that up. Not only was it a big game, but it was a big game for me, personally. It's funny because I played for three other teams besides the Reds, and I can't remember those other openers. But I remember the Reds openers. You always knew going into it that the day is going to be huge. You know the crowd is going to be there. *I don't care if TV tries to sneak in a game on Sunday night. I ignore it. It's stupid. There's one Opening Day, and that's in Cincinnati, and everybody here knows it.*

You also know that the next night—for your second game—there's going to be 15,000 people there and it's going to be cold as hell.

So, anyway, there I am in '89 thinking about Fred Merkle, and on the first play of the game, Willie Randolph is leading and he hits a ground ball to Chris Sabo. And Chris, who could never throw accurately to first base, anyway—just the opposite of Barry; Chris'd just throw it, and half the time it'd be in the dirt—and anyway, that's where his first throw goes, in the dirt, almost impossible to catch. So, anyway, I'm thinking, "That's OK, I have a chance to show them I'm a good first baseman," but I miss it. Now I'm thinking—and this is how fast the stuff is going through your mind on a day like that—that's OK, it's not my error, I tried. But after the ball hit off me and got past me, Willie hits the base and turns toward second, because he sees he can make it. I was trying to get the ball, I'm looking all over for it, and Willie and I collide and the umpire calls obstruction on me! And that's an error on me!

*My first play in Riverfront Stadium, and I've got an error! The first batter of the game, and we've*

Where's Dad? Family and friends of Todd Benzinger cheered Todd in his first Cincinnati opener in 1989 at Riverfront Stadium. But Benzinger's father had moved to a more secluded spot, too nervous to share his excitement. From left are Benzinger's sister, Lynn Kepf, mother Joan Benzinger and friend Mary Wagner.

*got two errors on us! That's not the kind of thing you envision!*

The night before you're thinking, "I'm going to hit a home run in my first at bat. It's going to be great." I just know it. I just have that feeling. So what happens? The first pitch Tim Belcher throws a fastball right down the middle, 88 miles an hour, a straight fastball, and I out-think myself and I take it. And right then and there I say, "That was the home-run pitch! Why didn't I swing at at that?"

And that's the at bat I remember the most, even though I got a hit in my next at bat.

The 1990 opener was even more memorable in one way, and that's because we didn't open at home. And yet it was the Reds best start ever in franchise history. We won our first eight games. It was strange to start that season on the road in Houston. Opening Day and no hoopla. It really stood out to me because there was nobody in the stands. It was in the Astrodome, and it was empty. But Lou Piniella was our new manager and he didn't know anything about Reds hoopla on Opening Day. And he didn't care. He was all business. "Let's get started—let's go," that was his attitude. And when you look back on it, it's probably good we opened that year on the road.

In '91, Opening Day was memorable because we got our World Series rings. So, I have three very memorable Opening Days as a Red. And that's pretty good, because I was only there for three of them.

# Danny Jackson

*Jackson pitched for 15 seasons in the major leagues, including three with Cincinnati (1988–1990). He never started an opener in Cincinnati, but he played for six different teams which gives him a variety of Opening Day experiences.*

I think Opening Day in Cincinnati is the best of all the Opening Days. Opening Day in Kansas City, the fans don't get jacked up as much as Cincinnati does. Coming over here, I noticed it seems like everyone's out of school, schools are shut down, every business is closed except the ones downtown. It's just one big, huge celebration. That's what I remember about Opening Day in Cincinnati.

It was amazing to come here and see what a big difference it is. Chicago's not the same, Pittsburgh wasn't quite the same, Philly is somewhat similar, St. Louis had a pretty good one. But there's something just a little more special in Cincinnati. *For so many years, this city always had the first game of the year, and it was special. And people still feel that way about it. The opening game of the baseball season is theirs.*

I never got an Opening Day start in Cincinnati. Would I have loved to have an Opening Day start? Sure! It's a special honor. If you're a pitcher who doesn't want that, there's something wrong with you. You always want the ball—on Opening Day, in the playoffs, in the World Series, closing it out.

A city gets wired for its World Series teams, and it was that way when we opened in Cincinnati in 1991, after our World Championship season. An Opening Day after a World Championship season is special. I feel privileged to have been a part of that.

# ROB DIBBLE

*Dibble came up through the Reds farm system and joined the big-league club in 1988. Along with Norm Charlton and Randy Myers, Dibble became one of the three "Nasty Boys" relievers in the 1990 World Championship season.*

The first opener I would have gotten into was '89, because I was called up in '88. I was setting up John Franco, and Johnny had almost 40 saves that year.

Pete Rose was one of those guys who went right to the bullpen when the starter got tired, because he had such a strong bullpen. When I came up, it was me, Frank Williams, Rob Murphy and Franco at the end of the game.

Same thing in the '90s; people remember the Nasty Boys, but we had Tim Birtsas and the late Tim Layana.

Opening Day was great because it meant the season was getting started, and it meant coming to the clubhouse every day. We had really good teams, really close teams, and it was great coming to the clubhouse. It was something you looked forward to.

*We used to laugh about the fact that there wasn't a bullpen at Riverfront. The relievers sat at the end of the bench. Who would set up a stadium where there isn't a bullpen? Who would set up stadium where the relievers would have to sit at the end of the bench? But you were into the game the whole time.*

And for TV games, there was even less space because a TV camera would take up the last 10 feet of the dugout. So now you've got guys sitting *behind* the starters. You were grouped together all the time! We were close—whether we wanted to be or not.

And when Marge owned the team, there was only one team bus! There weren't two team buses like we had when I went to the White Sox and the Brewers. We jammed two guys into the two seats; there was no extra room. But you know what? That was great, and it was a great time to be here.

*Rob Dibble appeared in three openers, earning saves in 1991 and 1993.*

# NORM CHARLTON

*Charlton came up with the Reds in 1988 and was a part of the infamous "Nasty Boys" bullpen of 1990. He appeared in the 1990 road opener in Houston and the home opener in Cincinnati.*

My first time in uniform for Opening Day was '89. I came up as a starter in the summer of '88, and then in spring training of '89, the Reds had traded Rob Murphy, and Pete needed a left-hander in the pen. Pete came to me in spring training and said, "Right now, you're my fifth starter. That means you're going to Triple-A for a couple of weeks. Can you pitch out of the bullpen?"

I said, "Well, I've pitched out of the 'pen only a couple of times, and that's when I was in college." He said, "Well, do you wanna try it?"

*I said, "Hell, yeah, I wanna try it. If it means me being there on Opening Day, yeah, I wanna try it."* I'm thinking to myself, "Hell, if I gotta cook the *meal* after the game, I wanna be there. I don't wanna go back to Triple-A." And I wound up in the bullpen the whole year.

I played with other clubs, but I think one reason Opening Day is so so great here is the tradition. And I'm not just talking about Cincinnati having the oldest franchise. I'm talking about the Big Red Machine. When all the hoopla is going on, you're thinking about the guys who played here before you. You'd look across the locker room and you'd see Tony Perez. Lee May, Johnny Bench, Joe Morgan; all these guys would have passed through the clubhouse.

The thing I remember clearly about Opening Day, especially about the first one, is that "OK, now I've arrived; I've made the team out of spring training. I established myself a little bit last year and they think enough of me that I've made the Opening Day roster." Making the Opening Day roster the first time is a big deal.

The other thing is that Opening Day is louder than any other regular-season game. There's more excitement surrounding Opening Day. When you're a reliever, most of the hoopla in the stands is over by the time you get in the game. Things have settled down. So it's different for us than it is for the position players or the starting pitcher.

*I distinctly remember Opening Day in Houston in '90. That's where the whole Nasty Boys thing started.* I remember throwing in that game. I remember Tom Browning hit Glenn Davis twice and Randy Myers hit him once. It tied a record.

People always ask me about the World Championship season, and they always remind me of that collision with Mike Scioscia of the Dodgers. The way I remember it is that the night before, we had a close game, and Eric Davis slid into the plate, but Scioscia had the plate blocked, and kept him off it. I remember sitting down there in the bullpen, and saying, "Man, if I ever get a chance to run over a catcher…" The next night, I think I reached base on a walk, and Joe Oliver doubled, and I was on first. Our third-base coach—Sammy Perlozzo—was holding me up. I ran right through that stop sign, and I got to the plate the same time the ball did. I think the most surprising thing to a lot of people was that it was a pitcher running into the catcher. But whether you're a pitcher or a position player or a coach, there's only one way to play the game. Every time you go out on the mound, you leave everything you have on the mound. That's the way I've always approached it.

It's funny that through my whole pitching career, that's the thing that people seem to bring up the most. *Oh, yeah, the Nasty Boys, that was great, but remember when you ran over Scioscia?* I think it typified the way that '90 team played the game. I think it typified the fact that anybody on our team was willing to do whatever it took to win a ballgame. We just played. And if you were in the lineup, you played as hard as you could as long as you could, and when Lou took you out, he took you out. That's pretty much the way we went about our business.

My shoulder was a little bit sore after the collision, but I pitched the next inning. I never missed any time. I guess pitchers probably ought to be saved, and play the game like a pitcher, but if I was on first again, and Scioscia was catching and Joe hit a double down there, I think I'd try to score again. If I'm on base, I'm a base runner.

*Opening Day in '91 was tremendous. We were World Champions! We got our rings. I didn't know at that time what a big deal getting a ring was. I was young and naïve. Dibs and I and Randy Myers thought we were the best thing since sliced bread.* It would probably mean a ton more to me now. I know now how special getting a ring is.

*Norm Charlton says he is remembered in Cincinnati as much for his nasty home plate collision with Mike Scioscia as for his role with the "Nasty Boys."*

Back then, I was young and stupid and didn't have to work hard; I had all the talent in the world. I just went out there and did it. Later, you come to realize how many people go through this grind, day in and day out, and don't ever get one. When I got my ring in '91, I wasn't as proud as I should have been. I didn't feel as lucky as I should have.

Don't get me wrong. I was very excited; it was a really cool thing. But every day now when I put it on that ring, it's more special to me now than it was then. I used to wear it every day. I'd be working on a tractor on the range, and I'd have it on. I decided, you know what, I probably shouldn't be beating it up like this. Now I wear it on special occasions. Other times, when I feel like I want to look at it, I'll pick it up in the bathroom and I'll put it on. Sometimes, I catch myself wearing it four or five days a week, for no other reason than just to wear it.

## LOU PINIELLA

*Piniella played for 18 seasons and began his managerial career in 1986 with the Yankees. He managed the Reds to a World Championship in his first year in Cincinnati in 1990.*

The only Opening Day I remember as a manager—and I'm sure it's because it was my first—is the first one I managed in New York in 1986. It was the first game I ever managed in the big leagues. It was against Kansas City and Dick Howser.

Kansas City had just won the World Championship the year before. I had played for Dick in New York, and he was the coach there for a long, long time. We won the opener and it was a big deal for me, because it was my first game as a manager, and I was trying to get myself established.

We had a huge crowd, 56,000 people. Robert Merrill—the opera star—sang the national anthem and threw out the first pitch. We were wearing black armbands because Roger Maris and Pete Sheehy—the old clubhouse man—had died during the off-season. I remember that '86 Opening Day well. But the rest of the Opening Days, I just don't remember.

But I remember my first one as a player with the Royals. That would have been in 1969. We opened at Municipal Stadium in Kansas City. We played the Minnesota Twins. I went 4-for-5. I was 24 years old. I never had a better opener as a hitter. My first one was my best one. We beat Minnesota; Billy Martin was their manager.

*You always get excited about Opening Day, no matter how long you've been in the game.* If you can't get excited for an opener, you don't belong in the business. You get goose bumps; the nervousness is all part of it. You know you're starting for real after seven weeks of spring training. There's a lot of antic-

Lou Piniella was the favorite of many interviewers in 1990, including Johnny Bench (left) who was a member of the Reds TV broadcast team.

ipation. As long as I'm in this business, Opening Day will be pretty special. There is no other day quite like it.

## JOSE RIJO

*Rijo was traded to the Reds in 1988, and soon established himself as the ace of the staff. He started four openers (1992–1995), winning one. He retired in 1995 because of arm injuries, and then returned in an emotional comeback with the Reds in 2001.*

Opening Day '93 was my favorite, by far. First of all, I was facing a Latin pitcher, and not just any Latin pitcher, but Dennis Martinez, *El Presidente*. Second of all, it was a great, exciting game that we won, 2–1. That's the kind of game you expect to see on Opening Day. People got what they deserve that day.

Any time you have a Dominican manager—Felipe Alou—against you, and a Spanish pitcher against you, it's a big deal. Same with a Latin batter. But you know what? That is relaxing to me. It relaxes me, because I know we're going to have fun. But it also makes me work harder, because I know I have to get them out.

I like to face Spanish players, because I know it is a thrill for me, because we can talk about it later. But I know I've got to get them out, because I know I don't want to hear about it later. Moises Alou and Wil Cordero were in the Expos lineup that day. That made it even more interesting for me. And Tony Perez was our manager.

*For that '93 opener, you had a Dominican and a*

*Nicaraguan on the mound, and a Dominican in one dugout, and a Cuban in the other. It was "Latin Day" at the ballpark.*

I talked with *El Presidente* after the game. He said, "I hate to face your ass, especially in Cincinnati." I remember one sequence in particular that day—I don't remember the name of the batter—but the umpire called an outside slider a strike, and the batter said, "F—! What the f— you helping Rijo for? Rijo don't need no f—ing help!"

It reminds me of the time another umpire, Frank Pulli, told me one day: "Josie, if you keep the ball right there, I will give you that pitch all day." I said, "Thank you very much." And he did give me that pitch all day, because I was right there with it.

I knew that Mario Soto had a great Opening Day record. What did he have? Four wins? I wanted to top him. There are some similarities in our careers. *["But," Rijo is told, "Soto is not as good-looking as you." Replied Rijo: "Nobody is!"]*

I grew up watching Soto pitch; we played against each other. The first time was when I was 15 years old, and he was in his prime. Then, seven years later—the day I was traded to Cincinnati in 1987—Soto was pitching that day in the Dominican. He was on his way out. He said, "Josie, you have been traded to a great organization. You are going to have fun." He told me what to expect, and what they were looking for. He was an amazing pitcher. He wasn't that big. He kind of reminds me of Pedro Martinez, guys who aren't very big, but throw very hard. I think I have a better body for a pitcher. Strong and big. Not because it means you're going to be able to throw any harder, but because your body can take more punishment. I'm 6-3, 230 pounds; I was 218 in my prime.

Back in those days, both when Soto was pitching and when I was pitching Opening Days, the Reds started first. All eyes were on Cincinnati. It was even better than opening on *Monday Night Football* because we were *first*.

*Nobody had as much fun with the fans as Jose Rijo, and they responded in kind with an outpouring of love for the Dominican pitcher.*

*Monday Night Football* is always *second*, the day after the first games on Sunday.

There was a time when the Reds had the only game on Opening Day. The other games were the next day. Every team, every player was watching you: "I wonder what the Reds got this year?" It was awesome. I always liked when I got attention. It gave me a chance to prove myself.

*Nobody does Opening Day like Cincinnati. I mean, where else but Cincinnati do you have a dog take a shit at home plate on Opening Day?*

Marge Schott's dog did that. Schottzie! I never saw anything like that in my life. I thought I saw everything in the Dominican that could happen on a baseball field. But I had to come to Cincinnati to see a dog take a shit at home plate on Opening Day!

You got a guy scooping up dog shit in front of 50,000 people. It's one thing to pitch in front of 50,000 people on Opening Day, to throw the first pitch of the season, but how about scooping up dog shit in front of 50,000 people? I'm telling you, shit happens on Opening Day in Cincinnati that don't happen nowhere else!

I love pitching in Cincinnati, especially Opening Day. People love the game over there. They love the Reds. They love baseball. They get into it. And when you've got them all together at once, you want to show them how good you are. Because you don't get to do that every day. But they're all there Opening Day. So, you'd better take advantage of it. They may watch a game on TV, or listen to it on the radio or read about it, but when they see it in person, they *know*.

It's a great feeling to be named the Opening Day pitcher. All the hard work, all the things you worked for, are rewarded that day. If you are healthy and you are pitching on Opening Day, you are the best pitcher not only on the team, but *in the game*. And that's a great beginning. When you're the Opening Day pitcher, you know you're No. 1. And when you know you're No. 1, it inspires you to work even harder, because that's what you want: to be No. 1. The whole world is looking at you. And you know you're going to have a full stadium that day—and that might be the only day that it gets full. You get pumped up. Very pumped up. Too pumped up.

In that sense I never liked to be the Opening Day pitcher. *I was never ready for Opening Day, and it was because of the weather. My head could take it, but my arm could not.* I came from all that hot weather in the Dominican, and all the hot weather in Florida, to the cold weather in Cincinnati. I don't like cold weather. I can take 100 degrees better than I can take 40 degrees, and I will guarantee you a better outing in 100 degrees. I was not my best. But I liked it because of all the fans, and because I

Schottzie's "work" on the field left many players with an enduring memory of Opening Day.

earned that spot, and because it made me concentrate better.

I always overthrew on Opening Day. I didn't feel loose, but I was always trying to "get it there." I overthrew and that is not good. The year I had the surgery on my elbow—1995—the year before that was the strike. I never went so long without pitching—September, October, November, December, January, February, March. That was the first time I ever got so much rest.

That spring training, I didn't give up a run—not one! On Opening Day, that's the first day my arm started feeling sore. Normally it gets sore after June, you know, all the throwing takes a toll on my elbow. But that day, Opening Day '95, that's when it got sore, and it was because of the weather.

*And then after the surgeries, I had to start changing the way I pitched. Especially when I had my comeback. I used to throw hard all the time, but I became a real estate pitcher: "Location, location, location."*

I have to tell you that my best regular-season game ever was my comeback game in 2001. I never saw so much excitement in a regular-season game. Standing ovations. People calling my name in the sixth inning. It was unbelievable! The fans were great. Six years without seeing me! They didn't expect to see me ever again. People love me in Cincinnati, and I love them. I'd be out doing my running downtown and people would say, "Jose, I haven't been to a game in so long, but I'm going to come out and see you." That was like a shot of motivation, every day. I wanted to give the people a show.

I think back to 1984, when I was 18 years old and in the big leagues with the Yankees. Dave Winfield was 32 years old. And I said to him one day, "Dave, you're fat!" And his exact words were, "Jose, you will wish you could be in my shape when you get to my age."

And as I got further along into my career, I began to think about that. Every year, when I gave away so much as a pound, I would think about that, and I would say to myself, in a good way, "I've got to make Dave look bad. I've got to show him that he was wrong about me." And now look at me! I have kept myself in shape—like Dave Winfield.

I am thankful for the words he used to me. You never know what are the words that are going to stick with a young guy. I saw Dave in Puerto Rico four years ago, and I told him that story, and he remembered it.

*I remember another time when Winfield had a team party in Minnesota, and I said, "Dave, how should I dress?" He said, "Jose, dress like you got money."* In other words: dress with class. Act with class.

The best thing that happened to me when I was traded to Cincinnati was Eric Davis. He did so much for me. I asked him one day, "Eric, how am I ever going to repay you?" He said, "Josie, there is only one way you can pay me back. What I do for you, you do for others." That is what I have tried to do. I have carried on.

You are asking me about Opening Day. Do you remember Hector Carrasco, who in '94 came out of A ball and wasn't supposed to make the team? I worked with him in spring training. He blew everybody away. I would call the pitches for him sometimes. And he made the team!

Davey Johnson brought Hector into that "second Opening Day" game in 1994—the Monday afternoon game after our Sunday night game on ESPN—and Hector got the win. I was calling the pitches from the dugout in the tough situations *1, 2, 3*. One a fastball, two a curveball, three a slider. He had an outstanding fastball: 96, 98. Hector said to me one day, "Jose, how do I pay you back for all this?" I said, "You're doing it now by learning. Later, you will pass it on to the kids who are coming up."

*Growing up in the Dominican, I use to dream about playing in the major leagues. I grew up in San*

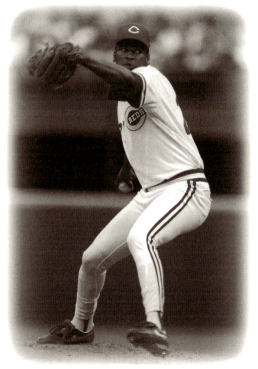

Rijo faced fellow Latin pitcher Dennis Martinez in the 1993 opener, and Jose bested "El Presidente" for his only Opening Day win.

*Cristobal. We were poor, like so many other families there. We played with cardboard gloves.* My brother used to slap me, because I used to borrow his leather glove and take it to the stadium. Sometimes I would forget the glove and leave it at the stadium, and my brother would say: "Where's my glove? You'd better run back and get it!" I owe my brother a lot, because of all he gave me. Today, he runs my baseball camp back home in the Dominican.

Here, look at these pictures of the camp! All these baseball fields! And here is a bird cage—I've got swans, peacocks, all that stuff—and here is a pool, and see? A water fountain. It is beautiful, isn't it? We had nothing like this when I was a kid.

I am trying to give back. I have been blessed. And I was blessed to be a Cincinnati Red.

# Joe Oliver

*Oliver started five openers in Cincinnati. He had a 12-year major league career and spent eight of those seasons in a Reds uniform. Oliver was the starting catcher for the Reds in their championship season of 1990.*

I didn't think of it at the time, but I should have known my career was going to be a little bit different, just from the way my first Opening Day in 1990 went.

Here I was, my first full season in the big leagues, a rookie, and all of a sudden, a tradition is being broken. *The Reds aren't opening at home.* Because the players had been locked out of spring training, we opened on the road, in Houston.

Lou Piniella had come in that year and he said I'd be his starting catcher on Opening Day—even though he wouldn't have been able to pick me out of a roomful of people, as he put it. He said he'd heard what I'd had done, read the reports and all that, but he had never seen me play before. It was a vote of confidence when he named me to start.

I was in awe to be getting that start—it was my first big-league Opening Day and we were facing Mike Scott in Houston. And then, *we came back home 6-and-0 after sweeping the Astros and the Braves, and I remember standing in front of 55,000 screaming maniacs in Cincinnati and that made it even sweeter.* We started out 9-and-0. Talk about being spoiled! I had just come up to the big leagues the previous July. Fortunately, I had enough good, quality people around me who didn't let me get too awestruck.

I look back on my 12 seasons in the major leagues and it seems like the 1990 season and the World Series were yesterday.

To be standing there on that line in the pre-game introductions before Game 1 of the World Series would have been special under any circumstances. But it was really special because of what we were going through as a country—the Gulf War. We had the flag on the chests of our uniforms.

That was one of the most exciting post-seasons I'd ever been a part of or saw on TV. In the NLCS, the Pirates and us were playing at the highest levels we could. The plays were unbelievable, on both sides of the field. Every outfielder on our team had an assist and they all meant something. Glenn Braggs in the last game, jumped above the wall and made that catch on Carmelo Martinez. Then there was Billy Hatcher jumping up against the wall and Eric Davis backing him up and throwing out Bobby Bonilla at third. And Paul O'Neill throwing out Andy Van Slyke at third when it didn't look like he had a chance of throwing anybody out.

*As for the World Series, well, that was just unbelievable. I can't remember a time when I've come to Cincinnati since then—even back when I was an opposing player coming in here with Pittsburgh—that people haven't stopped me and said, "Game 2, Dennis Eckersley, down the third-base line."*

I consider myself an average player, not at that superstar level. But in this area, people really know their Reds players—especially they know everybody on that World Championship team.

They remember Luis Quinones, making those big pinch hits; they know Billy Bates, who came up in September and had no hits as a Red and started that 10th inning in Game 2 by chopping one off the plate, and they know Glenn Braggs beating out a couple of balls by sliding headfirst across first base and swinging through a ball in Oakland and breaking his bat on his shoulder.

It's guys who didn't steal the headlines all the time who seemed to really rise to the occasion. Hal Morris drove in the last run in Game 4 in Oakland on a sac-fly; Herm Winningham who came in when Eric Davis went down and had a big bunt with two strikes. It wasn't always the go-to guys who got the job done for this club. Remember Game 2 of the World Series—well before the 10th inning—when Ron Oester was sent up to pinch-hit and hit the single that cut our deficit to 4-2 and got the comeback started?

It seemed like that's the way our whole team was. We believed that whoever got put into that situation, whether it was offense or defense, we believed that guy was going to do the job. Lou and his coaching

"Game 2, Dennis Eckersley, down the third-base line." Joe Oliver says he hears this refrain from Reds fans as they recall his game-winning hit against Oakland in the second game of the 1990 World Series.

I think the biggest compliment I've ever gotten as a baseball player was many years after the 1990 World Series. Dennis Eckersley was with the St. Louis Cardinals, and he walked up to me, shook my hand and said, "Thanks for screwing up my season." He'd had all those saves in '90—he'd only blown a couple of saves that whole year—and he said I screwed up his whole season with that one game.

That's the biggest compliment you can pay another player. It wasn't a line shot in the gap. I topped a back-up slider down the third-base line, and Carney Lansford wasn't playing the line. I can still see the ball in the air, tumbling down the line. I can still see Randy Marsh jumping out of the way, pointing fair, and it just seems like it was suspended in time, just seeing that ball, and just praying that it caught part of the baseline.

It's funny how my kids have handled it. That season was very memorable for me because my first child—D.J.—was born that year. He's 12 now, so when I look at him, I know that 1990 season wasn't yesterday even though it might feel like it. He was the baby in my wife's arms the night I got that double to win Game 2.

My kids have worn out the videotape of the Game 2-winning hit. They watch it all the time. When D.J. was five or six years old, he started watching the video, just about every night before he went to bed. And when Gavin—his younger brother— got old enough, he'd go in and watch it with him.

*On Opening Day, 2002, I told my wife it felt like I should be somewhere. It was my first season out of baseball. Any one of the 30 teams would have been fine with me!* I watched a little bit of an Opening Day game in 2002, but I couldn't even tell you which one it was. I was upset that I wasn't a part of it, but I had a lot going on with my three kids as well. I was in real life now; I wasn't in this fantasy land anymore.

I haven't missed the travel, but I miss the competition. I *love* to compete. I loved every aspect of it—whether I was overmatched or was equal to the challenge. I miss that. I miss thinking three innings ahead. *What pitcher's coming in? Who's that other manager going to use as a pinch hitter?* I miss being the quarterback. As catcher you knew when somebody was out of place in the infield or outfield. You knew the pitch selection. You'd gone over the scouting reports. You run the show. You tell the pitcher, "This is what I think is the best pitch." You're a used car salesman a lot of the time. You gotta sell the pitcher

staff had built us that way. Whether you were playing regularly or not, when you got your opportunity, you were going to be put into a situation that was best for you, and guys believed that. That's what winners are made of—they believe in themselves, and their teammates believe in them.

I remember saying after Game 2 that you dream about a hit like that when you're playing on the sandlot, and then being able to actually live it is an incredible feeling. The truth is, it didn't really sink in until many years down the road.

In that way, it's typical baseball. You have a big hit, you make a big pitch, but you're playing a game the next day. We got on a plane and we took off to Oakland. You can savor it, but the game's starting again. *You've got another game.* You don't get that opportunity to really let it soak in until years later. For me, it didn't fully hit me until three or four years down the road when I was far removed from being on a winning ball club. I was in Milwaukee, and I was starting to understand what it was all about. I'd been spoiled. I'd taken it for granted. Even though the Reds had the same players three years in row, we'd only reached the playoffs one time. Everything has to work out just right for you to get there. I understood then just how hard it was. Unless you're the Yankees, it just doesn't happen that often. I'm jealous of them. But I saw it firsthand in 2001 in that Yankee clubhouse. They understand just how lucky they have it. They are not an arrogant group of players. Mariano Rivera, Derek Jeter, Jose Posada. They know.

on it. On the other hand, I'm getting something I haven't had for 12 years now—I'm seeing my kids every day of their lives now. That's more rewarding than anything.

I've been on a lot of different clubs for Opening Day games—Cincinnati, Detroit, Yankees, Milwaukee, Seattle—although the only Opening Day starts I got were in Cincinnati and Milwaukee. At the time I signed with some of those other clubs, they had other catchers and I was platooning with them, but I beat them out after the season had started.

*A lot of clubs have great openers, especially the Yankees with all their history in Yankee Stadium, but I never saw an Opening Day that got the attention of an entire city the way the Reds opener does.* In New York, it's a big deal, but there are so many other things going on. You come to Cincinnati and you see what Opening Day is *really* meant to be—the entire city shuts down. People are calling in sick; they've planned this years in advance, each year.

Opening Day is a bigger deal in baseball than in other sports. You see the hoopla for the NFL, but it seems like they really get it all for the Super Bowl. They kick it off, but it doesn't seem like they really do it like baseball. Baseball is America's pastime; it's been around longest. I think more people can associate themselves with going out in the yard and playing baseball. You remember playing catch with your dad, or playing ball in the living room, or in your yard, or doing it as a kid in the sandlot. It seems like you're able to relate to the sport a little easier than some of the other ones. Who can go up and dunk a basketball? You can't play above the rim like those guys. But you can at least pick up a bat and try to hit a ball.

Baseball has the strongest thing of all associated with it—the coming of spring. It's been a long winter and you've got something new to look forward to. Spring, and then summer, is just around the corner. The shorts and short sleeves are about ready to break out. There's nothing like Opening Day.

# Hal Morris

*Morris played 10 seasons in Cincinnati and was a first baseman on the 1990 World Championship squad. He started in six openers in the 1990s.*

I was always happy to have Opening Day over with. I was always so anxious. There was tension building for Opening Day from the last three to four weeks of spring training. There was so much fanfare for Opening Day, it was just good to get it over with and settle into the grind.

*It is not like Cincinnati everywhere. The year I played for the Royals, we opened the season in Baltimore, and it was like any other game.*

Baseball is part of the American culture, but in certain cities—specifically, Cincinnati—it is part of the fiber of the entire community. There's a daily rhythm that develops around the Reds. You listen to the post-game wrap-ups and the reports the next day. The Reds are a topic of conversation at the water coolers around town.

In '90, it was still a real learning period for me. I was a rookie, having played with the Yankees just a little bit. I remember that with spring training cut short in '90 because of the lockout, we were just better prepared than a lot of clubs. We were young, and we didn't need long to get ready.

With Lou, there was emotion and a lot of energy in the dugout—especially that year. We had speed, good hitters and a good pitching staff—the type of baseball that lends itself more to energy, than trying to hit the ball out of the ballpark.

I think it was good we opened on the road that year. We were pretty young—not babes in the woods, by any means—but if we'd been put in Riverfront Stadium to open the season, we might have tried to do too much, tried to match the hype of the day. Instead, on the road, it was us against the world, and that suited us well.

# Barry Larkin

*Cincinnati native Larkin was drafted by the Reds in 1985 and debuted in 1986. Through 2003, he has played in 16 Reds openers, second to Pete Rose and Bid McPhee. He has hit .325 in his 16 openers.*

I never made it to an Opening Day when I was growing up. I probably asked my parents—one time—and they would've said, "Don't you have school?"

*I remember seeing the Opening Day parade on the TV news, and I knew all about the Big Red Machine players. In Wiffle Ball, I was Davey Concepcion. And on the field, I'd do the bounce throw—or least try to—the way he did off the Astroturf from shortstop.*

My first opener would have been in '87, but I don't remember the game itself. I remember being especially proud of being a Red that day. When I got called up in '86 is when the pride-in-Cincinnati thing started. That first night, against the Giants, I got called in to hit against Atlee Hammaker and hit a ground ball to the shortstop, Jose Uribe, and scored the runner from third base. I ran down the first-base line, and got a standing ovation. For making contact! That's when I knew, "These people really appreciate you being from Cincinnati."

I was supposed to start that day, but I arrived late because I flew in from Denver and was routed through Chicago, but they had bad weather and I was re-routed to Detroit. I walked into the clubhouse about 7:15 p.m.—this is back when played 7:35 games—and I went into Pete's office and he said, "You're starting!" But all my bags had been re-routed—I didn't have anything! Pete gave me shoes, and Dave Parker gave me bats, Eric Davis gave me this, and everybody else gave me that, but there wasn't time to get me in the starting lineup. When I got out to the bench, the game was already under way, and that's why I came in to pinch-hit, instead of starting.

When I first came up, Nolan Ryan was the toughest pitcher I faced. He had gotten word that this rookie shortstop from Cincinnati needed to be intimidated. I was leading off the game. At that time, I used to dig in, I used to bunt, I used to do all those things that Nolan Ryan supposedly doesn't like. And I had about 70 family members down there who were hollering at Nolan Ryan that I was going to take him deep! So, before the game had even barely started, my back was already dirty. Two times he knocked me down. So, yeah, Nolan Ryan was the most intimidating pitcher I ever faced—and the toughest.

*Barry Larkin has appeared in 16 openers, with a .325 batting average (21-for-56).*

*I think the players who are from Cincinnati appreciate Opening Day in Cincinnati in a way that's a little different from the guys who aren't from here.* I wear a lot of pride when I put on that "C". I don't know if guys who aren't from Cincinnati feel that same thing. Back in the '80s, we had Buddy Bell, and Ronnie Oester, Pete Rose and Dave Parker, so there were a lot of Cincinnati people here. I think there's a real pride associated with it.

I get butterflies before every game, but they're more pronounced before Opening Day, because I know everything's starting for real. It's an emotional day. And I always look forward to it. Everybody's hyped, and that lasts for a couple of innings, and then it's like, "OK, it's a baseball game, let's play!"

I remember doing some good things on Opening Day—a couple home runs against Montreal, a couple of hits to spark rallies, a couple of plays here and there—but I don't remember what years they happened. I just know they happened on Opening Day.

I remember 1990 because it was in Houston—the first time we'd opened on the road. I hit a bases-loaded triple in the 11th inning to win it. Off Charlie Kerfeld. I remember '94, the Easter Sunday Night Opener on ESPN, and how it didn't feel right. Monday felt more like the opener, even though we knew it was the second game, and we were 0-1 going into it.

It didn't feel right in '95, either, with the late start because of the strike. The electricity wasn't there that day, and it's a feeling that's lingered since. I think the strike has made a lot of people in Cincinnati kind of callous.

One opener I missed was 1998, and that was when Pokey Reese made the four errors. It was just part of the Opening Day experience. Guys get hyped, and under those situations, some guys struggle, and some other guys do things that make you say, "Whoa!" Pokey just happened to be on the other end of that spectrum. I didn't think it was any indication of what kind of year he was going to have—because he did well after that. I talked to him. I told him about three errors I had in LA—and should have had four, but they called time out. And I told him about the time that Ozzie Smith told me that he had three errors in a game.

The 2000 opener was special when Ken Griffey, Jr. got those big ovations. I remember that well. I was standing beside him on the foul line, for the first of two ovations—the second great ovation came when he stepped to home plate. What it said to me was, "We're glad to have one of ours back." It was tremendous.

# Billy Doran

*Doran was born and raised in Mt. Healthy, a Cincinnati suburb. He played ball at Mt. Healthy High School and Miami University. He made his major league debut with the Astros in 1982. He spent 2½ seasons with the Reds (1990–1992) and played in the 1991 opener.*

Do you know which of the Cincinnati openers I remember best? Not the one in Cincinnati. Nineteen ninety in Houston. I was with the

Astros.

I remember facing that Reds team, and after three games against them, we were absolutely deflated! The Reds ran us ragged. That team left such an impression on us, I'd never seen anything like it. It was like: *How on earth are we going to be able to compete with this team in our division?* The Reds started out the season by sweeping us in Houston, and they never looked back.

I remember the guys in our clubhouse—me included—after those games just shaking our heads. At their speed, with everything they had. It was obvious to us, after only three games, that that team right there was special. They were so athletic, so young, and they had that great bullpen.

You play against a lot of teams over the course of a season—a lot of teams that are hot, a lot of teams that are cold, but there was something different about that team right from the get-go.

I was traded to the Reds that August. I came over here, and the one thing that hit me was their *pace*. The Astros were a last-place team and our games just dragged. There was no pace to them. I got over here and suddenly—*Snap! Snap! Snap!*—things were moving. On and off the field. Get the ball, throw it. Catch the ball, throw it. *Snap! Snap! Snap!* Everything was moving. They were in such a rhythm.

I think it had a lot to do with Lou Piniella—his impatience, his desire. Everybody has desire, everybody wants to win. But Lou was a little different. He was so demanding, so on top of things all of the time. There was no time to breathe. Right from the get-go, he knew what had to be done with that club. He knew they had a lot of talent, and he wasn't going to settle for anything less than their best. That's all he cared about with them. He wasn't going to let them waste it.

Lou had established a sense of urgency right from the beginning in spring training. The guys knew, "Well, this is what it is." When they came down and opened up in Houston, they jumped out of the gate like nothing I'd ever seen before. I think that just carried over, and lasted the entire season. Boy, they had a lot of fuel in that tank. Geesh.

My first big-league game, I watched from the bench. I came up in September 1982. We were in Philadelphia. I remember just getting into town and going to the ballpark. In my first game, I watched Steve Carlton pitch against Nolan Ryan, and Mike Schmidt hit a home run in the bottom of the ninth or 10th inning to beat Ryan, 1-0. *I sat in the dugout and I remember thinking the entire time: "I may never get a hit in this league."*

I'll tell you a funny story about Barry Larkin. You gotta remember that Barry and I grew up in Cincinnati. And I had a little history with Barry even beyond that. Barry played college ball for the same guy that coached me at Miami—Bud Middaugh. I first met Barry at a camp up in Michigan. In fact, I've got a picture at my house—me in a Houston uniform, Barry in a Michigan uniform, with our coach.

When Barry first got called up to the Reds in 1986, some of the guys on the Reds told him, "Go ahead and bunt on Ryan. Don't worry about it." Well, Nolan *hated* people to bunt against him. So, Barry tries to drop one down. After that at bat, Nolan asked me, "Who the hell is this kid? Is he all right?" I said, "No, he's a pain in the ass. You might wanna just let him know you're out there."

The next time up, Nolan dusted him off. Barry picked himself up off the ground, and he's thinking, "What's this all about?" Nolan was known to do that sort of thing. I told Barry after the game about my conversation with Nolan, and Barry just shook his head with that grin of his. He knew I'd got him good. It was all in good fun.

*If I had to use one word to describe Opening Day in Cincinnati, I would say it is an event. In other towns, Houston included, Opening Day was different than normal games, but of all the places we opened, I never played in an Opening Day that was as big a deal as it was in Cincinnati. In Cincinnati, Opening Day is electric.*

Growing up in Cincinnati, and understanding the history of baseball here, gives you a different perspective. Had I not grown up here, I don't think I could have fully appreciated that. And then, on top of all that, playing here for the Reds, just adds another layer of perspective. You see it from the inside, and you realize how big a deal it is to be a player with all this going on around you. That's when I think I realized it was such a different thing here, in comparison to all the other places. Had I not actually been in a Reds uniform, I probably would have never noticed the difference.

# Jeff Reed

*Reed played for the Reds from 1987 to 1991. He is well-remembered for being the backup catcher on the '90 World Champions. He started the 1989 and 1991 openers.*

I was traded from Montreal to Cincinnati in '87, and I remember an opener in '89 when we beat the Dodgers in a close game. It was bitter cold. In the five years I was here—four Opening Days—we won all of them. We always played well on Opening Day. Of all the places I played—Colorado, San Francisco, Minnesota, Montreal, and with the Chicago Cubs—Cincinnati was just a little bit more pumped up about Opening Day. The fans were all dressed up in red, everybody downtown was in red. It was a real big deal here. *Opening Day with the Reds!*

*Jeff Reed (34) joins Reds starters on the foul line prior to the 1991 opener against the Astros. On the third-base line with the Astros are Craig Biggio and Jeff Bagwell, who made his major league debut at the 1991 opener.*

My first opener was in Minnesota as a Twin. It was in '84 when we played the Tigers. That was the year they jumped off to that ridiculous 20-and-4 record or something and they won it all. I had made the club out of camp—I was 20 years old—and I remember just watching those guys the Tigers and thinking, *"Oh my goodness, I'm in the big leagues. These guys look like they can play!"*

Fans have good memories, especially about home-plate collisions. They remember one I had here with Eric Yelding in 1991. We were playing Houston, close game, eighth inning. I was blocking the plate, but my left side was totally exposed because I was reaching out with my glove hand to receive the throw from Paul O'Neill in right field. Yelding hit me a split second after the ball was in my glove. But I have no recollection of catching it, and hanging onto it, even though I did. I remember Rob Dibble pulling the ball out of my glove—there were still runners on base and only two outs—but the only other thing I remember is I'd had the wind knocked out of me completely and I couldn't breathe. I remember thinking, "If I don't get a breath, I'm going to die." I got my breath, and I stayed in the game, even though it turns out I had three broken ribs. You never want a guy to think he knocked you out of the game!

I had a collision that was acutally worse but it wasn't as a Red. I got cut right here on my chin. It just laid me open. You could see my jawbone. But I didn't feel a thing. And I bled all over, and I didn't even know I was bleeding! It took 18 stitches to close. Then I got on the plate afterwards and ate a cheeseburger. That ended any chance of getting any sympathy from my wife. She told me, "You can't be hurt too bad if you're eating a cheeseburger!" But, I was hungry.

## CRAIG BIGGIO AND JEFF BAGWELL

*Biggio who has played for Houston since 1988, played in his first opener in Cincinnati in 1991. Bagwell made his major league debut at Riverfront Stadium on the same day.*

BIGGIO:   I remember Tom Browning pitched, and he was tough. *Opening Day is big everywhere, but it's not everywhere that you see a parade of horses and other animals coming onto the field through the center-field gate,* and then take a couple laps around the field. They definitely pull out all the stops here. I like that.

BAGWELL:   I was so nervous. I was on overload. The troops had just come back from Desert Storm, and some of them were being honored here. The Reds got their World Championship rings that day. The fans were jacked.

There was so much going through my mind: *"I can't believe I'm here. Am I good enough to be here? I'm going to play today, but am I good enough to stay here?"*

I remember standing up for the national anthem, and I was shaking. I couldn't stop myself from shaking. I remember my father was here. I can't remember if my mother was here.

I don't remember a thing that happened in the field, but I remember my at bats. Tom Browning was pitching. I walked my first time up. Then I made a couple of outs. Rob Dibble was pitching on my last at bat. I lined out to Barry Larkin to end the game. He was standing up the middle. He caught the guy off base. Double play.

## FRED MCGRIFF

*McGriff, who debuted in the major leagues in 1986, appeared in the 1992 Cincinnati opener with the Padres and the 2002 opener with the Cubs.*

Being with the visiting team in Cincinnati on Opening Day, I really couldn't appreciate what Opening Day here really meant. But I could tell it was a big deal, what with the parade. If I didn't have to play in the game, I'd have been able to absorb a lot more of it. But half the time on Opening Day, you're taking batting practice, getting ready to go play a game, so you don't really get to take it all in like a fan can.

The Reds have always been one of my favorite teams because I grew up in Tampa, where the Reds used to have spring training. *The season would start, and the Reds'd be the first team to open the season. And what a team! The Big Red Machine. You'd say, "Yeah, they should be first!" They had the tradition, and they had the team. They had it all.*

But being a left-handed hitter, I didn't have too many left-handers on the Reds to follow. Most of the Reds stars back then—other than Joe Morgan—were right-handed batters: George Foster, Johnny Bench, Tony Perez. And I didn't want to do the flapping chicken-wing thing with my arm like Joe. That was his thing. I couldn't make it mine. That's why I liked it when Dave Parker came along. He was my favorite Red. Big left-handed swinger. Great all-around player. Could do it all.

I've always liked Opening Day. By the end of the season, it's been a long year, and you're ready to go home. But, after you've been home for a while during the off-season and February comes around, you're like, "Yeah! I'm ready to play baseball again." You go to spring training, and pretty soon here comes Opening Day. And back come the butterflies. No matter how long you've been playing, on Opening Day you're going to have the butterflies.

## MARK GRACE

*Grace debuted in 1988 with the Chicago Cubs, and played in the 1995 opener in Cincinnati.*

I remember opening the season here in 1995 and we opened with a two-game series here, and actually swept it. And it was a good Reds club. They ended up winning the division, if I remember correctly. *We beat Jose Rijo in the opener. I remember Sammy Sosa got a hit off of Rijo. They're homeys.* So Rijo was all over his ass. This was before Sammy was the dominating power hitter he is now.

I think it's kind of a cool thing, actually, that the Reds get to open at home every year. Tradition is a part of baseball. The Reds playing at home is a tradition. Just like the Detroit Lions playing on Thanksgiving Day.

This was my 15th opening day this year, and I remember having butterflies and being nervous. I've had some crazy stuff happen on Opening Days. I've had Opening Days in Japan. The Mets and us opened there a few years ago. I hit a home run in Japan. I got a pop in Japan!

My first year in the big leagues was 1988, but my first Opening Day was '89. It still goes down as one of the more famous Opening Days in Chicago. We'd just made a trade: the Cubs' Rafael Palmeiro and a couple others for Mitch Williams and a few others. We had a one-run lead on the Phillies, and Williams proceeded to walk the bases loaded with nobody out, and then struck out the next three guys. It was Chris James, Mike Schmidt and a guy named Mark Ryal.

That's something how you remember stuff like that.

## GEORGE GRANDE

*Grande has been paired with former Reds pitcher Chris Welsh on the Reds TV broadcasts since 1993.*

My first Opening Day was at the Polo Grounds—I was a New York Giants fan, a Willie Mays fan.

To me, Opening Day is the best day of the year—rebirth, springtime, hope for a new year, fans believing this is finally their team's year; it's one of the most blessed days of any year—and the last day of the season is always one of the saddest.

I remember my first time doing a major league game: Yankee Stadium with the Yankees against the Cleveland Indians. Yankee Stadium is special, and there's nothing like being in Yankee Stadium at the start of a World Series game. Whenever I'm there for a World Series game, I always walk down behind home plate to listen to the anthem, to listen to the ovation, and then I go back upstairs. There's nothing like it. Yankee Stadium is *the* place to be in the post-season.

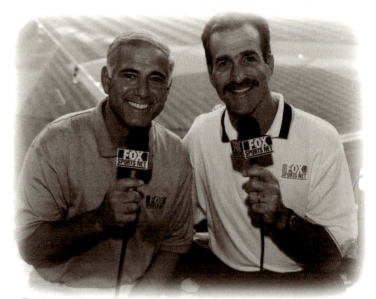

*The longest-running TV broadcast team in Reds history, George Grande (left) and Chris Welsh, have broadcast every opener since 1993.*

Opening Day in Yankee Stadium is great—especially after you've won a World Series—but year in and year out, the way Cincinnati embraces Opening Day, the way baseball is so much a part of the Cincinnati's history, it's unlike any other ballpark, any other city that I've ever been in for Opening Day. *For Opening Day I've been at Yankee Stadium, Shea Stadium, Fenway Park, Detroit after they won in '84, St. Louis, Cleveland Municipal Stadium, Dodger Stadium and the opening of the new ballparks in Pittsburgh, Milwaukee and San Francisco. And I'm telling you, there is no place that has an Opening Day like Cincinnati's.* People genuinely care for the history and tradition of the game here. They *know* it is their game, because the pro game started here, and, of course, the parade sets Cincinnati apart from all the other Opening Days. It really is a holiday here, a baseball holiday, and nobody else has that.

People also know the game is played *right* here. And they're proud of that. It's not just winning, it's winning the right way. The Big Red Machine reflected the way the game should be played, the way kids play Knothole baseball and high school baseball. There is no place for showboating here. The Reds have always played it that way. There's more of it in our society now, so yeah, there's a little bit of it with the Reds, but fortunately we don't have a lot of it here.

# Jim Tarbell

*Tarbell, a Cincinnati city councilman, has been playing the role of the legendary "Peanut Jim" Shelton for years, dressing up in a tux and tail and top hat and marching in the Findlay Market Opening Day parade.*

Peanut Jim Shelton.

The real Peanut Jim fresh-roasted nuts outside Crosley Field and Riverfront Stadium for about 50 years. He died in 1982, at 93.

At Findlay Market is where people really identify with Peanut Jim. Especially the older black folks, from the West End, who grew up with Peanut Jim around Crosley Field, and have the memory of him—not just as a guy who roasted peanuts outside the ballpark, but as a neighborhood character. He lived in the neighborhood. He lived a few blocks away from Crosley Field. He just rolled out of bed, and rolled his peanut cart on down to the front door of Crosley, and went into business.

*Jim Tarbell offers his tribute to Peanut Jim Shelton (below) each year in the Opening Day parade. Shelton sold roasted peanuts at Crosley Field and Riverfront Stadium.*

So, the older people in the neighborhood understand that kind of context. As soon as you walk by them in the parade, and they see that top hat and tail and they see that peanut cart, they start smiling. There's no words exchanged. They just know it.

But then, when you get south of Central Parkway, you can kind of feel it change a little bit. People then start to relate to me, Jim Tarbell, the council member. Above Central Parkway, they're really into Peanut Jim. South of Central Parkway, if they recognize me as a council member, why then they wave. Otherwise, they don't quite get the Peanut Jim connection.

I bought the outfit in a thrift store about 20 years ago. I've been doing the parade about 15 years. I got the peanut cart from a guy named "Walt" in Northside. He's got a neighborhood café called "The Fifth Amendment."

I was thinking about doing Peanut Jim in the parade. I had the top hat, and I had the tail, but I didn't have the peanut cart. I walked into Walt's one day and there's this peanut cart just sitting in the corner. So I met the owner and I said, "Walt, what's that doing there?" He said, "I just like it; I just kind of keep it around for furniture." And I said, "Could I borrow that for the Opening Day parade?" And he said, "Yeah!" So, I've been using it ever since.

Jeff Wehmeier, Herm's son, has been marching with me every year, wearing his dad's baseball uniform. That's been an integral part of the procession.

The peanut cart isn't set up to roast peanuts right now, but it could. And I could over-roast 'em as good, as Peanut Jim could over-roast 'em. They were always over-roasted with Peanut Jim.

# POKEY REESE

*Reese made his big-league debut in 1997 with the Reds. He remained with the club through the 2001 season and started in four openers. His most memorable Opening Day was also his worst—four errors in the 1998 opener, tying a major-league record.*

The thrill of Opening Day at Cinergy Field—whether you're a Red or a visiting player—is knowing you're playing on the same field as the great Reds players that came before you: the Morgans, the Roses, the Benches, the Perezes, the Concepcions.

Players around the league know how big Opening Day in Cincinnati is. They know how special this place is on that day. Just getting the chance to be in the major leagues, on the roster on Opening Day, is awesome. Knowing you're a big-leaguer is like walking on air. You're there with the best players in the game, and you're one of them! That's awesome in itself. You want to stay here; you don't want to even think about going back down to the minors.

I had butterflies that day, but it went away once I stepped out on the field and got the first play out of the way. I don't know what happened in the third inning, when I made the three errors, and four on the day. I remember hoping they would hit me another ground ball that inning—just to get it out of the way, out of my system. It was just one of those days.

Nerves didn't contribute to it. I was just making errors, not staying down on the ball. *The funny thing is, after those four errors on Opening Day, I didn't make an error in the next 50 chances or so.* Guys were saying stuff that day to pick me up. Even Tony Gwynn told me out there on second base: "Just keep playing hard. Forget about it. That play's over with." And that's the way I took it. I was embarrassed, sure, but deep down it didn't bother me, because I knew I was a good fielder.

Of course, it had to be in front of 50,000 people and on ESPN! Now, when I think back on it, it's like, "Wow." I can't believe it happened. But it did. It was just one of them things.

# SEAN CASEY

*Casey deserves the nickname, "Mr. Opening Day." He was traded on the eve of the 1998 opener for Reds pitcher Dave Burba, who was to have started. Casey has hit safely in all five of his openers, including home runs in 1999 and 2001. His first-day heroics continued in 2001 in Milwaukee and Pittsburgh where he christened new ballparks with the first hit.*

I didn't realize Opening Day in Cincinnati was that big of a deal until '99, with the parade and the sellout and the adrenaline I felt when I was coming out for the introductions. I could feel the crowd's energy. When I hit the home run that put us ahead, the excitement that was going on in that stadium was overwhelming. When I was rounding those bases, I felt like just jumping out of my shoes.

*I think that's when I realized that Cincinnati is a baseball town. I remember thinking, "It doesn't get any better than this."* Just to play in it, even if you're 0-for-4, is great, but to get three hits with a home run is unbelievable. And the fans are so excited, because of all the hoopla leading up to it.

I didn't even notice all that in '98, because the whole day was such a blur to me. I'd just been traded for Dave Burba. I got in, in the 8th inning, and managed to single off Kevin Brown. I was still in shock. I didn't know anything about the Reds, about Opening Day, or much about anything, really.

Two thousand one was cool too, because I hit a three-run homer to tie it in the sixth, against John Burkett of the Braves. I'm telling you, you get your adrenaline going in those openers, no doubt about it.

# KEN GRIFFEY, JR.

*Griffey, Jr. grew up in Cincinnati, the son of Big Red Machine outfielder, Ken Griffey, Sr. Junior graduated from Moeller High School, and joined the Seattle Mariners in 1989. He was voted to Major League Baseball's All-Century team. Junior came to the Reds in 2000.*

Opening Day is probably the most excitement that you have, until you're in the playoffs or World Series.

I kind of knew what it would be like in 2000. I was familiar with all the excitement in the air, because I grew up here going to Opening Day. It was not hard for me to get out of school. No! Everybody knew I was going to the ballpark for Opening Day to see my dad play. I'd go to school for a half-day, 8 to 12, and Mom would pick us up at 12, and we'd be at the ballpark by 12:30. By we, I mean my brother Craig and me. We weren't the only ones doing that. A *lot* of families did that; our dad just happened to play for the Reds, that's all.

*It's a holiday in Cincinnati. You have tickets, you go to the game. Built-in excuse, nobody questions it. You don't have to make up some excuse. Anything else, you need a doctor's excuse. Not Opening Day.*

Opening Day, when my Dad was playing, was a blast. First thing we'd do is go into Sparky's office and get a red pop—Sparky was still there—because he was the only one with red pop. And off we'd go. We'd go off into the tunnel, wander around, go to the batting cage, have the run of the place.

As a player, you look forward to Opening Day, because you know it's going to be a packed house, and you know the fans are going to be yelling and screaming the whole day. And, then, after that, after all that excitement of Opening Day, the feeling of the next game is like, "Oh, OK, Opening Day is over, let's play!"

Nothing could have prepared me for that standing ovation in 2000. I can't describe it, because it doesn't happen but once, or maybe twice in your career. Until you retire, and you have that last go-round to each city like Cal Ripken and Tony Gwynn, you aren't going to get any ovation like that.

For me, the feeling was "Welcome Home." I came home, and the fans were saying, "Welcome Home." It was awesome.

My very first opener was my major league debut. The Mariners opened in '89 in Oakland. I wore out the mirror before the game: that was my first big-league uniform. I went 1-for-3; first at bat, double in the left-center field gap, and then proceeded to go 3-for-the-next-17 at bats. Then we went to Seattle for the home opener; first pitch I saw, home run to left field.

I never got to play an Opening Dad with my dad. He came over to Seattle late in the '90 season. We would've in '91, but he was in a car accident, and hurt his neck. *But when Dad came over to Seattle from Cincinnati in '90 and we played together, that game felt like Opening Day!* He was in left, I was in center. Everybody on the team was excited that we were playing together, 19 years apart. Everybody was nervous. He was more nervous than I was. He was worse!

He got over it, though. I made him take me out to lunch every day. Oh yeah! He lived with me. And I had a house. I said, "You got to live by *my* rules now." That didn't go over too good. My mom started laughing. She told my dad, "Hey, *you* always told him, 'Until you get your own house, you have to abide by *my* rules!'"

I told him I was going to make him sign a contract. And at the end of the contract, I said, "Last but not least, you have to do everything that Mom says!"

## TODD WALKER

*Walker started only one opener as a Cincinnati Red, in 2002, but he made it memorable with a home run and two doubles.*

They boo you more here in Cincinnati than in Denver and Minnesota. But the good part about it is that when you do well, there's no better fans in the world.

I'm not a big fan of Opening Day. It's a football-game atmosphere. It's unbelievable. And I don't feel comfortable playing on Opening Day. Baseball's a game where you relax, and you play through the month of June, July and August, and there's not much hype to it. You just play your game.

But Opening Day is unusual, in that it's a big deal. *The reason you play so many games is that you have room for mistakes, but on Opening Day, you don't necessarily feel like you have that room. You feel like you've got to be perfect.* But one good thing about it is that with as many people as there are in the stands, and as much excitement as there is around the first day, you can use it for your advantage or disadvantage. For me, it makes me feel more focused. I try to use it to my advantage that way.

It's great to win a game like we did on Opening Day, 2002—I wish everybody could experience it—to win a game like that, in the bottom of the ninth. It's great, for that brief moment, to have everybody together.

## AARON BOONE

*Aaron Boone was drafted by the Reds in 1994, and was the starting third baseman from 1999 to 2003 when he was traded to the Yankees. He started in four Cincinnati openers.*

Opening Day is an exciting day, and even a little more so in Cincinnati. It's even more exciting if you're starting. I got called up in '97, had my first opener in '98, and my first start in an opener in '99.

I still have a framed picture signed by everyone, of the team on the line before the '99 opener. It's a pretty cool feeling. When you take the field, you're pretty pumped up. You certainly have a little bit of adrenaline. You have to ratchet yourself down, and that's not an easy thing to do. It's like that almost every first game. It's for real, and that's a different feeling. Everything has a heightened sense about it. There's an electricity to it. The switch has been flipped; the game is on.

*In 1998, I was an extra player, and here's what I remember: It seemed like about five minutes before the game was to start, an elephant relieved itself right there in front of our dugout. So there's* an Opening Day memory for you!

## ADAM DUNN

*Adam Dunn made his major league debut in 2001, and started in the 2002 and 2003 openers.*

The night before the 2002 opener I had trouble getting to sleep. I didn't get to bed until about 3 o'clock in the morning. Trying to get to sleep the night before your first Opening Day is like trying to get to sleep the night before your first day of school.

*I'm finally sleeping pretty good when the phone rang. It was Barry. He was calling to check on me and thank God he called me because I had my clock set for "p.m." instead of "a.m."* Maybe he figured I was the guy to check on, because I was the guy most likely to do something stupid—like having my clock set wrong.

He called at nine-something. We had to be there at 11. I was sleeping pretty good when that phone rang! If he didn't call, I would've slept right through the opener!

## AUSTIN KEARNS

*Kearns, a native of Lexington, Kentucky, played his first Opening Day as a Red in 2003 in the inaugural game at Great American Ball Park. The 22-year-old started in right field and batted cleanup.*

We flew in from spring training on Thursday night, four days before Opening Day. It wasn't quite dark yet; it was kind of twilight. The pilot flew right over the stadium and the lights were on, and we were able to look down and see inside. That was pretty awesome, knowing that on Monday afternoon it was all going to start for real.

When I was a kid growing up in Lexington, I never got to go to an Opening Day in Cincinnati, although I did come to games here in the summertime. We don't have that rule in Lexington that you can get out of school for Opening Day if you have a ticket to the game!

Getting to talk with former President Bush before the game was very cool. It's awesome that he visited our clubhouse. And it wasn't like he was just walking by shaking hands. He talked to everybody individually, and asked us where we were from. I told him that when I was 12 years old, our South Lexington "Bambino" team won the World Series and that we got to go to the White House when he was president. That was in 1992. I think it's pretty neat I got to meet him that long ago, and got to meet him again 11 years later, before my first Opening Day in the big leagues.

Brandon Larson, who's from Texas, gave him the "Hook 'em Horns" sign and Adam Dunn brought up the fact he's from New Caney, Texas, which is near Houston. The president told Adam, "Don't beat up on the Astros too bad this year, because I have to live down there!"

With everything going on in the world, it's easy to forget about a game of baseball. But I think Opening Day brings everybody together: the players, the fans, everybody. Having the former president here just made it all that more special.

## RICK STOWE

*Stowe is part of the Reds' "First Family of Baseball." Rick's dad, Bernie, has worked in the Reds clubhouse since 1947. Rick joined the "family business" as did his brother Mark. Rick's first job with the Reds was batboy, beginning in 1981.*

The best way I can describe Opening Day for me is "balls to the wall!" On the Sunday before the opener—Workout Day—everybody's uniform fits. And then the guys come up in the next morning, and *nothing* fits. Guys are swapping uniform pants left and right!

My dad tells me they were doing that even back when he came on board in the '40s, so I guess some things never change. Guys want them *just* right. In spring training when the guys are being fit for their uniforms, I'll say, "I want a witness here! Sean Casey says his pants fit!" because come Opening Day, I *know* he's going to be one of the guys who says his pants don't fit and he's going to be one of the guys flip-flopping them.

And the weather can cause problems, too. We've had days where it's been warm on the workout day, and then Opening Day is cold. All of a sudden, guys say, "I need the skull cap! I need the long johns!" We're running up to Koch's Sporting Goods on Fourth Street buying stuff.

See, everything on Opening Day is brand spanking new. Everything from spring training is obsolete—everything, that is, except the underwear, the jocks and the shoes, because of the blisters and all. Even the socks are new. The pants are new, the shirts are new and every shirt that goes underneath the uniform jersey, whether it's long sleeves or short sleeves, is new for Opening Day. We have new emblems every year, and we don't break them out till Opening Day, so everything's new. Jackets. Sweat shirts. Four or five different hats that we've got to fit them for.

Not to mention you gotta suit up Doc Tim Kremchek and the trainers and the therapists and the strength coach and the coaches. And you got batting-practice pitchers coming in and saying, "Hey, I need a uniform!" Which they do. So, it's not just 25 players. You've got 40 guys you're trying to get fixed up. And then sometimes you got a guy like Deion Sanders, and he decides on the Sunday before Opening Day, "Hey, I want this tailored," or "I want that tailored"—and now you're trying to find a tailor or a seamstress on a Sunday night! Jose Rijo liked his pants real tight around his calves. *You need to take it in down here, Rick.*

We used to use New Look Cleaners down on Queen City to launder our uniforms until we started doing them ourselves. I remember one year we had a big new washing machine, and it "extracted" too much, and the uniforms all looked wrinkled and we had to send them out and get them pressed on Sunday night! The day before the opener! The washing machine had been sitting there three or four months, unused. So, in subsequent years, we got smart and had the machines tested during the winter and had them ready to go.

You know what it's like to have the uniforms fit, and then we wash them and dry them and the player says, "Ohmigosh! This thing shrunk!" Well, no, it didn't shrink, but we've got to deal with it, make it right.

That's the other thing: *The mirrors in the clubhouse get worn out on Opening Day. The guys want to see themselves. They do the little turn, and all that. They give it everything.*

*New.* If I had to pick only one word to describe Opening Day, that'd be it. *New.* Even the catcher's gear is new! Brand-new! You're calling Nike up: "Hey, I need this, I need that, I need this." That's because the players gave away all their stuff to the minor-leaguers at the end of spring training: batting gloves, some of their shoes, wristbands, shorts, T-shirts.

And you also got guys saying to you: "I need this for my wife," or "I need this for a buddy." And tickets! *Tickets*! You gotta get guys their tickets. You know, make adjustments on the fly.

Another thing about Opening Day is the breakfast we have for them. We have breakfasts before other day games, too, but the Opening Day breakfast is always a little confusing.

Somebody'll ask, "Hey, where's the salt?" Or "Hey, where's the pepper?" I called Pokey Reese "the pepper guy." I remember him asking for pepper on Opening Day. I said, "Gee, I dunno Pokey, I can't find it; it's in one of these boxes we shipped home from spring training." We have a semi-trailer that leaves from Florida three or four days before we do with all our stuff in it. It'll pull up into the unloading bay at the stadium one day before the workout day. And I'll have a couple people up north unload it before we get there. And I have no idea where anything is. It's like when somebody else has packed your suitcase. You arrive at your destination, you open your suitcase, and you say, "Where the hell's my underwear?"

And Pokey's wondering where the *pepper* is? Hey, I'm not going to know where the pepper is until the second game, and that's because I got that off day in between to find it—and everything else that is in a box somewhere.

I think the pepper year was the year Pokey made the four errors – three of them in one inning—on Opening Day. I remember the headline the next day: "How many E's are in P-o-k-e-y R-e-e-s-e?" Classic!

And you get a ton of questions from the players on Opening Day: *Where I do I park? Where's a good place to live? How's this side of town? Where do I go eat? What bars are good around here? Where shouldn't I go? How do I get here? How do I get there?* *Usually, on Opening Day, the game's over early and guys want to go out. So you got to be like a concierge in a hotel. You got to have answers.*

Bip Roberts had a tendency to run us a little bit. You know, the clubhouse boys. *Go get me a cup coffee.* You know, stuff they could actually do themselves. But, we've had a good group of guys in here over the years. And I think it stems from Larkin. He gets his laundry and puts it in the basket. Griffey, same way. You aren't picking up stuff for those guys. The other guys see that. They see it in spring training, and they see it doesn't change on Opening Day.

And there's new ballboys and batboys to break in on Opening Day, every two years or so. We've gotta try to train them that morning. "OK, you have to go here, and to get there you have to take the elevator to three, and go down two offices…" and "OK, you're going to be down the line during the game, and you gotta be sure not to catch any fair balls that wind up going into foul territory."

Dave Parker always had a field day with the new ballboys on Opening Day. You remember how loud Parker was? Well, we'd get up to Cincinnati from spring training, and the players hadn't seen the new ballboys yet, and if one of them

*Rick Stowe (right) has worked in the Reds organization with his dad, Bernie, since 1981.*

has a blemish or wears glasses or anything at all like that, the players gotta come up with a nickname for them. And Parker was right in the middle of it. So, yeah, it's boisterous in there. Loud. Things are going a mile-and-a-half a minute.

*Yeah, it's balls to the wall, and then, all of a sudden, they're playing the national anthem, and you're like, "Whew! Thank God for that!"*

My first opener, I was a ballboy, 1981. We had a right-fielder named Jeff Jones. Big, strong, red-haired fella. I was down the right-field line. That was my job. You know, getting foul balls and playing catch with the right fielder between every half inning. And Jeff Jones, our brand-new right fielder, was just as jacked as I was! He must've been throwing about *85 miles an hour* to me. There's 55,000 people out there—I'm nervous, I'm down the line, out on the field for the very first time—and this guy is throwing *BBs!* And I'm doing everything I can not to catch it in the teeth!

So he's juicing it up, and I'm thinking, "Hey, *I'm* gonna juice it up! I ain't gonna throw rainbows into this guy!"

*And my very first throw sailed over his head! My very first throw! And it's bouncing along the warning track out there past the 375-foot mark, rolling along the wall. It was the only ball I would throw over an outfielder's head in the two years I was out there, and it was Opening Day my first year!*

I had to work my way up the ladder like my dad did. After working the right-field line, I moved behind home plate being ballboy for the umpires, and then I moved inside. Being ballboy for the umpires was a good workout back then. The umpire needs three balls, four balls, at all times.

Geez, the baseballs. My dad never told me about the guy mudding up the baseballs before the game. I remember being behind home plate the very first time, and I looked at the baseballs and I said, "Damn, these balls are muddy! What the hell—they gave me batting practice balls!" So, I cleaned them all up. You know, spit on them and rubbed all the mud off with a towel. And the home-plate umpire comes by and says, "Damn, tell Hank to put some more mud on the balls. Christ, there ain't no mud on the balls!" Oops, I realized I'd done something I shouldn't. So, trying to cover up for this, I say, "You're right! They're ain't no mud on the balls! Where the hell's the mud? I'll go tell Hank!"

When Dick Wagner was here, he didn't like us or anybody else giving balls away to people in the stands. So, if a ball was hit down the left-field line, you had one pitch to run all the way over there, and the ballboy down the left-field line would throw the ball to you, and then you'd have to run it back to the dugout and throw it in the used-ball bag, and that would be used for batting practice the next day. Wagner said, "That's four dollars." That's what a ball cost, four dollars.

The other thing about Wagner was he didn't want ballboys to be impersonating the players. So even though it was usually cold on Opening Day—or when it was *really* cold for the second game which was the first night game—Wagner didn't want any ballboys sitting out there with Reds jackets on. He wanted everybody to know it was a ballboy out there, not a player. I looked like the Michelin man out there, I had so many layers of clothes on underneath!

Even back then when I was working as a ballboy, I was immersed on Opening Day in getting the players ready for the game. I'm not going to divulge the player's name, but I'd leave this one guy a cup of beer to calm his nerves down before the game. At Riverfront there was a little spot in the walkway before you get to the bench in the dugout where I could hide a cup of beer. This guy was a starting pitcher, a good one. He was in lot of Opening Day games in the '80s. Opening Day was the only day he wanted it. I don't even know if he finished the whole thing; he probably didn't. He just needed something to calm him down.

All the players are nervous on Opening Day, whether they admit it or not. A couple of years ago, I asked Barry Larkin, "Hey, Lark, you don't get butterflies before the first game, do you?" The reason I asked him that, is I had just asked Junior if he got nervous, and he said, "Naw, man, naw. I don't get nervous. Just another game." Lark said, "Are you kidding me? Sure, I get butterflies. You bet I do. I always get butterflies before Opening Day."

I mean, how could you not get butterflies? It's a huge deal in Cincinnati. The newspaper puts out a special section on Opening Day, which is awesome. And we put the TV coverage of the parade on our TV sets in the clubhouse, because a lot of the guys haven't seen that. There's a tendency to think there's very little turnover on the team from one Opening Day to the next—fans tend to think of the established stars as being "the team" from one year to the next—but there really is a lot of turnover. *The new guys see the parade on TV, and they say, "What the hell is this? A parade?" They've never seen a parade associated with Opening Day before.*

Terry Francona was a new guy in '87. He was a nervous wreck on Opening Day. He wasn't even supposed to start the game. He wound up hitting a home run that day—he was the "Star of the Game"—and I think the next home run he hit was in September. I went out with him that night, you know, after the opener, and after he got home, sometime in the middle of that night his wife had a baby. What a day!

That was some year in '87. I think that was the year Eric Davis was on the covers of all those magazines. "The Next Willie Mays." He'd had a great season the year before. He had a great season that year, too, and he started in right away homering on Opening Day. That was Larkin's first Opening Day, too, I think. But it was Terry Francona who was "Star of the Game." He stole the show.

It wasn't just the new guys who were nervous on Opening Day. Soto had four straight Opening Day victories, and he was nervous as hell when he went out there, every single time!

Those were fun times back in the mid-'80s, when Pete was managing. We had Rob Murphy, Buddy Bell, Ron Oester, Johnny Franco, Frank Williams, Ron Robinson, Tom Browning, Bill Gullickson, Eric Davis, Dave Parker, Barry Larkin, Bo Diaz. That was the most fun team to work for—even though they never got out of second place. And the '99 team was a lot of fun, too.

Some of my favorite guys—I really got a kick out of Buddy Bell. I liked him and his family, his kids. Tom Browning was right up there. The best tipper I ever had was John Smiley. He was very, very generous with me. Jeff Brantley was right up there.

I remember Kevin Mitchell—now there was a character—and I remember him during one of the exhibition games sleeping on the trainer's table—"sicker'n a bitch," he said—and he'd roll off that table a day or two later and get a big hit or two on Opening Day. I saw him do that against Kansas City in a spring training game: rolled off the training table, rolled downstairs, took a swing, knocked it 423 feet and came back in and laid down.

*Mitch always said, "A sick hitter is a dangerous hitter."*

And Mitchell puked all the time. I remember one time on Opening Day he puked, and somebody else puked, or somebody else puked, and Mitchell puked, and I think he had a home run that day. And you know something else funny about Kevin

As recalled by Rick Stowe and others, Kevin Mitchell was one of the great clubhouse characters of all time.

Mitchell? He was usually the first one in the clubhouse, and that included Opening Day.

When he got hungry, it was time for donuts. He'd have one of the ballboys go out and get him "one of everything," and he'd give the ballboy a hundred bucks and the kid'd keep the change! We got a kid who works in the clubhouse—Junior loves to get him to go to Skyline or P.F. Chang's, or somewhere else—and he'll give the kid fifty bucks and the kid doesn't even *think* about giving him his change back anymore! He just pockets it. It's classic.

Tom Browning had a ritual he went through before every game he started, and it all began with Opening Day, if he had the start that day. He was as regimented as anybody I've ever seen. He called it "red drawer" day. He did things by the clock. You know, two hours and 33 minutes before the game, or whatever it was, the red drawers would go on. And an hour and a half before the game, or whatever it was, he'd go to the rest room. And then he'd come back and pull his pants up and pull up his stirrups, and he'd put on his shoes and buckle everything up.

Reds pitching coach Don Gullett has this thing he does before every game, and it starts on Opening Day, too. He puts two new baseballs in the starting pitcher's locker. That's what they go down to the bullpen with. I like the traditions that guys have.

My dad talks about the guys barnstorming north on the trains back in the 1940s and 1950s—playing games throughout the south on the way north. We had our version of that, too. We'd fly into Louisville or Nashville or Cleveland and play an exhibition game.

Different things would happen on the way north. I remember one year Deion Sanders had this boil underneath his armpit. We were playing an exhibition game in Richmond, Virginia. The clubhouse was no bigger than a small conference room. They brought in some doctor to lance Deion's boil, and the doctor said, "This is gonna hurt!" And there were about 20 guys around him when he lanced it—I mean, they had no choice; that's how small the room was—and everybody was like, "Arggggh!" when he lanced it. To this day, if you ask Deion what was the most pain he was ever in, I'll guarantee you he says that day.

In 1995, the year of the replacement players, we're on a charter plane with those clowns, heading north. We had everything—uniforms and all that—made up for those clowns, just like we'd have for the regular players every year. After the Sunday workout, it was announced that Major League Baseball had decided against using replacement players, and we were like, "OK, here's your garbage bag—now get out of here." Having those replacement players reminded me of fantasy camp—only we were paying them, instead of them paying us. And they were getting meal money, too.

Opening Day '98 stands out, too. That was the year we traded our Opening Day pitcher, Dave Burba, to Cleveland for Sean Casey—the day before Opening Day!

The day of the trade—Sunday, March 30, the workout day—Jim Bowden says to me, "Just act like you're your getting a phone list together for everybody on the team, but make sure you get Dave Burba's number," and Jim also gave me a couple of other guys to be sure to get. So, I'm going around acting like I'm getting a phone list. And I say, "Dave, where you gonna be tonight? I need a phone number. I'm compiling a phone list." I give it to Jim and next thing I know, *pffft!* Burba is traded! And oh yeah, I had to get the phone number of Mike Remlinger, so we could tell him was going to be starting the opener. Man, you talk about a shock to your system.

*Remlinger goes from thinking, "I'm gonna just sit back and enjoy this game," and the next thing you know he's the Opening Day starter!*

And we got no uniform for Casey! We called Cleveland—"How big is this guy, anyway?" But, we got the uniform made up.

Opening Day is just *different*, that's all. You can see what it means to the guys by all the hugs and handshakes and "have-a-good-years" that are going on. Casey or Larkin might get all the hugging started in the clubhouse. It just feeds on itself. And then the same thing goes on in the dugout before the game.

And the handshakes. They all got to go through their new handshakes on Opening Day. I think Barry has a different handshake for every guy.

Casey's something on Opening Day, ain't he? And not just here. I mean, we were "on the line" three times in 2001—Cincinnati, Pittsburgh and Milwaukee—and he had a great game every time! First dong in Pittsburgh; first hit in Milwaukee, a three-run dong in Cincinnati. Geesh! Some guys just got it. The cream usually rises to the top on Opening Day.

There's so much stuff going on, on Opening Day. Back before the installation of the grass field, the parade would come into the ballpark. That was cool.

The equipment managers get introduced. That's very neat. It's the one day the clubhouse guys always make a point to check out the beginning of the game. We always go out to the bench and watch a half inning or so, and then we go back inside. I mean, hey, *somebody's*

*Sean Casey has become something of an Opening Day legend, according to Rick Stowe.*

got to carry the fruit basket back in! You know, the big fruit basket the Findlay Market Association gives the Reds manager.

And somebody always sends down some "hitting cookies" on Opening Day. Pearl Ackerman did that. She sat behind home plate. And somebody would always send down a cake. The phone'd be ringing in the clubhouse from upstairs: "Hey, y'all got balloons up here!" Or, "Hey, so-and-so's got flowers up here for y'all."

There's no day like Opening Day! It's great to be able to open up at home every year. It is *soooo* much easier to open at home. All we gotta do is make sure the white uniforms fit.

Even before I started working Opening Day, I'd go down to the ballpark to hang out with my dad. And I'd also go to spring training. I'd have to get excused from Our Lady of Victory of School every year to go to spring training. I'd turn in my note to the principal Sister Mary Walters—and she'd always send a note home with me. The note said, *"Yes, Richard may be excused from school to go to spring training—provided you get me two tickets for Opening Day."*

# REMEMBERING JOHN McSHERRY

*In 1996, Opening Day in Cincinnati turned tragic. Umpire John McSherry collapsed and died of a heart attack behind home plate. The 1996 opener should have been one of the happiest days of Ray Knight's professional life. He was making his managerial debut for the Reds, the team that two decades earlier had drafted and signed and ultimately installed him at third base in 1980 to try to fill the shoes of the great Pete Rose. But April 1, 1996 turned out to be Ray Knight's, and everybody else's, saddest day in baseball. Here, Knight describes the buildup to Opening Day. Then he and other eyewitnesses—plus Randy Marsh, McSherry's friend and fellow umpire—recall "Big John's" death and its aftermath.*

# Ray Knight

I have so many feelings about that day. It was already such an emotional day for me. And a lot of that emotion started with a phone call from Davey Johnson who I had replaced in 1996. I was so moved by that telephone call. And then I ended up getting flowers from Davey and his wife.

And, of course, Sparky Anderson was there. The Reds front office had called me and asked, "Is it going to upset you if Sparky throws out the first pitch?"

Remember now, when I made my debut as a Reds player at third base at Riverfront Stadium, the fans were booing because Pete wasn't in there. And now, the greatest manager in Reds history is throwing out the first pitch, when I'm making my managerial debut.

Honestly, it was uncomfortable. By that Opening Day, I'd already had 30 articles written about how I had back-stabbed Davey to get the job, even though that was not true. I love Davey like a brother and I was always very loyal to him, always very protective of him. And now Sparky was here. But I loved Sparky. How could I not? I started my career with him in Cincinnati, and then he reacquired me a few years later, after he went to Detroit.

Then, we had to release the doves, like they always do. Sparky had a dove, Marge Schott had a dove, I had a dove. And these were little white doves, with their red, white and blue ribbons on, and I don't know how to hold this dove! I don't have a clue. I'm thinking, "Oh, boy, here's one *more* thing that management wants on Opening Day. What time does the game start?" All I wanted to do was play *baseball*! And we let these doves go, and mine gets all tangled up, and he finally gets out of there, and takes off.

So, now, *finally* they announce the lineups, and I run out there and Felipe Alou is the manager of the Expos, and we've always been buddies, and I shake his hand. I'm feeling good, and I get on the rail in the dugout. I hadn't even settled in and the first two guys are out and here's Rondell White. I don't even know what the count was, when John McSherry winced and reached out and Gully said, "Did you see that? He hurt his back!" And then John took his mask off, and he turned. Gully said, "Man, he really hurt his back!" John started to walk, real gingerly, and then I saw him motion to the attendants behind the plexiglass to come out, and then it was like he melted into the ground. We shot out there and, already, before we got there, his face was swelling.

Tom Hallion, one of the other umpires, started crying, and I put my arm around Hallion, and he was breaking down. John was supposed to go to the doctor the day before for some heart work, but he hadn't gone because he didn't want the National League officials to take him off the crew.

The medical personnel tried to resuscitate him and they took him out, and we went to the clubhouse. And I'm just overmatched. Now, the game doesn't mean anything. I mean nobody knew yet what John's condition was, but we knew it didn't look good. So, I immediately call Jim Bowden and we meet and he says, "Marge wants to play." Play? *Play?*

I call Larkin to the side—he's the team captain—and I say, "What do you think?" And he says, "There's no way I can play." And I say, "OK, let me make that decision. Don't just start telling everybody, 'I'm not going to play.'" I said, "Just keep everything together right here. There's a lot of things going on out there." I mean, this is all a matter of only 10 minutes having elapsed. It was a very emotional scene. There were a lot of guys crying.

I go into the umpire's room, and they are all just unbelievably shaken. And Jerry Crawford says, "John would want us to play." And he starts putting on his shin guards and all the equipment. So, we're sitting there deferring to Jerry Crawford, as the closest friend to John McSherry, thinking, "Well, if that's what he thinks would be the right thing to do, maybe it's the right thing to do."

Then, Felipe is saying his guys don't want to play, but he respects what the umpires want to do. So, this is like 10 or 12 minutes of confusion, and Marge comes bursting in and says, "Hey, we've got 55,000 people here! We're going to play this game, aren't we? You don't know if he's dead!" And that's just the way it happened.

Well, it's true, that we didn't know that John was dead. But now I'm being told, "Go to your clubhouse, and talk to your guys about playing."

*Moments before the first pitch of the 1996 opener, Ray Knight (center), Marge Schott and Sparky Anderson gathered for pre-game ceremonies.*

There's no way in heck I would have played. My personal feeling was we shouldn't be playing. We absolutely should not play. But I didn't feel I should convey that to the players at that time, because I'm getting from Marge, "Hey, we need to play." Jim and I finally got separated from everybody else and he said, "Do whatever you think is right." And I said, "Jim, I don't think we should play." And he said, "I don't think we should play, either." It was the right thing.

So, I say to the players, "What are we going to do?" And we explained the whole thing: "The umpires say that we should play." And half of the guys said, "We need to play," and other half said, "No way are we playing."

By this time, Moises Alou and some other guys from the Expos came over and talked, and the players decided they're not going to play. And I go back to the bosses and said, "We're not playing." And Marge was *furious*. She wanted to play that game.

Jerry Crawford had a conversation with the NL president, Leonard Coleman. Len asked, "What do you want to do, Jerry?" And Jerry said, "I think John would have wanted us to play." And Len asked, "Well, what kind of pressure are you getting there?"

And, truthfully, I think until Marge came in there and was forceful about wanting to play, I think if it was Jerry's decision, we would've played. But the way it unfolded with Marge saying, "We're gonna play, aren't we?" there is no doubt in my mind that there was a stiffening of resolve not to play.

The thinking was, "Hey, we're playing because John would have wanted us to play, not because *you* want us to play."

If I had it to do over again, I would have said, "Hey, we're not playing." Because, I'm the boss. But I never felt I had autonomy.

*Reds staff, fellow umpires and stadium personnel rushed to John McSherry seconds after he fell behind home plate in the first inning of the 1996 opener. McSherry was taken off the field on a stretcher moments later and rushed to a hospital.*

## BARRY LARKIN

Ray handled it right. It was a real personal issue for a lot of people. And I appreciated the fact that Ray asked us, and didn't tell us. That was part of his sensitivity. People were deeply disturbed by what had happened. Ray knew everybody had personal feelings and he wanted to respect those feelings.

Everybody was deeply affected. Certain guys felt "if we've got to play, we've got to play." And I think that was the overriding sentiment on the part of those guys. You know, "If they tell us we've got to play, we've got to go do our job." But I don't think there were very many guys who *wanted* to play.

Everybody was shaken up. It was like everybody was in shock.

## JOE OLIVER

Eddie Taubensee was behind the plate that day. I remember waking up that morning and there was snow on the ground. And then it warmed up and it was a beautiful day.

Then to have McSherry go down like that, I just lost it. Because, I have a camaraderie with those guys. Even though you get into the fights, you have the arguments, those guys are leaning over your shoulder, game in and game out, week after week, month after month, year after year, all the time. You build up a brotherhood, even though you don't see eye-to-eye on a lot of calls and decisions they make. We both have the masks on, both have the gear on. I protect him, he takes care of me.

I was very emotional that whole day, to see how tragic it was, to see a man lose his life at the ballpark, doing what he wanted to do. And, then, to know the next day that John had planned to go in and have an angioplasty. It was horrific.

I remember Ray coming and asking Pete Schourek if he could pitch, and Pete said he could. And then Ray said, "Guys, what do you want to do?" And we as a unit said, "We don't want to play." This man losing his life is more important than a ball game. He would probably want us to keep playing, but you can't do it. The focus is not there. It can't be. You just saw a man die. There's no way you could ask the umpires to get their composure back, and call a game.

I went and checked on my family. I was still in uniform. I was still in shock. I'd get myself back together and then I'd lose it again. It hit me very hard. I visited the umpires in their locker room. They were devastated, hysterical with grief.

I can't even imagine what it would be like to lose a close friend of mine in a situation like that. The only thing I can compare it to is the death of Darryl Kile, the St. Louis Cardinals pitcher. I don't know how those guys in St. Louis got through that.

Ray handled it correctly. He shouldn't feel guilty for that. If we had said we wanted to play, he could have interjected and said, "Guys, we really need to look at this." But I don't think there were many guys who wanted to go back out there and play. The Expos had already sent over word that they did not want to play, that they were ready to play the next day, the off day. I told Ray, and some other guys followed me, and we said, "If this games goes on, we're not playing. No disrespect to you, Ray, but this is out of respect to John."

## Rick Stowe

When John went down, the players came back in and there were guys crying. They had a meeting, and I remember them being asked, "What do you want to do?"

The stadium was full, and there was pressure from above that the game should be played, and there was some sense that John would have wanted the game to go on. And nobody knew what to do. I don't think *anybody* wanted to go back out there, but it was like, "We're the players. They pay us a lot of money. We don't want to play, but if they ask us to go back out there, we'll do it. It's our job."

And I remember Reggie Sanders got up to speak, and he was in tears. That was the most vocal I've ever heard him. He said, "A gentleman just died out there! And we are *NOT* going back out there! We are *NOT* going back out there!" And after that, there was no doubt in my mind what was going to happen. That turned it. And he was absolutely right, and everybody knew it.

## Randy Marsh

My umpiring crew was doing the game at Shea Stadium in New York, which is where John is from.

And about the sixth or seventh inning, Dave McKay, the first base coach for the Cardinals, came down to first base, which is where I was working. He said, "Big John went down in Cincinnati." And I said, "He did?" I knew right away what he was talking about. And Dave said, "We don't know the status just yet."

I went in and talked to Harry Wendelstedt and he said, "Oh, man, I hope he's all right." Then, when the game ended, I was jogging off the field, and McKay got me to the side, and said, "Randy, I didn't want to say anything to you during the game. John died."

The funeral was a couple of days later. And the league was really good about it. They moved a bunch of Triple-A umpires in and out, and the visitation was two days, so everybody who wanted to get there, could. It was the right thing to do, and the nice thing to do.

They let me stay there for the whole thing. I was kind of a director in the front of the church, helping out, because John didn't have much family. I knew John and I knew all his friends. They had a big wake for him at Doubleday's in the Bronx—a big party—and the church was packed for the funeral.

The authorities shut down the expressways in New York for his funeral procession. I mean to tell you, that funeral procession was *huge*. And the cops held the cars back from the expressway entrances all the way to the cemetery. John was buried in the same cemetery as Babe Ruth and Billy Martin. Gate of Heaven Cemetery.

*John McSherry umpired in the National League from 1971 to 1996. McSherry was 53 years old.*

What affects me the most when I recall all this, is the bagpipes. The church is at a big intersection, and the sound of those bagpipes was just beautiful, absolutely beautiful. It sends chills up your spine. It still does, just talking about it now.

## George Grande

No individual I have ever met in the game of baseball cared more about the game and what it meant to the people who played it and followed it—and what it meant to this country—than John.

That day, I walked into the umpires room, as I always do, and Big John was there. And the first thing he said to me was, "Isn't this great? Opening Day in Cincinnati! This is the best place to be." He *loved* Cincinnati; he idolized it.

He said, "It's the greatest day of the year. It's the start of a new season." And he looked at everybody in the room and he said, "Fellas, let's go out there and have fun."

And that's the way I remember John. That's who he was. Every year since then, I remember John and I remember him in my prayers. As tragic as that day was, I've turned it into a positive. I've remembered how much the game meant to John and how much he cared about the game. Those words—"Fellas, isn't this great? Let's go and have some fun"—will always ring in my ears.

*On the eve of the 1894 opener, the* Cincinnati Commercial Gazette *carried this cartoon on the front page. Leading the parade of fandom was drum major (and Reds president) John Brush. Next to Brush was business manager Frank Bancroft, the "Father of Opening Day." Dignitaries followed the Reds brass, while the Cincinnati players rode in the carriages. The Reds opened a new grandstand on Opening Day, 1894. For details of the game, see page 173.*

## Chapter 2
# History of Opening Day
## How One Game Became a Baseball Holiday

In the beginning, it was just another game.

Season openers were nothing special in the early years of professional baseball, and Cincinnati's home opener drew little attention from the press or from the public. Depending on the weather, the opener sometimes drew fewer fans than exhibition games held days earlier.

None of the traditions associated with Opening Day in modern times were present in the early years. There were no sellout crowds, no hoopla, no ceremonies and no parade. But beginning in the 1890s, the celebration of Opening Day began to grow, fed by the increasing popularity of baseball, and by the steady drumbeat of promotion led by the Reds new business manager, Frank Bancroft. Bancroft's efforts, ably supported by club owners John Brush and Garry Herrmann, transformed the first game of the season into a civic festival.

Over time, the opener became "Opening Day," a day with capital letters, just like any other recognized holiday. For even if Opening Day is not officially noted on any calendars, make no mistake: This is baseball's annual festival, and nowhere is it celebrated like it is in Cincinnati.

The customs and festivities of Opening Day are well-established today, but the Findlay Market Parade, the sellout crowds, the on-field ceremonies and the civic support for the opener developed slowly. The story of each of these elements will be told below, but we begin with the foundation for Opening Day—the schedule that places the Reds at home for every season inaugural.

### The Schedule: The Home Opener [1]

No other major league baseball team is granted the privilege of opening at home every season except the Cincinnati Reds. This is a custom of scheduling that Reds fans believe is probably found somewhere in the U.S. Constitution, or at the very least, in the hallowed rules of Major League Baseball.

The tradition of the home opener has existed so long that the facts of its beginning have been lost, and, further, the tradition is muddled by four widespread misconceptions that most Reds fan swear by.

First, it is widely held that Major League Baseball rules stipulate that the Reds open at home. Secondly, it is believed that this honor has always been granted since the Reds began playing in the National League (that is, since 1876). Third, there is a long-standing belief that the baseball schedule grants the Reds the honor of the home opener because Cincinnati is the home of professional baseball. Finally, there is a belief that the Reds were also granted the honor of playing the *first* game of each season (although this favor has been ignored in recent years by the schedule-makers).

Unfortunately, none of these widely recognized "facts" is true, although that in no way diminishes the significance of Opening Day. But if these commonly held beliefs are not true, how then do we answer the question, "Why do the Reds always open at home?"

Unfortunately, the answer cannot be found in any rule. There is no rule nor other written document guaranteeing the Reds a home opener that anyone can recall or find in the National League office.

The answer appears to be a combination of geography, opportunism, tradition and money. First, it was geography that dictated the schedule, putting the Reds at home every season because Cincinnati was the southernmost city in the league (except when Louisville was in the NL in the 1890s). Then the Reds, led by business manager Frank Bancroft, cleverly promoted the event and the city eagerly responded, transforming this annual schedule quirk into a major event and money-maker. Finally, when the home opener was threatened in 1935, the Reds rebuffed the schedule-makers, pointing to a 60-year tradition, and the economic loss to the club and city of a guaranteed sellout.

The evidence certainly does not support the theory the opener grew out of a National League tribute to the 1869 Red Stockings. In fact, the history of the early years of the National League argues that the NL would not have honored Cincinnati with a home opener for any reason in the first years of the league.

First, the opener carried no significance in the league's infancy, and opening at home would not have been seen as a special honor. Secondly, the Reds were hardly the NL's poster child in the early years of the league. The club went bankrupt in the middle of the 1877 season, and its new owners so muddled the club's re-entry into the league that the NL refused at first to even count the Reds games as official. The club folded again after 1879. New ownership formed in time to play the 1880 season, but the NL kicked the Reds out when the club persisted in selling beer at the ballpark and in renting the grounds to other clubs for Sunday ball.

Reds ownership then spearheaded a drive to form a competing league, the American Association, which started play in 1882. The Reds remained in the AA until 1889, when they rejoined the NL. All in all, this was not the kind of behavior that would have endeared the Reds to the National League.

The newspaper accounts of the first Opening Days also fail to add any evidence to support the Red Stocking theory. Although the Reds opened at home in 12 of the 13 seasons they played prior to 1890, it is clear from the newspaper accounts, or more precisely, what is *not* in the newspaper accounts, that the tradition of the home opener had not yet been established. If it was due to an honor bestowed by the NL (or by the American Association), it is never mentioned in the newspaper accounts. Nor do the papers report any pre-game ceremonies to honor the old Red Stockings.

More circumstantial evidence can be found in the coverage of the 1888 opener, the only time the Reds have been scheduled to open on the road. The Reds opened in Kansas City on April 18. As the opener approached, none of the Cincinnati daily papers carried stories bemoaning the break in tradition. There were no stories the following year, when the Reds opened at home, about the restoration of Cincinnati's right to a home opener. It appears that while the Reds had a habit of opening at home, there was no special significance attached to it.

Then how does one explain the fact that the Reds have been scheduled to open at home every year but one in their long history?

The schedule itself provides significant evidence. It is obvious from a quick examination of the accompanying chart of "Scheduled Opening Day Opponents," that there is a pattern to the schedule beginning around 1890 after the Reds rejoined the National League. By 1890, the NL had clearly defined eastern and western teams, and the league always started the season with eastern clubs playing eastern clubs and western teams playing western teams. The Reds always opened at home against another western club. From 1889 to 1957, Pittsburgh, Chicago and St. Louis (and Cleveland one time) were the opponents until Milwaukee, another western city, joined the league in 1953. The other southern teams—St. Louis and Louisville in the 1890s when Louisville had an NL franchise—also usually opened at home, while the northernmost western clubs—Chicago, Cleveland and Pittsburgh—always opened on the road.

The Pirates opened on the road for 60 straight years (1894–1953), usually alternating between Cincinnati and St. Louis. The Chicago Cubs opened on the road for 25 straight seasons from 1881 to 1906, then began alternating home openers with the Chicago White Sox of the American League. The Cardinals

## Scheduled Opening Day Opponents

| Year | Opponent |
|---|---|
| 1876 | St Louis |
| 1877 | Louisville |
| 1878 | Milwaukee |
| 1879 | Troy |
| 1880 | Chicago |
| 1881 | Reds Out of Baseball |
| 1882 | Columbus |
| 1883 | St. Louis |
| 1884 | Columbus |
| 1885 | Louisville |
| 1886 | Louisville |
| 1887 | Cleveland |
| 1888 | AT Kansas City |
| 1889 | St. Louis |
| 1890 | Chicago |
| 1891 | Cleveland |
| 1892 | Pittsburgh |
| 1893 | Chicago |
| 1894 | Chicago |
| 1895 | Cleveland |
| 1896 | Pittsburgh |
| 1897 | Chicago |
| 1898 | Cleveland |
| 1899 | Pittsburgh |
| 1900 | Chicago |
| 1901 | Pittsburgh |
| 1902 | Chicago |
| 1903 | Pittsburgh |
| 1904 | Chicago |
| 1905 | Pittsburgh |
| 1906 | Chicago |
| 1907 | Pittsburgh |
| 1908 | Chicago |
| 1909 | Pittsburgh |
| 1910 | Chicago |
| 1911 | Pittsburgh |
| 1912 | Chicago |
| 1913 | Pittsburgh |
| 1914 | Chicago |
| 1915 | Pittsburgh |
| 1916 | Chicago |
| 1917 | St Louis |
| 1918 | Pittsburgh |
| 1919 | St Louis |
| 1920 | Chicago |
| 1921 | Pittsburgh |
| 1922 | Chicago |
| 1923 | St Louis |
| 1924 | Pittsburgh |
| 1925 | St Louis |
| 1926 | Chicago |
| 1927 | Pittsburgh |
| 1928 | Chicago |
| 1929 | St Louis |
| 1930 | Pittsburgh |
| 1931 | St Louis |
| 1932 | Chicago |
| 1933 | Pittsburgh |
| 1934 | Chicago |
| 1935 | Pittsburgh |
| 1936 | Pittsburgh |
| 1937 | St Louis |
| 1938 | Chicago |
| 1939 | Pittsburgh |
| 1940 | Chicago |
| 1941 | St Louis |
| 1942 | Pittsburgh |
| 1943 | St Louis |
| 1944 | Chicago |
| 1945 | Pittsburgh |
| 1946 | Chicago |
| 1947 | St Louis |
| 1948 | Pittsburgh |
| 1949 | St Louis |
| 1950 | Chicago |
| 1951 | Pittsburgh |
| 1952 | Chicago |
| 1953 | Milwaukee |
| 1954 | Milwaukee |
| 1955 | Chicago |
| 1956 | St. Louis |
| 1957 | St. Louis |
| 1958 | Philadelphia |
| 1959 | Pittsburgh |
| 1960 | Philadelphia |
| 1961 | Chicago |
| 1962 | Philadelphia |
| 1963 | Pittsburgh |
| 1964 | Houston |
| 1965 | Milwaukee |
| 1966 | New York |
| 1967 | Los Angeles |
| 1968 | Chicago |
| 1969 | Los Angeles |
| 1970 | Montreal |
| 1971 | Atlanta |
| 1972 | Houston |
| 1973 | San Francisco |
| 1974 | Atlanta |
| 1975 | Los Angeles |

### Scheduled Opening Day Opponents

| Year | Opponent |
|---|---|
| 1976 | Houston |
| 1977 | San Diego |
| 1978 | Houston |
| 1979 | San Francisco |
| 1980 | Atlanta |
| 1981 | Philadelphia |
| 1982 | Chicago |
| 1983 | Atlanta |
| 1984 | New York |
| 1985 | Montreal |
| 1986 | Philadelphia |
| 1987 | Montreal |
| 1988 | St Louis |
| 1989 | Los Angeles |
| 1990 | Houston |
| 1991 | Houston |
| 1992 | San Diego |
| 1993 | Montreal |
| 1994 | St Louis |
| 1995 | Chicago |
| 1996 | Montreal |
| 1997 | Colorado |
| 1998 | San Diego |
| 1999 | San Francisco |
| 2000 | Milwaukee |
| 2001 | Atlanta |
| 2002 | Chicago |
| 2003 | Pittsburgh |

opened at home every year from 1892 to 1906, then began alternating home openers with the AL's St. Louis Browns. During Louisville's ten seasons in the National League, it opened at home nine of the ten years.

These distinct patterns in the NL's opening day schedule are best explained by geography. Western teams played western teams to start the season, and the southernmost western clubs opened at home more often. It seems likely that the Reds opened at home because the schedule makers believed the city's southern exposure gave it a better chance of good weather for the early spring game.

In article from Opening Day, 1910, a *Cincinnati Times-Star* reporter discussed the home opener with business manager Frank Bancroft. "Banny," who had been with the Reds since 1892, knew of no official reason the Reds always opened at home. But, the reporter noted, Reds officers believed that "Cincinnati is always the opening city because it is a Southern town and the weather has a lot to do with it." There is no mention of the first professional team, no mention of any official league policy.

Perhaps it was this lack of official policy that allowed the league to consider having the Reds open on the road in 1935. The longtime owner of the Pirates, Barney Dreyfuss, had been happy to forego starting the season at home all the years he had owned the club, believing that better weather in Pittsburgh and a bigger crowd would result from scheduling the home opener after the season started. But, in 1935, a new ownership group decided that after 41 years, it was time for Pirates to open in Pittsburgh. They requested a home opener from the National League. Figuring the Reds monopoly on home openers had gone on long enough, the NL released a preliminary schedule showing the Reds opening in Pittsburgh. Cincinnati's home opener may have become a tradition, but it was not sacrosanct as far as the NL was concerned.

Reds owner Powel Crosley and general manager Larry MacPhail immediately responded. The volatile MacPhail served as the point man. The defense? Economics. This was the middle of the Great Depression, and the Reds needed the revenue from the opener, which had become a guaranteed sellout. How could the league even consider taking it away from the financially strapped Reds? Further, why would Pittsburgh want to jeopardize its share of the cut from a sellout crowd? If the Reds opened on the road, who knew how much money would be lost? *Had the NL lost its mind?*

With MacPhail on the warpath, the NL quickly backed down. The official 1935 schedule had the Reds opening in Cincinnati.

Writing about the squabble in *The Sporting News*, Cincinnati sportswriter Tom Swope, went on to add his own rationale for keeping the opener in Cincinnati. The Reds deserved the honor because, after all, Cincinnati was where the professional game began.

The episode revealed two important details. First, the league's policy was not cast in stone before 1935. But it was after that, for 1935 was the last year the NL made a serious attempt to strip Cincinnati of its home opener.

Second, there was no mention by the NL or the Reds of any justification of keeping the home opener as a tribute to the original Red Stockings. Swope's linkage in *The Sporting News* was apparently the first time such a rationale for the opener had been made. Swope's argument made little impact at first. As late as 1947, veteran sportswriter Arthur Daley of the *New York Times*, had no idea why the league granted the Reds the honor: "For some reason that has never

*Reds general manager Larry MacPhail (third from left), owner Powel Crosley (third from right) and manager Bob O'Farrell accept a floral baseball from the Findlay Market Parade organizers before the 1934 opener. The next season, MacPhail and Crosley fought off a challenge to the Reds home opener from Pittsburgh and the National League.*

been clearly explained the Reds always open at home."

In 1949, the *Enquirer* explained that "Cincinnati unquestionably is the best opening day city in either league—that's why the Reds' first game perennially is scheduled on the home lot."

It was only in the 1950s and after that the Cincinnati press began to link Opening Day with the 1869 Red Stockings. What we think of today as the reason the Reds have always had a home opener—that Cincinnati is the home of professional baseball—developed as a justification for *defending* the custom of the home opener rather than as a reason for *establishing* the tradition in the first place.

### The Schedule: The First Game of the Season

In 1985, the American League audaciously scheduled two games to start before the first pitch was thrown in Cincinnati at 2:05. Seven years earlier, in 1978, the AL had done the same thing, beginning its season a full day before the Reds. No protest was raised, but the 1985 schedule inexplicably struck Cincinnati fans as a serious breach of tradition. Reds fans—blessed with short memories—had come to believe that not only did the Reds have the right to open at home every year, they had the right to start the season in the Queen City.

Loyal fans howled in protest. Members of Cincinnati City Council,

*Reds fans rose to the defense of tradition in 1985 and protested the AL's decision to schedule their games to start earlier than in Cincinnati. What Reds fan forgot was that this had been common practice prior to the 1970s. On Opening Day 1958 (above), as the Reds and Phillies gathered for pre-game ceremonies, the far right section of the scoreboard shows two AL games already underway.*

ever sensitive to grass-roots issues, fired off letters to the commissioner's office and passed resolutions decrying the outrage.

But in reality, the "tradition" of the Reds starting the season had a short history. (For a year-by-year rundown of the schedule of Opening Days, see the chart, "When Were We First?" on pages 147-148). Before 1948, the Reds opened the season first in the NL only one time, in 1939. Typically in the years prior to 1948, all the clubs—both in the AL and the NL—opened on the same day, and often an East Coast game was in progress before the first pitch in Cincinnati.

The perception that the Reds enjoyed the privilege of opening the season first came about as a side effect of a new scheduling arrangement the National League adopted in 1950. Some NL clubs began to demand a home opener on a more regular basis. With the Reds opening at home every season, the other NL clubs had fewer opportunities to open at home.

The NL's solution was to create a schedule that had the Reds opening on the road every other year, just like all the other clubs. But in order to protect Cincinnati's Opening Day tradition in these years, the league *added* a game in Cincinnati prior to the start of the season. Thus the Reds kept their home opener, and then immediately traveled to another city to open the next day with all the other NL clubs.

This pattern is evident in the early 1950s with the Reds opening a day earlier in 1951, 1953, and 1955. But in the even years, the Reds opened on the same day as every other club, and frequently one of the other NL clubs started earlier than the Reds. In 1954, for example, the Reds started at 2:30, a full hour after the Brooklyn Dodgers and New York Giants began play. No one raised a ruckus, however, because there was never any understanding or history of the Reds starting the season before everyone else.

Beginning in 1961, with the expansion of the NL to 10 teams, the schedule makers dropped this every-other-year pattern and the tacking on of a game at the beginning of the season. But the league continued to favor the Reds by scheduling Cincinnati to open a day early five times during the 1960s.

But even in the years the Reds played their opener a day before the rest of the NL in the 1950s and 1960s, they still did not necessarily *begin* the major league season in Cincinnati. The Reds shared the Opening Day date with the Washington Senators. This tradition began in 1955 and with few exceptions, continued until 1971 when the Senators relocated to Texas. During this time the Senators frequently started the season earlier than the Reds. First pitch in Washington was often at 1:30, while the Reds did not get underway until 2:30.

Not until the mid-1970s did the baseball season consistently open first in Cincinnati. Every year but one between 1976 and 1984, the first pitch of the season was thrown at Riverfront. The Reds often shared their opening date with an AL club, but the AL games either

# WHEN WERE WE FIRST?
## Cincinnati's Opening Day Schedule
### 1948–2003

From 1900 through 1947, the schedule-makers usually had all eight NL teams opening on the same day. The AL opened the same day, or a day later. In three years (1901, 1913, and 1937), the NL schedule had the Reds opening on the second day of the NL season. There was only one year (1939) in which the Reds opened a day before the other NL clubs.

Beginning in 1948, the schedule often had the Reds opening a day early. In the 38 seasons between 1948 and 1985, the Reds were scheduled to open a day before the rest of the National League 24 times, and in many of those years, the first pitch of the NL season, if not the major league season, was thrown here. It certainly happened often enough to explain how the misconception developed that the Reds always opened first.

| Year | Scheduled to Open Day Before Other NL Clubs | Scheduled to Start on Same Day/ or Day(s) Later Than Rest of NL | Notes |
|---|---|---|---|
| 1948 | ● | | 3 AL teams open on same day |
| 1949 | | ● | Phil vs. Bost (NL); Phil vs. Wash (AL) open day before |
| 1950 | | ● | All NL & AL teams open same day |
| 1951 | ● | | Reds first in MLB |
| 1952 | | ● | 3 NL, 3 AL openers on same day |
| 1953 | ● | | Reds 1st in MLB |
| 1954 | | ● | All NL & AL teams open same day |
| 1955 | ● | | Senators opens same day |
| 1956 | | ● | All NL & AL teams open same day |
| 1957 | | ● | Senators open day before; all other teams on same day |
| 1958 | | ● | Senators open day before; all other teams on same day |
| 1959 | ● | | Senators open same day |
| 1960 | | ● | All NL teams open same day; AL opens next day |
| 1961 | | ● | All NL & AL teams open same day |
| 1962 | ● | | Senators open same day |
| 1963 | ● | | Senators open same day |
| 1964 | ● | | Senators open same day |
| 1965 | | ● | All NL teams and 6 of 10 AL teams open same day |
| 1966 | ● (Reds rained out) | | Senators open same day. |
| 1967 | ● | | Senators open same day |
| 1968 | (All openers pp due to MLK Funeral) | ● | Pitts vs. Hous (NL) on same day; Senators open same day |
| 1969 | | ● | SF vs. Atl (NL) on same day; Senators open same day |
| 1970 | ● | | Senators open same day |
| 1971 | | ● | LA vs. Hous (NL) on same day; Senators open same day |
| 1972 | ● (All openers pp due to players' strike) | | |
| 1973 | ● | | Reds 1st in MLB |
| 1974 | ● | | Oak vs. Tex (AL) on same day |
| 1975 | | ● | Atl vs. Hous & Mon vs. StL on same day; KC vs. Cal same day |
| 1976 | ● | | NY vs. Milw in AL on same day |
| 1977 | ● | | Cal vs. Sea in AL on same day |
| 1978 | ● | | Min vs. Sea in AL open on previous evening |
| 1979 | ● | | Cal vs. Sea in AL on same day |

## WHEN WERE WE FIRST?
### Cincinnati's Opening Day Schedule
#### 1948–2003 (continued)

| YEAR | SCHEDULED TO OPEN DAY BEFORE OTHER NL CLUBS | SCHEDULED TO START ON SAME DAY/ OR DAY(S) LATER THAN NL | NOTES |
|---|---|---|---|
| 1980 | ● | | Tor vs. Sea in AL on same day |
| 1981 | ● | | Reds 1st in MLB |
| 1982 | ● | | KC vs. Balt on same day |
| 1983 | ● | | 3 AL games on same day |
| 1984 | ● | | 2 AL games on same day |
| 1985 | ● | | 4 AL games on same day—2 start earlier than Reds |
| 1986 | | ● | SD vs. LA on same day; 3 AL games same day—1 starts earlier |
| 1987 | | ● | 2 other NL games; 5 AL games—2 games start earlier |
| 1988 | | ● | 2 other NL games; 6 AL games—1 starts earlier |
| 1989 | | ● | 2 other NL games; 4 AL games—none start earlier |
| 1990 | | ● (All openers pp due to owners' lockout) | 2 other NL games; 2 AL games |
| 1991 | | ● | 2 other NL games; 5 AL games—1 starts earlier |
| 1992 | | ● | 3 other NL games; 5 AL games—1 starts earlier |
| 1993 | | ● | 4 other NL games; 4 AL games—1 starts earlier |
| 1994 | ● | | Reds 1st in MLB; ESPN Sunday night game |
| 1995 | | ● (All openers pp due to players' strike) | Reds scheduled to open on 2nd day of NL season |
| 1996 | | ● | All NL openers on same day; 1 AL opener day before |
| 1997 | | ● | All NL openers on same day; 5 AL openers—1 starts earlier |
| 1998 | | ● | 7 NL openers on same day; 4 AL openers on same day |
| 1999 | | ● | 1 NL game day before (in Mexico); 6 NL, 5 AL openers next day |
| 2000 | | ● | 1 NL game on 3/29 (in Japan); 7 NL, 6 AL openers on 4/3 |
| 2001 | | ● | 6 NL openers same day; 1 AL opener day before (Puerto Rico) |
| 2002 | | ● | 5 NL openers same day; 1 AL opener day before |
| 2003 | | ● | 7 NL openers same day; 1 AL opener day before |

started at night, or were played on the West Coast, and so started after Cincinnati. The lone exception in this stretch was 1978, when Seattle and Minnesota opened the day before the Reds.

The common perception in Cincinnati, however, was that the Reds had "always" launched the season in Cincinnati before the AL crashed the party in 1985. The misperception is understandable. In the 38 seasons between 1948 and 1985, the Reds were scheduled to open a day before the rest of the National League 24 times, and in many of those years, the first pitch of the NL season, if not the major league season, was thrown in Cincinnati. It certainly happened often enough to explain how the misconception developed that the Reds always opened *first*.

The annual furor over the schedule subsided in the early 1990s, but in 1994 the lingering resentment over the loss of the opening game of the season led to one of the more bizarre Opening Days in Cincinnati: The year of *two* openers. Reds owner Marge Schott had continued to lobby MLB to grant the Reds the first game, and baseball finally responded in 1994, scheduling the Reds to begin the season. The prize came with strings attached. ESPN and MLB scheduled the game for Easter Sunday evening. Schott, fully in tune with the sentiments of Reds fans, refused to treat the game as the official opener. The holiday evening start was disruptive of tradition and family gatherings, and Schott announced that the Reds would celebrate the second game of the season—scheduled for the next afternoon—as the true opener.

Baseball fans tuning in on ESPN that Sunday evening were treated to the unusual sight of an opening game with absolutely no fanfare, and an underwhelming crowd of 32,000 on hand. But Monday? For the "official" opener the next day, the club sold 55,000 tickets. The bunting was up, the dignitaries were on hand and the annual Findlay Market parade wound through downtown.

Since 1994, whatever expectation Cincinnati had to beginning the baseball season has been lost to the impact of television's growing influence over scheduling, and MLB's interest in promoting the game world-wide. In recent years, teams in both the NL and AL have enjoyed earlier starting times than Cincinnati. And the spate of international openers, beginning in 1999, forced Cincinnati to play its first game a day or more after the season began.

Although Cincinnati's claim to opening the baseball season never had the legitimacy nor the tenure of its claim to the annual home opener, it nonetheless came to symbolize the primacy of Cincinnati in the pageantry of baseball history. It gave order to the season, a routine to the schedule that hailed Cincinnati as the birthplace of professional baseball. The first pro team was the first to start the season.

Don Sutton, the Hall of Fame pitcher who started two openers in Cincinnati, recalled knowing about Cincinnati's opener even as a kid growing up in the south. "We all knew where Opening Day was going to be; it's a tradition," he said. "It's got to be there (Cincinnati). So when I came here for Opening Day, I remember thinking, "Yeah, this is the way America is supposed to go about baseball!"

It is a tradition worth *restoring* in the minds of most Reds fans.

## Festivities: From Canaries to Clydesdales

The earliest opening days in Cincinnati were void of any ceremony, a sharp contrast to the modern opener in which the festivities preceding the game last longer than the game itself. The Findlay Market parade, the kingpin of the Opening Day ceremonies, will be covered in the next chapter in more detail. Here we focus on the evolution of the other customs associated with Opening Day.

All the hoopla, all the pomp and circumstance that is Opening Day began with canaries.

In 1886, for the first time, the Reds treated the game as a festive occasion. As fans entered the ballpark, they were greeted by the chirping of canaries from cages located above the entrances. The club also hired the Cincinnati Orchestra Reed Band to play a medley of tunes including waltzes and popular "airs" to entertain the early arrivals before the game started.

Although the game drew an Opening Day record crowd of 5,460, the club did not repeat the effort in 1887 or 1888, the year the Reds opened on the road in Kansas City

But the next year—1889—marked the first year the Reds treated Opening Day as a truly special game. League Park sported decorations including banners, bunting and "flags of all nations." The full Cincinnati Orchestra provided a pre-game concert. Club president Aaron Stern gave a souvenir—a team photo—to every lady in attendance. The club advertised that "prominent business and social circles" would be present. The publicity and promotion paid off when over 10,410 "cranks"—as the fans were then called—filled the grandstand and the bleachers and stood in the outfield, the first standing-room-only Opening Day crowd.

The following year the Reds rejoined the National League which faced a challenge from the new Players League, playing its first and only season. The Players League placed teams in several NL cities (although not in Cincinnati), thus creating head-to-head showdowns for fan support. In the weeks leading up to the opening of the season, each league announced special promotions for Opening Day, including bands and street parades. Although the Reds did not have an intra-city rival, the club announced it, too, would kick off the season with a parade. The Chicago and Cincinnati teams rode in two carriages through the downtown streets, led by a marching band. They arrived at the gaily decorated ballpark 30 minutes before the game and paraded around the field before warming up.

Frank Bancroft became the Reds business manager in 1892, and the former theater-troupe promoter, circus-act manager and veteran baseball man soon put his stamp on Opening Day. Bancroft continued the pre-game band concert and made a special effort to invite local dignitaries and businessmen to the opener. Poor weather dampened the crowds in his first few years, including washing out a gala event he had scheduled for 1894, when the Reds opened a new grandstand.

But in 1895, the weather cooperated and Bancroft pulled off the prototype of the modern opener. Pre-game publicity and word-of-

*The first standing-room-only crowd at a Cincinnati Opening Day occurred in 1889 when over 10,000 spectators filled the wooden stands and the bleachers. This was the first time the team heavily promoted Opening Day as a unique event on the Reds baseball schedule.*

*This 1908 cartoon depicts the Opening Day enthusiasm of the rooters, complete with drums and megaphones. By the early 20th century, women were a familiar and welcome sight at the ballpark, and often came to the opener wearing the latest spring fashions.*

mouth created enormous interest and brisk advance ticket sales. He resurrected the street parade which had not been held since 1891. Dozens of dignitaries were on hand, including five men associated with the hallowed 1869 Red Stockings. For the first time, a Cincinnati paper referred to the day as a "half-holiday."

Weber's Band provided the pre-game concert, and just before the game started, local tobacco merchants presented two huge floral pieces to Cincinnati's new manager Buck Ewing and catcher Harry Vaughn. The clubs gathered before a box decorated with bunting and flags to hear brief remarks from Cincinnati Mayor John Caldwell. After his speech, Caldwell then tossed a ball to the umpire, the first "first pitch" at a Cincinnati opener.

With the master promoter Bancroft in charge, and with new Reds owner John Brush lending support, the Reds transformed Opening Day into the biggest game of the year. Sold-out crowds became the norm; ticket sales began to build several months in advance. Special excursion trains ran from Dayton and other cities. Local dignitaries *had* to be seen at Opening Day. A sure sign of the game's increasing popularity was the number of women in attendance, often sporting the finest in new spring fashions.

It must also be noted that Bancroft enjoyed a run of very good weather in the next few years, which certainly helped boost attendance. Cold weather could still trump the master promoter. The 1901 opener, possibly the coldest opener on record with temperatures in the mid-30s, drew only 4,900, the worst in Bancroft's 29-year run.

In 1902, the Reds opened the new Palace of the Fans grandstand, and added additional seating. In the 10 Palace openers, Opening Day attendance averaged 15,300 and reached a peak in 1910 when the Reds first drew more than 20,000 for Opening Day.

The schedule of Opening Day festivities remained fairly constant in the years after 1895. Mayors spoke and threw out first pitches from a grandstand box (except in 1897 when Mayor Caldwell arrived late and missed the ceremonies). Flowers were sometimes presented to players and managers. Weber's Band played a pre-game concert. The teams usually entered the ballpark through an outfield gate and marched across the field to the cheers of the crowd. In 1903, the Reds were led on this procession by a midget mascot, clad in a Reds uniform and sporting a large glove.

The streetcar parade featuring the Reds and their opponents continued until 1902 when the club cancelled the affair. Other major league cities were also discontinuing the custom. New York hosted a parade as late as 1905, and Pittsburgh sponsored one in 1908. But the team-sponsored parades faded away soon thereafter, not to resume. In Cincinnati, however, groups of fans, loosely organized into what were known as "rooters' groups," filled the void, staging their own noisy processions through downtown. The Findlay Market Parade would evolve from this rooters' group tradition some 20 years later.

It was these rooters' groups that first gave Opening Day its reputation as a day for partying. Many of the groups dressed in costumes, carried noisemakers and were often accompanied by their own bands. They began the day touring the downtown in large horse-drawn wagons, called tallyhos, stopping frequently at local drinking establishments for "nourishment" before the trek to the ballpark.

Although this description in the *Cincinnati Commercial Tribune* dates to 1923, it captured the spirit of the day as early as 1900: "It was Christmas, Fourth of July, Yo Kippur and St. Patrick's Day rolled all into one and with an added flavor only sensed on Cincinnati's day of

*The largest crowd to attend a baseball game in Cincinnati to that time filled new Redland Field on Opening Day, 1912. The attendance was 26,336, which meant nearly 5,000 standees were admitted. They can be seen standing in front of the main grandstand and the bleachers in right field.*

# Doubles Anyone? Field Seats and Ground Rules

After the 1959 opener, the Reds discontinued a tradition that reached back to the earliest days of the national pastime. The club discontinued placing temporary seats on the Crosley Field terrace for the Opening Day overflow crowd.

Up until the 1920s, the use of field seats was common throughout baseball. They were used not only on Opening Days, but for any games when sales far exceeded capacity. But by the 1950s, the Reds were the only club baseball allowed to use field seats, and Opening Day was the only day the Reds used them.

Fans stood behind ropes stretched around the outfield or sat on chairs. The conditions in the temporary seats were primitive compared to the grandstand seats. There were no concessions and no easy access to restrooms. If it rained, or if the field was wet, the chairs sunk into the turf and mud.

The temporary seats at Crosley also reduced the outfield dimensions by 25 feet or more. In an already cozy ballpark (328 feet to left field, 389 feet to center), the shrunken dimensions resulting from the temporary seats made a mockery of Opening Day offense. The front edge of the left-field seats was measured at 290 feet.

Hall of Fame pitcher Robin Roberts took one look at the seats on his first Opening Day appearance in Cincinnati in 1958 and said, "I know how you get those bleachers down after the game. The pitchers go out and take 'em down."

The temporary seats required special ground rules which were decided in the pre-game meetings between the umpires and the managers. In the early 20th century, when the dimensions of the Palace of the Fans and Redland Field were much bigger than Crosley Field in its later years, the rules awarded triples on balls that reached the crowd. In the late 1920s and early 1930s, a batter was awarded a home run on a fly ball over the ropes.

By the mid-1930s, the rules permitted doubles on balls that bounced or flew into the temporary seats, and that remained the rule up until 1959. In the 1950s, there were several high-scoring games that featured a rash of ground-rule doubles, most of them

*Fans stood in the outfield in front of the right-field bleachers for the 1912 opener, the first game at Redland Field. Balls hit into the crowd were ground-rule triples.*

easy outs on any day but Opening Day. *Cincinnati Post* sportswriter Pat Harmon wrote an annual column in the late 1950s blasting the club for allowing the field seats to turn the opener into a freak show where routine fly balls became extra-base hits.

In a 9–6 loss to the Cubs in 1950, the teams combined for 11 ground-rule doubles. In 1954, Jim Greengrass tied a major league record with four doubles in one game, all hit into the temporary seats. The Reds and the Braves totalled 13 doubles, tying the NL mark. In 1955, the two teams combined for nine doubles; they hit seven in 1956, nine in 1957 and eight in 1958.

The business manager of the Reds in the 1950s, John Murdough, recalled that the club discontinued the practice because of the uncomfortable conditions for the fans, and the problem of the ground-rule doubles.

days—the baseball getaway."

By 1900, the game had attained the status of an unofficial holiday. "Close up shop and come out," urged the *Commercial Tribune* in 1907. "Everybody will be there anyway, so what's the use of keeping open? Next year fans will circulate a petition to have the day declared a half-holiday, and if it's up to the Mayor you can gamble that he will O.K. the petition."

The next big boost for Opening Day came with the opening of Redland Field in 1912. The new park had a comfortable seating capacity of 20,000, almost twice that of the Palace of the Fans, which had thousands of wooden bleacher seats. Opening Day attendance boomed. The club sold out Redland almost every opener. As it had in the Palace era, the standing-room-only crowd lined the outfield behind ropes. "The great seating capacity of the of the splendid park was jammed to the limit an hour ahead before game time," noted the *Enquirer* in 1916, "and the crowd surged over the barriers and found standing rom on the outskirts of the field."

The fans on the field necessitated special ground rules. Typically,

# The Gong Sounds and the Lid-Lifter Begins

Today it is known as Opening Day, with a capital "O" and a capital "D," fitting for a day that has attained the status of a holiday.

But a review of advertisements, Reds yearbooks, and newspaper stories shows that "Opening Day" is a relatively late addition to the lexicon of the season's "lid-lifter" (a common phrase for many years).

In the beginning, the first game of the season followed soon after the final exhibition game, and the club and writers felt it important to note the distinction. The opener was the "first championship game," the "first League game," the "opening of the championship season."

An 1889 ad lumped the entire first series of games together, not bothering to call special attention to the opener. "THE EVENT OF THE BASE BALL SEASON—OPENING CHAMPIONSHIP CONTESTS—TOMORROW, NEXT DAY, FRIDAY AND SATURDAY," read the banner ad across the top of the page.

In the 1890s, the writers turned to more colorful phrases: "The Drum Tap," "The Gong Will Tap," "The Bell-Tap," "Prying Open the Season," and "The Lid-Lifter."

In the 1890s, the Reds actually had a gong that rang at the conclusion of pre-game practice on Opening Day and signaled time to start the game. It is not clear whether the gong was used for every game or just the opener, but a gong or bell reference was frequently used in the headlines for the Opening Day story.

In 1896, in a story in the *Cincinnati Commercial Gazette*, the phrase "opening day," appears for the first time, but it was not capitalized, nor did it immediately catch on. It was just one of many terms applied to the game.

By the 1940s, the most frequently used term for the game was the "opener," which when linked to the Reds' losing record on Opening Day, led to this familiar joke:

"The Reds won't be serving beer at Crosley Field this year."

"Why not?"

"They lost the opener."

Beginning in the 1950s, the phrases "opening day," "opening game" and "opener" appeared most often. All occasionally appeared in capital letters. In the early 1970s, perhaps as a reflection of the event becoming larger than just the game itself, the phrase "Opening Day," in capital letters, began to dominate. By the late 1970s, the term was used exclusively in headlines and the lead paragraphs of stories. Although other synonyms are used, "Opening Day" has become the official name of the old "Gong-Tap."

hitters were awarded doubles or triples on balls that reached the fans on the field, although for several years in the late 1920s and early 1930s, the rules awarded home runs on any ball hit over the ropes.

The Reds occasionally tinkered with the Opening Day festivities. Bancroft added a vocalist to the lineup in 1915. Miss Minnie Hammond sang several tunes, which in a time before amplified speakers, were barely heard. "The applause given the songstress was a matter of kindheartedness," noted the *Commercial Tribune*, "for not a note could be heard."

In 1911, the club eliminated the ceremonial first pitch and the mayor's speech. This earned Reds owner Garry Herrmann the thanks of most fans who could barely hear the often long-winded remarks. The next year, however, the ceremonies resumed for the Redland Field inaugural. A few years later the mayor's formal speech was finally discontinued (although it was gradually replaced by longer and longer informal remarks by assorted dignitaries).

The opening pitch ceremony was always handled by the mayor in the early years. His Honor would take a new ball and, from his box seat, toss it to the umpire to begin the game. The first mayor to throw off the mound was Henry T. Hunt in 1913. For the record, his toss was high and outside. Hunt's example did not catch on, however. It was not until 1930 that another city official—City Manager C. O. Sherrill—again took the mound. From that time on, a first pitch was almost always delivered from the mound, frequently preceded by a preliminary ceremonial pitch tossed out by another dignitary from the box seats in the lower grandstand.

The customary Opening Day festivities were pushed aside in 1917, 1918 and 1919 out of respect for America's involvement in World War I. Attendance was nearly normal, but, according to the *Enquirer* (from 1918), "There was not the customary noise and enthusiasm attending an opener, especially when the home team is victorious, but this was due to the absence of so many of the youngest rooters, the ones who ordinarily lead in the cheering and demonstrations."

Hundreds of soldiers in uniforms dotted the grandstand and fans

*In 1918, Weber's Band featured patriotic tunes during the pre-game ceremony, including the Star Spangled Banner, first played at an opener in 1917.*

*The 1944 opener saluted America's soldiers serving in World War II. The Findlay Market rooters presented the American flag.*

waved American flags. Military bands joined in the pre-game concert. One new tradition surfaced in 1917: the playing of the national anthem. John Weber's band played the Star Spangled Banner as its first selection and the fans stood at attention. When the song was played the next year, in 1918, the crowd cheered for five minutes.

The end of the war brought a more festive air to Opening Day. "There was the usual band concert, parade [around the field] and presentation of posies before the game," observed the *Commercial Tribune* in 1923. However, the frivolity of the rooters' groups had all but disappeared. Although business and civic delegations continued to attend the opener and parade around the field (in 1922 a delegation of stock yard businessmen, the "Hog & Cow" club showed up), the groups abandoned the elaborate get-ups, noisemakers and the pre-game, downtown tour of saloons.

Frank Grayson, Cincinnati newspaperman and author, lamented the decline of the rooters' groups in a 1930 story in the *Times-Star*: "The tallyho parties and the beer wagon club affairs have passed. There was a time when the entire morning was devoted to impromptu parades of these with a stop about every seventy feet to get the dust out of parched throats."

In 1920, however, a new rooters' group, representing the Findlay Market Association made its Opening Day debut. By 1922, the Findlay marketers along with the Rotary Club, had become the two largest organizations to be represented during the Opening Day ceremonies. In 1922, both groups, led by bands, paraded around the field, and made presentations to the Reds manager, Pat Moran.

Although other organizations continued to make an appearance on the field during the pre-game ceremonies, by the late 1920s the Findlay Market group was the biggest and best organized. Its annual presentation of huge floral pieces, in the shape of pennants or baseballs, became an Opening Day highlight. Then, in 1930, the Findlay Market marchers presented an American flag to the club, marking the beginning of this annual tradition. After the presentation, six boy scouts marched to the flagpole in center field and raised the Stars and Stripes.

The 1940s brought the revival of another custom, the participation of the governor of Ohio in the first-pitch ceremonies. The first governor to throw out a first pitch was Cincinnati native Governor Myers Cooper in 1929. Governors seldom attended in the 1930s, but by the 1940s, the Ohio governor, and occasionally the Kentucky governor, were on hand. The six-term governor of Ohio, Frank J. Lausche, set the all-time Cincinnati Opening Day record by appearing in nine first-pitch ceremonies between 1945 and 1956.

During World War II, the ceremonies again took on a somber tone.

## Opening Day with *The Today Show*

The quirky traditions of Opening Day drew the attention of *The Today Show* in 1956. Host Dave Garroway and 20 staff members broadcast the show live from Fountain Square.

The cast included Garroway, reporter Jack Lescoulie, weatherman Frank Blair, Lee Meriwether and Mr. Muggs, a chimpanzee mascot, (The last time a chimp had a starring role in Opening Day was in 1896 when the Reds debuted a mascot named Mose.)

The crew turned up at 4:30 a.m. to assemble the set for the show. Sound checks boomed through downtown before the sun was up. Flood lights bathed the Square and caught reflections of snow flakes drifting across the sky. Early morning temperatures hovered around the freezing mark.

But the temperatures failed to dim the enthusiasm of the Opening Day faithful. Mayor Charles Taft was on hand to lend the official welcome. Smitty's Band, outfitted in lederhosen, played several rousing tunes, and local entertainers from the Midwestern Hayride pranced through square dancing routines accompanied by a banjo-and-fiddle band. Lescoulie broadcast from Crosley Field in a Reds cap and jacket as he interviewed manager Birdie Tebbetts.

Local television also featured Opening Day in the 1950s. From 1957 through 1961, WLW-T aired a special on the eve of the opener. Reds managers and players were interviewed by Ruth Lyons, Bob Braun and Peter Grant. The show went by different names, including "Meet the Reds," and "Hi, Redlegs!"

After the presentation of the flag and the playing of the national anthem, the teams marched out to the flagpole to participate in the flag-raising. Short speeches by the Cincinnati mayor, Reds owner Powel Crosley, a representative from Findlay Market and other dignitaries saluted the war effort. In 1942, the Findlay Market group presented war bonds instead of flowers. And in 1945, the flag was raised only to half-mast, in honor of President Franklin D. Roosevelt, who had died five days earlier.

Through the Great Depression and World War II, Opening Day remained a sellout. Reserved seats were sold far in advance, leaving the bleacher and standing-room-only seats for sale the day of the game. Not only did many local businesses treat the day as a half-holiday, schools even closed in recognition of the annual rite of spring. "All the schools were let out [for Opening Day]," reported the *Enquirer* in 1933, "so the fatalities among grandmothers was much less than usual." In 1947, the Cincinnati Public Schools closed at 1 o'clock; however students were required to report an hour earlier the next day to make up for the half-day vacation.

Emptying the schools was not an annual event, nor did every school district participate. But many teachers would grant an excused absence if a student was lucky enough to have a ticket. Veteran *Enquirer* newsman Jim Schottelkotte recalled in a 1985 article, "It was sort of a tacit understanding at the parochial schools, anyway. If you had an Opening Day ticket and could show it, the nuns wouldn't say anything if you missed school and went to the ball game."

By the 1960s, the Opening Day festivities had been well established for three decades. In the '60s the club made a few additions. Marian Spelman, a star of local television, became the "official" singer of the national anthem, appearing every year into the mid-1970s. Two other groups joined the Findlay Market Association in annual presentations: the Rosie Reds and the Knothole Association, representing youth baseball.

*Marian Spelman of WLW-T sang the national anthem on Opening Day in the 1960s beginning a tradition of vocalists performing the anthem. Prior to the '60s, a band played the Star Spangled Banner. Reds manager Fred Hutchinson (1) led the Reds in honoring the flag.*

The biggest disruption to Opening Day since 1913—when rain delayed the opener two days—occurred in 1966. Three days of rain forced the Reds to open on the road for the first time since 1888, pushing the Reds home opener back 11 days to April 22. The game was held on a Friday evening—the first home opener ever to be held at night—and only 10,266 attended. No dignitaries were on hand. An abbreviated schedule of festivities included the Findlay Market rooters parading around the field and the presentation of flowers and the American flag.

The next significant change in Opening Day came in 1971 when the Reds played their first home opener at new Riverfront Stadium. Crowds of 50,000 and above became the standard. In the early 1970s, the club urged fans to "wear red" to the opener, and red shirts, dresses, blouses, sweaters, sweatshirts, blankets and coats became *de rigueur* for the well-dressed Opening Day afficionado. Reporters described a "sea of red" in the stands.

The fervor over the success of the Big Red Machine helped swell interest in the Reds and the opener. Regional interest was at an all-time high. Excursion trains no longer ran between Cincinnati and the nearby cities, but the interstate highway system delivered thousands of fans from Kentucky, Ohio and Indiana who made the annual Opening Day pilgrimage to Riverfront.

*The overflow crowd filled center and left fields in the 1950s at Crosley Field leading to many ground-rule doubles. In this 1955 opener, the Cubs' Dee Fondy had just doubled into the crowd at the base of the scoreboard. Ernie Banks headed around third base. The Cubs won the opener, 7–5. The last opener to feature field seating was in 1959.*

Reds management, under the direction of Bob Howsam and Dick Wagner, began expanding the first-pitch ceremony to include VIPs other than politicians. In 1971 and 1973, servicemen from Vietnam were involved in the ceremony. In 1979, the club began a five-year run of bringing the first-pitch ball to the park in an unusual fashion. A canoeist, raising money to build lights for a community baseball park in Morehead, Kentucky, paddled 200 miles with the ball to Riverfront in 1979. A hiker, raising money for the March of Dimes, walked 430 miles with the ball in 1980. In 1981, in support of the Red Cross, a bicyclist brought the ball from Washington D.C. The next year, astronauts Richard Truly and Joe Engle carried the ball into space, and delivered it in person to Riverfront where they threw out the first pitch. In 1983, the ball arrived after a trip aboard the nuclear submarine, the U.S.S. Cincinnati. The crew had to bring a backup ball since the original first-pitch ball had been lost after it was fired out of a torpedo tube and lost in the Atlantic.

Since the early 1900s, Opening Day had almost always been a sellout, and certainly in the heyday of the Big Red Machine, Opening Day crowds regularly topped 50,000. But in 1982, the Reds lost 100 games for the first time in club history under the direction of the president and pariah, Dick Wagner. Reds fans quickly figured out how to make their feelings known. In 1983 and in 1984, the opener failed to sell out. Thousands of upper-deck outfield seats sat empty in silent protest. The shock to the Reds organization was palpable. Opening Day sell-outs had come to be taken for granted. For this and several other reasons, Wagner was fired and the architect of the Big Red Machine, Bob Howsam, returned to power. In the mold of Opening Day's master promoter, Frank Bancroft, Howsam revitalized fan interest with bold moves. He signed free agent and native son Dave Parker, added fireworks after each home run, installed a beer garden and lowered the outfield fences from 12 feet to eight. Forty-six thousand came out to take a look on Opening Day, 1984. With the return of Pete Rose in August of '84, the magic returned to Riverfront and the opener. Despite miserable weather for the 1985 inaugural, nearly 53,000 were on hand. Every regularly scheduled opener since has been a sellout.

The most significant change to the Opening Day festivities generated by the move to Riverfront Stadium was the transformation in the Findlay Market parade. In the Crosley Field era, the Findlay Market Parade was actually *less* than met the eye. The event was limited to the market shopkeepers and their families and friends. There were few outside entries, and those were by invitation only. The parade included a handful of decorated vehicles, a band or two, and the mayor and other politicians leading the march. The parade began at Findlay Market and traveled the 10 blocks to Crosley Field. It attracted a few onlookers, primarily residents of Over-the-Rhine and the West End.

When the parade entered the ballpark, however, it found the spotlight. Now the star attraction, the marchers and vehicles circled the field to the applause of the crowd. When people referred to the Findlay Market Parade in the Crosley era, they usually meant the procession inside the ballpark, and not the trek over from the market.

With the Reds' move from the West End to the riverfront, the street parade soon became the focus. Now the march was nearly two miles, mostly through downtown Cincinnati. At first, the organizers kept it small trying to retain the focus on "Findlay Market." But by the mid-1970s, the parade had grown to 50 entries and it steadily expanded to 200 entries, including the famous Budweiser Clydesdales horses, which made their first appearance in 1980.

Ironically, as the street parade gained attention, the on-field presentation diminished. The club permitted fewer units to tour the interior of the stadium, and by the late 1990s, Findlay Markets' role in the opening ceremonies was limited to the traditional presentation of the flag and fruit baskets.

The decades of the '70s and '80s saw an increased admiration for the tradition and history of Opening Day. It was as though the city began to realize just how unique an event it had nourished over the years. One small but telling sign of the opener's increasing importance was a change in punctuation. The phrase went capital. No longer opening day, it was now *Opening Day*. Prior to the '70s, the event did not have an official name. It was referred to by a variety of terms, and it was seldom capitalized. But beginning in the 1960s, the phrase, "opening day," became the standard, and by the 1970s, it nearly always was written with a capital "O" and a capital "D."

The widespread support for Opening Day proved critical in the 1980s and 1990s when the event experienced some of its greatest chal-

Opening Day always a sellout? Not in 1983 and 1984 when fans signaled their anger with Reds management after a 100-loss season in 1982. Attendance fell to 42,000 in 1983, some 10,000 below the typical Opening Day crowd in the Riverfront Stadium era. The club held fans out of the red seats in center field.

lenges. These threats to the tradition came at a time when the new Reds president, Marge Schott, was one of the the most enthusiastic supporters Opening Day had ever had. In 1985—her first opener as owner of the Reds—she rode in the parade and threw out the first pitch. Along with her St. Bernard dogs, she starred in nearly every opener during her tenure with the club. The supporting cast often included a number of four-legged actors, including elephants and camels from the Cincinnati Zoo. Frank Bancroft, the "Father of Opening Day," may have been a long-time promoter of circus acts, but it was Marge Schott, 100 years later, who actually turned Opening Day into a circus.

Of course, the animals inevitably left their calling cards on the field, and handlers quickly scampered about removing the residue. The view of an elephant unburdening itself of a large load was a sight that fans and players never forgot. It remains for many a peculiar, but undeniable memory of Opening Day. As Lenny Harris, a Reds player from the 1980s and 1990s, recalled, "There are a lot of good Opening Days in baseball. But it's tough to top those elephants in Cincinnati!"

For Schott, the day was about ceremony and tradition, and the game came second. "There's nothing in the United States like Opening Day in Cincinnati," she told the crowd in 1997, "and there is nothing like the Findlay Market Parade."

Baseball's schedulers and labor problems threatened to interrupt Cincinnati's holiday. In the mid-1980s, the American League began schedule games earlier than the start of the opener in Cincinnati. Although the AL had done this as recently as 1978, and was free to set their schedule as they wished, many Cincinnati fans saw the move as an affront to tradition. Although Opening Day lost a little luster, the scheduling wars had no impact on attendance or civic support of the opener and the parade.

In 1990, the last-minute settlement of the owners' lockout of the players threw the opening week of the season into a turmoil. The new schedule had the Reds opening on the road, and returning for a home opener at night a week later. Schott sensed that a nighttime opener would jeopardize the tradition and she rescheduled the game for an afternoon start. The parade organizers, who were on the verge of cancelling the event, scrambled to throw together a new parade lineup and wound up having their biggest entry list to date as civic groups lined up to support the event. But the game failed to sell out.

In 1994, after Schott lobbied baseball to give the Reds the first game of the season, MLB indeed scheduled the season to begin in Cincinnati. But the game was set for Easter Sunday evening, and Schott immediately declared that the Reds would not treat a holiday night game as the traditional opener. Instead, said Schott, the Reds would honor the next afternoon as Opening Day. For the Reds owner, there was never any doubt she was making the right decision.

"That's when Opening Day is, honey!" she said. "Monday afternoon!" Schott was right. Only 32,000 turned out for the Sunday night game while the second game—er, Opening Day—sold out.

In 1995, another labor battle delayed the opener. This time the Findlay Market Parade organizers could not switch dates to accommodate the new schedule. The group met to consider cancelling the parade, but decided to carry on. If 1994's opener was bizarre with two Opening Days, 1995 topped that with an Opening Day parade with *no* opening game.

The crowd was slight by parade standards and the incongruity of a parade without a game made national news. But it was a victory for tradition. Schott lent her full support. "This is what Opening Day is all about," she gushed. "To me, this is the most important thing of Opening Day. Look at the excitement!"

The club held the usual on-field ceremonies for the opener 23 days later. The game was an official sellout but the delay had taken its toll; there were 15,000 no-shows.

After two years of Opening Day mix-ups, the 1996 opener appeared to be a return to normalcy. Ex-Reds manager Sparky Anderson threw out the first pitch—after receiving the ball from an elephant, of course—and a full house cheered the start of the the game. But seven pitches into the contest, home-plate umpire John McSherry suffered a fatal heart attack. The stunned crowd watched as McSherry was lifted onto a stretcher and rushed off the field. After considerable behind-the-scenes confusion about if and when to continue the game, the announcement was made to postpone the opener one day. The tragedy day became even uglier when some fans booed the decision.

Schott herself wanted the game to continue. Her reaction to the postponement—and the revelation that she had sent an old bouquet of flowers to the umpires dressing room—drew well-deserved criti-

*Opening Day was a circus in the Marge Schott era. Sparky Anderson accepts the ball for the first pitch on an assist from an elephant during the 1996 pre-game ceremonies.*

*Barry Larkin (11) trotted towards the mound to shake hands with President George Bush after Bush threw out the first pitch to open Great American Ball Park on Opening Day, 2003.*

cism. Unable to put the day's events into perspective, she had let her fondness for Opening Day override good judgment.

By 2000, Schott had sold her controlling interests in the Reds under pressure from Major League Baseball, and Opening Day lost one of its most public supporters.

The Reds new regime, led by owner Carl Lindner and chief operating officer John Allen, made two significant changes in the routines of Opening Day. Perhaps the most noticeable change from the Schott years was the end of appearances by the elephants and other zoo animals. The second major change has been the near disappearance of the Findlay Market Parade from the ballpark. Parade officials still present a fruit basket to the club prior to the game in brief ceremonies, but no parade entries are allowed on the field. In part, this decision was supported by the switch in the playing field surface from artificial turf to grass in 2001.

As a result, Opening Day has lost much of its unique Cincinnati flavor. In the pursuit of the "thrill of the grass," and tight field security, the club has suctioned much of the life out of what had made Cincinnati's Opening Day truly special. The christening of Great American Ball Park on Opening Day, 2003 was a memorable day, but it was not all that different a celebration from those held by other cities in recent years. Without the local flavor that has made Opening Day unique, Cincinnati experienced "McOpener."

Still, all those who attended saw the most historic Cincinnati opener since 1912. Fans arrived hours early to tour the new park with its views of the Ohio River, Mt. Adams and downtown Cincinnati. A full house waved small American flags—gifts of owner Lindner—in support of the recent invasion of Iraq. The war kept President George W. Bush from attending, but his father, President George Bush threw out the first pitch, "coming off the bench," he said, for his son. Each spectator received a commemorative GABP Opening Day lanyard.

Opening Day has survived many challenges over the years, from bad weather to lousy teams, to hard economic times and World Wars, to postponements and delays brought about by baseball's labor battles, to schedule changes, to the tragic death of an umpire. The game is no longer so often in the national spotlight, but this is still Cincinnati's special day. More than any other annual public event in the city, Opening Day brings the community together, bridging generations and geography. Beginning in Over-the-Rhine, finishing at the riverfront, young and old, black and white, salute the Cincinnati Reds.

In many ways, the opener is bigger than ever in the public mind. Media coverage blankets the region in the days leading up to the opener. The parade draws twice as many entries as it did a decade ago; the enthusiastic crowds number in the tens of thousands. The game remains a sellout. Employers not only grant time off to workers, they close up shop and take the staff to the game. A ticket can still excuse one from school. Opening Day has always been as much about the holiday as about the game.

The long-term success of Opening day depends on the Cincinnati Reds embracing their role as the protector of this rich and storied tradition, unique in baseball. It is a tradition one cannot sustain by promotion alone, nor inflate with 21st century hype. Opening Day in Cincinnati can be nourished only by the heartfelt hope of the fans and the deep, abiding love of a city for the national pastime, which has its professional roots in the Queen City.

1. Thanks to John Snyder who first proposed the geography theory to explain the patterns in the National League schedules from the late 19th and early 20th centuries. Snyder's theory that the Reds opened at home because of their southernmost location in the league was first published in **Redleg Journal** (Greg Rhodes and John Snyder, Road West Publishing, 2000) and continues to be supported as additional evidence is uncovered.

### Let's Play Two

An Opening Day doubleheader in Cincinnati? It's never happened, but during the early days of the Depression, Reds owner Sid Weil needed to maximize every revenue opportunity he could. Knowing the Reds always had a full house for the opener, Weil proposed to the National League that the Reds play two games on Opening Day, a morning-afternoon double header. Weil had visions of two sellouts. Sixty thousand joyful Reds loyalists clicking through the turnstiles! But the NL turned him down.

## Chapter 3
# Findlay Market Parade

Former Reds owner Marge Schott, who was wrong about so many things when she owned the club, was absolutely right when it came to Opening Day and the Findlay Market Parade.

"The Findlay Market Parade *is* Opening Day!" says Schott. "Without the Findlay Market Parade, we wouldn't even *have* Opening Day!"

Cincinnati would still have the opener of course, but without the parade, Opening Day in Cincinnati would not be distinguishably different from the inaugurals of Almost-Any-MLB-City, U.S.A.

Not that anyone would ever confuse the Findlay Market procession with the Rose Bowl Parade. This is not a pageant of majestic floats, extravagant musical productions and corporate underwriting. It is grass-roots Cincinnati, a red-convertible and pickup-truck brigade with a few modest floats, high school marching bands and more politicians than roses. It is, after all, a parade organized by shopkeepers and butchers. But their open-door policy has nourished the "people's parade." They have welcomed nearly every group who has wanted to celebrate Opening Day and the heritage of the national pastime. And the merchants of Findlay Market have been proudly stepping to the plate as organizers for over 75 years.

Findlay Market has been synonymous with Opening Day for so long it is hard to imagine it wasn't always part of the festivities. In fact, Opening Day was nearly 50 years old before the Findlay Market Association began participating. The parade organizers date their inaugural march to Opening Day, 1920. The first mention in the Cincinnati newspapers of the Findlay Market rooters comes in 1922. "The Findlay Market Rooters' Club, one hundred and fifty strong, carried an immense floral horseshoe around the park and upon reaching home plate presented it to Manager Moran," observed the *Enquirer*.

The Findlay Market rooters were not the only ones parading around Redland Field in the early 1920s. They were just one of several rooters' groups that invaded the baseball field every Opening Day. The tradition of the rooters' groups in Cincinnati dates to the early 1900s when they emerged after the Reds abandoned their annual team parade.

The Reds, along with several other major league clubs at the turn of the century, had staged parades on the morning of the home opener. In Cincinnati, the custom began in 1890. The Reds and the visiting team climbed aboard two streetcars or carriages and toured the downtown streets, often accompanied by a band. The main purpose of the parade was promotional: stir up interest in the afternoon's opener and sell tickets. The parade usually began in the heart of downtown on Fifth Street and wound through the central business area. In the mid-1890s, the parade detoured to include Eastern Avenue to greet the neighbors of Reds manager Buck Ewing, who lived in the East End. Sometimes the parade began after lunch and traveled directly to the ballpark, but in other years it started at 10:30 and stopped at noon on Fountain Square at the Gibson House where the Reds and their opponents ate lunch before heading to the park.

The club-sponsored parades faded away shortly after the turn of the century and the Reds held their last one in 1902.

*In the early 20th century, Reds rooters' clubs paraded through downtown streets and traveled to the ballpark in informal caravans that included automobiles and horse-drawn vehicles.*

But in Cincinnati, the Opening Day faithful did not mourn the loss of the parade. They simply started their own. For several years, loosely organized groups of fans had attended the game and sat together in the grandstands. By 1905, many of these troupes, called "rooters' groups," began to gather downtown in the late morning and tour the streets in their vehicles

Before sports bars and tailgate parties, there were rooters' groups. Waving flags, singing, and tooting horns and noisemakers, the merrymakers rode through downtown in decorated vehicles which included large horse-drawn wagons known as tallyhos. They also walked, rode in processions of carriages and chugged along in the newfangled "smoke wagons"—or automobiles. Some groups rented streetcars. Many wore costumes, and a few even had their own bands.

Unlike with the modern Findlay Market Parade, it would be incorrect to characterize the merrymaking of these groups as anything organized. The processions began in different places, started at different times and followed different routes to the ballpark, with scheduled and unscheduled stops for refreshments along the way. It was a grass-roots outpouring of support for the opening of the baseball season and the Cincinnati Reds.

While Opening Day had developed a holiday spirit, the proliferation of the rooters' groups turned it into a street party. In 1923, the *Commercial Tribune* described the impact of the rooters' groups: "It was Christmas, Fourth of July, Yo Kippur and St. Patrick's Day rolled all into one."

Typically, the groups would arrive at the ballpark an hour or more before the game began. They would alight from their vehicles, enter the ballpark, march around the field with noisemakers blaring and then take their seats in the grandstands. A few presented flowers and gifts to the manager or the players. For some groups, the party wasn't over with the start of the game. In 1912, the *Commercial-Tribune* reported that a group called the "Redlanders Baseball Club," carried a huge bell and rang out some tunes between innings, "but any melodies that came from it were anything but harmonious." In 1917, the *Enquirer* reported that a group of 200 rooters from Covington "added to the excitement with vociferous rooting and songs between innings."

The heyday of the rooters' groups lasted from about 1905 to 1918,

## Before The Findlay Market Parade and Tailgate Parties, There Were Rooters' Groups

The rooters' groups of the early 1900s—from which the Findlay Market Parade evolved—usually consisted of a few dozen fans who often dressed in costumes and operated noisemakers of various types. "Rube" bands and German get-ups were popular. Some of the groups paraded through downtown prior to the game in decorated vehicles, especially horse-drawn wagons called tallyhos. Others simply attended the game as a group.

In 1912, the *Cincinnati Commercial Tribune* offered this overview of the "Tallyho Brigade":

> They came in all sizes of of tallyhos, from two horses up to six, and though some only seated six people, others were capable of carrying and did carry thirty-five to forty rooters in them.
>
> In all there were a dozen big tallyhos with rooters and they came dressed in fantastic garbs and labeled with large streaming banners and badges.
>
> Every rooter that came in a tallyho also brought along some instrument to make a noise. Some carried bells, some whistles, some crickets and others various articles with which to add to the din.

Typically, the rooters consisted of members of a social club or business organization and were often named after the individual who organized the gathering.

In 1909, the *Commercial Tribune* described several rooters' clubs:

- "Lee Heine's party of rooters certainly took the premium. About thirty carriages had been engaged to carry them to the park after a parade through the business portion of the city."
- "William Brueggeman's rooters stormed the park in a tallyho."
- "The Carraro rooters were well supplied with megaphones and other instruments of noise."
- "Suthoff's rooters from Price Hill came down on a large haywagon. True to their masquerade, they played the part of green rubes throughout the game, keeping everybody within hearing on the broad grin."
- "The Storm Fishing club had Ed Weber's band on the leading tallyho playing on the entire trip through the city."
- "The Sting 'Em Apollo Rooters arrived at the park early in the special trolley car which had been engaged for the occasion."

when the entrance of America into World War brought a more patriotic and serious tone to Opening Day festivities. The amateur bands and outlandish costumes disappeared. Jack Ryder, baseball reporter of the *Enquirer*, observed in 1919, "The truckloads of wild-eyed enthusiasts who have sometimes paraded the downtown streets for hours before game time were busy elsewhere."

The participation of the rooters' groups resumed after the war, but there were fewer groups and a diminution of the outlandish merry-making that had characterized the earlier era.

The 1919 World Championship, however, motivated the Findlay Market shopkeepers to attend the 1920 Opening Day as a group to honor the champion Reds. The Findlay Market gang made it an annual event, and quickly became one of the biggest and best organized of the rooters' groups. By the mid-1920s, several hundred rooters marched around the field behind a band. Each year they carried in an elaborate floral piece to present to the Reds manager, an event that became a highlight of the pre-game ceremony.

The organization drew considerable attention with its appearance in 1924. "The annual parade of members of the Findlay Market Association was an affair that eclipsed all former parades in numbers and originality. More than 400 members of the association, each wearing a flower in his coat, wearing a large white hat and carrying a cane were in line when the parade passed through the gates at Redland Field and marched around the playing ground."

In 1930, the marketers presented an American flag for the club to fly during the season, a tradition that continued for 70 years. Although other groups continued to appear on the field before the opener to make presentations of gifts and flowers, by the early 1930s, the Findlay Market Association had captured the starring role in the Opening Day ceremonies.

The starring role, however, was limited largely to their appearance on the field. When people spoke of the Findlay Market Parade in the Crosley Field era, they referred primarily to the procession inside the ballpark, rather than the march to Crosley Field from the market.

The "parade" was a small affair, limited to the Findlay Market shop owners, their families, friends and loyal customers. They invited a band or two to accompany them, and often the mayor or other city dignitary would lead the march to the ballpark. The retinue usually included a few vehicles, some of which were decorated.

The parade circled the market twice and then struck out for Crosley Field, about 10 blocks away. They attracted sparse crowds, mostly folks living along the route in Over-the-Rhine and the West End. The spotlight did not really shine on the group until they entered the ballpark.

With the first Opening Day at Riverfront Stadium in 1971, the dynamics changed completely. Now, the line of march wound through the heart of downtown. The attention paid to the parade mushroomed, and the organization decided in the early 1970s to open up the event to outside organizations. Today it has grown to an entry list of more than 200.

In the oral history that follows, parade organizer Jeff Gibbs picks up the history and relates how the parade has grown since the 1970s. He also talks about financial issues, the organization's changing relationship with the Reds, and the serious questions these issues raise about the future of the Findlay Market Parade.

# JEFF GIBBS

*Gibbs, who owns and operates the Gibbs Cheese & Sausage store at the Findlay Market House, is a lifelong West Sider and longtime organizer of the parade.*

Every year, it's shoulder-to-shoulder from Findlay Market to the Taft Theater. The closer you get to town, the deeper the crowd gets. And when Opening Day falls on spring break for most of the school kids around here, we get enormous crowds, because everybody brings their kid down to see the Opening Day Parade.

*If you're an out-of-towner on Opening Day, you'd think it was a national holiday. The whole town goes nuts.*

*Jeff Gibbs, organizer of the Findlay Market Parade, presents Marge Schott with an American flag prior to the 1996 opener. Findlay Market presented a flag to the Reds from 1930 through 2000. Since 2001, the club has bucked the tradition.*

I'm entrenched in it. I'm 45 years old, and I bet I haven't missed the parade in 35 years. And even before that, I'm sure I was on beer duty, you know, "Go get your uncle so-and-so a beer."

Even before I took over the shop, I was just up here, running around, walking in the parade. Getting to go on the field was cool, because my uncle or my dad was always on the board. I've been going onto the field for Opening Day for most of my life. My uncle Russ and my dad Jim were the first ones in the family to be involved in the Findlay Market Parade. There are pictures of my Dad going back to the '40s, when he was a grand marshal.

One of my first recollections of the parade, and the memory that stands out the most, is from the '60s. My dad was a big man, not that tall, but big around, probably 250-275 pounds. We were standing at the field entrance to Crosley Field—a snowy Opening Day in the '60s—and Dad was so big, and wearing such a huge coat, he had four or five high school cheerleaders from the parade wrapped up in it. Cold…Opening Day…Crosley Field, and Dad having fun with it all.

*In those early years—early for me, that is—it was mostly a parade of walkers. The Roger Bacon Band always showed up. It was a short walk over to Crosley Field, ten blocks or so, and we'd do two laps around the market before heading to Crosley. My uncle was a big beer drinker, and he'd hit every bar in every other alley. It was basically a pub crawl.*

## Three Generations of Gibbs at Findlay Market

"This business (Gibbs Cheese & Sausage) dates back to a general store in Fairview, Indiana, in the 1840s. I'm the third generation here at Findlay Market and the fifth generation in the business. My uncle had the business before me, and before that, my grandfather," said Jeff Gibbs.

"It started even before that, at the old Sixth Street markethouse. My great-grandfather—they were selling stuff on the packet boats that came up river—came to Cincinnati to take the middleman out of it. And they opened a store down on Sixth Street, in the early 1900s across from the markethouse. They got into the Sixth Street market in the 'teens, and they moved up here to Findlay Market in 1922. And the Opening Day parade goes way back to those early years."

Even when we started going downtown in the '70s, and into the early '80s, it was still a big party. My favorite year was when I rode in the Budweiser truck. It's a motor home with a half barrel on tap in the back of it. We were hanging out the side of the truck, waving and shouting to spectators. It was like Mardi Gras!

I can remember one year back in '80 or '81 when the driver of the pickup that was pulling the official Findlay Market float, crashed into the service-entrance wall entering Riverfront Stadium off Mehring Way. That was back when we would take a lap around the field and stop at home plate. He hit it pretty hard. The driver was "Dirty Pierre," and they blew two half-barrels before they got to the Westin Hotel. On the way off the field, they ran over third base and home plate and missed the gate on the way out. We got a letter from the police after that. It said we had no socially redeeming qualities, and if we ever threw a parade like that again, "you'll never get a permit in this town again!"

In the late '60s at Crosley Field, we had 30 or 40 entries. Well, that's what we said, but back then they used to count every horse as an entry to make the number bigger!

The Al Schottelkotte noon-time TV report on Channel 9 put a spotlight on the parade beginning with the first Opening Day at Riverfront Stadium in 1971, and that really helped to start make it a bigger parade. Being downtown, and having the Big Red Machine, and everybody in town being nuts for the Reds all through the '70's, made it big, too.

Even when I was going to Miami University in the '70s, I was skipping classes to be involved in the parade. When I got *really* involved with it in the '80s, 75 or 100 entries was still a big parade.

*Surrounding a Crosley compact car, the Findlay Market Parade participants gathered at the market before heading to Crosley Field in 1950.*

I was in my 20s when I started helping organize the parade. Mike Luken had done a great job with it, but he'd pull it together in three weeks. He didn't even send out entry forms until the beginning March. He'd draw a map on a piece of paper, putting 75 floats and other marching groups in a half-block area. Me, being a computer geek, I said, "Let me do that; I want to do the map," and so I did. We started sending out letters in January and making it a little more official and more organized.

Nineteen ninety is when the parade really took off. There was a players' strike and they weren't going to have Opening Day. The powers-that-be in Major League Baseball said "We're locking 'em out," and we made the announcement: "The Opening Day Parade is cancelled." It had gotten to the point where we had to spend money on insurance and postage, and we didn't even have a date.

Tony Bare was the chairman back then, and I was just a computer guru, his right-hand man. Opening Day, of course, would've been on the Monday if there was going to be one—which there wasn't—and Tony was scheduled to go on vacation to Florida on Tuesday or Wednesday.

*Well, they settled the strike, and Marge called and said, "How many days you need to do a parade? We've got to have a parade. We've really got to have the parade when the Reds come back to town."*

*And I said, "I need 21 days." Well, I got 20. And in 20 days we did the whole thing from scratch, and it was the biggest parade we ever had.*

They put our phone number on WLW, WCPO and WKRC, from 6 to 9 p.m. four or five times a night: "Want to be in the Findlay Market Opening Day Parade? Call Jeff Gibbs at such-and-so number."

The opener was scheduled for Tuesday. Well, on Good Friday, I was still putting people in the parade. I picked up my telephone at 7 a.m.—and I swear to you as I am sitting on this stack of milk cartons—that with call waiting, I did not put the phone down until 1 o'clock in the afternoon! Good Friday is the busiest Friday of the year for my stand. And I'm trying to wait on customers, run my business, put people in the parade, and finally, I literally took the phone off of the wall, and said, "That's it, I can't do it anymore." I was just absolutely insane.

That's when it got huge. It was absolutely insane, the most insane two weeks of my life. I know it was damn near twice the size it had ever been before. We went from 85 or 90 entries the previous year to about 160 that year—and it was all because of the publicity.

By comparison, in 2003, we did the biggest one we've ever done, and we had over 200 entries. It was the new stadium that gave it the juice.

In '90, we had more marching bands than we ever had before—we were always looking for bands. A lot of common Joes came in, too. Guys with red convertibles who just wanted to be in the parade, and a lot of businesses—gas stations and tow truck companies.

We got people in '90 who've been here every year since. And we worked out a deal with WLW that they would televise the whole parade that year. We got on TV for five or six years, flag-to-flag coverage. There were a couple of years where I was actually sitting up on some scaffolding somewhere along the parade route, doing color commentary.

For the 75th anniversary of the parade—'94 I guess it was—we had all the dads, all the patriarchs in the market, eight or ten of them. That was a great year, a blast.

Ninety-five was a critical year, too, as far as what it meant to the parade. That was the year of the replacement players. Remember? The players were on strike and the teams were going to open the season on schedule with replacements. Our marshals' T-shirts had "Replacement" stamped across the front of them.

On Thursday or Friday before Opening Day, I already had half a parade in town—the Clydesdales were in town, I had made hotel arrangements for two or three out-of-town high school bands—and MLB postponed the opener! They settled the strike and were going to wait a few weeks before starting up to give the regular players a

*Findlay Market Parade floats circle Riverfront Stadium in 1993 during the Opening Game ceremonies. Reds owner Marge Schott, who enthusiastically supported the parade, was equally loved by the parade organizers. This float lent support to Schott during her first suspension by Major League Baseball.*

*Grand Marshals for the Findlay Market Parade have included baseball, football and basketball players, Findlay Market shop owners, Mickey Mouse and Jerry Springer (far left) in 1993.*

chance to get in shape.

I walked into the door here Friday morning when I got the news. There were a half-dozen people waiting for me: a guy from the *Enquirer*, a guy from the *Post*, and two TV stations, asking me what were going to do, because Opening Day had been postponed!

We got the parade committee together—I told everybody we'll have a meeting Saturday night after market. We went over to Yunger's—this is when Yunger's was still open—and we were sitting at this big table in the back. Of course, we're all drinking beer—it's Saturday night and we're all done—and anybody who works here knows what Saturday is like "at market."

There are three TV stations, TV reporters, and newspaper reporters waiting for us to make this decision. My first inclination was to cancel the parade. I stepped away from the table, and while they're talking, a cameraman from Channel 19 says to me, "You know, you run that parade next week and you're going to be the only show in town—everybody's gonna know. You'll make national headlines." And that sealed the deal for me. That made the decision.

Our company line became: "*Somebody* is playing baseball; we don't care who it is—we're gonna have a parade!"

And we did make national headlines. They were going to do a story in the *Wall Street Journal*, anyway, so the story just got better, that's all. I called the reporter and woke him up in California, and he revamped it, and it was on the front page of the *Journal*.

We had 75 to 80 percent of the parade show up. And the message it sent was: "Look, we're Cincinnati. We show up on Opening Day whether you clowns—MLB—do or not."

And I'm out there that day with the fire truck blowing the whistle, and I turned around and I counted nine TV cameras and 10 guys with microphones, sticking them in my face.

And I said, "It's only a *parade* guys!"

The parade is as blue-collar as it gets; it's a parade of the people. People in Cincinnati are always going to remember "Peanut Jim" in that big top hat, tux and tails, out there with his peanut wagon, selling his peanuts. It's as much a part of Opening Day as anything. And Jim Tarbell makes the connection now—marching in the parade in his Peanut Jim outfit, and you can see the way people react to him. They know; they *remember*.

"Opening Day in Cincinnati" still belongs to the people. And it is why Opening Day here is so special, even if some of the bloom is off the rose of the regular season because of all the strikes and free agency and all that.

*Funny, isn't it? In 1990 and 1995, the opening of the season was delayed by strikes, and what do people in Cincinnati rally around? The parade! Because the parade is theirs. It's what makes their Opening Day unique.*

*There's always been a feeling associated with it of "Don't rain on my parade—you can't rain on my parade. We're out here celebrating as a city—this is our city, this is our game—and nothin's gonna stop it. The show must go on." That was the attitude that came across in '90 and '95.*

*That's a great feeling, a great attitude, and I love it. No matter how much the game changes, Opening Day will always belong to the people here. And the parade is what reinforces that fact—every year, game or no game.*

I remember one year when I was sitting at Fifth and Race Streets, early '90s—I was getting golf carts for guys that are on the committee—and we had a *huge* crowd, and I said to myself, "Look at the party I just threw!" Seriously, I'm sitting down there and I said, "*I* can throw a party!"

Marge was always so much in favor of doing the parade, that she'd give us what we needed. *Marge we need some red convertibles,* and she'd send 'em down. *Marge, we need a better grand marshal,* and they'd helped us with that. We've been blessed to have had some great grand marshals. Sparky was huge. Oscar Robertson, Anthony Munoz, Chuck Harmon, Ken Griffey, Sr. Call them the people's champions. People relate to them.

Marge has never been the grand marshal—we've asked her—but I don't think she ever will. She'd rather be Marge. She always comes over and starts the thing. I ride in a golf cart in the parade every year because I'm haulin' Marge around! I get Marge duty because she likes me. One year, I got left holding Schottzie, and I said, "Would somebody take this goddamned dog from me, I've got a parade to run!"

Back when she was the owner of the team, we had three or four meetings with the Reds, just because she wanted to sit around in her office and have us drink Cokes, bulls—, and smoke cigarettes.

Marge built the elephant house up at the zoo, so she always arranged to have elephants in the parade in the past. Then a few years ago the zoo ran into insurance problems with their animals out in a public situation like that. So we were sitting down in Marge's office the next year and she was talking with Ed Maruska, who used to be the head guy at the zoo. He must have been telling her about these problems. Marge just said, *"You bring that goddamned elephant down here or I'm gonna take my $3 million and go someplace else!"*

People love that elephant in the parade. They want that. They want the giraffe. They want the animals from the zoo! And Marge knew that. Did you ever see that World Championship ring that she had made for the elephant? She kept it in her office in one of those great big stainless steel cases. She kept it under the couch and the goddamned thing was this big!

Marge was just great for us, fabulous. One year, back in the early '90s, St. Louis' Opening Day was the same as ours, and so the Clydesdales had to be in St. Louis. We went out and got Miller Beer; they had a big hitch. But Marge loved those Clydesdales. Later, she cornered Auggie Busch at a function in St. Louis and she raised hell with him. And he said, "Marge, as long as you're running that team, I promise you the Clydesdales will be there." And they were there, every year after that. They may've missed once since Marge has been out. But, because of Marge, Auggie made good!

The Clydesdales have always been one of the bigger draws. In 2003, we had three or four of the premier hitch teams in the country: the Budweiser Clydesdales, Ray Wegman's Belgian Drafts and Black Clydesdales—they're a breed of Clydesdales that are black, almost blue. All the big-hitch guys love coming here. They make a party out of it, too. They stay at Ray Wegman's out on the west side of town, and we throw a big party out there every year. They love the way we treat them, and they love the way they get treated by Ray. The guys look forward to coming here.

When Marge was suspended and her marketing guy, Chip Baker, got fired, that's when the Reds started squeezing us on the number of

*The Findlay Market Parade enters downtown on Fifth Street and passes by Fountain Square where thousands congregate to greet the marching bands and other participants.*

*The Findlay Market Parade kicks off in Over-the-Rhine and heads south down Race Street. The parade has more than doubled in size since 1990.*

*All eyes were on Cincinnati on Opening Day in 1976 in the heyday of Reds baseball. The Reds opened the NL season the day before the other teams every year but one from 1973 to 1985.*

Opening Day tickets the Reds would give us. We went from a high of about 1,500 tickets to whatever they'll sell us now, which is a few hundred.

We *have* to have those tickets. We've never made an issue of it, but that is what we use to pay for the parade. We pay cash, upfront, for the tickets, face value, no discount. We put a premium on them, and if we can get four or five dollars per ticket, times 1,000 tickets, that's four or five grand that we can use to pay for the parade. We solicit the parade entrants for donations—that was something Tony Bare and I started—but we've never charged an entry fee.

It got even leaner on tickets when the Reds took the "bite" out of Cinergy Field to make room for the building of Great American Ball Park. That meant 15,000 fewer seats for the ball club—including Opening Day, when they really needed them—and that meant fewer tickets for us, too.

We can understand that. It had to come out of somebody's hide. And now they've got a 42,000-seat stadium instead of 55,000, so I can understand that, too. But now we're down to 400 or 500 tickets—compared to three times what we used to have. So the result is that 2003 became the first year the parade cost us money out of the pocket of the Findlay Market Association. If Joseph Chevrolet hadn't bucked up, we'd have lost our ass.

Our biggest expense is the insurance. As long as I've been involved, there's always been an insurance bill, and we have to carry some sort of liability. And that might eventually be what kills this thing. Nobody wants to write this stuff after September 11th. The guy that'd been writing our insurance for years, in 2002 had a real problem finding somebody to write the insurance. In 2003 he said, "There are only two or three companies in the U.S. who'll write this kind of insurance, anymore. There was a time when I'd have five or six people competing for the business, but now I have to go looking for them."

*We could hardly get insurance in 2003 and it cost us four times as much as it did in 2000. It went from about $1,800 to $6,000 for 2003. So our expenses are going up, and the Reds have cut us back on tickets. I swear, I think the Reds would just as soon we went away. That's the impression we have.*

Since the move to a grass field in 2001, they won't let us take anything—floats or hitch teams—out on the field, but they were cutting down on it even before that. Part of that was our fault. One of the Findlay Market vendors always carried a big Findlay Market banner onto the field. And he probably took 150 or 200 people out there with him, and that didn't go over real well! But, heck, we just walked around. It was one of the perks we used to get people to help us with the parade.

It's been fun for me the last 20 years, getting on the field before the game and meeting people. Leaning up against the visitors' dugout, talking to the players, has been a ball. The opposing players can't believe all the stuff. *You do this s— every year?* They are just stunned

*The Clydesdales marched around Riverfront prior to the home opener in 1984. The Clydesdales first appeared in the Findlay Market Parade in 1980. Since the Reds began playing on grass turf in 2001, the Clydesdales and the other parade units have been barred from entering the ballpark.*

Opening Day 2003 at Great American Ball Park featured dozens of dignitaries and groups, including a brief presentation by the the Findlay Market Parade and its organizers. However, the parade no longer enters the ballpark, and the parade officials do not have a prominent role in the pre-game ceremonies as they did for over 70 years.

with the amount of stuff that goes on!

But that was "back in the day." There's a disconnection now. We're not allowed to come through the wall onto the field with the Clydesdales or any of the floats anymore. People in the ballpark aren't seeing us anymore, except for us giving the fruit basket to the manager. And in 2003 we weren't even invited up to the mike stand. That's the first time we weren't invited to do that.

What are the Clydesdales going to do? Eat the grass? I mean, horses walk on grass all the time! But, yes, I understand they could do some damage. Hopefully something can be worked out.

Since our presence on the field has gotten smaller, the fruit basket presentation is just one more part of the stuff that goes on down on the field. Nobody pays attention to it. *I think we're losing some of the connection to the parade that happens in town. I mean people sitting in the ballpark would never even know there's been a parade!*

And now, they don't even want us to give them the American flag anymore, like we used to do. That was part of the ceremony we'd been doing forever! We'd present them with a flag that they'd fly over the stadium every year. The last three years they told me, "No."

So, we're down to two guys on the field in the ceremony. Me and whoever carries in the fruit basket. Ten years ago we had seven or eight units on the field, waving to the fans and taking their victory lap: the Findlay Market float; the winning float of the float contest; the winner of the spirit contest—that's for somebody who was wearing a really great costume or somebody raising the most hell in the parade; the 20 to 50 parade marshals who carry the unfurled flags; the Air Force color guard; the Air Force Band; the Clydesdales and Wegman's Hitches.

And it *looked* like a parade. Basically, it was the "Best of the Findlay Market Parade" parade.

*Now, we're down to two people and a fruit basket. It's a little like having this great celebration, this great party on wheels headed somewhere, and when you get there, they won't let you in the door.*

Back when things were good, I had a big Findlay Market flag—emblem and everything, we'd carry it unfurled onto the field—and I said to the Reds, "Look, would you guys fly it on Opening Day with the American flag we've always given you?"

And they said, "Sure!" They thought it was great. The reason I wanted it up there was I wanted something everybody in the stadium could see, and from the red seats you could read it. The grand marshal would sign it. And the Reds loved it. I know that one year it flew above the stadium for a week.

All of that has changed.

I'm not going to sit here and tell you that the parade isn't good for Findlay Market and for me, because it is. I've made customers from the parade, and I know we all have. But not enough more that you'd say, "Oh, that parade more than makes it worth our while." No, the parade is fun and the biggest perk of it for us was being able to personally get on the field.

It'd be nice to work something out in the future to get some floats onto the field again, to restore that connection. Hopefully, something can be worked out.

CHAPTER 4

# Year-by-Year at Opening Day

Each Opening Day since 1876—the first year of the National League, and the first year the Reds belonged to an organized professional league—is included in this chapter.

Each opener was covered in the local newspapers. Our summaries are a compilation of that reporting. There have been at least two and often three Cincinnati papers covering Opening Day.

In the beginning years, the coverage was limited to just one story of the game itself. There was no pre-game coverage, no pre-season special sections. The papers usually ran a paragraph or two the day before the game, announcing the starting time and the lineups of the teams. By the 1890s, the coverage had increased dramatically, including cartoons and illustrations of the pre-game ceremonies and of key plays during the game. By the early 1900s, the first photographs of Opening Day were printed.

Our summaries typically include a short sample of the newspaper writing, using brief reports from one or more papers. These are highlighted in italics and are taken from the sources noted at the end of each summary.

One note about the box scores that accompany the summaries Up until 1884 in the American Association (and 1886 in the National League), the two captains had to agree which team would bat first. Beginning in 1885 (and in 1887 in the NL), the choice of first bats was determined by the home captain, which meant, in practice, that the home team almost always chose to bat last. However, the box scorers continued to place the home team on the top line of the line score. It was not until the mid-1930s that the box scores regularly listed the home team on the bottom line.

We have also included attendance and temperature reports for each opener. Opening Day attendance figures generally report tickets sold, not attendees. For many cold openers, less than a full house was on hand, even though the club reported a sellout. (Before 1900, attendance figures given in the papers were often rounded to the nearest thousand.)

Temperatures are not necessarily game-time temperatures. Temperature readings are either high temperatures reported for the day or mid-afternoon readings if available. Beginning in the 1950s, writers often reported the temperature from the ballpark. However, as any fan who has been at the ballpark on an early spring day knows, temperatures can vary widely depending on location of seats, and over the course of the game.

We have also rated each Opening Day on a scale of one to five. The most memorable or historic openers received a five. Our number one opener is 1974, the year of Hank Aaron's 714th home run which tied Babe Ruth on the career home-run list. Aaron's historic blast and a dramatic extra-inning comeback by the Reds gave the nod to 1974.

### Top 15 Opening Days

| | | |
|---|---|---|
| 1 | 1974 | Aaron's 714th home run; Reds comeback victory in 11 |
| 2 | 1975 | Reds beat arch-rival Dodgers in 14, 2-1 |
| 3 | 1912 | Opening of Redland Field; Reds rally to win, 10-6 |
| 4 | 1945 | Clay's grand slam home run; shoelace fiasco; Reds win in 11 |
| 5 | 1954 | Greengrass' 4 doubles; 13 doubles overall; Reds win, 9-8 |
| 6 | 1943 | Best pitcher's duel ever; Vandy beats Cooper in 11, 1-0 |
| 7 | 1934 | Lon Warneke's no-hit bid broken up in ninth; Reds lose |
| 8 | 1894 | League Park opens; Holliday's grand slam; Reds comeback win |
| 9 | 1895 | Ewing's homecoming; parade draws thousands; 10-9 win |
| 10 | 2002 | Reds win in 9th; last opener at Cinergy |
| 11 | 1977 | "They can't play!" Despite 4″ of snow, 38°, fans shine; Reds win |
| 12 | 1924 | Largest Crosley OD crowd; Reds win in 9th, 6-5; 79° |
| 13 | 1963 | Robinson homers; Rose debuts; Reds win |
| 14 | 1985 | Reds win; Rose's 1st OD since return; every season of weather |
| 15 | 2003 | Reds open GABP, but embarrassing 10-1 loss |

# Reds Open 1st NL Season With Win
## St. Louis Falls, 2–1

**Cincinnati Ball Park.**

GRAND OPENING GAME.
ST. LOUIS vs. CINCINNATI
TUESDAY, APRIL 25.
Game called at 3 p.m.
Tickets for sale at Hawley's, Perry & Morton's book stores, Davis', Kramer's, and Donovan's cigar stores. Trains leave Plum Street Depot 2, 2:30, and 3:30 p.m., railroad time. Cars reserved for ladies. 1t

*The Opening Day ad from 1876 announced special trains running from downtown to the ballpark on Spring Grove Avenue.*

### 1876 OPENING DAY SCHEDULE

| Date | League | Matchup |
|---|---|---|
| April 22 | National League | Phil v. Bost |
| April 24 | National League | Phil v. Bost |
| April 25 | National League | StL vs. Cin |
|  |  | Brkln v. Bost / Chic vs. Lou |
| April 27 | National League | Hrtfrd vs. Brkln |

Two months after the National League was formed, the Cincinnati Reds opened their first NL season at home against the St. Louis Browns with a 2-1 victory.

The game was not accompanied by any parades, ceremony or hoopla; in fact the game drew only 2,000 to the Avenue Grounds ballpark, which had about 4,000 seats. Among the spectators were 50 ladies who occupied a reserved section of the grandstand set aside for women and their escorts.

The Avenue Grounds field looked very unusual by modern standards. The infield was grass, while the outfield was bare dirt.

The game was tied, 1–1, in the eighth inning when the St. Louis defense collapsed. Two errors put the Reds shortstop, Henry Kessler, on third base. The next batter, Amos Booth, was struck in the head by a pitch, but under the rules of the day, he was not awarded a base. After a few groggy moments, Booth resumed batting and grounded out. But on the throw to first, Kessler broke for the plate and was safe when the St. Louis catcher could not handle the throw from the first baseman. Cherokee Fisher, the Reds pitcher, retired the Brown Stockings in the ninth inning and earned the victory. Fisher pitched a complete game—a typical performance in this era of underhand pitching—and gave up just six hits. The local press provided the following descriptions of the game:

*The grounds were in pretty good shape. The space inside the bases has been neatly covered with green turf, presenting a pleasing appearance in contrast with the remainder of the field which is bare of vegetation.*

*Nothing exciting occurred in the game until the close of the fourth inning. Battin drove a ball away to the limit of the left field, letting him as far as the third base, and Pike from first base to the home plate, thus earning the only run which the Browns made.*

*The visiting club appeared to have no difficulty in hitting Fisher's delivery, but were singularly unfortunate in the directions chosen by the balls after being struck. Kessler scored the unearned run made in the eighth inning [by the Reds] on a succession of bad errors by Battin, Clapp and Bradley. The St. Louis club was then retired in one, two, three order and the first of the championship games resulted in a victory for the Reds. The game was witnessed by a audience excellent in character, and numbering about 2,000.*
[Cincinnati Commercial and Cincinnati Enquirer]

### OPENING DAY TRIVIA

| | |
|---|---|
| Star of the Game | Reds Pitcher Cherokee Fisher |
| Weather | "Pleasant"; Pt. Cloudy |
| Attendance | 2,000 |
| Notable | First NL Game & First Opening Day |
| Rating | ◐◐◐◐ |

### APRIL 25, 1876

**CINCINNATI**

| | T. | 1B. | TB. | R. | O. | PO. | A. | E. |
|---|---|---|---|---|---|---|---|---|
| Kessler, s. s. | 4 | 2 | 2 | 1 | 2 | 1 | 1 | 1 |
| Booth, 3b. | 4 | 1 | 1 | 0 | 1 | 3 | 2 | 0 |
| Gould, 1b. | 4 | 1 | 1 | 0 | 3 | 6 | 0 | 0 |
| Clack, r. f. | 4 | 1 | 1 | 0 | 3 | 2 | 0 | 0 |
| Jones, c. f. | 4 | 2 | 2 | 0 | 3 | 3 | 0 | 0 |
| Snyder, l. f. | 4 | 1 | 1 | 0 | 3 | 3 | 0 | 0 |
| Sweasy, 2b | 4 | 1 | 1 | 0 | 3 | 2 | 0 | 0 |
| Pierson, c. | 4 | 0 | 0 | 0 | 4 | 2 | 0 | 1 |
| Fisher, p. | 3 | 0 | 0 | 0 | 5 | 0 | 0 | 1 |
| Totals | 35 | 8 | 8 | 2 | 27 | 27 | 3 | 3 |

**ST. LOUIS**

| | T. | 1B. | TB. | R. | O. | PO. | A. | E. |
|---|---|---|---|---|---|---|---|---|
| Cuthbert, l. f. | 4 | 0 | 0 | 0 | 3 | 2 | 0 | 0 |
| Clapp, c. | 4 | 1 | 1 | 0 | 4 | 5 | 1 | 1 |
| McGeary, 2b. | 4 | 0 | 0 | 0 | 3 | 1 | 0 | 0 |
| Pike, c. f. | 4 | 1 | 1 | 1 | 2 | 1 | 0 | 0 |
| Blong, r. f. | 4 | 0 | 0 | 0 | 4 | 1 | 1 | 0 |
| Battin, 3b. | 4 | 2 | 3 | 0 | 3 | 2 | 0 | 1 |
| Bradley, p. | 3 | 0 | 0 | 0 | 3 | 2 | 2 | 2 |
| Dehlman, 1b. | 3 | 0 | 0 | 0 | 2 | 9 | 0 | 2 |
| Mack, s. s. | 3 | 0 | 1 | 0 | 3 | 1 | 2 | 0 |
| Totals | 33 | 4 | 6 | 1 | 27 | 27 | 7 | 6 |

**RUNS SCORED**

| Innings | 1. | 2. | 3. | 4. | 5. | 6. | 7. | 8. | 9. |  |
|---|---|---|---|---|---|---|---|---|---|---|
| Cincinnati | 1 | 0 | 0 | 0 | 0 | 0 | 0 | 1 | 0 | —2 |
| St. Louis | 0 | 0 | 0 | 1 | 0 | 0 | 0 | 0 | 0 | —1 |

| | Cincinnati | St. Louis |
|---|---|---|
| Fly balls caught | 20 | 12 |
| Fly balls missed | 0 | 1 |
| First base on errors | 1 | 4 |
| Left on bases | 6 | 5 |
| Struck out | 5 | 0 |
| Runs earned | 1 | 0 |

# 1877 Miserable!
## Rain Delays Opener Three Times; Reds Finally Lose Home Opener, 24-6

*Opening Day ad, 1877; rain postponed the game until May 14*

In one of the most miserable openings in Reds history, rain postponed the opener three times, forcing the Reds to begin the 1877 season on the road. When the home opener was finally held, the Reds suffered their worst Opening Day defeat ever.

The schedule originally had the Reds opening at home against Louisville on May 3. Rains postponed the game, which was rescheduled the next day. But the field was too wet and the Reds postponed the game a second time. The rains came again, causing a third postponement. The schedule then called for the Reds and Louisville to play in Louisville on May 10, and the two teams headed downriver to play their opening game. The Reds clobbered their hosts, winning 15–9, and the teams returned to Cincinnati for what proved to be the home opener on May 14.

The weather was excellent and a "flattering attendance" of 3,000 turned out. It was probably the largest crowd of the year as the Reds drew an average of fewer than 1,000 per game in 1877.

But the large crowd could not bring the Reds victory. Louisville embarrassed Cincinnati, 24-6. The Reds trailed by only one run, 5–4, in the fifth inning before the pitching and fielding collapsed. Reds starter Bobby Matthews gave up seven runs on seven hits in the fifth. Relief pitcher Jack Manning fared no better, allowing 12 runs over the last four innings. Louisville batters had 30 hits.

The Reds defense shared much of the blame for the shellacking. The box score charged the Reds with 16 errors. Every player on the Reds, except for second baseman Jimmy Hallinan, was charged with at least one error.

Not surprisingly, the offensive show established several Cincinnati Opening Day records, including the odd coincidence of two players—George Hall of Louisville and Bob Addy of Cincinnati—setting the record for most hits (5).

The local papers provided this coverage: *Perhaps a few aching hearts will be relieved by the profoundly wise and philosophic reflection this morning that the commercial prosperity and artistic progress of Cincinnati are not dependent upon the success of the combination of ballplayers that bear her name.*

*The game, if remarkable for anything besides the disparity between the runs scored, was remarkable for the strong batting of the Louisville players. In this department, the honors of the day were won by [George] Hall whose record consists of two single base hits, two doubles and one triple. His rival was [Bob] Addy, of the Reds, who scored a single hit every time he went to the bat.*

*It was a long tiresome game.*
**[Cincinnati Commercial and Cincinnati Enquirer]**

### OPENING DAY TRIVIA

| | |
|---|---|
| STAR OF THE GAME | LOUISVILLE OUTFIELDER GEORGE HALL |
| WEATHER | 76°; FAIR SKIES |
| ATTENDANCE | 3,000 |
| NOTABLE | WORST OPENING DAY DEFEAT |
| RATING | ⚾ |

### 1877 OPENING DAY SCHEDULE

| | |
|---|---|
| APRIL 30 | NATIONAL LEAGUE |
| BOST vs. HARTFORD | |
| MAY 3 | NATIONAL LEAGUE |
| LOU VS. CIN (PP) | |
| MAY 8 | NATIONAL LEAGUE |
| BOST vs. STL | HRTFRD vs. CHI |

# 1878 McVey, White Lead Reds
## Umpire Threatens to Leave Field

Cal McVey, who played right field for the legendary 1869-1870 Cincinnati Red Stockings, had four hits in the 1878 opener.

As bad as the weather was in 1877, it was that gorgeous for the 1878 opener. But only a modest crowd of 2,500 took advantage and visited Avenue Grounds to watch the Reds defeat the visiting Milwaukee club, 6–4.

The Reds were led by the pitching of newcomer Will White and the offense of veteran third baseman Cal McVey. McVey and White's careers were heading in opposite directions on this Opening Day. McVey, who had four hits and scored twice in the opener, was a member of the original 1869 Red Stockings and was nearing the end of his career. For White, the victory was his first of 227 wins for the Reds, a total that ranks him as the Reds all-time leader.

Another highlight of this game was the appearance of White's brother, Jim "Deacon" White as the catcher, marking the first time a brother battery appeared for the Reds.

The Reds victory was tarnished, according to the reporter for the *Cincinnati Enquirer*, because of numerous delays, including an injury to Reds shortstop Joe Gerhardt, and a threat by umpire Robert Crandall to quit the game. Crandall was involved in two lengthy disputes. Crandall called Reds shortstop Billy Geer out on strikes, a decision that was hotly contested by the Reds. According to the paper, Crandall "sulked," and was finally coaxed into continuing the game.

In the fifth inning, Crandall and the crowd endured another long argument over a foul ball call. Crandall eventually reversed his decision after an extended discussion which involved a re-reading of the rule book. In the same inning, Gerhardt sprained his ankle and was removed from the game. The Reds only substitute, Bobby Mitchell, had not expected to play and was not in uniform. Another holdup resulted while Mitchell dressed. The delays lengthened the time of the game to three hours, a lengthy game for the era.

White allowed 11 hits, but good defense after the first inning kept Milwaukee from rallying. White went on to win 30 games for the Reds in 1878 and lead the Reds to a second-place finish in the six-team league.

### 1878 Opening Day Schedule
| May 1 National League |
|---|
| MLW'KEE VS. CIN |
| BOST VS. PROV   CHI VS. IND'POLIS |

### Opening Day Trivia
| | |
|---|---|
| Star of the Game | Reds Third Baseman Cal McVey |
| Weather | 77°; Clear Skies |
| Attendance | 2,500 |
| Notable | Will White's First Win as a Red |
| Rating | ◐◐◐ |

The local papers described the day: *A lovelier day for out-of-door sports never shone than our May day yesterday, and an immense throng of people took advantage of the clear sky and balmy air to go out and witness the first trial of our Nine in a league contest. The bright attires of the ladies, the throng of carriages beyond the field, and the quick movements of the players made a wonderfully animated and attractive scene.*

*It opened in a slovenly manner on both sides, and, though the record of the subsequent innings showed an improvement, yet there were few plays made that were peculiarly sharp, and none, save a fly catch or two, that were remarkable. This loose play was rather disappointing to the spectators.*

*[In the fifth inning, Joe] Gerhardt withdrew from the game because of a sprained ankle, and a halt had to be called until [Bobby] Mitchell could put himself into uniform and take Gerhardt's place. These delays were vexatious considering that there was no recompense in beautiful plays.*
**[Cincinnati Commercial and Cincinnati Enquirer]**

# 1879 Buttercup's Catch Saves the Game;
## Reds Hold on for 7–5 Victory

> **BASE BALL.**
> OPENING OF THE LEAGUE SEASON YESTERDAY.
> CINCINNATI, 7; TROY, 5.
> SYRACUSE, CLEVELAND AND BUFFALO DEFEATED BY CHICAGO, PROVIDENCE AND BOSTON RESPECTIVELY.

*Opening Day games in the 1870s received no more coverage than a regular-season game.*

### 1879 OPENING DAY SCHEDULE

| May 1 | National League |
|---|---|
| Troy vs. Cin | |
| Syr'cuse vs. Chi | Bost vs. Buff |
| Cleve vs. Prov | |

A sparse Opening Day crowd of just 1,200 traveled to Avenue Grounds to see their Reds win a tough battle with the lads from Troy, New York, a new entry in the National League for 1879. The Reds had fared poorly in several exhibition games in Cincinnati prior to Opening Day, and the game drew half the expected crowd.

The game was not decided until the last out, a daring circus catch with the bases full by the Reds young left fielder, Buttercup Dickerson. Will White, the Reds star pitcher, allowed nine hits and struck out four for the victory, his second consecutive Opening Day victory.

The Reds came from behind to win, rallying from a 4–2 deficit before taking the lead for good with three runs in the third inning. The batting leaders for the Reds were Cal McVey, Dickerson and King Kelly, who had two hits each.

The Reds led, 7–5, as White took the ball in the bottom of the ninth inning. (Troy had won the toss and elected to bat last.) White quickly disposed of the first two Troy batters, but then ran into trouble. Troy pitcher George Bradley singled, and moved to third on Charlie Reilly's hit. White then walked Al Hall and the bases were loaded. Ed Caskin lofted a long fly to left field, which drifted into foul territory. Dickerson, after a long dash, and sprinting at full speed, caught the ball for the final out.

The local papers offered the following coverage: *A brighter and prettier day for both playing and witnessing a game of base ball than was yesterday could not have been desired. In the grand stand were dozens of "old stand byes," who have attended the sport regularly since its introduction here in 1866. A like punctuality exhibited by these gentlemen in visiting church edifices on Sunday, would guarantee them front seats in the celestial choir and the ownership of a choice harp. A number of ladies encouraged the contestants by their presence, and were enthusiastic in exclamation of delight whenever a good play occurred. Every effort should be made by the Directors [of the ball club] to induce their attendance, as it adds to the respectability of the National pastime.*

*The Troy men looked admirably in their trim lavender suits and little round caps. Bradley, smiling Bradley, was in his position as pitcher, beaming that cast iron smirk on the batsman that must be aggravating in the extreme.*

*In the ninth inning the Reds were for the nonce threatened by disaster, but Dickerson saved the day. In this supreme moment, Caskins hit a long foul fly to left field, which Dickerson caught in some extraordinary manner, and saved the day.* **[Cincinnati Commercial and Cincinnati Enquirer]**

### OPENING DAY TRIVIA

| | |
|---|---|
| Star of the Game | Reds Outfielder Buttercup Dickerson |
| Weather | 62°; Clear Skies |
| Attendance | 1,200 |
| Notable | Will White Wins 2nd Straight Opener |
| Rating | ●●● |

### MAY 1, 1879

**THE SCORE.**

| CINCINNATI. | A.B. | R. | 1B. | R. | P.O. | A. | E. |
|---|---|---|---|---|---|---|---|
| Floating, m. | 5 | 1 | 1 | 2 | 0 | 0 | 1 |
| Barnes, 2b. | 5 | 2 | 1 | 3 | 7 | 3 | 1 |
| Burke, s. s. | 5 | 0 | 0 | 0 | 0 | 2 | 1 |
| McVey, 1b. | 4 | 2 | 2 | 4 | 8 | 0 | 1 |
| Dickerson, l. f. | 5 | 2 | 2 | 3 | 4 | 0 | 1 |
| Kelly, r. f. | 5 | 0 | 2 | 3 | 2 | 1 | 0 |
| J. White, c. | 5 | 0 | 1 | 1 | 5 | 6 | 3 |
| W. White, p. | 4 | 0 | 1 | 1 | 0 | 6 | 0 |
| Gerhardt, 3b. | 4 | 0 | 1 | 1 | 1 | 0 | 0 |
| Totals | 42 | 7 | 11 | 18 | 27 | 18 | 8 |

| TROY CITY. | A.B. | R. | 1B. | R. | P.O. | A. | E. |
|---|---|---|---|---|---|---|---|
| Hall, m. | 4 | 0 | 2 | 3 | 2 | 0 | 0 |
| Caskins, s. s. | 5 | 1 | 2 | 2 | 1 | 2 | 0 |
| Mansell, l. f. | 4 | 1 | 1 | 1 | 1 | 0 | 0 |
| Hawkes, 2b. | 4 | 0 | 0 | 0 | 2 | 3 | 3 |
| Evans, r. f. | 4 | 1 | 0 | 2 | 1 | 1 | 0 |
| Clapp, 1b. | 3 | 0 | 1 | 2 | 15 | 0 | 1 |
| Doescher, 3b. | 4 | 0 | 1 | 1 | 1 | 1 | 2 |
| Bradley, p. | 4 | 2 | 1 | 3 | 0 | 7 | 0 |
| Reilly, c. | 4 | 0 | 1 | 2 | 4 | 1 | 1 |
| Totals | 36 | 5 | 9 | 16 | 27 | 15 | 7 |

**RUNS MADE EACH INNING.**

| CLUBS. | 1. | 2. | 3. | 4. | 5. | 6. | 7. | 8. | 9. | T. |
|---|---|---|---|---|---|---|---|---|---|---|
| Cincinnati | 2 | 0 | 3 | 0 | 2 | 0 | 0 | 0 | — | 7 |
| Troy City | 3 | 1 | 0 | 0 | 0 | 1 | 0 | 0 | — | 5 |

Runs earned—Cincinnati, 1.
Bases on called balls—McVey, 1; Clapp, 1; Hall, 1.
First base on errors—Cincinnati, 7; Troy City, 6.
Left on bases—Cincinnati, 9; Troy City, 6.
Struck out—Burke, Kelly, Mansell, Hawkes, Clapp, Reilly.
Two base hits—Barnes, 1; Kelly, 1.
Passed balls—Reilly, 1.
Umpire—M. Walsh, Louisville.

# Opening Day for Bank Street Grounds
## Chicago Rallies in Ninth for 4–3 Win

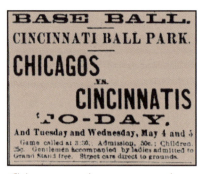

*Clubs encouraged women to attend games by offering the "ladies" and their escorts free admission.*

The Reds christened a new ball park on this Opening Day, inaugurating the Bank Street Grounds with a disheartening 4–3 loss to Chicago.

Chicago rallied for two runs in the bottom of the ninth inning (the Reds lost the toss and batted first) on two hits, two errors and a mad dash to home by shortstop Tom Burns. Chicago pitcher Larry Corcoran allowed the Reds only four hits and pitched a complete game, besting the Reds ace, Will White, who was attempting to pick up his third consecutive Opening Day win.

Chicago led, 2–1, until the eighth when the Reds rallied for two runs and a 3–2 lead. With one man on base, Reds catcher John Clapp smashed a long drive to center field for an inside-the-park home run (the first homer ever hit on Opening Day in Cincinnati). It was Clapp's second long hit of the day—he tripled in the sixth inning—and he graciously accepted the cheers of the spectators.

Will White whitewashed Chicago in the eighth inning, but his defense deserted him in the ninth. Pitcher Larry Corcoran led off the inning with a single. An error by shortstop Sam Wright on Tom Burns put runners on first and third. Second baseman Joe Quest earned a single to right that easily drove in Corcoran. Behind him came the rookie Burns at top speed.

Right fielder Jack Manning had time to throw Burns out, but his throw home sailed high over the catcher's head and Burns tallied the winning run.

Despite the attraction of a new facility and fine weather, the game drew only 2,038 spectators. The capacity of Bank Street Grounds is not known, but it is likely this was not a sellout, as most parks of this era could hold a much larger audience. However, the crowd was probably the largest of the season; the Reds drew only 21,000 in 39 games, an average of 538 a game.

The papers offered these descriptions of the game: *The day was extremely favorable for the game and the grand stand, with its north and west wings, was comfortably crowded with nearly two thousand spectators.*

*In the eighth inning Manning's single and Clapp's hit to center for a home run set the crowd wild, and they got upon their feet and made the air fairly ring with their cheers.*

*But the game was not yet won, for in the last inning Corcoran opened for his side with a hit to right. Then Sam Wright got rattled and fumbled Burn's hit allowing that young man to reach first. Quest's hit to right let in Corcoran, and Burns, who had kept booming right along to bring in the winning run for Manning, in trying to cut him off, threw the ball in home some six feet over Clapp's head.* [Cincinnati Commercial and Cincinnati Gazette]

### Opening Day Trivia

| | |
|---|---|
| Star of the Game | Reds Catcher John Clapp |
| Weather | 62°; Clear Skies |
| Attendance | 2,038 |
| Notable | First Opening Day Home Run |
| Rating | ●●● |

### 1880 Opening Day Schedule

| May 1 | National League |
|---|---|
| Chi vs. Cin | |
| Bost vs. Prov | Buff vs. Clev |
| Troy vs. Wor'ster | |

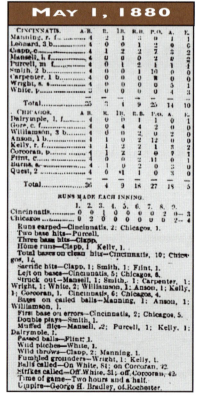

# Reds Lose First Game in New League

## 1882

*The 1882 Cincinnati Reds in their multi-colored uniforms, which they did not wear on Opening Day. Rookie and future Hall of Famer Bid McPhee is on the far right.*

After a year's absence from the major league ranks, the Reds opened the 1882 season in the new American Association. The Cincinnati club, which had been banned from the National League after the 1880 season for renting its ballpark for Sunday games, joined with five other clubs to create a second major league.

The Reds hosted Pittsburgh in the opening game and lost to the Allegheny boys, 10–9. This game marked the debut of Reds second baseman and Hall of Famer, Bid McPhee. Although McPhee went hitless in five at-bats, his fielding immediately set him apart. On a day the Reds made **nine** errors, the *Cincinnati Commercial* noted McPhee's six assists and six putouts with no errors, and commented, "McPhee's fielding…took the Chicago wheat market. Examine his score." McPhee would go on to play 18 seasons in Cincinnati; his 2000 induction into the Hall of Fame was a tribute to his fielding skill.

Reds pitcher Will White started his fourth consecutive Opening Day, but a sore arm put him at a disadvantage. He was unable to throw sidearm at full speed until the sixth inning. (Full overhand delivery was not yet legal.) In the early innings, he threw underhand. He gave up 15 hits, but only four of the Pittsburgh tallies were earned.

After leading early by three runs, the Reds entered the ninth inning trailing 10–8. Left fielder Joe Sommer started the inning with a single. After McPhee flied out, Hick Carpenter singled, and Pop Snyder then drove in Sommer with his fourth hit of the day. With the tying and winning runs on base, the crowd sent forth cheer after cheer. But Dan Stearns and Bill Tierney both flied out, and Pittsburgh claimed the victory.

### 1882 OPENING DAY SCHEDULE

| MAY 2 | AMERICAN ASSOCIATION |
|---|---|
| | PITTS VS. CIN |
| LOU VS. STL | PHIL VS. BALT |

The crowd of some 1,500 was probably something of a disappointment. The Reds had drawn more for an exhibition game a few days earlier. However the Reds would go on to win the pennant (their first championship) and set a club attendance record of 65,000 fans.

The local press found the opener a "decidedly interesting one": *There were nearly fifteen hundred people on the grounds, and though the home club was defeated it is safe to say that there was no one present who failed to get the worth of his money out of the game.*

*There is no use of singling out any one player and casting upon him the burden of the defeat of the team. It could in this instance be divided equally among the nine men. If they were strong in the field, they were weak at the bat, and vice versa.*

*It was plain to see that [Will] White's arm was not in good trim. He didn't get his hand up to his belt until the sixth inning. After that, the visitors didn't hit him so hard.*

*[Newly signed substitute Harry] McCormick took tickets at the grand stand. He needs some practice and will then be able to pitch.* **[Cincinnati Commercial and Cincinnati Enquirer]**

### OPENING DAY TRIVIA

| STAR OF THE GAME | REDS CATCHER POP SNYDER |
|---|---|
| WEATHER | 55°; CLEAR SKIES |
| ATTENDANCE | 1,500 |
| NOTABLE | HALL OF FAMER BID MCPHEE'S FIRST GAME |
| RATING | ◐◐◐ |

### MAY 2, 1882

| CINCINNATIS. | A.B. | R. | 1 B. | P.O. | A. | E. |
|---|---|---|---|---|---|---|
| Sommer, l. f. | 4 | 2 | 1 | 2 | 0 | 0 |
| McPhee, 2 b. | 5 | 1 | 0 | 6 | 6 | 0 |
| Carpenter, 3 b. | 5 | 3 | 3 | 0 | 4 | 0 |
| Snyder, c. | 5 | 1 | 4 | 3 | 0 | 2 |
| Stearns, r. f. | 5 | 0 | 0 | 0 | 0 | 2 |
| Tierney, 1 b. | 5 | 1 | 0 | 11 | 0 | 1 |
| Fulmer, s. s. | 5 | 0 | 1 | 0 | 5 | 2 |
| Mueller, m. f. | 4 | 0 | 3 | 2 | 0 | 1 |
| White, p. | 4 | 0 | 1 | 0 | 5 | 0 |
| **Total** | **41** | **9** | **14** | **27** | **21** | **9** |
| PITTSBURGS. | A.B. | R. | 1 B. | P.O. | A. | E. |
| Swartwood, r. f. | 6 | 2 | 1 | 0 | 0 | 0 |
| Taylor, 3 b. | 6 | 2 | 2 | 0 | 1 | 0 |
| Leary, p. | 5 | 1 | 1 | 0 | 7 | 0 |
| Mansell, l. f. | 5 | 1 | 1 | 5 | 0 | 0 |
| Goodman, 1 b. | 5 | 1 | 1 | 9 | 2 | 0 |
| Peters, s. s. | 4 | 1 | 1 | 0 | 8 | 0 |
| Morton, m. f. | 5 | 1 | 4 | 5 | 0 | 0 |
| Strief, 2 b. | 3 | 0 | 3 | 4 | 4 | 1 |
| Keenan, c. | 5 | 1 | 3 | 7 | 2 | 1 |
| **Total** | **44** | **10** | **15** | **27** | **22** | **2** |

| Innings | 1 | 2 | 3 | 4 | 5 | 6 | 7 | 8 | 9 |
|---|---|---|---|---|---|---|---|---|---|
| Pittsburgs | 0 | 0 | 4 | 0 | 0 | 3 | 2 | 1 | 0 — 10 |
| Cincinnatis | 2 | 0 | 0 | 5 | 0 | 0 | 0 | 1 | 1 — 9 |

Runs earned—Cincinnatis 2, Pittsburgs 4.
Three-base hits—Taylor 1, Morton 1.
Total bases on clean hits—Cincinnatis 14, Pittsburgs 19.
Left on bases—Cincinnatis 6, Pittsburgs 9.
Bases on called balls—Cincinnatis 1, Pittsburgs 6.
Struck out—Fulmer 2, Tierney 1, Sommer 1, Taylor 1, Mansell 1.
Double plays—McPhee and Tierney 1, Taylor, Strief and Goodman 1, McPhee, Fulmer and Tierney 1, Peters and Strief 1.
Wild throws—Snyder 2, Stearns 1, Fulmer 1.
Passed grounders—Stearns 1, Fulmer 1, Morton 1.
Muffed thrown balls—Tierney 2, Strief 1, Keenan 1.
Fumbled grounders—Taylor 1.
Wild pitches—White 2, Leary 1.
Passed balls—Keenan 1.
Foul catches—White 1, Leary 3.
Umpire—Harry Wheeler.
Time of game—Two hours and twenty minutes.

# A Glorious Opener
## Record Crowd Cheers Reds Win in 11

**1883**

### MAY 1, 1883

| Cincinnatis | A.B. | R. | 1B. | P.O. | A. | E. |
|---|---|---|---|---|---|---|
| Reilly, 1b | 4 | 0 | 0 | 8 | 0 | 1 |
| Carpenter, 3d | 5 | 0 | 0 | 3 | 4 | 1 |
| Jones, l.f | 5 | 1 | 1 | 4 | 2 | 1 |
| Sommer, r.f | 4 | 2 | 2 | 0 | 1 | 0 |
| Corkhill, m.f | 5 | 1 | 1 | 5 | 0 | 1 |
| Snyder, c | 5 | 0 | 2 | 6 | 4 | 0 |
| Fulmer, s.s | 5 | 1 | 1 | 3 | 3 | 3 |
| McPhee, 2b | 4 | 1 | 1 | 0 | 1 | 1 |
| White, p | 4 | 0 | 1 | 0 | 4 | 1 |
| **Totals** | **41** | **6** | **9** | **33** | **18** | **9** |
| ST. LOUIS | AB | R | 1B | P.O. | A | E |
| W. Gleason, s.s | 5 | 0 | 0 | 0 | 7 | 2 |
| Latham, 3d b | 5 | 0 | 2 | 1 | 4 | 0 |
| Comiskey, 1st b | 5 | 0 | 0 | 18 | 0 | 0 |
| Loftus, c.f | 5 | 0 | 1 | 1 | 0 | 0 |
| J. Gleason, l.f | 5 | 1 | 0 | 0 | 0 | 0 |
| McGinnis, p | 5 | 1 | 3 | 0 | 1 | 1 |
| Nichol, r.f | 5 | 1 | 2 | 2 | 0 | 1 |
| Dolan, c | 5 | 1 | 1 | 3 | 1 | 0 |
| Strief, 2d b | 4 | 0 | 0 | 6 | 3 | 0 |
| **Totals** | **44** | **5** | **9** | **31** | **16** | **7** |

Innings...... 1. 2. 3. 4. 5. 6. 7. 8. 9.10.11.
St. Louis.... 0 0 0 0 3 0 0 1 0 0 1—5
Cincinnati... 1 2 1 0 0 0 0 0 0 0 2—6

Runs earned—Cincinnatis 2.
Two-base hit—Corkhill 1.
Three-base hits—Dolan 1, Latham 1.
Double play—Jones and Snyder 1.
Left on bases—Cincinnatis 5, St. Louis 5.
Bases on called balls—By McGinnis 2.
Struck out—By White 2, McGinnis 1.
Passed balls—Deasley 1, Dolan 1.
Muffed flies—Jones 1, Corkhill 1, Fulmer 1, White 1, Nichol 1, W. Gleason 1, McGinnis 1.
Wild throws—Fulmer 1, Carpenter 1, Deasley 1, Dolan 1, W. Gleason 1.
Muffed thrown balls—McPhee 1, Fulmer 1, Reilly 1.
Time of game 2 hours and 40 minutes.
Umpire—W. H. Becannon.

The Reds opened the defense of their 1882 championship with a dramatic, 11-inning, 6–5 victory over St. Louis. The mix of ideal weather, a huge crowd and a Reds win in extra innings ranks this as one of the great all-time Opening Days.

Although small by today's standards, the crowd of 3,500 filled the main grandstand and all the bleacher seats. They arrived early, for precisely at 3 o'clock the championship banner was raised up the flagpole. The huge flag—measuring 18 feet by nine feet—carried the inscription, "Champions – 1883."

The Reds quickly jumped out to a 4–0 lead, and with the veteran Will White making his fifth straight Opening Day start, the Reds appeared on their way to an easy win. But three consecutive muffs of fly balls in the fifth inning by Reds Charlie Jones, Chick Fulmer and Pop Corkhill, and a triple by Tom Dolan, led to three runs for St. Louis. Several fly balls were dropped by both teams, the players having trouble judging the flight of the ball against the bright blue sky.

Jumbo McGinnis, the St. Louis pitcher, held the Reds scoreless over the next several innings, in part because of what the Reds claimed was an illegal delivery. The rules forbade the pitcher to release the ball above his shoulder. Cincinnati captain Pop Snyder protested to Umpire Becannon, but no reprimand was issued.

St. Louis tied the game, 4–4, in the eighth and had runners on first and second with one out in the ninth before the Reds defense halted the rally. Third baseman Hick Carpenter forced the lead runner at third after a dazzling stop of a hot grounder, and Reds catcher Pop Snyder picked off the runner at first for the final out.

St. Louis took the lead in the top of the eleventh, but the defending champs were not beat. Joe Summer led off with a single and Corkhill's double put runners on second and third. Snyder's "slow sacrifice" to second (likely what is now known as a squeeze play) scored Summer. Chick Fulmer then rapped a single to left and the crowd went "stark mad" as Corkhill scored the winning run.

The local press admired the crowd and criticized the umpire: *The concourse of people who attended was not only large numbers, but was of a class which gives tone to the sport. A large delegation of ladies and gentlemen from the Dramatic Festival stars were attentive spectators. There were thirty-six carriages and buggies on the grounds yesterday, and two ladies on horseback.*

*[St. Louis pitcher Jumbo] McGinnis openly violated the pitching rules by throwing on a level with his head during the last half of the game. Umpire Becannon was reminded of this several times by [Reds] Captain Snyder, but refused to enforce the rule. A rule was made to especially keep the arm below the shoulder, and made so it could be enforced. No umpire will do his sworn duty unless he enforces all the rules. He is under oath to enforce all of them. [**Cincinnati Commercial Gazette**]*

### 1883 OPENING DAY SCHEDULE

| MAY 1 | AMERICAN ASSOCIATION |
|---|---|
| StL vs. Cin | NY vs. Balt |
| Phil vs. Pitts | Lou vs. Col |

### OPENING DAY TRIVIA

| | |
|---|---|
| Star of the Game | Chick Fullmer |
| Weather | 67°; Clear Skies |
| Attendance | 3,500 |
| Notable | First Extra-inning Opener |
| Rating | ○○○○○ |

# 1884 Section of New Stands Collapses
## Injuries Minor; Reds Lose Opener

*The new stands under construction in April 1894. The platform that collapsed on Opening Day was located behind the main grandstand.*

The 3,200 spectators that filled the new Cincinnati ballpark for the home opener between the Reds and Columbus thought they had seen enough excitement in the final innings of the game as they cheered the Reds in a furious but futile comeback.

Moments after the last out was made and the final tally—Columbus 10, Cincinnati 9—posted on the scoreboard, a landing at the rear of the new stands collapsed as the spectators crowded onto the stairway leading to Western Avenue. A section of the platform suddenly gave way, dropping some 40 spectators 12 feet to the ground.

Despite the fall and the melee that resulted, only four injuries were reported, and only one of a serious nature, a fractured arm.

*The Cincinnati Enquirer*, which had thrown its support behind the new Union Association Reds, a new team in what proved to be an ill-fated league, reported the accident as a major tragedy and even reported a possible fatality among the injured, a rumor which persisted for many years. The other major Cincinnati daily, the *Cincinnati Commercial Gazette*, which supported the American Association Reds, downplayed the accident, calling it "harmless."

The confluence of significant events—Opening Day, the opening of a new ballpark, the accident and the playing of the first game on the future site of Crosley Field—combined to make this one of the most historic openers in Reds history.

And the game itself was not too bad, either. Cincinnati led, 6–2, before Columbus began its comeback. The visitors took the lead in the seventh with six runs aided by two Cincinnati errors.

The Reds picked up one run in the eighth and nearly tied the game in the ninth. Two hits scored one run and with a runner on third, the rookie Columbus pitcher, Ed Morris, was called for a balk on an illegal pitch (above the shoulder). The ruling sent the runner home, the batter to first, and nearly the entire Columbus team to home plate to argue with the umpire. The call stood, but Morris, unflustered by the episode, struck out the final two batters to preserve the win. Morris finished the game with 13 strikeouts, the record for a Cincinnati opener. Reds pitcher Will White took the loss, running his Opening Day record to 3–3.

The ballpark came in for considerable criticism, given the collapse of the landing and the odd dimensions of the field. The right field fence was apparently quite short, for when John Richmond, the Columbus shortstop hit a "terrific" drive over the fence, he was only given a double, for that was the ground rule in effect. The stands were also very close to the field and several foul balls went into the stands. By the customs of the day, play was halted each time while the ball was retrieved, delays which one reporter found "tiresome."

*[Cincinnati Commercial Gazette and Cincinnati Enquirer]*

### 1884 OPENING DAY SCHEDULE

| MAY 1 | AMERICAN ASSOCIATION |
|---|---|
| COL VS. CIN | INDPLS VS. STL |
| TOL VS. LOU | NY VS. BALT |
| BRKLYN VS. WASH | PHIL VS. PITTS |

### OPENING DAY TRIVIA

| | |
|---|---|
| STAR OF THE GAME | COLUMBUS PITCHER, ED MORRIS |
| WEATHER | 80°; CLOUDY & WINDY |
| ATTENDANCE | 3,200 |
| NOTABLE | FIRST GAME AT FUTURE SITE OF CROSLEY FIELD |
| RATING | ○○○○○ |

### MAY 1, 1884

| CINCINNATI | A.B. | R. | 1B. | P.O. | A. | E. |
|---|---|---|---|---|---|---|
| Mansell, l. f. | 5 | 1 | 1 | 2 | 0 | 2 |
| Carpenter, 3b. | 5 | 1 | 1 | 1 | 0 | 0 |
| Reilly, 1b. | 5 | 2 | 3 | 3 | 0 | 0 |
| Jones, m. f. | 4 | 2 | 1 | 3 | 1 | 0 |
| Corkhill, r. f. | 5 | 1 | 2 | 2 | 0 | 0 |
| McPhee, 2b. | 5 | 0 | 1 | 7 | 1 | 0 |
| Snyder, c. | 4 | 1 | 0 | 5 | 3 | 1 |
| Fulmer, s. s. | 4 | 1 | 0 | 1 | 1 | 3 |
| White, p. | 4 | 0 | 0 | 0 | 0 | 0 |
| Totals | 41 | 9 | 9 | 24 | 6 | 6 |

| COLUMBUS. | A.B. | R. | 1B. | P.O. | A. | E. |
|---|---|---|---|---|---|---|
| Brown, r. f. | 5 | 2 | 2 | 0 | 0 | 0 |
| Smith, l. f. | 4 | 1 | 1 | 3 | 1 | 0 |
| Kemmler, 1b. | 3 | 1 | 0 | 7 | 0 | 3 |
| Richmond, s.s. | 5 | 1 | 2 | 0 | 1 | 1 |
| Mann, m. f. | 4 | 2 | 1 | 1 | 0 | 0 |
| Carroll, c. | 4 | 1 | 1 | 13 | 2 | 1 |
| Kuehne, 3b. | 4 | 1 | 2 | 0 | 1 | 0 |
| Mountain, l. f. | 4 | 1 | 2 | 2 | 0 | 0 |
| Morris, p. | 3 | 0 | 2 | 0 | 2 | 3 |
| Totals | 37 | 10 | 11 | 27 | 7 | 9 |

| Innings | 1 | 2 | 3 | 4 | 5 | 6 | 7 | 8 | 9 | |
|---|---|---|---|---|---|---|---|---|---|---|
| Cincinnati | 2 | 0 | 0 | 4 | 0 | 0 | 0 | 1 | 2 | —9 |
| Columbus | 1 | 1 | 0 | 0 | 0 | 2 | 6 | 0 | — | —10 |

Runs earned—Cincinnati 1, Columbus 7. Two-base hits—McPhee 1, Smith 1, Richmond 1. Three-base hits—Kuehne 1, Carroll 1. Home runs—Brown 1, Mountain 1, Corkhill 1. Total bases on balls—Cincinnati 13, Columbus 25. Left on bases—Cincinnati 5, Columbus 7. Struck out—By White 5, Morris 13. Bases on balls—By White 4, Morris 1. Bases on balls—By Morris 2. Wild pitches—White 1, Morris 1. Passed balls—Carroll 1. Time of game—Two hours and ten minutes. Umpire—T. C. Connell, of Philadelphia.

# Reds Win Rain-Delayed Opener
## Will White Leads Cincinnati
### 1885

*Will White won four of the seven consecutive Opening Days he started.*

Will White, making his seventh straight Opening Day start, allowed only three hits, and his teammates generated just enough offense to give the Reds a 3–1 victory over Louisville.

This was the home opener for the Reds, but the second game between Cincinnati and Louisville. The Reds were forced to open in Louisville on Sunday, April 19 after rain cancelled the scheduled home opener on April 18.

The Reds won the road opener, 4–1, behind another strong pitching performance by Gus Shallix.

The crowd of 2,500 was somewhat less than would have attended the scheduled opener, but the *Commercial Gazette* noted that, as had become the custom at Opening Day, the throng contained "many of the best people of Cincinnati."

White recorded only three strikeouts, but he was dominant. The only threat Louisville mounted came in the second when two hits and an error on Pop Corkhill in right field produced an unearned run. Louisville had base runners in just two other innings—one on a single and one on an error—but both runners where thrown out trying to steal second. White faced the minimum of three batters in eight of the nine innings.

The Reds scored the winning runs in the fifth inning without a hit, breaking a 1–1 tie. Louisville pitcher Phil Reccius was victimized by poor fielding and his own wild pitch. Bid McPhee and Corkhill both reached base on errors by shortstop Billy Geer. Reccius then uncorked a wild pitch that moved the runners up to second and third. McPhee and Corkhill both scored on throwing errors.

White contributed to the Reds score by driving in the first run in the third inning with a single to center.

The *Commercial Gazette* lavished praise on the crowd and the team: *The Cincinnatis won their second championship game, this time on their own grounds. It was a victory well earned by splendid fielding and fine team work. Although it was Monday, the worst day of the week for attendance, there were nearly twenty-five hundred people on the grounds. It was a remarkably fine class of attendance, numbering many of the best people of Cincinnati, and the grand stand contained a large number of ladies. The spectators enjoyed the game very much and were liberal in their applause. It was a beautiful day, and the field was in the best kind of form.* [**Cincinnati Commercial Gazette**]

### 1885 OPENING DAY SCHEDULE

| APRIL 18 | AMERICAN ASSOCIATION |
|---|---|
| | LOU VS. CIN (PP) |
| PITTS VS. STL | NY VS. PHIL |
| APRIL 20 | AMERICAN ASSOCIATION |
| | BRKLYN V. BALT |

### OPENING DAY TRIVIA

| STAR OF THE GAME | REDS PITCHER WILL WHITE |
|---|---|
| WEATHER | 75°; PARTLY CLOUDY |
| ATTENDANCE | 2,500 |
| NOTABLE | WHITE'S 7TH STRAIGHT OPENING DAY START |
| RATING | ●●● |

### APRIL 20, 1885

| CINCINNATIS. | A.B. | R. | 1B. | P.O. | A. | E. |
|---|---|---|---|---|---|---|
| Fennelly, s.s. | 4 | 0 | 0 | 3 | 3 | 0 |
| Jones, l. f. | 4 | 0 | 1 | 2 | 0 | 0 |
| Clinton, m. f. | 4 | 0 | 1 | 3 | 0 | 1 |
| Reilly, 1b. | 4 | 0 | 1 | 13 | 0 | 0 |
| Carpenter, 3b. | 4 | 0 | 1 | 0 | 3 | 0 |
| McPhee, 2b. | 3 | 1 | 0 | 3 | 2 | 0 |
| Corkhill, r. f. | 3 | 1 | 0 | 0 | 0 | 1 |
| Baldwin, c. | 3 | 1 | 1 | 5 | 2 | 0 |
| White, p. | 3 | 0 | 2 | 1 | 5 | 0 |
| Totals. | 32 | 3 | 7 | 27 | 15 | 2 |
| **LOUISVILLES.** | **A.B.** | **R.** | **1B.** | **P.O.** | **A.** | **E.** |
| Browning, m.f. | 4 | 0 | 1 | 2 | 1 | 0 |
| Wolf, r.f. | 4 | 0 | 0 | 1 | 0 | 0 |
| Reccius, p. | 4 | 0 | 0 | 1 | 2 | 0 |
| Kerins, 1b. | 3 | 1 | 1 | 10 | 0 | 1 |
| Geer, s.s. | 3 | 0 | 1 | 0 | 7 | 2 |
| Maskrey, l.f. | 3 | 0 | 0 | 0 | 0 | 0 |
| Crotty, c. | 3 | 0 | 0 | 5 | 6 | 0 |
| Miller, 3b. | 2 | 0 | 0 | 1 | 0 | 0 |
| McLaughlin, 2b. | 3 | 0 | 0 | 8 | 1 | 2 |
| Totals. | 29 | 1 | 3 | 27 | 18 | 5 |

| Innings. | 1. | 2. | 3. | 4. | 5. | 6. | 7. | 8. | 9. |
|---|---|---|---|---|---|---|---|---|---|
| Cincinnatis | 0 | 0 | 1 | 0 | 2 | 0 | 0 | 0 | 0—3 |
| Louisvilles | 0 | 1 | 0 | 0 | 0 | 0 | 0 | 0 | 0—1 |

Left on bases—Cincinnatis 3, Louisvilles 2. Double plays—Reccius, McLaughlin and Kerins 1. Struck out—By Reccius 6, White 3. Bases on hit by pitcher—White 1. Wild pitches—Reccius 2. Time of game—One hour and a half. Umpire—John Kelly.

# Over 5,000 Watch Reds Drop Opener
## Louisville Quiets the Crowd, 5–1

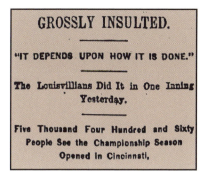

*The first Opening Day promotion helped bring out a record crowd of 5,460.*

A vast throng—a record Opening Day crowd of 5,460 spectators—jammed the Cincinnati Ball Park for the opening game of the 1886 season, but Louisville pitcher Guy Hecker was not impressed.

He limited the Reds to three hits and only one run as his Louisville club rang up a 3–1 defeat of the Cincinnatis.

The Reds scored their only run in the first and might have added more to the tally but for a disputed call by umpire Ben Young. Hick Carpenter tried to score all the way from second when John Reilly's ground ball was kicked around by the Louisville first baseman. Carpenter appeared to slide in safely before the throw arrived, but Young called him out for the first out of the inning.

Fred Lewis then smashed a double scoring Reilly. No one suspected at the time that the Reds offense was through, but Hecker allowed only two more hits after the first and the Louisville fielders supported Hecker with errorless ball over the last eight innings.

Larry McKeon matched Hecker's performance for most of the game, holding Louisville scoreless in eight of nine innings. But that left the disastrous fifth when Louisville scored all five of its runs. All the runs were earned.

Two scratch hits put runners on first and second. A double, a single and another double drove in the five runs.

The Opening Day crowd was treated to a most unusual sight at the entrances to the ballpark—bird cages filled with lively canaries. The birds kept up a brisk chatter, entertaining the spectators as they arrived.

A second innovation for Opening Day was a pre-game concert by the Cincinnati Orchestra Reed Band. Apparently this band had played prior to games in previous seasons, but never on Opening Day. The band had also developed a bad-luck reputation. The *Commercial Gazette* observed, "The concert was a splendid treat, but, as usual, a defeat followed the music. Is a band a Jonah?" (Jonah was slang for jinx.)

The *Commercial Gazette* lauded the audience: *The splendid crowd of 5,460 thoroughly enjoyed the game, in spite of the results. For it really was a game full of brilliant plays. The great crowd included in its numbers the very best representative men and ladies of Cincinnati. This is not a boast without truth. Every spectator in the grand stand knows that leading merchants, manufacturers and officials were plentifully scattered throughout the vast throng.*

*The lady attendants were out in large numbers. More than half the occupants of the south half of the grand stand were ladies, and the scene from the rear lobbies was a most brilliant one.*

*[However] there was no waiter in the grand stand. When the boys get thirsty, they must go down stairs.* [*Cincinnati Commercial Gazette*]

### 1886 OPENING DAY SCHEDULE

| APRIL 17 | AMERICAN ASSOCIATION |
|---|---|
| LOU VS. CIN | PITTS VS. STL |
| BRKLYN VS. BALT | NY VS. PHIL |

### OPENING DAY TRIVIA

| | |
|---|---|
| STAR OF THE GAME | LOUISVILLE PITCHER GUY HECKER |
| WEATHER | 75°; PARTLY CLOUDY |
| ATTENDANCE | 5,460 |
| NOTABLE | FIRST OPENING DAY CROWD OVER 5,000 |
| RATING | ●●● |

### APRIL 17, 1886

| CINCINNATIS. | A.B. | R. | 1B. | SB. | P.O. | A. | E. |
|---|---|---|---|---|---|---|---|
| Jones, l. f. | 3 | 0 | 1 | 1 | 3 | 0 | 0 |
| Reilly, 1b. | 4 | 1 | 0 | 0 | 6 | 0 | 0 |
| Lewis, m. f. | 3 | 0 | 1 | 0 | 1 | 1 | 0 |
| Fennelly, s. s. | 2 | 0 | 0 | 0 | 2 | 2 | 2 |
| Carpenter, 3b. | 3 | 0 | 1 | 0 | 2 | 2 | 3 |
| McPhee, 2b. | 3 | 0 | 0 | 0 | 2 | 1 | 0 |
| Corkhill, r. f. | 3 | 0 | 0 | 0 | 0 | 0 | 0 |
| Keenan, c. | 3 | 0 | 0 | 0 | 7 | 0 | 0 |
| McKeon, p. | 3 | 0 | 0 | 0 | 1 | 1 | 0 |
| Totals | 27 | 1 | 3 | 1 | 24 | 7 | 5 |

| LOUISVILLE. | A.B. | R. | 1B. | SB. | P.O. | A. | E. |
|---|---|---|---|---|---|---|---|
| Cook, l. f. | 4 | 1 | 1 | 0 | 1 | 0 | 0 |
| Kerins, 1b. | 4 | 1 | 1 | 0 | 11 | 0 | 0 |
| Hecker, p. | 4 | 0 | 1 | 0 | 1 | 3 | 0 |
| Browning, c. f. | 4 | 0 | 0 | 0 | 3 | 0 | 0 |
| Cross, c. | 4 | 0 | 1 | 0 | 3 | 1 | 0 |
| White, s. s. | 4 | 0 | 0 | 0 | 1 | 1 | 0 |
| Mack, 2b. | 4 | 1 | 1 | 0 | 4 | 6 | 1 |
| Werrich, 3b. | 4 | 1 | 1 | 0 | 1 | 1 | 0 |
| Reccius, r. f. | 2 | 1 | 1 | 0 | 3 | 0 | 0 |
| Totals | 34 | 5 | 7 | 0 | 27 | 12 | 1 |

| Innings | 1 | 2 | 3 | 4 | 5 | 6 | 7 | 8 | 9 | |
|---|---|---|---|---|---|---|---|---|---|---|
| Cincinnatis | 1 | 0 | 0 | 0 | 0 | 0 | 0 | 0 | 0 | —1 |
| Louisvilles | 0 | 0 | 0 | 0 | 5 | 0 | 0 | 0 | 0 | —5 |

Runs earned—Louisvilles 5. Two-base hits—Lewis 1, Reccius 1. Three-base hits—Kerins 1. Left on bases—Cincinnati 1, Louisvilles 5. Double plays—Mack and Kerins. Struck out—By Hecker 0, by McKeon 5. Bases on balls—By Hecker 1, by McKeon 1. Bases on hit by pitcher—Hecker 1. Wild pitches—Hecker 1. Passed balls—Cross 1. Time of game—One hour and thirty-five minutes. Umpire—Mr. Ben Young.

# 1887 Sixteen Runs for the Reds
## McPhee and Mullane Star

*Bid McPhee scored four runs to lead the Reds in the 1887 opener.*

Future Hall of Famer Bid McPhee scored four runs and handsome ladies' man Tony Mullane pitched a complete game and hit a home run to help the Reds down the visitors from Cleveland, 16–6.

George "White Wings" Tebeau, the Reds center fielder, had the decisive hit of the day, a three-run home run in the first inning. The Reds scored five in the first and two more in the second to take a 7–0 lead. Frank Fennelly, the Reds shortstop, added a three-run home run in the sixth inning, putting the Reds ahead at that point, 12–2.

McPhee seemed to be on base every inning, with four walks and a single. He kept the crowd cheering with his daring baserunning and headfirst slides.

Although Mullane gave up eight walks and seven hits, Cleveland never assembled a major threat. Mostly, this was the result of excellent defense. The Reds killed Cleveland rallies with three double plays in the first three innings.

The crowd of 2,700 was barely half of the 1886 attendance record, but the weather was to blame. The day grew increasingly colder and the skies threatened to dump rain or snow on the city. By 3:30 the temperature had dropped to the mid-30s.

The press lauded Ed Cuthbert for his umpiring. There were no disputes, despite many rule changes for 1887. Batters were no longer allowed to call for a high or low ball, and a strike out was extended to four strikes. The papers also enjoyed the Reds play and praised the opponents: The Cincinnati men, one and all, played a sharp and brilliant fielding game, and ran bases with the dash and skill for which they are fast becoming noted. The Cincinnatis played ball just as if it was a nice, warm, summer day. The Clevelands were defeated, and by a one-sided score at that, but their defeat is no discredit to them. They did not lose the game by any blundering work on their part, but by reason of the superior character of the ball played by the Cincinnatis.

McPhee played a great game both at the bat and on the bases. He accepted nine chances without an error and made nearly a clean record with the stick. He worked his way to first on balls no less than four times, made one clean single and scored four runs. He also made two or three pretty head-first slides to second.

The crowd numbered a few over 2,700 people, and it would have been much larger had it not been for he sudden and unfavorable change in the weather. The game was not called until 3:30 o'clock, when the boys from the Forest City took the field, attired in a neat gray checkered uniform, with dark blue stockings and belt.

*[Cincinnati Commercial Gazette and Cincinnati Enquirer]*

### 1887 OPENING DAY SCHEDULE

| APRIL 16 | AMERICAN ASSOCIATION |
|---|---|
| CLEV VS. CIN | STL VS. LOU |
| NY VS. BRKLYN | PHIL VS. BALT |

### OPENING DAY TRIVIA

| STAR OF THE GAME | REDS SECOND BASEMAN BID MCPHEE |
|---|---|
| WEATHER | MID-30S; CLOUDY |
| ATTENDANCE | 2,700 |
| NOTABLE | WALKS COUNTED AS HITS IN 1887 |
| RATING | ●●● |

### APRIL 16, 1887

| CINCINNATI | A.B. | R. | 1B. | S.B. | P.O. | A. | E. |
|---|---|---|---|---|---|---|---|
| McPhee, 2b | 6 | 4 | 5 | 3 | 3 | 6 | 0 |
| Fennelly, s. s. | 6 | 2 | 1 | 0 | 4 | 4 | 2 |
| Corkhill, r. f. | 5 | 1 | 3 | 0 | 5 | 0 | 0 |
| Jones, l. f. | 5 | 0 | 1 | 0 | 1 | 0 | 0 |
| Reilly, 1b | 5 | 1 | 0 | 0 | 11 | 0 | 0 |
| Carpenter, 3b | 5 | 2 | 2 | 1 | 2 | 2 | 0 |
| Tebeau, c. f. | 6 | 2 | 2 | 2 | 0 | 0 | 0 |
| Baldwin, c. | 5 | 1 | 2 | 1 | 1 | 2 | 1 |
| Mullane, p. | 5 | 3 | 2 | 1 | 0 | 5 | 0 |
| Totals | 47 | 16 | 18 | 8 | 27 | 17 | 3 |
| CLEVELAND. | A.B. | R. | 1B. | S.B. | P.O. | A. | E. |
| Hotaling, c. f. | 5 | 2 | 3 | 1 | 2 | 0 | 0 |
| McKeon, s. s. | 5 | 1 | 0 | 0 | 3 | 5 | 1 |
| Sweeney, 1b | 5 | 0 | 3 | 0 | 13 | 0 | 0 |
| Mann, l. f. | 5 | 0 | 1 | 0 | 4 | 0 | 1 |
| Allen, r. f. | 4 | 2 | 1 | 0 | 3 | 0 | 1 |
| Herr, 3b. | 4 | 0 | 2 | 0 | 2 | 2 | 1 |
| Stricker, 2b. | 4 | 1 | 1 | 0 | 1 | 3 | 0 |
| Reipschlager, c. | 4 | 0 | 1 | 0 | 2 | 2 | 1 |
| Pechiney, p. | 4 | 0 | 0 | 0 | 0 | 3 | 1 |
| Totals | 40 | 6 | 15 | 1 | 27 | 15 | 5 |

| Innings | 1. | 2. | 3. | 4. | 5. | 6. | 7. | 8. | 9. | |
|---|---|---|---|---|---|---|---|---|---|---|
| Cincinnati | 5 | 2 | 0 | 1 | 0 | 3 | 0 | 1 | 4 | 16 |
| Cleveland | 0 | 0 | 0 | 1 | 1 | 2 | 0 | 0 | 2 | 6 |

Runs earned—Cincinnati 9, Cleveland 2. Two-base hit—McKeon. Three-base hits—Corkhill and Mann. Home runs—Stricker, Tebeau, Mullane and Fennelly. Base on called balls—McPhee 4, Carpenter 2, Mullane, Hotaling 2, Sweeney 3, Allen, Herr, Reipschlager. Passed balls—Reipschlager 4. Wild pitches—Mullane 2. Time of game—One hour and fifty minutes. Umpire—Cuthbert.

# 1888 Reds Return From Road Opener to Crush Louisville

*Tony Mullane almost recorded a rare shutout in the 1888 home opener. He also won the road opener in Kansas City.*

For the first and only time in club history, the Reds were scheduled to open on the road. After traveling to Kansas City and defeating the Missouri nine, the Reds returned to Cincinnati and destroyed their chief rivals from Louisville in the home opener, 18–2.

The 18 runs set a record for runs scored by the Reds in a home opener, and the margin of victory was also a record.

Despite the offensive explosion, the laurels belonged to pitcher Tony Mullane, who won his second consecutive home opener. Mullane allowed only four singles and a walk. He struck out seven of the Colonels. Mullane, as polished as his handlebar moustache, nearly pitched a shutout, finally yielding two runs in the last inning.

The Reds turned the contest into a rout in the fifth inning. Cincinnati scored five in the fifth for a 9–0 lead, and then pounded Louisville's pitcher, "King" Ramsey, for seven earned runs in the eighth to settle any questions about the outcome.

There were several offensive stars, including John Reilly who banged out three singles and a triple. But the biggest cheers went to Hick Carpenter for his home run all the way to the picket fence in deep left field in the eighth inning.

The attendance was 2,200, a satisfactory crowd for the home opener, considering the very cool temperature and the late date of Opening Day. The Reds opened the season two weeks earlier on April 18th in Kansas City. Cincinnati soundly whipped Kansas City, 10–3. Mullane picked up the win in Kansas, giving him victories in both openers.

The Reds' opening road trip included stops in St. Louis and Louisville before returning home to play the May 1 opener.

The *Commercial Gazette* delighted in the punishment the locals laid on their rivals from Kentucky: *[Louisville manager John] Kelly and his aggregation of alleged ball-players came to Cincinnati yesterday with the avowed intention of drubbing the Red Stockings on their home grounds. They fell far short of victory, however. Kelly was beside himself with grief at the unexpected slaughter of his pets, and when the fifth inning closed he was seen to steal quietly away from the players' bench and sought seclusion in the Director's office beneath the grand stand.*

*From the time game was called, the Cincinnatis played with the greatest confidence, while their opponents on the other hand seemed to have a bad case of "rattles."*

*The visitors appeared upon the field in a rather odd uniform, though attractive, with maroon pants and shirts, and belts and stockings of a pale blue color.*

*Despite the inauspicious weather some twenty-two hundred enthusiasts paid admission and with their overcoats buttoned tightly around them, stood throughout the entire game, loudly cheering every creditable play.* [*Cincinnati Commercial Gazette*]

## OPENING DAY TRIVIA

| | |
|---|---|
| STAR OF THE GAME | REDS PITCHER TONY MULLANE |
| WEATHER | 45°; CLOUDY |
| ATTENDANCE | 2,200 |
| NOTABLE | REDS SCHEDULED OPENER ON ROAD |
| RATING | ●●● |

## 1888 OPENING DAY SCHEDULE

| APRIL 18 | AMERICAN ASSOCIATION |
|---|---|
| CIN VS. KC | LOU VS. STL |
| CLEV VS. BRKLYN | BALT VS. PHIL |

*This 1889 drawing is the first known illustration of a Cincinnati Opening Day game.*

# Gala Atmosphere for Opening Day
## But Reds Fall, 5–1

A record crowd of 10,410, the largest ever to see a baseball game in Cincinnati—a record that would stand until 1895—filled the grounds at Findlay and Western Avenue. But St. Louis pitcher Silver King was unruffled, leading his Browns to a 5–1 victory.

The grandstand, the covered pavilion and the uncovered bleachers of the Cincinnati Ball Park were packed, and a line of fans, three to four deep, stood behind ropes stretched along the foul lines and around the outfield.

Flags and bunting decorated the grandstand and early arrivals were entertained by a 90-minute concert by the full Cincinnati orchestra. Never had Opening Day been celebrated with such fanfare.

As *The Cincinnati Enquirer* bemoaned, "A home victory was all that was needed to complete the grandest testimonial ever paid the National game in the Queen City."

But the team, splendidly attired in their new black uniforms, was not up to the task. The Reds fell behind, 5–0, and only a lone marker in the eighth inning prevented an embarrassing Opening Day shutout.

Reds starter Tony Mullane matched King for most of the day, but finally broke down in the sixth inning when he allowed five hits and four runs.

King overpowered the Reds. He struck out six, and several batters could only manage weak pop-ups to the infield. "King's pitching was superb," said Reds first basemen John Reilly. "I never saw him use such speed as he showed today."

The papers devoted considerable coverage to the unprecedented crowd and festivities: *Cincinnati was base-ball crazy yesterday. The severe Third-street banker and the hustling broker dropped business to discuss base hits and base-ball averages. The street-car conductor, the restaurant waiters, the boot-blacks, the newsboy—in fact every body inside the corporate limits of Cincinnati gave up every thing else to speculate about the Reds' chances against the Browns.*

*It seemed as if every body were headed in the direction of Western avenue and Findlay street. All the street-cars were packed in suffocation. Car-load after car-load of humanity was dumped in front of the gates. These were reinforced by pedestrians from all quarters of the city.*

*The telegraph poles, the roofs of the adjoining buildings and the tops of box-cars on the side tracks west of the park furnished accommodations to bush whackers who had not made the acquaintance of the gentleman in the box-office.*

*[The Browns] Jumping Jack Latham was the life of the game. He kept the crowd in a good humor by his ready wit.* [**Cincinnati Commercial Gazette and Cincinnati Enquirer**]

### OPENING DAY TRIVIA

| | |
|---|---|
| STAR OF THE GAME | ST. LOUIS PITCHER SILVER KING |
| WEATHER | 71°; MOSTLY SUNNY |
| ATTENDANCE | 10,410 |
| NOTABLE | LARGEST CROWD, MOST FESTIVE DAY TO DATE |
| RATING | ○○○○ |

### 1889 OPENING DAY SCHEDULE

**APRIL 17   AMERICAN ASSOCIATION**

| StL vs. Cin | KC vs. Lou |
|---|---|
| Brklyn vs. Phil | Col vs. Balt |

# Reds Back in National League
## 1890
### Carriage Parade Opens Festivities; Reds Lose to Chicago

*The last line of this 1890 ad reads "Don't Miss Anson's Colts." "Colts" was the nickname of the Chicago club and they were captained by Hall of Famer Cap Anson.*

After a 10-year absence, National League baseball returned to the Queen City in 1890. But the Reds could not celebrate with a victory. The boys from Chicago stole the Opening Day laurels with a 5–4 victory.

| 1890 OPENING DAY SCHEDULE ||
|---|---|
| APRIL 19 | NATIONAL LEAGUE |
| CHI VS. CIN | CLEVE VS. PITTS |
| BRKLYN VS. BOST | PHIL VS. NY |

The 6,000 spectators were entertained with the usual Opening Day fanfare, which for the first time included the novelty of a carriage parade of the two teams through the downtown streets that reached the gates of the ballpark at 3 o'clock. Many of the other team's openers featured similar promotional activities, as the NL and the American Association prepared for the challenge from the new Players League, which opened its inaugural season in New York, Boston, Buffalo and Pittsburgh. (The Players League survived only one season.)

The Reds had every chance to open the 1890 season with a victory. They squandered leads of 2–0 and 4–2. They out hit Chicago eight to four. Jesse Duryea, the Reds leading pitcher from the 1889 season, pitched an outstanding game, racking up eight strikeouts, but five errors and timely hitting by Chicago made the difference.

Bug Holliday, the Cincinnati center fielder put the Reds ahead, 2–0, in the first inning with a home run to left over the outfielder's head. But Chicago evened the tally at 2–2 on two hits, a passed ball, a sacrifice and a ground out.

In the third, after the Reds had taken a 4–2 lead, the Colts countered with what proved to be the winning rally. A double, a three-base error by Reds left fielder Joe Knight, and a long home run to right-center by Chicago center fielder Walt Wilmot accounted for the three runs. Duryea did not give up a hit the rest of the game, but the Colts Bill Hutchinson matched him, goose egg for goose egg, and the big crowd went home cold and unhappy.

The papers gave close attention to the brisk weather and the parade:

*Before the game the Chicago and Cincinnati teams, in uniform and headed by the First Regiment Band, paraded the streets, and they did not arrive at the ball grounds until a few minutes to 3 o'clock. The players of both teams left the carriages at the gate, and marched upon the field. As the two teams with military-like precision came across the field to the strains of an inspiring march, every body was on their feet.*

*Men swung their hats and yelled themselves hoarse, while the ladies clapped their hands and waved their handkerchiefs. The crowd numbered more than six thousand, which must be estimated as a very large attendance for a week-day game with the weather so unfavorable. Chilling winds blew across the field, much to the discomfiture of the players and spectators alike. The air was pneumonia-breeding and many stayed at home on this account.*

*The victory should have belonged to the Cincinnatis but stupid base running and loose fielding allowed the Chicagos to carry off the prize.* [Cincinnati Commercial Gazette and Cincinnati Enquirer]

| OPENING DAY TRIVIA ||
|---|---|
| STAR OF THE GAME | CHICAGO CENTER FIELDER WALT WILMOT |
| WEATHER | 50°; CLEAR AND WINDY |
| ATTENDANCE | 6,000 |
| NOTABLE | FIRST PARADE & FIRST GAME BACK IN NL |
| RATING | ◐◐◐◐ |

# Rain and Spiders Spoil Opener
## Cleveland Wins, 6–3

Opening Day is referred to as as the "Opening Championship Game," in this 1891 headline.

In the mud and slop that passed for the Cincinnati Base Ball Park, the Cleveland Spiders defeated the home town club, 6–3, on an Opening Day better suited for rain gear and boots than uniforms and spikes.

The start of the opener was delayed for over 30 minutes by a mid-afternoon shower that began around 2 o'clock. Weber's Band entertained the spectators who gathered under the roofs of the stands and watched the water puddle on the field. The teams arrived at the park from their parade through the downtown streets just as the rains commenced.

As the game was about to be called off, the skies lightened, the rain stopped and the ground crew worked feverishly to make the field playable. Even the Reds players joined in, led by their captain, Arlie Latham, who sprinkled sawdust about the diamond.

Despite the mud and areas of standing water in the outfield, the umpire called, "Play ball" at 3:39, and Cincinnati came to the bat. The Reds set the pattern for the afternoon: They threatened, but failed to score. In the bottom of the first, Cleveland took a 3–0 lead, an advantage they would never surrender. George Davis, who had an outstanding game at the plate and in the field, singled in one run. Davis also had a run-scoring triple in the three-run sixth, which put the Spiders up, 6–0.

Breathtaking defensive plays by Cleveland stopped the Reds from scoring in the first and second innings. In the first inning, with two on, John Reilly hit a smash back through the middle with such force that pitcher Farmer Young nearly turned upside down trying to catch the ball. He recovered and threw out Reilly at first. In the second, with two on, Davis saved two and possibly three runs with a running one-handed catch of Bid McPhee's long drive into right-center. According to the *Commercial Gazette*, "The play was so brilliant and unexpected that it incited a great outburst of applause."

The papers gave as much attention to the weather as they did the game: *Just at the time when business men usually desert their desks and start for the base ball park rain was coming down in bucketfuls. At 3:15 there was a break in the clouds and the crowd began to cheer. When Superintendent Oehler and his corps of juvenile assistants marched on the field with brooms in their hands, they howled with delight. They worked with a will. Captain Latham rolled up his sleeves and lent a hand. They swept off the puddles and dumped sundry and copious wheelbarrow-loads of sawdust around the pitcher's box, third base and the home plate. The grounds were put in fair condition, and the game was started with the players standing ankle deep in mud and water.*
[*Cincinnati Commercial Gazette* and *Cincinnati Enquirer*]

### 1891 OPENING DAY SCHEDULE
| APRIL 22 | NATIONAL LEAGUE |
|---|---|
| CLEVE VS. CIN | CHI VS. PITTS |
| BRKLYN VS. PHIL | BOST VS. NY |

### OPENING DAY TRIVIA
| | |
|---|---|
| STAR OF THE GAME | CLEVELAND CENTER FIELDER GEORGE DAVIS |
| WEATHER | 63°; CLOUDY; DAMP |
| ATTENDANCE | 4,503 |
| NOTABLE | RAIN DELAYS START BY 30 MINUTES |
| RATING | |

# 1892 Beckley's Homer Leads Pittsburgh
## 3-Run Blast Dooms Reds

*The Pirates' Jake Beckley, who joined the Reds in 1897, hit a first-inning home run.*

The cool temperatures for Opening Day must have chilled the Reds bats, for Cincinnati was able to ring up only six hits against Pittsburgh's Mark Baldwin and lost the game, 7–5.

Baldwin allowed a mere two hits through the first eight innings, and only a four-run rally in the ninth made the final score respectable.

The opener drew 7,648, a fine crowd on such a cold afternoon. The club threw open the gates at 1 o'clock and hundreds streamed into the grounds and quickly claimed seats in the sun. Many more sought out "old Sol" behind the ropes in center field. The usual Opening Day concert preceded the game, but the club did not hold a street parade.

The beginning of the game was delayed briefly as a squadron of police swept the outfield, moving the standees back from the diamond.

The Reds took a brief, 1–0, lead in the first inning, but big Jake Beckley quickly put the Pirates ahead. With two runners on base, Beckley lined a drive deep over Billy Halligan's head. The ball rolled all the way to the base of the embankment in deep right field, and before Halligan could retrieve it, Beckley was around third and in for a home run.

The boys from the Smoky City added additional tallies in the third, sixth and eighth off starter Tony Mullane, to take a 7–1 lead. The dwindling crowd finally found reason to cheer in the ninth inning. After two were out, the Reds scored one run and then loaded the bases. Bug Holliday lifted a high fly ball to left that rolled all the way to the picket fence. Three runs scored and Bug wound up on third. The blow brought the crowd to life, but Reds left fielder Tip O'Neill flied out and the Reds had dropped their fourth opener in a row.

The papers highlighted Beckley's home run and the ninth-inning rally: *It was a characteristic Cincinnati base-ball opening. There was the same great crowd, the same concert by a grand orchestra, the same bright summer sky with a December temperature, and last, but by far the most undesirable, the same old hollow-eyed defeat.*

*[With two on] the dangerous 'Pirate,' Jake Beckley, then faced Mullane. Tony sent him a fast high ball just to suit his fancy, and a groan went up from the multitude as they heard the ominous crack of the bat. It passed Billy Halligan with the speed of the "Royal Blue" train, bounded through the line of spectators and rolled up on the embankment.*

*The crowd was weary and disappointed when the ninth inning rolled around. That rally in the ninth saved many a cuss word. Many of the spectators who would have gone forth breathing maledictions on the heads "of a lot of rotten charley horse stiffs, who ought to be behind a plow instead of masquerading as ball-players," were in high glee by reason of the four runs.*

[*Cincinnati Commercial Gazette* and *Cincinnati Enquirer*]

### 1892 OPENING DAY SCHEDULE

| APRIL 12 | NATIONAL LEAGUE |
|---|---|
| PITTS VS. CIN | CHI VS. STL |
| CLEVE VS. LOU | BOST VS. WASH |
| BRKLYN VS. BALT | NY VS. PHIL |

### OPENING DAY TRIVIA

| STAR OF THE GAME | PITTSBURGH FIRST BASEMAN JAKE BECKLEY |
|---|---|
| WEATHER | 44°; CLEAR |
| ATTENDANCE | 7,468 |
| NOTABLE | NO PARADE |
| RATING | ⚾ |

# Mullane in Relief
## Reds Trample Chicago, 10–1;
## No-Hit Wonder Jones Suffers Sore Arm

*Tony Mullane won his third Opening Day game in 1893.*

After a month of rain and snow, the clouds parted, the sun shone and the Reds won the Opening Day battle over Chicago, 10–1.

The victory broke the Reds' four-game losing streak on Opening Day and gave Tony Mullane his third victory in six Opening Day appearances.

Mullane did not start the game; that honor went to young Bumpus Jones, who had endeared himself with Reds fans with his no-hitter in the last game of the 1892 season. That was also Mr. Jones' first big league game and the Reds cranks were quite intrigued to see what Bumpus would do for an encore.

Jones complained of a sore arm prior to the game but Captain Charlie Comiskey started him as planned. That was a mistake as Jones lasted only one inning. Perhaps his injury was related to the new pitching rules which increased the pitching distance from 50 feet to the modern dimension of 60 feet, six inches. Mullane pinch-hit for him in the second inning and was masterful, allowing four hits.

Like Jones, Chicago's starting pitcher Willie McGill also faltered. After McGill gave up six walks, three hits and four runs through 1⅓ innings, Captain Anson brought in newcomer Gus McGinnis. But it was too late. Mullane kept the Colts off the bases, and timely hitting and poor defense by Chicago allowed the Reds to score six more runs.

The high point of the game came in the fifth, when a controversial play resulted in two Cincinnati tallies. With Farmer Vaughn on third and George Henry on first, Charlie Duffee hit a hard ground ball to the shortstop who threw home to stop Vaughn from scoring. Vaughn was caught in a rundown. Before Vaughn was tagged out, Henry ran past the play and headed for home plate. The Chicago third baseman, who had just tagged Vaughn, threw home to nab Henry, but the throw was wild and Henry and Duffee scored. Anson loudly protested the runs, but umpire Bob Emslie ruled both runs counted.

Emslie later admitted he had never seen such a play. He made the call based on his own judgment and thought that "the league should make a rule covering this point."

The papers were most appreciative of the win and the weather:
*Providence was kind to the Reds yesterday. The weather, crowd, music, and best of all, victory were with them. After two weeks of rain, snow and all other kinds of weather, Old Sol managed to get his face in front of the clouds and looked down kindly and smilingly on the Reds opening.*

*The Chicagos were the first to appear upon the field but the cheers that greeted the Chicagos were nothing in comparison with the grand ovation that was given the Reds when they moved with measured tread across the field attired in jackets of dazzling red.* [Cincinnati Commercial Gazette and Cincinnati Enquirer]

### 1893 Opening Day Schedule
**April 27  National League**
| | |
|---|---|
| Chi vs. Cin | Lou vs. StL |
| Clev vs. Pitts | Bost vs. NY |
| Brklyn vs. Phil | Balt vs. Wash |

### Opening Day Trivia
| | |
|---|---|
| Star of the Game | Reds Pitcher Tony Mullane |
| Weather | 55°; Sunny Skies |
| Attendance | 7,000 |
| Notable | First Opening Day Win in 4 Years |
| Rating | ●●●●  |

# 1894 League Park Opens
## It's a Holli-day!

*Bug Holliday hit the first Cincinnati Opening Day grand-slam home run in 1894.*

The Reds inaugurated a new grandstand with a come-from-behind victory over Chicago in one of the most glorious Opening Days in the history of Cincinnati baseball. The winning blow was a bases-full home run by Bug Holliday.

The only missing ingredient was sunshine, but the drama of the game and the grandeur of the new stands warmed the spectators. The game, which was postponed one day, drew 6,285 to the new facility, an excellent showing given the blustery, damp conditions. The weather caused the cancellation of the parade and dedication ceremonies scheduled for pre-game.

The players, however, did not seem affected by the conditions. They rapped out a total of 23 hits, including four home runs.

But the two everyone will remember came in the sixth inning. The Reds trailed, 6–5, when pitcher Tom Parrott stroked a long drive into the left-center field seats and trotted in with a home run that tied the game. Chicago pitcher Bill Hutchinson subsequently unraveled. He walked Dummy Hoy, Jack McCarthy beat out a bunt, Arlie Latham laid down a sacrifice, and Hutchinson threw wide to first, loading the bases. Holliday smashed a long fly into the left field seats bringing in four runs. The last innings were played in a drizzle, and the Colts never rallied.

The papers lavished praise on the crowd and Holliday, but found some fault with the layout of the new field: *The grounds were in miserable shape for a game, but [Reds] President [John] Brush was determined to have the opening. Until within half an hour of calling "play ball" a delegation of sponge manipulators moved over the diamond mopping up the moisture and squeezing it into tin cans.*

*The game was a model, one of those kind of games that has made baseball the national sport. Never was there any more excitement or enthusiasm displayed here or anywhere else as was in yesterday's game.*

*[With Holliday at bat] the ball came up, the bat met it and in a few seconds it was over among those seats near the carriage gate. Three runs had come in, and amid the shrieks, yells and applause of the multitude, the Bug came trotting home—a hero from Heroicville. For nearly two minutes the excitement continued and on his return to the field the sun gods gave another ovation to "The Bug," who had sent the Colts to the stable.*

*It is too late to speak of mistakes that were made in building the new stand at the Cincinnati Park. The bounds of the field have been diminished so much by the new stands and terrace seats that it is an easy matter to make a home run. The patrons of the club, however, are offered the best accommodations, and every one can't but appreciate the new and handsome stand, with its roomy seats.* [Cincinnati Commercial Gazette, Cincinnati Times Star, and Cincinnati Enquirer]

### OPENING DAY TRIVIA

| | |
|---|---|
| STAR OF THE GAME | CINCINNATI LEFT FIELDER BUG HOLLIDAY |
| WEATHER | 50°; CLOUDY, DAMP |
| ATTENDANCE | 6,285 |
| NOTABLE | FIRST GAME AT LEAGUE PARK |
| RATING | ●●●●● |

### April 20, 1894

| Cincinnati. | AB. | R. | BH. | SB. | SH. | PO. | A. | E. |
|---|---|---|---|---|---|---|---|---|
| Hoy, c. f. | 4 | 1 | 0 | 0 | 0 | 3 | 1 | 0 |
| McCarthy, r. f. | 5 | 1 | 2 | 0 | 0 | 3 | 0 | 0 |
| Latham, 3b. | 5 | 1 | 0 | 0 | 0 | 1 | 2 | 2 |
| Holliday, l. f. | 4 | 2 | 3 | 0 | 0 | 2 | 0 | 0 |
| McPhee, 2b. | 4 | 1 | 0 | 0 | 0 | 2 | 4 | 0 |
| Motz 1b | 5 | 1 | 4 | 0 | 0 | 11 | 0 | 0 |
| Murphy, c. | 4 | 2 | 2 | 0 | 0 | 5 | 0 | 0 |
| Smith, s. s. | 5 | 0 | 0 | 0 | 0 | 0 | 2 | 0 |
| Parrott, p. | 5 | 1 | 2 | 0 | 0 | 0 | 4 | 0 |
| Totals | 41 | 10 | 12 | 1 | 0 | 27 | 13 | 2 |

| Chicago. | AB. | R. | BH. | SB. | SH. | PO. | A. | E. |
|---|---|---|---|---|---|---|---|---|
| Camp, 2b. | 5 | 0 | 0 | 0 | 0 | 4 | 3 | 1 |
| Dahlen, 3b. | 4 | 0 | 0 | 0 | 0 | 3 | 2 | 0 |
| Wilmot, l. f. | 5 | 0 | 2 | 0 | 0 | 2 | 0 | 0 |
| Dungan, r. f. | 5 | 1 | 2 | 0 | 0 | 3 | 0 | 0 |
| Lange, c. f. | 4 | 2 | 2 | 0 | 0 | 2 | 0 | 0 |
| Decker, 1b. | 4 | 2 | 2 | 0 | 0 | 4 | 0 | 1 |
| Irwin, s. s. | 3 | 0 | 0 | 0 | 1 | 1 | 5 | 2 |
| Hutchinson, p. | 3 | 1 | 1 | 0 | 0 | 1 | 1 | 1 |
| Kittredge, c. | 4 | 0 | 2 | 0 | 0 | 4 | 2 | 0 |
| Totals | 37 | 6 | 10 | 0 | 1 | 24 | 13 | 5 |

| Innings. | 1 | 2 | 3 | 4 | 5 | 6 | 7 | 8 | 9 | |
|---|---|---|---|---|---|---|---|---|---|---|
| Cincinnati | 1 | 0 | 2 | 0 | 1 | 5 | 0 | 0 | — | 10 |
| Chicago | 0 | 4 | 0 | 1 | 1 | 0 | 0 | 0 | — | 6 |

Earned runs—Cincinnati 6, Chicago 6. Home runs—Holliday, Parrott, Decker, Hutchinson. Two-base hits—Motz 2, Wilmot, Dungan, Lange, Kittredge. Stolen base—Holliday. Bases on balls—By Parrott 2, Hutchinson 2. Left on bases—Cincinnati 10, Chicago 7. Struck out—By Parrott 3, Hutchinson 1. Time of game—One hour and fifty minutes. Umpire—Mr. Swartwood.

### 1894 OPENING DAY SCHEDULE

| APRIL 19 | NATIONAL LEAGUE |
|---|---|
| CHI VS. CIN (PP) | PITTS VS. STL |
| CLEV VS. LOU (PP) | NY VS. BALT |
| BRKLYN VS. BOST | PHIL VS. WASH |

# A Marvelous Opener in Cincinnati
## Ewing Leads the Reds

Mayor Caldwell tossed out the ceremonial first pitch—the first-ever at a Reds opener—and made a brief speech.

| 1895 OPENING DAY SCHEDULE | |
|---|---|
| **APRIL 18** | **NATIONAL LEAGUE** |
| CLEVE VS. CIN | CHI VS. STL |
| PITTS VS. LOU | BRKLYN VS. NY |
| PHIL VS. BALT | |
| **APRIL 19** | **NATIONAL LEAGUE** |
| WASH VS. BOST | |

| OPENING DAY TRIVIA | |
|---|---|
| STAR OF THE GAME | REDS FIRST BASEMAN AND CAPTAIN BUCK EWING |
| WEATHER | 65°; CLEAR |
| ATTENDANCE | 13,297 |
| NOTABLE | LARGEST CROWD TO DATE; PARADE RESUMES |
| RATING | ⚾⚾⚾⚾⚾ |

The great Buck Ewing returned to his hometown for the first time in a Cincinnati uniform, and led his teammates to a thrilling, 10–9, victory over Cleveland. An enormous crowd of 13,297, the largest Opening Day attendance to date, filled the stands and spilled out onto the grounds.

Many were there to usher in another season of baseball, but the main attraction was Ewing, one of the game's greatest players. The 35-year-old Ewing, who made his home in Cincinnati's East End, had played 15 seasons, but this was the first playing for the team in red stockings.

Ewing had the crowd buzzing in the first inning with a single and a steal of second base. He drove in a run in the third with another single. But he saved the best for last, a dramatic defensive play in the ninth inning that preserved the Reds win.

The Reds, who at one time led 10–4, watched the Cleveland boys rally in innings six through eight, and pull to within two runs. In the ninth, with runners on second and third and one out, Jimmy McAleer grounded back to the pitcher, who threw to Ewing for the out at first.

Ewing immediately saw that the runner on second, Cleveland captain Patsy Tebeau, had headed for third base, thinking Ed McKean was running home on the play. But McKean was still on third, and before Tebeau could retreat, Ewing dashed across the diamond and trapped Tebeau between bases. Ewing allowed McKean to run home and concentrated on Tebeau.

"Throw it home!" shouted Tebeau as he tried to dodge Ewing. But Ewing wisely ignored the advice and chased Tebeau back to second and tossed the ball to Bid McPhee who applied the putout. A roar burst forth from the stands, the fans tossed seat cushions into the air, and hundreds flooded onto the field to congratulate the winners.

The opener drew such interest that the streetcars became overcrowded and one man, hanging from the side, was pinned against a bridge railing and killed.

The papers commented on the big crowd and the Opening Day festivities, the most elaborate to date: *Cincinnati [took] a half holiday and paid a most eloquent tribute to the occasion by sending such another crush and jam of humanity to the park. The [street] cars were crowded early in the afternoon, and as the hour of the game approached, they were stuffed to their fullest capacity. In the crush, one man was killed at the Plum-street bridge.*

*The parade was an ovation. The idea of the club's making a car circuit of the city, headed by Weber's great band, showed that somebody in the management of the affair had a head on him! Gangs of boys ran the breath out of their bodies trying to keep up, and it was with some difficulty the cars could be got away from the Gibson House without running over somebody.*
[*Cincinnati Commercial Gazette and Cincinnati Enquirer*]

# 1896 Big Crowd; Big Let Down
## Pittsburgh Wins Easily, 9–1

*Political dignitaries began attending the opener in the 1890s, including George B Cox (left), the political "boss" of Cincinnati.*

### 1896 OPENING DAY SCHEDULE

| APRIL 16 | NATIONAL LEAGUE | |
|---|---|---|
| PITTS VS. CIN | | CHI VS. LOU |
| CLEV VS. STL | | BOST VS. PHIL |
| BRKLYN VS. BALT | | NY VS. WASH |

The Reds should have stayed on the streetcars.

The trolley parade, which had become one of the most popular features of the opening day festivities, drew thousands of well-wishers who cheered the teams at every stop along the downtown route.

But, as it turned out, those were the only cheers Buck Ewing's boys heard on this warm and sunny Opening Day. The Pittsburgh team trounced the Reds, 9-1, before another record crowd of over 14,000, the second consecutive year the opener broke an attendance record.

The Reds kept the game close for five innings, with Cincinnati's Billy Rhines matching Pittsburgh's Pink Hawley pitch-for-pitch. But Rhines tired, Reds substitute second baseman Bill Grey fumbled two plays, and Pittsburgh racked up eight runs over the final four innings.

The game might have ended more to the big crowd's satisfaction had the injured Bid McPhee been in his regular position at second base. Grey's error in the sixth led to one unearned run and his poor throw in the seventh led to two more unearned tallies.

The Reds' only run came in the second inning on back-to-back triples by Germany Smith and Charlie Irwin. Smith's triple created the most interesting play of the day. His long fly to right should have been caught by Patsey Donovan, who lost it in the sun at the last moment. Smith ran full speed to third with his eyes set on home. But Pittsburgh third basemen Denny Lyons pulled one of the oldest and cheapest tricks in the book. He backed into Smith and knocked him off-stride. Smith kicked at Lyons and the two scuffled briefly. Smith eventually scored on Irwin's triple. Lyons, a Cincinnati native, was loudly hissed by the fans during the remainder of the game.

The papers gave the contest itself little attention, focusing their coverage on the crowd, the pre-game ceremonies, and Mose, a monkey the Reds adopted as a mascot: *The day was a perfect one for baseball. The sun was as cordial as a long-lost friend. Early in the afternoon the tide set in toward the park, and by the time the Pittsburgs took the field for practice every available seat, and some that were not available, had been filled.*

*In spite of the fact that the mascot monkey Mose had a suit on something similar to the Reds' natty new uniforms, and all the players petted him before the game he could not pull the home team out of the hole....*

*Every man and boy was given a "Rooters' Button," and every lady a half-toned group [photograph] of the famous Champions of '69, as a souvenir of the opening of the league season of 1896.*

*Had the Reds but heeded Mayor Caldwell's advice, given just before he tossed the ball into he field before the games, there might have been several runs added to the Cincinnati team totals. His Honor said, "I now direct you to play ball." The Pittsburgs played the tip. The Reds did not.*
**[Cincinnati Commercial Gazette, Cincinnati Times-Star, and Cincinnati Enquirer]**

### OPENING DAY TRIVIA

| | |
|---|---|
| STAR OF THE GAME | PITTSBURGH PITCHER PINK HAWLEY |
| WEATHER | 86°; SUNNY |
| ATTENDANCE | 14,412 |
| NOTABLE | WARMEST OPENER ON RECORD |
| RATING | ⚾⚾ |

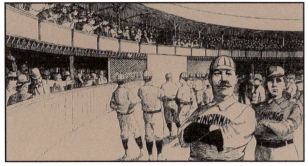

*Captains Buck Ewing (center) and Cap Anson (right) wait in vain for the mayor to arrive and throw out the first pitch.*

# 1897

# Reds Win in 10!

## Irwin's Hit Clinches Comeback

### April 22, 1897

| Cincinnati. | AB. | R. | BH. | SB. | SH. | SO. | BB. | PO. | A. | E. |
|---|---|---|---|---|---|---|---|---|---|---|
| Burke, l.f. | 4 | 1 | 0 | 0 | 0 | 1 | 1 | 3 | 0 | 0 |
| Hoy, c.f. | 5 | 1 | 1 | 1 | 0 | 0 | 0 | 5 | 0 | 1 |
| McPhee, 2b. | 4 | 0 | 1 | 0 | 0 | 0 | 1 | 2 | 3 | 0 |
| Miller, r.f. | 5 | 1 | 1 | 0 | 0 | 0 | 0 | 2 | 0 | 1 |
| Peitz, c. | 4 | 0 | 0 | 0 | 1 | 2 | 0 | 3 | 2 | 0 |
| Vaughn, 1b. | 5 | 1 | 2 | 0 | 0 | 0 | 0 | 11 | 0 | 0 |
| Irwin, 3b. | 4 | 3 | 2 | 4 | 0 | 0 | 1 | 1 | 5 | 1 |
| Richey, s.s. | 4 | 2 | 3 | 0 | 0 | 0 | 0 | 3 | 5 | 1 |
| Ehret, p. | 3 | 0 | 0 | 0 | 0 | 1 | 0 | 0 | 3 | 0 |
| *Schriver | 1 | 0 | 0 | 0 | 0 | 0 | 0 | 0 | 0 | 0 |
| Rhines, p. | 0 | 0 | 0 | 0 | 0 | 0 | 0 | 0 | 1 | 0 |
| Totals | 39 | 8 | 16 | 0 | 1 | 4 | 3 | 30 | 15 | 6 |

| Chicago. | AB. | R. | BH. | SB. | SH. | SO. | BB. | PO. | A. | E. |
|---|---|---|---|---|---|---|---|---|---|---|
| Everitt, 3b. | 6 | 0 | 1 | 0 | 0 | 0 | 0 | 0 | 1 | 1 |
| Dahlen, s.s. | 4 | 2 | 2 | 1 | 0 | 0 | 1 | 3 | 6 | 1 |
| Lange, c.f. | 5 | 1 | 1 | 0 | 1 | 0 | 0 | 2 | 0 | 0 |
| Ryan, r.f. | 6 | 1 | 3 | 0 | 0 | 0 | 0 | 0 | 0 | 0 |
| Decker, 1b. | 4 | 0 | 1 | 0 | 1 | 1 | 0 | 16 | 0 | 0 |
| Thornton, l.f. | 4 | 3 | 2 | 1 | 0 | 0 | 1 | 2 | 0 | 1 |
| Pfeffer, 2b. | 3 | 0 | 0 | 0 | 1 | 1 | 0 | 0 | 1 | 2 |
| Griffith, p. | 5 | 0 | 0 | 0 | 0 | 0 | 0 | 4 | 3 | 0 |
| Kittredge, c. | 4 | 0 | 1 | 0 | 0 | 0 | 1 | 5 | 1 | 0 |
| Totals | 42 | 7 | 11 | 2 | 3 | 2 | 3 | †28 | 13 | 5 |

| Innings | 1 | 2 | 3 | 4 | 5 | 6 | 7 | 8 | 9 | 10 | |
|---|---|---|---|---|---|---|---|---|---|---|---|
| Cincinnati | 0 | 0 | 4 | 0 | 0 | 0 | 0 | 0 | 2 | 2 | —8 |
| Chicago | 1 | 1 | 3 | 0 | 1 | 1 | 0 | 0 | 0 | 1 | —7 |

*Batted for Ehret.
†One man out when winning run was scored.
Earned Runs—Off Ehret 2, off Griffith 5.
Two-base Hits—Richey, Lange, Dahlen.
Three-base Hits—Vaughn, Thornton.
Double Plays—Dahlen and Decker; Irwin and Vaughn.
Bases on Balls—By Ehret, Dahlen, Thornton; by Rhines, Kittredge; by Griffith, Irwin, Burke, McPhee.
Hit by Pitcher—By Ehret, Lange.
Left on Bases—Cincinnati 7, Chicago 4.
Passed Balls—None.
Wild Pitch—None.
Innings Pitched—By Ehret 9, by Rhines 1, by Griffith 10.
No. Hits Made—Off Ehret 10, off Rhines 1, off Griffith 16.
Reached First on Errors—Cincinnati 2, Chicago 3.
Time of Game—Two hours and ten minutes.
Weather—Fair.
Condition of Ground—Fast.
Umpire—Mr. Sheridan.

In one of their most thrilling openers ever, the Reds rallied three times to catch the Cubs and finally passed them in the bottom of the 10th inning for a 8–7 victory.

With one out in the 10th, Charlie Irwin cracked out a single to left field that brought in Harry Vaughn from third base with the winning run. The crowd erupted in a roar and surged onto the field.

"That was one of the finest games of baseball I have ever seen in my life," said Reds owner John T. Brush.

The crowd had every reason to fear another Opening Day defeat as the Reds and starter Red Ehret quickly fell behind, 4–0.

But in the third, with a little help from Chicago second baseman Fred Pfeffer, the Reds tied the score. With one out and the bases full, Dummy Hoy sent what looked like a double-play to Pfeffer. But the wickets were open and the ball rolled into right field. Two runs scored and when shortstop Bill Dahlen overthrew third base, the third run tallied. Hoy came in minutes later on a Bid McPhee single.

The Colts tallied twice more to take a 6–4 margin into the bottom of the ninth. But another error by Pfeffer, a double by rookie Claude Ritchey and a single by Hoy tied the score.

Again, the Colts took the lead, this time off of relief pitcher Billy Rhines. A triple and a sacrifice fly put Chicago ahead, 7–6.

But these Reds knew how to rally. Dusty Miller singled, Vaughn tripled and Irwin finished the day with his game-winner to left field.

The fantastic finish let Mayor Caldwell off the hook. At game time, the mayor, who was to deliver the opening remarks and the first pitch, was missing. After a short wait, the umpire called for the game to begin, sans ceremony. Business manager Frank Bancroft had dispatched a carriage to pick up the mayor, but by some misunderstanding the vehicle never arrived.

The annual streetcar parade, however, was a grand success. Three decorated cars carrying the Reds, the Chicago players and Weber's Band paraded through the downtown streets before the game. The boys disembarked at at the Gibson House about noon for a light lunch before heading to the ballpark.

Rookie shortstop Claude Ritchey had a brilliant debut and received considerable praise in the press (Ritchey played just this one season with the Reds, but he went on to have a fine 13-year career): *Ritchey's work in yesterday's game was the talk of the town last night. The youngster was as cool as a cucumber at all times. Two of his three hits came at times when they were most needed. It was Ritchey's safe bunt that started that rally in the third, and it was his two-bagger that started the rally in the ninth. All through the game Ritchey was the recipient of applause. The crowd was pleased with his earnest efforts, and took pains to show it.* ***[Cincinnati Commercial Tribune, Cincinnati Times-Star, and Cincinnati Enquirer]***

### Opening Day Trivia

| | |
|---|---|
| Star of the Game | Reds Third Baseman Charley Irwin |
| Weather | 74°; Partly Cloudy |
| Attendance | 11,448 |
| Notable | Mayor Misses Opening Pitch Ceremony |
| Rating | ⚾⚾⚾⚾⚾ |

### 1897 Opening Day Schedule

| | |
|---|---|
| April 19 | National League |
| Phil vs. Bost | |
| April 22 | National League |
| Chi vs. Cin | Cleve vs. Lou |
| Pitt vs. StL | Brklyn vs. Wash |
| Bost vs. Balt | NY vs. Phil |

# 1898
# Breitenstein Bests Cy Young
## Reds Defeat Cleveland, 3–2

*Ted Breitenstein (on right in second row) was a small left-hander with a big curveball.*

| 1898 OPENING DAY SCHEDULE ||
|---|---|
| APRIL 15 NATIONAL LEAGUE ||
| CLEV VS. CIN | PITTS VS. LOU |
| CHI VS. STL | BALT VS. WASH |
| BRKLYN VS. PHIL | BOST VS. NY |

The great Cy Young allowed only seven hits and one earned run, but the Reds' Ted Breitenstein bested the Cleveland ace, as the Reds pulled out a 3–2 victory.

Some 10,000 spectators filled the grounds and watched Breitenstein, who won 23 games in 1897, dominate Cleveland. He allowed five hits, walked four and used his curve ball to escape trouble.

The day's festivities began in the late morning with the downtown trolley parade. The players enjoyed a sumptuous spread at noon at the Gibson House, and Weber's Band delighted the early arrivals at the ball park with a concert. Mayor Gustav Tafel, from his box in the grandstand, deftly handled his opening remarks and tossed out the first pitch.

The only blemish on the day was the poor condition of the field. Five feet of flood water covered the surface a week earlier. The floodwaters left a line on the grandstand beams that drew the attention of many spectators. That the game was played as scheduled was a testament to the laying on of hands by field superintendent John Schwab and his sons.

The Reds scored first in the top of the third inning without a hit. Charlie Irwin walked, Heinie Peitz sacrificed him to second, a passed ball moved him to third, and Breitenstein brought Irwin home with a short sacrifice fly to left. The Reds added a second run in the fourth, but the Indians tied the game in their half of the inning on hits by Jimmy McAleer and Patsy Tebeau. The Reds scored the winning run in the sixth, when Elmer Smith, Miller and Bid McPhee singled off Young.

A rash of rowdy behavior in the 1897 season prompted some changes in 1898. The league assigned two umpires to each game. A new warning sign from Reds management greeted Cincinnati "cranks": "Any spectator who insults a player or umpire by use of profane or obscene language will be expelled from this ball park." The Reds' opener went off with no problems. The spectators, umpires and club officials enjoyed a game played without kicking or squabbles.

Cy Young averted one possible incident when he stopped from running over Breitenstein along the first base line. Young had hit a weak grounder toward first and Breitenstein's fielding effort put him directly in Young's path. But rather than run Breitenstein over, Young—who had 50 pounds on the smaller Reds pitcher—avoided the collision. The *Commercial Tribune* noted, "Little exhibitions of manhood of that sort do not go by unnoticed, and Cy was complimented on all sides in the stands."

The papers praised the crowd: *It was a representative baseball crowd, including many of the best known men of the city with their wives and daughters. Music, sunshine, enthusiasm, a concourse of well-dressed people and above all, glorious victory.*
[*Cincinnati Commercial Tribune, Cincinnati Times-Star, and Cincinnati Enquirer*]

| OPENING DAY TRIVIA ||
|---|---|
| STAR OF THE GAME | REDS PITCHER TED BREITENSTEIN |
| WEATHER | 67°; SUNNY |
| ATTENDANCE | 10,000 |
| NOTABLE | FLOOD WATERS COVERED FIELD A WEEK EARLIER |
| RATING | ●●● |

**APRIL 15, 1898**

| CINCINNATI | AB | R | BH | SH | PO | A | E |
|---|---|---|---|---|---|---|---|
| McFarland, m. | 3 | 0 | 0 | 0 | 3 | 0 | 0 |
| Smith, l. | 4 | 1 | 2 | 0 | 1 | 0 | 0 |
| Beckley, 1. | 4 | 1 | 0 | 0 | 11 | 0 | 0 |
| Miller, r. | 4 | 0 | 2 | 0 | 1 | 0 | 0 |
| McPhee, 2. | 4 | 0 | 1 | 0 | 2 | 5 | 0 |
| Corcoran, s. | 4 | 0 | 0 | 0 | 2 | 1 | 0 |
| Irwin, 3. | 2 | 1 | 0 | 0 | 1 | 0 | 0 |
| Peitz, c. | 3 | 0 | 1 | 1 | 2 | 3 | 1 |
| Breitenstein, p. | 3 | 0 | 0 | 0 | 2 | 3 | 0 |
| Totals | 31 | 3 | 7 | 1 | 27 | 12 | 1 |
| CLEVELAND. | AB | R | BH | SH | PO | A | E |
| Burkett, l. | 4 | 0 | 2 | 0 | 1 | 0 | 0 |
| McKean, s. | 3 | 0 | 0 | 1 | 2 | 2 | 1 |
| Childs, 2. | 3 | 1 | 0 | 0 | 4 | 2 | 0 |
| Wallace, 3. | 4 | 0 | 0 | 1 | 1 | 1 | 0 |
| McAleer, m. | 3 | 1 | 1 | 0 | 4 | 0 | 0 |
| Blake, r. | 3 | 0 | 0 | 0 | 1 | 0 | 0 |
| Tebeau, 1. | 4 | 0 | 1 | 0 | 11 | 0 | 1 |
| O'Connor, c. | 3 | 0 | 0 | 0 | 4 | 1 | 0 |
| Young, p. | 3 | 0 | 0 | 0 | 3 | 3 | 1 |
| Totals | 29 | 2 | 4 | 1 | 27 | 15 | 3 |

Innings        1 2 3 4 5 6 7 8 9
Cincinnati     0 0 1 1 0 1 0 0 0—3
Cleveland      0 0 0 2 0 0 0 0 0—2

Two-base Hits—Burkett, McAleer.
Three-base Hits—Miller, Burkett.
Struck Out—By Breitenstein 2, by Young 1.
Bases on Balls—By Breitenstein 4, by Young 1.
Hit by Pitcher—By Young 1.
Passed Ball—O'Connor.
Time of Game—One hour and forty minutes.
Umpires—Swartwood and Wood.

*Bid McPhee played the last of his 17 openers in 1899.*

# 1899 Reds Late Rally Falls Short
## Pittsburgh Pulls Away for 5–2 Win

### April 15, 1899

| CINCINNATI | AB | R | BH | SH | PO | A | E |
|---|---|---|---|---|---|---|---|
| McBride, r. f. | 4 | 1 | 2 | 0 | 1 | 0 | 0 |
| Selbach, c. f. | 4 | 0 | 1 | 0 | 1 | 0 | 1 |
| Smith, l. f. | 4 | 1 | 1 | 0 | 4 | 0 | 1 |
| Corcoran, s. s. | 4 | 0 | 1 | 0 | 1 | 5 | 0 |
| McPhee, 2b | 4 | 0 | 2 | 0 | 1 | 6 | 0 |
| Beckley, 1b | 3 | 0 | 1 | 0 | 16 | 0 | 0 |
| Steinfeldt, 3b | 4 | 0 | 0 | 0 | 0 | 4 | 0 |
| Peitz, c | 4 | 0 | 2 | 0 | 2 | 1 | 0 |
| Hawley, p | 3 | 0 | 0 | 0 | 1 | 1 | 0 |
| Totals | 34 | 2 | 11 | 0 | 27 | 16 | 2 |

| PITTSBURG | AB | R | BH | SH | PO | A | E |
|---|---|---|---|---|---|---|---|
| Donovan, r. f. | 5 | 1 | 1 | 0 | 2 | 0 | 0 |
| McCarthy, l. f. | 5 | 1 | 1 | 0 | 2 | 0 | 0 |
| McCreery, c. f. | 5 | 1 | 2 | 0 | 2 | 0 | 1 |
| Clarke, 1b | 2 | 0 | 1 | 1 | 11 | 0 | 0 |
| Williams, 3b | 3 | 0 | 0 | 0 | 1 | 1 | 0 |
| Reitz, 2b | 4 | 0 | 1 | 0 | 4 | 5 | 0 |
| Ely, s. s. | 4 | 1 | 2 | 0 | 2 | 4 | 0 |
| Schriver, c | 3 | 0 | 1 | 1 | 3 | 1 | 0 |
| Tannehill, p | 4 | 1 | 2 | 0 | 0 | 6 | 0 |
| Totals | 34 | 5 | 10 | 2 | 27 | 17 | 1 |

| Innings | 1 | 2 | 3 | 4 | 5 | 6 | 7 | 8 | 9 |
|---|---|---|---|---|---|---|---|---|---|
| Cincinnati | 0 | 0 | 0 | 0 | 0 | 0 | 0 | 2 | 0 — 2 |
| Pittsburg | 0 | 0 | 0 | 0 | 1 | 0 | 0 | 2 | 2 — 5 |

Stolen Base—McPhee.
Two-base Hits—McCreery 2, Schriver.
Home Run—McCarthy.
Double Plays—Ely to Reitz to Clarke; Reitz to Clarke; McPhee to Corcoran.
Struck Out—By Hawley 2, by Tannehill.
Bases on Balls—By Hawley 2, by Tannehill 1.
Hit by Pitcher—By Hawley 1.
Passed Ball—Schriver.
Time of Game—Two hours and fifteen minutes.
Umpires—Swartwood and Warner.

Maybe it was the uniforms.

The Reds new white shirts did not arrive in time for the opener, so the players took the field wearing their dark blue road shirts and white pants, an unusual sight for the home crowd.

Apparently the Reds never felt comfortable in their blues, for the visitors from Pittsburgh walked off with the Opening Day victory, 5–2. Pink Hawley was not sharp, but he pitched well enough to keep the Reds in the game until the ninth. But defensive lapses and poor baserunning did in the home club.

Despite their gaffes, the Reds rallied late to pull within one run in the eighth inning, and threatened to take the lead. But Tommy Corcoran was thrown out at the plate on the front end of a double steal, and the rally died. The Pirates tacked on two insurance runs in the ninth, and the big throng of 9,148 went home disappointed.

Dayton, Kentucky native Jesse Tannehill pitched a complete-game victory for Pittsburgh. He allowed 11 hits, but all were singles. The hero of the game for Pittsburgh was left fielder Jack McCarthy, the former Red, who made two dazzling catches in deep left field and knocked a home run over the center-field fence in the eighth inning.

While McCarthy dazzled the crowd with his outfield play, Reds left fielder Elmer Smith did not have an Opening Day to remember. Smith misplayed a long fly in the fifth into a double, allowing one run to score. In the ninth, Smith's failure to field Patsy Donovan's single permitted Tannehill to score all the way from first.

The papers were critical of the Reds: *One might as well be candid and say that the Reds were outplayed at every point of the game. The shivering enthusiasts who filled all the stands stomped their feet to keep warm, and rooted with might and main to [Cincinnati captain Buck] Ewing's men to get off in the lead, but their rooting was all for naught. There was something lacking in the Cincinnati's team work. There was a dearth of coaching, and they did everything in a purely mechanical way that did not carry any enthusiasm with it. In short, the Reds played a game that is best described by the expressive word, "dopey."*

*Everything the Reds did seemed to go wrong. They made every amateurish showing at the bunting game. It was what might be expected of a Millcreek bottom team, but from the Reds it was disgusting.*

*McCarthy made a splendid home-run. The ball cleared the center-field fence almost on a line with the home plate. It passed over the top board, with three or four feet to spare, and fell in the [street] car tracks on Western avenue. McCarthy was forced to doff his cap in acknowledgment of the applause that followed the home run.* [*Cincinnati Commercial Tribune, and Cincinnati Enquirer*]

### 1899 Opening Day Schedule

| April 14 | National League | |
|---|---|---|
| Chi vs. Lou | | Wash vs. Phil |
| **April 15** | **National League** | |
| Pitts vs. Cin | | Clev vs. StL |
| | Bost vs. Brklyn | |

### Opening Day Trivia

| | |
|---|---|
| Star of the Game | Pittsburgh Left Fielder Jack McCarthy |
| Weather | 62°; Cloudy |
| Attendance | 9,148 |
| Notable | Reds Wear Road Uniforms |
| Rating | ◠◠ |

# 1900 Reds Pitching Collapses
## Reds Fall to Chicago, 13–10

*The Reds argued umpire Hank O'Day's call in the sixth inning.*

**1900 OPENING DAY SCHEDULE**

| April 19 | National League | |
|---|---|---|
| Chi vs. Cin | | Pitts vs. StL |
| Phil vs. Bost | | Brklyn vs NY |

The Reds started the season and the century on the wrong foot with a 13–10 loss to Chicago on Opening Day, 1900.

For the first half of the contest, the Reds controlled things. Bill Phillips, who won 17 times for the Reds in 1899, was sailing along with a 5–2 lead going into the sixth inning.

The Reds had pecked away at Chicago starter Clark Griffith for five runs, and Phillips had the Colts off-balance with his change of pace and curves. But in the sixth, an error by Phillips allowed one run to score. That seemed to rattle the Reds pitcher, who surrendered three straight hits as the Colts took the lead.

The Reds retaliated, scoring three runs off relief pitcher Jack Menefee, two on a Tommy Corcoran single to move back in front, 8–6. The Colts answered with a five-run barrage in the seventh.

Rookie Ed Scott replaced Phillips and walked the first two batters. He might have escaped the inning, but Jack McCarthy doubled down the right field line to drive in two runs.

The Reds claimed the ball bounced foul just before it crossed the bag. Umpire Hank O'Day, who was calling balls and strikes from behind the pitcher, did not reverse his call, but admitted he was not in the best position to see the play.

"It is an impossibility for an umpire, standing behind the pitcher in the middle of the diamond to say positively whether a ball which goes right over or near the bag is safe or foul," said O'Day. "He just has to guess…. I am certain, however, that McCarthy's ball was fair, for I could see it bounding all the way."

The Colts scored three more runs in the seventh, then two more off Scott in the eighth. Although the Reds scored in the eighth and ninth, their efforts fell short. The nearly 12,000 spectators headed home, shaking their heads over one that slipped away.

The Opening Day ceremonies consisted of the familiar streetcar parade, the team luncheon at the Gibson House, the pre-game concert by Weber's Band and remarks by the mayor. It was the last opener held at League Park; the main stands were destroyed in a fire on May 28.

The papers paid particular attention to the fairer sex: *Merchants, bankers, brokers, doctors, lawyers, ministers, employers and employees, not forgetting the omnipresent small boy, were there. But one must not forget the ladies. They were present in such force as has never been seen before at League Park. Crowds of four and five hurried in to the grand stand, usually accompanied by some obliging male escort. The bright new spring garments and bonnets of the ladies added color and beauty to the occasion, and, to say the least, they made a brave and sparkling showing.* **[Cincinnati Commercial Tribune, and Cincinnati Enquirer]**

**OPENING DAY TRIVIA**

| | |
|---|---|
| Star of the Game | Reds Outfielder Jimmy Barrett |
| Weather | 70°; Clear |
| Attendance | 11,920 |
| Notable | 23 Combined Runs Most Since 1900 |
| Rating | ⚾⚾⚾ |

*The frigid conditions for the 1901 opener brought out the best in the local cartoonists. Bid McPhee and Fred Clarke captained the two nines.*

# A Frigid Opener
## 1901 Cold Conditions Contribute to Reds Defeat

They played ice ball at League Park to begin the 1901 season. The damp, windy and very cold weather that delayed the opener for two days failed to take the hint and leave town. Instead it lingered like a shroud and made this one of the coldest openers ever.

Pittsburgh provided no comfort to the 4,800 frozen "cranks," defeating the home team, 4–2. At least it was over quickly; the game lasted just over 90 minutes.

Frank "Noodles" Hahn pitched a strong game for the Reds, but three triples in the sixth inning yielded four runs and the Reds could not rally off Pittsburgh's Sam Leever, the Goshen, Ohio, schoolmaster.

The cold weather contributed to the Pirates rally. Hahn had allowed only one hit through the first five innings and had a 2–0 lead. He scored the second run in the fifth after he had tripled. But the Reds fifth inning was the longest of the game, and Hahn's noodle went cold.

"My arm was stiff from sitting on the bench when I started to pitch in the sixth and I lacked speed," Hahn explained.

Hahn attempted to warm up, tossing the ball to his first baseman, but new rules prohibited any warm-up tosses once the batter stepped to the plate. Hahn continued to toss to Beckley after Fred Clarke came to bat. Umpire Dwyer promptly called one ball, and Hahn was forced to stop tossing and pitch. Clarke smashed a triple to right and the triple parade began. Honus Wagner and Kitty Bransfield followed with triples into the ruins of the League Park grandstand in deep left. Two errors brought in the final tallies.

At least four balls rolled into the debris from the old grandstand which had burned in 1900. After the fire, the Reds constructed a new diamond in what was deep right field and played the entire last half of the 1900 season and all the 1901 season under this makeshift arrangement, while a new grandstand (Palace of the Fans) rose from the ruins.

The weather caused the cancellation of the trolley parade and dominated the newspaper coverage: *With the thermometer bobbing around freezing point and a chilly northwest wind sweeping the field continuously, there was not a comfortable spot anywhere within the enclosure of League Park. Had the local management given away hot tamales, seasoned with tabasco sauce, turtle soup [and] ear muffs it would have made a ten-strike. It was the coldest baseball opening Cincinnati has experienced in years.*

The papers reported that Pittsburgh star Honus Wagner stirred up the crowd whenever he came to the plate: "*Get out, get out, here comes Hannes!*" was the order given the local outfielders every time Wagner came to the bat. "*Soak him in the noodle, Hahn! That's the only way to get the butcher boy out of the road!*" [**Cincinnati Commercial Tribune, and Cincinnati Enquirer**]

### OPENING DAY TRIVIA

| | |
|---|---|
| STAR OF THE GAME | PITTSBURGH SHORTSTOP HONUS WAGNER |
| WEATHER | 35°; WINDY, CLOUDY |
| ATTENDANCE | 4,800 |
| NOTABLE | ONE OF COLDEST OPENERS EVER |
| RATING | ○ |

### 1901 OPENING DAY SCHEDULE

| | |
|---|---|
| APRIL 18 | NATIONAL LEAGUE |
| PITT VS. CIN (PP) | CHI VS. STL (PP) |
| NY VS. BOST (PP) | BRKLYN VS. PHIL |

# 1902 Palace of Fans Opens
## But Reds Fall to Chicago, 6–1

*The new Palace of the Fans grandstand provided the backdrop for this cartoon critical of off-season bickering between players and owners.*

### 1902 OPENING DAY SCHEDULE

| April 17 | National League |
|---|---|
| Chi vs. Cin | Pitts vs. StL |
| Bost vs. Brklyn | Phil vs. NY |

Cincinnati and Chicago christened the 1902 season and a new grandstand at Findlay and Western before 10,000 fans. The trolley parade, pre-game concert and ceremonies made it a festive occasion, although the Reds players threw their usual wet blanket on it. The 6–1 defeat to Chicago was the fourth straight Opening Day loss.

The new stands brimmed with "cranks," and all 38 boxes were filled. The "Rooters' Row" area at field level under the grandstand was jammed with spectators, including club owner John Brush. The stands were not quite finished, and neither was the playing field. Reporters noticed some uneven spots, and the outline of the temporary diamond (where the club played in 1901 and 1902) in deep right field was still visible. In fact, the Reds practiced on the old diamond the day before the opener, while Matty Schwab and his crew worked on the new infield.

Manager Bid McPhee started Cincinnati native Len Swormstedt on the strength of Swormstedt's strong showing in exhibition games. But the Cubs banged out 10 solid hits and worked Swormstedt for four walks. Meanwhile, Chicago's Jack Taylor surrendered only five hits, and smacked two of his own.

The Reds took the lead in the first, and might have made the day more interesting had Tommy Corcoran not hit into a double play with the bases loaded. It only got worse. Corcoran went hitless and made two errors.

The Cubs added two runs in the fourth and two in the seventh for a 5–1 lead, and the cranks knew the end was near. Taylor turned Reds bats into kindling and excised the rooters from Rooter's Row.

Perhaps the biggest cheer of the day came when Reds first baseman Jake Beckley pulled off the hidden ball trick in the third inning. Chicago first baseman Frank Chance hustled out a slow roller to shortstop. Beckley discreetly held the ball, and when Swormstedt stepped to the mound, Chance danced off first. Beckley surprised him with the tag.

The trolley parade, band concert and mayor's remarks preceded the game.

The papers offered their comments on the new ball park: *The new grandstand, while not entirely completed, showed its full advantage yesterday. Not only is it the most beautiful structure of the kind, but every play can be seen from every seat in it. The new diamond, still rough and lumpy, made it a difficult matter to judge ground balls.*

*The crowd was a living demonstration of what a ball team is worth to a city, for in it were people from no less than 50 of Cincinnati's sister cities and villages in the three states, and even as far away as West Virginia.* [**Cincinnati Commercial Tribune, and Cincinnati Enquirer**]

### OPENING DAY TRIVIA

| | |
|---|---|
| Star of the Game | Chicago Pitcher Jack Taylor |
| Weather | 62°; Cloudy |
| Attendance | 10,000 |
| Notable | Opening of Palace of the Fans |
| Rating | ○○○○ |

# 1903 New Owners; Same Old Results
## Reds Lose Fifth Straight Opener

*On Opening Day, Reds owner Garry Herrmann entertained Pittsburgh club president Barney Dreyfuss in these box seats behind home plate.*

### 1903 OPENING DAY SCHEDULE
**APRIL 16 NATIONAL LEAGUE**
| PITTS vs. CIN | CHI vs. STL |
|---|---|
| BOST vs. PHIL (PP) | BRKLYN vs. NY (PP) |

The 1903 season dawned with new ownership in Cincinnati, but the Opening Day results were glumly the same. The Reds lost the opener, 7–1, to Pittsburgh on a dreary and damp day. Deacon Phillippe was in mid-season form, throwing curve after curve past the hapless Reds, who managed only two hits.

For the first time since 1895, the trolley parade was not held. However the club continued its long tradition of providing an Opening Day concert. Weber's Band entertained the crowd with pre-game music.

Despite the miserable conditions, some 12,000 souls filled the grounds, a tribute to the growing tradition of Opening Day and the popularity of baseball in the Queen City. Among the faithful was new Reds president Garry Herrmann, who purchased the Reds in 1902. He was joined in his front-row box by Pittsburgh club president Barney Dreyfuss, who no doubt enjoyed the game more than his host.

The day belonged to Phillippe, the tall veteran pitcher who had won 20 games in 1902, and who would go on to win 25 games in 1903. Phillippe had a perfect game through six innings. In the seventh, the faithful had their first chance to cheer, when Cy Seymour laid down a bunt single and scooted to third on Phillippe's wild throw. Seymour scored on a ground out, which resulted in the day's wildest cheering, but that was all the Reds could muster. Tom Corcoran made the only other hit, a sharp single in the eighth.

Meanwhile, Reds starter Jack Harper had a live arm, but lacked control. "I had all my speed today," explained Harper, "but somehow or other, when I wanted to use it the ball would shoot out on me, and I had myself in a hole all the time."

Harper walked eight and gave up 11 hits. The Pirates scored in the second, fourth, eighth and ninth innings, and threatened to score in nearly every other inning.

The Reds looked as though they had never seen a curveball, which was not far wrong. Pitchers in this era did not rely on breaking balls much in the early spring. Coaches believed it would ruin the arm. But Phillippe fooled the Reds with a steady delivery of curves and "slants."

Reds manager Joe Kelley admitted the Reds weren't prepared. "I have been playing ball a few years, but I never knew a pitcher to use as many curveballs at this season of the year as Phillippe did today. We have not been up against any curve pitching. Our pitchers have not dared use them in practice."

Reds outfielder Mike Donlin was also amazed: "He [Phillippe] certainly must be in great shape to be able to do that, for if he ain't, I'll bet his arm will be sorer than a boil tomorrow."

*[Cincinnati Commercial Tribune, Cincinnati Times-Star, and Cincinnati Enquirer]*

### OPENING DAY TRIVIA
| STAR OF THE GAME | PITTSBURGH PITCHER DEACON PHILLIPPE |
|---|---|
| WEATHER | 51°; HEAVY OVERCAST, SPRINKLES |
| ATTENDANCE | 12,000 |
| NOTABLE | REDS DISCONTINUE OFFICIAL TROLLEY PARADE |
| RATING | ◐ |

### APRIL 16, 1903

| CIN'TI. | AB. | R. | BH. | SB. | SH. | SO. | BB. | PO. | A. | E. |
|---|---|---|---|---|---|---|---|---|---|---|
| Kelley, l.f. | 4 | 0 | 0 | 0 | 0 | 1 | 0 | 4 | 0 | 0 |
| Seymour, c.f. | 4 | 1 | 1 | 0 | 0 | 0 | 0 | 1 | 0 | 0 |
| Donlin, r.f. | 4 | 0 | 0 | 0 | 0 | 0 | 0 | 2 | 1 | 0 |
| Beakley, 1b. | 4 | 0 | 0 | 0 | 0 | 1 | 0 | 8 | 0 | 0 |
| Morrissey, 3b. | 3 | 0 | 0 | 0 | 0 | 1 | 1 | 1 | 1 | 0 |
| Corcoran, s.s. | 3 | 0 | 1 | 0 | 0 | 1 | 0 | 1 | 4 | 1 |
| Steinfeldt, 2b. | 3 | 0 | 0 | 0 | 0 | 0 | 0 | 3 | 4 | 1 |
| Peitz, c. | 2 | 0 | 0 | 0 | 0 | 1 | 0 | 7 | 3 | 0 |
| Harper, p. | 3 | 0 | 0 | 0 | 0 | 1 | 0 | 0 | 4 | 0 |
| Totals | 30 | 1 | 2 | 0 | 0 | 5 | 1 | 27 | 16 | 2 |

| PITTS. | AB. | R. | BH. | SB. | SH. | SO. | BB. | PO. | A. | E. |
|---|---|---|---|---|---|---|---|---|---|---|
| Beaumont, c.f. | 4 | 2 | 1 | 0 | 0 | 0 | 1 | 2 | 0 | 0 |
| Clarke, l.f. | 5 | 1 | 2 | 1 | 0 | 1 | 0 | 3 | 0 | 0 |
| Leach, 3b. | 5 | 1 | 1 | 1 | 0 | 1 | 0 | 2 | 1 | 0 |
| Wagner, s.s. | 3 | 0 | 2 | 1 | 0 | 0 | 2 | 1 | 1 | 0 |
| Bransfield, 1b. | 4 | 1 | 1 | 0 | 0 | 0 | 0 | 9 | 0 | 0 |
| Sebring, r.f. | 4 | 1 | 0 | 0 | 0 | 1 | 0 | 2 | 0 | 0 |
| Ritchey, 2b. | 4 | 0 | 1 | 0 | 0 | 1 | 1 | 0 | 4 | 0 |
| Phelps, c. | 5 | 0 | 3 | 0 | 0 | 0 | 0 | 7 | 0 | 0 |
| Phillippi, p. | 2 | 2 | 0 | 0 | 0 | 0 | 3 | 0 | 3 | 1 |
| Totals | 36 | 7 | 11 | 3 | 1 | 3 | 5 | 27 | 8 | 1 |

Cincinnati ..... 0 0 0 0 0 1 0 0—1
Pittsburg ..... 0 1 0 3 0 0 2 1—7

Two-base Hits—Bransfield, Ritchey, Phelps.
Three-base Hits—Clarke, Leach.
Left on Bases—Cincinnati 2, Pittsburg 11.
Wild Pitches—Phillippi, Harper.
First on Errors—Pittsburg 2.
Time of Game—1:50.
Attendance—12,000.
Umpire—Emslie.

# 1904
# Ninth-Inning Rally Beats the Cubs
## Joe Kelley Slides Home with Final Run

*Reds manager and first baseman Joe Kelley was the hero of the 1904 opener.*

Old "Kel's" daring dash home with the winning run from second base in the bottom of the ninth broke the Reds' five-year Opening Day losing streak.

Joe Kelley, the Reds manager and first baseman, slid across home plate just ahead of Johnny Evers throw. It was all that was needed to give the Reds a 3–2 victory in the opener.

The stands erupted with a roar. Despite chilly conditions, over 13,000 filled the Palace of the Fans. Thousands sitting in the bleachers and standing behind the ropes swarmed onto the field to celebrate.

Pre-game ceremonies included Weber's Band concert and the mayor's opening address. With that concluded, the Reds Jack Suthoff took the mound and immediately faced trouble in the first inning. The Cubs scored twice and the "cranks" anticipated another Opening Day disappointment. But Suthoff shut out the Cubs over the final eight innings, thanks to some excellent outfield defense by center fielder Cy Seymour, and shortstop Tommy Corcoran.

The Reds were not having much better luck with Jake Weimer, but some well-timed hits and costly Chicago errors let the Reds draw even.

In the first, the Reds scored an unearned run. In the sixth, a triple by Seymour and a single by Mike Donlin tied the score. Chicago put runners on second base in the both the eighth and ninth, but failed to score.

Kelley led off the Reds ninth with a single and Harry Steinfeldt sacrificed him to second. Corcoran then smashed a hard ground ball at shortstop Joe Tinker. Tinker moved in front of the ball, but it struck his foot and bounded out beyond second base. Kelley was on the move. Donlin, who was coaching third, gave him the stop sign, but the Reds manager overruled him and kept on running.

Evers picked up the ball and threw home, but his aim was high and wide. Kelley slid past the catcher, rolled over and knocked down umpire James Johnstone. But Johnstone bore no grudge, and quickly called Kelley safe, setting off the wild jubilation.

The papers delighted in the victory: *No more interesting game, and no more exciting finish was ever seen at League Park. Gray-haired men stood up and cheered, women nervously applauded with their gloved hands, while the real fans exclaimed their joy as only a fan can.*

*And the bleachers—what a sight! Like a huge wave creeping up the beach thousands of men and boys came out of their seats and in an instant flooded the field, anxious to get a closer look at their heroes. For fully five minutes one could not hear himself talk. Every face indicated joy and contentment, for the Reds had won the first game of 1904.*
*[Cincinnati Commercial Tribune, Cincinnati Times-Star, and Cincinnati Enquirer]*

### 1904 OPENING DAY SCHEDULE

| APRIL 14 | NATIONAL LEAGUE | |
|---|---|---|
| CHI vs. CIN | | BRKLYN vs. NY |
| BOST vs. PHIL | | |
| APRIL 15 | NATIONAL LEAGUE | |
| PITTS vs. StL | | |

### OPENING DAY TRIVIA

| STAR OF THE GAME | REDS 1ST BASEMAN & MANAGER JOE KELLEY |
|---|---|
| WEATHER | 48°; PARTLY CLOUDY |
| ATTENDANCE | 13,000 |
| NOTABLE | FIRST OPENING DAY WIN IN 5 YEARS |
| RATING | ●●●●● |

# Hapless Reds Give One Away
## Big Throng Endures 9–4 Loss

*Men in dark coats and derbies dominated this grandstand scene at the Palace of the Fans.*

The largest Opening Day crowd to date—15,118—would have settled for a five-inning opener. Their Reds led, 4–2, and starter Jack Harper seemed to have the better of his opponent, Pat Flaherty.

But in the disastrous sixth, the Reds simply forgot how to play baseball. The Pirates scored six runs without one solid hit. Walks and fielding lapses gave Pittsburgh every advantage, and when the dust had settled, Pittsburgh led, 8–4. Flaherty shut down the Reds the rest of the way, and the Reds had let the Opening Day victory slip away.

Reds shortstop Tommy Corcoran was largely responsible for the early lead of the Reds. He singled in two runs in the second, and tripled home two more in the fourth. But that was all the offense the Reds could pile up; after that, the game belonged to Pittsburgh.

The Pirates tallied two in the fifth, and in the sixth they loaded the bases on two walks and a bunt single. Tommy Leach lifted a short fly to left that appeared to be catchable, but it fell between Fred Odwell and Corcoran. One run scored, and a second run scored on a fielder's choice.

With two out, it appeared the Reds would survive the inning, but another shallow fly ball fell between center fielder Cy Seymour and second baseman Miller Huggins, and the Pirates took the lead. After another walk loaded the bases, Fred Clarke dribbled a slow roller toward second. Huggins made a mad dash for the ball, grabbed it and looked toward first. But first baseman Mike Dolan had come off the bag, and Huggins had no throw. In desperation, Huggins threw home to cut down the runner trying to score from second, but his throw was high. A double steal added the sixth and final run of a disastrous inning.

The crowd filled every nook and cranny in the ballpark, and even some it wasn't supposed to fill. A new upper deck atop the left field stands was still under construction and posted as "off-limits," but before club officials could react, some 500 fans had invaded the space and no one bothered to eject them.

The papers gave the big crowd considerable coverage: *At 12:40 o'clock, twenty minutes before the gates were due to open, 500 men were lined up in Western Avenue. Rooters' clubs came in with a whirlwind of shouts and fierce noises. The Geneva Club rode in on two hay wagons. The members wore straw hats a yard across. In the first half-hour the bleacherites [in right field] began dropping over the fence from the lowest row of seats and hustled out on the field to the rope boundary. There they congested and began to sway back and forth in a great line that soon took crescent form and veered around toward center field and gave Cy Seymour a background of humans in a solid line when he went out to practice.* [*Cincinnati Commercial Tribune, Cincinnati Times-Star,* and *Cincinnati Enquirer*]

### OPENING DAY TRIVIA

| | |
|---|---|
| STAR OF THE GAME | REDS SHORTSTOP TOMMY CORCORAN |
| WEATHER | 63°; SUNNY |
| ATTENDANCE | 15,118 |
| NOTABLE | A RECORD-SETTING CROWD |
| RATING | ☺☺ |

### APRIL 14, 1905

| CIN'TI. | AB | R | BH | SB | SH | SO | BB | PO | A | E |
|---|---|---|---|---|---|---|---|---|---|---|
| Huggins, 2b | 4 | 0 | 0 | 0 | 0 | 0 | 3 | 6 | 1 |
| Dolan, 1b | 4 | 0 | 0 | 0 | 0 | 0 | 0 | 11 | 1 | 0 |
| Seymour, c.f. | 4 | 0 | 0 | 0 | 0 | 0 | 0 | 1 | 0 | 0 |
| Sebring, r.f. | 3 | 1 | 1 | 0 | 0 | 0 | 1 | 2 | 0 | 0 |
| Odwell, l.f. | 4 | 2 | 0 | 0 | 0 | 0 | 0 | 0 | 0 | 0 |
| Steinfeldt, 3b | 3 | 1 | 1 | 0 | 1 | 0 | 0 | 3 | 2 | 0 |
| Corcoran, s.s. | 4 | 0 | 3 | 0 | 0 | 0 | 0 | 3 | 2 | 0 |
| Schlei, c. | 4 | 0 | 0 | 0 | 0 | 0 | 0 | 4 | 6 | 1 |
| Harper, p. | 2 | 0 | 0 | 0 | 0 | 1 | 0 | 0 | 2 | 0 |
| Chech, p. | 1 | 0 | 0 | 0 | 0 | 0 | 0 | 0 | 1 | 0 |
| Totals | 33 | 4 | 5 | 0 | 1 | 1 | 2 | 27 | 20 | 2 |
| PITTS. | AB | R | BH | SB | SH | SO | BB | PO | A | E |
| Clymer, r.f. | 5 | 1 | 3 | 1 | 0 | 0 | 0 | 3 | 0 | 0 |
| Clarke, l.f. | 5 | 0 | 2 | 1 | 0 | 0 | 0 | 2 | 0 | 0 |
| Beaumont, c.f. | 4 | 1 | 0 | 0 | 0 | 0 | 1 | 1 | 0 | 0 |
| Wagner, s.s. | 4 | 1 | 0 | 0 | 1 | 1 | 3 | 6 | 1 |
| Clancy, 1b | 4 | 2 | 1 | 0 | 0 | 0 | 1 | 16 | 0 | 1 |
| Leach, 3b | 5 | 1 | 3 | 0 | 0 | 0 | 0 | 1 | 1 |
| Ritchey, 2b | 4 | 2 | 1 | 0 | 0 | 0 | 0 | 1 | 2 | 0 |
| Peitz, c. | 3 | 0 | 0 | 0 | 1 | 1 | 0 | 0 | 9 | 1 |
| Flaherty, p. | 3 | 1 | 1 | 0 | 0 | 0 | 0 | 1 | 0 | 1 |
| Totals | 37 | 9 | 12 | 3 | 0 | 2 | 5 | 27 | 18 | 4 |

Cincinnati ....... 0 2 0 2 0 0 0 0 0—4
Pittsburg ........ 0 0 0 0 2 6 0 0 1—9

Three-base Hit—Corcoran.
Double Plays—Corcoran, Dolan and Steinfeldt; Wagner and Clancy.
Bases on Balls—By Harper 4, by Chech 1.
Left on Bases—Cincinnati 4, Pittsburg 6.
Passed Ball—Peitz.
Wild Pitch—Flaherty.
Innings Pitched—By Harper 6, by Chech 3.
Number Hits Made—Off Harper 9, off Chech 3.
Struck Out—By Harper 1, by Chech 1.
Time of Game—1:50.
Umpire—Klem.
Attendance—15,118.

### 1905 OPENING DAY SCHEDULE

| APRIL 14 NATIONAL LEAGUE | |
|---|---|
| PITTS VS. CIN | CHI VS. STL |
| NY VS. BOST | PHIL VS. BRKLYN |

# 1906 Record Crowd Sees Reds Lose

*The Reds hired extra policemen for the 1906 opener to cut down on the vile insults hurled by fans. This group of spectators was seated in the right-field bleachers.*

### 1906 OPENING DAY SCHEDULE

| APRIL 12 | NATIONAL LEAGUE |
|---|---|
| CHI VS. CIN | PITTS VS. STL |
| BOST VS. BRKLYN | NY VS. PHIL |

If the Reds could only put as many good players on the field as they do loyal fans in the seats, they would surely have won a few more openers.

For the second year in a row, a record-setting crowd filled the Palace of the Fans for Opening Day, and for the second straight year, the Reds embarrassed themselves with a poor showing. Chicago, behind the pitching of Carl Lundgren, downed the Reds, 7–2. It was the Reds seventh loss in the last eight openers.

Perhaps the faithful had an inkling of what was to come when Mayor Dempsey made a wild toss on his ceremonial first pitch. Certainly they had a premonition when Reds starter, big Orval Overall, struggled through the first inning, showing the first signs of the wildness that would plague him all afternoon.

The Reds did take a short-lived 1–0 lead in the third, but Chicago retaliated with three runs in the fourth. Overall contributed mightily to his demise with a throwing error that brought in two runs.

The Reds mounted feeble efforts at a rally in the next few innings, but Lundgren shut the door. As late as the eighth inning, fans still had reason to hope. The Reds trailed by only two as Chicago batted with two out and none on. But Overall walked Joe Tinker and then gave up a triple and a double for two more runs. Although they weren't needed, Chicago added two more tallies in the ninth.

The Reds finally picked up their second run in the ninth, but the rally died and the Cubs walked off with the Opening Day win.

Although the team had to be disappointed in its showing, business manager Frank Bancroft was pleased with the huge throng. The gross receipts were the largest ever taken in at a Cincinnati game.

The Reds announced before the game that they would take measures to remove anyone who used abusive language to harass visiting or local players. The *Cincinnati Times-Star* announced the new policy: *Rooters, be careful, or the policemen will get you. For years Cincinnati has had the reputation among visiting players of being one of the most disagreeable places on the circuit in which to [play]. This reputation was gained through the abuse that was heaped upon the players, not only of visiting teams, but also of the home team.*

*In the [exhibition] game last Saturday a few abusers made [their] presence known by roasting some of the Detroit players, and following it up by saying mean things to several of the Reds. This aroused the ire of President [Garry] Herrmann. [The] Chief of Park Police was instructed to hire two extra policemen to patrol the grounds in front of the grandstand. "And if they hear anyone abusing the players of either team,"* said Mr. Herrmann, *"have them warn the offenders that it must cease or they can get their money back at the box office. If they persist in roasting the players, the police must use the strong-arm method."*

[*Cincinnati Commercial Tribune, Cincinnati Times-Star, and Cincinnati Enquirer*]

### OPENING DAY TRIVIA

| STAR OF THE GAME | CHICAGO PITCHER CARL LUNDGREN |
|---|---|
| WEATHER | 70°; FAIR SKIES |
| ATTENDANCE | 17,241 |
| NOTABLE | ANOTHER RECORD OPENING DAY CROWD |
| RATING | ⚾⚾ |

Groups of loyal Reds rooters climbed aboard horse-drawn "tally-hos" and horseless carriages to form informal processions through downtown on the way to the ballpark for Opening Day.

# 1907 Ganzel's Hit Wins the Game
## Noisy Crowd Cheers Rally

### 1907 OPENING DAY SCHEDULE

| April 11 | National League |
|---|---|
| Pitts vs. Cin | StL vs. Chi |
| Phil vs. NY | Brkly vs. Bost (pp) |

It was not the biggest crowd at an Opening Day, but it was the loudest. And the happiest, as their beloved Reds staged a terrific ninth-inning rally to defeat Pittsburgh, 4–3.

The boisterous throng of 10,000 ignored the 45-degree weather and kept up a constant barrage of clatter with noisemakers of all types throughout the game to cheer on the Queen City boys.

The Reds didn't give the revelers much to cheer about through the first five innings. The Pirates scored first off starter Bob Ewing in the second, and added another run in the third when Ewing walked home a run. Ewing was plagued by wildness all day, handing out eight free passes.

The Reds finally scored in the sixth, tying the score at 2–2. Johnny Kane scored on a wild throw by Honus Wagner, and Mike Mitchell tripled in another run.

Both teams threatened in the final innings, but the Pirates broke through first in the ninth on a walk, a sacrifice and a single to take a 3–2 lead.

Reds manager Ned Hanlon sent up burly Larry McLean to pinch-hit for Ewing and McLean rose to the occasion. He doubled off Pittsburgh reliever Lefty Leifield. Miller Huggins sacrificed him to third. But then Leifield lost his control. He walked pinch hitter Ed Tiemeyer and Kane. With the crowd hollering for a hit, John Ganzel delivered. His soft fly fell into short right field for a single, sending home two runs for the victory.

Ganzel was immediately mobbed by fans who rushed the field, but he found a way to keep the crowd at bay. The *Commercial Tribune* reported: "Some of the rooters wanted to carry him off the field, but the big Captain would not listen to it. In fact, to keep the overanxious fans away from him, the Captain picked up the keg of ice water and commenced dousing the crowd with it."

The crowd arrived early, many groups of rooters riding in the horse-drawn tallyhos: *Tallyho parties seemed to be the order of the day. They came in all sizes from two horses up to six, and though some only seated six people, others were capable of carrying thirty-five to forty rooters in them. In all there were a dozen big tallyhos with rooters and they came dressed in fantastic garbs and labeled with large streaming banners.*

*At two o'clock the tallyhos and various other kinds of rigs started to put in their appearance, and from that time on it appeared as though every man in the park was trying to outdo his neighbor in the matter of noisemaking. Megaphones were too weak and horns and rattles were employed. Cornets, bugles and other instruments were also on hand. It was seldom that umpire Hank O'Day's voice could be heard above the din.* [Cincinnati Commercial Tribune, Cincinnati Times-Star, and Cincinnati Enquirer]

### OPENING DAY TRIVIA

| Star of the Game | Reds First Baseman John Ganzel |
|---|---|
| Weather | 45°; Cloudy |
| Attendance | 10,000 |
| Notable | Reds Win in Last At Bat |
| Rating | ●●●● |

# 1908 Nearly 20,000 See Reds Lose in 9th
## 5–0 Lead is Wiped Out

*The teams gathered to hear Mayor Markbreit deliver the annual Opening Day address, a tradition begun in 1895.*

Chicago overcame a five-run deficit, scoring the winning run in the top of ninth to edge the Reds, 6–5, and ruin what had been shaping up to be one of the most glorious openers in history.

All reserved seats were sold prior to the game, ensuring a big crowd. The papers exhorted fans to visit the ballpark. "Close up shop and come out," urged the *Commercial Tribune*. "Everybody will be there anyway, so what's the use of keeping open? Next year fans will circulate a petition to have the day declared a half-holiday, and if it's up to the Mayor you can gamble that he will O.K. the petition."

Summer-like temperatures convinced any stragglers to head for the grounds. Last-minute walk-up sales topped all expectations. The crowd became so large that business manager Frank Bancroft ordered the ticket windows closed shortly after 2 o'clock. Bancroft announced the official tally at 19,257, the largest Opening Day crowd to date.

After the usual ceremonies, the Reds rudely greeted their ex-teammate, Orval Overall, scoring five runs in the first inning before anyone was out.

### 1908 OPENING DAY SCHEDULE

| APRIL 14 | NATIONAL LEAGUE |
|---|---|
| CHI vs. CIN | PITTS vs. StL (PP) |
| BRKLYN vs. BOST | PHIL vs. NY |

Overall gave up five hits, but three errors contributed significantly to the rally. It was hardly a representative performance from the defending World Champions, and over the next eight innings they redeemed themselves. Overall and reliever Mordecai Brown only allowed the Reds three more hits. The Chicago defense stiffened, and the offense kept banging away at Reds starter Bob Ewing and reliever Billy Campbell, who took the loss. The Cubs tied the score in the sixth, and pushed across the winning run in the ninth on a single by pinch hitter Heinie Zimmerman.

The papers once again focused on the crowd, and the growing popularity of the automobile as a way to reach the ballpark: *Every regular [street]car on all the lines leading to Western Avenue was packed and jammed for three solid hours before the game. Hundreds walked out from Fountain Square rather than push their way onto the crowded cars.*

*More automobiles were seen at the park yesterday than ever before. So numerous were the motor cars that the spacious ground set apart for them [beneath the stands] proved insufficient, and many had to be left outside the yard.*

*Scores of automobiles scurried through the streets of the West End carrying happy fans of both sexes. Sheriff Nagle of Campbell County, Ky., was there with bells on. He brought a big crowd over in his automobile. Another bunch of noisy and happy fans was in the delegation of the Wooden Shoe Fishing Club. They wore grotesque and fantastic costumes.* [*Cincinnati Commercial Tribune, Cincinnati Times-Star, and Cincinnati Enquirer*]

### OPENING DAY TRIVIA

| | |
|---|---|
| STAR OF THE GAME | CHICAGO PINCH HITTER HEINIE ZIMMERMAN |
| WEATHER | 76°; PARTLY CLOUDY |
| ATTENDANCE | 19,257 |
| NOTABLE | LARGEST OD CROWD TO THAT TIME |
| RATING | ◐◐◐ |

*Cincinnati "bugs" who didn't have tickets for the opener could follow the game on scoreboards at Fountain Square.*

# 1909 Reds Shut Out by Pirates
## Camnitz Hurls a Gem

Opening Day drew near-record numbers to the Palace of the Fans, and the 18,000 "bugs" brought with them a seemingly record-breaking number of noise-makers. The *Commercial Tribune* reported, "Cow bells, rattles attached to skillets, horns of every size and description, bugles, drums and a peculiar little whistle that was a novelty…made a humdrum during the entire afternoon."

The pre-game concert even featured a new tune: "Take Me Out to the Ball Game."

But while the faithful may have raised a racket at the Palace, Pittsburgh starter Howie Camnitz ignored the din and pitched the Pirates to a 3–0 win over the Reds.

This was the first shutout in Opening Day history. The victory proved to be no fluke. Camnitz won 25 games (five shutouts) in 1909.

The Pirates scored all the runs they needed in the first on a triple and a sacrifice fly. Camnitz, a native of Covington, Kentucky, stopped the Reds on six hits. The Reds didn't threaten until the fifth when the first two hitters reached base. But Camnitz retired the next three in order. The Reds put a runner on third with one out in the sixth, but again failed to take advantage.

Reds starter Art Fromme was the victim of the Reds' inability to hit in the clutch. He gave up only four hits, and pitched as well as Camnitz.

Mayor Galvin delivered the annual speech and then showed off a pretty fair throwing arm. His ceremonial first pitch sailed far over the heads of the players gathered below his box.

The papers gave considerable attention to the many organized groups of rooters which paraded through downtown on their way to the ball park: *Especially noticeable were the Rooters' clubs, of which there were a dozen or more. Some went out in special [street] cars, others in tally-hos, some in sight-seeing autos and some in carriages. All were furnished with flags, banners and all kinds of noise-making devices. The clubs paraded the city before going out to the park and attracted an immense amount of attention.*

*In point of numbers, Lee Heine's party of rooters certainly took the premium, for among all the parties organized none had managed to turn out in such numbers. About thirty carriages had been engaged to carry them to the park after a parade through the business portion of the city. [They carried] an enormous bell to toll the knell of the Pirates, but which had to be switched to another purpose, as the Pirates refused to be tolled for.*

*New flags adorned the park and it made the park look like it had been dressed up in its "Sunday-go-to-meetin'" clothes. There have been many opening games, but for wild enthusiasm the one of yesterday copped off first prize and had something to spare.* [Cincinnati Commercial Tribune, Cincinnati Times-Star, and Cincinnati Enquirer]

### 1909 OPENING DAY SCHEDULE

| APRIL 14 | NATIONAL LEAGUE |
|---|---|
| PITTS. VS. CIN | STL VS. CHI |
| PHIL VS. BOST | BRKLYN VS. NY (PP) |

### OPENING DAY TRIVIA

| | |
|---|---|
| STAR OF THE GAME | PITTSBURGH PITCHER HOWIE CAMNITZ |
| WEATHER | 50°; CLEAR |
| ATTENDANCE | 18,000 |
| NOTABLE | FIRST OPENING DAY SHUTOUT |
| RATING | ◯◯ |

# "The Finish Most Delightful"
## 1910
### Beebe Shuts Out Cubs; Reds Win in 10th, 1–0

*The Enquirer cartoonist "skinned" the Cubs in honor of the Reds victory.*

In one of the best pitchers duels ever on Opening Day, Cincinnati's Fred Beebe outlasted Chicago's Orval Overall in 10 innings as the Reds beat Chicago, 1–0.

| OPENING DAY TRIVIA | |
|---|---|
| STAR OF THE GAME | REDS PITCHER FRED BEEBE |
| WEATHER | 79°; PARTLY CLOUDY |
| ATTENDANCE | 21,221 |
| NOTABLE | LARGEST CROWD IN PALACE HISTORY |
| RATING | ○○○○○ |

Beebe allowed only three hits; Overall gave up just five, but two came in the 10th—the only inning in which either team had two hits—and that was enough for the Reds to push across the one and only run of the game.

Another huge crowd, the largest in the history of the Palace of the Fans, attended the opener. Business manager Frank Bancroft was forced to close the 25-cent ticket window at the bleacher gate on Western Avenue 30 minutes early. Over 8,000 bleacher seats and standing room-only tickets had been sold—as many as the ballpark could handle.

Festivities included the traditional pre-game band concert and the Mayor's opening remarks.

Both pitchers proved so tough that neither team provided any offensive fireworks for the crowd until the 10th inning. In the top of the 10th, Reds left fielder Bob Bescher earned the biggest cheers to that point with a spectacular catch of a long drive by Joe Tinker. The Cubs third baseman had launched a rocket toward the crowd in left. It looked like a sure triple—the ground rules permitted three bases on all balls hit into the standees behind the rope—but Bescher never gave up the chase. The *Cincinnati Enquirer* described the catch: "Big Bob went back with long strides, and as he reached the edge of the crowd, jumped high in the air, got his bare right hand on the ball and held it in a vicelike grip. He stumbled and fell backward over the ropes as he made the catch, but held the ball." No photograph or movie reel highlights this catch, but from all description, it was the most spectacular in Opening Day history.

| 1910 OPENING DAY SCHEDULE | |
|---|---|
| APRIL 14 NATIONAL LEAGUE | |
| CHI VS. CIN | PITTS VS. STL |
| BOST VS. NY | BRKLYN VS. PHIL |

Bescher's catch lit up the crowd and it ignited the Reds bats. In the bottom of the 10th, Mike Mitchell led off with a clean single to center field. Then the Cubs defense stumbled. Johnny Egan bounded slowly to third. Harry Steinfeldt had a play on Egan, but threw low to first and the Reds had the first two runners on.

Left fielder Sandy McCabe hit a long fly to the edge of the crowd in right that was caught. Mitchell tagged up and went to third. That brought up Tom Downey who hit a bullet down the third-base line, past Steinfeldt, and Mitchell scored the game-winner. The crowd rushed the field and carried Downey on their shoulders to the Reds clubhouse, a glorious end to the opener.

Said Reds President Garry Herrmann after the game, "This beats anything I have seen since I have been in baseball. The weather was ideal, the crowd large and orderly, the playing perfect and the finish most delightful. It was made to order for Cincinnati."

*[Cincinnati Commercial Tribune, Cincinnati Times-Star, and Cincinnati Enquirer]*

### APRIL 14, 1910

| CINCIN'TI. | AB | R | 1B | SH | SB | PO | A |
|---|---|---|---|---|---|---|---|
| Bescher, lf | 4 | 0 | 0 | 0 | 0 | 2 | 0 |
| Lobert, 3b | 4 | 0 | 0 | 0 | 0 | 5 | 2 |
| Hoblitzell, 1b | 4 | 0 | 1 | 0 | 0 | 9 | 0 |
| Mitchell, cf | 4 | 1 | 1 | 0 | 0 | 1 | 0 |
| Egan, 2b | 4 | 0 | 0 | 0 | 0 | 1 | 2 |
| McCabe, rf | 4 | 0 | 1 | 0 | 0 | 2 | 0 |
| Downey, ss | 3 | 0 | 2 | 0 | 0 | 4 | 3 |
| Clarke, c | 3 | 0 | 0 | 0 | 0 | 6 | 3 |
| Beebe, p | 3 | 0 | 0 | 0 | 0 | 0 | 0 |
| Totals | 33 | 1 | 5 | 0 | 0 | 30 | 10 |
| CHICAGO. | AB | R | 1B | SH | SB | PO | A |
| Evers, 2b | 3 | 0 | 0 | 0 | 0 | 1 | 1 |
| Beaumont, lf | 3 | 0 | 1 | 0 | 0 | 4 | 0 |
| Schulte, rf | 4 | 0 | 3 | 0 | 0 | 2 | 1 |
| Chance, 1b | 3 | 0 | 0 | 0 | 0 | 9 | 2 |
| Steinfeldt, 3b | 3 | 0 | 0 | 0 | 0 | 1 | 0 |
| Hofman, cf | 4 | 0 | 0 | 0 | 0 | 2 | 0 |
| Tinker, ss | 4 | 0 | 0 | 0 | 0 | 1 | 5 |
| Archer, c | 4 | 0 | 0 | 0 | 0 | 7 | 1 |
| Overall, p | 3 | 0 | 0 | 1 | 0 | 1 | 1 |
| Totals | 32 | 0 | 3 | 2 | 0 | 28 | 10 |

One out when winning run was scored.

| Innings | 1 | 2 | 3 | 4 | 5 | 6 | 7 | 8 | 9 | 10 |
|---|---|---|---|---|---|---|---|---|---|---|
| Cincinnati | 0 | 0 | 0 | 0 | 0 | 0 | 0 | 0 | 0 | 1–1 |
| Chicago | 0 | 0 | 0 | 0 | 0 | 0 | 0 | 0 | 0 | 0–0 |

Three-Base Hits—Downey, Schulte 2. Left on Bases—Cincinnati, 5; Chicago, 6. Struck Out—By Beebe, 3; by Overall, 7. Bases on Balls—By Beebe, 2; by Overall, 1. Time—1:51. Umpires—O'Day and Brennan.

# 1911 Pirate Triples Rain on Big Crowd
## Reds Humbled, 14–0

*The Opening Day throng filled the outfield stands and temporary seating areas in center and left field. Four of the Pirate's five triples landed in the left-field crowd.*

Hoist the white flag. The Reds surrendered to the Pirates, 14–0, in the second-worst Opening Day loss in Reds history, and the worst defeat after 1900.

Fortunately, the 18,000 spectators who descended on the ballpark could not guess the final outcome, or they would have stayed home. But beginning in the late morning, even as skies threatened rain, the "bugs" headed for the Palace of the Fans. They came by streetcar, by automobile, in carriages and on foot. By early afternoon the bleachers were full and the crowd had begun to stake out the best standing room seats.

The weather was questionable up to the last moment, as dark clouds hovered above the field, but by the second inning, the sun emerged and the rest of the game was played under near-perfect conditions.

There was nothing "near-perfect" about the Reds. Cincinnati starter Arthur Fromme lasted only 4⅔ innings, giving up 10 hits and 10 runs. His replacement, Jesse Tannehill, allowed seven hits and four runs in the final 4⅓ innings. The defense was no help. The usually dependable first baseman, Dick Hoblitzell, made two errors, as did second baseman Tom Downey.

And the offense, thanks to Pittsburgh starter Babe Adams, took the day off as well. Adams gave up only four hits. The lone time a Cincinnati runner reached third base was in the ninth inning on Bob Bescher's triple.

Adams would have earned the day's laurels, but for the record-tying five-for-five performance of Pirate third baseman, Bob Byrne. He had a double and a triple among his five hits.

The low point of the game for the Reds came in the disastrous fifth inning when Pittsburgh scored seven runs to take a 10–0 lead. The first three hitters smacked long drives into the crowd in left field and were awarded ground-rule triples. Three more singles and a walk loaded the bases. With two out Fred Clarke bounced to Downey for what should have been the final out. But Downey fumbled the ball and then threw late to Hoblitzell. In his haste to throw home to cut off the second run, "Hobby" threw wild, and all three Pirates scored.

Among the Pirates' 17 hits were five triples, tying a Cincinnati Opening Day record.

The papers made no excuses for the Reds: *There was no joy in Redville last night. There are a good many headaches in Bugville this morning. What else is there to do but extend Manager Clarke's peppery Pirates our warmest congratulations? You kicked us to within an inch of our lives. Spare us, Pirates, spare us! We don't mind being "shown up," but we do object to being humiliated before so many home fans. Begging your pardons for furnishing you such poor practice, we close our case without a single further plea.* **[Cincinnati Commercial Tribune, Cincinnati Times-Star, and Cincinnati Enquirer]**

### OPENING DAY TRIVIA

| | |
|---|---|
| STAR OF THE GAME | PITTSBURGH THIRD BASEMAN BOB BYRNE |
| WEATHER | 64°; DAMP; RAIN IN MORNING |
| ATTENDANCE | 18,000 |
| NOTABLE | 5 HITS BY BYRNE; 5 TRIPLES BY THE PIRATES |
| RATING | ⚾ |

### 1911 OPENING DAY SCHEDULE

| APRIL 12 | NATIONAL LEAGUE |
|---|---|
| PITTS VS. CIN | STL VS. CHI |
| BOST VS. BRKLYN | PHIL VS. NY |

# 1912 Redland Opens in Winning Style
## 26,336 Watch Reds Rally, 10–6

*Redland Field (renamed Crosley Field in 1934) opened on April 11, 1912.*

| 1912 OPENING DAY SCHEDULE | |
|---|---|
| April 11 | National League |
| Chi vs. Cin | Pitts vs. StL |
| NY vs. Brklyn | Phil vs. Bost |

"With a record-breaking crowd cheering out its numerous lungs in gleeful support…[the] Reds, with a wonderful exhibition of aggressiveness and up-hill fighting, captured the opening game of the championship season in the shadow of the finest grand stand in the country."

So began the report of *Cincinnati Enquirer* scribe Jack Ryder on the Reds 10–6 Opening Day victory, the inaugural game at Redland Field. The Reds rallied from a 5–1 deficit with six runs in the fourth inning and never gave up the lead.

Superlatives were as plentiful as the 24 hits that whizzed around the spacious yard. "Thrilling," "the swellest," "immense," and "grandest," said the fans. "Great" was all one spectator needed. "Great day, great stands, great crowds and a great game. What more could we ask?"

It didn't start out great, with Reds starter Frank Smith treated roughly by Chicago. He gave up five runs in the third inning on two singles, a double, a triple, two walks and an error. Manager Hank O'Day then made his best move of the afternoon, bringing in Bert Humphries to replace Smith. Humphries' slow tantalizing curves were far more effective than Smith's rapid spit balls. Over the last six innings, Humphries relinquished three hits and one run.

The Reds reclaimed the lead in the fourth, sending 11 men to the plate and scoring six times. The big hits were a triple by third baseman Art Phelan, and a two-run triple by left fielder Bob Bescher. Bescher scored three times and drove in two runs.

The Cubs hit Humphries hard in the seventh, scoring once, but the Reds answered with two more in the bottom of the seventh and one final tally in the eighth. The Reds fought off one last rally in the ninth. The Cubs had runners on first and third with none out, but Humphries retired the next three hitters and the Reds had won the historic opener.

Pre-game ceremonies included the band concert, a flag-raising ceremony by both clubs at the center-field flagpole and a brief opening address by the mayor.

The papers gave extensive coverage to the new field: *Wonder and amazement were written on the faces of the people as they took their first look at the new plant and the exclamations of pleasure and surprise at its beauty and magnificence would have made an emperor proud.*

Downtown, city hall, courthouse and business houses were as deserted as on a legal holiday. When the gates were opened at noon, three hours before game time, there was a big rush of the early birds for the front benches, and in half an hour all the unreserved seats were alive with humanity. [*Cincinnati Commercial Tribune, Cincinnati Times-Star,* and *Cincinnati Enquirer*]

| OPENING DAY TRIVIA | |
|---|---|
| Star of the Game | Reds Left Fielder Bob Bescher |
| Weather | 75°; Partly Cloudy |
| Attendance | 26,336 |
| Notable | First Game at Redland/Crosley Field |
| Rating | ●●●●● |

# 1913 Floodwaters Conquered
## But Not Pirates, Who Win 9–2

**BUGS AND BUGESSES BRAVE WINTRY WINDS**
To Sport Their Glad Rags and See Those Dear Reds Get Walloped.
**FANTASTIC COSTUMES SEEN**
Which Cause Crowd To Laugh and Get a Little Warmer—

*Fans, or "bugs" as they were called in the 1910s, received their share of attention on Opening Day.*

What the Reds faithful needed on this cold, blustery, damp Opening Day was a Reds victory to warm them up, but instead the Pirates dumped more cold water on an already soggy Cincinnati, and walloped the Reds, 9–2.

The game was postponed two days by rain and could easily have been put off for several more but for the herculean efforts of the ground crew. A week before the scheduled opener, 12 feet of water covered the ballpark. Groundskeeper Matty Schwab washed the mud off the field with hoses, and then put a crew to work with a steamroller and sponges to "wring" out the sod. Schwab's roller broke down midway through the job, which was not surprising considering it had been sitting under water for several days. Finally, Schwab resorted to lighting fires around the field to burn off the rest of the water. By game time, the water was gone, but so was the grass.

A white line on the left-field fence marked the height of the flood at its peak on April 1.

Despite the field conditions and the damp, dreary ambience, 20,000 "bugs" turned out. The traditional pre-game concert went on as scheduled, and the mayor threw out the first pitch from the mound (rather than from the seats), a first for the Reds.

Art Fromme started for the home club and suffered his third Opening Day loss without a victory (a mark later tied by Bucky Walters). In five innings, Fromme gave up four runs, nine hits and two walks.

Charlie Adams held the Reds in check all day and picked up the complete-game victory. He allowed seven hits. The Reds had only one hit through five innings, but finally broke through in the sixth with their first tally. But Reds reliever Joe McManus was hit hard in the seventh, giving up a single, a double, a triple and two walks, for four Pirate runs, dashing any hope of a Reds comeback.

The fans were quite surprised at the sight of the ebony infield: *Many were the gasps of amazement as the people flocked in at the strange appearance of the ballyard. From home plate to second and from first to third the once green turf had entirely disappeared and as black as the proverbial inside of a Derby hat showed the surface. For Matty Schwab had rolled and burnt and dried the diamond, finishing the process with the placing of black, dry loam over the entire space.*

*In the outer garden the dull green of the sod was splotched in a score of places where sawdust had been put on the spots especially soft. Back of the catcher's box and in the coacher's position the ground was very wet and oozy, but the infield, while slow, was dry.* [Cincinnati Commercial Tribune, Cincinnati Times-Star, and Cincinnati Enquirer]

### OPENING DAY TRIVIA

| | |
|---|---|
| STAR OF THE GAME | PITTSBURGH STARTER CHARLIE ADAMS |
| WEATHER | 52°; CLOUDY, DAMP |
| ATTENDANCE | 20,000 |
| NOTABLE | 12 FEET OF WATER ON FIELD WEEK BEFORE GAME |
| RATING | ☾ |

### 1913 OPENING DAY SCHEDULE

| | |
|---|---|
| APRIL 9 | NATIONAL LEAGUE |
| | PHIL VS. BRKLYN |
| APRIL 10 | NATIONAL LEAGUE |
| | PITTS VS. CIN (PP)  STL VS. CHI (PP) |
| | BOST VS. NY |

# 1914
# A Drizzly Opener
## Reds Behind Benton Route Cubs, 10–1

*The Reds warmed up prior to the start of the opener. Weber's Band (lower left) entertained the crowd with its pre-game concert.*

The Reds proved to be the better mudders in the 1914 opener, easily defeating Chicago, 10–1 on a very sloppy track, otherwise known as "Lake Redland."

The precipitation began just after one o'clock, alternating between a mist and a drizzle. The bleacher seats were already full when the rains started and the club officials hoped in vain for a letup. The gates remained open and the grandstand continued to fill. The heavy gray skies kept some rooters at home, but nearly 16,000 refused to yield to the raindrops.

As game time (2:30) approached, club President Garry Herrmann conferred with his manager Buck Herzog and decided not to call the game and disappoint the crowd. Despite the steady rain, no one had left the park. Herrmann ordered the canvass tarpaulin removed from the diamond to the cheers of the crowd, and the game began some 25 minutes late.

Reds starter Rube Benton seemed oblivious to the conditions. He gave up only two hits. The lone run he allowed came in the ninth when a brief spate of wildness ruined his shutout.

The Cubs pitchers, on the other hand, could not control the slippery ball. The Reds managed only six hits, but Chicago starter Larry Cheney and reliever Elmer Koestner threw in a generous gift of nine walks, seven wild pitches and two hit batters. The wildness culminated in two farcical innings, the sixth and seventh, when the Reds scored six runs without a hit.

The Reds scored three in the sixth on an error, two wild pitches, a sacrifice fly, a hit batter, a stolen base, another hit batsman, another wild pitch and another sacrifice fly. One reporter called it "burlesque."

If it was theater, the seventh provided the encore. The Reds scored on a walk, a sacrifice, three straight walks, a wild pitch and a sacrifice fly. Shortly thereafter, the crowd began to head for the exits.

Weber's Band performed its annual pre-game concert, but the mayor's ceremony was cancelled. There were no opening remarks, and no "first" pitch delivered.

The papers focused on the weather and the hardy fans: *[The fans] could not be held back by the certainty of a wetting, but kept on coming in great numbers. Hundreds of the fair sex were game enough to face the ruin of their Easter finery in order not to miss the opening game of the season.*

*The bleacherites sprouted umbrellas almost from the first and everybody got very wet in spite of the rain sticks. But there is the habitat of the real fan and it takes more than fire or flood or sword to make him stay away.*

*The Reds' new white suits were a sight to wring any heart except a dry cleaner's three minutes after play commenced.* [Cincinnati Commercial Tribune, Cincinnati Times-Star, and Cincinnati Enquirer]

### 1914 OPENING DAY SCHEDULE

| APRIL 14 NATIONAL LEAGUE | |
|---|---|
| CHI VS. CIN | PITTS VS. STL |
| BOST VS. BRKLYN | NY VS. PHIL |

### OPENING DAY TRIVIA

| | |
|---|---|
| STAR OF THE GAME | REDS PITCHER RUBE BENTON |
| WEATHER | 53°; LIGHT RAIN |
| ATTENDANCE | 15,728 |
| NOTABLE | GAME PLAYED IN STEADY DRIZZLE |
| RATING | ⚾⚾ |

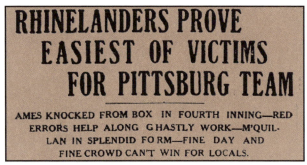

*The Opening Day headline referred to the Reds as the "Rhinelanders," a popular nickname for the team in the 1910s and 1920s*

# 1915 Easy Win for Pittsburgh
## Herzog Survives Choking Fit

The Reds lost the opener and almost lost their manager.

Buck Herzog nearly choked to death in the seventh inning, when he inadvertently swallowed a large wad of gum. Herzog, who was standing in the dugout, was rendered speechless by the incident and began motioning to his players for help. Several pounded on his back to no avail. According to a reporter, Herzog's face turned "black" and he began to go into convulsions.

The Reds team physician, who had been summoned, arrived just in time to help Herzog dislodge the gum.

The commotion drew the attention of the players on the field and play stopped for a few moments. Herzog took several minutes to regain his senses, and when he ventured onto the field to coach in the bottom of the seventh, he was quite wobbly. But he gradually recovered and seemed at full strength after the game.

The near-tragic episode provided the only moment of drama of the 1915 opener, as the Pirates easily won the game, 9–2. Reds starter Red Ames was hit freely and his "defense" committed four errors. Reliever Pete Schneider, who took over in the fifth, gave up five runs over the last four innings.

The Reds had their chances against Pirates starter George McQuillan, who gave up eight hits and walked three. But McQuillan pitched out of trouble, especially in the fourth when the Reds had the bases loaded with only one out. McQuillan got the last two outs on a pop-up and a roller back to the mound.

The Pirates ended any hope of a Reds rally with four runs off Schneider in the ninth.

The listless play of the Reds ruined an otherwise beautiful Opening Day. For the first time in two years, the day was dry and sunny. Among the 21,000 in attendance was guest of honor Charlie Gould. The first baseman for the 1869 Red Stockings joined the mayor in the center box behind home plate. The mayor delivered his brief address and tossed out the first pitch.

John Weber's Band provided the pre-game concert, accompanied by a soloist, whose vocal talent was lost in the hum of the large crowd. The *Commercial Tribune* offered this review: "The applause given the songstress was a matter of kindheartedness and belief in [club president] Garry Herrmann's musical taste, for not a note could be heard."

The press noted that the automobile had become the favored means of transportation to the game: *The age of gasoline and rubber tires is truly with us. Motors large and motors small, trucks and delivery wagons, [and] motorcycles honked and hissed and purred and splattered down town from every hilltop, from over the river cities, from heaven knows where.*

*There were the usual number of rube and farmer bands, German bands and parties in costumes, while the Carraro bunch opened up a new feature with the letting loose of countless red balloons.* [Cincinnati Commercial Tribune and Cincinnati Enquirer]

### OPENING DAY TRIVIA

| | |
|---|---|
| STAR OF THE GAME | PITTSBURGH PITCHER GEORGE MCQUILLAN |
| WEATHER | 62°; CLEAR AND CRISP |
| ATTENDANCE | 21,000 |
| NOTABLE | REDS MANAGER NEARLY CHOKES TO DEATH |
| RATING | ◐◐ |

### 1915 OPENING DAY SCHEDULE

| APRIL 14 | NATIONAL LEAGUE |
|---|---|
| PITTS vs. CIN | StL vs. CHI |
| BRKLYN vs. NY | PHIL vs. BOST |

### APRIL 14, 1915

| PITTSBURG. | AB. | R. | 1B. | PO. | A. | E. | CINCINNATI. | AB. | R. | 1B. | PO. | A. | E. |
|---|---|---|---|---|---|---|---|---|---|---|---|---|---|
| Carey, lf. | 4 | 1 | 1 | 0 | 0 | 0 | Leach, cf. | 5 | 1 | 0 | 3 | 0 | 0 |
| Johnston, 1b. | 4 | 1 | 1 | 9 | 0 | 0 | Herzog, ss. | 3 | 0 | 2 | 3 | 3 | 1 |
| Viox, 3b. | 3 | 2 | 1 | 1 | 1 | 0 | Killifer, lf. | 4 | 0 | 1 | 3 | 0 | 0 |
| Wagner, 2b. | 5 | 1 | 1 | 5 | 2 | 0 | Griffith, rf. | 3 | 0 | 0 | 2 | 0 | 0 |
| Hinchman, rf. | 5 | 2 | 3 | 0 | 0 | 0 | Groh, 3b. | 3 | 0 | 1 | 0 | 1 | 0 |
| Lejeune, cf. | 3 | 1 | 1 | 4 | 0 | 0 | Olson, 2b. | 4 | 0 | 1 | 1 | 4 | 1 |
| Gerber, ss. | 4 | 0 | 2 | 6 | 5 | 1 | Mollwitz, 1b. | 4 | 0 | 0 | 11 | 0 | 1 |
| Gibson, c. | 3 | 1 | 0 | 2 | 1 | 0 | Dooin, c. | 4 | 0 | 2 | 4 | 3 | 1 |
| McQuillan, p. | 3 | 0 | 0 | 0 | 4 | 0 | Ames, p. | 1 | 0 | 0 | 0 | 2 | 0 |
| | | | | | | | Schneider, p. | 2 | 0 | 0 | 0 | 2 | 1 |
| | | | | | | | *Wagner | 0 | 1 | 0 | 0 | 0 | 0 |
| | | | | | | | †Twombly | 1 | 0 | 1 | 0 | 0 | 0 |
| Totals | 36 | 9 | 10 | 27 | 14 | 2 | Totals | 34 | 2 | 8 | 27 | 14 | 4 |

*Ran for Dooin in the ninth.
†Batted for Schneider in the ninth.

Pittsburg............0 0 3 0 0 2 0 0 4—9
Cincinnati...........0 0 0 0 1 0 0 0 1—2

Two-Base Hits—Wagner, Olson and Viox.
Three-Base Hit—Hinchman.
Stolen Bases—Hinchman, Lejeune, Gerber, Joe Wagner, Twombly.
Earned Runs—Pittsburg 3.
Sacrifice Hits—Lejeune, McQuillan.
Double Plays—Olson, Herzog to Mollwitz; Gerber, Wagner to Johnston.
Left on Bases—Pittsburg 5, Cincinnati 8.
First Base on Errors—Pittsburg 2, Cincinnati 1.
Bases on Balls—Off McQuillan 3, off Ames 1, off Schneider 2.
Hits—Off Ames 5 in four innings, off Schneider 5 in five innings.
Struck Out—By McQuillan 4, by Ames 2, by Schneider 2.
Passed Balls—Gibson 1, Dooin 1.
Umpires—Klem and Emslie.
Time—1:59.

# 1916
## Spitballer Beats Reds
### Chicago Wins, 7–1

*Fans filled the 25¢ bleacher seats at Redland Field (in the background), an area known as the Sun Deck in the Crosley Field era. Late arrivals settled for standing-room-only space in front of the bleachers.*

### 1916 OPENING DAY SCHEDULE

| April 12 | National League |
|---|---|
| Chi vs. Cin | Pitts vs. StL |
| Bost vs. Brklyn | NY vs. Phil |

Summer-like weather brought out an enormous Opening Day crowd of 24,607, including the many rooters' groups that arrived after parading through the downtown streets.

The Reds failed to welcome the big crowd, however, falling meekly to Chicago, and the spitball master, George McConnell, 7–1.

The best show came before the game. Several of the rooters' groups circled the field after arriving at the ballpark. The Rotary club drew particular notice as they followed a brass band across the field, and then marched up through the stands to their seats. Every member carried a small banner which read "First Place or Bust."

Fred Toney, the Reds starter, gave up two runs in the first, but the Reds came back with a lone tally in the second. With none out, Heinie Groh doubled and Baldy Louden sent him home with a single. A wild pitch put Louden on second with one out, but McConnell quickly ended the threat. It proved to be the Reds last gasp, as McConnell had excellent control of his trademark spitball.

McConnell earned the start with an impressive performance during pre-game practice. Chicago manager Joe Tinker chose McConnell over Claude Hendrix after watching the pair throw warmup pitches.

Toney kept the Reds in the game until the fifth, when two misplays seemed to rattle the Reds starter. Reds left fielder Ken Williams misplayed a single into a double, and catcher Ivy Wingo made a throwing error, putting runners on first and third with none out. Three straight Cub singles brought in three runs. The Cubs had a 5–1 lead and McConnell never gave the Reds a chance to rally.

On the day before the opener, the Chamber of Commerce's "Minute Men" club, an organization of 500 businessmen, hosted a luncheon for the team and club officials. Manager Buck Herzog took the opportunity to plead for more civility in the stands, noting that the Reds were often the victims of taunts and insults. He asked for more "boosts" instead of "knocks," and noted that other cities, such as Boston and Philadelphia, seemed to give their players more respect. The luncheon concluded with songs by Reds outfielder Tommy Griffith. The event was hailed as the first of its kind in Cincinnati, and the Reds continued the tradition for several years.

As for the opener, the press made no excuses for the Reds: *The Cubs played fast and aggressive ball at the bat, hit when hits were needed, took advantage of all Red wobbles, and rolled home on the high gear in the smoothest possible manner. Our boys had trouble with carburetor, the clutch, the transmission and the steering gear, and came up to the finish line limping, coughing and demoralized.*

*John C. Weber and his prize military band was on the job as usual between third and home plate. They played all their selections in that old dashing style, and when "America" was finally reached both fans as well as players, arose and heads were bared.*

[*Cincinnati Commercial Tribune* and *Cincinnati Enquirer*]

### OPENING DAY TRIVIA

| Star of the Game | Chicago Pitcher George McConnell |
|---|---|
| Weather | 76°; Partly Cloudy |
| Attendance | 24,607 |
| Notable | Big Luncheon for Reds Day Before Game |
| Rating | ⚾⚾ |

### APRIL 12, 1916

| CHICAGO. | AB. | R. | H. | O. | A. | E. |   | CINCINNATI. | AB. | R. | H. | O. | A. | E. |
|---|---|---|---|---|---|---|---|---|---|---|---|---|---|---|
| Mulligan, ss. | 5 | 0 | 0 | 1 | 5 | 2 |   | Killifer, c. f. | 4 | 0 | 1 | 1 | 0 | 0 |
| Flack, r. f. | 3 | 2 | 2 | 0 | 0 | 0 |   | Herzog, ss. | 4 | 0 | 2 | 0 | 2 | 1 |
| F. Williams, c. f. | 4 | 1 | 2 | 3 | 0 | 0 |   | K. Williams, L. f. | 4 | 0 | 1 | 2 | 0 | 0 |
| Zimmerman, 3b | 4 | 1 | 2 | 1 | 1 | 0 |   | Griffith, r. f. | 4 | 0 | 0 | 1 | 2 | 0 |
| Saier, 1b | 3 | 1 | 1 | 14 | 0 | 0 |   | Groh, 3b | 4 | 1 | 1 | 0 | 1 | 1 |
| Schulte, l. f. | 3 | 0 | 0 | 2 | 0 | 0 |   | Louden, 2b | 4 | 0 | 3 | 4 | 2 | 0 |
| Mann, l. f. | 1 | 0 | 0 | 0 | 0 | 0 |   | Mollwitz, 1b | 4 | 0 | 1 | 10 | 1 | 0 |
| Yerkes, 2b | 2 | 0 | 1 | 5 | 0 | 0 |   | Wingo, c. | 4 | 0 | 0 | 6 | 1 | 1 |
| Archer, c. | 4 | 1 | 1 | 5 | 0 | 0 |   | Toney, p. | 1 | 0 | 0 | 1 | 0 | 0 |
| McConnell, p | 3 | 1 | 0 | 0 | 2 | 0 |   | Schulz, p. | 1 | 0 | 0 | 1 | 2 | 0 |
|  |  |  |  |  |  |  |   | *Neale | 1 | 0 | 0 | 0 | 0 | 0 |
| Totals | 32 | 7 | 9 | 27 | 14 | 2 |   | Totals | 35 | 1 | 7 | 27 | 11 | 2 |

Cincinnati ............. 0 1 0 0 0 0 0 0 0—1
Chicago ............... 2 0 0 0 3 0 0 2 0—7

*Batted for Toney in the fifth.
Two-base Hits—F. Williams, Groh, Archer. Stolen Bases—Mollwitz, Neale. Sacrifice Hit—McConnell. Double Plays—Herzog, Louden and Mollwitz; Yerkes and Saier. Left on Bases—Chicago 4, Cincinnati 7. First Base on Errors—Cincinnati 2, Chicago 2. Bases on Balls—By Toney 4, by Schulz 1. Hits and Earned Runs—Off Toney, hits 5, runs 3 in five innings; off Schulz, hits 4, runs 2, in four innings; off McConnell, hits 7, runs 1, in nine innings. Struck Out—By Toney 3, by McConnell 5, by Schulz 3. Wild Pitches—Toney, McConnell. Passed Ball—Archer. Time—1:54. Umpires—Byron and Quigley.

# Patriotic Crowd Enjoys Victory
## Defense Shines in 3–1 Victory

*Heinie Groh's defense and hitting made him the star of the 1917 opener.*

Before a immense crowd flush with patriotic fervor, Cincinnati defeated St. Louis, 3–1, in the 1917 home opener. The game was played five days after America entered World War I.

Never had Opening Day occurred at a time of national emergency. The traditionally festive half-holiday was accompanied by the colorful sights and melodious sounds of support for the war effort. Bunting and flags, martial music and patriotic signs were the order of the day.

The game itself, played in staccato time (92 minutes), also provided plenty to cheer about. The Reds and Cardinals, meeting on Opening Day for the first time, flashed plenty of defense and pitching, but in the end it was the Reds "leather," the bats of Heinie Groh and Hal Chase, and the arm of Pete Schneider that made the difference. This was the first game—and the first victory—for the Reds new manager, Christy Mathewson.

The Reds defense gave the crowd a show in almost every inning. Shortstop Larry Kopf started it off with two outstanding plays behind second base in the first inning. Manuel Cueto, Cuban-born left fielder, and Hoosier-bred center fielder Edd Roush took away two triples with spectacular catches. Cueto's catch was acrobatic; at the edge of the crowd in deep left field he jumped and stopped a line drive with his glove hand, juggled it, and reclaimed it with both hands as he was falling down. Roush's catch, also near the crowd in deep left-center field, saved two runs in the sixth.

The beneficiary of these gems was Reds starter Pete Schneider. The willowy right hander did not have his best control, giving up five walks along with four hits, but the Reds defense sprang him from "jail" more often than a Friday night bail bondsman.

The Reds put two runs on the board in the fourth and that was all they would need. After a single by Bill McKechnie—who would later manage the Reds in the 1930s and 1940s—Groh tripled and scored on a Hal Chase single. They reversed roles in the sixth, Groh singling and scoring on a Chase triple.

The papers described the war-time atmosphere at Redland: *[There was] a great display of American flags and bunting, giving the assemblage the air of a patriotic meeting. Nearly every rooter carried a flag and waved it gaily at every opportunity. The band concert before the game delighted the gathering with its program of American airs. When the Rotary Club arrived [with its band] the two bands played in harmony, while the 25,000 fans stood with bared heads, a most impressive sight.*

*When the "Star Spangled Banner" was rendered there was a demonstration that lasted nearly five minutes. Some of the most enthusiastic patriots were the kids in the bleachers.*

*There were hundreds of soldiers in uniform. A recruiting station was opened at the park, but not many rookies were secured.*

*An enthusiastic rooter presented each of the Reds with a flag just before the game started.* [**Cincinnati Commercial Tribune and Cincinnati Enquirer**]

### Opening Day Trivia

| | |
|---|---|
| Star of the Game | Reds Third Baseman Heinie Groh |
| Weather | 70°; Fair Skies |
| Attendance | 24,938 |
| Notable | Two Circus Catches By Reds Outfielders |
| Rating | ◐◐◐◐ |

### 1917 Opening Day Schedule

| April 11 | National League |
|---|---|
| StL vs. Cin | Pitts vs. Chi |
| NY vs. Bost (pp) | Phil vs. Brkyn |

# 1918
# One-Hitter!
## Pete Schneider Dominates Cubs; Stengel Raps Lone Hit

*Pete Schneider won his second straight opener with his one-hitter over Chicago.*

| 1918 OPENING DAY SCHEDULE | |
|---|---|
| APRIL 16 | NATIONAL LEAGUE |
| PITTS VS. CIN | STL VS. CHI |
| NY VS. BRKLYN | PHIL VS. BOST |

Pete Schneider, who won 20 games for the Reds in 1917, earned his spot in Opening Day lore with a one-hitter over Pittsburgh in the 1918 inaugural. This was the only one-hitter by a Red in a Cincinnati opener.

Pirate right fielder Casey Stengel stroked the lone hit, a double in the fourth inning. His drive carried just beyond the reach of left fielder Sherwood Magee. One reporter opined that if the speedy left fielder Greasy Neale had been in the lineup, he would have caught up with the rocket before it landed.

Schneider also walked five, but none came home to roost. Not a single Pirate—not even Stengel—reached third base.

The Reds needed every bit of Schneider's pitching skill, for the Pirates veteran left-hander, Wilbur Cooper, also pitched well. Cooper allowed a mere three hits through seven innings. The two runs he allowed were unearned, the result of two errors and a Eddie Roush single in the fourth inning.

Cooper had to be replaced after the seventh when he sprained an ankle on a play at first base. Cooper tripped over the bag, wrenching his foot, and fell so hard he was knocked unconscious. He was quickly revived and carried off the field.

With American troops fighting in France, the game was played in a patriotic atmosphere. Flags sprouted from the grandstand, and the pre-game concert featured stirring military marches. The crowd of 19,000 came to their feet for the playing of "America" and "The Star Spangled Banner."

| OPENING DAY TRIVIA | |
|---|---|
| STAR OF THE GAME | REDS PITCHER PETE SCHNEIDER |
| WEATHER | 68°; SUNNY |
| ATTENDANCE | 19,000 |
| NOTABLE | THIRD FASTEST OPENER EVER: 1:20 |
| RATING | ○○○○○ |

The press noted the effect of the war on the opener: *It was the first opening game since our armies have been actively hurled against the heartless Hun on the fields of France, and under the circumstances the interest shown was a remarkable tribute to the undying popularity of America's national pastime. The paid attendance [was] not quite a capacity gathering for Redland Field, but a great turnout, considering the large number of fighting men who are no longer here.*

*In the stands were hundreds of officers and men of the national army giving a distinctly military tinge to the spectacle.*

*There was not the customary noise and enthusiasm attending an opener, especially when the home team is victorious, but this was due to the absence of so many of the youngest rooters, the ones who ordinarily lead in the cheering and demonstrations.*

*The game was rushed through in an hour and twenty minutes. Both pitchers worked fast and effectively.*
[Cincinnati Commercial Tribune and Cincinnati Enquirer]

# 1919 Eighth-Inning Comeback
## Reds Rally to Beat St. Louis, 6–2

*Greasy Neale, who battled a St. Louis catcher during pre-game practice, hit a two-run single in the eighth inning to put the Reds ahead, 5–2.*

Combining a penchant for grandiose ceremony with a flair for the patriotic, the Reds arranged for an Army plane from Dayton, Ohio to buzz Redland Field and drop the Opening Day baseball into the outfield prior to the Cincinnati–St. Louis opener. Reds fans thought they might also catch a glimpse of club President Garry Herrmann circling the field in a plane, but the Reds chief caught a case of cold feet at the last moment. Herrmann, his chilly dogs firmly on terra firma, motored by car to the ballpark.

Weber's Band again entertained the big crowd of 22,462 with a foot-stomping pre-game concert heavy on John Phillips Sousa marches. Perhaps infected by the militaristic melodies—but more likely remembering some past feud—Reds outfielder Greasy Neale came to blows with St. Louis catcher Frank Snyder before the game. Teammates soon separated them.

The game managed to top the pre-game highlights. The Reds, trailing 2–1 entering the eighth, exploded for five runs after two out to whip the Cardinals, 6–2.

It was a thoroughly entertaining eighth because after the Reds edged ahead, 3–2, thunder and lightning rolled across the sky, and the wind picked up.

The Cardinals resorted to delay tactics, hoping the game would be called, and the score would revert to the tally at the end of the seventh. But the umpire refused to call off play, and Greasy Neale ended the cat-and-mouse game with a two-out, two-run single that all but clinched the Reds victory. Hod Eller, the Reds third pitcher, retired the Cardinals in the ninth.

The papers noted that some of the customary pre-game hoopla had disappeared. Since the U.S. entered World War I two years before, there had understandably been a falling off of some of the frivolity which had come to characterize Opening Day in Cincinnati: *There were lacking some of the features from the past. The amateur bands, the coteries of bugs in outlandish costumes, and the noisy rooting brigades equipped with horns and rattles were noticeable by their absence. The truckloads of wild-eyed enthusiasts who have sometimes paraded the downtown streets for hours before game time were busy elsewhere.*

*There may not have been the clown bands and there certainly were not the "German" bands of yore but there certainly was in evidence a big, clean, healthy and over-whelming desire for the national game that bespeaks much for its brilliant future.*

*Previous to the contest Manager Pat Moran [and] Captain Heinie Groh were presented with beautiful bouquets of cut flowers by local admirers. [Club president Garry] Herrmann threw out the first ball and the season was on.*

[*Cincinnati Commercial Tribune and Cincinnati Enquirer*]

### 1919 Opening Day Schedule

| April 19 | National League |
| --- | --- |
| | Brklyn vs. Bost (2) |
| April 23 | National League |
| | StL vs. Cin   Chi vs. Pitts (pp) |
| | NY vs. Phil |

### Opening Day Trivia

| Star of the Game | Reds Left Fielder Greasy Neale |
| --- | --- |
| Weather | 74°; Partly Cloudy |
| Attendance | 22,462 |
| Notable | Time of Game Considered "Long" at 2:37 |
| Rating | ○○○○ |

# 1920 Roush and Ruether Lead the Reds

*Edd Roush's home run was the first Opening Day homer for the Reds since 1894.*

In weather better suited for football, the Reds opened the defense of their 1919 championship with a rousing, 7–3, victory over Chicago.

Edd Roush and Larry Kopf were the batting stars, while Dutch Ruether out-pitched Grover Cleveland Alexander to earn the victory.

Over 24,000 braved the 48° weather, including many "bugs" who traveled from out of town. As had become a recent custom, excursion trains from Indiana and central Ohio arrived in Cincinnati the evening before the opener and on the morning of the big day. A large steamer from Portsmouth also brought hundreds of fans from upriver.

The most prominent visitor was industrialist John D. Rockefeller, who sat in a box behind third base. After Ruether made the first pitch, Rockefeller signed the ball, and presented it to Reds president Garry Herrmann.

Several local rooters' groups attended the game, including the Rotary Club, which brought its own band and paraded across the field. One group represented Findlay Market—the first appearance by this organization on Opening Day.

One conspicuous absence was that of 73-year-old Frank Bancroft, the longtime business manager of the club. The popular "Banny," who helped build Opening Day into a gala event, was recovering from an illness and missed the game. Bancroft never made another opener. He died in March 1921.

Another off-field episode also drew attention. On the eve of Opening Day, the Board of Directors of the Reds voted not to issue the customary season passes to stockholders. Several stockholders loudly protested. In defense of the move, one club officer explained that the previous year, a stockholder had purchased 10 shares and put each in the name of a different family member, thus receiving 10 season passes. The directors were not pleased at what they considered a violation of club etiquette, and passed the new resolution.

As for the game, the Reds took a 3–0 lead in the first inning. With one out and two on, Edd Roush drove a long drive to center field for an inside-the-park home run. After the Cubs tied the score in the fifth, the Reds continued their assault on Alexander. Ruether drove in the go-ahead run in the seventh, and the Reds put the game away with three more runs in the eighth, two scoring on Kopf's single.

Roush's homer was described in epic terms: *Putting all he had into his swing, timing it to the utmost limits of perfection, he met that oncoming sphere with might and main. Like a bullet it went on a line towards the green painted concrete of the center field fence. The pandemonium was ear-rendering, and everybody screamed for Eddie to make it the full circuit. The coacher waved him on but it was unnecessary as [Roush] knew better than anyone else just how brutally he had murdered that ball.*
[*Cincinnati Commercial Tribune* and *Cincinnati Enquirer*]

### OPENING DAY TRIVIA

| | |
|---|---|
| STAR OF THE GAME | REDS CENTER FIELDER EDD ROUSH |
| WEATHER | 48°; CLOUDY |
| ATTENDANCE | 24,822 |
| NOTABLE | JOHN D. ROCKEFELLER ATTENDS GAME |
| RATING | ●●●● |

### 1920 OPENING DAY SCHEDULE

| APRIL 14 | NATIONAL LEAGUE |
|---|---|
| CHI VS. CIN | PITTS VS. STL |
| PHIL VS. BRKLYN | BOST VS. NY |

### APRIL 14, 1920

| CHICAGO. | AB. | R. | BH. | PO. | A. | E. |
|---|---|---|---|---|---|---|
| Flack, r. f. | 3 | 0 | 1 | 2 | 0 | 0 |
| Hollocher, s.s. | 4 | 0 | 0 | 1 | 3 | 0 |
| Herzog, 2b. | 4 | 0 | 0 | 0 | 3 | 0 |
| Barber, 1b. | 4 | 0 | 0 | 9 | 1 | 0 |
| Paskert, c.f. | 3 | 0 | 0 | 5 | 0 | 0 |
| Deal, 3b. | 4 | 0 | 1 | 2 | 0 | 0 |
| Twombly, l. f. | 4 | 1 | 1 | 2 | 0 | 0 |
| Killefer, c. | 4 | 2 | 1 | 3 | 0 | 0 |
| Alexander, p. | 3 | 0 | 2 | 0 | 3 | 0 |
| Totals | 32 | 3 | 5 | 24 | 10 | 0 |
| CINCINNATI. | AB. | R. | BH. | PO. | A. | E. |
| Rath, 2b. | 5 | 0 | 2 | 6 | 3 | 0 |
| Daubert, 1b. | 3 | 0 | 1 | 9 | 0 | 0 |
| Groh, 3b. | 4 | 3 | 3 | 1 | 1 | 0 |
| Roush, c. f. | 4 | 1 | 1 | 2 | 0 | 0 |
| Duncan, l. f. | 4 | 0 | 2 | 0 | 0 | 0 |
| Kopf, s.s. | 4 | 0 | 2 | 1 | 5 | 0 |
| Neale, r. f. | 4 | 1 | 1 | 3 | 0 | 0 |
| Wingo, c. | 3 | 0 | 0 | 5 | 2 | 0 |
| Ruether, p. | 3 | 0 | 2 | 0 | 2 | 0 |
| Totals | 34 | 7 | 13 | 27 | 13 | 0 |

Chicago .................. 0 0 2 0 1 0 0 0 0—3
Cincinnati ............... 3 0 0 0 0 0 1 3 *—7

Two-base Hits—Groh, Killefer 2. Three-base Hit—Alexander. Home Run—Roush. Double Play—Ruether, Kopf and Daubert. Left on Bases—Chicago 5, Cincinnati 7. Bases on Balls—By Ruether 1, by Alexander 4. Hit by Pitcher—Ruether 2. Struck Out—By Ruether 1, by Alexander 5. Time—1:48. Umpires—Rigler and Moran.

*Lou Fonseca was one of three first-time Opening Day starters to star in the 1921 opener.*

# Substitutes Pull Out Victory
## Holdouts Forgotten in 5–3 Win

Edd who? Heinie who? Larry who?

Edd Roush, Heinie Groh and Larry Kopf, the Reds starting center fielder, third baseman and second baseman, respectively, staged holdouts over contract disputes and missed the 1921 opener. In their place, manager Pat Moran started three relative unknowns: Charlie See, Sam Bohne and Lou Fonseca.

The three combined for five of Cincinnati's nine hits and drove in four of the Reds five runs, in the 5–3 win over Pittsburgh. All three drove in runs in the Reds' four-run eighth inning, which clinched the victory.

Dolf Luque had battled the Pirates Babe Adams over the first seven innings to a 1–1 draw. The Pirates racked up 12 hits, but the Havana native managed to squeeze out of every difficulty to ultimately earn the win.

"He was hit rather hard," admitted manager Moran, "but pitched fine ball in the pinches. I was sure that Luque could deliver the goods."

Luque also scored the Reds first run in the third inning after tripling into the standing-room-only section in deep left field.

The Pirates tied the score in the seventh and the 29,963 Redland rooters began to think about an extra-inning contest. But the Reds broke through against Adams in the eighth. With two on and one out, Bohne struck the first big blow, a two-run ground-rule triple into the crowd in left.

After the veteran Jake Daubert fouled out, the fresh-faced recruits struck again. See singled Bohne home, and Fonseca whacked another drive into the left-field crowd for the Reds' third triple of the day and a 5–1 lead. The Pirates tallied two in the ninth off a tiring Luque, but the "Pride of Havana" sucked it up for his first Opening Day win.

The 1921 opener was short on hoopla. There was no mention of pre-game motorcades through downtown, and there were no formal opening ceremonies. But tickets were sold out weeks in advance and the game attracted a distinguished crowd: *[Ohio] Governor Harry L. Davis occupied a box near the Reds bench with Mayor John Galvin and [Reds] President [Garry] Herrmann. The Governor keeps his own score and watches every play from the standpoint of an expert.*

*John C. Weber and his prize Military Band were on hand as usual and rendered many splendid selections previous to the game. "Doc" Howard's Cabaret made its annual appearance on the big field and the singers, fifteen in number, mixed some harmony, jazz and melody to their latest numbers.*

*Many fans spoke with regret of the absence of [long-time business manager] Frank Bancroft. His genial countenance was sadly missed by the regulars. And how Banny would have delighted in handling that big crowd!* [**Cincinnati Commercial Tribune and Cincinnati Enquirer**]

### 1921 OPENING DAY SCHEDULE

| APRIL 13 | NATIONAL LEAGUE |
|---|---|
| PITTS VS. CIN | StL VS. CHI |
| BRKLYN VS. BOST | NY VS. PHIL |

### OPENING DAY TRIVIA

| | |
|---|---|
| STAR OF THE GAME | REDS THIRD BASEMAN SAM BOHNE |
| WEATHER | 70°; CLEAR |
| ATTENDANCE | 29,963 |
| NOTABLE | RECORD CROWD FOR OPENING DAY |
| RATING | ●●●● |

### APRIL 13, 1921

| CINCIN'TI | AB. | R. | BH. | PO. | A. | E. | PITTS'H | AB. | R. | BH. | PO. | A. | E. |
|---|---|---|---|---|---|---|---|---|---|---|---|---|---|
| Paskert, r. f. | 3 | 1 | 0 | 3 | 0 | 0 | Bigbee, l. f. | 5 | 1 | 2 | 1 | 0 | 0 |
| Daubert, 1b. | 4 | 1 | 2 | 7 | 1 | 0 | Carey, c. f. | 4 | 1 | 3 | 2 | 0 | 0 |
| Bohne, 3b. | 4 | 1 | 2 | 3 | 2 | 0 | Maranville, s. s. | 5 | 0 | 2 | 1 | 2 | 1 |
| Duncan, l. f. | 4 | 0 | 0 | 3 | 0 | 0 | Barnhart, 3b. | 5 | 0 | 0 | 3 | 0 | 0 |
| See, c. f. | 4 | 1 | 1 | 2 | 0 | 1 | Whitted, r. f. | 4 | 1 | 3 | 0 | 0 | 0 |
| Fonseca, 2b. | 4 | 0 | 2 | 0 | 0 | 0 | Tierney, 2b. | 3 | 0 | 3 | 1 | 6 | 0 |
| Crane, s. s. | 4 | 0 | 1 | 4 | 0 | 0 | Grimm, 1b. | 3 | 1 | 1 | 13 | 0 | 0 |
| Wingo, c. | 3 | 0 | 0 | 4 | 2 | 0 | Schmidt, c. | 3 | 0 | 0 | 3 | 0 | 0 |
| Luque, p. | 3 | 1 | 1 | 1 | 3 | 0 | Adams, p. | 3 | 0 | 0 | 0 | 1 | 0 |
| | | | | | | | Hamilton, p. | 1 | 0 | 0 | 0 | 0 | 0 |
| | | | | | | | *Rohmer | 1 | 0 | 0 | 0 | 0 | 0 |
| Totals | 33 | 5 | 9 | 27 | 8 | 1 | Totals | 36 | 3 | 12 | 24 | 12 | 1 |

*Batted for Hamilton in ninth.

Pittsburgh .......... 0 0 0 0 1 0 0 0 2—3
Cincinnati .......... 0 0 1 0 0 0 0 4 x—5

Two-base Hits—Bohne, Bigbee 2 Maranville. Three-base Hits—Luque, Grimm, Bohne, Fonseca. Sacrifice—Schmidt. Double Plays Maranville, Tierney and Grimm. Left on Bases—Cincinnati 5, Pittsburgh 10. Bases on Balls—By Luque 3, by Adams 1. Hits—Off Adams 9 in 7 2-3 innings. Struck Out—By Luque 3, by Adams 1. Balk—Luque. Winning Pitcher—Luque. Losing Pitcher—Adams. Time—1:31 Umpires—Rigler and Moran. Attendance—30,444.

# Alexander Too Much for Reds

## Chicago Vet Topples Rixey and Reds, 7–3

*Grover Cleveland Alexander (left) and Eppa Rixey shake hands before the 1922 opener.*

In a battle of two future Hall of Fame pitchers, Grover Cleveland "Pete" Alexander bested Eppa Rixey, as Chicago walked off with the opener, 7–3.

This was one of only two times in Reds history that two Hall of Fame pitchers opposed one another on Opening Day. (The other was a Tom Seaver–Steve Carlton matchup in 1981.) Alexander was in the 12th year of a 20-year career that would produce 373 victories. Rixey was a 10-year veteran, not quite halfway through his 266-win, 21-year career.

But on this day, Alexander was superior. "The prince of right-handers," as one local reporter dubbed Alexander, held the Reds to seven hits. He struck out four and walked one. The Reds managed a two-run rally in the eighth which served only to make the score respectable.

Rixey kept the game close through the sixth inning, down just 3–1. But "Eppa Jeptha" failed to survive the seventh. He gave up five hits, including a double to his counterpart, Alexander, that drove in one run. Rixey was relieved and John Couch stopped the hit parade, but the Cubs' 7–1 lead was all but unassailable.

The crowd of 27,095 and would have been even bigger if the weather had been more settled. Overnight rain left the ground saturated and the temperatures cool. Although the sun shone for most of the game, chilly breezes swept across the field and kept the overcoats buttoned.

After what seems to have been a somewhat subdued opener in 1921, the merrymakers were back: *Judging from the crowds congregated in the lobbies of the downtown hotels, this opening attracted more out-of-town fans than any other.*

*Upon the streets the crush of motors was almost unbelievable. On every hand horns tooted, rattles rattled and unusually exuberant bugs howled to the highest of heavens. Rooters' clubs adorned the inside and out of strings of autos. Clown bands and other bands, and lone musicians let loose early. Business may not have stopped, but it certainly slackened up, and Cincinnati and its environs hearkened to the diamond call. For it was Baseball's Day!*

*Every street within four blocks of the park was filled to its allowed capacity with automobiles. There were in the neighborhood of five thousand autos parked on the thoroughfares.*

*The Cincinnati Rotary Club turned out in an impressive manner. Fifty automobiles, showingly decorated, conveyed the Rotarians to Redland Field. The Findlay Market Rooters' Club, one hundred and fifty strong, carried an immense floral horseshoe around the park and upon reaching home plate presented it to Manager Moran.*

*The peanut and candy venders and the soft drinks and cigarette peddlers were out in double force. The roofs of buildings surrounding the park were packed with fans.*

*There was no throwing out the first ball or speeches. Governor Davis could not make the grade on account of sudden and important business.* [*Cincinnati Commercial Tribune and Cincinnati Enquirer*]

### APRIL 12, 1922

| CHICAGO. | AB. | R. | BH. | PO. | A. | E. |
|---|---|---|---|---|---|---|
| Statz, cf. | 5 | 1 | 1 | 1 | 0 | 0 |
| Hollocher, ss. | 5 | 1 | 1 | 2 | 5 | 0 |
| Kelleher, 3b. | 4 | 1 | 2 | 1 | 4 | 0 |
| Grimes, 1b. | 4 | 1 | 2 | 15 | 0 | 0 |
| Friberg, rf. | 3 | 1 | 1 | 1 | 0 | 0 |
| Miller, lf. | 4 | 0 | 1 | 3 | 0 | 0 |
| Krug, 2b. | 4 | 1 | 2 | 0 | 4 | 0 |
| Hartnett, c. | 2 | 0 | 0 | 5 | 0 | 0 |
| Alexander, p. | 3 | 1 | 1 | 0 | 3 | 0 |
| Totals | 34 | 7 | 11 | 27 | 16 | 0 |

| CINCINNATI. | AB. | R. | BH. | PO. | A. | E. |
|---|---|---|---|---|---|---|
| Burns, cf. | 4 | 0 | 1 | 2 | 0 | 0 |
| Neale, rf. | 4 | 1 | 2 | 2 | 0 | 0 |
| Duncan, lf. | 3 | 0 | 1 | 4 | 1 | 1 |
| Bohne, 2b. | 3 | 1 | 0 | 5 | 3 | 0 |
| Daubert, 1b. | 4 | 0 | 0 | 9 | 0 | 0 |
| Caveney, ss. | 4 | 0 | 0 | 3 | 3 | 0 |
| Pinelli, 3b. | 4 | 0 | 2 | 1 | 3 | 1 |
| Wingo, c. | 3 | 0 | 0 | 0 | 1 | 0 |
| Rixey, p. | 2 | 0 | 0 | 0 | 4 | 0 |
| Couch, p. | 0 | 0 | 0 | 1 | 1 | 0 |
| *Harper | 1 | 1 | 1 | 0 | 0 | 0 |
| Gillespie, p. | 0 | 0 | 0 | 0 | 1 | 0 |
| Totals | 32 | 3 | 7 | 27 | 17 | 2 |

Cincinnati .......... 0 1 0 0 0 0 2 0—3
Chicago ............ 0 2 0 0 1 4 0 0—7

*Batted for Couch in eighth.
Two-base Hits—King, Alexander. Three-base Hits—Pinelli, Neale. Stolen Bases—Bohne, Pinelli, Kelleher, Friberg. Sacrifices—Friberg, Hartnett 2, Duncan. Double Plays—Kelleher, Hollocher and Grimes; Couch and Bohne. Left on Bases—Cincinnati 4, Chicago 6. Base on Balls—By Rixey 1, by Couch 1, by Alexander 1. Struck Out—By Alexander 4. Hits—Off Rixey 10 in 6 1-3 innings, off Couch 1 in 1 2-3 innings. Hit by Pitcher—Grimes by Couch. Wild Pitch—Alexander. Losing Pitcher—Rixey. Time—1:47. Umpires Klem and Sentelle.

### OPENING DAY TRIVIA

| | |
|---|---|
| STAR OF THE GAME | CUBS PITCHER GROVER CLEVELAND ALEXANDER |
| WEATHER | 52°; PARTLY CLOUDY |
| ATTENDANCE | 27,095 |
| NOTABLE | TWO FUTURE HALL OF FAMERS START GAME |
| RATING | ●●● |

### 1922 OPENING DAY SCHEDULE

| APRIL 12 | NATIONAL LEAGUE |
|---|---|
| CHI VS. CIN | STL VS. PITTS |
| BRKLYN VS. NY | PHIL VS. BOST |

# Triumph in 11; Reds Edge Cards
## First Opener to Top 30,000

*Many players were honored prior to home openers, including Reds veteran first baseman Jake Daubert, here receiving a bouquet from an unidentified admirer.*

### 1923 OPENING DAY SCHEDULE

| APRIL 17 | NATIONAL LEAGUE |
|---|---|
| StL vs. Cin | Pitts vs. Chi |
| Phil vs. Brklyn | NY vs. Bost |

It was a perfect ending to a perfectly raucous day at Redland Field. Cincinnati scored the winning run in the bottom of the eleventh inning to beat St. Louis, 3–2.

The crowd of 30,338 was the first to break the 30,000 barrier for Opening Day, and although a chilly wind blew for much of the afternoon, the bugs kept themselves warm with their noisemakers and cheers.

Pete Donohue pitched the entire game and contributed to the winning rally with a sacrifice bunt. Donohue was not sharp; he gave up 13 hits and one walk. But Pete scattered the hits (all were singles) and benefitted from two double plays and error-free defense. Pete also held the reigning batting champion, Rogers Hornsby, hitless.

The Reds scored first off Cardinal starter Ed Pfeffer, with single runs in the second and sixth. But the Cardinals broke through against Donohue in the seventh and eighth and the game rolled into extra innings.

The Reds started the winning rally in the eleventh. The first batter, Jimmy Caveney walked. Ivy Wingo then shot a hot grounder between first and second that hit Caveney, which put him out and put Wingo on first. Donohue then laid down a perfect sacrifice bunt which brought up outfielder George Burns. Burns rolled a single into left field, and Wingo beat the throw to score the winning run.

Once again, the Reds faithful turned the opener into a holiday. Rooters' groups filled the streets: *The slowly moving streams of motors were punctuated ever so often by huge busses, each crammed with scores of Rooters' clubs. Many of the passengers in this assorted series of procession wore fancy costumes. Clowns and "Dutchmen" and pierotts and tramps abounded. It was Christmas, Fourth of July, Yom Kippur and St. Patrick's Day rolled all into one and with an added flavor only sensed on Cincinnati's day of days—the baseball getaway.*

*By 11 o'clock there were fully 12,000 people within the fences and hundreds more poured in every few minutes. Having nothing else to do save sit and wait and watch their neighbors, the early birds found the usual panacea of idle mankind and burst into various sorts of song.*

*Ropes were stretched all the way around the field and the rooters stood 20 deep for more than three hours. All ceremonies were omitted from the program. No dignitary threw out the first ball and no one made a speech, for which kindness the management be praised.*

*Staff photographers and movie men roamed swiftly from point to point. Bouquets of flowers were showered upon the famous performers of both clubs. The athletes sped nimbly through their practice stunts. And then the game was on.* **[Cincinnati Commercial Tribune and Cincinnati Enquirer]**

### OPENING DAY TRIVIA

| | |
|---|---|
| Star of the Game | Reds Pitcher Pete Donohue |
| Weather | 52°; Cloudy |
| Attendance | 30,338 |
| Notable | First Opener to Draw 30,000 |
| Rating | ○○○○ |

### APRIL 17, 1923

| ST. LOUIS. | AB. | R. | H. | O. | A. | E. | | CINCIN'TI. | AB. | R. | H. | O. | A. | E. |
|---|---|---|---|---|---|---|---|---|---|---|---|---|---|---|
| Blades, l. f. | 4 | 0 | 1 | 4 | 0 | 0 | | Burns, r. f. | 6 | 0 | 2 | 1 | 0 | 0 |
| Smith, r. f. | 5 | 0 | 2 | 2 | 0 | 0 | | Harper, c. f. | 4 | 0 | 0 | 4 | 0 | 0 |
| Hornsby, 2b. | 5 | 0 | 0 | 2 | 4 | 0 | | Duncan, l. f. | 5 | 0 | 2 | 0 | 0 | 0 |
| Bottomly, 1b. | 5 | 1 | 4 | 16 | 1 | 0 | | Bohne, 2b. | 4 | 1 | 0 | 5 | 4 | 0 |
| Stock, 3b. | 5 | 0 | 0 | 2 | 0 | 0 | | Fonseca, 1b. | 3 | 1 | 1 | 15 | 0 | 0 |
| Mueller, c. f. | 4 | 0 | 0 | 2 | 0 | 0 | | Pinelli, 3b. | 5 | 0 | 2 | 1 | 5 | 0 |
| Freigau, ss. | 5 | 0 | 2 | 1 | 3 | 1 | | Caveney, ss. | 2 | 0 | 0 | 2 | 3 | 0 |
| Ainsmith, c. | 3 | 0 | 2 | 1 | 1 | 0 | | Wingo, c. | 3 | 1 | 2 | 5 | 0 | 0 |
| *Dyer | 0 | 1 | 0 | 0 | 0 | 0 | | Donahue, p. | 4 | 0 | 0 | 0 | 4 | 0 |
| Clemons, c. | 2 | 0 | 1 | 2 | 1 | 0 | | Totals | 36 | 3 | 9 | 33 | 17 | 0 |
| Pfeffer, p. | 2 | 0 | 0 | 1 | 2 | 0 | | | | | | | | |
| †Flack | 1 | 0 | 1 | 0 | 0 | 0 | | | | | | | | |
| ‡Mann | 0 | 0 | 0 | 0 | 0 | 0 | | | | | | | | |
| Sell, p. | 2 | 0 | 0 | 0 | 2 | 0 | | | | | | | | |
| Totals | 43 | 2 | 13 | 31x | 16 | 1 | | | | | | | | |

St. Louis .......... 0 0 0 0 0 1 0 0—2
Cincinnati ........ 0 1 0 0 0 1 0 0 0 0 1—3

*Ran for Ainsmith in seventh. †Batted for Pfeffer in seventh. ‡Ran for Flack in seventh. xCaveney out, hit by batted ball. Two out when winning run was scored.

Two-base Hits—Duncan, Fonseca, Wingo. Sacrifices—Harper, Fonseca, Caveney, Donahue. Double Plays—Pinelli to Bohne to Fonseca; Bohne to Fonseca; Hornsby to Freigau. Left on Bases—St. Louis 10, Cincinnati 11. Bases on Balls—Off Donahue 1, off Pfeffer 3, off Sell 1. Hits—Off Pfeffer 5 in six innings, off Sell 4 in four and two-thirds innings. Hit by Pitcher—By Donahue 1. Losing Pitcher—Sell. Time of Game—2:31. Umpires—Quigley and Pfirman.

# 1924
# Over 35,000 Cheer Reds Comeback
## Reds Down Pittsburgh in 9th, 6–5

*Bubbles Hargrave was the hitting star of the 1924 opener, going four-for-four with two triples.*

### 1924 OPENING DAY SCHEDULE

| APRIL 15 | NATIONAL LEAGUE |
|---|---|
| PITTS VS. CIN | CHI VS. STL |
| BOST VS. PHIL | BRKLYN VS. NY |

Cheered on by 35,000 fans at Redland Field and thousands more listening to the game at home on their radio sets, the Reds rallied to beat Pittsburgh, 6–5, in the 1924 opener. The crowd of 35,747 set the all-time Opening Day attendance mark at Redland/Crosley Field.

This was the first Opening Day to be broadcast in Cincinnati, carried simultaneously by WLW and WSAI. The Crosley Broadcasting Corporation installed a temporary microphone on top of the roof of the grandstand where announcer Eugene Mittendorf handled the play-by-play. The only complaint from listeners was that the screaming of the crowd occasionally drowned out the announcer's voice.

Mr. Mittendorf must have grown hoarse, for it was an opener worthy of much cheering. The Reds took a comfortable, 4–1, lead into the sixth inning. Pete Donohue had given up only one hit through the first five innings, but the Pirates figured him out in the sixth. They scored four runs on five hits and two sacrifice flies.

The Reds began their comeback in the eighth. Bubbles Hargrave, who had four hits on the day, belted one of his two triples to lead off the inning. He scored moments later on Sammy Bohne's sacrifice fly to left, tying the score.

In the ninth, reliever Tom Sheehan started the winning rally with a one-out walk. George Burns singled and Jake Daubert drew another walk, loading the bases with one out. Edd Roush then drove a long fly to Carson Bigbee in left, but it was so deep he did not even make a throw home, and pinch runner Ed Hock scored the winning run. (This was the highlight of Hock's year; he appeared in only two games.)

The big crowd, the pre-game concert and the many rooters' groups again added to the Opening Day atmosphere: *In the hotels, crowded to the window sills with visiting Red rooters from towns within a radius of two hundred miles, the hopes and fears of myriads were broadcast. Ignoring vociferous calls of "Front," bellhops gathered in knots with "the latest dope from [Reds manager Jack] Hendricks" or proudly showed priceless jewels—tickets to the opening game!*

*On the street corners it was the same. Forgotten was business, and if the fatigued princes of the marts of trade did enter their offices, it was to grant permission for a thousand office boys to "enjoy" the funerals of a thousand grandmothers!"*

The annual parade of members of the Findlay Market Association was an affair that eclipsed all former parades in numbers and originality. More than 400 members of the association, each wearing a flower in his coat, wearing a large white hat and carrying a cane were in line when the parade passed through the gates at Redland Field and marched around the playing ground. [**Cincinnati Commercial Tribune and Cincinnati Enquirer**]

### APRIL 15, 1924

| Pittsburgh. | AB. | R. | H. | O. | A. | E. |
|---|---|---|---|---|---|---|
| Maranville, 2b. | 3 | 1 | 1 | 5 | 3 | 1 |
| Carey, c. f. | 5 | 1 | 2 | 0 | 0 | 0 |
| Bigbee, l. f. | 4 | 1 | 1 | 3 | 0 | 0 |
| Traynor, 3b. | 3 | 1 | 0 | 0 | 3 | 0 |
| Barnhart, r. f. | 4 | 1 | 2 | 3 | 0 | 0 |
| Wright, s.s. | 4 | 0 | 1 | 1 | 2 | 2 |
| Grimm, 1b. | 3 | 0 | 1 | 9 | 1 | 0 |
| Schmidt, c. | 3 | 0 | 1 | 2 | 4 | 0 |
| Morrison, p. | 3 | 0 | 0 | 0 | 2 | 0 |
| *Mueller | 1 | 0 | 0 | 0 | 0 | 0 |
| Meadows, p. | 0 | 0 | 0 | 0 | 0 | 0 |
| Totals | 34 | 5 | 8 | 26 | 15 | 3 |
| Cincinnati. | AB. | R. | H. | O. | A. | E. |
| Burns, r. f. | 4 | 1 | 1 | 1 | 0 | 0 |
| Daubert, 1b. | 3 | 0 | 1 | 12 | 0 | 0 |
| Roush, c. f. | 4 | 0 | 0 | 5 | 0 | 0 |
| Duncan, l. f. | 4 | 0 | 0 | 1 | 1 | 0 |
| Hargrave, c. | 4 | 2 | 4 | 2 | 1 | 0 |
| Bohne, 2b. | 3 | 0 | 1 | 1 | 2 | 0 |
| Pinelli, 3b. | 3 | 1 | 1 | 1 | 4 | 0 |
| Caveney, s.s. | 4 | 0 | 1 | 1 | 0 | 2 |
| Donohue, p. | 2 | 0 | 0 | 0 | 4 | 0 |
| †Harper | 0 | 0 | 0 | 0 | 0 | 0 |
| Sheehan, p. | 0 | 1 | 0 | 0 | 0 | 0 |
| §Hock | 0 | 1 | 0 | 0 | 0 | 0 |
| Totals | 31 | 6 | 9 | 27 | 12 | 2 |

Pittsburgh .... 0 1 0 0 0 4 0 0 0—5
Cincinnati .... 0 1 0 1 2 0 0 1 1—6

*Batted for Morrison in ninth.
†Two out when winning run was scored. ‡Batted for Donohue in seventh. §Ran for Sheehan in ninth.

Two-base Hit—Burns. Three-base Hits—Hargrave 2, Bigbee. Stolen Base—Maranville. Sacrifices—Burns, Daubert, Roush, Bohne, Traynor, Grimm. Double Plays—Burns and Daubert; Morrison Traynor and Grimm. Left on Bases—Pittsburgh 6, Cincinnati 7. Base on Balls—By Donohue 1, by Sheehan 1, by Morrison 2, by Meadows 2. Struck Out—By Donohue 1, by Sheehan 1, by Morrison 2. Hits—Off Donohue 6 in seven innings, off Morrison 8 in eight innings off Sheehan 2 in two innings, off Meadows 1 in two-thirds inning. Wild Pitch—Morrison. Winning Pitcher—Sheehan. Losing Pitcher—Meadows. Time—1:49. Umpires—Klem and Wilson.

### OPENING DAY TRIVIA

| STAR OF THE GAME | REDS CATCHER BUBBLES HARGRAVE |
|---|---|
| WEATHER | 79°; SUNNY |
| ATTENDANCE | 35,747 |
| NOTABLE | RECORD CROWD; FIRST OPENER ON RADIO |
| RATING | ●●●●● |

*Pete Donohue won his second Opening Day game in 1925 with a four-hitter.*

# 1925
# Peter The Great
## Donohue Blanks Cardinals, 4–0

| OPENING DAY TRIVIA | |
|---|---|
| STAR OF THE GAME | REDS PITCHER PETE DONOHUE |
| WEATHER | 76°; MOSTLY SUNNY |
| ATTENDANCE | 31,888 |
| NOTABLE | TIME OF GAME: 1:26 |
| RATING | ○○○○ |

For the first time in three years, the Reds did not have to resort to late-inning heroics to win the opener. This time they turned matters over to Pete Donohue, who picked up his second Opening Day victory, a masterful six-hit shutout.

Redland Field sported a new flag for the opener. The National League gave each team a 50th anniversary banner to display. The blue flag had the words "National Jubilee, National League, 1875–1925" in gold letters.

Cardinal starter Jess Haines held Cincinnati to six hits in six innings, but it was a weak start that did him in. Two walks and a hit loaded the bases in the first before a Red was out. Then came the critical play of the game. Rube Bressler lofted a high fly into left-center field that Wattie Holm caught after a long run. Hughie Critz came in easily after the catch and Babe Pinelli headed to third. Holm's throw was way off target and rolled over to the stands, allowing Pinelli to score the second run.

The two tallies were all that Donohue needed. No runner reached third against him, and only one reached second. He walked none. The Cardinal's only threat came in the seventh when the first two runners reached base. But a force out and two strike outs ended the inning.

The Reds added runs in the fourth and fifth. Three singles produced one run in the fourth, and the Reds appeared to ring up more runs when Bubbles Hargrave launched a deep drive to center field. But Heinie Mueller made a sensational catch. "As vicious a case of highway robbery as was ever witnessed," wrote one reporter. Mueller dove for the ball and held on as he somersaulted across the turf. Hargrave had to be cursing his luck. Mueller's catch was one of three great outfield plays that robbed the Reds catcher of extra-base hits.

Donohue's sharp control and the Cardinals steady pitching kept the innings short, and the game ended in one hour and 26 minutes, the third fastest Reds' Opening Day game on record.

The increasingly familiar traffic jams caught the reporters' attention: *As early as 11 o'clock the streets leading to Redland Field were made to know the coming of acute congestion. It was, of course, a motor caravan. Cars of every make, hue and description soon grew more and more numerous. By noon the movement grew slower as from the hill-top suburbs, from over the river and from near-by towns the crammed autos came honking and snorting.*

*With 1 o'clock came pandemonium. The rusty noses of a horde of Hen Ford's international pests thrust brazenly into fenders that scowled above the wheels of lordly Rolls-Royces. Headlights were crunched with sickening sound.*

*From the long lines of street cars came the proletariat, knocking over those who stood in their way. But good nature held sway in almost every dilemma.* [**Cincinnati Commercial Tribune and Cincinnati Enquirer**]

| 1925 OPENING DAY SCHEDULE | |
|---|---|
| APRIL 14 | NATIONAL LEAGUE |
| STL VS. CIN | PITTS VS. CHI |
| PHIL VS. BRKLYN | NY VS. BOST |

### APRIL 14, 1925

| St. Louis | AB | R | H | PO | A | E |
|---|---|---|---|---|---|---|
| Flack, r. f. | 4 | 0 | 2 | 1 | 0 | 0 |
| Mueller, c. f. | 4 | 0 | 3 | 0 | 0 | 0 |
| Hornsby, 2b | 4 | 0 | 0 | 2 | 3 | 0 |
| Bottomley, 1b | 4 | 0 | 2 | 10 | 0 | 0 |
| Bell, 3b | 4 | 0 | 1 | 0 | 2 | 0 |
| Holm, l. f. | 3 | 0 | 0 | 5 | 0 | 1 |
| Schmidt, c. | 3 | 0 | 0 | 3 | 2 | 0 |
| Thevenow, s. s. | 3 | 0 | 1 | 0 | 4 | 0 |
| Haines, p. | 1 | 0 | 0 | 0 | 1 | 0 |
| *Smith | 1 | 0 | 0 | 0 | 0 | 0 |
| Day, p. | 0 | 0 | 0 | 0 | 0 | 0 |
| †Blades | 1 | 0 | 0 | 0 | 0 | 0 |
| Sherdel, p. | 0 | 0 | 0 | 0 | 0 | 0 |
| Totals | 32 | 0 | 6 | 24 | 12 | 1 |
| Cincinnati | AB | R | H | PO | A | E |
| Critz, 2b | 2 | 1 | 0 | 1 | 6 | 0 |
| Pinelli, 3b | 4 | 1 | 1 | 1 | 2 | 0 |
| Roush, c. f. | 3 | 0 | 1 | 5 | 0 | 0 |
| Bressler, 1b | 3 | 1 | 1 | 11 | 0 | 0 |
| Walker, r. f. | 3 | 0 | 1 | 3 | 0 | 0 |
| Zitzmann, l. f. | 3 | 0 | 1 | 1 | 0 | 0 |
| Caveney, s. s. | 3 | 0 | 0 | 2 | 2 | 0 |
| Hargrave, c. | 3 | 0 | 0 | 3 | 0 | 0 |
| Donohue, p. | 3 | 1 | 1 | 1 | 1 | 0 |
| Totals | 27 | 4 | 6 | 27 | 11 | 0 |

St. Louis ...... 0 0 0 0 0 0 0 0 0—0
Cincinnati ... 2 0 0 1 1 0 0 0 *—4

*Batted for Haines in sixth. †Batted for Day in eighth.

Three-base Hit—Roush. Sacrifices—Critz, Bressler. Double Play—Critz, Caveney and Bressler. Left on Bases—St. Louis 5, Cincinnati 3. Bases on Balls—By Haines 2. Struck Out—By Donohue 2, by Haines 2, by Day 1, by Sherdel 1. Hits—Off Haines 6 in six innings, off Day none in two innings, off Sherdel none in one inning. Losing Pitcher—Haines. Time—1:26. Umpires—O'Day, Pfirman and Sweeney.

# "May" Day in April
## Reds Reliever Earns Victory; Scores Winning Run

*Jakie May picked up the victory in the 1926 opener in relief when he scored the winning run.*

Maybe they were lucky hats.

The Reds unveiled new blue lids with their new home uniforms for the 1926 opener and came away with a wild 10-inning victory over Chicago. The seesaw affair resulted in four lead changes, three in the last three innings. A great crowd of over 32,000 cheered itself hoarse as the Reds finally pushed over the winning tally in the bottom of the 10th for a 7–6 win. It was the ninth Opening Day victory in 10 years for the Reds, a string of success second only to the Reds of the 1970s and '80s, who won 16 of 18 openers.

The roly-poly North Carolinian, Jakie May, earned the victory with two scoreless innings of relief, and he scored the winning run on a single by shortstop Sammy Bohne.

Chicago tiptoed to a 1–0 lead off Pete Donohue, who was starting his fourth consecutive opener. But the Reds leaped ahead after scoring three runs in the fifth and two in the sixth off veteran Wilbur Cooper. Two errors fueled the Reds fifth. In the next inning, catcher Val Picinich clobbered a two-run home run into the temporary seats.

For reasons unrecorded, the teams agreed to a ground-rule home run on balls hit into this area, which in past years had been limited to a triple.

Donohue failed to hold the 5–1 lead, giving up five runs in the eighth, highlighted by a two-run triple by Hack Wilson and a two-run homer (into the same left field seats) by Dayton native Howard Freigau.

But the Reds would not go gently. Edd Roush drove in the tying run in the bottom of the eighth, forcing extra innings. Bohne delivered the final blow in the tenth, sending May streaking across the plate.

Another overflow crowd had jammed Redland Field. Two youngsters were first in line: *As the sun's rays fell on Redland Field [on the morning of the game] the forms of two young boys huddled beside a bonfire were revealed. They arrived at the bleacher wall at 10:30 [the night before] and waited for the ticket window to open. Both are in the eighth grade.*

*Every available location in the big stands was filled, with thousands standing on their weary dogs throughout the long afternoon rather than miss the thrill of the getaway. Long lines of patient observers surrounded the entire playing field from one foul line to the other.*

*Several sections of rooters marched around the field to display their hot Reds patriotism. The Findlay Market Rooters made a fine showing as they paraded around the field before the game, headed by a band and marching like real soldiers. There was the usual shower of bouquets for those players whose special friends were numerous in the crowd, but no gifted statesmen threw out the first ball and the contest was only five minutes late in getting underway.*

*[Reds] President [Garry] Herrmann gave a jolly party at the Elks Temple immediately after the game.*
*[Cincinnati Commercial Tribune and Cincinnati Enquirer]*

### Opening Day Trivia

| | |
|---|---|
| Star of the Game | Reds Pitcher Jakie May |
| Weather | 60° |
| Attendance | 32,304 |
| Notable | Ninth Opening Day Win in Ten Years |
| Rating | ◇◇◇◇◇ |

### 1926 Opening Day Schedule

| April 13 | National League |
|---|---|
| Chi vs. Cin | Pitts vs. StL |
| Brklyn vs. NY | Bost vs. Phil |

*The Findlay Market rooters presented manager Jack Hendricks a floral baseball prior to the first pitch.*

# Donohue, Reds Lose Pitcher's Duel
## 1927 Pirates Win Opener, 2–1

| 1927 OPENING DAY SCHEDULE ||
|---|---|
| APRIL 12 | NATIONAL LEAGUE |
| PITTS VS. CIN | STL VS. CHI |
| BRKLYN VS. BOST | NY VS. PHIL |

The 1927 opener was billed as a magnificent matchup of two of the top right-handers in baseball. Cincinnati's Pete Donohue and Pittsburgh's Ray Kremer lived up to the promotion.

Unfortunately for the 34,758 who crammed into Redland Field, Donohue had one more wobble than his opponent, and Pittsburgh walked off with the opener, 2–1.

The opening round was the downfall for the Reds. Donohue gave up three hits and two runs, and then shut out Pittsburgh the rest of the way. Reliever Red Lucas pitched a perfect ninth. But the first inning outburst put the Pirates up, 2–0, and that was all Mr. Kremer needed. He gave us just six hits and walked none. He retired the side in order in five innings, and allowed only three runners to reach second base.

In the Pirate first, George Grantham lined a single to right. Lloyd Waner then laid down a perfect bunt which went for a single. Another bunt put both runners in scoring position, and Paul Waner came through, knocking a sharp single to center.

Donohue, making his fifth consecutive Opening Day start, faced scoring threats in the second and third, but pitched out of both jams. The right-hander allowed only two more hits over his last five innings.

The Reds finally put up a run in fifth. Bubbles Hargrave singled and moved to second when the left fielder bobbled Bubbles' ball. Hargrave scored moments later on a single by Hod Ford. In the sixth, the Reds mounted another rally and nearly scored the tying run. Walter Christensen singled and Charlie Dressen sent him to third with another single. Curt Walker then grounded to first and Christensen was thrown out attempting to score.

The Reds had one last gasp in the ninth, putting the tying run on second with one out, but Kremer retired the final two outs on fly balls.

Although the club added 5,000 new box seats, the attendance far outstripped the supply of chairs, and the standees lined the outfield. The day was highlighted by the usual festivities: *There were many rooting parties, but the biggest public display was made by the Findlay Market boys, who marched around the field as usual, headed by Esberger's Band, and carrying a huge floral baseball, supported on crossed bats. This was presented to Manager Hendricks and the team just before the game started.*

*WLW had two microphones at the field and they started broadcasting fully half an hour before the first ball was pitched. Several leading players of both teams said a few reassuring words to the fans and then Powel Crosley, Jr., owner of WLW, began to interpret the game play by play.*

[Reds] President [Garry] Herrmann was not too much depressed over the defeat to organize a big baseball dinner after the game. Dancing was continued until a late hour. **[Cincinnati Commercial Tribune and Cincinnati Enquirer}**

### APRIL 12, 1927

| Cincinnati. | AB | R | H | PO | A | E |
|---|---|---|---|---|---|---|
| Christensen, c.f. | 4 | 0 | 1 | 4 | 0 | 0 |
| Dressen, 3b | 4 | 0 | 3 | 0 | 0 | 0 |
| Walker, r.f. | 3 | 0 | 0 | 3 | 0 | 0 |
| Bressler, l.f. | 4 | 0 | 0 | 2 | 1 | 0 |
| Kelly, 1b | 4 | 0 | 0 | 9 | 1 | 0 |
| Hargrave, c. | 3 | 1 | 1 | 3 | 0 | 0 |
| Ford, s.s. | 3 | 0 | 1 | 1 | 3 | 1 |
| Pittenger, 2b. | 3 | 0 | 0 | 4 | 4 | 0 |
| Donohue, p. | 2 | 0 | 0 | 1 | 3 | 1 |
| Lucas, p. | 1 | 0 | 0 | 0 | 0 | 0 |
| *Zitzmann | 0 | 0 | 0 | 0 | 0 | 0 |
| Totals | 31 | 1 | 6 | 27 | 13 | 2 |

*Ran for Dressen in ninth.

| Pittsburgh. | AB | R | H | PO | A | E |
|---|---|---|---|---|---|---|
| Grantham, 1b | 4 | 1 | 1 | 9 | 1 | 0 |
| L. Waner, l.f. | 4 | 1 | 1 | 4 | 0 | 1 |
| Cuyler, c.f. | 3 | 0 | 2 | 6 | 0 | 0 |
| P. Waner, r.f. | 3 | 0 | 1 | 1 | 0 | 0 |
| Wright, s.s. | 4 | 0 | 1 | 0 | 2 | 0 |
| Traynor, 3b | 4 | 0 | 1 | 1 | 2 | 0 |
| Rhyne, 2b | 3 | 0 | 0 | 2 | 4 | 0 |
| Smith, c. | 4 | 0 | 4 | 1 | 0 | 0 |
| Kremer, p. | 2 | 0 | 0 | 0 | 4 | 0 |
| Totals | 31 | 2 | 7 | 27 | 12 | 1 |

Cincinnati...... 0 0 0 0 1 0 0 0 0—1
Pittsburgh..... 2 0 0 0 0 0 0 0 0—2

Two-base Hit—Cuyler. Sacrifices—Cuyler, Rhyne, Walker. Double Plays—Ford, Pittenger and Kelly 2, Rhyne and Grantham. Struck Out—By Kremer 4, by Donohue 2. Bases on Balls—By Donohue 2. Hits—Off Donohue 7 in eight innings, off Lucas 0 in one inning, off Kremer 6. Left on Bases—Cincinnati 4, Pittsburgh 5. Time—1:29. Umpires—Moran, Quigley and Jorda.

| OPENING DAY TRIVIA ||
|---|---|
| STAR OF THE GAME | PITTSBURGH PITCHER RAY KREMER |
| WEATHER | 65°; CLEAR |
| ATTENDANCE | 34,758 |
| NOTABLE | CLUB ADDS 5,000 FIELD-LEVEL BOX SEATS |
| RATING | ⚾⚾ |

# 1928 Luque Leads Reds To 5–1 Win
## Cub Star Hack Wilson Injured

*Dolf Luque won his third Opening Day game in 1928.*

Who needs Cy Young when you have Dolf Luque?

Cy Young, the legendary pitcher, was to have tossed out the ceremonial first pitch at the 1928 opener, but his motorcade arrived moments too late, and the game began without the fanfare.

While many fans were disappointed, Luque was up to the first pitch and nearly every one after that. He out-pitched long-time Reds nemesis Charlie Root for the victory, 5–1.

The game was marred by a serious injury to the National League's reigning home run champion, Chicago outfielder Hack Wilson. Wilson broke a small bone in his left ankle when he fell chasing a long drive in right-center field in the eighth inning. He was carried off the field by his teammates, and wound up missing several games.

Neither team scored until the fifth, when the Reds pushed two runs across, aided by a Chicago error. With runners on first and third, the Reds attempted a double steal. Cub catcher Gabby Hartnett bluffed the throw to second and had Bubbles Hargrave trapped off third. But Hartnett's throw was so wild it sailed all the way to the left-field wall and both runners scored.

It was all Luque asked. The Cuban right-hander was touched for seven hits and he faced serious scoring threats in the late innings, but wriggled out of each situation. The Cubs only run came on a ground-rule home run by Freddie Maguire.

The attendance of 30,517 was less than in previous years, and for the first time in many openers, the standees did not fill up the entire outfield, the center-field area being empty. The reporters blamed the chilly weather and threatening skies in the early afternoon for keeping many fans at home. The dignitary list included the Governor of Ohio, Cincinnati Mayor Seasongood and baseball commissioner Judge Landis. The commissioner admitted he enjoyed every game he watched. "They are all my teams," he said, "so my team always wins."

Wilson's injury drew considerable attention from the writers: *Chasing a puzzling fly Wilson overran the course of the ball a bit, tried to reverse himself suddenly and, crossing his legs, the weight of his husky body proved too much for the distorted ankles and down to the sward he crashed in intense agony. He tore at his cap and flung it far from him and then writhed and flopped about on the grass. All of the athletes rushed out to him and he was finally carried out of the park and rushed to a hospital.*

*The [x-ray] showed a splintering of the bone, so the doctor took Hack to the Hotel Sinton and put him to bed at once.*

*The Findlay Market Rooters, as usual, made a fine showing. They marched around the field headed by a band and a decorated automobile and were quite the life of the party for a while.*

*Several members of both teams tried their hands at broadcasting through Station WLW with microphones located at both dugouts.*

[Cincinnati Commercial Tribune and Cincinnati Enquirer]

### OPENING DAY TRIVIA

| | |
|---|---|
| STAR OF THE GAME | REDS PITCHER DOLF LUQUE |
| WEATHER | 54°; CLEAR |
| ATTENDANCE | 30,517 |
| NOTABLE | CY YOUNG ARRIVES TOO LATE FOR 1ST PITCH |
| RATING | ◐◐◐ |

### 1928 OPENING DAY SCHEDULE

| APRIL 11 | NATIONAL LEAGUE |
|---|---|
| CHI VS. CIN | PITTS VS. STL |
| PHIL VS. BRKLYN | BOST VS. NY |

### APRIL 11, 1928

| Cincinnati | A.B. | R. | H. | O. | A. | E. |
|---|---|---|---|---|---|---|
| Dressen, 3b. | 4 | 0 | 0 | 1 | 5 | 0 |
| Allen, c. f. | 4 | 0 | 0 | 3 | 0 | 0 |
| Purdy, l. f. | 3 | 1 | 1 | 5 | 0 | 0 |
| G. Kelly, 1b. | 1 | 0 | 0 | 13 | 0 | 0 |
| Walker, r. f. | 4 | 0 | 0 | 1 | 0 | 0 |
| Critz, 2b. | 4 | 1 | 1 | 4 | 3 | 0 |
| Ford, s. s. | 4 | 0 | 2 | 0 | 3 | 0 |
| Hargrave, c. | 3 | 1 | 0 | 3 | 0 | 0 |
| Luque, p. | 2 | 0 | 1 | 0 | 2 | 0 |
| Totals | 29 | 5 | 5 | 27 | 14 | 0 |

| Chicago | A.B. | R. | H. | O. | A. | E. |
|---|---|---|---|---|---|---|
| English, s s. | 5 | 0 | 0 | 2 | 0 | 1 |
| Maguire, 2b. | 4 | 1 | 1 | 3 | 4 | 1 |
| Cuyler, r.-c. f. | 3 | 0 | 1 | 2 | 0 | 0 |
| Wilson, c. f. | 4 | 0 | 1 | 1 | 0 | 0 |
| Webb, r. f. | 0 | 0 | 0 | 0 | 0 | 0 |
| Stephenson, l. f. | 4 | 0 | 1 | 2 | 0 | 0 |
| Grimm, 1b. | 3 | 0 | 1 | 7 | 1 | 0 |
| Hartnett, c. | 3 | 0 | 0 | 7 | 0 | 1 |
| Butler, 3b. | 3 | 0 | 1 | 0 | 1 | 0 |
| Root, p. | 2 | 0 | 0 | 0 | 1 | 0 |
| Bush, p. | 0 | 0 | 0 | 0 | 0 | 0 |
| †Heathcote | 0 | 0 | 0 | 0 | 0 | 0 |
| ‡J. Kelly | 1 | 0 | 1 | 0 | 0 | 0 |
| Totals | 33 | 1 | 7 | 24 | 7 | 3 |

Cincinnati  0 0 0 0 2 1 0 2 *—5
Chicago     0 0 0 0 0 1 0 0 0—1

†Batted for Root in seventh ‡Batted for Bush in ninth.

Two-base Hits—Butler, Wilson, Ford. Home Run—Maguire. Stolen Base—Cuyler. Sacrifices—Grimm, G. Kelly. Struck Out—By Root 5, by Luque 1, by Bush 2. Bases on Balls—By Root 3, by Luque 3. Hit by Pitcher—Hargrave by Root. Hits—Off Root 2 in six innings, off Bush 3 in two innings. Losing Pitcher—Root. Time—1:49. Umpires—Quigley, Pfirman and Stark.

*The bleachers were full, but there were no standees in right field for the chilly 1929 opener.*

# Brrrr!! Cold Day at Redland
## Shivering Fans See St. Louis Topple the Reds

### 1929

| OPENING DAY TRIVIA | |
|---|---|
| STAR OF THE GAME | CARDINAL LEFT FIELDER CHICK HAFEY |
| WEATHER | 42°; WINDY, DAMP |
| ATTENDANCE | 24,822 |
| NOTABLE | TIED FOR FASTEST OPENER EVER: 1:17 |
| RATING | ⚾ |

If the frozen denizens of Redland Field had a crystal ball on Opening Day, they could have gone home after the first inning and saved themselves a few shivers.

The Cardinals pushed across three runs in the first and downed the Reds, 5–2, in one of the coldest openers anyone could recall. The 42-degree temperature did not set a record, but every account had it as bone-chilling cold.

The day did produce one greatly appreciated milestone: the game was completed in one hour and 17 minutes, which ties it with the 1944 opener as the fastest opener on record.

Grover Cleveland "Pete" Alexander won his second Opening Day game in Cincinnati, besting Red Lucas, who pitched well enough to win most games. Each pitcher gave up only five hits, but a streak of wildness by Lucas in the first inning proved the difference.

A lead-off single, hit batsman, sacrifice and walk loaded the bases with one out. Lucas wild-pitched the first run home. Chick Hafey's single easily scored runs two and three.

The Reds scored in the second, giving the fans some hope for a rally against Alexander. But the old veteran held steady, while the Cardinals touched up Lucas for two more in the fifth. Chick Hafey drove in his third and fourth runs with a two-run homer into the temporary seats on the left-field terrace.

The Reds mounted one final effort in the seventh. They scored once, but the rally ended quickly with a double play. Alexander retired the last eight men.

Reds president C.J. McDiarmid congratulated the crowd on braving the conditions. "We could not have played at all if it had been any worse, and it was a great tribute to the game that more than 25,000 fans turned out to inaugurate the season."

One of the groups that turned out in full force was the Findlay Market rooters. They had become the most prominent of the rooter groups during the 1920s and had taken center stage at the pre-game ceremony: *The Findlay Market Rooters made their annual appearance in a body. They paraded around the field, led by a big band and then stopped at the plate, where Manager Hendricks was presented with a huge baseball made of posies.*

*Station WLW, as its first step toward daily broadcasting, aired the entire proceedings, with Bob Burdette, sports announcer, in charge.*

*A stunting airman roared over the field during the third inning and put on a real circus, looping the loop, banking, [and] doing the falling-leaf.*

*Never has a crowd been so slow in arriving at the field. Not until after 2 did the main body start pouring in and then the rush was tremendous. The intense cold had evidently made all the folks put off the suffering as long as possible.*
[*Cincinnati Commercial Tribune and Cincinnati Enquirer*]

| 1929 OPENING DAY SCHEDULE | |
|---|---|
| APRIL 16 | NATIONAL LEAGUE |
| StL vs. Cin | Pitts vs. Chi |
| Brklyn vs. Bost (PP) | NY vs. Phil (PP) |

### APRIL 16, 1929

| Cincinnati. | AB. | R. | H. | O. | A. | E. |
|---|---|---|---|---|---|---|
| Critz, 2b | 4 | 0 | 1 | 2 | 1 | 0 |
| Purdy, l.f. | 4 | 0 | 3 | 0 | 0 | 0 |
| Kelly, 1b | 4 | 1 | 1 | 12 | 0 | 0 |
| Walker, r.f. | 3 | 1 | 2 | 2 | 0 | 0 |
| Allen, c.f. | 3 | 0 | 1 | 4 | 0 | 0 |
| Pittenger, 3b | 3 | 0 | 0 | 3 | 0 | 0 |
| Ford, s.s. | 3 | 0 | 0 | 1 | 1 | 0 |
| Sukeforth, c. | 3 | 0 | 0 | 3 | 1 | 0 |
| Lucas, p. | 3 | 0 | 0 | 0 | 6 | 0 |
| Totals | 30 | 2 | 5 | 17 | 12 | 0 |
| St. Louis. | AB. | R. | H. | O. | A. | E. |
| Douthit, c.f. | 4 | 1 | 2 | 2 | 0 | 0 |
| Haney, 3b | 3 | 1 | 0 | 2 | 4 | 0 |
| Frisch, 2b | 3 | 1 | 0 | 4 | 3 | 0 |
| Bottomley, 1b | 3 | 1 | 0 | 12 | 0 | 0 |
| Hafey, l.f. | 4 | 1 | 2 | 3 | 0 | 0 |
| Roettger, r.f. | 4 | 0 | 0 | 0 | 0 | 0 |
| Gelbert, s.s. | 4 | 0 | 2 | 2 | 2 | 0 |
| Jonnard, c. | 4 | 0 | 2 | 1 | 0 | 0 |
| Alexander, p. | 3 | 0 | 0 | 1 | 6 | 0 |
| Totals | 29 | 5 | 5 | 27 | 15 | 0 |

Cincinnati .....0 1 0 0 0 0 1 0 0—2
St. Louis .....3 0 0 0 2 0 0 0 0—5

Two-base Hit—Kelly. Three-base Hit—Walker. Home Run—Hafey. Sacrifices—Frisch, Bottomley. Double Plays—Alexander, Frisch and Bottomley. Struck Out—By Lucas, 3; by Alexander, 1. Bases on Balls—By Lucas 3. Hit by Pitcher—Haney by Lucas. Wild Pitch—Lucas. Left on Bases—Cincinnati 1, St. Louis 3. Time—1:17. Umpires—Quigley, Moran and McLaughlin.

# 1930
## Sunshine Is a "Hit"
### Clubs Rap Out 32 Bingles; Pirates Take Opener on Warm Day

*Red Lucas lost his second straight Opening Day decision.*

The Findlay Market rooters weren't the only ones holding a parade on Opening Day.

Batters on both sides staged a "hit" parade, pounding out a total of 32 bingles. The combination of torrid bats and tropical temperatures turned the mound into a sweatshop, and neither starter—Pittsburgh's Ray Kremer nor Cincinnati's Red Lucas—survived it.

But Pirate reliever Steve Swetonic allowed the Reds only one run over the final five innings, and that was the difference as the Pirates won, 7–6.

It was an exciting game with four lead changes and a number of fielding highlights that kept the crowd of 30,000 roaring throughout. Two ground-rule home runs into the temporary seats on the left-field terrace put the Pirates up, 3–2, in the second, but the Reds held the lead, 5–3, entering the fifth.

A three-run rally in the fifth pushed the Pirates back ahead and Paul Waner singled in what proved to be the winning run in the sixth. Archie Campbell relieved Lucas, and he and Benny Frey blanked the Pirates the rest of the way, but Swetonic was able to hold off the Reds final threats.

Cincinnati scored one in the seventh, and threatened to rally in the eighth when the first two men reached on singles. But a botched sacrifice and a double play killed the threat.

The papers captured the pageantry of the day: *Into the various hostelries poured the thousands who had taken advantage of excursions from other towns or who had motored in from practically every city in Ohio, Indiana, Kentucky and West Virginia. The congestion filled every street leading toward the Mecca of all Meccas, Redland Field.*

*The traction company, bus lines and the Cincinnati Police Department went into carefully-planned and rehearsed action and never has so large a throng been so speedily and well-handled.*

*There were the customary ceremonies. Some hours before starting time, the loud speakers were turned on, and the bleacherites and other early arrivals were entertained with music and song.*

*A big feature was the parade of the Findlay Market rooters, always loyally on the job. They marched around the field, preceded by a band and presented the club with a handsome United States flag, which was immediately run up on the tall pole in right-center.*

*Just before the teams took the field, City Manager Sherrill went to the middle of the diamond and pitched the first ball in the general direction of Mayor Russell Wilson.*

*[Reds] President Sidney Weil took care of the announcing over the radio during the sad and fatal fifth inning, but gamely stuck to the "mike."* **[Cincinnati Commercial Tribune and Cincinnati Enquirer]**

### OPENING DAY TRIVIA

| | |
|---|---|
| STAR OF THE GAME | PITTSBURGH RIGHT FIELDER PAUL WANER |
| WEATHER | 80°; PARTLY CLOUDY |
| ATTENDANCE | 30,112 |
| NOTABLE | 32 HITS, INCLUDING 26 SINGLES |
| RATING | ●●●● |

### 1930 OPENING DAY SCHEDULE

| APRIL 15 | NATIONAL LEAGUE |
|---|---|
| PITTS VS. CIN | CHI VS. STL |
| BOST VS. NY | PHIL VS. BRKLYN |

### April 15, 1930

| Cincinnati | AB | R | H | PO | A | E |
|---|---|---|---|---|---|---|
| Crits, 2b | 4 | 1 | 1 | 2 | 2 | 0 |
| Callaghan, c.f. | 4 | 1 | 2 | 2 | 0 | 0 |
| Meusel, l.f. | 5 | 0 | 3 | 2 | 0 | 0 |
| Heilmann, r.f. | 5 | 1 | 2 | 3 | 0 | 0 |
| Kelly, 1b | 5 | 0 | 2 | 7 | 1 | 0 |
| Cuccinello, 3b | 5 | 0 | 1 | 1 | 4 | 0 |
| Ford, s.s. | 5 | 1 | 2 | 5 | 3 | 0 |
| Gooch, c. | 4 | 1 | 2 | 3 | 3 | 0 |
| Sukeforth, c. | 1 | 0 | 0 | 1 | 0 | 0 |
| Lucas, p. | 3 | 1 | 2 | 1 | 0 | 0 |
| Campbell, p. | 0 | 0 | 0 | 0 | 0 | 0 |
| Frey, p. | 0 | 0 | 0 | 0 | 0 | 0 |
| *Dressen | 0 | 0 | 0 | 0 | 0 | 0 |
| †Walker | 0 | 0 | 0 | 0 | 0 | 0 |
| Totals | 40 | 6 | 17 | 27 | 15 | 0 |

| Pittsburgh | AB | R | H | PO | A | E |
|---|---|---|---|---|---|---|
| Brickell, c.f. | 5 | 0 | 2 | 0 | 0 | 1 |
| Grantham, 2b. | 4 | 1 | 2 | 5 | 2 | 0 |
| P. Waner, r.f. | 4 | 1 | 4 | 0 | 0 | 0 |
| Comorosky, l.f. | 4 | 1 | 1 | 1 | 0 | 0 |
| Suhr, 1b. | 5 | 0 | 2 | 10 | 2 | 0 |
| Bartell, s.s. | 3 | 1 | 1 | 2 | 5 | 0 |
| Hemsley, c. | 4 | 1 | 1 | 7 | 1 | 1 |
| Engle, 3b. | 5 | 1 | 2 | 0 | 3 | 0 |
| Kremer, p. | 2 | 0 | 0 | 1 | 0 | 0 |
| Swetonic, p. | 2 | 1 | 0 | 0 | 1 | 0 |
| Totals | 38 | 7 | 15 | 27 | 16 | 2 |

Cincinnati... 1 1 2 1 0 0 1 0 0—6
Pittsburgh... 0 3 0 0 3 1 0 0 —7

*Ran for Gooch in seventh. †Batted for Campbell in seventh.

Two-base Hits—Engle, Heilmann, Comorosky, Gooch. Home Runs—Bartell, Hemsley. Stolen Base—Meusel. Sacrifices—Callaghan, Critz, Bartell 2. Double Plays—Bartell, Grantham and Suhr; Engle, Grantham and Suhr. Struck Out—By Lucas 1, by Swetonic 6, by Frey 1. Bases on Balls—By Lucas 3, by Swetonic 2, by Campbell 1. Wild Pitch—Swetonic. Hits—Off Kremer 11 in three and two-thirds innings, off Swetonic 6 in five and one-third innings, off Lucas 13 in five and two-thirds innings, off Campbell none in one and one-third inning, off Frey 2 in two innings. Winning Pitcher—Swetonic. Losing Pitcher—Lucas. Left on Bases—Cincinnati 11, Pittsburgh 9. Time—2:19. Umpires—Klem, Stark and Clarke.

*The prescription for the country's "Depression" on Opening Day was to "take" one baseball game daily.*

# 1931 Pitching Falters
## Cardinals Rally Wipes Out Reds' Early Lead

For the first six innings, the 1931 opener had everything the fans could ask: perfect weather and a Reds lead.

But the Cardinals ruined the party with six runs in the last three innings off starter Larry Benton and reliever Ray Kolp to capture the inaugural, 7–3.

The winning pitcher was Cardinal starter Flint Rhem, who gave up two runs in six innings. Reliever Jim Lindsey pitched the final three innings, allowing the Reds a harmless tally in the ninth.

The beautiful day helped attract more than 29,000 to the park, and they watched the Reds and Cardinals trade the lead three times in the first seven innings. St. Louis began the scoring with one in the fourth. The Reds grabbed the lead in the sixth on a two-run home run by Joe Stripp, a slashing line drive to the temporary seats on the left-field terrace.

Ground rules stipulated a double on a ball bouncing into these seats, but Stripp's ball flew into the crowd in the air.

Benton and the Reds defense quickly lost the lead. In the seventh, the Cardinals tied the game and had the bases loaded with one out. Then came the decisive play. Cardinal outfielder Taylor Douthit grounded sharply to Charley Dressen at third base. Dressen stepped on third for the force and threw to first to try to complete the double play. But the throw to first was wild and two runs scored, giving St. Louis a lead the Reds could not overcome.

There were a minimum of festivities surrounding the game, probably due to the increasingly difficult economic times. The Findlay Market delegation was the only group to attract newspaper attention: *The Findlay Market rooters, who never fail, were out in force, with their usual parade around the field before the game. Following their band came a car bearing an immense floral ball, which was presented to the Reds as a token of good luck.*

*The opening ceremonies were quite simple, consisting of a band concert and the remarkable sight of three high government officials performing an athletic stunt out in public view. Mayor Russell Wilson opened the championship season by pitching two balls, one to Cincinnati manager Dykstra and the other to Governor George White, of Ohio. The Mayor had good control. There was not a wild pitch or a passed ball among the whole three of them.*

*The three arbiters in charge of the contest were remembered by the Greater Cincinnati Umpires Association, each being presented with a handsome red bouquet.*

*The game started out briskly enough, but the last three innings dragged a bit after the defense of the Reds went haywire, and so the contest lasted just two minutes over two hours.* [Cincinnati Enquirer and Cincinnati Times-Star]

| OPENING DAY TRIVIA | |
|---|---|
| STAR OF THE GAME | ST. LOUIS PITCHER FLINT RHEM |
| WEATHER | 82°; SUNNY |
| ATTENDANCE | 29,343 |
| NOTABLE | THIRD OPENING DAY LOSS IN A ROW |
| RATING | ◐◐ |

| 1931 OPENING DAY SCHEDULE | |
|---|---|
| APRIL 14 | NATIONAL LEAGUE |
| STL VS. CIN | PITTS VS. CHI |
| BRKLYN VS. BOST | NY VS. PHIL |

# 1932 What A Finish! Reds Rally in 9th
## Reds Score Four to Win

*Reds outfielder Taylor Douthit drove in the tying and winning runs in the bottom of the ninth inning.*

Lightning struck not once, but twice, in the bottom of the ninth inning as the Reds, led by Red Lucas and Taylor Douthit, rallied for four runs to edge Chicago, 5–4.

This was the largest ninth-inning deficit ever overcome by the Reds on Opening Day. Only 25,869 were on hand to see it however, as 44-degree temperatures kept many of the last-minute crowd at home.

Lucas and Douthit each drove in two runs in the ninth to rescue a game the Reds seemed certain to lose. Many in the crowd of 25,869 had long left frigid Redland Field before the Reds began the comeback.

The early innings all belonged to Chicago. The Cubs grabbed a 2–0 lead in the first inning off Reds starter Si Johnson. Johnson then settled down and gave up only one more run on back-to-back doubles in the fifth. But these three runs—and a fourth added in the eighth off reliever Larry Benton—seemed more than Cubs starter Charlie Root would need. The Reds had only one hit through the first four innings, and managed to squeeze out one run in the sixth on two singles and a fielder's choice. Root seemed to have the game well in hand heading to the ninth.

But George Grantham started the comeback with a single. Root then walked Mickey Heath. Ernie Lombardi smashed a hot drive up the middle that Root deflected, but the lumbering Lombardi crossed the bag before the ball was retrieved. With the bases loaded, Root gave way to reliever Guy Bush. Bush struck out the first batter and the crowd grew uneasy.

Then came the fireworks. Pinch hitter Red Lucas drove a double into the crowd at the base of the flagpole in deep right-center. After an intentional walk to load the bases, Douthit sent a drive into right-center that reached the edge of the crowd. Two runs scored easily and the improbable victory belonged to the Reds.

Despite the chilly weather and the continuing economic gloom, this opener was a festive one: *The parades [around the field] were watched with much interest by the big crowd, which assembled early despite the cold. The Lower Cincinnati Business Men's Association was the first to appear headed by a band. Then came the famous drum corps of the Bentley Post of the American Legion, which played several stirring tunes in front of the grandstand, and marched off amid great applause. Last to appear were the faithful Findlay Market rooters. There was more enthusiasm before the game than has been the case for several years.*

All the Reds wore mourning bands on their sleeves out of respect to the memory of the late Louis C. Widrig, for many years the popular Treasurer of the Cincinnati club. The flag in center field was at half-mast. [***Cincinnati Enquirer and Cincinnati Times-Star***]

---

**1932 OPENING DAY SCHEDULE**

| APRIL 12 | NATIONAL LEAGUE |
|---|---|
| CHI VS. CIN | PITTS VS. STL |
| BOST VS. BRKLYN | PHIL VS. NY |

---

**OPENING DAY TRIVIA**

| STAR OF THE GAME | REDS CENTER FIELDER TYLER DOUTHIT |
|---|---|
| WEATHER | 44°; CLOUDY |
| ATTENDANCE | 25,869 |
| NOTABLE | REDS OVERCOME 3-RUN DEFICIT IN 9TH |
| RATING | ◯◯◯◯◯ |

---

**APRIL 12, 1932**

| CINCINNATI. | AB. | R. | 1B. | SH. | SB. | PO. | A. | E. |
|---|---|---|---|---|---|---|---|---|
| Douthit, cf. | 5 | 0 | 1 | 0 | 0 | 3 | 0 | 0 |
| Gilbert, 3b. | 4 | 1 | 1 | 0 | 0 | 0 | 1 | 1 |
| F. Herman, rf. | 4 | 0 | 1 | 0 | 0 | 2 | 0 | 0 |
| Grantham, 2b. | 4 | 1 | 1 | 0 | 0 | 2 | 2 | 0 |
| Heath, 1b. | 3 | 1 | 0 | 0 | 0 | 11 | 0 | 0 |
| Lombardi, c. | 4 | 0 | 2 | 0 | 0 | 6 | 0 | 0 |
| *Durocher | 0 | 1 | 0 | 0 | 0 | 0 | 0 | 0 |
| Crabtree, lf. | 4 | 0 | 2 | 0 | 0 | 3 | 0 | 0 |
| Morrissey, ss. | 3 | 0 | 1 | 0 | 0 | 0 | 2 | 0 |
| †Lucas | 1 | 0 | 1 | 0 | 0 | 0 | 0 | 0 |
| ‡Bluege | 0 | 1 | 0 | 0 | 0 | 0 | 0 | 0 |
| Johnson, p. | 2 | 0 | 0 | 0 | 0 | 0 | 4 | 1 |
| §High | 1 | 0 | 0 | 0 | 0 | 0 | 0 | 0 |
| Benton, p. | 0 | 0 | 0 | 0 | 0 | 0 | 0 | 0 |
| ¶Roettger | 1 | 0 | 0 | 0 | 0 | 0 | 0 | 0 |
| Totals | 35 | 5 | 10 | 0 | 0 | 27 | 9 | 2 |

*Durocher, ran for Lombardi in ninth inning.
†Lucas, batted for Morrissey in ninth inning.
‡Bluege, ran for Lucas in ninth inning.
§High, batted for Johnson in seventh inning.
¶Roettger, batted for Benton in ninth inning.

| CHICAGO. | AB. | R. | 1B. | SH. | SB. | PO. | A. | E. |
|---|---|---|---|---|---|---|---|---|
| Hack, 3b. | 5 | 1 | 1 | 0 | 0 | 1 | 1 | 0 |
| W. Herman, 2b. | 5 | 1 | 2 | 0 | 0 | 2 | 3 | 0 |
| Cuyler, cf. | 4 | 1 | 1 | 0 | 0 | 1 | 0 | 0 |
| Barton, rf. | 4 | 0 | 1 | 0 | 0 | 1 | 0 | 0 |
| Stephenson, lf. | 3 | 0 | 0 | 0 | 0 | 4 | 0 | 0 |
| Moore, lf. | 0 | 1 | 0 | 0 | 0 | 0 | 0 | 0 |
| Hartnett, c. | 4 | 0 | 1 | 0 | 0 | 5 | 0 | 0 |
| Grimm, 1b. | 4 | 0 | 2 | 0 | 0 | 7 | 1 | 0 |
| Jurges, ss. | 4 | 0 | 0 | 0 | 0 | 3 | 2 | 0 |
| Root, p. | 4 | 0 | 0 | 0 | 0 | 1 | 1 | 0 |
| Bush, p. | 0 | 0 | 0 | 0 | 0 | 0 | 0 | 0 |
| Totals | 37 | 4 | 8 | 0 | 0 | 25* | 7 | 0 |

*One out when winning run was scored.

| Innings... | 1 | 2 | 3 | 4 | 5 | 6 | 7 | 8 | 9 | |
|---|---|---|---|---|---|---|---|---|---|---|
| Cincinnati... | 0 | 0 | 0 | 0 | 1 | 0 | 0 | 4 | —5 | |
| Chicago... | 2 | 0 | 0 | 1 | 0 | 0 | 1 | 0 | —4 | |

Two-Base Hits—Douthit, Lucas, Hack, W. Herman.
Left on Bases—Cincinnati, 7; Chicago, 7.
Struck Out—By Johnson, 6; by Root, 4; by Bush, 1.
Bases on Balls—Benton, Root, Bush.
Base Hits—Off Johnson, 7; off Benton, 1; off Root, 8; off Bush, 2.
Time of Game—2:06.
Umpires—Rigler, Quigley and Donnelly.

*The end of Prohibition meant that Reds fans could enjoy beer at the opener for the first time in 13 years.*

# Prohibition Repealed, But Not Pirates
## 1933
### Pittsburgh Takes Opener, 4–1

Cincinnati continued to build its tradition as a great baseball town, when more than 25,000 turned out for the 1933 opener in defiance of those who had predicted that the Depression, a recent flood and a miserable ball club would result in a low turnout for Opening Day.

Oh, and there was also beer. As a result of the repeal of Prohibition, Reds fans enjoyed spirits at the game for the first time in 13 years. The club set up a rathskeller-like setting—on the concourse beneath the main grandstand—with benches and long tables, and served hamburgers smothered in onions along with the regular hot dog fare.

Every seat was filled, with the overflow wedged behind the ropes in deep right field. Unfortunately, the Reds, who had finished last in 1931 and 1932, failed to convince anyone they were yet worthy of such an outpouring. The Pirates walked off with everything but the hamburgers, winning 4–1.

Pittsburgh's Bill Swift dominated the Reds, allowing four hits and walking one. His opponent, Si Johnson, pitched well, but his teammates literally dropped the ball on several occasions.

The Pirates scored first, gathering two runs on a single, a triple by Paul Waner and a double by Gus Suhr, all in the first inning. The Pirates should have had only one run, but the Reds botched a run-down play after they had Waner trapped off third. Suhr made them pay with the first of his three hits.

The Cincinnati defense faltered again in the fourth. With one out and one on, George Grantham fumbled a double-play ball that would have ended the inning. Paul Waner then singled home two runs and the Pirates had a 4–0 lead.

The Reds roused the crowd in the bottom of the fourth on a triple by Jim Bottomley. He scored on a fielder's choice, but that proved to be the Reds only uprising until the ninth, when a single and an error put two on. That brought up Ernie Lombardi. The big catcher grounded into a double play to end the threat and the game.

The papers noted the annual festivities: *The Findlay Market rooters made their usual admirable showing, with a band leading the way and a large delegation in line. They presented the club with an American flag and Manager [Donnie] Bush with an elaborate stand of flowers.*

*All the schools were out yesterday afternoon, so the fatality among grandmothers was much less than usual.*

*[The crowd] came from all walks of life and from all sections of the city, the county and state. It was a democratic gathering, indicating to a certainty that baseball still remains the leading pastime of the nation.*
[Cincinnati Enquirer and Cincinnati Times-Star]

### OPENING DAY TRIVIA

| | |
|---|---|
| STAR OF THE GAME | PITTSBURGH PITCHER BILL SWIFT |
| WEATHER | 64°; SUNNY |
| ATTENDANCE | 25,305 |
| NOTABLE | BEER AVAILABLE FOR THE FIRST TIME IN 13 YEARS |
| RATING | ◉◉◉ |

### 1933 OPENING DAY SCHEDULE

| APRIL 12 | NATIONAL LEAGUE |
|---|---|
| PITTS VS. CIN | STL VS. CHI |
| NY VS. BOST (PP) | BRKLYN VS. PHIL (PP) |

### APRIL 12, 1933

| CINCINNATI | AB | R | 1B | PO | A | E |
|---|---|---|---|---|---|---|
| Grantham, 2b | 4 | 0 | 0 | 7 | 3 | 2 |
| Morrissey, 3b | 4 | 0 | 0 | 2 | 3 | 1 |
| Bottomley, 1b | 4 | 1 | 1 | 8 | 1 | 0 |
| Hafey, lf | 4 | 0 | 1 | 1 | 0 | 0 |
| Moore, cf | 3 | 0 | 0 | 1 | 1 | 0 |
| Lombardi, c | 4 | 0 | 0 | 5 | 1 | 0 |
| Rice, rf | 3 | 0 | 2 | 0 | 0 | 0 |
| Durocher, ss | 3 | 0 | 0 | 3 | 3 | 0 |
| Johnson, p | 2 | 0 | 1 | 0 | 1 | 0 |
| *High | 1 | 0 | 0 | 0 | 0 | 0 |
| Benton, p | 0 | 0 | 0 | 0 | 0 | 0 |
| **Totals** | 32 | 1 | 4 | 27 | 13 | 3 |

| PITTSBURGH | AB | R | 1B | PO | A | E |
|---|---|---|---|---|---|---|
| L. Waner, lf | 5 | 1 | 0 | 3 | 0 | 0 |
| Lindstrom, cf | 5 | 1 | 3 | 5 | 0 | 0 |
| P. Waner, rf | 5 | 1 | 2 | 3 | 0 | 0 |
| Traynor, 3b | 4 | 0 | 0 | 0 | 2 | 0 |
| Suhr, 1b | 4 | 0 | 3 | 8 | 0 | 0 |
| Vaughan, ss | 3 | 0 | 0 | 1 | 2 | 1 |
| Piet, 2b | 4 | 0 | 1 | 1 | 1 | 1 |
| Grace, c | 4 | 0 | 1 | 6 | 0 | 0 |
| Swift, p | 4 | 1 | 0 | 0 | 0 | 0 |
| **Totals** | 38 | 4 | 9 | 27 | 5 | 2 |

*High batted for Johnson in eighth inning.

```
Innings...... 1 2 3 4 5 6 7 8 9
Cincinnati... 0 0 0 1 0 0 0 0 0—1
Pittsburgh... 2 0 0 2 0 0 0 0 0—4
```

Two-Base Hits—Suhr 2.
Three-Base Hits—Bottomley, P. Waner.
Stolen Base—Rice.
Left on Bases—Cincinnati, 5; Pittsburgh, 10.
Double Play—Vaughan to Piet to Suhr.
Struck Out—By Johnson, 3; by Swift, 4.
Base on Balls—Off Johnson, 3; off Swift, 1.
Base Hits—Off Johnson, 8 in 8 innings; off Benton, 1 in 1 inning.
Time of Game—2:02.
Umpires—Moran, Reardon and McGrew.

# Warneke Loses No-Hitter in Ninth
## Comorosky's Single Lone Hit in 6–0 Loss

*Si Johnson lost both the 1933 and 1934 openers.*

By the time the ninth inning began, even the Cincinnati fans were rooting for Lon Warneke. The Cubs pitcher began the last of the ninth needing three outs for a no-hitter, the first-ever in the history of Opening Day in Cincinnati.

The Reds trailed, 6–0, and Warneke's pitching gem was all that held the attention of the Cincinnati faithful. Appreciating the historical nature of the moment, they cheered as pinch-hitter Ernie Lombardi whiffed for the first out of the ninth.

Adam Comorosky, the veteran outfielder the Reds acquired from the Pirates in a trade in the off-season, then took the first pitch for strike one. Comorosky swung at the next pitch and grounded a sharp single up the middle into center field. The no-hitter was gone, but after Warneke retired the next two hitters, several of his teammates put him on their shoulders and carried him off the field. Warneke walked two, and one man reached on an error.

It was the closest any pitcher came to a no-hitter in a Cincinnati opener. The Reds' Pete Schneider tossed a one-hitter in 1918, with the lone hit coming in the fourth inning.

The 1934 opener was close until the sixth inning, when Chicago scored four runs off starter Si Johnson, two on a home run into the right-field bleachers by Chuck Klein. This was the first over-the-fence home run on Opening Day in Redland/Crosley Field.

In the broadcast booth, Walter "Red" Barber made his debut as a major league announcer for WSAI. It was also the debut for Powel Crosley as the owner of the Reds, and the first time the park was called "Crosley Field."

Warneke's performance, new uniforms and the festivities drew praise from the press: [*Warneke*] *had everything—speed, finely breaking curves, a magnificent change of pace, control, courage, nonchalance and what not. He was superb.*

*The new Red uniforms attracted much attention. There is a touch of blue on the sleeves and also on the stockings, making them the snappiest suits the team has ever had.*

*Several loyal organizations displayed their wares before the game. The Findlay Market Rooters paraded around the field, with ponies, automobiles and a band, and presented a floral ball of enormous size to the Reds. The McTavern Bowlers of Bellevue, Ky., staged a burlesque act, and the Lackner Rooters were in evidence in the left-field stands.*

*Suitcases were presented to General Manager [Larry] MacPhail, Manager [Bob] O'Farrell and Captain Jim Bottomley by the Findlay Market Boosters. Maybe they think these boys are going somewhere this summer.* [**Cincinnati Enquirer and Cincinnati Times-Star**]

### OPENING DAY TRIVIA

| | |
|---|---|
| STAR OF THE GAME | CUBS PITCHER LON WARNEKE |
| WEATHER | 67°; SUNNY |
| ATTENDANCE | 30,247 |
| NOTABLE | RED BARBER'S FIRST MAJOR LEAGUE BROADCAST |
| RATING | ●●●●● |

### 1934 OPENING DAY SCHEDULE

| APRIL 17 | NATIONAL LEAGUE |
|---|---|
| CHI vs. CIN | PITTS vs. STL |
| BOST vs. BRKLYN | PHIL vs. NY |

### APRIL 17, 1934

| CINCINNATI | AB | R | 1B | PO | A | E |
|---|---|---|---|---|---|---|
| Comorosky, lf | 4 | 0 | 1 | 2 | 0 | 0 |
| Koenig, 3b | 3 | 0 | 0 | 0 | 0 | 0 |
| Piet, 2b | 3 | 0 | 0 | 4 | 0 | 0 |
| Hafey, cf | 3 | 0 | 0 | 3 | 0 | 0 |
| Bottomley, 1b | 3 | 0 | 0 | 5 | 0 | 0 |
| Shiver, rf | 3 | 0 | 0 | 3 | 0 | 0 |
| O'Farrell, c | 3 | 0 | 0 | 12 | 1 | 0 |
| Slade, ss | 2 | 0 | 0 | 0 | 0 | 0 |
| Si Johnson, p | 1 | 0 | 0 | 0 | 0 | 0 |
| *Adams | 1 | 0 | 0 | 0 | 0 | 0 |
| Benton, p | 0 | 0 | 0 | 0 | 0 | 0 |
| †Lombardi | 1 | 0 | 0 | 0 | 0 | 0 |
| Totals | 27 | 0 | 1 | 27 | 1 | 0 |

| CHICAGO | AB | R | 1B | PO | A | E |
|---|---|---|---|---|---|---|
| English, 3b | 5 | 0 | 0 | 0 | 1 | 0 |
| W. Herman, 2b | 4 | 1 | 2 | 2 | 2 | 0 |
| Klein, lf | 5 | 1 | 1 | 1 | 0 | 0 |
| F. Herman, rf | 5 | 0 | 1 | 0 | 0 | 0 |
| Stainback, cf | 4 | 2 | 3 | 1 | 0 | 0 |
| Grimm, 1b | 3 | 1 | 2 | 7 | 0 | 1 |
| Jurges, ss | 4 | 0 | 0 | 3 | 2 | 0 |
| Hartnett, c | 5 | 1 | 2 | 13 | 1 | 0 |
| Warneke, p | 4 | 0 | 1 | 0 | 1 | 0 |
| Totals | 37 | 6 | 11 | 27 | 7 | 1 |

*Adams batted for Si Johnson in sixth inning.
†Lombardi batted for Benton in ninth inning.

| Innings | 1 | 2 | 3 | 4 | 5 | 6 | 7 | 8 | 9 |
|---|---|---|---|---|---|---|---|---|---|
| Cincinnati | 0 | 0 | 0 | 0 | 0 | 0 | 0 | 0 | 0 — 0 |
| Chicago | 0 | 0 | 0 | 0 | 0 | 4 | 0 | 2 | 0 — 6 |

Two-Base Hit—Stainback.
Home Run—Klein.
Left on Bases—Cincinnati, 3; Chicago, 7.
Struck Out—By Si Johnson, 5; by Benton, 1; by Warneke, 13.
Passed Ball—O'Farrell.
Bases on Balls—By Si Johnson, 1; by Benton, 2; by Warneke, 2.
Base Hits—Off Si Johnson, 8; off Benton, 3.
Time of Game—1:53.
Umpires—Klem and Pfirman.

# 1935
## Unlucky Seven
### Pirates Score Seven in Seventh; Hoyt Picks Up Victory, 12–6

*Catcher Ernie Lombardi watches Arky Vaughn (21) score the first run of the 1935 opener. Tom Padden waves in Pie Traynor from third. Both runs scored on Harry Lavagetto's single.*

Reds owner Powel Crosley and General Manager Larry MacPhail rescued the 1935 opener from the league schedule-makers, but the Reds couldn't save the game from the attack of the Pittsburgh Pirates, who rattled four Cincinnati pitchers for a 12–6 win on a frigid day at Crosley Field. Veteran Waite Hoyt picked up the victory.

The National League originally scheduled the Reds to open in Pittsburgh, but MacPhail and Crosley adamantly opposed the idea, citing the nearly 60-year tradition the city had in hosting and supporting the opener. Since the 1890s, Opening Day in Cincinnati had been a sell-out, and was one of the best-attended of all the NL openers. Only New York teams would draw bigger crowds.

However, the Reds must have wondered if they would have been better off in Pittsburgh. A thin blanket of snow covered the field on the morning of the game, and MacPhail seriously considered postponing the game. But with the Reds heading to Pittsburgh the next day, the opener would have had waited nearly a week to be played. Not wanting to risk losing a guaranteed sellout crowd, MacPhail, with the approval of the managers, put the word out at 9:45 a.m. that the game was on. Despite the cold, dreary conditions, 27,400 in furs and overcoats made the trek to Findlay and Western.

Tony Freitas started for the Reds and immediately ran into trouble, none of his own making. In the second inning, Lew Riggs bobbled a double play ball, and Chick Hafey dropped a fly in center field, leading to four Pirate tallies. However, the Reds refused to fold, scoring one in the second and three in the fifth to tie the game. Two of the fifth inning runs came on a Sammy Byrd home run, an over-the-fence jolt to left field.

Then came the unlucky seventh. Three Reds pitchers gave up eight singles and two walks for seven Pirate runs. The stands emptied out after the rally as the shivering congregation had seen enough.

Hoyt pitched a complete game, although he gave up 13 hits. He also singled twice and drove in two runs. Hoyt was one of eight future Hall of Famers on the field, the most at any Cincinnati opener. He joined teammates Arky Vaughn, Lloyd and Paul Waner, and Pie Traynor, and Ernie Lombardi, Jim Bottomley and Hafey of the Reds.

Even with freezing conditions, the pre-game ceremony proceeded as usual: *Mayor [Russell] Wilson observed a time-honored custom by pitching the first ball, with City Manager Dykstra on the receiving end. The Mayor's control was good and he was credited with a strike on Honus Wagner, who took his well-known batting position at the plate.*

*The Findlay Market Rooters arrived at the park shortly after two o'clock and made a great impression as they paraded around the field, headed by a forty-piece band.*
**[Cincinnati Enquirer, Cincinnati Post, and Cincinnati Times-Star]**

### OPENING DAY TRIVIA

| | |
|---|---|
| STAR OF THE GAME | PITTSBURGH PITCHER WAITE HOYT |
| WEATHER | 38°; CLOUDY; SNOW ON FIELD IN AM |
| ATTENDANCE | 27,400 |
| NOTABLE | REDS ORIGINALLY SCHEDULED TO OPEN ON ROAD |
| RATING | ◎◎ |

### 1935 OPENING DAY SCHEDULE

| APRIL 16 | NATIONAL LEAGUE |
|---|---|
| PITTS VS. CIN | STL VS. CHI |
| BRKLYN VS. PHIL | NY VS. BOST |

### APRIL 16, 1935

| CINCINNATI. | AB. | R. | H. | PO. | A. | E. |
|---|---|---|---|---|---|---|
| Myers, ss | 5 | 0 | 3 | 1 | 3 | 0 |
| Byrd, lf | 5 | 1 | 1 | 2 | 0 | 0 |
| Riggs, 3b | 4 | 1 | 2 | 2 | 3 | 0 |
| Bottomley, 1b | 4 | 0 | 2 | 9 | 0 | 0 |
| Hafey, cf | 4 | 1 | 1 | 4 | 0 | 1 |
| Goodman, rf | 4 | 0 | 1 | 0 | 0 | 0 |
| Lombardi, c | 4 | 0 | 1 | 5 | 1 | 0 |
| *Piet | 0 | 1 | 0 | 0 | 0 | 0 |
| Kampouris, 2b | 4 | 2 | 2 | 1 | 1 | 0 |
| Freitas, p | 1 | 0 | 0 | 2 | 1 | 0 |
| Frey, p | 1 | 0 | 0 | 0 | 0 | 0 |
| Schott, p | 0 | 0 | 0 | 0 | 0 | 0 |
| †Pool | 0 | 0 | 0 | 0 | 0 | 0 |
| Hollingsworth, p | 0 | 0 | 0 | 0 | 0 | 0 |
| ‡Campbell | 1 | 0 | 0 | 0 | 0 | 0 |
| Totals | 37 | 6 | 13 | 27 | 9 | 1 |

*Piet ran for Lombardi in ninth inning.
†Pool batted for Schott in seventh inning.
‡Campbell batted for Hollingsworth in ninth inning.

| PITTSBURGH. | AB. | R. | H. | PO. | A. | E. |
|---|---|---|---|---|---|---|
| L. Waner, cf | 6 | 1 | 3 | 1 | 0 | 0 |
| P. Waner, rf | 3 | 1 | 2 | 6 | 0 | 0 |
| Herman, lf | 5 | 1 | 1 | 1 | 0 | 0 |
| Vaughan, ss | 4 | 2 | 2 | 2 | 4 | 0 |
| Traynor, 3b | 6 | 2 | 2 | 1 | 0 | 0 |
| Suhr, 1b | 3 | 2 | 0 | 9 | 0 | 0 |
| Lavagetto, 2b | 5 | 1 | 2 | 3 | 3 | 0 |
| Padden, c | 4 | 1 | 1 | 3 | 1 | 0 |
| Hoyt, p | 4 | 1 | 2 | 1 | 1 | 0 |
| Totals | 40 | 12 | 14 | 27 | 11 | 0 |

Innings..  1 2 3 4 5 6 7 8 9
Cincinnati.. 0 1 0 0 3 0 0 0 2—6
Pittsburgh.. 0 4 0 0 0 0 7 0 1—12

Two-Base Hits—Riggs, Hafey, Lombardi, Kampouris.
Home Run—Byrd.
Left on Bases—Cincinnati, 6; Pittsburgh, 12.
Double Plays—Freitas to Myers to Bottomley; Vaughan, to Lavagetto to Suhr.
Struck Out—By Freitas, 4; by Hollingsworth, 3; by Hoyt, 2.
Bases on Balls—By Freitas, 4; by Frey, 1; by Schott, 1; by Hollingsworth, 3; by Hoyt, 1.
Wild Pitch—Hollingsworth.
Base Hits—Off Freitas, 5; off Frey, 2; off Schott, 1; off Hollingsworth, 2.
Time of Game—2:20.
Umpires—Klem, Magerkurth, and Barr.

# 1936 "Doubled" Up
## Pirates Smack 8 Doubles in 14 Hits; Hoyt Grabs Second Win, 8–6

Nine thousand seats were available in the days before the 1936 Opening Day.

The Pirates and the Reds kicked off the 1936 baseball season with a rousing contest that featured heavy hitting, some outstanding relief pitching and extraordinary defensive plays, all of which added up to a 8–6 Pittsburgh victory.

Veteran Waite Hoyt, who in five years would be manning the microphone as the Reds play-by-play announcer, picked up the win in relief for his second straight Opening Day victory in Cincinnati. Hoyt is the only visiting pitcher to win two Cincinnati openers in a row.

The nearly perfect weather drew over 32,000 fans, which as it turned out, worked against the hometown Reds. The overflow filled the temporary seats in the outfield and the Pirates took advantage by striking eight balls into the crowd, all of which went for ground-rule doubles.

Both starting pitchers were hit hard. Paul Derringer was relieved in the third after giving up five runs on five hits. Pirate starter Cy Blanton allowed eight hits and six runs, before giving way to Hoyt with one out in the fourth.

After four innings, the score stood, 7–6, in favor of the Pirates, but the relievers put an end to the flood of runs. Hoyt shut the Reds out over the last 5 2/3 innings. He survived several threats, including a two-on, no-out rally in the bottom of the ninth. But Hoyt easily retired the final three batters on a ground out and two fly balls and the Reds dropped their fourth opener in a row.

The warm weather allowed the female fans to display the latest in spring fashions. "Everything was hotsy-totsy for the femmes in their Easter finery," wrote one sportswriter. And the fans were not the only ones dressed for the day. The papers noted a number of "new looks" at the ballpark:

*The fans got their first glimpse of revamped Crosley Field. The seats have been repainted and are quite colorful. The field boxes are done in salmon-color paint. Other seats are medium brown and chocolate color. The railings separating the boxes are in apple green, while the remainder of the park is dark green, with silver trimmings. Ouch, my eyes!*

*The new concessionaire believes in going in for loud colors. The peanut and soft drink barkers looked like French Admirals in their blue and white silky-looking uniforms, while the bevy of good-looking girls that dispense hamburgers and seat cushions, are eye filling in their long panties and snappy-looking coats.*

*Early arrivals in the terrace seats that surrounded the entire playing field were treated to balls batted in by members of both teams. As an added treat, several members of the Pirates tossed in a few dozen before the game.* [**Cincinnati Enquirer and Cincinnati Post**]

### OPENING DAY TRIVIA

| | |
|---|---|
| STAR OF THE GAME | PITTSBURGH PITCHER WAITE HOYT |
| WEATHER | 76°; CLOUDY |
| ATTENDANCE | 32,243 |
| NOTABLE | DEBUT OF DISTINCTIVE SALMON-COLORED SEATS |
| RATING | ◐◐ |

### 1936 OPENING DAY SCHEDULE

| APRIL 14 | NATIONAL LEAGUE |
|---|---|
| PITTS VS. CIN | CHI VS. STL |
| BRKLYN VS. NY | BOST VS. PHIL |

# 1937
# 13 Hits; 0 Runs
## Reds Pound Dean, But Fail to Score

Umpires separated the Reds' Hub Walker (top left) and the Cardinals' Leo Durocher (top, second from right). Their spat emptied the dugouts in the seventh inning. Other Reds in the debate included Ernie Lombardi (2) and Billy Myers (5).

The Reds knocked out 13 hits off St. Louis star Dizzy Dean, but none of the base runners crossed home plate. When the curtain finally fell after ten innings, the Cardinals had a 2–0 victory in the 1937 opener.

Ray "Peaches" Davis, the Reds starter, was the hard-luck victim, as he out-pitched Dean through nine innings, holding the Cardinals to five hits. Not one runner reached third base; only one reached second.

The Reds, on the other hand, had no trouble finding their way to first, second and third. But the hitters couldn't deliver a timely blow. Dean also benefitted from excellent defense, including a game-saving play in the bottom of the ninth. The Reds had runners on first and second with one out. Jimmy Outlaw smashed what appeared to be a single up the middle, but Leo Durocher snagged the bounder, and turned it into a 6-4-3 double play.

Davis tired in the tenth, giving up back-to-back doubles to Joe Medick and Johnny Mize. Durocher singled in the final run.

Ernie Lombardi started the Reds 10th with a double, but Dean retired the next three batters to preserve the win. The victory ran Dean's record against the Reds to 23–4.

The game had enough excitement to keep the 34,374 fans delighted, including a near-brawl in the seventh inning. The Reds' Hub Walker, a reserve outfielder, took offense at some remarks of Durocher and went out to discuss the matter. Both benches emptied, but the umpires quickly gained control of the debate.

Perhaps it was presence of "Ol' Diz" that set the tone, but the day seemed to have more than its share of light-hearted moments:

*Best comedy of the day was in the seventh inning when [St. Louis center fielder] Terry Moore leaped high in the air against the center field terrace fence to snag Lombardi's long drive and so astonished several dozen front row spectators that they leaned too hard against the railing, mashed it down and fell sprawling into the playing field.*

*[Reds pitcher] Lefty Grissom stepped out in front of Henry Fillmore's band to swing a baton and chew gum in time to "The Organ Grinder's Swing."*

*A red-haired lady and two gentlemen who remained in the upper right-field grandstand long after the last out had been made [did] a series of adagio dances between the seats.*

*Grandstand beams had markers on them to indicate the heighth of flood waters in January. There was also a mark on the flagpole in center field, indicating that the water was higher than the center field barrier. The announcer blared forth at the start of the game, informing everybody about the markings.*

*The Wild Bricklayer from Oxford dragged his aging legs around the bases and strutted in front of the stands. Airplanes flew overhead carrying advertisements for stoves and beer.* [*Cincinnati Enquirer and Cincinnati Post*]

### OPENING DAY TRIVIA

| | |
|---|---|
| STAR OF THE GAME | ST. LOUIS PITCHER DIZZY DEAN |
| WEATHER | 73°; PARTLY CLOUDY |
| ATTENDANCE | 34,374 |
| NOTABLE | PAINTED LINES MARK HEIGHT OF 1937 FLOOD |
| RATING | ○○○ |

### 1937 OPENING DAY SCHEDULE

| APRIL 19 | NATIONAL LEAGUE | |
|---|---|---|
| PHIL VS. BOST (2) | | |
| APRIL 20 | NATIONAL LEAGUE | |
| StL VS. CIN | PITTS VS. CHI | |
| NY VS. BRKLYN | | |

# Disputed Call Costs Reds

## 1938

### Reds Rally in 9th Ends in Controversy; Cubs Win, 8–7

*Frank McCormick slides into third base in the seventh inning. Stan Hack, the third baseman, was spiked on the play and had to leave the game. McCormick scored the Reds sixth run moments later when Billy Myers doubled.*

| 1938 OPENING DAY SCHEDULE |  |
|---|---|
| **April 19 National League** | |
| Chi vs. Cin | Pitts vs. StL |
| Brklyn vs. Phil | Bost vs. NY |

Before the start of the opener, Cincinnati native and umpire Larry Goetz received a handsome floral bouquet.

After the game, Goetz received the raspberries.

With two out in the ninth, and the Reds trailing by one run, Goetz called Reds right fielder George Davis out for running wide of the base line while avoiding a tag. The Reds erupted in protest and, when last seen, new manager Bill McKechnie was still jawing with Goetz as the crowd filed out of the stands.

McKechnie lost and Chicago won, 8–7. It was the Reds' sixth Opening Day loss in a row.

The ninth-inning rhubarb capped a wild day at the yard. The teams combined for 29 hits including nine ground-rule doubles and two ground-rule home runs. Neither starting pitcher lasted past the sixth inning. Chicago's Clay Bryant headed for the showers in the fourth, and Gene Schott, unable to hold a big lead, followed in the sixth.

The Reds jumped out to an early 5–1 advantage, then saw the Cubs tie it in the sixth and go ahead in the seventh. Chicago led, 7–6, heading into the ninth, and they added an insurance run on a two-out double by rookie Coaker Triplett. That proved to be the winning run when the Reds rallied for one in the controversial ninth.

Two walks and an error loaded the bases. Cub catcher Gabby Hartnett then attempted to pick Willard Hershberger off second. His throw hit Hershberger and bounded into right field, allowing Billy Myers to score from third, and Hershberger and Davis to move up one base.

Lew Riggs popped to first for the second out, and then came the disputed play. Dusty Cooke grounded to Tony Lazzeri at third. Hershberger headed home, and Davis, who was running on the play, neared third. Lazzeri swiped at the runner. Davis dodged the tag, and Lazzeri then threw to first, but too late to get Cooke. It appeared Hershberger had scored the tying run and all hands were safe. But Goetz quickly pointed to third base and signalled Davis out for running more than three feet out of the base line.

The Reds squawked, and McKechnie could barely contain himself, but Goetz remained steadfast, and the game was over.

The hitting star of the game for the Reds was shortstop Myers, who had three hits, including two doubles, and drove in three runs.

The pre-game ceremonies included the usual festivities: *The Findlay Market Association was on hand in all its glory, and Bill McKechnie got a gorgeous bunch of posies and Powel Crosley, Jr., an American flag. After the flag raising in center field, the two teams made an impressive sight as they paraded, fan-like, across the field with the band playing "Happy Days Are Here Again."*

*A large part of the ushering was taken care of by high school boys. Athletes from Hughes, Purcell, Roger Bacon, and Western Hills donned their monogram sweaters for the occasion.* **[Cincinnati Enquirer and Cincinnati Post]**

| OPENING DAY TRIVIA | |
|---|---|
| Star of the Game | Reds Shortstop Billy Myers |
| Weather | 81°; Sunny |
| Attendance | 34,148 |
| Notable | Game Ends on Disputed Play |
| Rating | ⚾⚾⚾ |

### April 19, 1938

| CHICAGO. | AB. | R. | H. | P.O. | A. |
|---|---|---|---|---|---|
| Hack, 3b | 3 | 1 | 2 | 0 | 1 |
| Lazzeri, 3b | 1 | 0 | 0 | 2 | 0 |
| Herman, 2b | 5 | 1 | 1 | 5 | 3 |
| Collins, 1b | 5 | 3 | 4 | 7 | 0 |
| Demaree, rf | 4 | 0 | 3 | 0 | 0 |
| Marty, cf | 5 | 1 | 2 | 2 | 1 |
| Triplett, lf | 5 | 1 | 2 | 2 | 0 |
| Jurges, ss | 4 | 1 | 1 | 1 | 5 |
| Hartnett, c | 3 | 0 | 1 | 5 | 0 |
| Bryant, p | 1 | 1 | 0 | 1 | 0 |
| Root, p | 2 | 0 | 0 | 0 | 1 |
| Logan, p | 1 | 0 | 0 | 0 | 0 |
| Totals | 40 | 8 | 15 | 27 | 12 |
| CINCINNATI | AB. | R. | H. | P.O. | A. |
| Goodman, rf | 4 | 2 | 2 | 1 | 0 |
| G. Davis, rf | 1 | 0 | 0 | 0 | 0 |
| Riggs, 3b | 4 | 0 | 0 | 0 | 3 |
| Cooke, lf | 6 | 1 | 3 | 3 | 0 |
| Craft, cf | 3 | 1 | 0 | 3 | 1 |
| McCormick, 1b | 5 | 2 | 2 | 10 | 2 |
| Lombardi, c | 3 | 0 | 3 | 4 | 0 |
| *Outlaw | 0 | 0 | 0 | 0 | 0 |
| V. Davis, c | 1 | 0 | 0 | 1 | 1 |
| Kampouris, 2b | 5 | 0 | 3 | 4 | 4 |
| Myers, ss | 4 | 1 | 3 | 3 | 4 |
| Schott, p | 2 | 0 | 0 | 1 | 0 |
| R. Davis, p | 1 | 0 | 1 | 0 | 0 |
| †Jordan | 0 | 0 | 0 | 0 | 0 |
| Hollingsworth, p | 0 | 0 | 0 | 0 | 2 |
| ‡Hershberger | 1 | 0 | 0 | 0 | 0 |
| Totals | 40 | 7 | 14 | 27 | 18 |

*Ran for Lombardi in seventh.
†Batted for R. Davis in seventh.
‡Batted for Hollingsworth in ninth.

| Innings: | 1 2 3 4 5 6 7 8 9 |
|---|---|
| Chicago | 0 0 1 2 0 2 2 0 1—8 |
| Cincinnati | 1 0 4 0 0 0 1 0 1—7 |

Errors—Hack, Jurges 2, Hartnett, Riggs, Myers.
Runs Batted In—Collins 2, Marty, Triplett, Jurges 2, Bryant, Cooke, McCormick 2, Myers 3.
Two-Base Hits—Collins, Marty, Triplett 2, Goodman, Cooke, McCormick, Myers 2.
Home Runs—Collins, Bryant. Sacrifices—Demaree, Riggs.
Double Plays—Hack to Herman to Collins; Jurges to Herman to Collins; Schott to Myers to McCormick; Myers to Kampouris to McCormick.
Left on Bases—Chicago, 8; Cincinnati, 14.
Bases On Balls—Off Bryant, 3; off Root, 1; off Logan, 3; off Schott, 1; off R. Davis, 1.
Struck Out—By Bryant, 2; by Root, 1; by Logan, 2; by Schott, 1; by Hollingsworth, 1.
Hits—Off Bryant, 3 in 3⅓ innings; off Root, 5 in 3 innings; off Logan, 1 in 2⅔ innings; off Schott, 8 in 3⅓ innings; off R. Davis, 2 in 1⅔ innings; off Hollingsworth, 4 in 2 innings.
Winning Pitcher—Root.
Losing Pitcher—R. Davis.
Umpires—Reardon, Pinelli, and Goetz.
Time—2:25.
Paid Attendance—34,148.

# Pirates at Home on the Crosley Ark
## Flood Threatens Opener

*Frank McCormick hit a long home run and drove in three runs in the 7–5 loss to Pittsburgh.*

| OPENING DAY TRIVIA | |
|---|---|
| STAR OF THE GAME | REDS FIRST BASEMAN FRANK MCCORMICK |
| WEATHER | 69°; SUNNY WITH A BRIEF SHOWER |
| ATTENDANCE | 30,644 |
| NOTABLE | RISING FLOODWATERS NEARLY POSTPONE GAME |
| RATING | ●●● |

The Red and Pirates battled not only each other, but rising floodwaters which threatened to cancel the opener.

The ballpark was in danger of inundation, because as the Millcreek rose, floodwater backed up into the park through sewer lines that normally drained water away from Crosley Field. A few inches of water did creep into the area beneath the stands and filled one ramp leading to the Reds dugout. Boards were placed over the "moat" and the Reds navigated the walkway.

The surrounding streets were dry except for the large parking lot just west of Crosley Field. A small puddle at game time had grown into a small pond by game's end, although there were no reports of stranded cars. Concern over the floodwaters and a threat of afternoon rain held the crowd to under 31,000, the smallest crowd in several years.

Fans were rewarded with an entertaining game, if not a Reds victory. The club lost its seventh straight opener, a 7–5 setback to Pittsburgh. This was the longest losing streak in Cincinnati's Opening Day history.

The Reds took an early lead on Frank McCormick's home run over the left-field wall in the first. The Pirates tied it in the third, sending starter Johnny Vander Meer to a quick shower. Behind the relief work of Bucky Walters, the Reds rebuilt their lead to 5–2 after seven innings. But the Pirates replied with a four-run eighth that won the game. Pittsburgh roughed up Walters and Ray "Peaches" Davis in the inning for five hits, a walk, and four runs.

One scary moment came in the second inning, when popular shortstop Billy Myers was hit in the head by an infielder's throw. Myers, who had hit a slow roller to third base, was struck on the back of the head by the throw just as he neared the bag. His momentum carried him across the base and he fell unconscious just beyond first.

Four teammates lifted the limp Myers off the ground and carried him to the clubhouse. He was quickly rushed to the hospital, and soon regained consciousness. Myers did take some consolation from the incident, telling reporters that since he had been credited with a hit on the play, his average stood at 1.000.

"I'm the batting king of the National League," Myers kidded the press. Myers returned to the lineup a few days later.

For the first time in the 20th century, the Reds inaugurated the NL season by playing the first game of the year.

The usual ceremonies were held before the game: *The Findlay Market merchants were there in all their glory; state and city pooh-bahs were on hand and the presentation of floral offerings and the blare of bands added to the fanfare. When Smitty's Band swung into a hot number [Reds] Whitey Moore and Wally Berger "got into the groove" with a little jitterbugging in the dugout.* **[Cincinnati Enquirer and Cincinnati Post]**

| 1939 OPENING DAY SCHEDULE | |
|---|---|
| APRIL 17 | NATIONAL LEAGUE |
| STL VS. CIN | |
| APRIL 18 | NATIONAL LEAGUE |
| CHI VS. CIN | STL VS. PITTS |
| NY VS. BRKLYN | PHIL VS. BOST |

### APRIL 17, 1939

```
PITTSBURGH.   AB.R. H. P.A.E
L. Waner, cf..  4 1 1 3 0 0
Bell, rf......  5 0 1 1 0 0
Rizzo, lf.....  3 1 0 0 0 0
Vaughan, ss...  5 2 2 2 3 0
Suhr, 1b......  4 1 3 17 1 0
Young, 2b.....  5 1 3 3 1 0
Brubaker, 3b..  4 0 2 1 3 2
Mueller, c....  3 0 0 0 0 0
*Manush.......  1 0 0 0 0 0
†Berres, c....  1 0 0 0 0 0
Blanton, p....  3 1 1 0 3 0
‡P. Waner.....  1 0 1 0 0 0
Brown, p......  0 0 0 0 0 0
                _____
Totals ..     39 7 15 27 17 2
*Batted for Mueller in eighth.
†Batted for Blanton in eighth.
CINCINNATI    AB R. H. P.O.A.E
Werber, 3b....  4 1 2 2 1 0
Berger, lf....  4 0 0 0 2 0
Goodman, rf...  5 1 1 3 0 0
McCormick, 1b.  4 2 3 7 0 0
Lombardi, c...  4 0 1 7 1 0
Craft, cf.....  4 0 1 1 1 0
Joost, 2b.....  4 0 0 4 3 0
Myers, ss.....  1 0 1 1 0 1
Richardson, ss  3 0 0 1 3 0
Vander Meer, p  1 0 0 0 0 0
Walters, p....  2 1 1 0 0 0
Davis, p......  0 0 0 0 0 0
Grissom, p....  0 0 0 0 0 0
*Scarsella....  1 0 0 0 0 0
                _____
Totals ....   37 5 10 27 12 1
*Batted for Grissom in ninth.
Innings.      1 2 3 4 5 6 7 8 9
Pittsburgh .. 0 0 2 0 0 0 0 4 1—7
Cincinnati .. 2 0 0 0 1 1 1 0 0—5
Runs Batted In—L. Waner, Suhr
2, Young 2, Brubaker, Manush, Mc-
Cormick 3, Craft.
Two-Base Hits—Vaughan, Young
2, Brubaker, Werber, Walters.
Home Run—McCormick.
Sacrifice—Suhr, Walters.
Double Plays—Suhr to Vaughan
to Suhr, Richardson to Joost to Mc-
Cormick.
Left on Bases—Pittsburgh 10, Cin-
cinnati 7.
Bases on Balls—Off Blanton 1,
Vander Meer 2, Walters 1.
Struck Out—By Vander Meer 2,
Walters 4, Grissom 1.
Hits—Off Blanton 9 in 7 innings,
Brown 1 in 1; Vander Meer 4 in
2⅓, Walters 7 in 4⅓ (none out in
eighth), Davis 2 in 1, Grissom 2 in 1.
Wild Pitch—Blanton.
Winning Pitcher—Blanton.
Losing Pitcher—Walters.
Umpires—Klem, Barr, and Camp-
bell.
Time of Game—2:16.
Attendance—30,644.
```

# Derringer + Goodman = Win
## Paul's Pitching, Ival's Homer Gives Reds 2–1 Victory over Chicago

**1940**

*Paul Derringer earned his only Opening Day win in 1940.*

The Reds opened defense of their 1939 National League championship with good pitching and timely hitting, producing a 2–1 victory over Chicago. It was the first Opening Day win for Cincinnati since 1932, and 34,342 enthusiastic rooters savored the outcome.

Perhaps the only disappointment of the day was the club's decision to postpone the raising of the 1939 NL championship pennant. Many fans had hoped the Reds would unfurl it on Opening Day, but the club elected to wait until the second home stand.

The early arriving fans enjoyed a long-ball exhibition by the Reds during batting practice, and the crowd took the opportunity to greet Ernie Lombardi with loud cheers. The ovation was an "all-is-forgiven" tribute directed at the big catcher who had received considerable criticism for his fielding gaffe—often referred to as the "Snooze"—in Game Four of the 1939 World Series.

The game featured a stirring pitcher's duel between Chicago's Bill Lee and Cincinnati's Paul Derringer. Both men worked fast and the game was completed in only 93 minutes. Lee gave up only eight hits, but two were back-breakers, a home run to Frank McCormick in the third, and the game-winner by Ival Goodman in the eighth. Goodman's blast just carried over the right-field bleacher wall. There was some initial confusion if the ball had cleared the barrier beyond the temporary seats, but the umpires quickly gave the home run signal.

Derringer allowed only six hits and walked none. The only run came on a Augie Galan home run in the sixth. It was Derringer's 11th straight victory dating back to the 1939 season.

Many people expected a record-breaking crowd in honor of the reigning NL champs, but threatening skies in the morning may have kept the attendance under the 35,000 mark. Nonetheless, the crowd of 34,342 was the fourth-largest in Opening Day history to that point, which was a box-office winner: *The opener grossed an estimated $50,000 for the Redleg business office. That's almost enough to keep the team in eatin' tobacco for the whole year.*

*Marchers of the Findlay Market Business Men's Association took the town with canes and miniature baseball bats. Mayor Stewart and Smitty's Band were leaders of the parade. The line of march was east on Elder to Vine, south to 12th, west to Elm, north to Findlay thence to Crosley Field.*

*Out-of-towners came here early for the game. There were scores from Hamilton, Dayton and Richmond, Ind. On all streets surrounding the stadium, new hot dog stands were open for business. Vendors with pennants acclaiming the 1939 league champs were on the scene at dawn.*

*Frank McCormick's third-inning homer was a mighty sock. It sailed over the center-field fence like a well-hit No. 1 iron shot.*

[Cincinnati Enquirer and Cincinnati Post]

### 1940 Opening Day Schedule

| April 16 | National League | |
|---|---|---|
| Chi vs. Cin | | Pitts vs. StL |
| Brklyn vs. Bost | | Phil vs. NY |

### Opening Day Trivia

| | |
|---|---|
| Star of the Game | Reds Right Fielder Ival Goodman |
| Weather | 69°; Cloudy |
| Attendance | 34,342 |
| Notable | First Opening Day Win Since 1932 |
| Rating | ●●●● |

# Defending Champs Drop Opener
## McCormick's Two Home Runs Not Enough To Save Reds

**1941**

*Ernie Lombardi (left) greets Frank McCormick after the first of his two home runs on Opening Day, 1941.*

All that was missing was the victory.

The Cincinnati Reds, baseball's defending World Champions, began the defense of their crown on a nearly perfect day, with a pre-game ceremony that included the raising of the World Champion-ship pennant and the presentation of the World Series rings.

A gate-crunching mob of 34,490 flocked to Crosley Field, including an All-Star cast of VIPS: Ohio Governor John Bricker—who threw out the first pitch—Mayor James Stewart, baseball Commissioner Kenesaw M. Landis, National League president Ford Frick and Senator A.B. (Happy) Chandler of Kentucky.

But the visiting St. Louis Cardinals threw cold water on the party with a 7–3 victory over the Reds.

The Reds' Frank McCormick gave the fans plenty to cheer about early, when he walloped his first home run of the game over the left-field wall. Moments later, an RBI-double by Eddie Joost gave the Reds and starter Paul Derringer a 2–0 lead. But Big Paul couldn't hold the lead, and the Cardinals edged ahead in the fourth on home runs by Ernie Koy and Enos Slaughter. They took a 5–2 lead in the eighth, sending Derringer to the showers. Johnny Mize hit a two-run homer in the ninth off reliever Joe Beggs.

After giving up the two runs in the second, St. Louis starter Lon Warneke shut the Reds out until the ninth when McCormick hit his second home run. The clubs combined for five home runs, a Cincinnati Opening Day record (tied in 1999).

Although few fans were aware of the episode, one spectator, 64-year-old Harry Shaft, suffered a fatal heart attack in the stands in the third inning. He was pronounced dead at the scene by two doctors who were sitting nearby.

The club announced the attendance of 34,940 as an Opening Day record, but it actually fell short of the 35,747 in 1924. The temporary seats were up all around the outfield. The scribes took note of the home runs and the ceremonies: *Frank McCormick's ninth-inning round-tripper [carried] over close to the left-field corner of the scoreboard and bounded over a streetcar on Western Avenue. Mize's ninth-inning homer was the longest of the day. It carried like a shot over the fence at the center-field corner of the bleachers and hit on the far side of Western Avenue.*

*Judge Kenesaw M. Landis, high commissioner of baseball, presented diamond rings to each of the Reds on last season's championship team. He kidded a few of the veterans like Jim Turner, Bill McKechnie and Coach Hank Gowdy. After the game each of the Reds slipped on his ring and was proudly displaying it to friends.* **[Cincinnati Enquirer, Cincinnati Post and Cincinnati Times-Star]**

### 1941 OPENING DAY SCHEDULE

| APRIL 15 | NATIONAL LEAGUE |
|---|---|
| StL vs. Cin | Pitts vs. Chi |
| Bost vs. Phil | NY vs. Brklyn |

### OPENING DAY TRIVIA

| | |
|---|---|
| STAR OF THE GAME | REDS FIRST BASEMAN FRANK McCORMICK |
| WEATHER | 76°; PARTLY CLOUDY |
| ATTENDANCE | 34,940 |
| NOTABLE | REDS PRESENTED WORLD SERIES RINGS |
| RATING | ◊◊◊◊ |

# DiMaggio's Catch Rescues the Pirates
## Ninth-Inning Grab Protects 4–2 Lead

*Ival Goodman, who had two hits on Opening Day, 1942, hit .419 in his seven Cincinnati openers (13-for-31), tops on the all-time club list.*

Joe DiMaggio had nothing on his brother Vince. With two on and two out in the bottom of the ninth, Pittsburgh center fielder Vince DiMaggio did his best imitation of the "Yankee Clipper" by snaring Ival Goodman's bid for a hit that would have tied the game.

Racing in at full speed, DiMaggio snatched the ball off his shoe tops, and preserved the Opening Day victory for Pittsburgh, 4–2.

Max Butcher earned the win, although he walked seven, including four to Lonny Frey. He limited the Reds to six hits, but with the exception of Goodman's triple in the fifth, none of the hits came with runners in scoring position.

Bucky Walters pitched well enough to win most games, holding the Pirates to seven hits and walking only two. But his defense deserted him in the first and fourth innings, as the Pirates picked up four runs, three unearned.

Walters gathered steam as the game progressed, allowing only two base runners in the final five innings. He retired the last nine Pirates in a row.

But Butcher was his equal, teasing the Reds with flashes of wildness that put runners on base, then coaxing harmless ground balls to end the innings.

The lone exception came in the fifth, with the Reds trailing, 4–0. After Walters and Frey walked, Goodman drove in both runners with a triple to right field.

In the ninth, Goodman nearly tied the game with another bid for an extra-base hit. Two more Butcher walks had put the tying runs on base. Goodman worked the count to three and two, then lined hard to center where DiMaggio caught it for the final out.

Nearly perfect baseball weather lured 34,104 fans to Crosley Field to see the first wartime opener since 1918. The pre-game ceremonies, coming five months after the attack on Pearl Harbor, were somber: *The men, with their hats held reverently over their hearts, stood in military fashion. They didn't simply hold their hats and stand first on one foot, then the other or with their backs to the flag. The women were just as attentive and solemn. It was indicative that the crowd realized there are more important things happening on the various battlefronts and throughout the country's defense plants.*

*But once the "Play Ball" signal was given, the crowd, at least to all outward appearances, became the same jovial, carefree gathering of other years. The Findlay Market Association paraded, as usual, once around the park [and] presented Manager Bill McKechnie with two war bonds. One bond went to the Red scoring the first run and the other to the player driving in the first run. Walters and Goodman were the winners of [the] $25 war bonds.*

In the radio booth, the sportscasters blast away selling beer, cigars, gasoline, bug powder, laundry service and, above all, the Reds.

[*Cincinnati Enquirer* and *Cincinnati Post*]

### OPENING DAY TRIVIA

| | |
|---|---|
| STAR OF THE GAME | REDS RIGHT FIELDER IVAL GOODMAN |
| WEATHER | 72°; SUNNY |
| ATTENDANCE | 34,104 |
| NOTABLE | FIRST OPENER AFTER PEARL HARBOR |
| RATING | ◐◐ |

### 1942 OPENING DAY SCHEDULE

| APRIL 14 | NATIONAL LEAGUE |
|---|---|
| PITTS VS. CIN | CHI VS. STL |
| BOST VS. PHIL | BRKLYN VS. NY |

# Vandy and Max
## Vander Meer and Marshall Lead Reds over Cards in 11

*Johnny Vander Meer pitched an 11-inning two-hitter to beat the Cardinals in the 1943 opener.*

### 1943 OPENING DAY SCHEDULE

| APRIL 21 | NATIONAL LEAGUE | |
|---|---|---|
| StL vs. Cin | | Pitts vs. Chi |
| Bost vs. Brklyn (PP) | Phil vs. NY (PP) | |

It was the greatest pitcher's duel in a Cincinnati opener.

Johnny Vander Meer and Mort Cooper battled for 11 innings before Cincinnati right fielder Max Marshall knocked in the game-winner to beat the defending World Champion St. Louis Cardinals, 1–0.

Only the chilly temperatures put a damper on the day. For the first time in many years, the bleachers in right field were not full. The temporary seats were up in the outfield, but were sparsely populated. The standees preferred the warmth of the grandstand to the exposed conditions in the outfield seats. A few fans in the left-field stands fought off the chill with a small bonfire.

The cool, damp weather postponed half the openers around baseball. None of the cities that did host games (Washington, Chicago, Cleveland and St. Louis) had a capacity crowd. Cincinnati's opener drew, by far, the largest crowd.

The 27,709 loyal Cincinnati fans who braved the elements more than received their money's worth. Vander Meer was nearly perfect. He gave up only two hits, both singles, and he held St. Louis hitless over the last eight innings. Only two Cardinals reached second base, and none reached third. Vandy walked five, but St. Louis never mounted a serious threat.

And when the Cardinals did hit the ball hard, center fielder Eric Tipton was there to make the catch. Tipton robbed three St. Louis hitters of extra-base hits.

Cardinal starter Mort Cooper matched Vander Meer zero for zero, although he had to stifle scoring threats in the second, sixth and ninth innings to send the game into extra innings. Finally, in the eleventh, the Reds assembled a classic rally. Speedy Lonny Frey began the inning with an infield single and Mike McCormick laid down a perfect sacrifice bunt. Marshall, who had gone hitless in four at-bats, smacked Cooper's first pitch into center field to drive home Frey and give the Reds the win.

The papers noted the war-time atmosphere, and the stellar play of Tipton: *Private John Decker of the United States Marines, who was wounded in action in the Pacific, threw out the first ball.*

*Crosley Field was decked out tastily in the customary inaugural day flags and bunting. Smitty's Band entertained the early arrivals with popular tunes of the day.*

*The Findlay Market Association, as usual, played a prominent part in the pre-game ceremonies. The annual parade was led by Mayor James Garfield Stewart.*

*[Tipton's] catch in the eleventh was one of the finest witnessed in many a day at Crosley Field. He timed the drive perfectly and leaped high into the air to make a gloved-hand catch of the stitched onion just as it appeared certain to drop safely.*

**[Cincinnati Enquirer and Cincinnati Post]**

### OPENING DAY TRIVIA

| | |
|---|---|
| STAR OF THE GAME | REDS PITCHER JOHNNY VANDER MEER |
| WEATHER | 48°; CLOUDY |
| ATTENDANCE | 27,709 |
| NOTABLE | BEST PITCHERS' DUEL ON OPENING DAY |
| RATING | ☆☆☆☆☆ |

### APRIL 21, 1943

| ST. LOUIS | AB | R | H | PO | A | E |
|---|---|---|---|---|---|---|
| Brown, 2b | 2 | 0 | 0 | 5 | 5 | 0 |
| Demaree, rf | 5 | 0 | 1 | 4 | 0 | 0 |
| Musial, lf | 4 | 0 | 0 | 1 | 0 | 0 |
| Kurowski, 3b | 3 | 0 | 0 | 2 | 3 | 0 |
| W. Cooper, c | 4 | 0 | 0 | 4 | 1 | 0 |
| Adams, cf | 2 | 0 | 0 | 11 | 1 | 0 |
| Hopp, 1b | 4 | 0 | 0 | 0 | 0 | 0 |
| Klein, ss | 4 | 0 | 0 | 0 | 2 | 0 |
| M. Cooper, p | 4 | 0 | 1 | 0 | 1 | 0 |
| Totals | 33 | 0 | 2 | a31 | 13 | 0 |

a-One out when winning run was scored.

| CIN'TI | AB | R | H | PO | A | E |
|---|---|---|---|---|---|---|
| Frey, 2b | 5 | 1 | 2 | 1 | 6 | 1 |
| M. McCormick cf | 3 | 0 | 1 | 2 | 0 | 0 |
| Marshall, rf | 4 | 0 | 1 | 3 | 1 | 0 |
| F. M'Cormick 1b | 4 | 0 | 1 | 16 | 1 | 0 |
| Miller, ss | 4 | 0 | 0 | 3 | 1 | 0 |
| Haas, 3b | 4 | 0 | 1 | 5 | 0 | 0 |
| Tipton, lf | 4 | 0 | 0 | 3 | 0 | 0 |
| Mueller, c | 3 | 0 | 0 | 3 | 0 | 0 |
| Vander Meer, p | 4 | 0 | 0 | 0 | 5 | 0 |
| Totals | 34 | 1 | 6 | 33 | 17 | 1 |

| | | | |
|---|---|---|---|
| St. Louis | 000 000 000 00 | — | 0 |
| Cincinnati | 000 000 000 01 | — | 1 |

Run Batted In—By Marshall. Two-base Hits—Frey, Tipton. Sacrifices—M. McCormick, Marshall. Double Plays—Klein Brown and Hopp; Haas, Frey and F. McCormick; Marshall and F. McCormick. Struck Out—By M. Cooper 4, Vander Meer 8. Bases on Balls—By M. Cooper 2, Vander Meer 5. Hit Batsman—Miller. Left on Bases—St. Louis 5, Cincinnati 7. Time—Two hours and 13 minutes. Umpires—Reardon, Ballanfant and Goetz. Paid Attendance—27,709.

# Walters Loses Three-Hitter
## 1944
### Young Joe Nuxhall Watches Game from Dugout

*Bucky Walters held the Cubs to three hits in the 1944 opener, but lost the game. Walters, one of the greatest pitchers in Reds history, was 0-3 on Opening Day.*

Veteran Bucky Walters out-pitched second-year Cubs hurler Henry Wyse in the 1944 opener, but lost the game, 3–0. Walters allowed only three hits over nine innings, but Chicago made every one of them count. The Reds squandered their opportunities and left eight men on base.

Wyse, whose nickname was "Hooks," spun his curve ball so deftly that the Reds managed only five hits. He and Walters pitched as though walks and minutes were part of war-time rationing. Wyse walked two, Walters one. The game was played in the record time of 1:17, tying the Cincinnati Opening Day mark set in 1929. Perhaps the pitching was too sharp and the game too fast. One sportswriter called the opener "dull."

The crowd of 30,154 included 505 service men who came as guests of the club.

One other non-paying spectator was 15-year-old Joe Nuxhall, whom the Reds had just signed to a contract. Joe was granted an excuse from Wilson Junior High in Hamilton to attend the game. He sat on the Reds bench, in uniform, but manager Bill McKechnie had no intention of playing Nuxhall in this game. (Nuxhall made his famous debut later in the 1944 season.)

### OPENING DAY TRIVIA

| | |
|---|---|
| STAR OF THE GAME | REDS PITCHER BUCKY WALTERS |
| WEATHER | 65°; PARTLY CLOUDY |
| ATTENDANCE | 30,154 |
| NOTABLE | TIED FOR FASTEST OPENER EVER: 1:17 |
| RATING | ☺ |

The Cubs cobbled together two hits in the fourth inning and a sacrifice fly for their first two runs. They added a final tally in the ninth on a sacrifice fly by Bill Nicholson, his second RBI of the game.

The usual ceremonies preceded the wartime opener, with Mayor James Garfield Stuart tossing out a wild pitch to start the game. The papers discussed the pageantry and the appearance of young Mr. Nuxhall: *The Findlay Market boys, as usual, did a splendid job of supplying the pre-game color. Old Glory was flung to the breeze in an impressive ceremony before the game as Smitty's 30-piece Victory Band played the Star Spangled Banner.*

*The teams paraded across the field to the cheers of the crowd and the strains of martial music with President Powel Crosley, Jr., General Manager Warren Giles and [manager] Deacon McKechnie striding jauntily at their head.*

*Joe [Nuxhall] said he told his principal he'd like to skip classes for a day so he could come down and get in a day's work with the Reds and the principal—John Elwell—said it would be okay just this once, seeing as how it was opening day and all that.*

*Joe made the trip down to Cincinnati alone and by bus. He went right back after the game. Joe's a likeable youngster and doesn't appear to be the kind who'd get excited very easily. He looks big and loose-jointed. When he sits down, he sort of folds up. Something about the way he moves makes you think of Eppa Rixey.* **[Cincinnati Enquirer and Cincinnati Post]**

### APRIL 18, 1944

| CHICAGO. | AB. | R. | H. | PO. | A. |
|---|---|---|---|---|---|
| D. Johnson, 2b. | 4 | 1 | 1 | 1 | 1 |
| Cavaretta, 1b. | 3 | 2 | 2 | 5 | 0 |
| Nicholson, rf. | 4 | 0 | 1 | 5 | 0 |
| Goodman, lf. | 4 | 0 | 0 | 1 | 0 |
| Pafko, cf. | 3 | 0 | 0 | 3 | 0 |
| York, 3b. | 3 | 0 | 0 | 1 | 4 |
| Schuster, ss. | 3 | 0 | 0 | 0 | 0 |
| Holm, c. | 3 | 0 | 0 | 1 | 0 |
| Wyse, p. | 3 | 0 | 0 | 0 | 2 |
| Totals | 30 | 3 | 3 | 27 | 7 |

| CINCINNATI. | AB. | R. | H. | PO. | A. |
|---|---|---|---|---|---|
| Clay, cf. | 4 | 0 | 0 | 1 | 0 |
| Williams, 2b. | 4 | 0 | 1 | 0 | 3 |
| Walker, rf. | 3 | 0 | 1 | 4 | 0 |
| McCormick, 1b. | 4 | 0 | 0 | 13 | 0 |
| Tipton, lf. | 4 | 0 | 2 | 1 | 0 |
| Miller, ss. | 4 | 0 | 0 | 2 | 3 |
| Mesner, 3b. | 3 | 0 | 0 | 1 | 3 |
| †Crabtree | 1 | 0 | 0 | 0 | 0 |
| Mueller, c. | 3 | 0 | 0 | 3 | 0 |
| †Fansett | 1 | 0 | 0 | 0 | 0 |
| Walters, p. | 3 | 0 | 1 | 2 | 2 |
| Totals | 23 | 0 | 5 | 27 | 12 |

*Batted for Mesner in ninth.
†Batted for Mueller in ninth.

| Innings | 1 | 2 | 3 | 4 | 5 | 6 | 7 | 8 | 9 | | |
|---|---|---|---|---|---|---|---|---|---|---|---|
| Chicago | 0 | 0 | 0 | 2 | 0 | 0 | 0 | 0 | 1 | – | 3 |
| Cincinnati | 0 | 0 | 0 | 0 | 0 | 0 | 0 | 0 | 0 | – | 0 |

Error—Schuster.
Runs Batted In—Nicholson 2, Goodman.
Two-Base Hit—Tipton.
Three-Base Hit—Cavaretta.
Left On Bases—Chicago 1, Cincinnati 8.
Bases On Balls—Wyse 2, Walters 1.
Struck Out—By Wyse 1, Walters 2.
Umpires—Barr, Sears and Conlan.
Time—1:17.
Attendance—30,154.

### 1944 OPENING DAY SCHEDULE

| APRIL 18 | NATIONAL LEAGUE |
|---|---|
| CHI VS. CIN | PITTS VS. STL |
| BRKLYN VS. PHIL | BOST VS. NY |

# Clay the Hero of Wild Opener
## Shoestring Fiasco Wipes Out Pittsburgh Home Run

*Dain Clay set a Cincinnati Opening Day record with five RBIs, four coming on a grand slam home run.*

### April 17, 1945

| PITTSB'GH. | AB. | R. | H. | PO. | A. | E. |
|---|---|---|---|---|---|---|
| Zak, ss | 5 | 2 | 2 | 1 | 5 | 0 |
| Barrett, cf | 4 | 1 | 2 | 4 | 0 | 0 |
| Russell, lf | 5 | 1 | 2 | 1 | 1 | 0 |
| Elliott, 3b | 4 | 1 | 1 | 3 | 5 | 0 |
| Colman, rf | 4 | 0 | 1 | 1 | 0 | 0 |
| Dahlgren, 1b | 5 | 0 | 0 | 18 | 1 | 0 |
| Gustine, 2b | 5 | 0 | 0 | 2 | 1 | 0 |
| Lopes, c | 4 | 1 | 1 | 7 | 2 | 0 |
| Ostermueller, p | 2 | 0 | 0 | 1 | 0 | 0 |
| Rescigno, p | 0 | 0 | 0 | 1 | 0 | 0 |
| a-Gionfriddo | 1 | 0 | 1 | 0 | 0 | 0 |
| Sewell, p | 2 | 0 | 0 | 0 | 0 | 0 |
| Totals | 42 | 6 | 11 | b-31 | 17 | 0 |

a-Gionfriddo singled for Rescigno in seventh.
b-One out when winning run was scored.

| CIN'TI. | AB. | R. | H. | PO. | A. | E. |
|---|---|---|---|---|---|---|
| Clay, cf | 5 | 1 | 2 | 2 | 0 | 0 |
| Tipton, lf | 4 | 1 | 1 | 3 | 0 | 0 |
| Walker, rf | 5 | 0 | 1 | 5 | 0 | 0 |
| McCormick, 1b | 4 | 0 | 2 | 12 | 0 | 0 |
| Mesner, 3b | 5 | 0 | 0 | 1 | 3 | 0 |
| Williams, 2b | 4 | 1 | 1 | 3 | 4 | 0 |
| Wahl, ss | 3 | 1 | 1 | 5 | 1 | 0 |
| Just, c | 3 | 1 | 1 | 1 | 0 | 0 |
| Walters, p | 3 | 1 | 0 | 0 | 4 | 1 |
| Lisenbee, p | 0 | 0 | 0 | 0 | 0 | 0 |
| c-Flager | 1 | 1 | 0 | 0 | 0 | 0 |
| Totals | 37 | 7 | 9 | 33 | 15 | 1 |

c-Flager walked for Lisenbee in the eleventh.

Pittsburgh ....... 100 010 400 00—6
Cincinnati ....... 000 060 000 01—7

Runs Batted In—By Barrett, Russell 2, Elliott 2, Dahlgren, Clay 5, Walters (Tipton scored while Walker was being run down in fifth). Two-Base Hits—Zak, Elliott, Tipton, McCormick 2. Home Run—Clay. Sacrifices—Tipton, Wahl, Just. Double Plays—Walters, Wahl and McCormick; Williams, Wahl and McCormick. Struck Out—By Ostermueller 2, Sewell 3, Walters 3, Lisenbee 1. Bases on Balls—By Ostermueller 3, Sewell 3, Walters 3, Lisenbee 1. Off Ostermueller, 5 runs, 4 hits in 4 innings (none out in fifth); Rescigno, 1 run, 2 hits in 2; Sewell, 1 run, 3 hits in 4⅔; Walters, 6 runs, 11 hits in 9; Lisenbee, no runs, no hits in 2. Winning Pitcher—Lisenbee. Losing Pitcher—Sewell. Left on Bases—Pittsburgh 7, Cincinnati 8. Time—Two hours and 38 minutes. Umpires—Barr, Sears and Conlan. Paid Attendance—30,069.

### 1945 Opening Day Schedule

| April 17 | National League | |
|---|---|---|
| Pitts vs. Cin | | StL vs. Chi |
| Phil vs. Brklyn | | NY vs. Bost |

Reds fans toasted Frankie Zak's shoestring and Dain Clay's lumber in the aftermath of Cincinnati's thrilling, 7–6, win over Pittsburgh. Clay drove in five runs, including the game-winner in the 11th. His other four RBIs came on a grand slam home run in the fifth inning.

As for the shoestring, it might as well have been a noose. It cost the Pirates three runs in their half of the fifth. Zak, who was on first, signalled for time out to tie his shoe just as Bucky Walters was in his windup. Second base umpire Ziggy Sears waved his arms, but Walters finished his delivery and Jimmy Russell smashed a three-run homer.

The crowd groaned and the Pirates celebrated, but Sears ruled the play dead, and sent Russell back to the plate. There was no explanation given over the loudspeaker, and many fans were left confused over the ruling.

The Pirates wound up with only one run in the fifth, which gave them a 2–0 lead. But a feat of Clay in the bottom of the inning helped propel the Reds to a 6–2 lead. Two walks and a single loaded the bases with none out. Walters then drew a walk to force in the first run. Clay, who was no power hitter, surprised everyone with a drive over the left-field fence for his first major league home run, and his only homer of the 1945 season. (Clay finished his four-year career with three homers.)

The Pirates tied the score in the seventh, taking advantage of a Reds fielding lapse. With one on in the seventh, Zak bounced backed to the mound. Walters fired it to second to start a double play, but rookie shortstop Kermit Wahl was slow to cover the base, and the ball—along with Walter's concentration—sailed into center field. The Pirates went on to score four runs.

The game remained tied until the 11th when the Reds loaded the bases with one out. With the outfield drawn in, Clay delivered the game-winner, a long fly to left that sailed over the fielder's head. The hit made a winner of Hod Lisenbee, a 44-year-old pitcher who was the oldest player in the major leagues. This was his only win in 1945.

The flags over the ballpark stood at half-mast in tribute to President Franklin D. Roosevelt, who had passed away five days before the opener. Some reporters found the mood subdued; others thought the crowd was "carefree:" *It was a large crowd and a surprisingly gay crowd and a fellow couldn't help but wonder if maybe the people have learned to take the war in stride. It was a long game, which was a fine break for the boys who were hoping for an excuse to stay around for just one more beer or snort. A fellow needed only to walk through the grandstand to discover that quite a few of them were pretty well buzzed up.*

*The usual throng of politicians and officeholders were present, indicating that business at City Hall and the Courthouse must have been almost at a standstill.*
**[Cincinnati Enquirer and Cincinnati Post]**

### Opening Day Trivia

| | |
|---|---|
| Star of the Game | Reds Right Fielder Dain Clay |
| Weather | 61° |
| Attendance | 30,069 |
| Notable | 44-Year-Old Lisenbee Earns Win |
| Rating | ●●●●● |

# Good Start, Lousy Finish
## 1946
### Reds Lose Three-Run Lead In Ninth to Cubs

*Ohio Governor Frank Lausche (right) and baseball commissioner Happy Chandler were familiar faces at Cincinnati openers in the 1940s and 1950s.*

### OPENING DAY TRIVIA

| | |
|---|---|
| STAR OF THE GAME | REDS THIRD BASEMAN GRADY HATTON |
| WEATHER | 51°; CLOUDY |
| ATTENDANCE | 30,699 |
| NOTABLE | CLUBS USE 37 PLAYERS |
| RATING | ◐◐ |

In the first Opening Day since VJ-Day, Cincinnati fans celebrated baseball without the heavy shadow of world war looming over the ballpark. The mood was light and celebratory.

Ohio Governor Frank Lausche led the parade of dignitaries, which included Commissioner Happy Chandler. Another noted "celebrity" was the new compact Crosley car, which circled the field during pre-game ceremonies.

The most unusual sight in the Reds dressing room before the game was a half-dressed Eddie Miller, the Reds shortstop. When the new uniforms were handed out, Miller's came without pants. Embarrassed uniform representatives found a last-minute replacement.

For eight innings, Joe Beggs and the Reds had a victory in the opener all wrapped up and ready to present to the 30,699 fans. Beggs had limited Chicago to one hit and the Reds—behind the clutch hitting of rookie Grady Hatton—had crept out to a 3–0 lead.

But Chicago made them play the ninth inning, and the lead slipped away. A four-run rally off Beggs and reliever Ed Huesser put the Cubs ahead, and they survived a stirring Cincinnati rally in the bottom of the ninth to walk away with a 4–3 win.

The Cubs uprising began with a single, a double and two more singles which produced two runs. After a walk loaded the bases, Bob Scheffing lined a two-run single over short and the Cubs had the lead.

In the bottom of the ninth, the Reds loaded the bases on two hits and a walk. But pinch hitter Ray Lamano struck out, bringing Hatton to the plate with two outs. Hatton, who already had three hits in his debut, hit the ball hard, but right at the shortstop. The Reds had seized an Opening Day loss from the jaws of victory.

The club unveiled a new seating section in front of the right-field bleachers, which reduced the distance down the right-field line from 366 feet to 342 feet. This section later became known as the "Goat Run," and it remained in place (except for 1951 and 1952) through the 1958 season. It also added enough extra seats that, for the first time since Crosley Field opened in 1912, the club did not use temporary seating in the outfield for the opener.

Despite the cool weather, the opener again sold out: *There were young people and old people. There were flashy blondes and housewives. There were dignified men with conservatively dressed women. There were kids excused from school. There were men in neckties from the bookie fraternity. There were plain, weather-beaten men from the farms. They wanted to see a baseball opener and the show that goes with it. They wanted to be able to say they were there. They were out to make a day out of it. Some of the gayer blades were ready to make a night of it.* [*Cincinnati Enquirer and Cincinnati Post*]

### 1946 OPENING DAY SCHEDULE

| APRIL 16 | NATIONAL LEAGUE |
|---|---|
| CHI VS. CIN | PITTS VS. STL |
| BRKLYN VS. BOST | PHIL VS. NY |

# Cardinals Can't Solve Blackwell
## Reds Win, 3–1; Local High Schools Close

### 1947

*Ewell Blackwell's three-hitter beat St. Louis on Opening Day, 1947.*

Ewell Blackwell, the rangy, side-arming right-hander of the Reds, teased the big Opening Day crowd with visions of a no-hitter through the first five innings before finally surrendering a single in the sixth. That was about all the offense the defending World Champion St. Louis Cardinals could muster, and the Reds kicked off the 1947 campaign with a 3–1 victory.

Blackwell finished with a three-hitter. He lost his shutout in the ninth when the Cardinals scored on two singles and a walk. With the tying run at the plate and one out, "Blackie" coaxed Marty Marion into a double-play grounder to end the game.

The Reds staked Blackie to a two-run lead in the third when rookie Frankie Baumholtz singled in one run. He drew oohs and aahs from the crowd for his inspiring at-bat. After St. Louis starter Howie Pollet sent Baumholtz sprawling in the dirt with a knockdown pitch, he jumped to this feet and promptly lined the next pitch into right field. Bobby Adam's single drove in the second run. Eddie Miller added the final run in the seventh on a home run over the left-field wall.

Although the attendance of 33,383 far exceeded Crosley Field's capacity of 29,000, the club did not seat any of the overflow in temporary outfield seats. However, a few youngsters found their own temporary perch, right on top of the center-field wall. They were run off by the umpires in the fifth inning.

The crowd, which was the biggest since 1942, may have been swelled by more students than ever before. Such was the futility of keeping students focused on schoolwork, the local high schools closed at one o'clock. However, the students had to make up for it the next day. School began an hour early (7:30) and students gave up their lunch hour to make up for the two-hour mini-vacation on Opening Day afternoon.

The papers focused on Blackwell and the crowd: *The giant right-hander, with the windmill windup and blazing fast ball, was never better. He made the Cardinals look like a collection of lettuce and tomato hitters. He had them popping up or beating the ball into the dirt.*

*In the fifth the umpires stopped the game and asked Announcer Al Stephan to chase a couple of dozen boys off the top of the center field wall. The boys were sitting in row like sparrows on a telephone wire.*

*A little later a fight broke out in the right-field bleachers and the park cops had to wade in and stop it.*

*Before the inning ended another bleachers fight broke out and while it was going on a couple of fire engines came tearing down Western Avenue with their sirens screaming. Some excitement! This riotous business must have unnerved right fielder Enos Slaughter for he immediately fell flat on his face in trying to field Baumholtz' fly ball.* [Cincinnati Enquirer and Cincinnati Post]

### April 15, 1947

| ST. LOUIS | AB | R | H | PO | A | E |
|---|---|---|---|---|---|---|
| Schoendienst, 2b | 3 | 0 | 0 | 4 | 1 | 0 |
| Walker, cf | 2 | 0 | 0 | 1 | 0 | 0 |
| Musial, 1b | 4 | 0 | 0 | 3 | 1 | 0 |
| Slaughter, rf | 3 | 0 | 0 | 0 | 0 | 0 |
| Kurowski, 3b | 3 | 0 | 1 | 4 | 2 | 0 |
| a-Cross | 0 | 0 | 0 | 0 | 0 | 0 |
| Sisler, lf | 4 | 0 | 1 | 3 | 0 | 0 |
| Marion, ss | 3 | 0 | 0 | 3 | 3 | 0 |
| Garagiola, c | 3 | 0 | 0 | 5 | 0 | 0 |
| Pollet, p | 2 | 0 | 1 | 1 | 1 | 0 |
| b-Diering | 1 | 0 | 0 | 0 | 0 | 0 |
| Wilks, p | 0 | 0 | 0 | 0 | 1 | 0 |
| Totals | 28 | 1 | 3 | 24 | 9 | 0 |

a-Cross ran for Kurowski in ninth.
b-Diering fanned for Pollet in eighth.

| CINCINNATI | AB | R | H | PO | A | E |
|---|---|---|---|---|---|---|
| Baumholtz, rf | 4 | 0 | 2 | 0 | 0 | 0 |
| Adams, 2b | 4 | 0 | 2 | 3 | 3 | 0 |
| Hatton, 3b | 4 | 0 | 1 | 1 | 1 | 0 |
| Vollmer, cf | 3 | 0 | 0 | 2 | 0 | 0 |
| Galan, lf | 4 | 0 | 0 | 1 | 0 | 0 |
| Lamanno, c | 4 | 0 | 1 | 6 | 2 | 0 |
| Haas, 1b | 2 | 1 | 1 | 11 | 1 | 0 |
| Miller, ss | 2 | 2 | 1 | 3 | 4 | 0 |
| Blackwell, p | 3 | 0 | 1 | 0 | 1 | 0 |
| Totals | 30 | 3 | 9 | 27 | 12 | 0 |

St. Louis     0 0 0  0 0 0  0 0 1—1
Cincinnati    0 0 2  0 0 0  1 0 x—3

*Runs Batted In—By Sisler, Baumholtz, Adams, Miller. Two-Base Hits—Baumholtz, Lamanno. Home Run—Miller. Sacrifice—Vollmer. Double Plays—Pollet, Marion and Musial; Marion and Schoendienst; Haas, Miller and Haas; Hatton, Adams and Haas. Struck Out—By Pollet 4, Blackwell 6. Bases on Balls—By Pollet 2, Blackwell 8. Off Pollet, 3 runs, 8 hits in 7 innings; Wilks, no runs, 1 hit in 1. Losing Pitcher—Pollet. Left on Bases—St. Louis 5, Cincinnati 6. Time—Two hours and 18 minutes. Umpires—Barr, Ballanfant and Boggess. Paid Attendance—33,384.

### Opening Day Trivia

| | |
|---|---|
| Star of the Game | Reds Pitcher Ewell Blackwell |
| Weather | 72°; Sunny |
| Attendance | 33,383 |
| Notable | Local Schools Close at one o'clock |
| Rating | ●●●● |

### 1947 Opening Day Schedule

| April 15 | National League |
|---|---|
| StL vs. Cin | Pitts vs. Chi |
| Bost vs. Brklyn | NY vs. Phil |

# Rhubarb Adds Flavor to Opener
## Reds Win, 4–1, Behind Sauer and Blackwell

**1948**

*Hank Sauer drove in two runs with an eighth-inning homer in the Reds 4–1 win over Pittsburgh.*

### 1948 OPENING DAY SCHEDULE

| April 19 | National League |
|---|---|
| | Pitts vs. Cin |
| **April 20** | **National League** |
| Cin vs. StL | Chi vs. Pitts |
| Brklyn vs. NY | Bost vs. Phil |

### OPENING DAY TRIVIA

| Star of the Game | Reds Left Fielder Hank Sauer |
|---|---|
| Weather | 81°; Sunny |
| Attendance | 32,147 |
| Notable | First Televised Opener |
| Rating | ◍◍◍◍◍ |

Plenty of sunshine, two Reds home runs, a gutty Ewell Blackwell performance and a near-brawl involving fans, players, photographers and umpires gave the 32,147 Opening Day fans plenty to rave about.

The temperature was a sunny 81 degrees, Bobby Adams and Hank Sauer hit home runs, "Blackie" kept pitching in and out of jams, and a photographer and a fan were kicked out of the ballpark after an eighth-inning ruckus.

And, oh yes. The Reds won, 4–1, over the Pirates for their fourth straight Opening Day victory.

No doubt most fans were talking about the episode in the eighth, a rhubarb that began after Sauer had unloaded his two-run blast to give the Reds a 4–1 lead. Babe Young followed with a double, but apparently was not greeted cordially at second base by Pirate shortstop Stan Rojek. Young stepped off the base to confront Rojek, but failed to call time out. Pitcher Vic Lombardi ran over and tagged Young. Umpire Jocko Conlan called Young out and the ruckus was underway. Young went after Conlan and Rojek, Reds manager Johnny Neun went to rescue the angry Young, and the Pirates and Reds started jawing at one another.

Four photographers, stationed behind third base, moved out to take photos. Conlan felt their presence wasn't necessary and he shoved *Cincinnati Enquirer* shutterbug Herbert Heise off the field. A fan, apparently a friend of Heise's, jumped over the railing and headed for Conlon. A police officer wrestled the would-be rescuer to the ground, and order was soon restored.

Fortunately, the delay did not affect Blackwell, who needed to stay on task in the ninth. After a lead-off double and an error by Grady Hatton, Rojek came to the plate as the tying run, but Blackie retired him on a grounder back to the mound. It was Blackie's 128th pitch of the day, just enough for the complete-game victory.

Reporters, who made an annual ritual of interviewing the first fans in line for bleacher tickets, featured two Kentucky high school students who arrived at the ballpark at 7 o'clock the night before the game—just hours after they had retired from sandbag duty along the Newport levee: *Jerry Ready and Roger Cook, students at Newport High School, were the first to camp outside the bleachers last night. With blankets, a few breakfast rolls, fruit juices and time, they took their places at 7 p.m.*

Ready and Cook, 15, were among the thousands in Newport who carried sand bags to fortify the floodwall. However, after the river crested, and their homes no longer were endangered, they headed for the ball park.

Truants? Not Ready and Cook, who said the teacher just requested a peek at their ticket stubs. [**Cincinnati Enquirer** and **Cincinnati Post**]

# 1949 Raffensberger Downs Cards
## Stallcup Injury Results in Two Redleg Runs

Ken Raffensberger earned the MVP honors for the 1949 opener with a brilliant five-hitter against St. Louis.

| 1949 OPENING DAY SCHEDULE | |
|---|---|
| APRIL 18 NATIONAL LEAGUE | |
| PHI VS. BOST | |
| APRIL 19 NATIONAL LEAGUE | |
| STL VS. CIN | PITTS VS. CHI |
| NY VS. BRKLYN | |

Virgil "Red" Stallcup took one on the chin for the Reds on Opening Day, and it turned into a two-run rally that won the game from St. Louis, 3–1.

With the Reds clinging to a 1–0 lead in the sixth inning, Stallcup came to bat with one out and runners on second and third. Stallcup took a weak swing at the offering of Cardinal starter Harry Breechen and tapped a slow roller toward shortstop. Third baseman Tommy Glaviano raced in, scooped up the ball and flung it wildly toward first. The ball struck Stallcup on the side of the face as he was nearing the bag.

Stallcup fell in a heap as the ball bounded away from first baseman Stan Musial. Both base runners scored as Stallcup lay motionless at first base. He was finally able to walk off the field, and was taken to Christ Hospital. Although X-Rays proved negative, Stallcup remained overnight at the hospital, with a large bruise and a black eye.

The play resulted in two runs, and the Reds needed them both after Enos Slaughter homered in the seventh. That was all Reds starter Ken Raffensberger permitted the Cardinals. He gave up only three hits, with Slaughter the only Cardinal to make it past second base. Raffensberger had to be sharp; Breechen surrendered only eight hits, and no earned runs.

Despite the cool weather, Crosley Field was again sold out: 32,188. The papers commented on the festivities and the latest fad which: It seemed like most everybody in Cincinnati was on hand and those who did not go to the park were elbowing their way to choice tavern seats or viewing their television sets in crowded living rooms throughout a radius of more than 100 miles. It is safe to assume that more people listened to and saw yesterday's contest than ever in the history of Redleg games.

Smitty's Band was on hand two hours before the game, and right there with the musicians was Harry Thobe, the Oxford, Ohio bricklayer. Thobe, as always, was rigged out in the white Palm Beach suit with the red umbrella.

Crosley Field, as usual, was in perfect shape. It was cleared of both teams almost a half hour before starting time for the traditional Findlay Market parade, flag-raising and such.

It was plenty chilly yesterday, especially in the late innings, and topcoats and furs were in order. *[Cincinnati Enquirer and Cincinnati Post]*

| OPENING DAY TRIVIA | |
|---|---|
| STAR OF THE GAME | REDS PITCHER KEN RAFFENSBERGER |
| WEATHER | 57° |
| ATTENDANCE | 32,118 |
| NOTABLE | THREE OPENING DAY WINS IN A ROW |
| RATING | ●●● |

# 1950 Reds Lose Slugfest to Cubs
## Teams Combine for 27 Hits

*Outfielder Johnny Wyrostek led the Reds 14-hit attack in the 1950 opener with three hits.*

| OPENING DAY TRIVIA | |
|---|---|
| STAR OF THE GAME | CHICAGO CENTER FIELDER ANDY PAFKO |
| WEATHER | 72°; SUNNY |
| ATTENDANCE | 31,213 |
| NOTABLE | ORGAN MUSIC DEBUTS AT CROSLEY FIELD |
| RATING | ◉◉◉ |

Gorgeous sunshine and live organ music greeted the 31,213 fans as they filed into Crosley Field, but there were 1,500 empty seats in the Sun Deck, a rarity on Opening Day. One too many a second-division finish had apparently taken its toll on diehard Cincinnati fans.

The Reds looked like an improved team in the inaugural, collecting 14 hits and gamely battling down to the final inning. But the Redlegs still lost to Chicago, 9–6.

Starter Ken Raffensberger, the winning pitcher in the 1949 opener, failed to last the third inning. He gave up a solo home run to Andy Pafko in the second, and a three-run blast to rookie Preston Ward in the third. The Reds trailed, 5–0, before they finally broke through against Cub starter Johnnie Schmitz. in the sixth. The Reds scored three runs on five hits including a double by Johnny Wyrostek, who led the Reds attack with three hits.

After the Cubs stretched the lead to 6–3 in the seventh, the Reds Johnny Usher hit a two-run homer in the eighth to again bring the Reds within one run.

But Pafko put an end to Reds hopes with a mammoth three-run homer in the ninth. Pafko had three hits on the day, including two home runs and a double, and four RBIs.

The clubs banged out 27 hits, including 11 doubles. Nine were into the temporary seats that stretched from left field to center field, for ground-rule doubles.

Opening Day fans were treated to the usual pre-game ceremonies—featuring the Findlay Market rooters—and enjoyed a new "player" in the lineup. The Reds debuted live organ music before and during the game. The only other NL park to feature an organ was Ebbetts Field, home of the Dodgers.

The papers reported on everything from concessions to home runs: *Ushers and vendors who have been working the opening game for years called it a "typical" crowd. They downed a little more beer and soft drinks than usual but didn't consume as many hot dogs.*

*The bleacher crowd appeared more colorful, perhaps because many sat shirt-sleeved and the white was reflected in the sun. In the grandstand green appeared the dominating color among the women as many wore suits or spring coats of that hue.*

*Pafko's smash [in the second inning] went over the "L" section in the temporary seats, which is one way of demonstrating how to knock the "L" out of the ball.*

[*Cincinnati Enquirer and Cincinnati Post*]

| 1950 OPENING DAY SCHEDULE | |
|---|---|
| APRIL 18 | NATIONAL LEAGUE |
| CHI VS. CIN | PITTS VS. STL |
| BRKLYN VS. PHIL | BOST VS. NY |

### APRIL 18, 1950

| CHICAGO | AB | R | H | PO | A | E |
|---|---|---|---|---|---|---|
| Terwilliger, 2b | 5 | 1 | 2 | 1 | 4 | 0 |
| Jeffcoat, rf-lf | 5 | 2 | 2 | 2 | 0 | 0 |
| Ward, 1b | 4 | 2 | 2 | 14 | 0 | 0 |
| Sauer, lf | 4 | 0 | 2 | 2 | 0 | 0 |
| a-Ramazzotti | 0 | 1 | 0 | 0 | 0 | 0 |
| Mauro, rf | 0 | 0 | 0 | 0 | 0 | 0 |
| Pafko, cf | 4 | 2 | 3 | 1 | 0 | 0 |
| Serena, 3b | 5 | 0 | 0 | 0 | 1 | 1 |
| Smalley, ss | 5 | 0 | 1 | 5 | 1 | 1 |
| Owen, c | 4 | 0 | 0 | 1 | 0 | 0 |
| Schmitz, p | 4 | 1 | 1 | 0 | 0 | 0 |
| Leonard, p | 0 | 0 | 0 | 1 | 0 | 0 |
| **Totals** | **40** | **9** | **13** | **27** | **16** | **2** |

a—Ran for Sauer in ninth.

| CINCINNATI | AB | R | H | PO | A | E |
|---|---|---|---|---|---|---|
| Hatton, 3b | 5 | 0 | 1 | 1 | 4 | 0 |
| Lowrey, lf | 5 | 0 | 1 | 1 | 0 | 0 |
| Wyrostek, cf | 5 | 2 | 3 | 1 | 0 | 0 |
| Cooper, c | 5 | 1 | 1 | 11 | 0 | 0 |
| Litwhiler, rf | 4 | 0 | 1 | 1 | 0 | 0 |
| b-Rackley | 1 | 0 | 1 | 0 | 0 | 0 |
| Klusewski, 1b | 5 | 0 | 2 | 8 | 0 | 0 |
| Bloodworth, 2b | 3 | 1 | 1 | 2 | 1 | 0 |
| Stallcup, ss | 3 | 1 | 2 | 1 | 3 | 0 |
| Raffensberger, p | 1 | 0 | 0 | 1 | 0 | 0 |
| Hetki, p | 2 | 0 | 0 | 0 | 1 | 0 |
| Smith, p | 0 | 0 | 0 | 0 | 0 | 0 |
| c-Usher | 1 | 1 | 1 | 0 | 0 | 0 |
| Erautt, p | 0 | 0 | 0 | 0 | 0 | 0 |
| **Totals** | **40** | **6** | **14** | **27** | **9** | **0** |

b—Singled for Litwhiler in ninth.
c—Homered for Smith in eighth.

Chicago       0 1 3   0 1 0   1 0 3—9
Cincinnati    0 0 0   0 0 3   0 2 1—6

Runs Batted In—By Ward 3, Sauer 2, Pafko 4, Cooper, Rackley, Bloodworth, Stallcup, Usher 2. Two-Base Hits—Terwilliger, Jeffcoat 2, Ward, Sauer, Pafko, Smalley, Wyrostek 2, Bloodworth, Stallcup. Home Runs—Ward, Pafko 2, Usher. Double Plays—Schmitz, Owen and Ward; Schmitz, Smalley and Ward. Struck Out—By Schmitz 1, Raffensberger 4, Hetki 1, Smith 2, Erautt 2. Bases on Balls—By Schmitz 2, Hetki 2, Erautt 1. Balks—Schmitz, Leonard. Off Schmitz, 5 runs, 12 hits in 8 innings; Leonard, 1 run, 2 hits in 1; Raffensberger, 4 runs, 6 hits in 2 2-3; Hetki 2 runs, 5 hits in 4 1-3 (none out in eighth); Smith no runs, no hits in 1; Erautt, 3 runs, 2 hits in 1. Winning Pitcher—Schmitz. Losing Pitcher—Raffensberger. Left On Bases—Chicago 7, Cincinnati 9. Time—Two hours and 26 minutes. Umpires—Stewart, Conlan and Gore. Paid Attendance—31,213.

# 1951
# Snowflakes!
## Pirates Down Reds Before 30,000 Frozen Fans

*Frank Smith pitched two scoreless innings in the 1951 opener. He appeared in relief in four openers with one save.*

White flakes fluttered in the first, and the Reds fell in the ninth, losing the Opening Day battle to Pittsburgh, 4–3.

Despite the coldest conditions in years, the opener featured a full house of loyal and shivering fans. Over 30,000 filled Crosley Field. They downed some 15,000 cups of coffee and hot chocolate, according to the manager of Sports Service, the Crosley concessionaire.

Frost froze out the annual all-night vigil outside the Reds ticket office on the eve of the opener. The first frigid fans didn't arrive until 8:40 a.m.

The unlikely hero of the opener was 30-year-old George Metkovich, a five-year veteran of the American League who spent the 1950 season in the minors. He had three hits, and made two outstanding defensive plays that shut down Reds rallies.

The Pirates "ushered" out starter Ewell Blackwell in the third inning (four runs, seven hits). Two of the runs scored on two errors by Reds center fielder Bob Usher on one play in the third inning. With runners on first and second, Usher charged a line-drive single, failed to pick the ball up cleanly and fired wildly to second base, allowing both runners to score.

Three Reds relievers—Harry Perkowski, Howard Fox and Frank Smith—blanked the Pirates the rest of the way.

The Reds began chipping away at Pittsburgh starter Cliff Chambers, and drew within one on Usher's two-run homer in the seventh.

Metkovich's mitt kept the Reds in check. With two out and Ted Kluszewski on first in the fourth, Metkovich made a leaping catch of Joe Adcock's long drive to rob him of a double. In the fifth, Metkovich's perfect throw nailed Grady Hatton at the plate.

The papers admired the fortitude of the fans: *The temperature was 44 at the start of the game and dropped to 41 at the conclusion of hostilities. A light snow swept over the field with the Pirates at bat in the opening round.*

*The temperature didn't keep the early spectators away. They appeared in the right-field bleachers four hours before game time. Most of them were school kids playing hooky. Few had overcoats, but a couple of bobby-soxers brought blankets.*

"Listen to 'em," moaned Bob (Red) Sobol, Cincinnati Manager of Sports Service, Inc. *Usually I hear 'em yelling, 'We want a hit,' but today all I get is, 'We want coffee.' I swear I think they're more interested in keeping warm than in who wins the game."*

[Former Red] William "Dummy" Hoy, at 89 threw out the first pitch (underhand, with an encore).

The Pirates got $7,001.43 as their cut of the gate. Visiting teams in the National League get 23 cents a head for each paid admission. [*Cincinnati Enquirer and Cincinnati Post*]

### 1951 OPENING DAY SCHEDULE

| APRIL 16 | NATIONAL LEAGUE | |
|---|---|---|
| | PITTS VS. CIN | |
| APRIL 17 | NATIONAL LEAGUE | |
| CIN VS. CHI | | STL VS. PITTS |
| PHIL VS. BRKLYN | | NY VS. BOST |

### OPENING DAY TRIVIA

| STAR OF THE GAME | PIRATE CENTER FIELDER GEORGE METKOVICH |
|---|---|
| WEATHER | 44°; CLOUDY |
| ATTENDANCE | 30,441 |
| NOTABLE | "DUMMY" HOY THROWS OUT 1ST PITCH |
| RATING | ⚾ |

# Another Frigid Opener
## 1952
### Below Capacity Crowd Bemoans Redleg Defeat in 10 Innings

*Cincinnati native Herm Wehmeier started the 1952 opener, but was sent to an early shower.*

| 1952 OPENING DAY SCHEDULE ||
|---|---|
| APRIL 15 | NATIONAL LEAGUE |
| CHI VS. CIN | STL. VS. PITTS |
| BRKLYN VS. BOST | PHIL VS. NY |

The band played "Jingle Bells" when the Findlay Market paraders marched up to home plate for the pre-game ceremonies.

A press box denizen suggested the Cubs trade center fielder Hal Jeffcoat for an overcoat. By game's end there were a dozen small bonfires burning in the grandstand aisles and in the temporary seat areas in center and left field.

Yep, you guessed it: For the second year straight, frigid temperatures invaded Crosley Field on Opening Day. The thermometer read 40 degrees at game time.

Too bad the weather was so miserable, because the Reds and Cubs staged quite a battle, with the Cubs finally prevailing in the 10th inning, 6–5.

The crowd was lively enough to agonize over the Reds failure to win the game in the bottom of the ninth. With the scored tied, Cincinnati loaded the bases on two singles and an intentional walk to Ted Kluszewski. Wally Post pinch-hit and ran the count to 3-0 off reliever Joe Hatten. The Reds were just one pitch from victory, but Hatten rallied, striking out Post and then retiring Andy Seminick on a fly to center.

| OPENING DAY TRIVIA ||
|---|---|
| STAR OF THE GAME | CHICAGO LEFT FIELDER HANK SAUER |
| WEATHER | 40°; CLOUDY |
| ATTENDANCE | 28,517 |
| NOTABLE | FROZEN FANS LIGHT BONFIRES IN STANDS |
| RATING | ◐◐ |

The Cubs then picked up the winning run in the top of the 10th off Frank Hiller. Hiller balked the eventual winning run to second base, and then gave up an RBI-single to Gene Hermanski.

The Cubs jumped out to a 5–0 lead off starter Herm Wehmeier. a native of Price Hill. The big blow was a grand slam home run by Hank Sauer in the third. The former Red would go on to win the MVP that season. Reliever Harry Perkowski then held the Cubs scoreless while the Reds mounted a comeback, finally tying the score at 5–5 on a Seminick home run in the eighth.

The reporters devoted considerable ink to the crowd on this cold day: *At 1:45 p.m. the Findlay Market band and all its angels marched in. They looked very cold. It was gray and cloudy. The band played, "Wait Till the Sun Shines, Nellie."*

*There was one bonfire, then six, then 12. A peanut vendor leaned against the fire to warm his backside. It was so cold the Cubs danced up and down in their dugout.*

But the best story of the '52 opener belonged to fan James McElhaney, 30. McElhaney spent much of the night locked in Crosley Field after he fell asleep in a bathroom.

"When Post struck out [in the ninth], that was enough for me. The washroom was the only place to get warm," explained McElhaney.

He called friends from a pay phone, but they didn't believe his plight. He finally called the police, who threw a ladder over the left-field wall, and McElhaney escaped the friendly confines. *[Cincinnati Enquirer and Cincinnati Post]*

### APRIL 15, 1952

| CHICAGO | AB | R | H | PO | A | E |
|---|---|---|---|---|---|---|
| Miksis, 2b | 2 | 0 | 0 | 2 | 1 | 0 |
| a-Ramazzotti, 2b | 0 | 1 | 0 | 2 | 0 | 1 |
| b-Hardin, 2b | 0 | 0 | 0 | 0 | 0 | 0 |
| Fondy, 1b | 4 | 1 | 2 | 12 | 0 | 0 |
| Baumholtz, rf | 4 | 1 | 1 | 0 | 0 | 0 |
| Sauer, lf | 5 | 1 | 2 | 1 | 0 | 0 |
| Jackson, 3b | 4 | 1 | 2 | 1 | 5 | 0 |
| Atwell, c | 3 | 0 | 1 | 5 | 0 | 0 |
| Jeffcoat, cf | 3 | 0 | 0 | 1 | 0 | 0 |
| Smalley, ss | 4 | 0 | 1 | 1 | 6 | 0 |
| Minner, p | 2 | 0 | 0 | 0 | 0 | 0 |
| Klippstein, p | 2 | 0 | 0 | 1 | 1 | 0 |
| Hatten, p | 0 | 0 | 0 | 0 | 0 | 0 |
| c-Hermanski | 1 | 0 | 1 | 0 | 0 | 0 |
| Leonard, p | 0 | 0 | 0 | 0 | 0 | 0 |
| Totals | 41 | 6 | 12 | 30 | 13 | 1 |

a-Ran for Miksis in third.
b-Grounded to Hatton for Ramazzotti in fourth.
c-Singled for Hatten in tenth.

| CINCINNATI | AB | R | H | PO | A | E |
|---|---|---|---|---|---|---|
| Hatton, 2b | 4 | 2 | 2 | 3 | 2 | 0 |
| Adams, 3b | 4 | 1 | 2 | 3 | 1 | 0 |
| Wyrostek, rf | 2 | 0 | 1 | 5 | 0 | 0 |
| Adcock, lf | 5 | 0 | 2 | 1 | 0 | 0 |
| Kluszewski, 1b | 4 | 0 | 0 | 10 | 0 | 1 |
| Borkowski, cf | 2 | 0 | 0 | 0 | 0 | 0 |
| d-Edwards | 1 | 0 | 0 | 0 | 0 | 0 |
| e-Post, cf | 1 | 0 | 0 | 0 | 0 | 0 |
| Seminick, c | 5 | 1 | 1 | 3 | 1 | 0 |
| McMillan, ss | 3 | 0 | 0 | 2 | 5 | 0 |
| Wehmeier, p | 2 | 0 | 0 | 0 | 0 | 0 |
| f-Temple | 1 | 0 | 0 | 0 | 0 | 0 |
| Perkowski, p | 1 | 0 | 0 | 0 | 3 | 0 |
| g-Maier | 1 | 0 | 0 | 0 | 0 | 0 |
| Hiller, p | 1 | 0 | 0 | 1 | 0 | 0 |
| h-Pellagrini | 1 | 0 | 0 | 0 | 0 | 0 |
| Totals | 40 | 5 | 12 | 30 | 10 | 1 |

d-Went to bat for Borkowski in ninth.
e-Fanned for Edwards in ninth.
f-Filed to Jeffcoat for Wehmeier in third.
g-Walked for Perkowski in sixth.
h-Filed to Sauer for Hiller in tenth.

```
Chicago     0 1 4 0 0 0 0 0 0 1—6
Cincinnati  0 0 2 0 1 0 1 1 0 0—5
```

Runs batted in—By Sauer 4, Jackson, Hermanski, Wyrostek, Adcock, Kluszewski, Seminick. Adams scored on wild throw by Ramazzotti in third. Two-base hits—Miksis, Baumholtz, Smalley, Hatton, Adams, Adcock. Home runs—Sauer, Jackson, Seminick. Sacrifice—Wyrostek. Double play—Fondy, unassisted. Struck out—By Minner 1, Klippstein 3, Hatten 1, Wehmeier 2, Perkowski 1, Hiller 1. Bases on balls—By Minner 2, Klippstein 4, Leonard 2, Wehmeier 1, Perkowski 1, Hiller 3. Balk—Hiller. Passed ball—Atwell. Off Minner, 3 runs, 7 hits in 4 2/3 innings; Klippstein, 2 runs, 4 hits in 4; Hatten, no runs, no hits in 2 1/3; Leonard, no runs, 1 hit in 1; Wehmeier, 5 runs, 8 hits in 3; Perkowski, no runs, 1 hit in 3; Hiller, 1 run, 3 hits in 4. Winning pitcher — Hatten. Losing pitcher—Hiller. Left on bases—Chicago 10, Cincinnati 14. Time—3:07. Umpires—Pinelli, Boggess, Robb and Warneke. Paid attendance—28,517.

# Milwaukee Opens With Win
## New Milwaukee Braves Win First Game Behind Surkont, 2–0

### 1953

Bud Podbleian was the hard-luck loser in the 1953 opener, losing a 2–0 duel to Milwaukee's Max Surkont.

| 1953 OPENING DAY SCHEDULE ||
|---|---|
| APRIL 13 | NATIONAL LEAGUE |
| MILW vs. CIN ||
| APRIL 14 | NATIONAL LEAGUE |
| CIN vs. CHI | STL vs. MILW |
| PITTS vs. BRKLYN | NY vs. PHIL |

The Braves, formerly of Boston, played their first game representing Milwaukee in Cincinnati on Opening Day, 1953. The Wisconsin lads curdled the Reds, 2–0.

It was the first time since 1898 the Reds did not play one of their traditional Opening Day opponents: Chicago, St. Louis or Pittsburgh.

The mound match-up generated a cacophony of consonants between Milwaukee's Max Surkont and the Reds Bud Podbleian. Podbleian allowed only eight hits in his eight innings. Surkont was even better—three hits in nine innings, with six of those nine going 1-2-3. He walked none and threw only 98 pitches.

Braves center fielder Bill Bruton provided the defense, hard by the temporary seats in center field. He robbed Willard Marshall and Bobby Adams of extra-base hits.

Bruton jump-started the Braves in the first with a single and steal of second. He scored the first run on a single by Sid Gordon. The Braves' final run came in the fifth on a double by Del Crandall and a single by Cliff Dittmer.

Also debuting this day was Reds batboy Bernie Stowe, the future clubhouse legend. Stowe, who had been the visiting batboy for three and a half seasons, later became the Reds clubhouse manager.

Cincinnati Mayor Carl Rich and Governor Frank Lausche, who was on hand for his seventh opener, took turns throwing out the ceremonial first pitch. Cold conditions brought out the wool.

Owner Powel Crosley was outfitted in a heavy coat with a fur collar. All he lacked was a blizzard. No snow fell, but the raw wind and gloomy skies made this an uncomfortable afternoon.

Reporters detailed the pre-game ceremonies and the effects of the weather: *The temperature at game time was a coolish 51. A biting wind, however, made it feel at least 10 degrees colder. Midwest Sports Service reported a brisk business in coffee and hot chocolate. Other observers reported that a large number of those on the grounds had taken the necessary anti-freeze precautions by raiding the family cellar before reaching the ball park.*

Ted Kluszewski obligingly supplied early arrivals with a sample of his power. He rammed at least one ball out of the park every time he took his turn in batting practice.

When Paul Summerkamp said on the public address system in the eighth inning, "Now's the time to give your blood to the Red Cross," someone piped up, "The temperature's 50 degrees. And they want blood!"

*[Cincinnati Enquirer, Cincinnati Post and Cincinnati Times-Star]*

| OPENING DAY TRIVIA ||
|---|---|
| STAR OF THE GAME | MILWAUKEE PITCHHER MAX SURKONT |
| WEATHER | 51°; WINDY |
| ATTENDANCE | 30,103 |
| NOTABLE | FIRST GAME EVER FOR MILWAUKEE BRAVES |
| RATING | |

### APRIL 13, 1953

| Milwaukee | AB | R | H | O | A | E |
|---|---|---|---|---|---|---|
| Bruton, cf | 4 | 1 | 2 | 4 | 0 | 0 |
| Logan, ss | 4 | 0 | 0 | 2 | 2 | 0 |
| Mathews, 3b | 2 | 0 | 0 | 2 | 2 | 0 |
| Gordon, lf | 4 | 0 | 2 | 0 | 0 | 0 |
| Pafko, rf | 4 | 0 | 0 | 2 | 0 | 0 |
| Adcock, 1b | 4 | 0 | 1 | 9 | 1 | 0 |
| Crandall, c | 4 | 1 | 1 | 4 | 0 | 0 |
| Dittmer, 2b | 4 | 0 | 1 | 1 | 3 | 0 |
| Surkont, p | 4 | 0 | 1 | 0 | 1 | 1 |
| Totals | 34 | 2 | 8 | 27 | 8 | 1 |

| Cincinnati | AB | R | H | O | A | E |
|---|---|---|---|---|---|---|
| Temple, 2b | 4 | 0 | 0 | 3 | 2 | 0 |
| Adams, 3b | 4 | 0 | 1 | 1 | 4 | 0 |
| Marshall, rf | 4 | 0 | 0 | 1 | 0 | 0 |
| Kluszewski, 1b | 4 | 0 | 2 | 6 | 1 | 0 |
| Greengrass, lf | 3 | 0 | 0 | 2 | 0 | 0 |
| Bell, cf | 3 | 0 | 0 | 1 | 0 | 0 |
| McMillan, ss | 3 | 0 | 0 | 3 | 3 | 0 |
| Landrith, c | 3 | 0 | 0 | 5 | 1 | 0 |
| Podbleian, p | 2 | 0 | 0 | 0 | 1 | 0 |
| *Easton | 1 | 0 | 0 | 0 | 0 | 0 |
| Smith, p | 0 | 0 | 0 | 0 | 0 | 0 |
| Totals | 31 | 0 | 3 | 27 | 12 | 0 |

*Flied out for Podbleian in eighth

| Innings | 1 | 2 | 3 | 4 | 5 | 6 | 7 | 8 | 9 |
|---|---|---|---|---|---|---|---|---|---|
| Milwaukee | 1 | 0 | 0 | 0 | 1 | 0 | 0 | 0 | 0—2 |
| Cincinnati | 0 | 0 | 0 | 0 | 0 | 0 | 0 | 0 | 0—0 |

E—Dittmer, McMillan. RBI—Gordon, Dittmer. 2B—Bruton, Crandall, Bell, Landrith, Surkont, Adcock. 3B—Bruton. DP—Kluszewski and McMillan. Left—Milwaukee 7, Cincinnati 4. BB—Podbleian 1, Surkont 1. SO—Podbleian 2, Surkont 1, Smith 1. HO—Podbleian 8 in 8 innings, Smith 1 in 1. R and ER—Podbleian 2-1, Smith 0-0, Surkont 0-0. HRP—Podbleian (Mathews). Winner—Surkont (1-0). Loser—Podbleian (0-1). U—Ballanfant, Barlick, Gore, Jackowski. T—1:58. A—30,103.

# Reds Win Thrilling Opener, 9–8
## Greengrass Leads Slugfest with Four Doubles

*Jim Greengrass' four doubles on Opening Day tied a major league record. All landed in the temporary outfield seats.*

It took 26 hits, 13 doubles, 17 runs and three hours and four minutes for the Braves and Reds to decide the 1954 opener, a thrilling 9–8 victory for Cincinnati. Perfect weather conditions lured a near-record crowd of over 33,000 to Crosley Field.

The day was a record-setter. The 81-degree temperature made it the second warmest opener in the 20th century. Vice Mayor Dorothy Dolby became the first woman to throw out a ceremonial first pitch at a Cincinnati opener. The game was also the first to be played under the new major league rule which forbid players to leave their gloves on the field between innings.

The game saw two major league records tied, although both were tainted by the short field required by the overflow crowd. The clubs tied the mark for most doubles in one game (13) and Jim Greengrass tied the record for most doubles by an individual hitter in one game (4). All the doubles fell in the temporary outfield seats, and many would have been caught on a normal day.

The game also ended with a record: it was the first nine-inning Cincinnati opener to break the three-hour barrier.

But no one was complaining about the length of this game. The barrage of hits and runs kept the crowd roaring. The clubs scored in seven of the nine innings. Neither starter, Cincinnati's Bud Podbleian nor Milwaukee's Bob Buhl, survived the first few innings of this slugfest. The Braves jumped off to a 5–1 lead after three innings and Podbleian gave way to Joe Nuxhall. In six-plus innings, Nuxhall gave up nine hits and four runs—including two home runs to Eddie Mathews—but picked up the win.

The Reds took the lead in the fourth, the Braves came back to tie it at 6–6 in the top of the sixth, and the Reds then retaliated with a three-spot in the bottom of the sixth. Wally Post drove in what proved to be the winning run with a two-run single.

The game's only disturbing moment came in the eighth when Nuxhall beaned Andy Pafko. Teammates carried Pafko off the field on a stretcher. He was taken to Christ Hospital, where X-rays proved negative. Frank Smith relieved Nuxhall after the beaning and Smith retired the last four Braves, earning him the save.

Future Hall of Famer Hank Aaron made his major league debut in the 1954 opener, starting in right field. Aaron had an inauspicious beginning: He was hitless in five at-bats.

Years later, Greengrass recalled he was not aware that he had set a major league record with his four doubles. But he knew he had had a good day. After the game, Reds general manager Gabe Paul congratulated Greengrass and asked him how he was feeling.

"Ready to negotiate," came the quick reply.

*[Cincinnati Enquirer, Cincinnati Post and Cincinnati Times-Star]*

| OPENING DAY TRIVIA | |
|---|---|
| STAR OF THE GAME | REDS LEFT FIELDER JIM GREENGRASS |
| WEATHER | 81°; SUNNY |
| ATTENDANCE | 33,185 |
| NOTABLE | HANK AARON MAKES MAJOR LEAGUE DEBUT |
| RATING | ◐◐◐◐◐ |

**1954 OPENING DAY SCHEDULE**

| APRIL 13 | NATIONAL LEAGUE |
|---|---|
| MILW VS. CIN | CHI VS. STL |
| PHIL VS. PITTS | BRKLYN VS. NY |

*Ted Kluszewski hit his only Opening Day home run in 1955.*

# Klu's Homer Not Enough
## Redlegs Fall to Chicago, 7–5;

Even the home-run king couldn't save the Reds in the 1955 opener. Ted Kluszewski, who was honored in the pre-game ceremonies as the reigning National League home-run champ, smashed a two-run homer in the third inning, but it wasn't enough to catch Chicago. The Reds lost, 7–5.

The wet weather of the preceding week gave way to sunny skies at game time, but the clubs did not take any fielding or batting practice on the rain-soaked field. Even the Findlay Market parade around the field was canceled.

The big tarpaulin covering the infield was not removed until just moments before the ceremonial first pitch.

Art Fowler started for the Reds and lasted only two innings, giving up three runs. His replacement, Joe Nuxhall, fared no better, also surrendering three runs in his two innings.

However, the Reds were also scoring freely off Chicago starter Bob Rush. Klu's homer in the third was followed by a four-hit outburst in the fourth that scored two more to bring the Reds within two runs, at 6–4.

But the Reds were unable to take the lead. Reliever Sam Jones, who replaced Rush in the fourth, earned the win. He kept the Reds off the scoreboard until the ninth. By that time the Reds trailed by three and their last-inning heroics fell just short. With the bases loaded and two out, Wally Post hit a hard bouncer up the middle. But shortstop Ernie Banks raced behind second, gloved the ball, and flipped to second for the final out.

In the dressing room after the game, Post gave Banks credit. "They played us right. We'd hit the ball hard and there they were, right in front of it."

In the abbreviated pre-game ceremonies, the Findlay Market Association honored Kluszewski, who led the majors in home runs and RBIs in 1954: *He was the "crunch king" of baseball last year and yesterday the citizenry gathered for the coronation. And a regal ceremony it was, too, for Ted Kluszewski, Crosley Field's most popular tenant. There before him were the crown and scepter. Doing the honors were Chester A. Lathrop, who crowned the big fellow "King Klu," and Jean Cohen, who made presentation of a huge bat on which were inscribed Ted's achievements of 1954.*

Mayor Carl W. Rich presented a huge American flag to Powel Crosley, Jr. and declared "we are sure the National League pennant will fly under this flag next October." [*Cincinnati Enquirer, Cincinnati Post and Cincinnati Times-Star*]

### OPENING DAY TRIVIA

| | |
|---|---|
| STAR OF THE GAME | CHICAGO PITCHER SAM JONES |
| WEATHER | 70°; PARTLY CLOUDY |
| ATTENDANCE | 32,195 |
| NOTABLE | KLU HONORED IN PRE-GAME CEREMONY |
| RATING | ☺☺ |

### 1955 OPENING DAY SCHEDULE

| APRIL 11 | NATIONAL LEAGUE | |
|---|---|---|
| | CHI VS. CIN | |
| APRIL 12 | NATIONAL LEAGUE | |
| CIN VS. MILW | PITT VS. BRKLN (PP) | |
| NY VS. PHIL (PP) | STL VS. CHI | |

### APRIL 11, 1955

| CHICAGO | AB | R | H | PO | A | E |
|---|---|---|---|---|---|---|
| Wade, cf | 3 | 0 | 0 | 0 | 0 | 0 |
| Baker, 2b | 4 | 2 | 3 | 3 | 6 | 0 |
| Kaiserholtz, rf | 5 | 0 | 0 | 1 | 0 | 0 |
| Sauer, lf | 4 | 0 | 1 | 3 | 0 | 0 |
| Jackson, 3b | 4 | 1 | 1 | 1 | 0 | 0 |
| Banks, ss | 4 | 1 | 1 | 0 | 3 | 0 |
| Fondy, 1b | 4 | 2 | 3 | 12 | 1 | 0 |
| Chiti, c | 4 | 1 | 2 | 6 | 2 | 0 |
| Rush, p | 2 | 0 | 1 | 1 | 1 | 0 |
| Jones, p | 2 | 0 | 0 | 0 | 0 | 0 |
| Jeffcoat, p | 0 | 0 | 0 | 0 | 0 | 0 |
| Totals | 36 | 7 | 11 | 27 | 13 | 0 |
| CINCINNATI | AB | R | H | PO | A | E |
| Temple, 2b | 5 | 0 | 0 | 3 | 1 | 0 |
| McMillan, ss | 3 | 0 | 2 | 1 | 1 | 0 |
| Bell, cf | 5 | 2 | 3 | 1 | 0 | 0 |
| Klusze'ski, 1b | 5 | 1 | 1 | 9 | 3 | 0 |
| Jablonski, 3b | 5 | 0 | 1 | 2 | 3 | 1 |
| Greengrass, lf | 4 | 0 | 0 | 2 | 0 | 0 |
| a-Harmon | 0 | 0 | 0 | 0 | 0 | 0 |
| Bailey, c | 4 | 0 | 1 | 4 | 2 | 0 |
| Post, rf | 5 | 1 | 2 | 2 | 0 | 0 |
| Fowler, p | 0 | 0 | 0 | 1 | 1 | 0 |
| b-Gorbous | 1 | 0 | 0 | 0 | 0 | 0 |
| Nuxhall, p | 0 | 0 | 0 | 1 | 0 | 0 |
| c-Landrith | 1 | 1 | 1 | 0 | 0 | 0 |
| Minarcin, p | 0 | 0 | 0 | 1 | 3 | 0 |
| d-Adams | 1 | 0 | 0 | 0 | 0 | 0 |
| Collum, p | 0 | 0 | 0 | 0 | 0 | 0 |
| Totals | 39 | 5 | 12 | 27 | 14 | 1 |

a-Ran for Greengrass in ninth.
b-Grounded to Baker for Fowler in second.
c-Doubled for Nuxhall in fourth.
d-Doubled for Minarcin in eighth.

Chicago ____ 031 200 100—7
Cincinnati __ 002 200 001—5

RBI—Baker, Sauer, Fondy 2, Chiti 3, Temple, Bell, Kluszewski, Bailey. 2B—Baker, Sauer, Fondy 2, Chiti, Bell, Post, Landrith, Adams. HR—Baker, Chiti, Kluszewski. CS—Wade, Banks. SH—Wade. SO—By Jones 5, Fowler 1, Nuxhall 1, Minarcin 1. BB—By Jones 4, Fowler 1, Nuxhall 1. HB—Bailey, by Jeffcoat. PB—Bailey. Off Rush, 4 earned runs, 10 hits in 3 2/3 innings; Jones, 1 earned run, 2 hits in 5; Jeffcoat, 0 hits in 1/3; Fowler, 3 earned runs, 4 hits in 2; Nuxhall, 3 earned runs, 4 hits in 2; Minarcin, 1 earned run, 3 hits in 4; Collum, 0 hits in 1. Winner—Jones. Loser—Fowler. LOB—By Chicago 5, Cincinnati 12. T—2:42. U—Goetz, Dascoli, Warneke and Secory. PA—32,195.

# Musial KOs Nuxhall in 9th
## 2-Run Homer Beats Redlegs, 4–2

*Joe Nuxhall took the loss, and took out one water cooler in the dugout after giving up a ninth-inning homer to Stan Musial.*

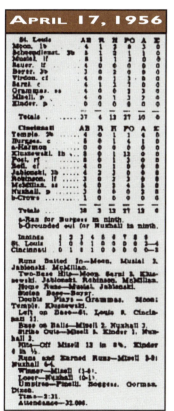

Stan Musial never should have made it to the plate in the ninth inning. But given the opportunity, the St. Louis star belted a Joe Nuxhall slider into the Sun Deck to win the opener for the Cardinals, 4–2.

Nuxhall, bidding for a complete-game victory, retired the first two batters in the ninth, but then bobbled Red Schoendienst's come-back grounder. Schoendienst was awarded a hit, but Nuxhall knew he should have had it.

"I never missed one of those in my life," a disgusted Nuxhall said later. "My little boy could have fielded it."

That brought up Musial who Nuxhall had retired four times, all on sliders. But this time Musial was ready. "If the pitch came inside, I was going for it. The slider broke, but it was inside," explained Musial. It landed in row 14 of the bleachers.

The Reds put the tying runs on base in the bottom of the ninth off a tiring Vinegar Bend Mizell. With two on and two out, Ellis Kinder came on in relief and struck out Wally Post on four pitches.

The cool temperatures did not prevent another Sold-out crowd for the Cincinnati opener. The annual outpouring of civic support for Opening Day had drawn national attention, and NBC-TV sent *The Today Show* to Cincinnati to cover the game. Dave Garroway and his cast arrived on Fountain Square at 4:30 a.m. to prepare for the morning telecast. Local person- alities, including Willie Thall and Mayor Charles Taft, made appearances. Smitty's Band, which later played their usual pre-game concert at Crosley Field, showed up to play "oompah" music. The most popular star on the set was Garroway's mascot, a monkey named Mr. Muggs.

There were a number of highlights for the 1956 opener, including the debut of 20-year-old Frank Robinson, who had two hits: *"Heck,"* confidently smiled Robinson, *"I saw no difference in this big league pitching than in the minors. That Mizell didn't bother me."*

*Robinson won himself a lot of friends during batting practice by bouncing three drives into the temporary seats in left.*

*When the Redlegs took the field at 12:40 for their half-hour of batting practice, there was but a handful of topcoated spectators in the stands and Sun Deck, which was scarcely the place to get a heavy tan in the 50-degree temperature. The first patron through the bleacher gate was Jerry Rohn, 12. He carried a baseball glove and his lunch—three cookies and two sandwiches.*

*Mayor Charles P. Taft and Judge Ralph Kohnen, representing the Findlay Market Association, landed in center field [in a helicopter] 20 minutes before the game started. Mayor Taft made a perfect catch of Governor Frank J. Lausche's toss, but the mayor's pitch to City Manager C.A. Harrell was short and wide of the plate. This was the tenth time [in fact, the ninth time] Lausche had thrown out the first ball as governor.*

### 1956 OPENING DAY SCHEDULE

| APRIL 17 | NATIONAL LEAGUE |
|---|---|
| StL vs. Cin | Chi vs. Milw |
| Phil vs. Brklyn | Pitts vs. NY |

### OPENING DAY TRIVIA

| | |
|---|---|
| STAR OF THE GAME | ST. LOUIS FIRST BASEMAN STAN MUSIAL |
| WEATHER | 48°; CLOUDY |
| ATTENDANCE | 32,095 |
| NOTABLE | FRANK ROBINSON'S MAJOR LEAGUE DEBUT |
| RATING | ●●● |

[Cincinnati Enquirer, Cincinnati Post and Cincinnati Times-Star]

# Wehmeier, Musial Lead Cardinals
## Redlegs Trounced, 13–4

*(From left in Reds jackets) Johnny Temple, Roy McMillan and Frank Robinson are honored in pre-game ceremonies.*

Reds manager Birdie Tebbetts wasted no time summing up the 1957 opener: "We just got the hell kicked out of us."

Tebbetts had it right. St. Louis manhandled his Reds, 13–4, on a day already made gloomy by dark skies and cool temperatures. The 32,554 faithful fans that made the trek to Crosley certainly hoped their Reds would brighten up the day, and for the first five innings, the game was close, the Cardinals holding a 3–2 lead.

But St. Louis broke the game open with five runs in the sixth, and dumped four more on the Reds in the eighth. It was the worst Opening Day loss since the Pirates mauled the Reds, 14–0, in 1911.

Ex-Red and Cincinnati native Herm Wehmeier picked up the complete-game victory. It was a satisfying win for Wehmeier, who was often booed during his eight years with the Reds.

The Cardinals kept the boys busy in the new Crosley Field scoreboard with their offensive show. St. Louis peppered Reds pitching for 17 hits, four by Stan Musial. None of the Cincinnati pitchers were effective. Starter Johnny Klippstein gave up five runs, Art Fowler three, Herschel Freeman four and Don Gross one.

A morning drizzle put a damper on the early arrivals. Smitty's Band, its members clad in overcoats, once again put on a fine pre-game concert. Two governors participated in the Opening Day ceremonies, causing some confusion over who would have the honor of tossing out the first pitch. Kentucky Governor Happy Chandler, baseball's former commissioner, solved the problem by agreeing to serve as "umpire." He donned a chest protector as Ohio Governor William O'Neill threw the first ball out from the stands, and Cincinnati Mayor Charles Taft tossed out one from the mound.

One longtime Opening Day attendee was conspicuously absent. Former Red pitcher Eppa Rixey watched the game from his hospital bed, where he was recovering from a slight stroke. Rixey had played in or attended 46 consecutive opening days.

The weather and the crowd drew the attention of the press: *A light rain fell all morning at Crosley Field. This caused cancellation of batting practice. The infield was a huge tarpaulin pockmarked by pools of water. But one event that went off as scheduled was the parade of the Findlay Market Association. Marian Spelman of WLW-T sang the Star Spangled Banner.*

*Seats had been at a premium for months, which left a lot of people in unlikely places. Shivering high up in the 37th row of the bleachers was the staff of the Cincinnati Art Museum with their boss, Philip R. Adams. "I applied last November," said Adams. "This was all we could get."* [Cincinnati Enquirer, Cincinnati Post and Cincinnati Times-Star]

### 1957 OPENING DAY SCHEDULE

| APRIL 16 | NATIONAL LEAGUE |
|---|---|
| StL vs. Cin | Milw vs. Chi |
| Brklyn vs. Phil | NY vs. Pitts |

### OPENING DAY TRIVIA

| | |
|---|---|
| Star of the Game | St. Louis First Baseman Stan Musial |
| Weather | 52°; Gloomy |
| Attendance | 32,554 |
| Notable | New Scoreboard |
| Rating | |

### APRIL 16, 1957

```
ST. LOUIS              CINCINNATI
         ab.r.h.po.a            ab.r.h.po.a
Blas'game,2b 6 2 2 4   Robinson,lf 3 1 1 4 0
Dark, ss   5 4 3 0 0   Hoak, 3b    3 0 2 1 2
Musial, 1b 4 1 4 12 1  Bell, cf    3 0 0 1 0
Ennis, rf  5 1 2 1 0   Post, rf    4 0 1 4 0
Boyer, 3b  3 0 0 1 2   Temple, 2b  4 2 2 3 2
Moon, lf   5 2 2 2 0   Kluszewski,1b 4 1 1 7 0
H. Smith, c 5 2 2 6 0  Bailey, c   4 0 1 6 1
B. Smith, cf 5 1 2 2 0 McMillan,ss 4 0 0 1 0
Wehmeier,p 4 0 0 1 2   Klippstein,p 2 0 0 0 0
                       Fowler, p   0 0 0 0 0
Total    42 13 17 27 9 Gross, p    0 0 0 0 0
                       aLynch      1 0 0 0 0
                       Freeman, p  0 0 0 0 1
                       bSchult     1 0 0 0 0
                       Total      33 4 8 27 6
```

aGrounded out for Gross in seventh.
bStruck out for Freeman in ninth.

St. Louis ...... 1 0 1 0 1 5 1 4 0—13
Cincinnati ..... 0 0 0 2 0 1 1 0 0— 4

Error—Hoak. Runs batted in—Musial 2, Ennis 3, B. Smith 2, H. Smith, Bailey 3, Wehmeier, Boyer, Bell, Moon 3. Two-base hits—Musial 2, Ennis, Moon, Dark, Hoak 2, Kluszewski, Temple. Home runs—B. Smith, Moon. Stolen base—Blasingame. Sacrifice—Hoak. Sacrifice flies—Wehmeier, Bell, Boyer. Double play—Temple and Kluszewski. Left on bases—St. Louis 7, Cincinnati 6. Bases on balls—Off Klippstein 3, Wehmeier 2. Struck out—By Klippstein 5, Wehmeier 4, Gross 1. Hits—Off Klippstein 8 in 5 innings (faced two batters in sixth), Fowler 3 in 1-3, Gross 2 in 1 2-3, Freeman 4 in 2. Runs and earned runs—Off Klippstein 5 and 5, Fowler 3 and 3, Gross 1 and 0, Wehmeier 4 and 4, Freeman 4 and 4. Wild pitch—Wehmeier. Winning pitcher—Wehmeier (1–0). Losing pitcher—Klippstein (0–1). Umpires—Conlan, Donatelli, Delmore and Smith. Time of game—2:44. Attendance—32,554.

# Tebbetts Protests Phillies Win

## But NL Rules Against Reds; Phillies' 5–4 Win Stands

Reds manager Birdie Tebbetts (1) argues with umpires in the seventh inning. Catcher Ed Bailey (6) and Roy McMillan (11) eavesdrop.

The Reds lost the 1958 opener. Or did they?

No one knew for several days. National League president Warren Giles finally tossed out a protest filed by the Reds, making the 5–4 Phillies win official.

Redleg manager Birdie Tebbetts filed the protest after a seventh-inning rally by the Phillies tied the game, 4–4. The Reds had just put four runs on the big scoreboard to take a 4–3 lead. In the Philadelphia seventh, with Richie Ashburn on first, Granny Hamner shot a bullet down the left-field line where a fan reached out and touched it. Roy McMillan chased the ball down in the bullpen, and held Hamner to a double. But Ashburn scored all the way from first, which brought Tebbetts out of the dugout. He argued that once the fan touched the ball it was a ground-rule double, and Ashburn had to return to third. However, the umpires ruled that while the fan did touch the ball, the fan's action did not benefit Ashburn. In their judgment he would have scored anyway.

Tebbetts and the Reds filed a protest after the game, but after reviewing the play and talking to the umpires, NL president Giles denied it.

The rhubarb and the uncertainty over the official outcome marred what was otherwise a fine game. Brooks Lawrence started for the Reds, but he failed to match the string of zeroes put up by Robin Roberts, who took a 3–0 lead into the sixth. But the Reds exploded for three doubles and two singles to take the lead, 4–3.

Then came the disputed run in the seventh that tied the score. The Phillies took the lead in the eighth on three undisputed singles, the winning run coming on a hit by Ted Kazanski.

Former Reds star Wally Post knocked out two hits. According to reporters, Post was his usual wise-cracking self before the game: *Looking around at the crowd assembling a half-hour before the game, Post commented, "Well, I see ol' Wally still packs them in."*

*The old stadium itself had been spruced up with a paint job. Venerable iron posts now wear stockings of orange-red. The Findlay Market fellows, wearing their traditional cardboard hatbands, came down the third-base line, preceded by a Marine Corps Color Guard.*

*Smitty's Band, in black uniforms and gold braid, set the pace with a spirited march. And in the stands, more than 32,000 Opening Day buffs sat on their raincoats and welcomed the Reds and baseball back to Cincinnati for another season.*

*All over town, the familiar voice of Waite Hoyt could be heard from the cars pausing at stop lights, from stereos, restaurants, shine parlors and barber shops. The weather cooperated beautifully, and so did the people. But, as usual, detectives picked up a handful of ticket scalpers outside the park.* [*Cincinnati Enquirer, Cincinnati Post and Cincinnati Times-Star*]

### OPENING DAY TRIVIA

| | |
|---|---|
| STAR OF THE GAME | PHILLIES SECOND BASEMAN TED KAZANSKI |
| WEATHER | 68°; SUNNY |
| ATTENDANCE | 33,849 |
| NOTABLE | GAME PLAYED UNDER PROTEST |
| RATING | ⚾⚾ |

### 1958 OPENING DAY SCHEDULE

| APRIL 15 | NATIONAL LEAGUE |
|---|---|
| PHIL VS. CIN | CHI VS. STL |
| PITTS VS. MILW | LA VS. SF |

*Frank Robinson had three RBIs to lead the Redlegs in the 1959 opener.*

# 1959 Redlegs Down Pirates, 4–1
## Purkey's Pitching, Robinson's RBIs Delight Opening Day Crowd

| 1959 OPENING DAY SCHEDULE | |
|---|---|
| APRIL 9  NATIONAL LEAGUE | |
| PITTS VS. CIN | |
| APRIL 10  NATIONAL LEAGUE | |
| CIN VS. PHIL | MILW VS. PITTS |
| LA VS. CHI | SF VS. STL |

| OPENING DAY TRIVIA | |
|---|---|
| STAR OF THE GAME | REDS FIRST BASEMAN FRANK ROBINSON |
| WEATHER | 53°; CLOUDY |
| ATTENDANCE | 32,190 |
| NOTABLE | LAST YEAR THAT FANS SIT ON FIELD |
| RATING | ○○○ |

The temperature was cool, but the bat of Frank Robinson sizzled in the 1959 opener. Robinson drove in three runs, two on a fourth-inning home run, to lead the Reds to a 4–1 victory over Pittsburgh.

It was the Reds first Opening Day win in four years. No wonder Ronnie Dale, the Crosley Field organ player, struck up "Happy Days Are Here Again," after the final out.

Bob Purkey also deserved "Star-of-the-Game" honors with his eight-hit, complete-game performance. It took the right-hander only 93 pitches to beat his former teammates.

Purkey gave up just two extra-base hits, and both were ground-rule doubles that landed in the temporary seats. He walked only one.

Robinson's homer in the fourth, a line drive over the left field wall, put the Reds ahead, 2–1. Pirate starter Ron Kline gave up another pair of runs in the fifth. Purkey lifted a fly into the center-field seats for a ground-rule double and scored on a single by Vada Pinson. After an infield out moved Pinson to second, he scored on a Robinson single.

The pre-game activities included all the usual ceremonies and VIPs, except Ohio Governor Michael DiSalle. For the first time in many years, Ohio's heaviest hitter was not present. DiSalle claimed he was too busy. DiSalle failed to make any Cincinnati opener during his four-year term. However, Kentucky's number one fan, Governor Happy Chandler, was on hand.

Pittsburgh coach Jimmy Dykes, a former Reds manager, kept the press entertained with stories before the game: *Dykes, one of baseball's most popular men, says the biggest thrill for him, like most players, comes on opening day. "The opener means that all the hard training is over," Jimmy mused. "And there's always a lot of ceremony, big crowds. It's also a great day for all the players, because, after all, it's the day their salary starts."*

*A chilled but cheering crowd jammed their way into the old ball park yesterday under what looked like an imminent threat of rain or, who knows, snow. The dark sky looked mean. The temperature stayed stubbornly around 50 degrees. A stiff unfriendly breeze swept the upper deck.*

*The colorful pre-game ceremonies got underway at 1:40 p.m. when the Findlay Market group made its appearance. Accompanied by the Color Guard, Smitty's Band, and the Boy Scouts, the Findlay Market members marched around the outfield to the left-field line where they paraded to home plate. The traditional flag-raising ceremony ended with a couple of Knothole League boys who presented Gabe Paul, Reds General Manager, with a good luck message in red carnations.* [*Cincinnati Enquirer and Cincinnati Post and Times-Star*]

### APRIL 9, 1959

```
PITTSBURGH           CINCINNATI
            ab.r.h.rbi              ab.r.h.rbi
Virdon, cf  ..4 0 0 0   Temple, 2b...3 0 0 0
Clemente, rf .4 0 1 1   Pinson, cf...4 2 2 1
Skinner, lf  .4 0 0 0   Bell, rf.....3 0 0 0
Stuart, 1b   .3 0 0 0   Robinson, 1b.4 1 2 3
Hoak, 3b     .4 0 1 0   Thomas, 3b...4 0 1 0
Mazeroski, 2b 3 0 1 0   Lynch, lf....3 0 1 0
Groat, ss    .3 0 1 0   Bailey, c....3 0 1 0
Foiles, c    .3 1 1 0   McMillan, ss.3 0 0 0
Kline, p     .1 0 0 0   Purkey, p....3 1 1 0
Smith, p     .0 0 0 0                ────────
aBurgess     .1 0 1 0   Total ....30 4 8 4
bSchofield   .0 0 0 0
Porterfield, p 0 0 0 0
   ────────
Total ....30 1 6 1
aDoubled for Smith in 8th; bRan for Burgess in 8th.
Pittsburgh  ......0 0 1  0 0 0  0 0 0—1
Cincinnati  ......0 0 0  2 2 0  0 0 x—4
E—None. A—Pittsburgh 11, Cincinnati 12.
DP—Groat, Mazeroski; McMillan, Temple,
Robinson (2). LOB—Pittsburgh 4, Cincinnati 6.
2B Hits—Mazeroski, Burgess, Thomas, Lynch,
Purkey. HR—Robinson. Sacrifice—Kline, Temple.
              IP.  H.  R. ER. BB. SO.
Kline (L, 0–1)... 5   7   4  4   2   2
Smith ...........2   1   0  0   1   0
Porterfield .....1   0   0  0   0   0
Purkey (W, 1–0)..9   6   1  1   1   3
Umpires—Conlan, Donatelli, Burkhart, Venzon. Time—2:05. Attendance—32,190.
```

# 1960 Little Mac Powers Reds
## McMillan Leads Way to 9–4 Win

*Roy McMillan's home run in the opener was one of 10 he hit in 1960.*

Sometimes it's the little guys who supply the power. Roy McMillan, the Reds diminutive shortstop, proved to be the power booster the Reds needed in the 1960 opener.

"Little Mac's" four RBIs led the Redlegs to a 9–4 victory over Robin Roberts and the Philadelphia Phillies.

The game was played on a perfect day—75 degrees under sunny skies.

And the times, they were a-changin'. The Reds abolished the familiar and distinctive overflow seating in the outfield. Why? No restrooms and rowdyism were concerns on the terrace, to say nothing of the epidemic of cheap extra-base hits caused by the truncated field dimensions. Some of the 30,073 fans found standing-room-only spots scattered throughout the rear of the grandstand.

The game started poorly for Reds starter (and Elder High graduate) Jim Brosnan. He spotted the Phillies four runs in the first two innings and gave way to Brooks Lawrence, who finished the second.

The Reds were not awed by Roberts, however. They rallied from a 4–0 deficit in the second inning with five runs, three coming on McMillan's homer. Reds relievers shut down the Phillies (two hits, no runs over the final seven innings) while the offense added four more runs.

Jim O'Toole pitched six scoreless innings and was awarded the victory by official scorer Lou Smith. Months later, however, National League President Warren Giles reversed the decision, awarding the win to Lawrence, because the Reds had taken the lead while he was still the pitcher of record.

For the second straight year, Ohio Governor Mike DiSalle stiffed the Reds as a no-show. However, Kentucky Governor Bert Combs arrived in a last-minute rush. There was no rush at the ticket office: For the first time on Opening Day, all tickets, including bleacher seats, were sold in advance. The only game-day tickets available were SRO.

As usual, the Findlay Market Association paraded over from Findlay Street and marched around the field. In the dugout, Joe Nuxhall provided his own pre-game festivities: *Joe Nuxhall, the Reds veteran left-hander, who has treated the water cooler in the Reds dugout with a celebrated harshness over the last few years, decided to "test kick" the cooler before [the] game. The kick loosened one of the connecting pipes, and water sprayed out over Nuxhall and several of his teammates. And just think: He wasn't even mad.*
[*Cincinnati Enquirer and Cincinnati Post and Times-Star*]

### OPENING DAY TRIVIA

| | |
|---|---|
| STAR OF THE GAME | REDS SHORTSTOP ROY MCMILLAN |
| WEATHER | 75°; SUNNY |
| ATTENDANCE | 30,073 |
| NOTABLE | O'TOOLE'S WIN LATER GIVEN TO LAWRENCE |
| RATING | ●●●● |

### APRIL 12, 1960

| PHILADELPHIA (N.) | ab | r | h | rbi | CINCINNATI (N.) | ab | r | h | rbi |
|---|---|---|---|---|---|---|---|---|---|
| Koppe, ss | 4 | 2 | 2 | 1 | McMillan, ss | 3 | 1 | 1 | 4 |
| Dark, 3b | 2 | 1 | 0 | 0 | Pinson, cf | 4 | 0 | 0 | 0 |
| H. Robinson, p | 0 | 0 | 0 | 0 | Bell, lf | 4 | 1 | 1 | 0 |
| fPost | 1 | 0 | 0 | 0 | F.Robinson, 1b | 4 | 1 | 1 | 0 |
| Curry, rf | 2 | 0 | 1 | 1 | Gonzalez, rf | 4 | 2 | 2 | 2 |
| bWalters, rf | 3 | 0 | 1 | 0 | Bailey, c | 3 | 1 | 0 | 0 |
| Bouchee, 1b | 4 | 0 | 1 | 2 | Martin, 2b | 3 | 1 | 1 | 1 |
| Herrera, 2b | 4 | 0 | 0 | 0 | Kasko, 3b | 4 | 1 | 2 | 0 |
| H.Anderson, lf | 1 | 0 | 0 | 0 | Brosnan, p | 0 | 0 | 0 | 0 |
| Gomez, p | 0 | 0 | 0 | 0 | Lawrence, p | 0 | 0 | 0 | 0 |
| dLepico, 3b | 1 | 0 | 0 | 0 | aLynch | 1 | 1 | 1 | 2 |
| Del Greco, cf | 3 | 0 | 0 | 0 | O'Toole, p | 1 | 0 | 0 | 0 |
| Coker, c | 4 | 1 | 1 | 0 | dNewcombe | 1 | 0 | 0 | 0 |
| Roberts, p | 2 | 0 | 0 | 0 | Henry, p | 0 | 0 | 0 | 0 |
| Short, p | 0 | 0 | 0 | 0 | | | | | |
| cSmith, lf | 2 | 0 | 0 | 0 | Total | 32 | 9 | 9 | 9 |
| Total | 33 | 4 | 6 | 4 | | | | | |

aDoubled for Lawrence in 2d; bSingled for Curry in 4th; cPopped out for Short in 6th; dFouled out for Gomez in 7th; eGrounded out for O'Toole in 8th; fStruck out for H. Robinson in 9th.

Philadelphia ......... 2 2 0  0 0 0  0 0 0 — 4
Cincinnati ........... 0 5 1  0 2 1  0 0 .. — 9

E—Koppe 2, Gomez. A—Philadelphia 10, Cincinnati 5. LOF—Philadelphia 8, Cincinnati 3. 2B Hits—Martin, Lynch. 3B—Coker. HR—McMillan, Gonzalez. SB—Koppe, F. Robinson. Sacrifice—O'Toole. SF—McMillan.

| | IP | H | R | ER | BB | SO |
|---|---|---|---|---|---|---|
| Roberts (L, 0–1) | 1⅓ | 7 | 8 | 8 | 2 | 0 |
| Short | ⅔ | 0 | 0 | 0 | 0 | 0 |
| Gomez | 1 | 1 | 1 | 0 | 0 | 0 |
| H. Robinson | 2 | 1 | 0 | 0 | 0 | 1 |
| Brosnan | 1⅔ | 4 | 4 | 4 | 3 | 1 |
| Lawrence | ⅓ | 0 | 0 | 0 | 0 | 0 |
| O'Toole (W, 1–0) | 6 | 2 | 0 | 0 | 2 | 4 |
| Henry | 1 | 0 | 0 | 0 | 0 | 2 |

HBP—By O'Toole (H. Anderson). Wild pitch—Brosnan. Umpire—Dascoli, Secory, Crawford, Venzon. Time—2:34. Attendance—30,075.

### 1960 OPENING DAY SCHEDULE

| APRIL 12 | NATIONAL LEAGUE | |
|---|---|---|
| PHIL vs. CIN | | PITT vs. MILW |
| STL vs. SF | | CHI vs. LA |

# No Taking This Win From O'Toole

## Post and Robinson Homers Back Up O'Toole's Four-Hitter

*Jim O'Toole (right) and Wally Post celebrated after the 1961 opener. Post homered and O'Toole pitched a complete-game win.*

Jim O'Toole wasn't going to let anyone rob him of this Opening Day victory. After losing his win in the 1960 opener to a ruling by National League President Warren Giles, the young left-hander pitched a complete-game masterpiece to down Chicago, 7–1.

"I'd like to see Giles or anyone else take it away," challenged O'Toole after the game.

This victory was secure. Frank Robinson blasted a first-inning home run and O'Toole needed only 102 pitches to finish off the Cubs. The only run he allowed came on a third-inning home run by Andre Rogers.

That blow tied the score, 1–1, but Wally Post quickly turned the game in the Reds favor. With two on in the bottom of the third, Post smashed a three-run homer off the new screen atop the left-field wall. The Reds bunched three singles, a double and a walk in the fifth for three more runs.

The day belonged to O'Toole. He retired the last 10 batters in a row. He struck out three and walked one. And, he rapped out two singles.

"All he has to do now," said his manager Fred Hutchinson, "is work on his baserunning." O'Toole was out by 20 feet in the third inning trying to move from first to third on a single to center.

Opening Day attendance was under 30,000 for the first time since 1952. All the 30,274 seats had been sold, but the cool temperatures kept many at home. Not among the faint of heart was 98-year-old Dummy Hoy, the former Red and oldest-living ex-major leaguer. Hoy threw out the first pitch from a grandstand box. He also threw out a first pitch six months later, before Game Three of the 1961 World Series in Cincinnati.

Perhaps some fans stayed away fearing significant traffic problems. Construction on I-75 (then called the Millcreek Expressway) had altered traffic patterns around the ballpark. The construction and the addition of several new parking lots resulted in the demolition of several buildings surrounding Crosley Field. The commercial laundry beyond the left-field wall was razed for a parking lot, and a 30-foot-high screen was placed atop the wall to prevent home runs from hitting cars. And that wasn't the only change: *When the fans arrived at Crosley Field they found a new color scheme. The outside wall of the ball park had been turned from the old dark green into white. The white walls stood out brilliantly in the midst of flat parking lots.*

*Pre-game ceremonies began promptly at 2 p.m. Marian Spelman, the golden voice of WLW, sang "The Star Spangled Banner." Then all was quiet as the crowd stood in tribute to the late Powel Crosley. The flag then was lowered to half staff.*

[Cincinnati Enquirer and Cincinnati Post and Times-Star]

### 1961 OPENING DAY SCHEDULE

| APRIL 11 | NATIONAL LEAGUE |
|---|---|
| CHI vs. CIN | StL vs. MILW |
| PITTS vs. SF | PHIL vs. LA |

### OPENING DAY TRIVIA

| | |
|---|---|
| STAR OF THE GAME | REDS PITCHER JIM O'TOOLE |
| WEATHER | 56°; CLOUDY |
| ATTENDANCE | 28,713 |
| NOTABLE | POWEL CROSLEY DIED ON MARCH 28 |
| RATING | ◐◐◐◐ |

### APRIL 11, 1961

| CHICAGO | ab r h rbi | CINCINNATI | ab r h rbi |
|---|---|---|---|
| Ashburn, lf | 4 0 1 0 | Kasko, ss | 4 1 1 0 |
| Zimmer, 2b | 4 0 1 0 | Pinson, cf | 4 2 3 0 |
| Williams, rf | 4 0 0 0 | Robinson, lf | 4 1 1 1 |
| Banks, ss | 2 0 0 0 | Post, rf | 3 2 1 3 |
| Santo, 3b | 3 0 1 0 | Freese, 3b | 4 1 1 1 |
| Heist, cf | 3 0 0 0 | Coleman, 1b | 4 0 2 1 |
| Rodgers, 1b | 3 1 1 1 | Bailey, c | 4 0 3 1 |
| Thacker, c | 2 0 0 0 | Baumer, 2b | 4 0 0 0 |
| Anderson, p | 0 0 0 0 | O'Toole, p | 4 0 2 0 |
| bWill | 1 0 0 0 | | |
| Brewer, p | 0 0 0 0 | Total | 35 7 14 7 |
| Hobbie, p | 1 0 0 0 | | |
| Wright, p | 0 0 0 0 | | |
| aBertell, c | 2 0 0 0 | | |
| Total | 29 1 4 1 | | |

aGrounded out for Wright in 6th; bFlied out for Anderson in 8th.

Chicago .............. 001 000 000—1
Cincinnati ........... 103 030 00x—7

E—None. A—Chicago 10, Cincinnati 7. DP—Santo, Zimmer, Rodgers; Coleman, Kasko; Freese, Baumer, Coleman. LOB—Chicago 2, Cincinnati 5.

2B Hits—Freese. HR—Rodgers, Robinson, Post.

| | IP | H | R | ER | BB | SO |
|---|---|---|---|---|---|---|
| Hobbie (L, 0–1) | 4 1/3 | 11 | 7 | 7 | 1 | 3 |
| Wright | 2/3 | 2 | 0 | 0 | 0 | 0 |
| Anderson | 2 | 1 | 0 | 0 | 0 | 0 |
| Brewer | 1 | 0 | 0 | 0 | 0 | 0 |
| O'Toole (W, 1–0) | 9 | 4 | 1 | 1 | 1 | 3 |

Umpires—Boggess, Gorman, Landes, Smith.
Time—1:56. Attendance—28,713.

# 1962 NL Champs Open With Loss
## Phillies Maul Reds, 12–4; West Hi Grad Mahaffey Gets Win

*Joey Jay, making his only Opening Day start, failed to survive the third inning.*

| OPENING DAY TRIVIA | |
|---|---|
| STAR OF THE GAME | PHILLIES PITCHER ART MAHAFFEY |
| WEATHER | 55°; GUSTY WINDS |
| ATTENDANCE | 28,504 |
| NOTABLE | EARLIEST OPENER TO THIS DATE |
| RATING | ◯ |

On a blustery, cold Opening Day in Cincinnati, the Reds began their defense of the National League pennant with a surprising loss to Philadelphia, 12–4.

Surprising because the defending champs had beaten Philadelphia 19 of 22 times in 1961. On this day, however, the Phillies simply outplayed the Reds. Five Reds pitchers relinquished 15 hits and 10 walks.

Phillies starter Art Mahaffey, a Cincinnati native and graduate of Western Hills High School, pitched a complete-game victory. Mahaffey admitted he didn't have his best stuff, but he didn't need it. By the time the Reds found the scoreboard, they were already down, 7–0.

"We had lousy pitching and lousy hitting," barked Reds manager Fred Hutchinson.

Reds starter Joey Jay began the debacle, giving up five runs and five hits. He was reaching for the Dial soap before the third inning was over. What followed was equally ugly: Bob Miller, Johnny Klippstein and Dave Hillman surrendered seven runs, 10 hits and seven walks.

The stage was set for a glorious opener. For the first time in 21 years, the Reds were the defending National League champions and they had a new owner in Bill DeWitt. But Mother Nature and the Reds pitchers mangled their roles.

| 1962 OPENING DAY SCHEDULE | |
|---|---|
| APRIL 9 | NATIONAL LEAGUE |
| PHIL VS. CIN | |
| APRIL 10 | NATIONAL LEAGUE |
| CIN VS. LA | PITTS VS. PHIL |
| HOUS VS. CHI | SF VS. MILW |
| NY VS. STL | |

The weather hurt attendance: The 28,504 was the lowest Opening Day crowd since 1943. There were 2,500 no-shows. They were the lucky ones. By the seventh inning, a lot of sad shoes were shuffling up Findlay Street on the long trip home.

The only good news? Vada Pinson recovered quickly from his nasty collision with the outfield wall in the seventh inning. He had banged his head hard against the wall robbing Johnny Callison of extra bases. After the game, Pinson showed reporters his cap, smudged with green paint where he had collided with the concrete.

With the Reds hitting all the wrong notes, the reporters turned to the musicians: *When the fans came in they found four six-piece bands, part of Barney Rapp's group, playing at four different spots in front of the box seats. George Smith, whose Smitty's Band had played for 32 consecutive openers, came in with the Findlay Market Parade at 1 p.m. Smitty's Band, 18 pieces, had marched with the Findlay Market Assn. through the streets, since noon. All the bands combined for the playing of the national anthem, and then the four small Rapp groups sprinted into the stands to make music during the game.* [**Cincinnati Enquirer and Cincinnati Post and Times-Star**]

### APRIL 9, 1962

```
PHILADELPHIA          CINCINNATI
         ab.r.h.rbi.           ab.r.h.rbi.
Taylor, 2b.  3 0 0 1   Bl's'g'm, 2b  4 1 1 1
Callison, rf 6 1 2 0   Kasko, ss     5 0 3 1
Gonz'lez, cf 5 3 3 0   Pinson, cf    4 0 1 2
Sievers, 1b  2 0 0 0   Rob's'n, rf   4 0 0 0
cConsolo     0 1 0 0   Lynch, lf     5 0 0 0
Torre, 1b    1 0 0 0   Colem'n, 1b   3 1 3 0
Cov'gton, lf 2 1 1 1   Edwards, c    4 0 0 0
aSavage, lf  3 1 2 2   Harper, 3b    4 1 1 0
Dem't'r, 3b  6 2 2 3   Jay, p        0 0 0 0
D'Ir'mple, c 4 2 2 2   Miller, p     1 0 0 0
Amaro, ss    3 1 2 1   bGaines       0 1 0 0
Mahaffey, p  2 0 1 2   Klipps'n, p   0 0 0 0
                       dKeough       1 0 0 0
 Total      37 12 15 12 Hillman, p   0 0 0 0
                       eCardenas     0 0 0 0
                       Brosnan, p    0 0 0 0
                        Total       35 4 9 4
aHit into force for Covington in 4th;
bWalked for Miller in 4th; cRan for Sievers
in 6th; dGrounded out for Klippstein in
6th; eWalked for Hillman in 8th.
Philadelphia......0 1 6 2 0 1  1 0 1—12
Cincinnati........0 0 1 3 0 0  0 0 0— 4
 E—None. A—Philadelphia 6, Cincinnati 14.
LOB—Philadelphia 12, Cincinnati 10.
 2B Hits—Gonzalez. HR—Demeter, Dal-
rymple. SB—Gonzalez. Sacrifice—Savage,
Mahaffey. SF—Taylor, Pinson.
                IP.  H. R. ER.BB.SO.
Mahaffey (W, 1–0)... 9  9  4  4  4  2
Jay (L, 0–1)....... 2⅓  5  5  5  3  2
Miller............. 1⅔  4  4  4  1  1
Klippstein......... 2   1  1  1  5  0
Hillman............ 2   2  1  1  0  0
Brosnan............ 1   3  1  1  1  1
 HBP—By Mahaffey (Robinson), by Miller
(Gonzalez). Wild Pitch—Klippstein. Um-
pires—Donatelli, Secory, Venzon, Pryor. Time
—3:17. Attendance—28,506.
```

# 1963 O'Toole Mows Down Pirates
## Robby, Cardenas Supply Power

*Gordy Coleman greets Frank Robinson (20) after his first-inning home run put the Reds ahead, 2–0. Robinson holds the major league record with eight Opening Day homers (three came with the Reds).*

New grass, new billboards and a new second baseman were among the highlights of the 1963 Opening Day, made all the more enjoyable by the Reds victory over the Pirates, 5–2.

Jim O'Toole pitched a complete-game, six-hitter for the win. Frank Robinson hit a two-run homer, and Leo Cardenas had a two-run single in the second to give O'Toole a comfortable four-run lead.

The new second baseman, Cincinnati native Pete Rose, failed to collect a hit, but walked and scored the first run of the season on Robinson's homer in the first. "It was like being a bit player in the greatest movie ever made," Rose said.

Rose had one error, but started two double plays. The Reds bailed O'Toole out of trouble in each of the first four innings with twin-killings.

Rose made the leap to the majors from the Class A team in Macon, Georgia. He had a strong spring training. Not until he saw the "14" on the scoreboard before the game, however, did he know he would start.

Threatening skies may have kept some fans away from the park. The attendance (28,896) was just shy of a full house. Rain drops fell until 45 minutes before game time, and the field lights flared on as the game began.

Crosley Field was in tip-top shape for the big day. Groundskeeper Mike Dolan had supervised a complete re-sodding of the field in the off-season. And for the first time since the early 1930s, the club placed advertising signs on the outfield fence. Three new painted billboards stretched across the left-field wall.

Reporters noted the field and the ceremonies: *Crosley Field never looked better. New sod brought from Gate of Heaven Cemetery. There were no bare spots and it all looked like, and felt like, a green carpet, wall to wall.*

*Upstairs, the front of the green deck had been painted a new red and white. There's a wooden fence in left field, made of plywood, in front of the hard rock wall, that lets an outfielder crash and bounce. He won't be knocked out.*

*The pre-game ceremonies had all the hoop-de-la of previous openers, with a shirt-sleeved Governor [James] Rhodes, arms bare, pitching the first ball past Mayor Walton H. Bachrach, which City Manager C. A. Harrell caught; marching by the Findlay Market group; band playing by Smitty's unit and others. and the speechifying.*

*But there were poignant moments, too. They came when Susan Schroeder, the Easter Seals child, stood on her crutches and tossed the first ball to the governor.* **[Cincinnati Enquirer and Cincinnati Post and Times-Star]**

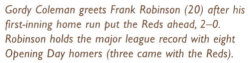

### 1963 Opening Day Schedule

| April 8 | National League | |
|---|---|---|
| | **Pitts vs. Cin** | |
| April 9 | National League | |
| Cin vs. Phil | | Milw vs. Pitts |
| LA vs. Chi | | SF vs. Hous |
| | StL vs. NY | |

### Opening Day Trivia

| | |
|---|---|
| Star of the Game | Reds Pitcher Jim O'Toole |
| Weather | 58°; Heavy Clouds |
| Attendance | 28,896 |
| Notable | Pete Rose Makes Major League Debut |
| Rating | ●●●●● |

# Smallest Crowd Since 1943
## 1964 Houston Wins Opener, 6–3, Behind Johnson and Wynn

*The Reds (foreground) and the Houston Colts line the bases before the start of the 1964 opener.*

Maybe it was a good thing the smallest crowd in 20 years was on hand to watch this opener.

The Reds, despite starting their ace Jim Maloney, were soundly trounced by the Houston Colts. Houston's Ken Johnson, the former Red, held his former team to only two hits in the first eight innings. Relying mainly on his curve and knuckleball, Johnson never faced a serious threat until the last inning.

By then, the Reds trailed by six runs. Maloney gave up three in the fifth and three in the sixth, although only two were earned.

A two-out error by Chico Ruiz led to three unearned runs in the fifth. Two scored on a single by Nellie Fox. Cincinnati native and Taft High School graduate Jim Wynn hit a two-run homer in the sixth off the left-field screen. The "Toy Cannon" also dazzled the home-town crowd with a diving catch in center field that saw him slide 10 feet on the wet turf.

The Reds finally found their offense in the ninth. Until then, they had failed to advance a runner beyond second base. Vada Pinson and Frank Robinson singled. Gordy Coleman forced Robinson, but Pinson scored. Bob Skinner hit a two-run homer, eliciting the first—and last—roar from the crowd. Johnny Edwards bounced out to end it.

Fans noticed two obvious changes at the ballpark, and one not-so-obvious. The club added an extension to the center-field wall to hide the distraction of passing traffic on I-75. And, for the first time, the Reds placed names on the back of the uniforms.

The sharp-eyed fan may have also noticed an absence of cigarette smoke in the dugouts. The National League posted a new rule forbidding players to light up on the bench.

The highly changeable weather may have kept the crowd down to 28,110, the smallest Opening Day crowd since 1943. At one point, it was sunny and raining at the same time. Play was halted briefly in the seventh when the clouds let loose. But the downpour stopped before the players could reach the dugouts, and the game quickly resumed.

Reporters noted the first-day traditions: *The Findlay Street Market Association marched. The mayor threw out the first ball. The first spectator dropped the first foul ball amid the first wave of laughter.*

And the wits trotted out the old joke after the home-town boys lost. "The Reds can't have beer at Crosley Field anymore. Why? They've lost the opener." Haw, Haw.

Governors James Rhodes of Ohio and Edward T. Breathitt of Kentucky, were at the park for the ceremonies. **[Cincinnati Enquirer and Cincinnati Post and Times-Star]**

### OPENING DAY TRIVIA

| | |
|---|---|
| STAR OF THE GAME | HOUSTON PITCHER KEN JOHNSON |
| WEATHER | 66°; RAIN, SUNSHINE AND GUSTY WINDS |
| ATTENDANCE | 28,110 |
| NOTABLE | SMALLEST OPENING DAY CROWD SINCE 1943 |
| RATING | ⚾ |

### 1964 OPENING DAY SCHEDULE

| APRIL 13 | NATIONAL LEAGUE |
|---|---|
| HOUS VS. CIN | |
| APRIL 14 | NATIONAL LEAGUE |
| LA VS. STL | PHIL VS. NY |
| CHI VS. PITTS | SF VS. MILW |

### APRIL 13, 1964

```
HOUSTON          AB  R  H  RBI  E
Kasko, ss         5  0  1   0   1
Fox, 2b           4  0  1   2   0
Runnels, 1b       4  0  1   1   0
Bond, lf          4  0  1   0   0
Stoub, rf         4  1  1   0   0
Wynn, cf          4  1  1   2   0
Aspromonte, 3b    3  1  1   0   0
Bateman, c        3  1  2   0   0
Johnson, p        2  1  2   0   0
Woodeshick, p     0  0  0   0   0
Totals           33  6  7   3   1

CINCINNATI       AB  R  H  RBI  E
Ross, 2b          4  0  1   0   0
Ruiz, 3b          4  0  1   0   1
Pinson, cf        4  1  1   0   0
Robinson, rf      4  0  1   0   0
Coleman, 1b       3  0  0   1   0
Skinner, lf       4  1  1   2   0
Edwards, c        4  0  0   0   0
Cardenas, ss      3  0  0   0   0
Maloney, p        1  0  0   0   0
a-Queen           1  0  0   0   0
Ellis, p          0  0  0   0   0
b-Keough          1  1  1   0   0
Nichols, p        0  0  0   0   0
Totals           33  3  5   3   2

a-Flied out for Maloney in sixth;
b-Reached first on error for Ellis.

HOUSTON      000  033  000 — 6
CINCINNATI   000  000  003 — 3

Putout-Assists—Houston 27-8. Cincinnati
27-11. Double Play — Cardenas to Ross.
Left On Base—Houston 8, Cincinnati 4.
Home Runs—Wynn, Skinner. Stolen Base—
Ruiz. Sacrifice—Johnson 2.

PITCHING SUMMARY
               IP    H  R  ER BB SO
Johnson (W, 1-0) 8⅔  5  3   3  1  3
Woodeshick       ⅓   0  0   0  0  0
Maloney (L, 0-1) 6   7  6   2  3  2
Ellis            2   0  0   0  0  1
Nichols          1   0  0   0  0  0

Wild Pitch—Maloney. Umpires—Jackow-
ski, Crawford, Vargo and Forman. Time—
2:19. Attendance—28,110.
```

# Two Hits All Reds Can Muster

## Cloninger Out-Duels O'Toole and Reds Lose, 4–2

### 1965

*Announcer Waite Hoyt (right) and manager Dick Sisler participate in the pre-game program. At left is a plaque dedicated to the late Reds manager, Fred Hutchinson.*

### 1965 OPENING DAY SCHEDULE

| APRIL 12 | NATIONAL LEAGUE |
|---|---|
| MILW vs. CIN | StL vs. CHI |
| SF vs. PITTS | LA vs. NY |
| PHIL vs. HOUS | |

Jim O'Toole was bruised and battered, and the game had just begun.

The Reds 1965 Opening Day starter took a hard ground ball on the knee off the bat of the first Milwaukee batter, Lee Maye. O'Toole recovered from Maye's hit, but he and his teammates could not overcome the pitching of Tony Cloninger, and the long balls of Joe Torre and Eddie Mathews. Cincinnati lost the opener, 4–2, to the Braves.

On a windy day—"The windiest I can remember ever here," said O'Toole—Cloninger mastered the elements and the Reds, holding Cincinnati to only two hits.

O'Toole pitched nearly as well until the winds and Mathews ganged up on him in the sixth. To that point, O'Toole was nursing a 1–0 lead, courtesy of a Deron Johnson home run in the third. But with one on in the sixth, Mathews jet-streamed a pitch over the left-field wall. Moments later, Joe Torre hit a solo blast for a 3–1 lead.

Mathews wasn't surprised his ball carried so well. "Crosley Field is a home run hitters' park, especially when the wind is blowing out. Balls were flying out during batting practice like aspirin tablets."

The Reds never caught up. They scored once in the sixth to close to 3–2, but Torre added the final run in the eighth on his second homer.

Pete Rose picked up his first hit on opening day, a single in the first inning.

The 1965 opener began with a moment of respect for the Reds late manager Fred Hutchinson.

### OPENING DAY TRIVIA

| | |
|---|---|
| STAR OF THE GAME | MILWAUKEE PITCHER TONY CLONINGER |
| WEATHER | 76°; SUNNY, WINDY |
| ATTENDANCE | 28,467 |
| NOTABLE | PLAQUE HONORING FRED HUTCHINSON |
| RATING | ●●● |

"Hutch" as he was fondly known, died of cancer during the off-season. Reds owner William O. DeWitt accepted a plaque from the Findlay Market Association and the crowd stood in silence before Marian Spelman sang the national anthem.

Cincinnati's opener again drew crowds from near and far: *Opening game and Cincinnati reflect a carnival spirit. And opening game, 1965, was no different. Reds' rooters streamed into Cincinnati from such points as Louisville, Ky.; Huntington, W.Va.; Muncie, Ind., and Portsmouth, Ohio. For Cincinnatians, the sounds of opening day were heard early when the Central Trust chimes played "Take Me Out To The Ball Game," for the fans who were just strolling the streets of [down]town.*

*Out at the ballpark Smitty's Band, an opening day tradition, played "Hello Dolly" and "Happy Days Are Here Again."*

*The Rosie Reds, women's rooting society, presented floral bouquets to the managers. The first ball of the 1965 season was thrown by Mayor Walton Bachrach, who can't pitch, to City Manager William Wichman, who can't catch.*
[*Cincinnati Enquirer* and *Cincinnati Post and Times-Star*]

### APRIL 12, 1965

| CINCINNATI | AB | R | H | RBI | E |
|---|---|---|---|---|---|
| Rose, 2b | | | 1 | 0 | 0 |
| Harper, lf | 4 | 0 | 0 | 0 | 0 |
| Pinson, cf | 3 | 0 | 0 | 0 | 0 |
| Robinson, rf | 3 | 0 | 0 | 1 | 0 |
| Coleman, 1b | 3 | 0 | 0 | 0 | 0 |
| Johnson, 3b | 4 | 1 | 1 | 1 | 0 |
| Edwards, c | 3 | 0 | 0 | 0 | 0 |
| Cardenas, ss | 3 | 0 | 0 | 0 | 1 |
| O'Toole, p | 2 | 0 | 0 | 0 | 0 |
| **Totals** | **28** | **2** | **2** | **2** | **1** |

| MILWAUKEE | AB | R | H | RBI | E |
|---|---|---|---|---|---|
| Maye, cf | 5 | 0 | 1 | 0 | 0 |
| Cline, cf | | | | | |
| Alou, rf | 4 | 0 | 2 | 0 | 1 |
| Mathews, 3b | 4 | 1 | 1 | 2 | 0 |
| Torre, c | 4 | 2 | 2 | 2 | 0 |
| Jones, lf | 3 | 0 | 0 | 0 | 0 |
| T. Aaron, 1b | 4 | 0 | 1 | 0 | 0 |
| Menke, ss | 3 | 0 | 0 | 0 | 0 |
| Alomar, 2b | 3 | 1 | 0 | 0 | 1 |
| Cloninger, p | 3 | 0 | 0 | 0 | 0 |
| **Totals** | **33** | **4** | **7** | **4** | **2** |

```
MILWAUKEE ....... 000  003  010 — 4
CINCINNATI ...... 001  001  000 — 2
```

Double Plays—Cincinnati: Cardenas to Rose to Coleman. Left On Bases—Milwaukee 6, Cincinnati 4. Two Base Hits—Alou. Home Runs—Torre (2), Mathews, Johnson. Sacrifice—Harper. Sacrifice Fly—Robinson.

PITCHING SUMMARY

| | IP | H | R | ER | BB | SO |
|---|---|---|---|---|---|---|
| Cloning. (W, 1-0) | 9 | 2 | 2 | 1 | 5 | 2 |
| O'Toole (L, 0-1) | 9 | 7 | 4 | 4 | 3 | 2 |

WP—O'Toole. Time—2:28. Attendance—28,467.

# Rain Forces Reds to Open on Road
## Home Opener Finally Held 11 Days Later on a Friday Night

*Three days of rain postponed the Reds opener, forcing Cincinnati to open on the road in Philadelphia. It was the first time the Reds had opened on the road since 1888.*

It was almost worth the wait.

The Reds did not play their home opener until Friday evening, April 22, after rain had forced the postponement of Opening Day on April 11.

Three days of rain washed out the entire opening series with the New York Mets, and sent the Reds on the road, where they played their first game against the Phillies on April 15—and lost, 4–3. By the time they returned to Cincinnati for the postponed home opener, the team had lost five games in a row, and stood a disappointing 1-6. The off-season trade of Frank Robinson to Baltimore for Milt Pappas and Jack Baldschun had already begun to unravel, and with the team in ninth place the fans were in not in much of a mood for the opening night festivities. The 10,266 who showed up were full of boos instead of good cheer.

But even the 1–6 start could not deter the Findlay Market Association. The group staged their annual pre-game parade of the field. Ceremonies included the presentation of an American flag and flowers to manager Dick Sisler. The event, which had always taken place during the day, seemed out-of-place under the lights of Crosley Field.

Joe Nuxhall started for the Reds, and took the loss. It was a wild game. The Reds were up, 5–4, after five innings, but the Phillies rallied for five runs in the final three innings to outlast the Reds, 9-7.

The game featured five lead changes, 16 runs and 28 hits.

The Reds took a 3–1 lead in the second on a three-run home run by Johnny Edwards. The Phillies regained the advantage with three in the fourth, an inning that saw Nuxhall give way to Don Nottebart.

The Reds rallied for two in the eighth, and would have scored more but for an outstanding defensive play by first baseman Bill White, who knocked down Edwards' bid for a double down the line.

Edwards wound up the game with four RBIs.

The anticlimactic opener drew little additional coverage from the newspapers. The small crowd and the dismal start to the season dampened whatever enthusiasm the postponed opener might have generated. It was the first time Opening Day had been postponed since 1913. That opener was played two days later in Cincinnati.

The last time the Reds played their first game on the road was 1888. The string of 78 years was remarkable given the uncertain weather conditions in Cincinnati in April. Many of those years passed under the watchful eye of the late owner Powel Crosley, of whom it was said brought "Crosley" luck to the opener. In his 26-year tenure, there were no Opening Day postponements, which prompted one longtime newspaper editor to remark: "If Powel Crosley were alive, it wouldn't have dared rain!" *[Cincinnati Enquirer and Cincinnati Post and Times-Star]*

### OPENING DAY TRIVIA

| | |
|---|---|
| STAR OF THE GAME | REDS CATCHER JOHNNY EDWARDS |
| WEATHER | 70° |
| ATTENDANCE | 10,266 |
| NOTABLE | FIRST POSTPONEMENT SINCE 1913 |
| RATING | ⚾ |

### 1966 OPENING DAY SCHEDULE

| APRIL 11 | NATIONAL LEAGUE |
|---|---|
| NY vs. CIN (PP) | |
| APRIL 12 | NATIONAL LEAGUE |
| HOUS vs. LA | PHIL vs. StL (PP) |
| CHI vs. SF | PITTS vs. ATL |

*Pete Rose greets Vada Pinson after Pinson's home run in the first inning of the 1967 opener.*

# Behind Maloney, Reds Down LA
## New Owners Cheer Victory

The 1967 opener featured new owners, new uniforms, new grass, and a convincing 6–1 win for the Reds over the Los Angeles Dodgers. A near-capacity crowd of 28,422 filled the park on a near-perfect day for baseball. Jim Maloney picked up the win with seven innings of five-hit pitching. Ted Abernathy finished the game with two scoreless innings of relief.

The Reds gave Maloney all the runs he needed in the first on solo home runs by Vada Pinson and Deron Johnson that landed in the Sun Deck in right field. Los Angeles tallied one in the fifth, but the Reds responded with one in the seventh and two in the eighth for the 6–1 margin.

Abernathy gave up one hit in the final two innings, but his catcher, Johnny Edwards, thought the submarining right-hander was nearly untouchable.

"I couldn't hit Abernathy, and I can't catch him," joked Edwards. A third strike from Abernathy got by him for a passed ball.

It was an auspicious beginning for the Reds new owners and the team's new general manager, Bob Howsam. An investment group headed by Frank Dale, publisher of *The Cincinnati Enquirer*, had purchased the Reds in the off-season from Bill DeWitt. The group hired Howsam from St. Louis.

| OPENING DAY TRIVIA | |
|---|---|
| STAR OF THE GAME | REDS PITCHER JIM MALONEY |
| WEATHER | 72°; CLOUDY |
| ATTENDANCE | 28,422 |
| NOTABLE | DEBUT OF BOB HOWSAM AS REDS GM |
| RATING | ●●●● |

Howsam made several changes at Crosley Field. Most noticeable to the fans were the new uniforms. The vest-style jersey was replaced by a shirt with sleeves.

Howsam also made it a little more difficult on the hitters by extending the home run height 10 feet in center field to the very top of the fence. No longer was it merely enough to clear the 10-foot high yellow line in center field atop the old concrete wall to be awarded a home run. Now, hitters would have to clear the wall and the wooden extension above it—an additional nine feet for a home run.

Groundskeeper Mike Dolan was responsible for the other new look at Crosley: *The field for opening day was a bright green. Dolan explained the park has a new grass called Zoysia. It comes from the Orient and is supposed to be especially good in hot weather.*

*It was the 47th annual occasion of the parade of the Findlay Market Association. The parade moved through the gates of Crosley Field at 1:55 p.m. and went right up to home plate. The parade group included a parade marshall, color guards, Smitty's Band, the Linkettes (baton twirlers) and Roger Bacon High School Band and Boy Scouts.*

*Paul Sommerkamp, the field announcer, called the players to the center of the arena, with the Reds along the third-base line. Marian Spelman of WLW-T sang the national anthem, and the game was ready to go.* **[Cincinnati Enquirer and Cincinnati Post and Times-Star]**

| 1967 OPENING DAY SCHEDULE | |
|---|---|
| APRIL 10 | NATIONAL LEAGUE |
| LA VS. CIN | |
| APRIL 11 | NATIONAL LEAGUE |
| ATL VS. HOUS | PHIL VS. CHI |
| SF VS. STL | PITTS VS. NY |

### APRIL 10, 1967

```
LOS ANGELES (N.)      CINCINNATI (N.)
           ab.r.h.bi              ab.r.h.bi
Parker, cf   3 0 0 0   Harper, rf   2 0 0 1
Hunt, 2b     3 0 0 0   Pinson, cf   4 1 1 1
L. Johnson, rf 4 0 1 0 Rose, lf     3 1 1 0
Fairly, 1b   4 0 1 0   D. J'hns'n, 3b 4 2 2 1
Lefebvre, 3b 4 0 0 0   Perez, 1b    3 0 1 1
Roseboro, c  4 1 2 0   Helms, 2b    4 0 0 0
Bailey, lf   4 0 0 0   Cardenas, ss 4 0 2 1
Michael, ss  2 0 2 1   Edwards, c   3 1 1 0
Hickman      1 0 0 0   Maloney, p   2 0 1 0
Schofield, ss 0 0 0 0  Simpson      1 1 1 1
Miller, p    1 0 0 0   Abernathy, p 1 0 0 0
Ferrara      1 0 0 0
Perranoski, p 0 0 0 0   Totals     31 6 10 6
Werhas       1 0 0 0
Regan, p     0 0 0 0
Totals      32 1 6 1

Los Angeles ............ 0 0 0 0 1 0 0 0 0—1
Cincinnati ............. 2 1 0 0 0 0 1 2 x—6
DP—Los Angeles 1, Cincinnati 2. LOB—
Los Angeles 6, Cincinnati 6. 2B—Roseboro,
Cardenas. HR—Pinson (1), D. Johnson (1),
Simpson (1). SB—Harper. SF—Perez.
                IP.  H.  R. ER.BB.SO.
R. Miller (L, 0-1)  4  7  3   3  0  5
Perranoski          3  1  1   1  1  2
Regan               2  2  2   2  2  0
Maloney (W, 1-0)    7  5  1   1  2  1
Abernathy           2  1  0   0  0  4
   PB—Edwards.
   T—2:14. A—28,422.
```

# Openers Delayed for King Tribute
## Reds Drop Cubs, 9–4, After Pause for MLK Funeral

**1968**

*Tony Perez receives congratulations from Lee May and Vada Pinson after his fifth-inning home run.*

### 1968 OPENING DAY SCHEDULE
**(ALL GAMES POSTPONED TO APRIL 10)**

| APRIL 8 | NATIONAL LEAGUE |
|---|---|
| CHI VS. CIN | PITTS VS. HOUS |
| **APRIL 9** | **NATIONAL LEAGUE** |
| PHIL VS. LA | ATL VS. STL |
| NY VS. SF | |

After a postponement of two days to honor the late Dr. Martin Luther King, Major League Baseball opened the 1968 season on Wednesday, April 10. (King had been assassinated in Memphis, Tennessee, on April 4; his funeral was held on April 9, which was designated a national day of mourning by President Lyndon Johnson.)

In Cincinnati, the game was played in the aftermath of urban rioting which struck the city on Monday, April 8. Rioters ravaged the city in response to King's murder.

Despite rumors of trouble at the ballpark, 28,111 attended the opener—nearly a full house. The club announced there would be a ban on liquor, but they lifted this decree on the morning of the game. Other than the dozens of extra police on the scene, the opener went off as usual. There was an interruption in the fourth inning, but not due to anything out of the ordinary—just a rain delay of 43 minutes.

The Reds defeated the Chicago Cubs, 10–4, behind the pitching of Milt Pappas and George Culver, and the power of Tony Perez. Joe Niekro started for the Cubs, but failed to finish the fifth inning, when the Reds broke a 1–1 tie with a five-run rally.

With the bases loaded, Vada Pinson hit a two-run double, and Perez followed with a towering drive high off the left-field screen for a three-run home run. That put the Reds up, 6–1, and seemingly secured the victory. But the Cubs scored three in the sixth and put the tying run at the plate. George Culver relieved Pappas and struck out Dick Nen with the tying runs on base.

The Reds insured the victory with three runs in the eighth, two on a Tommy Helms homer.

The sportswriters covered everything from the weather to the pre-game ceremonies: *The rain, with heavy black clouds, hit in the third inning. When the rain passed, a brilliant sun came back, [but it was] a chilling shower that dropped a balmy 67 degrees to 52.*

Reporters recognized a number of plainclothes officers circulating throughout the stands.

During the pre-game ceremonies, Chester A. Lathrop, president of the Findlay Market Association, crowned the day's queen, Donna Tangeman, introduced the celebrities, predicted a victory for the Reds in the game, and presented Marian Spelman to sing "The Star Spangled Banner."

What's new at the ball park? Ushers dressed in new Palm Beach red jackets. Pennants on the roof that fly the names of National League teams. A beer garden under the stands behind the third-base line.

Making the rounds in the clubhouse [after the game] was general manager Bob Howsam, shaking hands, offering congratulatory remarks, smiling at everyone. It was hard to remember the last time the "big brass" ever did this. [**Cincinnati Enquirer and Cincinnati Post and Times-Star**]

### APRIL 10, 1968

| CHICAGO | AB | R | H | RBI | E |
|---|---|---|---|---|---|
| L. Johnson, rf | 5 | 1 | 1 | 0 | 0 |
| Kessinger, ss | 4 | 1 | 3 | 0 | 1 |
| Williams, lf | 4 | 0 | 1 | 0 | 1 |
| Santo, 3b | 3 | 1 | 1 | 0 | 0 |
| Banks, 1b | 4 | 1 | 1 | 0 | 0 |
| Hundley, c | 4 | 0 | 2 | 3 | 0 |
| Arcia, 2b | 2 | 0 | 0 | 0 | 0 |
| Nen, ph | 1 | 0 | 0 | 0 | 0 |
| Elia, 2b | 0 | 0 | 0 | 0 | 0 |
| Phillips, cf | 4 | 0 | 0 | 0 | 0 |
| Niekro, p | 1 | 0 | 0 | 0 | 0 |
| Mikkelsen, p | 2 | 0 | 0 | 0 | 0 |
| Spangler, ph | 1 | 0 | 0 | 0 | 0 |
| Tiefenauer, p | 0 | 0 | 0 | 0 | 0 |
| Stevenson, ph | 1 | 0 | 0 | 0 | 0 |
| Totals | 36 | 4 | 8 | 4 | 3 |
| **CINCINNATI** | **AB** | **R** | **H** | **RBI** | **E** |
| Rose, rf | 4 | 1 | 1 | 0 | 0 |
| A. Johnson, lf | 5 | 1 | 0 | 0 | 0 |
| Pinson, cf | 4 | 2 | 2 | 2 | 0 |
| Perez, 3b | 4 | 2 | 2 | 3 | 0 |
| May, 1b | 4 | 1 | 1 | 0 | 0 |
| Pavletich, c | 3 | 0 | 2 | 0 | 0 |
| Helms, 2b | 4 | 2 | 2 | 2 | 0 |
| Cardenas, ss | 4 | 1 | 1 | 0 | 0 |
| Pappas, p | 2 | 0 | 0 | 0 | 0 |
| Culver, p | 0 | 0 | 0 | 0 | 0 |
| Totals | 34 | 9 | 11 | 8 | 3 |

```
CHICAGO       000  013  000—4
CINCINNATI    000  150  03x—9
```

Double Play—Cincinnati 2. Left On Base—Chicago, 6, Cincinnati 5. Two-Base Hit—Banks, Pinson, May. Three-Base Hit—Hundley. Home Runs—Perez 1, Helms 1. Sacrifice—Culver. 2. Pavletich. Sacrifice Fly—Rose.

**PITCHING SUMMARY**

| | IP | H | R | ER | BB | SO |
|---|---|---|---|---|---|---|
| Niekro (L,0-1) | 4 1/3 | 6 | 5 | 3 | 2 | 1 |
| Mikkelson | 1 2/3 | 2 | 1 | 0 | 2 | 1 |
| Tiefenauer | 2 | 3 | 3 | 2 | 0 | 2 |
| Pappas (W, 1-0) | 5 1/3 | 4 | 3 | 3 | 0 | 2 |
| Culver | 3 2/3 | 1 | 0 | 0 | 1 | 2 |

Time—2:26. Attendance—28,111.

### OPENING DAY TRIVIA

| STAR OF THE GAME | REDS THIRD BASEMAN, TONY PEREZ |
|---|---|
| WEATHER | 67°; RAIN AND SUNSHINE |
| ATTENDANCE | 28,111 |
| NOTABLE | KING FUNERAL DELAYS OPENER 2 DAYS |
| RATING | ◉◉◉ |

# 1969
# Happy 100th, But Reds Lose
## Rose, Tolan Homer in 1st; Drysdale & Singer Slam Door

*Pete Rose hit Don Drysdale's third pitch of the game for a home run in the first inning of the 1969 opener. Bobby Tolan homered on the very next pitch.*

### 1969 OPENING DAY SCHEDULE

| April 7 | National League | |
|---|---|---|
| LA vs. Cin | | SF vs. Atl |
| **April 8** | **National League** | |
| Hous vs. SD | | Mont vs. NY |
| Phil vs. Chi | | Pitts vs. StL |
| | SF vs. Atl | |

The 1969 season marked the 100th anniversary of the birth of the professional Cincinnati Red Stockings. A standing-room-crowd of 30,111 filled Crosley for the party. They had barely settled into their seats when Pete Rose and newcomer Bobby Tolan had them up and cheering. Rose homered on the third pitch of the game from Los Angeles starter Don Drysdale, and Tolan—in his first at-bat as a Red—homered on the next pitch.

That set the home-town crowd to rocking. But that was the end of the festivities. Drysdale gave up only two more hits, and his offense posted three runs to give the Dodgers a 3–2 victory.

After the game, Al Campanis, the Dodgers vice president, said, "In 30 years of baseball, I've never seen anything like it. The first two batters get home runs, and the team loses, 3–2."

Drysdale pitched six innings for the win, and Bill Singer finished with three perfect innings of relief. Twenty-year-old Gary Nolan started for the Reds and picked up the loss. He struck out 12 in his seven innings of work, but walked four and gave up seven hits. Nolan's 12 strikeouts rank him second in Cincinnati Opening Day history.

The Dodgers scored their first run in the second on a double by Jim Lefebvre. Ron Fairly tripled into the right-field corner to score two runs in the third and give the Dodgers the lead.

### OPENING DAY TRIVIA

| | |
|---|---|
| Star of the Game | Los Angeles Pitcher Don Drysdale |
| Weather | 77°; Sunny |
| Attendance | 30,111 |
| Notable | Tolan Homers on 1st Pitch as Red |
| Rating | ●●● |

There wasn't much to cheer about after that, except for a Pete Rose headfirst slide in the third inning. Rose also drew applause in the sixth when he made an over-the-shoulder catch in front of the center-field wall. Rose started in center, giving him five different starting positions in the seven openers he had played to that time (second, third, and all three outfield positions).

As the game settled into a pitcher's duel, the fans evidently turned their attention to the concession stands. Vendors reported that hot dogs and cold drinks were selling at record levels.

The festive day was duly noted by the reporters and commemorated in pre-game ceremonies: *The Reds celebrated their 100th birthday and 30,000 fans turned kids for a day to celebrate. Gray-flanneled businessmen, playing hooky from the office, stripped to shirt sleeves under 77-degree sunny skies and slurped beer. Hearty matrons came in red knit suits, Easter chapeaux and corsages—and gripped scorecards in their teeth as they applauded Pete Rose. Tow-headed youngsters in T-shirts and baseball caps pounded their mitts.*

*Officials of Findlay Market Assn. led the parade. Representatives of the Knothole Association carried a four-layer cake about five feet tall, commemorating the 100th birthday of the Cincinnati Reds.* **[Cincinnati Enquirer and Cincinnati Post and Times-Star]**

### April 7, 1969

| LOS ANGELES | AB | R | H | RBI | E |
|---|---|---|---|---|---|
| Crawford, cf | 5 | 1 | 1 | 0 | 0 |
| Gabrielson, rf | 4 | 1 | 1 | 0 | 1 |
| Russell, rf | 1 | 0 | 1 | 0 | 0 |
| Sudakis, 3b | 5 | 0 | 0 | 0 | 0 |
| Fairly, 1b | 5 | 0 | 1 | 2 | 0 |
| Kosco, lf | 4 | 0 | 0 | 0 | 0 |
| Parker, cf | 0 | 0 | 0 | 0 | 0 |
| Haller, c | 4 | 0 | 1 | 0 | 0 |
| Lefebvre, 2b | 2 | 1 | 1 | 1 | 0 |
| Sizemore, ss | 2 | 0 | 0 | 0 | 0 |
| Drysdale, p | 3 | 0 | 0 | 0 | 0 |
| Singer, p | 1 | 0 | 0 | 0 | 0 |
| Totals | 36 | 3 | 8 | 3 | 1 |
| **CINCINNATI** | **AB** | **R** | **H** | **RBI** | **E** |
| Rose, cf | 3 | 1 | 2 | 1 | 0 |
| Tolan, rf | 3 | 1 | 1 | 1 | 0 |
| A. Johnson, lf | 4 | 0 | 1 | 0 | 0 |
| Perez, 3b | 3 | 0 | 0 | 0 | 0 |
| L. May, 1b | 4 | 0 | 0 | 0 | 0 |
| Bench, c | 4 | 0 | 0 | 0 | 0 |
| Helms, 2b | 3 | 0 | 0 | 0 | 0 |
| Woodward, ss | 3 | 0 | 0 | 0 | 1 |
| Nolan, p | 2 | 0 | 0 | 0 | 0 |
| Granger, p | 0 | 0 | 0 | 0 | 0 |
| Whitfield, ph | 1 | 0 | 0 | 0 | 0 |
| Merritt, p | 0 | 0 | 0 | 0 | 0 |
| Totals | 30 | 2 | 4 | 2 | 2 |

LOS ANGELES .... 012 000 000—3
CINCINNATI ..... 200 000 000—2

Double Play—Los Angeles 1. Left On Bases—Los Angeles 10, Cincinnati 4. Two-Base Hits—Lefebvre, Russell. Three-Base Hits—Fairly. Home Runs—Rose (1), Tolan (1). Stolen Base—Lefebvre.

**PITCHING SUMMARY**

| | IP | H | R | ER | BB | SO |
|---|---|---|---|---|---|---|
| Drysdale (W., 1-0) | 6 | 4 | 2 | 2 | 2 | 4 |
| Singer | 3 | 0 | 0 | 0 | 1 | 1 |
| Nolan (L., 0-1) | 7 | 7 | 3 | 3 | 4 | 12 |
| Granger | 1 | 0 | 0 | 0 | 0 | 0 |
| Merritt | 1 | 1 | 0 | 0 | 0 | 1 |

Save—Singer. Time—2:29. Attendance—30,111.

# Reds Win Last Crosley Opener

## Merritt Gives Anderson First Win as Manager, 5–1

*Sparky Anderson was victorious in his first game as a major league manager on Opening Day, 1970.*

### 1970 OPENING DAY SCHEDULE

| APRIL 6 | NATIONAL LEAGUE | |
|---|---|---|
| | MONT VS. CIN | |
| APRIL 7 | NATIONAL LEAGUE | |
| CIN VS. LA | | ATL VS. SD |
| CHI VS. PHIL | | NY VS. PITTS |
| APRIL 8 | NATIONAL LEAGUE | |
| | STL VS MONT | |

### OPENING DAY TRIVIA

| | |
|---|---|
| STAR OF THE GAME | REDS PITCHER JIM MERRITT |
| WEATHER | 52°; OCCASIONAL DRIZZLE |
| ATTENDANCE | 30,124 |
| NOTABLE | LAST CROSLEY OPENER; SPARKY DEBUTS AS MNGR |
| RATING | ◐◐◐◐◐ |

Crosley Field's long good-by began with a Cincinnati win in the 1970 home opener, a 5–1 victory over Montreal. Crosley would host another 35 games before it closed the gates for the final time on June 24.

The Reds, who were beginning to answer to the nickname "Big Red Machine," defeated the Expos before a capacity crowd of 30,124. Jim Merritt pitched one of the best openers ever at Crosley, taking a no-hitter into the seventh inning. He allowed only three hits, striking out eight and walking two.

"I'm real happy with the way things turned out," Merritt said after the game. "I'm glad because it gets Sparky out on top."

"Sparky" was Sparky Anderson and this was his debut as a major league manager. He had played one season for the Phillies in 1959. Anderson admitted he was anxious before the game, but the three-hitter by his starter, and three home runs in one inning made the job easier.

Merritt and Montreal starter Joe Sparma pitched scoreless ball until the bottom of the fourth. But then Lee May shot one over the scoreboard for a two-run homer, and rookie Bernie Carbo and Bobby Tolan followed with solo home runs.

That was more than Merritt needed, and Sparky knew it. "I just sat on the bench and enjoyed a nice relaxed time," laughed the new skipper.

The full house endured some nasty mid-day weather. Early arrivals sat through two showers in 40-degree temperatures, and rain fell intermittently throughout the game. "*Pluie torrentielle*," said a Montreal reporter. Roughly translated, "Damn rain."

Scribes reflected on Crosley's final opener:

### APRIL 6, 1970

| Montreal | AB | H | Rbi | Cincinnati | AB | H | Rbi |
|---|---|---|---|---|---|---|---|
| Suth'land,2b | 4 | 1 | 0 | Tolan,cf | 5 | 1 | 1 |
| Staub,rf | 4 | 0 | 0 | Helms,2b | 4 | 0 | 0 |
| Fairly,1b | 4 | 1 | 1 | Rose,rf | 2 | 2 | 0 |
| Bailey,lf | 3 | 0 | 0 | Perez,3b | 3 | 0 | 0 |
| Laboy,3b | 3 | 0 | 0 | Bench,c | 4 | 1 | 0 |
| Phillips,cf | 3 | 0 | 0 | May,1b | 3 | 1 | 3 |
| Boccabella,c | 3 | 0 | 0 | Carbo,lf | 3 | 2 | 1 |
| Wine,ss | 2 | 0 | 0 | Concep'on,ss | 4 | 0 | 0 |
| Sparma,p | 1 | 0 | 0 | Merritt,p | 4 | 1 | 0 |
| Herrera,ph | 1 | 0 | 0 | | | | |
| Morton,p | 0 | 0 | 0 | Totals | 32 | 8 | 5 |
| Brand,ph | 1 | 0 | 0 | | | | |
| Waslewski,p | 0 | 0 | 0 | | | | |
| Totals | 29 | 3 | 1 | | | | |

Montreal .......... 000 000 100—1
Cincinnati .......... 000 410 00x—5

E—Laboy. LOB—Montreal 3, Cincinnati 9. 2B—Rose, Bench. 3B—Rose, Staub. HRS—May (1), Carbo (1), Tolan (1).

| Pitching | IP | H | R | ER | BB | SO |
|---|---|---|---|---|---|---|
| Sparma (L, 0-1) | 5 | 7 | 5 | 5 | 3 | 4 |
| Morton | 2 | 1 | 0 | 0 | 2 | 1 |
| Waslewski | 1 | 0 | 0 | 0 | 0 | 0 |
| Merritt (W, 1-0) | 9 | 3 | 1 | 1 | 2 | 8 |

T—2:06. A—30,124.

On this last opening day, with the sun occasionally poking its way through a gray sky, the stadium sparkled in its splendid decor, and the red-white-and-blue bunting hung from the bleacher decks in a festive, salutatory mood. Hooky-playing kids and politicians, civic leaders and middle-aged housewives, truck drivers and executives—they all came—and they yelled, "Let's Go Reds!"

The opener drew 30,000 fans and they never cheered louder. They saw the pre-game ceremonies. They had a multiple pitch of the first ball. Governor [James] Rhodes was in the stands. Charles Feeney, new president of the National League, was in the stands. So was the old president, Warren Giles. Montreal sent not only its team but some of its rooters and its mayor.

It was a glad day. But sad, too, for the fans who had come to love the openers in the quaint, little old ball park. [**Cincinnati Enquirer and Cincinnati Post and Times-Star**]

# 1971: Record Crowd at Riverfront
## 51,702 Endure Cold, Errors and Reds' Defeat

*A well-bundled crowd took in the inaugural opener at Riverfront in 45-degree temperatures.*

It wasn't much of a coming-out party.

Riverfront Stadium was all decked out for its first opener, and 51,702 fans attended—the largest baseball crowd to that time in Cincinnati history. But the Reds and the frigid weather spoiled the stadium's Opening Day debut.

In conditions better suited for the Cincinnati Bengals (the stadium's other tenant), the Reds committed six errors and lost to the Atlanta, 7–4.

Despite all the miscues, the game was tied going into the eighth inning, when the Reds' final error pushed across the go-ahead run. With a runner on third, Clete Boyer grounded to third baseman Woody Woodward. Woodward, who had already committed two errors, accomplished the hat trick with a wild throw into the Reds dugout.

"I wish I knew what happened," Woodward said after the game. "I know 50-some-thousand had something to say about it."

Woodward, normally a shortstop, started at third base for Tony Perez, who had been shifted to first for the injured Lee May.

With starter Gary Nolan struggling in the second inning, the Reds fell behind, 4–0. Nolan recovered, holding the Braves scoreless through the sixth when he departed for Wayne Granger.

Phil Niekro started for the Braves, but couldn't hold the lead. The Reds finally tied the score at four with three runs in the sixth, led by Tony Perez's two-run homer. Cecil Upshaw relieved Niekro and shut out the Reds the rest of the way.

After scoring the go-ahead run in the eighth, Atlanta added two more in the ninth, and what was left of the big, cold crowd filled the exits.

After the game, Sparky Anderson cautioned the reporters about making too much of the loss. "If this game had been played in July, nobody would have thought anything about it," joked Sparky. "[But] here, Opening Day is like the World Series."

The big crowd and the weather kept the reporters busy:

*"The biggest baseball crowd in Cincinnati history was at Riverfront Stadium today. The Reds ticket office said their orders came mainly from Cincinnati and then the regional cities. They had huge orders from Columbus, Indianapolis, Louisville, Lexington, Dayton, Huntington, Middletown, Hamilton, and Lima.*

*Ceremonies began at 2 p.m. The Findlay Market Assn., for the 51st year, paraded onto the field. And on came three marching bands—Roger Bacon High School, The Queen City Drum and Bugle Corps, and the Wright-Patterson Air Force Base band.*

*The temperature was a breezy 46 degrees at game time and falling. "By the sixth inning," cracked Reds' reliever Clay Carroll, "we'll be pitchin' snowballs."*

*"I've never been this cold at a football game," one fan noted as her husband guided her into a Walnut Street bar for something warming.*
**[Cincinnati Enquirer and Cincinnati Post and Times-Star]**

### 1971 Opening Day Schedule

| April 5 | National League | |
|---|---|---|
| ATL vs. CIN | | HOUS vs. LA |
| **April 6** | **National League** | |
| MONT vs. NY | | StL vs. CHI |
| SF vs. SD | | PHIL vs. PITTS |

### Opening Day Trivia

| | |
|---|---|
| Star of the Game | Reds First Baseman Tony Perez |
| Weather | 46°; Overcast |
| Attendance | 51,702 |
| Notable | Parade Changes Route; Marches Downtown |
| Rating | ◐◐◐ |

### April 5, 1971

| Atlanta | ab | h | bi | Cincinnati | ab | h | bi |
|---|---|---|---|---|---|---|---|
| Jackson, cf | 4 | 2 | 1 | Rose, rf | 5 | 0 | 0 |
| Garr, lf | 5 | 1 | 0 | Helms, 2b | 5 | 2 | 0 |
| Aaron, rf | 4 | 0 | 0 | T. Perez, 1b | 4 | 2 | 2 |
| Cepeda, 1b | 5 | 1 | 1 | Bench, c | 3 | 1 | 0 |
| King, c | 4 | 2 | 0 | Carbo, lf | 3 | 1 | 0 |
| Millan, 2b | 4 | 4 | 1 | McRae, cf | 4 | 1 | 1 |
| Boyer, 3b | 1 | 1 | 1 | Duffy, ss | 3 | 1 | 1 |
| M. Perez, ss | 5 | 1 | 1 | Stewart, ph | 1 | 0 | 0 |
| Niekro, p | 2 | 0 | 1 | Woodw'd, 3b | 3 | 0 | 0 |
| Upshaw, p | 1 | 0 | 0 | Nolan, p | 2 | 0 | 0 |
| | | | | Smith, ph | 1 | 0 | 0 |
| Totals | 38 | 12 | 6 | Granger, p | 0 | 0 | 0 |
| | | | | Gullet, p | 0 | 0 | 0 |
| | | | | Carroll, p | 0 | 0 | 0 |
| | | | | Bravo, ph | 1 | 0 | 0 |
| | | | | Totals | 35 | 9 | 4 |

Atlanta ................ 040 000 012—7
Cincinnati ........... 000 103 000—4
E—Carbo, Duffy, Woodward 3, Gullet. DP—Atlanta 1, Cincinnati 2. LOB—Atlanta 10, Cincinnati 7. 2B—King, Jackson, Duffy, Carbo. 3B—Millan. HR—T. Perez (1). S—King. SF—Niekro.

| Pitching | ip | r | er | bb | so |
|---|---|---|---|---|---|
| Niekro | 5 | 4 | 4 | 2 | 1 |
| Upshaw (W, 1-0) | 4 | 0 | 0 | 1 | 2 |
| Nolan | 6 | 4 | 3 | 2 | 2 |
| Granger (L, 0-1) | 1-3 | 1 | 1 | 0 | 1 |
| Gullet | 2-3 | 2 | 2 | 1 | 0 |
| Carroll | 2-3 | 0 | 0 | 0 | 0 |

T—2:24. A—51,702.

# Fans Stay Home in Protest
## Thousands of Empty Seats at Reds Opener; LA Wins, 3–1

*Pete Rose collided with Dodger catcher Duke Sims in the first inning of the 1972 opener. Rose was out and, he admitted later, "out" on his feet after the home plate get-together.*

The Los Angeles Dodgers beat the Reds, 3–1, in the 1972 opener. Amazingly, by the end of the game, the fans actually cared.

They certainly weren't supportive at first. A two-week players' strike delayed the start of the season by 10 days and fans were angry. Only 37,695 attended the opener, leaving thousands of empty seats as a silent protest.

But the Cincinnati fans who were at the ballpark were not silent. The players heard boos as they were introduced, especially Reds player representative Jim Merritt and Johnny Bench, who was outspoken in support of the strike. The only cheers were reserved for ex-Red Frank Robinson, who started in right field for the Dodgers, and singled in a run in the first.

But once the fans made their protest statement, the game was soon the center of attention. It didn't take long for the fans to come to their feet. In the first inning, Pete Rose, on third, dashed for home when LA pitcher Don Sutton bobbled a comeback grounder. Sutton quickly retrieved the ball and threw home. In a reprise of the 1970 All-Star Game collision, Rose slammed into catcher Duke Sims, but this time it was Rose who took the brunt of the impact. Sims hung onto the ball and Pete was out. He was also knocked loose of his senses. "I was dizzy the entire next inning," Pete later explained. "If anyone had hit me a fly ball [in left field] I would have seen four balls coming at me."

As it turned out, Rose's dash was one of the few scoring opportunities the Reds had. Newly acquired Denis Menke, playing in his first game after coming to the Reds in the blockbuster off-season trade with Houston, homered in the second. That was the only offense the Reds could manage off future Hall of Famer Sutton and reliever Jim Brewer.

Reds starter Jack Billingham, who was another of the players acquired in the Houston trade, took the loss, but pitched well (two runs). Jim Lefebvre doubled in the go-ahead run in the sixth inning to knock Billingham out of the game. Two other new Reds, Joe Morgan and Cesar Geronimo failed to get a hit, although Geronimo made a diving catch in right-center field.

Despite the "boycott" by Reds fans, Cincinnati still led the majors in opening day attendance. Reporters noted the hostile mood:

*It was sort of like opening day and sort of like an other game, with several thousand empty seats offering silent testimony that this was not the usual Reds' opener. Johnny Bench [took] the brunt of the boos until player representative Jim Merritt was introduced. Rarely has even an umpire been treated to more boos and catcalls. But he took it gracefully with a shrug and a smile.* **[Cincinnati Enquirer and Cincinnati Post and Times-Star]**

### APRIL 15, 1972

| LOS ANGELES (N.) | | | | | CINCINNATI (N.) | | | | |
|---|---|---|---|---|---|---|---|---|---|
| | ab. | r. | h. | bi | | ab. | r. | h. | bi |
| Wills, ss | 4 | 0 | 0 | 0 | *Rose, lf | 3 | 0 | 2 | 0 |
| Buckner, 1b | 4 | 1 | 1 | 0 | Morgan, 2b | 3 | 0 | 0 | 0 |
| Davis, cf | 4 | 1 | 1 | 0 | Tolan, cf | 4 | 0 | 0 | 0 |
| Robinson, rf | 4 | 0 | 1 | 1 | Bench, c | 4 | 0 | 0 | 0 |
| Lefevre, 2b | 4 | 0 | 1 | 1 | Perez, 1b | 4 | 0 | 0 | 0 |
| Crawford, lf | 4 | 0 | 1 | 0 | Menke, 3b | 3 | 1 | 1 | 1 |
| Brewer, p | 0 | 0 | 0 | 0 | Geronimo, rf | 3 | 0 | 0 | 0 |
| Sims, c | 4 | 1 | 1 | 1 | Concepcn, ss | 3 | 0 | 0 | 0 |
| Grabarkowitz, 4 | 0 | 0 | 0 | | Billinghm, p | 2 | 0 | 0 | 0 |
| Garvey, 3b | 0 | 0 | 0 | 0 | Hall, p | 0 | 0 | 0 | 0 |
| Sutton, p | 3 | 0 | 0 | 0 | Javier, ph | 1 | 0 | 0 | 0 |
| Mota, lf | 1 | 0 | 0 | 0 | MGlothin, p | 0 | 0 | 0 | 0 |
| Total | 36 | 3 | 6 | 3 | Total | 30 | 1 | 3 | 1 |

*Rose awarded first on catcher's interference.

Los Angeles ......... 1 0 0  0 0 1  1 0 0 — 3
Cincinnati ........... 0 1 0  0 0 0  0 0 0 — 1

E—Mogran, Sims, Hall, Grabarkowitz. DP—Los Angeles 1. LOB—Los Angeles 6, Cincinnati 4. 2B—W. Davis, Rose, Bruckner, Lefebvre. HR—Menke (1), Sims (1).

| | IP | H | R | ER | B.B. | SO |
|---|---|---|---|---|---|---|
| Sutton (W, 1-0) | 7 | 3 | 1 | 1 | 1 | 5 |
| Brewer | 2 | 0 | 0 | 0 | 0 | 2 |
| Billingham (L, 0-1) | 5⅔ | 5 | 2 | 2 | 0 | 1 |
| Hall | 2⅓ | 1 | 1 | 1 | 0 | 2 |
| MGlothin | 1 | 0 | 0 | 0 | 0 | 0 |

Save (Brewer (1). Wild pitch—Sutton.
T—2:13. A—37,895.

### OPENING DAY TRIVIA

| | |
|---|---|
| STAR OF THE GAME | LA PITCHER DON SUTTON |
| WEATHER | 68°; CLOUDY |
| ATTENDANCE | 37,695 |
| NOTABLE | PLAYER STRIKE DELAYS START OF SEASON |
| RATING | ◐◐ |

### 1972 OPENING DAY SCHEDULE (ALL GAMES POSTPONED TO APRIL 15)

| APRIL 5 | NATIONAL LEAGUE |
|---|---|
| HOUS VS. CIN | |
| APRIL 6 | NATIONAL LEAGUE |
| NY VS. PITTS | HOUS VS. ATL |
| SD VS. SF | |
| APRIL 7 | NATIONAL LEAGUE |
| CHI VS. MONT | PHI VS. STL |
| CIN VS. LA | |

# 1973
# Marichal Beats Cold and Reds
## Gullett Loses Pitchers' Battle

*Despite temperatures in the low 40's, thousands of Opening Day rooters poured into Riverfront for the 1973 opener.*

Some loyal Reds fans compare the anticipation of Opening Day to the excitement of Christmas morning. For the 1973 opener, they had December weather as well.

The San Francisco Giants, behind Juan Marichal's complete-game performance, beat Don Gullett and the Reds, 4–1, in one of the coldest openers ever. Game time temperature was 42 degrees.

Despite the chill, the attendance was announced as a sellout: 51,179. However, many empty seats dotted the stands as hundreds of the faithful decided not to brave the weather.

Those who did enjoyed a masterful pitching duel between future Hall of Famer Marichal and the young gun of the Reds staff.

The two battled to a 1–1 tie through the sixth inning. The Reds took an early 1–0 lead in the second inning on Gullet's sacrifice fly. The Giants tied it in the fifth. The score remained 1–1 until the Giants rally in the seventh. Two walks, one to Marichal, put the go-ahead run at second. Bobby Bonds boomed a double to center for one run, and Chris Speier's single drove in runs three and four.

The Reds could not mount any threat against Marichal. He retired the last 14 hitters he faced. Not that many fans were left to see it. Most of them begin heading for the exits after the Giants three-run rally in the seventh. For those who did sit through the entire nine innings, the game was over in a quick two hours and ten minutes.

The press considered the cold and celebrated the fans: *It is Opening Day, 1973. [It] belongs to the fans. The long-enduring, never-say-die, always-tomorrow, we-love-you-no-matter-what fans. They are as traditional to Cincinnati as beer, Sundays in the park, the tuba's "oom-pa," and the crack of the bat.*

*Even representatives of the Goodyear Tire & Rubber Co. and the United Rubber Workers [in contract negotiations] met eye-to-eye on one item. They are holding talks in "abeyance" so negotiators can attend the game.*

*If you ever wondered who sits in the very top row behind the scoreboard, be advised that on [Opening Day] it was Liz Shepherd and Mark Schmidt. Liz, a senior at Middletown High School, was celebrating her 18th birthday. She played hooky to see the game.*

*So did the whole senior class from Grant County, Ky., High School. Truants all (with the principal's sanction), they attended the game en masse to root for Johnny Bench and the Reds. Alas—in vain.*

*It was a holiday. You could get out of school for the asking and out of work whether your grandmother died again or not. "The whole town takes it on,"* said Ted Kluszewski, *who knows about this town.* [**Cincinnati Enquirer and Cincinnati Post**]

### APRIL 5, 1973

| SAN FRANCISCO | ab | r | h | bi | CINCINNATI | ab | r | h | bi |
|---|---|---|---|---|---|---|---|---|---|
| Bonds, rf | 5 | 1 | 1 | 1 | Rose, lf | 4 | 0 | 2 | 0 |
| Fuentes, 2b | 5 | 0 | 2 | 1 | Morgan, 2b | 4 | 0 | 1 | 0 |
| Speier, ss | 4 | 0 | 1 | 2 | Tolan, rf | 4 | 0 | 1 | 0 |
| McCovey, 1b | 3 | 0 | 1 | 0 | Bench, c | 3 | 0 | 0 | 0 |
| Maddox, cf | 4 | 0 | 1 | 0 | Perez, 1b | 4 | 0 | 1 | 0 |
| Gallagher, 3b | 4 | 0 | 1 | 0 | Geronimo, cf | 4 | 1 | 1 | 0 |
| Matthews, lf | 4 | 0 | 0 | 0 | Chaney, ss | 3 | 0 | 0 | 0 |
| Rader, c | 3 | 2 | 1 | 0 | Locklear, ph | 1 | 0 | 0 | 0 |
| Marichal, p | 2 | 1 | 1 | 0 | Menke, 3b | 2 | 0 | 1 | 0 |
| Total | 34 | 4 | 9 | 4 | Gullet, p | 1 | 0 | 0 | 1 |
| | | | | | Stahl, ph | 1 | 0 | 0 | 0 |
| | | | | | Borbon, p | 0 | 0 | 0 | 0 |
| | | | | | Total | 31 | 1 | 7 | 1 |

San Francisco ......... 000 010 300—4
Cincinnati ............ 010 000 000—1

E—Rader. DP—San Francisco 1. LOB—San Francisco 7, Cincinnati 6. 2B—Bonds, Geronimo, Perez. SB—Tolan. S—Marichal. SF—Gullett.

| | IP | H | R | ER | BB | SO |
|---|---|---|---|---|---|---|
| Marichal (W, 1-0) | 9 | 7 | 1 | 1 | 2 | 2 |
| Gullett (L, 0-1) | 7 | 8 | 4 | 4 | 3 | 3 |
| Borbon | 2 | 1 | 0 | 0 | 0 | 1 |

PB—Bench. T—2:10. A—51,179.

### 1973 OPENING DAY SCHEDULE

| APRIL 5 | NATIONAL LEAGUE | |
|---|---|---|
| | SF vs. CIN | |
| APRIL 6 | NATIONAL LEAGUE | |
| HOUS vs. ATL | | PHIL vs. NY |
| MONT vs. CHI | | StL vs. PITTS |
| | LA vs. SD | |

### OPENING DAY TRIVIA

| STAR OF THE GAME | SAN FRANCISCO PITCHER JUAN MARICHAL |
|---|---|
| WEATHER | 42°; CLOUDY |
| ATTENDANCE | 51,179 |
| NOTABLE | ACTOR DAVID HARTMAN WARMS UP WITH SF |
| RATING | ⚾⚾ |

# Greatest Opener Ever?
## 1974 — Aaron's Historic Blast, Reds Extra-Inning Win Thrill Fans

*Atlanta's Hank Aaron tied Babe Ruth's career home-run mark of 714 on his first swing of the 1974 season.*

### 1974 OPENING DAY SCHEDULE

| APRIL 4 | NATIONAL LEAGUE |
|---|---|
| ATL vs. CIN | |

| APRIL 5 | NATIONAL LEAGUE |
|---|---|
| HOUS vs. SF | PITTS vs. STL |
| SD vs. LA | |

| APRIL 6 | NATIONAL LEAGUE |
|---|---|
| NY vs. PHIL | CHI vs. MONT |

Was there ever a better Opening Day?

Baseball history, a come-from-behind win by the hometown Reds, a record crowd, and good weather to boot. Even a streaker. What a day.

The headlines belonged to Henry "Hank" Aaron, who tied Babe Ruth's career home run record in the first inning with a three-run shot over the left-center field wall. Aaron's history-making home run chase had been followed closely by the entire nation, and Aaron received a lengthy standing ovation from the 52,154 (the largest Opening Day crowd to date) at Riverfront Stadium. Vice-president Gerald Ford, who threw out the game's first pitch, joined baseball dignitaries to honor Aaron.

And the rest of the game? The Reds trailed until the bottom of the ninth when they tied the score, 6–6. The won it in the 11th when Pete Rose scored all the way from second on a wild pitch.

But in the early going, Aaron was the center of attention. He had hit his 713th homer at the end of the 1973 season, and some in the Atlanta Braves organization wanted to hold him out of the opener in Cincinnati so he could tie and break the record at home. But Commissioner, Bowie Kuhn, intervened and ordered the Braves to start Aaron in two of the three games in Cincinnati.

Hitting cleanup, Aaron's first at-bat came with two on in the first. Starter Jack Billingham threw three balls and then a called strike. Aaron swung at the next pitch—his first swing of the game—and the ball shot like a tracer over the left-center field wall. "A good pitch," said catcher Johnny Bench. "But not good enough to get Henry Aaron."

The game was stopped for seven minutes for on-field ceremonies. Aaron received congratulations from Ford and Kuhn, and was handed the home run ball. It had been retrieved by Cincinnati policeman Clarence Williams from the walkway between the outfield wall and the stands.

The Reds trailed, 6–1, before they began their comeback. Tony Perez hit a three-run homer in the eighth to make it 6–5. "They didn't stop the game for mine," Perez joked.

Rose knocked in George Foster with the tying run in the bottom of the ninth on a controversial play. The home plate umpire called Foster out, but was overruled by the first base umpire who saw the catcher drop the ball.

In the bottom of the 11th, Rose doubled, and with two out, Buzz Capra threw a wild pitch. Rose never hesitated rounding third, and scored easily. Sparky knew Rose was going all the way. "I knew Alex (third base coach Alex Grammas) would stop him and I knew Pete wouldn't stop."

Just like the Reds couldn't stop Hank Aaron. And if the day needed one more distraction, stadium security arrested a 24-year-old in the left field stands for "streaking." He had undressed in the rest room and walked naked back to his seat, smoking a cigar.

What a day! *[Cincinnati Enquirer and Cincinnati Post]*

### OPENING DAY TRIVIA

| | |
|---|---|
| STAR OF THE GAME | ATLANTA LEFT FIELDER HANK AARON |
| WEATHER | 68°; SUNNY |
| ATTENDANCE | 52,154 |
| NOTABLE | MARTY BRENNAMAN'S FIRST REDS BROADCAST |
| RATING | ⚾⚾⚾⚾⚾ |

### APRIL 4, 1974

| ATLANTA | AB | R | H | RBI | E |
|---|---|---|---|---|---|
| Garr, lf | 4 | 1 | 0 | 0 | 0 |
| Lum, cf | 5 | 2 | 3 | 0 | 0 |
| Evans, 3b | 4 | 0 | 2 | 0 | 0 |
| Aaron, lf | 3 | 2 | 1 | 3 | 0 |
| Office, cf | 0 | 0 | 0 | 0 | 0 |
| Murrell, ph | 1 | 0 | 0 | 0 | 0 |
| Tepedino, 1b | 0 | 0 | 0 | 0 | 0 |
| Baker, rf | 5 | 1 | 1 | 0 | 0 |
| Johnson, 2b | 3 | 0 | 0 | 0 | 0 |
| Oates, c | 4 | 0 | 0 | 0 | 0 |
| Robinson, ss | 5 | 0 | 0 | 0 | 0 |
| Morton, p | 3 | 0 | 0 | 0 | 0 |
| House, ph | 1 | 0 | 0 | 0 | 0 |
| Aker, p | 0 | 0 | 0 | 0 | 0 |
| Miller, ph | 1 | 0 | 0 | 0 | 0 |
| Capra, p | 0 | 0 | 0 | 0 | 0 |
| **Totals** | **38** | **6** | **6** | **3** | **0** |

| CINCINNATI | AB | R | H | RBI | E |
|---|---|---|---|---|---|
| Rose, lf | 5 | 3 | 3 | 1 | 0 |
| Morgan, 2b | 4 | 0 | 2 | 0 | 0 |
| Driessen, 3b | 4 | 0 | 1 | 2 | 0 |
| Gagliano, ph | 1 | 0 | 0 | 0 | 0 |
| Hall, p | 0 | 0 | 0 | 0 | 0 |
| Carroll, p | 0 | 0 | 0 | 0 | 0 |
| Geronimo, ph | 0 | 0 | 0 | 0 | 0 |
| Perez, 1b | 5 | 1 | 2 | 4 | 0 |
| Bench, c | 5 | 0 | 0 | 0 | 0 |
| Griffey, rf | 4 | 0 | 0 | 0 | 0 |
| Rettenmund, cf | 5 | 1 | 2 | 0 | 0 |
| Concepcion, ss | 5 | 1 | 2 | 1 | 0 |
| Billingham, p | 1 | 0 | 0 | 0 | 0 |
| Kosco, ph | 1 | 0 | 0 | 0 | 0 |
| Nelson, p | 0 | 0 | 0 | 0 | 0 |
| Crowley, ph | 1 | 0 | 0 | 0 | 0 |
| Borbon, p | 0 | 0 | 0 | 0 | 0 |
| Foster, ph | 1 | 1 | 1 | 0 | 0 |
| Chaney, 3b | 1 | 0 | 0 | 0 | 0 |
| **Totals** | **42** | **7** | **13** | **6** | **1** |

Two out when winning run scored.
ATLANTA.........300 120 000 00—6
CINCINNATI.....100 010 03: 01—7
DP—Atlanta 3, Cincinnati 1. LOB—Atlanta 6, Cincinnati 8. 2B—Driessen, Concepcion, Rose (2). HR—Aaron (1), Concepcion (1), Perez (1). SB—Morgan. S—Oates, Evans.

PITCHING SUMMARY

| | IP | H | R | ER | BB | SO |
|---|---|---|---|---|---|---|
| Morton | 7 | 8 | 3 | 2 | 6 | |
| Niekro | 1½ | 4 | 3 | 3 | 1 | 2 |
| House | 0 | 0 | 0 | 0 | 1 | 0 |
| Aker | 1⅓ | 0 | 0 | 0 | 0 | 3 |
| Capra (L 0-1) | ⅓ | 1 | 1 | 1 | 1 | |
| Billingham | 5 | 6 | 4 | 4 | 3 | |
| Nelson | 2 | 0 | 0 | 0 | 0 | 1 |
| Borbon | 2 | 0 | 0 | 0 | 1 | 0 |
| Hall | ½ | 0 | 0 | 0 | 0 | 0 |
| Carroll (W 1-0) | 1½ | 0 | 0 | 0 | 1 | 0 |

Morton pitched to one batter in eighth; House pitched to one batter in ninth.
WP—Capra. PB—Bench.
T—3:09. A52,154.

# 1975 Reds Win Longest Opener
## Reds, Dodgers Duel 14 Innings

*George Foster drove home Cesar Geronimo with the winning run in the bottom of the 14th inning.*

The 52,526 who attended Opening Day, 1975, could be excused if they thought it was September rather than April. The Red and the Los Angeles Dodgers staged an opener as fiercely contested as any late-season pennant-race game, before the Reds finally prevailed in 14 innings, 2–1.

It was the longest Opening Day game ever played in Cincinnati.

The two teams, who battled for the National League Western Division title in 1973 and 1974, played to form: outstanding pitching, great defense and plenty of emotion. The Reds won on a controversial play in the 14th when George Foster was judged safe at first on an infield hit that allowed the winning run to score.

The Dodgers were as upset as if the game had decided the NL West. Steve Garvey ranted and Davey Lopes hurled his glove to the ground. "He missed the call," moaned Ron Cey. "The umpire blew it," wailed Lopes. But television replay showed that first-base umpire Paul Pryor had the play right.

Don Gullett and Don Sutton, the starting pitchers, staged a terrific duel, each allowing only one run. Mike Marshall relieved Sutton in the eighth and pitched five scoreless innings. Gullett pitched 9 2/3 innings before Sparky hooked him. Clay Carroll, Pedro Borbon and Pat Darcy pitched scoreless ball over the final 4 1/3 innings.

Darcy faced the biggest threat in the top of the 14th. With runners on first and third and no one out, he struck out Steve Yeager and then coaxed Bill Russell to ground into a double play.

In the bottom of the 14th, with two out and a runner on third, Foster nubbed a bouncer toward Cey who was playing deep. Foster barely beat the throw, as Cesar Geronimo scored the winning run.

Despite temperatures in the 50s, the city enjoyed the opener and the parade: *Three bands kicked off the biggest opening day celebration in Cincinnati history. It was the most musicians and the most noise ever given in the start of the baseball season. Accompanying the big brass [was] 76-year-old grand marshal, Waite Hoyt. Mayor Ted Berry presided at the special program at Fountain Square to give those people who didn't have baseball tickets some kind of a show.*

*The Reds were able to keep their hands warm in the dugout by means of a trio of hibachi grills that Sparky Anderson had bought before the game. The charcoal burning accounted for the smoke emitting from the Reds' bench.*

*The boos were reserved for Anderson when he removed Don Gullett after 9 2/3 strong innings. The fans, in fact, showed great versatility, somehow booing Anderson while giving Gullett a standing ovation as he left.* [Cincinnati Enquirer and Cincinnati Post]

### OPENING DAY TRIVIA

| | |
|---|---|
| STAR OF THE GAME | REDS PITCHER DON GULLETT |
| WEATHER | 53°; SUNNY |
| ATTENDANCE | 52,526 |
| NOTABLE | LONGEST OPENER AT 14 INNINGS |
| RATING | ●●●●● |

### APRIL 7, 1975

```
LOS ANGELES           CINC.
         ab r h bi              ab r h bi
Lopes 2b   5 0 2 0  Rose lf    5 1 2 0
Buckner lf 4 0 0 0  Morgan 2b  5 0 2 0
MMota ph   1 0 0 0  Bench c    5 0 0 0
Paciorek lf 1 0 0 0 TPerez 1b  6 0 0 0
Wynn cf    5 1 1 0  Cncpcion ss 6 0 2 1
Hough p    0 0 0 0  Geronimo cf 5 1 0 0
Ferguson rf 5 0 1 0 Griffey rf 5 0 1 0
Garvey 1b  6 0 3 1  Vukovich 3b 3 0 1 0
Cey 3b     6 0 1 0  Chaney 3b  3 0 0 0
Yeager c   6 0 0 0  Gullett p  3 0 0 0
Russell ss 5 0 0 0  CCarroll p 0 0 0 0
Sutton p   2 0 0 0  Crowley ph 1 0 0 0
Marshall p 0 0 0 0  Borbon p   0 0 0 0
Crawford rf 1 0 0 0 Rttmund ph 0 0 0 0
                    Darcy p    0 0 0 0
                    GFoster ph 1 0 1 1
Total     47 1 8 1  Total     48 2 9 2

Dodgers  ... ... ... 000 100 000 000 00— 1
Reds     ... ... ... 000 001 000 000 01— 2
  E—Concepcion. DP—Cincinnati 2.
LOB—Los Angeles 10, Cincinnati 11. 2B—
Vukovich, Morgan, Garvey. SB—Morgan
2. S—Marshall, Rettenmund, Griffey.
              IP   H  R ER BB SO
Sutton         7   5  1  1  1  5
Marshall       5   2  0  0  2  3
Hough (L,0-1)  1 2-3 2  1  0  1
Gullett        9 2-3 5  1  1  1  5
CCarroll       2-3  0  0  0  0  0
Borbon         1 2-3 0  0  0  0  0
Darcy (W,1-0)  2   3  0  0  0  3
Two out when winning run scored.
  WP—Sutton. PB—Yeager. T—3:23. A—
52,526.
```

### 1975 OPENING DAY SCHEDULE

| APRIL 7 | NATIONAL LEAGUE |
|---|---|
| **LA vs. CIN** | |
| ATL vs. HOUS | MONT vs. STL |
| APRIL 8 | NATIONAL LEAGUE |
| PHIL vs. NY | SF vs. SD (PP) |
| APRIL 9 | NATIONAL LEAGUE |
| PITTS vs. CHI | |

# 1976 World Champs Rule Astros
## Perez, Rose, Foster Lead Reds Past Astros, 11–5

*Tony Perez had 14 RBIs in Cincinnati openers, including four in 1976.*

For the first time in 35 years, the Reds opened the season as the defending World Champs, and they played like it, demolishing the Houston Astros, 11–5, in the 1976 opener.

Chilly temperatures in the 50s did not discourage the ticket holders; the Reds announced the attendance at 52,949 and there were few "no-shows." Over 900 $3 standing-room-only tickets were sold the morning of the game.

The Findlay Market Parade wound through downtown to Fountain Square for a noon-time rally. Eleven of the units then proceeded to Riverfront, where they were cheered as they circled the field. Manager Sparky Anderson received the traditional Opening Day gifts, and then promised the cheering throng that his Reds would defend the championship flag all year, "so that flag will be there again next year."

The Reds banged out 15 hits against Houston starter J.R. Richard and five relievers. Tony Perez led the way with two hits and four RBIs. Pete Rose added three hits. But the "knock" of the day belonged to Pedro Borbon who lifted a bunt attempt over the mound that landed just beyond second base for a single. It left Anderson shaking his head.

"I'm always wondering what's going to happen when I tell Borbon to do something."

The Reds also delighted the big crowd with their daring baserunning. They stole four bases and picked up two additional bases on wild throws by catcher Cliff Johnson.

The wacky weirdness of Opening Day continued to amuse the reporters: *Would you believe red mesh underwear? Jack Murphy, Kettering, Ohio, wore a red sportcoat, pants, shirt, shoes and hat like many fans, but he was the first fan to wear red underwear. "See?" said Murphy lowering his belt line. "The shoes are a little tight, though," Murphy said, looking down at this red-and-white squirming feet. "I only wear them on Opening Day."*

*A factory worker, who wished to remain anonymous, acknowledged the city-wide mourning as he ferried an ocean of beer back to his seat.*

*"Yes," he admitted, with moist eye, "my grandmother was buried today. Mine, and the grandmothers of my companions."*

*Downtown Cincinnati had an atmosphere of Christmas, Fourth of July, and a Mardi Gras all wrapped into one. The parade moved to Fifth Street, then east to Fountain Square where fans gathered to listen to a band and the remarks of emcee Jim Labarbara of WLW.*

*Marian Spelman sang the national anthem; dignitaries from national and local government were introduced; Lou Nippert, chairman of the board of the Reds, threw out the first ball; and the game was on.*
**[Cincinnati Enquirer and Cincinnati Post]**

### OPENING DAY TRIVIA

| | |
|---|---|
| STAR OF THE GAME | REDS FIRST BASEMAN TONY PEREZ |
| WEATHER | 56°; SUNNY |
| ATTENDANCE | 52,949 |
| NOTABLE | REDS OWNER LOUIS NIPPERT TOSSES 1ST PITCH |
| RATING | ⚾⚾⚾⚾⚾ |

### APRIL 8, 1976

| HOUSTON | ab | r | h | bi | CINCINNATI | ab | r | h | bi |
|---|---|---|---|---|---|---|---|---|---|
| Howard lf | 5 | 0 | 0 | 0 | Rose 3b | 5 | 0 | 3 | 2 |
| Cabell 3b | 5 | 1 | 2 | 1 | Griffey rf | 5 | 2 | 1 | 0 |
| Cedeno cf | 5 | 1 | 1 | 2 | Morgan 2b | 4 | 3 | 3 | 1 |
| Watson 1b | 4 | 1 | 1 | 1 | Bench c | 4 | 1 | 0 | 0 |
| Johnson c | 2 | 1 | 1 | 0 | Perez 1b | 3 | 1 | 2 | 4 |
| Gross rf | 4 | 0 | 2 | 0 | Foster lf | 5 | 0 | 1 | 2 |
| Milbourne 2b | 4 | 0 | 1 | 1 | Concepcin ss | 5 | 1 | 1 | 1 |
| Metzger ss | 4 | 1 | 2 | 0 | Geronimo cf | 4 | 1 | 2 | 0 |
| Richard p | 1 | 0 | 0 | 0 | Nolan p | 2 | 1 | 1 | 1 |
| Boswell ph | 1 | 0 | 0 | 0 | Borbon p | 2 | 1 | 1 | 0 |
| Sosa p | 0 | 0 | 0 | 0 | | | | | |
| Cosgrove p | 0 | 0 | 0 | 0 | | | | | |
| Andujar p | 0 | 0 | 0 | 0 | | | | | |
| Cruz ph | 1 | 0 | 1 | 0 | | | | | |
| Barlow p | 0 | 0 | 0 | 0 | | | | | |
| Forsch p | 0 | 0 | 0 | 0 | | | | | |
| Roberts ph | 0 | 0 | 0 | 0 | | | | | |
| Totals | 36 | 5 | 11 | 5 | Totals | 39 | 11 | 15 | 11 |

Houston     000 013 100—5
Cincinnati  031 025 00x—11

E-Johnson 2, Gross 2. DP-Houston, Cincinnati 2. LOB-Houston 7, Cincinnati 8. 2B-Milbourne, Perez, Geronimo. 3B-Rose. HR-Cedeno (1), Watson (1). SB-Griffey 2, Morgan 2.

| | IP | H | R | ER | BB | SO |
|---|---|---|---|---|---|---|
| Richard L 0-1 | 4 | 5 | 4 | 4 | 1 | 2 |
| Sosa | 1 | 6 | 5 | 5 | 0 | 1 |
| Cosgrove | 1-3 | 1 | 1 | 1 | 0 | 0 |
| Andujar | 2-3 | 1 | 1 | 1 | 2 | 0 |
| Barlow | 1 | 1 | 0 | 0 | 1 | 0 |
| Forsch | 1 | 1 | 0 | 0 | 1 | 0 |
| Nolan W 1-0 | 5 1-3 | 6 | 4 | 4 | 2 | 3 |
| Borbon | 3 2-3 | 5 | 1 | 1 | 1 | 0 |

Sosa pitched to 3 batters in 6th.
Save-Borbon. WP-Richard, Sosa. T-2:42.
A-52,949.

### 1976 OPENING DAY SCHEDULE

| APRIL 8 | NATIONAL LEAGUE |
|---|---|
| | HOUS VS. CIN |
| APRIL 9 | NATIONAL LEAGUE |
| LA VS. SF | MONT VS. NY |
| CHI VS. STL | ATL VS. SD |
| APRIL 10 | NATIONAL LEAGUE |
| | PITTS VS. PHIL |

# 1977
# "Sn-opening Day"
## Four Inches Fails to Stop Game, Crowd or Reds

*With the precision of a well-drilled military platoon, Dick Wagner's ground crew cleared the field of snow before the 1977 opener.*

The Reds defeated San Diego, 5–3, in the frigid opener of 1977, behind the hitting of Cesar Geronimo and the relief pitching of Rawly Eastwick, but the day belonged to the Reds general manager Dick Wagner.

The prescient Wagner proved to be quite a long-range weather forecaster. While the Reds were in spring training in Tampa, on March 23, Wagner noticed the unusual cold weather hanging on in the midwest and he sent his ground crew a message: "Be prepared for rain or two inches of snow. I want to see a game-plan."

Well, he was off a couple of inches. There were *four* inches of snow on the ground on Opening Day. But the heads-up alert had the crew ready. An expanded staff of 60 pushed and shoveled and hauled snow off the field. They even had snow removal trucks on stand-by to carry it away. The only glitch in the Wagner plan came when the trucks were held up by pre-game traffic. But there was not a snowflake to be seen on the Riverfront turf by 2:34 p.m., when the first pitch was thrown.

Typical of Cincinnati openers, the game was officially sold out, but an estimated 4,500 stayed home to avoid the game-time temperature of 38 degrees and the 15-mile-per-hour winds.

There were no shirkers at the Opening Day Parade, however. The Findlay Market marchers braved the elements, although one reporter noted the bands had trouble keeping in step, dodging snow drifts and staggering through the gusting winds.

At Riverfront, the few early arrivals wrapped themselves in quilts, sipped coffee and hot chocolate, and cheered the ground crew. One delightful benefit of the frigid weather was that the dignitaries for once got it right: They mercifuly completed their pre-game orations in record time.

All the players complained of cold hands and numb feet. However, Ceasar Geronimo, a native of the Dominican Republic, who had seen snow only once before, found the conditions to his liking. He hit a two-run homer in the fourth inning off Randy Jones to put the Reds ahead, 4–2. Superb relief work by Eastwick in support of Woody Fryman (acquired from Montreal in the Tony Perez trade) shut out the Padres over the final three innings.

The reporters marveled at the fortitude of the crowd: *The weather did not hamper the festivities in the least. It all added to the unique aura of Opening Day.*

*"Who else would go out and play baseball on a day like today except the Reds? Mayor James T. Luken said. "This day is almost a religion."*

*As [fans] herded in, there was an ocean of red coats, red pants, red shirts, red hats, red blankets covering red people.*

*Mr. and Mrs. James Baldwin, Portland, Ind., claimed Cincinnati "is the best baseball town. Today we drove through a blizzard to get here—105 miles. We would have come through anything."*

[*Cincinnati Enquirer* and *Cincinnati Post*]

### 1977 OPENING DAY SCHEDULE

| Date | League | Games |
|---|---|---|
| April 6 | National League | SD vs. Cin |
| April 7 | National League | StL vs. Pitts; NY vs. Chi; SF vs. LA |
| April 8 | National League | Atl vs. Hous |

### OPENING DAY TRIVIA

| | |
|---|---|
| Star of the Game | Reds Center Fielder Ceasar Geronimo |
| Weather | 38°; Cloudy |
| Attendance | 51,917 |
| Notable | Four Inches of Snow in Morning |
| Rating | ○○○○○ |

### APRIL 6, 1977

| SAN DIEGO | ab | r | h | bi | CINCINNATI | ab | r | h | bi |
|---|---|---|---|---|---|---|---|---|---|
| G Rchrds lf | 3 | 0 | 1 | 0 | Rose 3b | 4 | 0 | 0 | 0 |
| Chmpn 2b | 5 | 1 | 3 | 0 | Griffey rf | 4 | 2 | 3 | 0 |
| Winfld rf | 3 | 1 | 0 | 0 | Morgan 2b | 4 | 0 | 1 | 0 |
| Hndrck cf | 3 | 0 | 1 | 0 | G Foster lf | 2 | 0 | 1 | 2 |
| Tenace c | 5 | 0 | 1 | 2 | Cncpcn ss | 4 | 1 | 2 | 0 |
| Ivie 1b | 5 | 1 | 3 | 1 | Drssen 1b | 4 | 0 | 0 | 0 |
| DoRder 3b | 4 | 0 | 0 | 0 | Plummer c | 4 | 1 | 2 | 1 |
| Almon ss | 4 | 0 | 0 | 0 | Grnlmo cf | 4 | 1 | 1 | 2 |
| RJones p | 1 | 0 | 0 | 0 | Frymn p | 2 | 0 | 0 | 0 |
| RVltne ph | 1 | 0 | 0 | 0 | Borbon p | 0 | 0 | 0 | 0 |
| Tomlin p | 0 | 0 | 0 | 0 | Arbst- ph | 1 | 0 | 0 | 0 |
| Bernal p | 0 | 0 | 0 | 0 | Eastwick p | 0 | 0 | 0 | 0 |
| Turner ph | 1 | 0 | 0 | 0 | | | | | |
| Fingers p | 0 | 0 | 0 | 0 | | | | | |
| Total | 35 | 3 | 9 | 3 | Total | 33 | 5 | 10 | 5 |

San Diego .................. 002 010 000— 3
Cincinnati ................. 011 210 00x— 5

E—G. Richards, Ivie. DP—Cincinnati 1. LOB—SanDiego 12, Cincinnati 6. 2B—Ivie, Concepcion, Champion, Griffey, Morgan. 3B—Foster. HR—Geronimo (1), Ivie (1). SB—G. Richards, Concepcion 2. SF—G. Foster.

| | IP | H | R | ER | BB | SO |
|---|---|---|---|---|---|---|
| R. Jones (L, 0-1) | 5 | 9 | 5 | 4 | 0 | 0 |
| Tomlin | 2-3 | 1 | 0 | 0 | 0 | 0 |
| Bernal | 1-3 | 0 | 0 | 0 | 1 | 0 |
| Fingers | 1 | 0 | 0 | 0 | 0 | 2 |
| Fryman (W, 1-0) | 5 1-3 | 7 | 3 | 3 | 6 | 2 |
| Borbon | 2-3 | 1 | 0 | 0 | 0 | 0 |
| Eastwick | 3 | 1 | 0 | 0 | 1 | 0 |

Save—Eastwick (1). Balk—R. Jones. T—2:27. A—51,937.

# 1978
# Rain, Runs and a Triple Play
## Reds Win Wacky Opener

*Three rain delays did not bother Joe Morgan, who had one of the best offensive performances ever in a Reds opener.*

The Reds defeated the Astros on a rainy Opening Day, 11–9. The fans who endured three rain delays, saw the teams combine for 20 runs on 28 hits, and a most unusual triple play, the only one in Cincinnati's Opening Day history.

Morning-long rain dampened the parade route of the Findlay Market rooters, but they stepped out right on schedule in the drizzle at 11 a.m. Thousands of onlookers, huddled under umbrellas, cheered them on as they headed down Race to Fifth and onto Fountain Square. They were greeted by dignitaries, and a gorilla—a fan dressed in a gorilla mask with a red cape, a Reds cap and a transistor radio around his large furry neck.

There were few empty seats at game time; the Reds announced the attendance at 52,378, another soldout opener.

With Tom Seaver and J.R. Richard the starters, fans had reason to expect a low-scoring affair, but the rain delays seem to bother both pitchers. Houston scored four in the fourth to take a 5–1 lead and Seaver headed to the showers. But the Reds struck for five in the bottom of the fifth and Richard joined Seaver on the sidelines. The Reds extended their lead to 11–5, but then had to hang on in the ninth when Houston scored four runs and had the tying run at the plate. Dave Tomlin recorded the final out.

Joe Morgan was the hitting star with a home run and two doubles, five RBIs and a stolen base in one of the best offensive performances ever on Opening Day.

In the seventh, Danny Driessen struck out into a triple play, an odd set of circumstances that had all the players momentarily confused. With Driessen up, and George Foster on first and Morgan on third, Anderson flashed the steal sign to Foster. Driessen struck out, but Foster slipped and scrambled back to first. The throw went to second base, and Morgan broke for the plate, but then hesitated. The shortstop threw to third to nab Morgan. During the Morgan rundown, Foster took off for second, and was thrown out for the 2-6-5-6 triple play. "That was a fluke," admitted Roger Metzger, the Astros shortstop. "A strikeout and two tags—you won't see that very often." It was so unusual, several of the Astros did not realize what had happened and were slow to leave the field.

The three rain delays totaled one hour and thirty nine minutes which kept the concession lines long. *Cincinnati Post* sportswriter Pat Harmon opined, "This may have been the greatest beer drinkers' baseball game of all time." The long afternoon finally came to a close at 7:07, with about 10,000 people left in the ballpark. *[Cincinnati Enquirer and Cincinnati Post]*

### 1978 Opening Day Schedule

| April 6 | National League |
|---|---|
| Hous vs. Cin | |

| April 7 | National League | |
|---|---|---|
| Mont vs. NY | | StL vs. Phil |
| Chi vs. Pitts | | LA vs. Atl |
| | SD vs. SF | |

### Opening Day Trivia

| | |
|---|---|
| Star of the Game | Reds Second Baseman Joe Morgan |
| Weather | 71°; Rainy |
| Attendance | 52,378 |
| Notable | Astros Pull off Triple Play |
| Rating | ●●●●○ |

### April 6, 1978

```
Houston           Cincinnati
        ab r h bi         ab r h bi
Puhl lf  4 2 2 1  Rose 3b  4 1 1 0
Cabell 3b 5 1 1 1 Knight 3b 0 0 0 0
Cedeno cf 4 1 2 2 Griffey rf 4 2 2 0
JCruz rf  5 1 3 2 Morgan 2b 4 3 3 5
Watson 1b 5 1 1 1 GFoster lf 5 2 2 0
Fergusn c 4 1 1 2 Driessn 1b 4 2 2 0
Howe 2b   4 1 1 0 Bench c   5 0 2 2
RMtzgr ss 3 0 0 0 Cncpcn ss 4 0 1 1
Brgmn ph  1 0 0 0 Geronm cf 4 0 2 1
Richard p 2 0 0 0 Seaver p  1 0 0 0
Pentz p   0 0 0 0 Borbon p  0 0 0 0
Walling ph 1 0 1 0 DaCns ph 1 1 1 1
Dixon p   0 0 0 0 DMurry p  1 0 0 0
Sambito p 0 0 0 0 Bair p    0 0 0 0
Howard ph 0 1 0 0 Tomlin p  0 0 0 0
Total    38 9 12 9 Total   37 11 16 10

Houston       1 0 0 4 0 0 0 0 4 — 9
Cincinnati    1 0 0 1 5 2 2 0 x — 11

E—Howe, Cruz. TP—Houston. LOB—
Houston 5, Cincinnati 9. 2B—JCruz, Gero-
nimo, Rose, Morgan 2, GFoster, Howe.
HR—Puhl (1), Cedeno (1), Ferguson (1),
Morgan (1). SB—Cedeno, Driessen, Ca-
bell, Morgan, Griffey.

                IP   H  R ER BB SO
Houston
Richard L,0-1  4 2-3 11  7  7  3  8
Pentz          1 1-3  2  2  1  3  1
Dixon            0    3  2  2  1  0
Sambito          2    0  0  0  0  2
Cincinnati
Seaver           3    6  5  5  0  3
Borbon W,1-0     2    2  0  0  0  0
DMurray        3 2-3  4  4  1  4
Bair             0    0  0  0  1  0
Tomlin         1-3    1  0  0  0  0

Save—Tomlin (1). HBP—Howard (by
DMurray). WP—Richard. Balk—Richard.
PB—Ferguson. T—2:53. A—52,378.
```

# Welcome to the McNamara "Error"
## 1979
### New Manager's Debut Game Marred by Five Miscues

*The press zeroed in on new manager John McNamara prior to the 1979 opener. This was McNamara's first game after replacing the popular Sparky Anderson.*

The calendar said "Opening Day," but the Reds played as though it was the opening of spring training.

With Tom Seaver on the mound for the Reds, the visiting San Francisco Giants scored eight times in the second inning, aided by three Cincinnati errors and a wild pitch. The final score was 11–5. Vida Blue picked up a complete-game victory for the Giants.

The Reds committed five errors, giving the Giants five unearned runs. The sloppy play and lopsided score, combined with the damp and cold weather, sent many of the 52,115 home early.

Many had *arrived* in a foul mood, still upset with the Reds for two unpopular off-season moves, the jettisoning of Pete Rose and Sparky Anderson. A few fans carried signs demanding the ouster of Reds President and General Manager Dick Wagner, who had elected not to re-sign Rose and fire Anderson.

New manager John McNamara and Wagner hoped to start the season on a positive note. With Seaver making his second Opening Day start for the Reds, they had reason for optimism. But for the second straight year, Seaver was rocked early.

The nightmarish second began with two singles. Roger Metzger then laid down a sacrifice; Seaver grabbed the bunt and threw to third, but Rick Auerbach, filling in for the injured Ray Knight at third base, failed to cover the bag.

The throw rolled down the foul line, allowing the first run to score. A sacrifice, an infield out, two singles and a wild pitch produced three more runs. After another RBI single, Bench threw wildly to third and two more runs scored. Paul Moskau replaced Seaver, and promptly gave up a home run to Mike Ivy, his second hit of the inning.

What little offense the Reds could muster off Blue was due largely to Cesar Geronimo, who singled and scored in the third, and drove in two runs in the fourth with a double. But Blue shutout the Reds over the last four innings.

Three of the four umpires at this opener were local amateurs, called in as last-minute replacements for the regular umpires, who walked a picket line outside Riverfront Stadium.

Early morning rain threatened the start of the Findlay Market Parade, but the pre-game ceremonies went off as scheduled: *It poured rain almost all morning but that didn't matter. Cincinnati's Opening Day parade went on. And a rather unusual parade it was. People dressed as 6-feet-tall beer cans swerved through downtown streets. After a high school band had whipped past playing a peppy version of "Disco Inferno," an old man leaped from the curb and pranced alongside the band.*

*A group of young women said they represented the DOWN movement— Dispose of Wagner Now."* [Cincinnati Enquirer and

### APRIL 4, 1979

| SAN FRAN | | | | | CINCINNATI | | | | |
|---|---|---|---|---|---|---|---|---|---|
| | ab | r | h | bi | | ab | r | h | bi |
| North cf | 5 | 0 | 0 | 1 | Griffey rf | 4 | 0 | 2 | 0 |
| Whitfild lf | 5 | 1 | 4 | 2 | Cncpcn ss | 3 | 0 | 1 | 1 |
| Madlck 2b | 4 | 1 | 1 | 1 | Morgan 2b | 4 | 1 | 1 | 0 |
| Clark rf | 3 | 3 | 1 | 0 | Foster lf | 4 | 0 | 1 | 0 |
| Evans 3b | 5 | 1 | 2 | 2 | Bench c | 3 | 1 | 1 | 0 |
| Ivie 1b | 4 | 2 | 2 | 1 | Driessn 1b | 4 | 1 | 1 | 1 |
| Hill c | 4 | 1 | 1 | 1 | Aurbch 3b | 4 | 0 | 0 | 0 |
| Metzger ss | 4 | 2 | 0 | 0 | Geronm cf | 4 | 2 | 2 | 2 |
| Blue p | 3 | 0 | 0 | 0 | Seaver p | 0 | 0 | 0 | 0 |
| | | | | | Moskau p | 1 | 0 | 0 | 0 |
| | | | | | DeFrts p | 0 | 0 | 0 | 1 |
| | | | | | Capilla p | 0 | 0 | 0 | 0 |
| | | | | | Tomlin p | 0 | 0 | 0 | 0 |
| | | | | | Collins ph | 1 | 0 | 0 | 0 |
| | | | | | Pastore p | 0 | 0 | 0 | 0 |
| | | | | | Keonny ph | 1 | 0 | 0 | 0 |
| Total | 37 | 11 | 11 | 8 | Total | 33 | 5 | 9 | 5 |

San Francisco 0 8 1 1 0 1 0 0 0 — 11
Cincinnati 0 0 1 3 1 0 0 0 0 — 5

E—Seaver, Auerbach, Bench, Morgan, Foster. DP—San Francisco. LOB—San Francisco 8, Cincinnati 7. 2B—Whitfield, Clark, Griffey 2. 3B—Geronimo. HR—Ivie (1). S—Blue 2, Metzger, Evans. SF—Concepcn, DeFreites.

| San Francisco | IP | H | R | ER | BB | SO |
|---|---|---|---|---|---|---|
| Blue W,1-0 | 9 | 9 | 5 | 5 | 4 | 2 |
| **Cincinnati** | | | | | | |
| Seaver L,0-1 | 1 2-3 | 6 | 7 | 4 | 1 | 0 |
| Moskau | 2 1-3 | 3 | 3 | 1 | 1 | 0 |
| Capilla | 1 1-3 | 1 | 1 | 1 | 2 | 0 |
| Tomlin | 0 2-3 | 0 | 0 | 0 | 0 | 1 |
| Pastore | 3 | 1 | 0 | 0 | 0 | 0 |

WP—Seaver. T—2:45. A—52,115.

### 1979 OPENING DAY SCHEDULE

| APRIL 4 | NATIONAL LEAGUE |
|---|---|
| SF vs. CIN | |
| APRIL 5 | NATIONAL LEAGUE |
| NY vs. CHI | SD vs. LA |
| APRIL 6 | NATIONAL LEAGUE |
| MONT vs. PITTS | ATL vs. HOUS |
| PHIL vs. STL | |

### OPENING DAY TRIVIA

| STAR OF THE GAME | SAN FRANCISCO PITCHER VIDA BLUE |
|---|---|
| WEATHER | 47°; DAMP AND CLOUDY |
| ATTENDANCE | 52,115 |
| NOTABLE | UMPIRES ON STRIKE |
| RATING | ☁ |

# Pastore Paints a Masterpiece
## Reds Shutout Atlanta, 9–0

*Frank Pastore (35) and Johnny Bench walk off the field after Pastore's Opening Day shutout.*

Frank Pastore made history in the 1980 opener, leading the Reds to a 9–0 shutout of the Atlanta Braves.

It was one of the most dominant performances by a Reds pitcher on Opening Day, and only the fifth shutout by a Reds pitcher in an opener.

Perhaps the most amazing detail of the day was that the 22-year-old Pastore wasn't even supposed to start. Tom Seaver was a late scratch due to illness. That ended Seaver's 13-year streak of starting the opener, both in New York and Cincinnati.

When Pastore reported to the clubhouse at 10:15, he discovered the Opening Day nod was his. "Oh boy, gimme the ball," responded the right-hander after he was told the news.

And when he got the ball, he knew just what to do with it. Pastore gave up three hits and walked none; Atlanta never moved a runner past second base. Pastore needed only two hours and seven minutes to finish the game; he threw 96 pitches.

Pastore's performance was brilliantly supported by the offensive fireworks of George Foster. The Reds left fielder had a home run, a double, a single and four RBIs. Reds second baseman Junior Kennedy added two hits and three RBIs.

The Reds started their scoring blitz in the first off knuckleballer Phil Niekro with four runs, two scoring on a Foster double.

In the top of the second, Atlanta mounted their only threat, putting two runners on base. But Pastore escaped the jam, and Foster struck again in the second with a two-run homer to left. By the end of the third, the Reds were up, 8–0. The dank day, combined with the Reds blowout sent many of the 51,774 home early.

For the second year in a row, the Reds staged a promotional stunt by having the Opening Day baseball arrive in an unusual fashion. In 1979, the ball came by canoe; in 1980, Procter & Gamble employee Keen Babbage hiked 430 miles from St. Louis with the first ball. He handed it to the March of Dimes poster child, Jason Edwards of Cincinnati. Jason tossed it to Johnny Bench and the game was on. The scribes covered the pageantry: *A baseball fan may forget his wedding anniversary. He might not greet Christmas with the same eager anticipation he once did. But this morning—ahh, this morning—this is different. It is the day in Cincinnati, festive, joyful and for people of all ages.*

*The dress of the day was mostly blankets, coats, umbrellas. The wind kept blowing, the temperature kept falling and by the end of the game the rain was falling.*

The Findlay Market Association orchestrated the Opening Day Parade, a spectacle that began with the band from St. Leon and ended with the horses from St, Louis, eight Clydesdales of the Anheuser-Busch Brewing Co. **[Cincinnati Enquirer and Cincinnati Post]**

### OPENING DAY TRIVIA

| | |
|---|---|
| STAR OF THE GAME | REDS PITCHER FRANK PASTORE |
| WEATHER | 56°; CLOUDY |
| ATTENDANCE | 51,774 |
| NOTABLE | FIRST SHUTOUT BY REDS PITCHER SINCE 1943 |
| RATING | ●●●●○ |

### 1980 OPENING DAY SCHEDULE

| APRIL 9 | NATIONAL LEAGUE |
|---|---|
| ATL vs. CIN | |
| **APRIL 10** | **NATIONAL LEAGUE** |
| LA vs. HOUS | SF vs. SD |
| CHI vs. NY | PITTS vs. STL |
| **APRIL 11** | **NATIONAL LEAGUE** |
| MONT vs. PHIL | |

### APRIL 9, 1980

| ATLANTA | ab r h bi | CINCINNATI | ab r h bi |
|---|---|---|---|
| Miller cf | 4 0 0 0 | Collins cf | 5 1 0 0 |
| Royster 2b | 4 0 0 0 | Griffey rf | 4 1 1 0 |
| Matthws rf | 4 0 0 0 | Concpcn ss | 5 1 1 0 |
| Horner 3b | 3 0 1 0 | Foster lf | 5 2 3 4 |
| Chmbls 1b | 3 0 2 0 | Driessn 1b | 2 1 0 0 |
| Murphy lf | 3 0 0 0 | Bench c | 3 1 1 1 |
| Pocorob c | 3 0 0 0 | Knight 3b | 3 1 0 0 |
| Gomez ss | 3 0 0 0 | Kennedy 2b | 3 1 2 3 |
| Niekro p | 0 0 0 0 | Pastore p | 3 0 1 1 |
| Assistn ph | 1 0 0 0 | | |
| Camp p | 0 0 0 0 | | |
| Lum ph | 1 0 0 0 | | |
| Bradford p | 0 0 0 0 | | |
| Brrghs ph | 1 0 0 0 | | |
| Hannah p | 0 0 0 0 | | |
| Boggs p | 0 0 0 0 | | |
| Totals | 30 0 3 0 | Totals | 33 9 9 9 |

Atlanta          000 000 000—0
Cincinnati       422 000 10x—9

E—Horner, Matthews. DP—Atlanta 1. LOB—Atlanta 3, Cincinnati 7. 2B—Foster, Bench, Kennedy. 3B—Kennedy. HR—Foster (1). S—Griffey. SF—Kennedy.

| | IP | H | R | ER | BB | SO |
|---|---|---|---|---|---|---|
| **Atlanta** | | | | | | |
| Niekro (L 0-1) | 2 | 5 | 6 | 4 | 3 | 2 |
| Camp | 2 | 2 | 2 | 1 | 0 | 0 |
| Bradford | 2 | 2 | 0 | 0 | 0 | 3 |
| Hannah | 1 | 0 | 1 | 1 | 2 | 0 |
| Boggs | 1 | 0 | 0 | 0 | 0 | 1 |
| **Cincinnati** | | | | | | |
| Pastore (W 1-0) | 9 | 3 | 0 | 0 | 0 | 5 |

WP—Hannah. PB—Pocoraba. T—2:07. A—51,774.

# Seaver Wins Duel with Carlton
## Bases-Loaded Walk in 9th Gives Reds Victory

*Tom Seaver failed to pick up a victory in any of his three Opening Day starts as a Cincinnati Red.*

For only the second time in history, two Hall of Famers faced each other as starting pitchers in a Cincinnati opener. Tom Seaver opposed Steve Carlton of the Phillies, and Seaver and the Reds eked out a 3–2 win with a tense ninth-inning rally. (The first two Hall of Famers to square off were Grover Cleveland Alexander and Eppa Rixey in 1922.)

Neither Seaver nor Carlton figured in the decision. Carlton left after seven innings, with the score, 1–0, in favor of the Reds. The run scored in the third on a single by Dave Collins and a double by Dave Concepcion.

It looked like that would be all the runs the Reds would need. Seaver allowed only six hits through eight innings, but gave up the tying run in the eighth on three singles—one by Pete Rose, who was back in Cincinnati on Opening Day for the first time since he left the Reds.

Tom Hume relieved Seaver in the ninth, but the Reds defense faltered. Dave Concepcion booted a ground ball and—after a sacrifice bunt—a single by Keith Moreland put the Phillies up, 2–1.

Unlike past years, when cold and rainy weather had chased many fans home early, most of the 51,716 at Riverfront were still in their seats, thanks to the close score and pleasant 73-degree weather. They stomped their feat and yelled "Charge!" and the Reds responded.

Collins blooped a double to left and scored on a single by Ken Griffey, Sr. Griffey stole second and went all the way to third on catcher Moreland's throwing error. After intentional walks to George Foster and Johnny Bench, reliever Tug McGraw faced Danny Driessen with one out and the bases loaded. Driessen worked the count full and with the crowd on its feet, McGraw threw low and outside for ball four, and the winning run walked home.

President Ronald Reagan was to throw out the first pitch, but he was sidelined in Washington, recovering from an assassination attempt on March 30. The Reds have never had a sitting president throw out the first pitch on Opening Day.

As always, the parade and the fans drew the attention of the reporters: *If you rate Opening Days by the sound of music, today's a record. It's a nine-bander. That is the number of bands lined up for the annual Findlay Market Parade. The previous record was six.*

*At Riverfront Stadium for the pre-game show were Gov. James Rhodes, U.S. Rep. Thomas Luken, baseball commissioner Bowie Kuhn, National League President Charles Feeney, and two former Iranian hostages.*

*Some 52,000 soaked in the sun and ate hot dogs and peanuts and drank beer. Some drank too much beer and fought in the upper decks. Police showed up quickly. That ended that.*
[*Cincinnati Enquirer and Cincinnati Post*]

### 1981 OPENING DAY SCHEDULE

| APRIL 8 | NATIONAL LEAGUE |
|---|---|
| PHIL VS. CIN | |
| APRIL 9 | NATIONAL LEAGUE |
| MONT VS. PITTS | HOUS VS. LA |
| NY VS. CHI | SD VS. SF |
| APRIL 10 | NATIONAL LEAGUE |
| CIN VS. ATL | |
| APRIL 11 | NATIONAL LEAGUE |
| PHIL VS. STL | |

### OPENING DAY TRIVIA

| STAR OF THE GAME | REDS PITCHER TOM SEAVER |
|---|---|
| WEATHER | 73°; PARTLY CLOUDY |
| ATTENDANCE | 51,716 |
| NOTABLE | TWO HALL OF FAMERS START OPENER |
| RATING | ◯◯◯◯ |

### APRIL 8, 1981

| PHILADELPHIA | | | | | CINCINNATI | | | | |
|---|---|---|---|---|---|---|---|---|---|
| | ab | r | h | bi | | ab | r | h | bi |
| Rose 1b | 5 | 0 | 3 | 0 | Collins rf | 5 | 2 | 3 | 0 |
| Trillo 2b | 5 | 0 | 1 | 1 | Griffey cf | 5 | 1 | 2 | 1 |
| McGraw p | 0 | 0 | 0 | 0 | Concepcion ss | 5 | 0 | 3 | 1 |
| McBride rf | 4 | 0 | 0 | 0 | Foster lf | 3 | 0 | 1 | 0 |
| Lyle p | 0 | 0 | 0 | 0 | Bench c | 2 | 0 | 0 | 0 |
| Reed p | 0 | 0 | 0 | 0 | Driessen 1b | 3 | 0 | 1 | 1 |
| Aviles 2b | 0 | 0 | 0 | 0 | Knight 3b | 3 | 0 | 2 | 0 |
| Schmidt 3b, ss | 2 | 0 | 0 | 0 | Oester 2b | 4 | 0 | 0 | 0 |
| Matthews lf | 3 | 0 | 0 | 0 | Seaver p | 3 | 0 | 0 | 0 |
| Maddox cf | 4 | 1 | 1 | 0 | Vail ph | 1 | 0 | 0 | 0 |
| Bowa ss | 3 | 0 | 0 | 0 | Hume p | 0 | 0 | 0 | 0 |
| Boone c | 2 | 0 | 0 | 0 | | | | | |
| Gross rf | 1 | 0 | 0 | 0 | | | | | |
| Carlton p | 2 | 0 | 0 | 0 | | | | | |
| Unser ph | 1 | 0 | 1 | 0 | | | | | |
| Smith pr | 0 | 1 | 0 | 0 | | | | | |
| Moreland c | 1 | 0 | 1 | 1 | | | | | |
| Totals | 33 | 2 | 7 | 2 | Totals | 34 | 3 | 12 | 3 |

One out when winning run scored
Philadelphia 000 000 011—2
Cincinnati 001 000 002—3
E—Moreland, Collins, Concepcion. DP—Philadelphia 1, Cincinnati 1. LOB—Philadelphia 9, Cincinnati 14. 2B—Concepcion, Knight, Driessen, Collins. SB—Schmidt, Bowa, Matthews, Griffey. S—Bowa, Knight.

| Philadelphia | IP | H | R | ER | BB | SO |
|---|---|---|---|---|---|---|
| Carlton | 7 | 9 | 1 | 1 | 4 | 6 |
| Lyle (L 0-1) | 1 | 3 | 2 | 2 | 0 | 1 |
| Reed | 1-3 | 0 | 0 | 0 | 2 | 1 |
| McGraw | 0 | 0 | 0 | 0 | 1 | 0 |
| Cincinnati | | | | | | |
| Seaver | 8 | 6 | 1 | 1 | 3 | 4 |
| Hume (W 1-0) | 1 | 1 | 1 | 1 | 0 | 1 |

Lyle pitched to 2 batters in 9th.
WP—Carlton 3. T—2:43. A—51,716.

# Reds Lose Rain-Shortened Opener
## Even Peanut Jim and Astronauts Can't Save the Day

*The king of roasted peanuts, Jim Shelton, was by honored by the Findlay Market parade organizers in 1982.*

Peanut Jim Shelton, the legendary vendor from the West End, was the Grand Marshal of the Findlay Market parade.

Astronauts Dick Truly and Joe Engle delivered the first ball, which had flown with them on a space shuttle flight.

The "Mr. Red Race" debuted on the scoreboard.

But even with all that going for them, the Reds still couldn't beat the Cubs, losing to Chicago, 3–2. The game was halted after the eighth inning due to rain. The Reds announced the attendance at 51,864, but there were hundreds of empty seats at the start of the game, no doubt due to the damp conditions and temperatures in the low 40s.

Mario Soto started for the Reds and gave up solo home runs in the first and second. He then allowed only four more hits, while striking out 10. His mound opponent, journeyman Doug Bird, was keeping the Reds off the scoreboard. The Reds finally pushed a run across in the seventh, but the Cubs came right back with what proved to be the game-winner on a disputed play in the top of the eighth.

With runners on first and second and two out, Reds reliever Bob Shirley threw high and inside to Leon Durham. Durham threw up his hands; the ball struck his bat and rolled towards Ron Oester, who threw to first for the final out.

But home plate umpire John Kibler ruled the ball had hit Durham. Reds manager John McNamara was ejected after a long argument with Kibler. Rain was falling and one reporter estimated at least an inch fell while the two debated the call. The next batter, Keith Moreland, then singled home a run, giving the Cubs a 3–1 lead. The Reds scored one in the eighth, but with the rain falling heavily, Kibler called a halt to the action after the final out of the inning. Fifty-one minutes later, with only 42 fans left in the stands, the game was officially declared over.

The poor weather conditions didn't detract from the usual Opening Day hoopla: The 62nd and largest Findlay Market Parade made its festive way down Race Street and through Fountain Square on schedule. Mike Luken, parade chairman, said there "about 3000 marchers, a few more than last year."

Luken owns Brighton Poultry, Fish and Seafood in the market, and he had fixed a 28-foot float in the form of a shrimp boat. "It's a dandy," admired Luken. "It's going to take the best float award. I'm the boss [of the parade], so I give it to myself."

You can't call Dick Grunden a fair-weather fan. The 81-year-old from Celina, Ohio, might have been excused for staying home instead of braving 42-degree temperatures, rain and gusty winds that buffeted Riverfront Stadium. "This will be 61 years without missing an opening day," he said. "I don't want to break my streak." [*Cincinnati Enquirer and Cincinnati Post*]

## Opening Day Trivia

| | |
|---|---|
| Star of the Game | Chicago Pitcher Doug Bird |
| Weather | 44°; Cloudy |
| Attendance | 51,864 |
| Notable | Debut of Mr. Red Race on Scoreboard |
| Rating | ☹ |

## April 5, 1982

| CHICAGO | ab | r | h | bi | CINCINNATI | ab | r | h | bi |
|---|---|---|---|---|---|---|---|---|---|
| Wills 2b | 4 | 1 | 2 | 1 | Oester 2b | 4 | 0 | 1 | 1 |
| Bowa ss | 4 | 1 | 1 | 0 | Driessn 1b | 3 | 0 | 0 | 0 |
| Bucknr 1b | 4 | 0 | 3 | 0 | Cncpcn ss | 4 | 0 | 1 | 0 |
| Durham rf | 3 | 0 | 1 | 0 | Cedeno cf | 4 | 0 | 0 | 0 |
| Morelnd c | 4 | 1 | 3 | 2 | Bench 3b | 4 | 1 | 1 | 0 |
| S.Hdrsn lf | 2 | 0 | 0 | 0 | Hshldr rf | 4 | 0 | 2 | 0 |
| Sndbrg 3b | 3 | 0 | 0 | 0 | Hurdle lf | 3 | 0 | 0 | 0 |
| Waller cf | 3 | 0 | 0 | 0 | Vail ph | 1 | 0 | 1 | 1 |
| Bird p | 2 | 0 | 0 | 0 | Mlinerpr | 0 | 0 | 0 | 0 |
| Morals ph | 1 | 0 | 0 | 0 | Trevino c | 3 | 0 | 0 | 0 |
| L.Smith p | 0 | 0 | 0 | 0 | Soto p | 1 | 0 | 0 | 0 |
| Hernndz p | 0 | 0 | 0 | 0 | Barrnc ph | 1 | 1 | 1 | 0 |
| | | | | | Shirley p | 0 | 0 | 0 | 0 |
| | | | | | Kern p | 0 | 0 | 0 | 0 |
| | | | | | Lndsty ph | 1 | 0 | 0 | 0 |
| Total | 30 | 3 | 10 | 3 | Total | 33 | 2 | 7 | 2 |

Chicago 110 000 01—3
Cincinnati 000 000 11—2
E—Buckner, Wills. DP—Cincinnati 1. LOB—Chicago 5, Cincinnati 10. 2B—Barranca. HR—Wills (1), Moreland (1). SB—Durham.

| | IP | H | R | ER | BB | SO |
|---|---|---|---|---|---|---|
| **Chicago** | | | | | | |
| Bird W, 1-0 | 7 | 5 | 1 | 1 | 2 | 1 |
| L.Smith | ⅔ | 1 | 1 | 0 | 0 | 0 |
| Hernandez S, 1 | ⅓ | 1 | 0 | 0 | 1 | 0 |
| **Cincinnati** | | | | | | |
| Soto L, 0-1 | 7 | 6 | 2 | 2 | 1 | 10 |
| Shirley | ⅔ | 3 | 1 | 1 | 0 | 0 |
| Kern | ⅓ | 1 | 0 | 0 | 0 | 0 |

Game called after 8 innings, rain.
HBP—Shirley (Durham). Wild Pitch—Soto. T—2:19. A—51,864.

## 1982 Opening Day Schedule

| April 5 | National League | |
|---|---|---|
| | **Chi vs. Cin** | |
| **April 6** | **National League** | |
| SF vs. LA | | StL vs. Hous |
| Mont vs. Pitts (PP) | | Atl vs. SD |
| NY vs. Phil (PP) | | |

# A Shocker! Opener Fails To Sell Out
## Only 42,892 See Reds Defeat Braves

**1983**

*In 1983, Cincinnati fans saw a most unusual sight on Opening Day: thousands of empty seats in the upper deck of Riverfront Stadium.*

### 1983 OPENING DAY SCHEDULE

| APRIL 4 | NATIONAL LEAGUE | |
|---|---|---|
| | ATL vs. CIN | |
| APRIL 5 | NATIONAL LEAGUE | |
| MONT vs. CHI | | PHIL vs. NY |
| SD vs. SF | | PITTS vs. STL |
| | LA vs. HOUS | |

For the first time since Riverfront Stadium opened, the Reds failed to sell out a regularly scheduled opener. Only 42,892 bought tickets, some 10,000 short of the usual sellout crowd.

The 1972 opener drew only 37,695, but that Opening Day was delayed by a strike.

In 1983, the club had no excuse. The team's worst season ever the year before (a record 101 losses), combined with anger over President and General Manager Dick Wagner, whom fans blamed for dismantling the Big Red Machine, kept thousands of fans home in protest. Eight red-seat sections in center field stood empty at game time. No one could blame the weather. It was 57 degrees and sunny.

For much of the 1983 opener, the Reds played as though it was still 1982. They fell behind 3–0, and committed two errors, a balk and a baserunning blunder. But in the end, they prevailed over the Atlanta Braves, 5–4.

Ron Oester started the Reds comeback with a two-run homer in the bottom of the third. The Braves still led, 4–2, when the Reds rallied to tie the score in the sixth. Gary Redus homered, Concepcion walked and stole second, and scored on a single by Johnny Bench.

In the eighth, Eddie Milner singled, stole second and scored the go-ahead run on Concepcion's single. Tom Hume pitched the ninth inning in relief of Mario Soto and earned a save. Soto picked up the win, the first of what would be four straight Opening Day victories.

The game was delayed several minutes in the second inning when Redus crashed into the center-field wall after catching a long drive off the bat of Glenn Hubbard. Racing back, Redus lost track of where the wall was and just as he turned his back to the field to catch the ball, he hit the wall face first. He held onto the ball, but suffered abrasions about the mouth. After treatment, he remained in the lineup.

One of the notable absences at the opener was field announcer Paul Sommerkamp, who missed his first game after 2,470 consecutive games. Sommerkamp was ill and returned to duty a few days later.

Despite the lack of a sellout, the Opening Day ceremonies proceeded as usual: *The pre-game parade [was] described by Findlay Market Association officials as the largest ever. Units in the parade ranged from an elaborate "Wizard of Oz" set to an ordinary bread truck, from politicians in convertibles to a person dressed as an oyster.*

*Before the game, fans were entertained by the Roger Bacon High School Band and the Lakota High School Chorale.* [*Cincinnati Enquirer and Cincinnati Post*]

### OPENING DAY TRIVIA

| STAR OF THE GAME | REDS SHORTSTOP DAVE CONCEPCION |
|---|---|
| WEATHER | 57°; SUNNY |
| ATTENDANCE | 42,892 |
| NOTABLE | 10,000 EMPTY SEATS |
| RATING | ◐◐◐ |

### APRIL 4, 1983

| Atlanta | ab | r | h | rbi | Cincinnati | ab | r | h | rbi |
|---|---|---|---|---|---|---|---|---|---|
| Butler, cf | 5 | 1 | 1 | 0 | Redus, lf | 4 | 1 | 1 | 1 |
| Ramirez, ss | 4 | 0 | 1 | 0 | Milner, cf | 4 | 1 | 1 | 0 |
| Wash'ton, rf | 3 | 0 | 0 | 1 | C'cepcion, ss | 3 | 1 | 1 | 1 |
| Murphy, lf | 2 | 0 | 0 | 0 | Bench, 3b | 4 | 1 | 2 | 1 |
| Horner, 3b | 3 | 1 | 0 | 0 | Hume, p | 0 | 0 | 0 | 0 |
| Chambliss, 1b | 4 | 1 | 1 | 2 | Driessen, 1b | 3 | 0 | 0 | 0 |
| Hubbard, 2b | 3 | 1 | 0 | 0 | Oester, 2b | 3 | 1 | 1 | 2 |
| Bedrosian, p | 0 | 0 | 0 | 0 | Jones, rf | 3 | 0 | 0 | 0 |
| Benedict, c | 3 | 0 | 1 | 0 | Trevino, c | 2 | 0 | 0 | 0 |
| Niekro, p | 3 | 0 | 1 | 0 | Soto, p | 2 | 0 | 0 | 0 |
| Royster, 2b | 1 | 0 | 0 | 0 | Landestoy, ph | 1 | 0 | 0 | 0 |
| | | | | | Kr'chicki, 3b | 0 | 0 | 0 | 0 |
| Totals | 31 | 4 | 5 | 3 | Totals | 29 | 5 | 6 | 5 |

Atlanta............1 2 0  0 0 1  0 0 0—4
Cincinnati........0 2 0  0 0 2  0 1 x—5

| Atlanta | IP. | H. | R. | ER. | BB. | SO. |
|---|---|---|---|---|---|---|
| Niekro | 7 | 4 | 4 | 4 | 2 | 2 |
| Bedrosian (L. 0-1) | 1 | 2 | 1 | 1 | 0 | 0 |

| Cincinnati | IP. | H. | R. | ER. | BB. | SO. |
|---|---|---|---|---|---|---|
| Soto (W. 1-0) | 8 | 5 | 4 | 2 | 4 | 5 |
| Hume (Save 1) | 1 | 0 | 0 | 0 | 0 | 1 |

Game-winning RBI—Concepcion.
E—Concepcion, Oester. DP—Atlanta 1. LOB—Atlanta 7, Cincinnati 2. 2B—Butler, Benedict, Bench. HR—Chambliss (1), Oester (1), Redus (1). SB—Concepcion, Milner. SH—Ramirez. SF—Washington. HBP—By Soto (Hubbard). Balk—Soto. T—2:22. A—42,892.

# 1984 It's a Blast!
## New Fireworks Celebrate Reds Win over Mets

*Catcher Dan Billardello greets Mario Soto after his Opening Day shutout. This was the second of four consecutive Opening Day wins for Soto.*

The Cincinnati Reds made wholesale changes in the off-season, including the removal of the unpopular President and General Manager Dick Wagner, but none of the changes delighted the Opening Day crowd like the new fireworks display that filled the sky in a colorful salute to the first victory of the year, an 8–1 win over the Mets.

The fireworks, the innovation of interim club president (and former president in the 1970s) Bob Howsam, also followed each Cincinnati home run. Eddie Milner was the first to be saluted with a blast following his second-inning home run.

The fireworks came as a surprise to the fans—and the players.

"It kind of scared me at first," admitted Milner. "I thought they were shooting at me."

Despite the changes, thousands of Reds fans skipped Opening Day for the second consecutive year, leaving the Reds short of a sellout. The club announced the attendance as 46,000.

The stay-at-homes missed a convincing Opening Day win, and the many other attractions Howsam introduced for the 1984 season. One change—the lowering of the outfield fences from 12 feet to 8 feet—immediately affected the game. Milner's second-inning homer, and Dave Concepcion's four-bagger in the seventh would have hit off the top of the old wall. Mets outfielder Darryl Strawberry reached above the wall in the sixth to rob Milner of his second home run.

Other innovations included a beer garden behind the blue seats in left field, and a pitching simulation for fans that featured a radar gun.

Mario Soto pitched a complete game for the Reds, allowing seven hits, and striking out eight. The Reds scored seven runs in the first two innings to give Soto all the help he needed. Newly acquired Dave Parker singled in two runs in his first at-bat as a Red.

Opening Day was also a big day for Tony Perez, back with the Reds since the infamous trade of 1976, and Johnny Bench: *[Bench] wasn't in uniform for the first time in 15 years. But he wore a spectacular plush purple sports jacket and led the Opening Day parade as grand marshal. Bench rode in the parade just ahead of Cincinnati Mayor Arnold Bortz. While everybody recognized Bench and applauded, few people recognized the mayor.*

*The biggest ovation at the ballpark went to a player who didn't even get in the game. When the Reds were introduced in pre-game ceremonies, Tony Perez received a thunderous 30-second standing ovation.*

*Dave Parker left 20 Opening Day passes for his family and friends. He had them scattered throughout the park, including right field, where his sister Betsy was located. "She's the most verbal one in the family," he chuckled. "I wanted her out there to keep me on my toes."*

**[Cincinnati Enquirer and Cincinnati Post]**

### OPENING DAY TRIVIA

| | |
|---|---|
| STAR OF THE GAME | REDS PITCHER MARIO SOTO |
| WEATHER | 60°; PARTLY CLOUDY |
| ATTENDANCE | 46,000 |
| NOTABLE | FIRST FIREWORKS FOLLOWING HRs & VICTORY |
| RATING | ●●●○ |

### APRIL 2, 1984

```
NEW YORK              CINCINNATI
            ab r h bi            ab r h bi
Backman 2b   3 0 1 0  Redus lf    5 1 1 0
Oquendo ss   3 0 0 0  Milner cf   4 2 3 3
Hernandz 1b  4 0 0 0  Concepcin ss 3 2 1 1
Foster lf    4 0 1 0  Parker rf   4 1 2 2
Strawbry rf  4 1 2 1  Househldr rf 0 0 0 0
Wilson cf    4 0 2 0  Driessen 1b 3 0 1 1
Brooks 3b    4 0 1 0  Esasky 3b   4 0 1 1
Hodges c     3 0 0 0  Oester 2b   4 0 0 0
Torrez p     0 0 0 0  Billardello c 4 1 2 0
Lynch p      1 0 0 0  Soto p      4 1 1 0
Jones ph     1 0 0 0
Swan p       0 0 0 0
Staub ph     1 0 0 0
Tidrow p     0 0 0 0
Totals      32 1 7 1  Totals     35 8 12 8

New York.........010 000 000—1
Cincinnati.......340 000 10x—8

Game-winning RBI—Parker (1).
DP—New York 1, Cincinnati 2. LOB—New York 6, Cincinnati 5. 2B—Redus, Esasky, Billardello, Milner, Driessen. HR—Strawberry (1), Milner (1), Concepcion (1). SB—Milner (1).

New York         IP   H   R  ER  BB  SO
Torrez (L 0-1).. 1 1-3 6   6   6   1   0
Lynch .......... 2 2-3 4   1   1   1   1
Swan ...........  3    2   1   1   1   1
Tidrow .........  1    0   0   0   0   1
Cincinnati
Soto (W 1-0)....  9    7   1   1   1   8
HBP—by Soto (Oquendo). T—2:12. A—46,000.
```

### 1984 OPENING DAY SCHEDULE

| APRIL 2 | NATIONAL LEAGUE | |
|---|---|---|
| | **NY vs. CIN** | |
| APRIL 3 | NATIONAL LEAGUE | |
| StL vs. LA | | Mont vs. Hous |
| Chi vs. SF | | Phil vs. Atl |
| | Pitts vs. SD | |

# Rose Blooms in Snow Showers
## Full House Cheers Pete as Reds Down Expos

*1985*

*Cesar Cedeno sprints off the field during the fifth inning blizzard. The wild day of weather also included rain and sunshine.*

After two years of failing to sell out the traditional home opener, the fans returned in full force for the 1985 opener, and were rewarded with a 4–1 Cincinnati victory over the Montreal Expos, highlighted by two hits and three RBIs by Pete Rose. The attendance of 52,971 set a new record (later broken).

Credit the fans' return to renewed interest sparked by Rose's homecoming (in August 1984) that resurrected a dead franchise. The novelty of the new distaff owner, Marge Schott, also made headlines. Schott made her love of the team well known, and in particular she championed the traditions of Opening Day. She sent the new baseball commissioner, Peter Ueberroth, an invitation to the opener from her pet St. Bernard, Schottzie, and Ueberroth was on hand to help Schott throw out the first pitch.

The newfound enthusiasm was not marred by the news that the American League had violated the long-standing tradition of the baseball season beginning in Cincinnati. The AL scheduled two games to start earlier than the Reds 2:05 start. But the Reds publicity department announced that they had still granted 285 press credentials, 50 more than normal.

The only thing that dampened the enthusiasm of the crowd was one of the more schizophrenic weather days in Opening Day history. Riverfront experienced sunshine, snow, hail, wind gusts and rain.

By the end of the fifth inning, which was delayed nearly an hour by two snow delays, only a scattering of fans were left.

But they had seen the Reds score three times in the fifth, to take a 3–0 lead. With two out, starter and winner Mario Soto singled and went to third on a double by Eric Davis. Rose then doubled down the left-field line to drive in two runs. He scored on a single by Dave Parker. Rose picked up another RBI in the seventh.

Soto lost his shutout bid in the seventh and retired to the bench on this cold day. Carl Willis earned the save with two shutout innings.

Quips about the amazing weather filled the newspapers: *When was the last time you went to a game that was interrupted by snow? There were two such delays and it was snowing again as the game ended. They should have abandoned "Take Me Out to the Ballgame" for "Jingle Bells."*

Press box idlers drew up a lineup that included Mario Snowto, Dave Parka, and St. Nick Esasky. Marty Brennaman could hardly have been blamed had he ended his broadcast by announcing: "This one belongs to the sleds."

Hot dogs and beer, rock 'n roll and baseball in the snow. That was Opening Day. The game began with thermometers reading 39 degrees. Almost an hour into the game, rain came down in sheets, then abruptly turned to snow. From time to time, the sun shone brilliantly. [**Cincinnati Enquirer and Cincinnati Post**]

### April 8, 1985

| MONTREAL | ab | r | h | bi | CINCINNATI | ab | r | h | bi |
|---|---|---|---|---|---|---|---|---|---|
| Raines lf | 4 | 0 | 0 | 0 | EDavis cf | 3 | 2 | 1 | 0 |
| Winningham cf | 2 | 0 | 0 | 0 | Rose 1b | 3 | 1 | 2 | 3 |
| Dawson rf | 4 | 0 | 0 | 0 | Milner cf | 0 | 0 | 0 | 0 |
| Driessen 1b | 4 | 0 | 1 | 0 | Parker rf | 3 | 0 | 2 | 1 |
| Brooks ss | 4 | 1 | 1 | 0 | Cedeno lf | 4 | 0 | 2 | 0 |
| Law 2b | 3 | 0 | 0 | 0 | Esasky 3b | 4 | 0 | 0 | 0 |
| Wallach 3b | 3 | 0 | 2 | 1 | Concepcion ss | 3 | 0 | 1 | 0 |
| Fitzgerald c | 3 | 0 | 0 | 0 | Oester 2b | 3 | 0 | 0 | 0 |
| Rogers p | 2 | 0 | 0 | 0 | Bilardello c | 4 | 0 | 1 | 0 |
| Burke p | 0 | 0 | 0 | 0 | Soto p | 3 | 1 | 2 | 0 |
| Dilone ph | 0 | 0 | 0 | 0 | Willis p | 1 | 0 | 0 | 0 |
| Roberge p | 0 | 0 | 0 | 0 | | | | | |
| Totals | 29 | 1 | 4 | 1 | Totals | 31 | 4 | 11 | 4 |

Montreal  000 000 100—1
Cincinnati 000 030 10x—4

Game Winning RBI—Rose (1).
DP—Montreal 2. LOB—Montreal 5, Cincinnati 8. 2B—Wallach, Driessen, EDavis, Rose, Cedeno. 3B—Brooks. SB—EDavis 2 (2), Milner (1).

| | IP | H | R | ER | BB | SO |
|---|---|---|---|---|---|---|
| **Montreal** | | | | | | |
| Rogers L,0-1 | 4⅔ | 8 | 3 | 3 | 1 | 3 |
| Burke | 2⅓ | 2 | 1 | 1 | 3 | 1 |
| Roberge | 1 | 1 | 0 | 0 | 1 | 1 |
| **Cincinnati** | | | | | | |
| Soto W,1-0 | 7 | 4 | 1 | 1 | 2 | 5 |
| Willis S,1 | 2 | 0 | 0 | 0 | 2 | 1 |

T—2:32. A—52,971.

### Opening Day Trivia

| | |
|---|---|
| Star of the Game | Reds First Baseman Pete Rose |
| Weather | 39°; Snow, Sun, Sleet, You Name It |
| Attendance | 52,971 |
| Notable | AL Starts Games Before Cincinnati |
| Rating | ●●●● |

### 1985 Opening Day Schedule

| April 8 | National League | |
|---|---|---|
| | **Mont vs. Cin** | |
| April 9 | National League | |
| LA vs. Hous | | StL vs. NY |
| SD vs. SF | | Pitts vs. Chi |
| | Atl vs. Phil | |

# Soto Struggles But Wins Again
## Fourth Straight Victory Sets All-Time Opening Day Record

*Facing the threat of cancellation of the Findlay Market Parade, community donors gave $4,000 to cover insurance costs and preserve the annual rite.*

Mario Soto extended his Opening Day win streak to four straight as the Reds beat the Phillies, 7–4.

For several days before the opener, another streak was in jeopardy. The Findlay Market Parade, which was celebrating its 66th annual appearance, was nearly derailed by insurance expenses. Cincinnati attorney lawyer Stanley Chesley and Blue Cross/Blue Shield combined to contribute $4,000 to cover the liability insurance and the parade went on as scheduled.

| OPENING DAY TRIVIA | |
|---|---|
| STAR OF THE GAME | REDS CENTER FIELDER ERIC DAVIS |
| WEATHER | 77°; SUNNY |
| ATTENDANCE | 54,960 |
| NOTABLE | PARADE RESCUED AT LAST MOMENT |
| RATING | ◍◍◍◍ |

Another Opening Day tradition could not be saved. For the second straight year, the American League scheduled an opener to begin before the first pitch at Riverfront. Despite pleas from the club and even the Cincinnati City Council, the schedule-makers were not swayed, and the major league season officially began in Detroit at 1:30. The Reds and Phillies kicked off the NL season at 2:05.

For the second year in a row, the club set an Opening Day attendance record. On a perfect day for baseball, 54,960 jammed Riverfront. They cheered Governor Richard Celeste, decked out in a Schottzie cap as he threw out the first pitch, but then groaned as the Phillies jumped out to a quick lead. A double, an error by Soto, an intentional walk, a sacrifice fly and a double by Von Hayes gave the Phillies three runs. But the Reds took the lead in the bottom of the second, the big blow a three-run homer by Eric Davis.

A home run by Mike Schmidt tied it at 4–4 in the third, but Bo Diaz drove in Tracy Jones with the Reds' fifth run in the bottom of the third, and Soto and reliever Ron Robinson shut down the Phillies over the last six innings.

The Reds added two final tallies in the fifth on a solo homer by Dave Parker and an RBI single by Dave Concepcion. All the Reds runs were charged to Steve Carlton.

The controversy over the early starting time of the opener in Detroit drew considerable attention: *Cincinnati vice-mayor J. Kenneth Blackwell led a tongue-in-cheek war of words* against the Tigers for upstaging Cincinnati. One of Blackwell's suggestions was that Greater Cincinnati International Airport suspend all landing rights for planes from the Detroit area.

The City Hall controversy did not raise the same response from the Reds. "We have so many things planned," [Owner Marge Schott] said, "I don't know when we'll start the game. We're going to turn our clocks back."

"Who cares if they play a half hour before us?" [said player/manager Pete Rose] "Maybe they'll get a rain delay." **[Cincinnati Enquirer and Cincinnati Post]**

| 1986 OPENING DAY SCHEDULE | |
|---|---|
| APRIL 7 | NATIONAL LEAGUE |
| PHIL VS. CIN | SD VS. LA |
| APRIL 8 | NATIONAL LEAGUE |
| MONT VS. ATL | CHI VS. STL |
| NY VS. PITTS | SF VS. HOUS |

### APRIL 7, 1986

| Phila'phia | ab | r | h | rbi | Cincinnati | ab | r | h | rbi |
|---|---|---|---|---|---|---|---|---|---|
| Redus, lf | 5 | 1 | 1 | 0 | Davis, cf-lf | 5 | 1 | 1 | 3 |
| Thompson, cf | 3 | 1 | 0 | 0 | Bell, 3b | 4 | 0 | 1 | 0 |
| Samuel, 2b | 4 | 0 | 0 | 0 | Parker, rf | 4 | 1 | 3 | 1 |
| Schmidt, 3b | 3 | 2 | 2 | 1 | Esasky, 1b | 3 | 1 | 0 | 0 |
| Wilson, rf | 3 | 0 | 0 | 1 | Jones, lf | 2 | 1 | 1 | 0 |
| Hayes, 1b | 4 | 0 | 2 | 2 | Milner, cf | 1 | 0 | 0 | 0 |
| Daulton, c | 3 | 0 | 0 | 0 | C'cepcion, ss | 4 | 1 | 2 | 1 |
| Jeltz, ss | 3 | 0 | 2 | 0 | Diaz, c | 4 | 1 | 3 | 1 |
| Carlton, p | 2 | 0 | 0 | 0 | Oester, 2b | 4 | 0 | 2 | 1 |
| Andersen, p | 0 | 0 | 0 | 0 | Soto, p | 2 | 1 | 0 | 0 |
| Lefebvre, ph | 1 | 0 | 0 | 0 | Robinson, p | 2 | 0 | 0 | 0 |
| Hudson, p | 0 | 0 | 0 | 0 | | | | | |
| G. Gross, ph | 1 | 0 | 0 | 0 | | | | | |
| Totals | 32 | 4 | 7 | 4 | Totals | 35 | 7 | 13 | 7 |

Philadelphia........3 0 1 0 0 0 0 0 0—4
Cincinnati...........0 4 1 0 2 0 0 0 x—7

| Philadelphia | IP. | H. | R. | ER. | BB. | SO. |
|---|---|---|---|---|---|---|
| Carlton (L, 0-1) | 4* | 9 | 7 | 7 | 2 | 0 |
| Andersen | 1 | 1 | 0 | 0 | 0 | 1 |
| Hudson | 3 | 3 | 0 | 0 | 0 | 0 |

| Cincinnati | IP. | H. | R. | ER. | BB. | SO. |
|---|---|---|---|---|---|---|
| Soto (W, 1-0) | 5⅔ | 6 | 4 | 1 | 3 | 0 |
| Robinson (Save 1) | 3⅓ | 1 | 0 | 0 | 0 | 2 |

*Pitched to three batters in fifth.

Game-winning RBI—Diaz.
E—Soto. DP—Philadelphia 2, Cincinnati 1. LOB—Philadelphia 6, Cincinnati 6. 2B—Redus, Hayes 2, Schmidt, Parker 2. HR—Schmidt (1), Davis (1), Parker (1). SB—Thompson, Jones. SH—Thompson. SF—Wilson. T—2:21. A—54,960.

# Nine-Run Inning Buries Expos
## Davis Leads Charge in 11–5 Win

*Eric Davis led the big day of offense with a home run, two RBIs, two stolen bases and three runs scored.*

On a cool, cloudy and drizzly Opening Day, it was up to the Reds to provide the sunshine, and they did with a nine-run rally in the fourth inning that clinched an 11–5 win over Montreal.

The nine-run inning was the biggest ever for the Reds on Opening Day.

Up until the fateful fourth, the game and the day offered little to cheer about. The thermometer topped out at 47 degrees and rain drizzled on the Findlay Market parade. And the Reds fell behind almost immediately.

Tom Browning started for the Reds and gave up eight hits and five runs, including a home run to the second batter he faced. He left after three innings with the fans booing and the Reds trailing, 5–2.

The Reds historic fourth began innocently with a walk to Eric Davis, who had homered in the second. Davis worked his way to third on a stolen base and a ground out, and he scored on a Bo Diaz single. Terry Francona then homered to tie the game at 5–5. But the Reds were just beginning. Ron Oester walked and scored on Paul O'Neill's pinch-hit double. O'Neill came home on a single by Kal Daniels. Daniels scored moments later when Barry Larkin—making his Opening Day debut—homered to make the score 9–5.

Dave Parker doubled and scored on Davis' single. Davis stole second and eventually scored on a wild pitch. On a day of offense, Davis was the star. He had one hit, stole two bases, scored two runs and had one RBI, and that was just in the fourth inning.

The Reds bullpen then took charge, shutting out the Expos over the final six innings. The quartet of Bill Landrum, Frank Williams, Ron Robinson and John Franco gave up only four hits.

For the third year in a row, the American League preempted the Reds start by scheduling two games to begin before the opening pitch in Cincinnati. The Cincinnati City Council again rose up in protest. But the Reds faithful did not let the audacity of the AL—or the miserable weather—ruin their day: *Hundreds braved rain and temperatures in the 40s to watch the Findlay Market parade on Fifth and Race streets. Grand Marshal [was] Walt Disney World's Mickey Mouse.*

*Joe Dippong, also called "Mr. Spoons," danced and slapped a pair of kitchen spoons. A big rig of horses tugged a beer carriage and then came a familiar, unmistakable mug. Dave Rose, Pete Rose's brother and lookalike, aimed a giant beer can car down the street.*

*A.B. "Happy" Chandler, a former baseball commissioner, [threw] out the ceremonial first pitch. The Opening Day game was broadcast over the Armed Forces Radio Network.*

**[*Cincinnati Enquirer* and *Cincinnati Post*]**

### 1987 Opening Day Schedule

| April 6 | National League |
|---|---|
| Mont vs. Cin | SD vs. SF |
| | LA vs. Hous |

| April 7 | National League |
|---|---|
| Phil vs. Atl | StL vs. Chi |
| | Pitts vs. NY |

### Opening Day Trivia

| | |
|---|---|
| Star of the Game | Reds Center Fielder Eric Davis |
| Weather | 47°; Damp, Cloudy |
| Attendance | 55,166 |
| Notable | Reds Score 9 Runs in the Fourth |
| Rating | ●●●● |

### April 6, 1987

| Montreal | ab | r | h | rbi | Cincinnati | ab | r | h | rbi |
|---|---|---|---|---|---|---|---|---|---|
| Powell, lf | 5 | 1 | 1 | 1 | Daniels, lf | 5 | 1 | 2 | 1 |
| Webster, rf | 5 | 1 | 2 | 2 | Larkin, ss | 4 | 1 | 1 | 2 |
| Galarraga, 1b | 4 | 1 | 2 | 0 | Parker, rf | 5 | 1 | 1 | 0 |
| Brooks, ss | 4 | 0 | 1 | 0 | Davis, cf | 3 | 3 | 3 | 2 |
| Wallach, 3b | 4 | 1 | 3 | 1 | Bell, 3b | 5 | 0 | 0 | 0 |
| Law, 2b | 4 | 0 | 1 | 0 | Diaz, c | 4 | 1 | 1 | 1 |
| Reed, c | 4 | 0 | 1 | 0 | Francona, 1b | 4 | 1 | 2 | 2 |
| Nichols, cf | 2 | 1 | 1 | 0 | Oester, 2b | 3 | 2 | 1 | 0 |
| W'ham, ph-cf | 1 | 0 | 0 | 0 | Browning, p | 0 | 0 | 0 | 0 |
| Youmans, p | 2 | 0 | 0 | 0 | Garcia, ph | 0 | 0 | 0 | 1 |
| Campbell, p | 0 | 0 | 0 | 0 | Landrum, p | 0 | 0 | 0 | 0 |
| McGaffigan, p | 0 | 0 | 0 | 0 | O'Neill, ph | 1 | 1 | 1 | 1 |
| Foley, ph | 1 | 0 | 0 | 0 | Williams, p | 1 | 0 | 0 | 0 |
| Sorensen, p | 0 | 0 | 0 | 0 | McC'don, ph | 1 | 0 | 0 | 0 |
| Parrett, p | 0 | 0 | 0 | 0 | Robinson, p | 0 | 0 | 0 | 0 |
| Candaele, ph | 1 | 0 | 0 | 0 | Franco, p | 0 | 0 | 0 | 0 |
| Totals | 37 | 5 | 12 | 4 | Totals | 36 | 11 | 12 | 10 |

Montreal .......... 2 2 1 0 0 0 0 0 0 — 5
Cincinnati ........ 0 1 1 9 0 0 0 0 x — 11

| Montreal | IP | H | R | ER | BB | SO |
|---|---|---|---|---|---|---|
| Youmans (L, 0-1) | 3⅓ | 5 | 7 | 7 | 2 | 0 |
| Campbell | 0 | 3 | 3 | 3 | 0 | 0 |
| McGaffigan | 1⅔ | 3 | 1 | 1 | 1 | 2 |
| Sorensen | 2 | 1 | 0 | 0 | 0 | 0 |
| Parrett | 1 | 0 | 0 | 0 | 1 | 1 |

| Cincinnati | IP | H | R | ER | BB | SO |
|---|---|---|---|---|---|---|
| Browning | 3 | 8 | 5 | 5 | 1 | 3 |
| Landrum (W, 1-0) | 1 | 0 | 0 | 0 | 0 | 0 |
| Williams | 3 | 4 | 0 | 0 | 0 | 3 |
| Robinson | 1 | 0 | 0 | 0 | 0 | 0 |
| Franco | 1 | 0 | 0 | 0 | 0 | 0 |

Pitched to three batters in fourth.
Game-winning RBI—O'Neill.
E—Brooks, Nichols, Daniels. DP—Cincinnati 2. LOB—Montreal 6, Cincinnati 6. 2B—Galarraga, Wallach, Powell, Law, O'Neill, Parker, Daniels. 3B—Oester. HR—Webster (1), Davis (1), Larkin (1), Francona (1). SB—Davis 2, Daniels. SF—Garcia. WP—McGaffigan. T—2:33. A—55,166.

# 1988 Reds Win Comedy of Errors
## Even Clocks Have "Setback"

*Manager Pete Rose greets Kal Daniels after his sixth-inning home run. Daniels had the game-winning hit in the 12th inning.*

### APRIL 4, 1988

| ST LOUIS | | | | | CINCINNATI | | | | |
|---|---|---|---|---|---|---|---|---|---|
| | ab | r | h | bi | | ab | r | h | bi |
| Coleman lf | 6 | 0 | 1 | 0 | Larkin ss | 5 | 1 | 2 | 0 |
| OSmith ss | 5 | 0 | 2 | 0 | Cncpcn 2b | 3 | 0 | 1 | 0 |
| Herr 2b | 4 | 0 | 0 | 0 | RMrphy p | 0 | 0 | 0 | 0 |
| Horner 1b | 4 | 0 | 0 | 0 | ONeill 1b | 2 | 0 | 0 | 0 |
| McGee cf | 6 | 1 | 1 | 0 | Daniels lf | 4 | 1 | 2 | 2 |
| Pndltn 3b | 3 | 1 | 1 | 1 | EDavis cf | 5 | 0 | 0 | 0 |
| Dayley p | 0 | 0 | 0 | 0 | TJones rf | 5 | 1 | 2 | 0 |
| Worrell p | 0 | 0 | 0 | 0 | BDiaz c | 5 | 0 | 1 | 0 |
| Pagnozzi c | 2 | 0 | 0 | 0 | Esasky 1b | 3 | 0 | 0 | 0 |
| McWlms p | 0 | 0 | 0 | 0 | Franco p | 0 | 0 | 0 | 0 |
| TPena c | 4 | 0 | 0 | 0 | McCInd ph | 0 | 0 | 0 | 0 |
| Peters p | 0 | 0 | 0 | 0 | PPerry p | 0 | 0 | 0 | 0 |
| Forsch p | 0 | 0 | 0 | 0 | Sabo 3b | 5 | 1 | 1 | 0 |
| Lake c | 0 | 0 | 0 | 0 | Soto p | 1 | 0 | 0 | 0 |
| Lindmn rf | 5 | 1 | 1 | 0 | Collins ph | 1 | 0 | 0 | 0 |
| Magrane p | 2 | 1 | 1 | 3 | Rijo p | 0 | 0 | 0 | 0 |
| Terry p | 0 | 0 | 0 | 0 | Tredwy 2b | 2 | 1 | 1 | 0 |
| Oquend 3b | 2 | 0 | 1 | 0 | | | | | |
| Totals | 43 | 4 | 8 | 4 | Totals | 41 | 5 | 10 | 2 |

StLouis      010 300 000 000—4
Cincinnati   001 002 100 001—5

Two outs when winning run scored.
Game Winning RBI — Daniels (1).
E—Soto 2, Concepcion, Pendleton, Horner. DP—StLouis 3. LOB—StLouis 11, Cincinnati 8. HR—Magrane (1), Daniels (1). SB—Larkin (1), Coleman 2 (2), OSmith (1), Sabo (1). S—Herr, Larkin.

| | IP | H | R | ER | BB | SO |
|---|---|---|---|---|---|---|
| **StLouis** | | | | | | |
| Magrane | 6 | 9 | 4 | 3 | 2 | 2 |
| Terry | 2/3 | 0 | 0 | 0 | 0 | 0 |
| Dayley | 0 | 0 | 0 | 0 | 1 | 0 |
| Worrell | 2 1/3 | 0 | 0 | 0 | 0 | 1 |
| Peters | 1/3 | 0 | 0 | 0 | 1 | 1 |
| Forsch L,0-1 | 2 | 0 | 1 | 1 | 2 | 0 |
| McWilms | 1/3 | 1 | 0 | 0 | 0 | 1 |
| **Cincinnati** | | | | | | |
| Soto | 5 | 6 | 4 | 3 | 4 | 1 |
| Rijo | 2 | 1 | 0 | 0 | 1 | 2 |
| RMurphy | 2 | 1 | 0 | 0 | 0 | 1 |
| Franco | 2 | 0 | 0 | 0 | 0 | 0 |
| PPerry W,1-0 | 1 | 0 | 0 | 0 | 2 | 0 |

Magrane pitched to 2 batters in the 7th, Dayley pitched to 1 batter in the 7th. WP—McWilliams. BK—Soto 2, Magrane 2. Umpires—Home, Weyer; First, McSherry; Second, Montague; Third, Brocklander. T—3:43. A—55,438.

### OPENING DAY TRIVIA

| | |
|---|---|
| STAR OF THE GAME | REDS LEFT FIELDER KAL DANIELS |
| WEATHER | 69°; SUNNY |
| ATTENDANCE | 55,438 |
| NOTABLE | 12-INNING GAME |
| RATING | ○○○○ |

The baseball season—and the silly season—began with the Reds beating St. Louis, 5–4, in 12 innings. This farce of a game featured five errors, four balks, a three-run homer by a pitcher and a starting time that only Cincinnatians recognized.

For the fourth straight year, the American League showed its junior league status—some would say bush-league status—by scheduling openers before the first pitch was thrown in Cincinnati. Cincinnati City Council railed against the insolence of the schedule-makers. Council voted to have the clock in the Reds clubhouse set back to 12:05 at game time (which according to official time keepers was 2:05).

No matter what the time of the start of the game, it was soon apparent the players were not quite ready. In the St. Louis second, Willie McGee singled and then made his way to third on a botched pick-off play by Reds starter Mario Soto, and a balk. He scored on a ground out. A balk by St. Louis starter Joe Magrane helped the Reds to the tying run in the second.

Magrane then put his team ahead with a three-run home run in the fourth. Kal Daniels made it 4–2 with a home run in the sixth, and the Reds tied it with two unearned runs, courtesy of Cardinal miscues. The tying run scored after first baseman Bob Horner fielded a bunt and threw to an empty first base. No one covered.

Fortunately, the Reds bullpen was immune from all the daffiness, and four relievers combined to hold the Cardinals scoreless over the final eight innings. The Reds finally pushed over the winning run in the bottom of the 12th on a single by Daniels.

The start was Mario Soto's last Opening Day appearance. He finished his career with a 4-1 record in openers. His six starts, four victories and five decisions remain Cincinnati Opening Day records.

Columnists and reporters mused on the annual spring rituals of Opening Day: Lights! Camera! Schottzie! Opening Day! On the scoreboard they listed the names of longtime Opening Day fans. More than one had been to 60 openers.

*There is spring in the air, happy chatter in the streets and Soto on the mound. It's Opening Day in Cincinnati and, on that account, all's right with the world.*

*Despite numerous reports to to Greater Cincinnati employers of the deaths of loved ones, local funeral homes found it to be a normal day. "We haven't had any deaths at all," said Marilyn Holt of the Gump-Holt Funeral Home in Western Hills. "I'd let you talk to my husband, but he's down at the stadium." [Cincinnati Enquirer and Cincinnati Post]*

### 1988 OPENING DAY SCHEDULE

| APRIL 4 | NATIONAL LEAGUE | |
|---|---|---|
| STL vs. CIN | | SF vs. LA |
| | NY vs. MONT | |
| APRIL 5 | NATIONAL LEAGUE | |
| PITTS vs. PHIL | | CHI vs. ATL |
| | SD vs. HOUS | |

# 1989
## Ovations Greet Pete
### Betting Scandal Forgotten in Reds Win Over LA; O'Neil(l) Goes 4–4

*Paul O'Neill beats the throw from Los Angeles right fielder Mike Marshall to score the Reds' first run in the second inning. Mike Scioscia's tag was a split-second late.*

### 1989 OPENING DAY SCHEDULE

| April 3 | National League | |
|---|---|---|
| LA vs. Cin | | SF vs. SD |
| | StL vs. NY | |
| April 4 | National League | |
| Atl vs. Hous | | Phil vs. Chi |
| | Pitts vs. Mont | |

Paul O'Neill was the star of the 1989 opener, with four hits, including a home run and a double and three RBIs, as he powered the Reds past the defending world champions Los Angeles Dodgers, 6–4.

O'Neill upstaged his manager, Pete Rose, who was clearly the star of the pre-game ceremonies. The fans voiced their support for their beleaguered and beloved manager who was under investigation for tax and gambling violations. This was Rose's first appearance in Cincinnati since the story broke in the off-season and he received two thunderous ovations from the 55,438 on hand for Opening Day.

Rose's teammate on the Big Red Machine, Johnny Bench, threw out the first pitch and the attention of the spectators turned to the game.

O'Neill's big day began with two blunders. First, when O'Neill tried on his new 1989 uniform, he discovered his name was spelled with just one "l" on the back of his jersey. Then, in his first at-bat in the bottom of the second, O'Neill thought he had drawn a walk and trotted down to first, only to be met by a smiling Eddie Murray. The Dodger first baseman notified O'Neill that it was only ball three.

As it turned out, the Dodgers might have been better off with the walk, for an embarrassed "O'Neil" then doubled and started a three-run rally that put wiped out an early 2–0 Dodger lead.

In the bottom of the third, O'Neill launched a three-run homer that put the Reds up, 6–2.

The O'Neill performance in his misspelled jersey prompted *Cincinnati Enquirer* sportswriter Tim Sullivan to observe, "Paul O'Neill had one L of an Opening Day."

After giving up two more runs, Reds starter Danny Jackson, who earned the win, gave way to the Reds bullpen of Rob Dibble and John Franco who pitched four scoreless innings.

Opening Day drew another sell-out crowd: *[Gregory] Lynn of New Richmond, Ohio, was among eight determined fans who braved the elements Sunday and early [Monday] in an all-night vigil to get some of the 220 standing room only tickets that went on sale at 9 a.m. Most of the more than 200 people who joined the line left empty-handed. The tickets were sold out by about 9:15 a.m. Meanwhile, the ticket scalpers along Third Street near the stadium were asking $75 per ticket.*

*By 10 a.m. the parade route was beginning to fill with baseball fans and red was the color of the day. Slogans like "We're Reds Hot!" and "Turn Dem Dodgers Blue" were painted on banners, signs and car windows all over town.* **[Cincinnati Enquirer and Cincinnati Post]**

### April 3, 1989

| LOS ANGELES | ab | r | h | bi | CINCINNATI | ab | r | h | bi |
|---|---|---|---|---|---|---|---|---|---|
| Randolph 2b | 4 | 1 | 1 | 0 | Larkin ss | 4 | 0 | 1 | 1 |
| Griffin ss | 4 | 0 | 0 | 0 | Sabo 3b | 5 | 0 | 1 | 0 |
| Gibson lf | 4 | 2 | 2 | 2 | EDavis cf | 3 | 0 | 0 | 0 |
| Murray 1b | 4 | 0 | 0 | 0 | Daniels lf | 3 | 1 | 0 | 0 |
| Marshall rf | 2 | 1 | 0 | 0 | Benzinger 1b | 4 | 1 | 1 | 0 |
| Shelby cf | 4 | 0 | 0 | 0 | ONeill rf | 4 | 2 | 4 | 3 |
| Hamilton 3b | 4 | 0 | 1 | 0 | Franco p | 0 | 0 | 0 | 0 |
| Scioscia c | 4 | 0 | 1 | 1 | Reed c | 4 | 1 | 2 | 1 |
| Belcher p | 1 | 0 | 0 | 0 | Oester 2b | 2 | 1 | 0 | 0 |
| Morgan p | 0 | 0 | 0 | 0 | Dibble p | 0 | 0 | 0 | 0 |
| MHatcher ph | 1 | 0 | 0 | 0 | Winningham rf | 1 | 0 | 0 | 0 |
| Crews p | 0 | 0 | 0 | 0 | DJackson p | 2 | 0 | 0 | 0 |
| Stubbs ph | 1 | 0 | 0 | 0 | LHarris 2b | 2 | 0 | 1 | 0 |
| Horton p | 0 | 0 | 0 | 0 | | | | | |
| Totals | 33 | 4 | 5 | 3 | Totals | 34 | 6 | 10 | 5 |

Los Angeles.................. 200 110 000—4
Cincinnati.................... 033 000 00x—6

E—Sabo, Benzinger, Reed, Belcher, Murray. DP—Los Angeles 1. LOB—Los Angeles 4, Cincinnati 8. 2B—ONeill. HR—ONeill (1), Gibson (1). SB—Gibson (1), Marshall (1), LHarris (1). SF—Larkin.

| Los Angeles | IP | H | R | ER | BB | SO |
|---|---|---|---|---|---|---|
| Belcher L,0-1 | 2⅓ | 6 | 6 | 4 | 2 | 1 |
| Morgan | ⅔ | 0 | 0 | 0 | 0 | 1 |
| Crews | 3 | 2 | 0 | 0 | 1 | 2 |
| Horton | 2 | 2 | 0 | 0 | 0 | 1 |
| **Cincinnati** | | | | | | |
| DJackson W,1-0 | 5 | 4 | 4 | 2 | 2 | 3 |
| Dibble | 2 | 1 | 0 | 0 | 0 | 2 |
| Franco S,1 | 2 | 0 | 0 | 0 | 0 | 2 |

Umpires—Home, Kibler; First, Quick; Second, Davis; Third, Gregg.
T—2:47. A—55,385.

### OPENING DAY TRIVIA

| | |
|---|---|
| Star of the Game | Reds Right Fielder Paul O'Neill |
| Weather | 69°; Sunny |
| Attendance | 55,385 |
| Notable | "O'Neil" Goes 4-for-4 |
| Rating | ○○○○ |

# And on the Seventh Game...
## Opening Day Finally Arrives After Reds Open on Road

*Marge Schott refused to allow baseball's labor problems interfere with the tradition of Opening Day in Cincinnati.*

| OPENING DAY TRIVIA | |
|---|---|
| STAR OF THE GAME | REDS PITCHER TOM BROWNING |
| WEATHER | 57°; CLOUDY |
| ATTENDANCE | 38,384 |
| NOTABLE | REDS OPEN ON ROAD |
| RATING | ○○○○ |

What baseball's labor problems taketh away, Marge Schott taketh back.

On the verge of losing the traditional Opening Day game and parade to the month-long labor squabble that forced baseball to delay the start of the season, the Reds owner and the Findlay Market parade organizers forged a makeshift Opening Day that contained all the familiar festivities.

The Reds did their part by winning the delayed opener, 2–1, over San Diego. It was the Reds' seventh game—and seventh straight win—under new manager Lou Piniella. Scheduled to open at home on April 2 against the Astros, the Reds opened on April 9 in Houston. It was only the fifth time in Reds history the club opened on the road.

The April 17 home opener was originally scheduled as a 7:35 start, but Schott changed the time to 2:05. The parade organizers, who had announced the parade would have to be cancelled, scrambled to make last-minute arrangements and wound up having their biggest parade ever, with 125 entries.

All that was missing was the sold-out crowd. Only 38,384 attended on a cool Tuesday afternoon; most observers blamed the lack of a sellout on the lingering anger over baseball's labor problems.

The Reds opened the scoring in the second inning. Two walks and two singles gave Cincinnati a 2–0 lead. Tom Browning pitched shutout baseball until the seventh when he gave up one run on a Benito Santiago home run. That brought in the bullpen and the first home appearance of the self-proclaimed "Nasty Boys." Norm Charlton and Randy Myers pitched three scoreless innings, with Meyers picking up the save.

The papers played up the unusual aspects of celebrating "Opening Day" seven games into the schedule and role of owner Marge Schott: *All right, it wasn't really Opening Day. It was really Marge's day. The Reds president kicked the whole circus into gear, walking up and down Race Street during the morning parade, greeting children, accepting the well wishes of senior citizens and feeling generally victorious that she salvaged some of the tradition connected with the Reds' home opener.*

*On-field pregame ceremonies at Riverfront Stadium [included] entertainment from the U.S. Army Reserves 100th Division Band, a special pigeon release, and a parade featuring Princess Schottzie, the elephant.*

*Reds management went all out for this game, dressing the hustling grounds crew and blue-seat-level ushers in tuxedos.*

*Joyce [Bless] took the day off from her job at McAlpin's. "It's not hard getting the day off," Mrs. Bless said. "Opening Day is a holiday here—isn't it?"* **[Cincinnati Enquirer and Cincinnati Post]**

| 1990 OPENING DAY SCHEDULE (ALL GAMES DELAYED TO APRIL 9TH) | |
|---|---|
| APRIL 2 | NATIONAL LEAGUE |
| HOUS vs. CIN | ATL vs. SF |
| SD vs. LA | |
| APRIL 3 | NATIONAL LEAGUE |
| NY vs. PITTS | STL vs. MONT |
| CHI vs. PHIL | |

### APRIL 17, 1990

| SAN DIEGO | ab | r | h | bi | CINCINNATI | ab | r | h | bi |
|---|---|---|---|---|---|---|---|---|---|
| Roberts 3b | 4 | 0 | 0 | 0 | Sabo 3b | 5 | 0 | 0 | 0 |
| Schiraldi p | 0 | 0 | 0 | 0 | BHatchr lf | 4 | 0 | 3 | 1 |
| Cora ph | 1 | 0 | 0 | 0 | Larkin ss | 4 | 0 | 3 | 0 |
| Alomar 2b | 3 | 0 | 3 | 0 | EDavis cf | 3 | 0 | 0 | 0 |
| TGwynn rf | 4 | 0 | 0 | 0 | ONeill rf | 4 | 0 | 0 | 0 |
| JaClark 1b | 3 | 0 | 1 | 0 | Bnzngr 1b | 1 | 1 | 1 | 0 |
| JCarter lf | 4 | 0 | 0 | 0 | Oliver c | 3 | 1 | 0 | 0 |
| Santiago c | 4 | 1 | 3 | 1 | Duncan 2b | 4 | 0 | 2 | 1 |
| Jackson cf | 4 | 0 | 0 | 0 | Brownng p | 3 | 0 | 0 | 0 |
| Tmpltn ss | 3 | 0 | 0 | 0 | Charlton p | 0 | 0 | 0 | 0 |
| Benes p | 1 | 0 | 0 | 0 | Wnghm ph | 1 | 0 | 0 | 0 |
| Abner ph | 1 | 0 | 1 | 0 | Myers p | 0 | 0 | 0 | 0 |
| Grant p | 0 | 0 | 0 | 0 | | | | | |
| JeClark ph | 1 | 0 | 1 | 0 | | | | | |
| Pglrulo 3b | 0 | 0 | 0 | 0 | | | | | |
| Parent ph | 1 | 0 | 0 | 0 | | | | | |
| Totals | 34 | 1 | 9 | 1 | Totals | 32 | 2 | 9 | 2 |

San Diego      000 000 100—1
Cincinnati     020 000 00x—2

DP—San Diego 1. LOB—San Diego 9, Cincinnati 11. HR—Santiago (2). SB—BHatcher (3), Larkin (3).

| San Diego | IP | H | R | ER | BB | SO |
|---|---|---|---|---|---|---|
| Benes L,1-1 | 5 | 7 | 2 | 2 | 4 | 6 |
| Grant | 1 | 1 | 0 | 0 | 0 | 1 |
| Schiraldi | 2 | 1 | 0 | 0 | 1 | 2 |
| Cincinnati | | | | | | |
| Browning W,2-0 | 6 | 7 | 1 | 1 | 1 | 2 |
| Charlton | 2 | 1 | 0 | 0 | 1 | 4 |
| Myers S,3 | 1 | 1 | 0 | 0 | 1 | 1 |

Browning pitched to 1 batter in the 7th.
BK—Benes, Schiraldi. Umpires—Home, Williams; First, McSherry; Second, Montague; Third, Davidson. T—2:46. A—38,384.

# 1991
# Rings Around the Astros
## Browning Stars as Ring-Laden Champs Bury Houston, 6–2

*Jose Rijo, MVP of the 1990 World Series, shows off his World Series ring on Opening Day, 1991.*

The defending World Champions ruled over baseball and the airwaves on Opening Day, 1991. There were four Opening Day preview shows on local TV stations, complete coverage of the Findlay Market parade, and of course the game itself. It was "All Reds, All the Time" coverage, appropriate for the "Wire-to-Wire" winners of 1990.

And the Reds did not disappoint the huge crowd of 55,205, defeating the Astros, 6–2, behind the pitching—and hitting—of Tom Browning. Browning had one of the best overall performances by a Cincinnati Opening Day starter, pitching 8⅓ innings of five-hit baseball, and driving in three runs with a bases-loaded double.

A crew of replacement umpires filled in for the regular umpires who had reached agreement on a new contract only a few hours before the game began.

The opener began with more than the usual pomp and circumstance. With a light drizzle falling, Reds owner Marge Schott handed out the 1990 World Series rings to the players. She announced each by last name only. Picking up Rob Dibble's ring, she introduced him with, "Another little cutie, named Dibble." More than one observer believed Schott simply did not know the players' full names.

Ohio Governor George Voinovich joined the festivities by serving as Schott's umbrella-holder, keeping the rain off the Reds "first lady."

Mrs. Schott also took time to continue an unusual Opening Day tradition, rubbing a tuft of Schottzie's fur on manager Lou Piniella's chest before the game began. Schott had first tried the same good-luck charm prior to the 1990 season.

The Astros scored first in the fourth inning on a Craig Biggio home run, but the Reds quickly responded in their half of the inning. Barry Larkin tied the game with a lead-off home run. Chris Sabo put the Reds ahead with a double that drove in Paul O'Neill. Then, with two outs and the bases loaded, Browning shot one into the right-field corner for a bases-clearing double and a 5–1 Reds lead.

The Opening Day crowd dodged the occasional rain drops and enjoyed the festive day: *The 71st annual parade was the largest—165 entries—and best ever. It included 14 marching bands (up from a mere two last year), a handful of decorated floats and "Captain Bingo," an elderly gent in a blue cape; a "Free Pete Rose" float; and the Lakota High School band wearing Reds hats.*

*[Marge Schott] wore a big white sweater celebrating the Reds 1990 World Championship.*

*David and Karen Barker of Loveland were playing hooky. Her explanation to her bosses: "Personal business.". "I'm on sick leave," said her husband, laughing. "I got better, though, this morning."* **[Cincinnati Enquirer and Cincinnati Post]**

### 1991 OPENING DAY SCHEDULE

| April 8 | National League | |
|---|---|---|
| Hous vs. Cin | | Phil vs. NY |
| | Mont vs. Pitts | |
| April 9 | National League | |
| SF vs. SD | | StL vs. Chi |
| | LA vs. Atl | |

### OPENING DAY TRIVIA

| | |
|---|---|
| Star of the Game | Reds Pitcher Tom Browning |
| Weather | 74°; Partly Cloudy with Drizzle |
| Attendance | 55,205 |
| Notable | Record 9th Straight Opening Day Win |
| Rating | ●●●●○ |

### April 8, 1991

| Houston | ab | r | h | bi | Cincinnati | ab | r | h | bi |
|---|---|---|---|---|---|---|---|---|---|
| Yelding ss | 4 | 1 | 1 | 0 | Hatcher rf | 4 | 0 | 0 | 0 |
| Finley cf | 3 | 0 | 0 | 1 | Larkin ss | 4 | 2 | 2 | 1 |
| Biggio c | 4 | 1 | 2 | 1 | O'Neill lf | 4 | 1 | 1 | 0 |
| Gonzalez lf | 3 | 0 | 0 | 0 | Davis cf | 4 | 0 | 2 | 0 |
| Caminiti 3b | 3 | 0 | 1 | 0 | Morris 1b | 4 | 0 | 1 | 1 |
| Bagwell 1b | 3 | 0 | 0 | 0 | Sabo 3b | 4 | 1 | 1 | 1 |
| Rhodes lf | 3 | 0 | 1 | 0 | J Reed c | 2 | 1 | 1 | 0 |
| McLe 2b | 3 | 0 | 0 | 0 | Duncan 2b | 1 | 1 | 0 | 0 |
| Scott p | 1 | 0 | 0 | 0 | Doran 2b | 2 | 0 | 1 | 0 |
| Rohde ph | 1 | 0 | 0 | 0 | Browning p | 3 | 0 | 1 | 3 |
| Clancy p | 0 | 0 | 0 | 0 | Myers p | 0 | 0 | 0 | 0 |
| Rmirez ph | 1 | 0 | 0 | 0 | Dibble p | 0 | 0 | 0 | 0 |
| Kile p | 0 | 0 | 0 | 0 | | | | | |
| Totals | 29 | 2 | 5 | 2 | Totals | 32 | 6 | 10 | 6 |

| | | | | | | |
|---|---|---|---|---|---|---|
| Houston | 0 0 0 | 1 0 0 | 0 0 1—2 |
| Cincinnati | 0 0 0 | 5 1 0 | 0 0 X—6 |

DP—Houston 1, Cincinnati 2. E—McLemore (1). LOB—Houston 4, Cincinnati 5. 2B—O'Neill (1), Sabo (1), Browning (1). 3B—Yelding (1). HR—Biggio (1), Larkin (1). SB—Hatcher. SF—Finley.

| | IP | H | R | ER | BB | SO |
|---|---|---|---|---|---|---|
| **Houston** | | | | | | |
| Scott L,0-1 | 4 | 5 | 5 | 5 | 1 | 1 |
| Clancy | 3 | 3 | 1 | 1 | 1 | 1 |
| Kile | 1 | 2 | 0 | 0 | 1 | 1 |
| **Cincinnati** | | | | | | |
| Browning W,1-0 | 8⅓ | 5 | 2 | 2 | 1 | 4 |
| Myers | 0 | 0 | 0 | 0 | 2 | 0 |
| Dibble S,1 | ⅔ | 0 | 0 | 0 | 0 | 1 |

Myers pitched to 2 batters in the 9th.
Umpires—Home, Ballino; First, Floras; Second, Bruns; Third, Urlage.
T—2:21. A—55,205.

# All Good Things Come to an End

## Reds Lose First Opener in 10 Years as Padres Win in 9th, 4–3

*Elephants were a regular attraction on Opening Day during Marge Schott's tenure as Reds CEO.*

Joe Nuxhall, fresh off a victory over prostate cancer, threw out the first pitch of the 1992 season, a one-bouncer to Reds catcher Joe Oliver. The 55-foot change of pace still earned the "Old Left-Hander" a standing ovation from the crowd.

Jose Rijo, the Reds starter, wasn't so lucky. Rijo pitched a complete game, but took the loss, 4–3, as San Diego defeated the Reds and snapped Cincinnati's nine-year Opening Day winning streak.

Padre outfielder Darrin Jackson hit a solo home run in the top of the ninth to break a 3–3 tie. Former Reds reliever, Randy Myers, pitched the ninth inning and saved the win for starter Bruce Hurst.

As had been the case nearly every year since 1985, the American League started its season before the first pitch of the Reds opener. But unlike in years past, the Cincinnati City Council and the print media gave little attention to the transgressors, apparently resigned to this breach of Opening Day protocol. The Reds did, however, continue the practice of playing the first game in the National League season.

The Reds took a 2–0 lead in the fourth inning on RBI singles by Glenn Braggs and Reggie Sanders. The Padres tied it in the fifth, and led, 3–2, after a Fred McGriff home run in the sixth.

In the seventh, the Reds tied the score and had Jacob Brumfield on third and Rijo on second with no outs. Bip Roberts grounded to third baseman Gary Sheffield who trapped Brumfield off third and tagged him out. Sheffield then threw back to second to nab Rijo who had wandered too far off the bag. That was the Reds last scoring threat.

Reds owner Marge Schott invited not one, but two elephants—Princess Schottzie and Mai Tai—to the pre-game ceremonies. Neither the elephants, the fans, nor Joe Oliver were discouraged by the damp and windy conditions: *Throngs of people gathered downtown in the early-morning chill, jockeying for the best spot to watch the Findlay Market Parade. High school bands entertained early arrivals on Riverfront Plaza. Ushers in the blue seats were decked out in tuxedos.*

*Chip Goff was first in line at the west plaza ticket office at 4:30 a.m.—7 ½ hours before 700 standing-room-only tickets went on sale. "It was pretty lonely out here at 4:30," Goff said. "Pretty cold, too. But I couldn't take a chance on missing this."*

*When Reds catcher Joe Oliver climbed out of bed at 5 a.m. his temperature was 100, his body ached and he was overtaken by nausea. For a moment, Oliver considered begging out of the lineup. Then he came to his senses.*

*"You start thinking about Opening Day," Oliver said, "and they'd have to wheel you off the field in a gurney."* **[Cincinnati Enquirer and Cincinnati Post]**

### OPENING DAY TRIVIA

| | |
|---|---|
| STAR OF THE GAME | PADRES CENTER FIELDER DARRIN JACKSON |
| WEATHER | 60°; DAMP AND BREEZY |
| ATTENDANCE | 55,356 |
| NOTABLE | END OF 9-YEAR OPENING DAY WIN STREAK |
| RATING | ●●● |

### 1992 OPENING DAY SCHEDULE

| APRIL 6 | NATIONAL LEAGUE |
|---|---|
| SD vs. CIN | SF vs. LA |
| MONT vs. PITTS | NY vs. STL |
| **APRIL 7** | **NATIONAL LEAGUE** |
| CHI vs. PHIL | ATL vs. HOUS |

# 1993 Reds Win Opener for Tony
## New Reds Skipper Pops the Bubbly After 2–1 Win

*New manager Tony Perez stands with his starting lineup prior to the 1993 opener.*

It was a perfect day to cool the champagne. With temperatures in the low 40s, the Reds beat the Expos in the opener, 2–1, and retired to the clubhouse to open the bubbly to celebrate this first win for new manager Tony Perez.

"Why not champagne?" asked a happy Perez. "The first win as a manager? That's a big one."

Perez was named manager in the off-season, replacing Lou Piniella. As it turned out, he had few chances to drink more champagne as the Reds fired him after 44 games (20-24).

But on Opening Day, 1993, all was smiles around the Reds clubhouse and in the grandstand where a then-record Opening Day crowd of 55,456 watched the game. (It ranks second all time, behind the 2000 opener.)

The game began on a cheerful note for the Perez family with Pituka Perez, Tony's wife, throwing out the first pitch. Then the Reds played nearly flawless ball to keep her husband happy the rest of the way. Jose Rijo pitched eight shut-out innings for the win.

The Reds new left fielder, Kevin Mitchell, made his Reds debut memorable with the game-winning hit in the fifth inning and by throwing out a runner at the plate in the eighth.

Chris Sabo started the scoring in the second with a solo home run off Montreal starter Dennis Martinez. Martinez matched zeros with Rijo until the Reds fifth, when the Reds loaded the bases with two out. Mitchell hit a hard grounder to third base that Frank Bolick backhanded. The rotund "Mitch," not known for his speed, barreled down the line and beat the throw with a last-second lunge across the first base bag that left the spent Red sprawled on the turf. The run scored, giving the Reds a 2–0 lead.

Montreal finally scored in the ninth when Larry Walker hit a two-out home run off reliever Rob Dibble.

Marge Schott, who had been placed on suspension by Major League Baseball for insensitive remarks, did not participate in the on-field activities, but she was not forgotten by the fans. *Marge Schott and Pete Rose may be banned from baseball—but they found plenty of supporters in [the] annual Opening Day parade. The parade's sponsor—The Findlay Market Association—displayed a big "We Love Marge" sign on its float near the front of [the] 155-unit parade. Cincinnati radio station WARM 98 [handed] out more than 10,000 cardboard fans emblazoned with Mrs. Schott's likeness.. Charlotte Jones of Western Hills wore a No. 14 uniform jersey in honor of Pete Rose as she stood on a float. Jerry Springer was grand marshall.*

*Skies were murky gray and the temperature a cool 40 degrees when the parade began at 11 a.m.* **[Cincinnati Enquirer and Cincinnati Post]**

| OPENING DAY TRIVIA | |
|---|---|
| STAR OF THE GAME | REDS PITCHER JOSE RIJO |
| WEATHER | 45°; CLOUDY |
| ATTENDANCE | 55,456 |
| NOTABLE | 2ND-LARGEST OPENING DAY CROWD EVER |
| RATING | ◐◐◐◐ |

| 1993 OPENING DAY SCHEDULE | |
|---|---|
| APRIL 5 | NATIONAL LEAGUE |
| MONT VS. CIN | LA VS. FLA |
| COL VS. NY | ATL VS. CHI |
| | PHIL VS. HOUS |
| APRIL 6 | NATIONAL LEAGUE |
| SD VS. PITTS | SF VS. STL |

### April 5, 1993

| MONTREAL | ab | r | h | bi | CINCINNATI | ab | r | h | bi |
|---|---|---|---|---|---|---|---|---|---|
| DeShields 2b | 4 | 0 | 1 | 0 | Roberts 2b | 4 | 1 | 1 | 0 |
| Alou lf | 4 | 0 | 0 | 0 | Kelly cf | 4 | 0 | 2 | 0 |
| Grissom cf | 4 | 0 | 0 | 0 | Larkin ss | 3 | 0 | 0 | 0 |
| Walker rf | 4 | 1 | 1 | 1 | Mitchell lf | 3 | 0 | 1 | 1 |
| Bolick 3b | 4 | 0 | 0 | 0 | Hernandez lf | 0 | 0 | 0 | 0 |
| Vanderwal 1b | 3 | 0 | 1 | 0 | Sabo 3b | 4 | 1 | 2 | 1 |
| Cordero ss | 3 | 0 | 0 | 0 | Milligan 1b | 4 | 0 | 2 | 0 |
| Laker c | 3 | 0 | 2 | 0 | Dibble p | 0 | 0 | 0 | 0 |
| DeMartinez p | 2 | 0 | 1 | 0 | RSanders rf | 3 | 0 | 0 | 0 |
| Wood ph | 1 | 0 | 0 | 0 | Oliver c | 1 | 0 | 0 | 0 |
| Fassero p | 0 | 0 | 0 | 0 | Rijo p | 3 | 0 | 0 | 0 |
| | | | | | Costo 1b | 0 | 0 | 0 | 0 |
| Totals | 32 | 1 | 6 | 1 | Totals | 29 | 2 | 8 | 2 |

Montreal  0 0 0 0 0 0 0 0 1—1
Cincinnati  0 1 0 0 1 0 0 0 x—2

E—De Martinez (1), Larkin (1). DP—Montreal 2, Cincinnati 1. LOB—Montreal 4, Cincinnati 7. 2B—Milligan (1). 3B—Laker (1). HR—Walker (1), Sabo (1). SB—DeShields (1), Roberts (1). CS—Kelly (1).

| | IP | H | R | ER | BB | SO |
|---|---|---|---|---|---|---|
| **Montreal** | | | | | | |
| DeMartinez L,0-1 | 7 | 8 | 2 | 2 | 3 | 5 |
| Fassero | 1 | 0 | 0 | 0 | 1 | 0 |
| **Cincinnati** | | | | | | |
| Rijo W,1-0 | 8 | 5 | 0 | 0 | 0 | 5 |
| Dibble S,1 | 1 | 1 | 1 | 1 | 0 | 2 |

WP—De Martinez. Umpires—Home, Tata; First, Gregg. Second, Davis. Third, Bonin. T—2:19. A—55,456.

# 1994 The Year of Two Openers
## Game One: The Easter Sunday Night Opener That Marge Doesn't Count

*Reggie Sanders' home run was one of the few highlights for the Reds in 1994 Sunday night opener.*

It was the first game of the year, but it wasn't "Opening Day."

The Reds opened the 1994 season against the St. Louis Cardinals at Riverfront, but the Reds owner Marge Schott refused to consider it the traditional opener since the game was on Easter Sunday evening.

"It's a holy day and people complained about it," she explained. She held back the bunting, pre-game ceremonies and the parade for the following day, a Monday afternoon game which she declared the real opener.

The Reds had lobbied to have the first game of the season when MLB and ESPN announced there would be a Sunday game. But soon after the Reds-Cardinals game was announced, Schott considered the ramifications of a Sunday night opener and declared the Reds would not honor it as the club's traditional Opening Day.

ESPN, and its game announcer Jon Miller, couldn't believe Schott had slammed the door shut on the baseball establishment. "Here is Major League Baseball's showcase game, on national TV, and they're allowing this person (Schott) for no logical reason to make it less than that," Miller complained. No doubt it looked that way to outsiders, but Miller, an outstanding broadcaster, was simply clueless about what made Opening Day so special in Cincinnati.

The fans of Cincinnati agreed with their owner. The Sunday opener didn't sell out—only 32,803 showed up for the evening game. With snow falling earlier in the day and temperatures in the 30s, the low turnout was not surprising, but Schott's decision was well received by a city that was used to celebrating its opener on a weekday afternoon.

Of course, the record books consider Sunday the official opening game, and so the Reds must be considered the losers of the 1994 opener. The Cardinals, behind the pitching and hitting of Bob Tewksbury, defeated Cincinnati, 6–4.

The Reds took a brief 3–1 lead in the second inning, but starter Jose Rijo gave up the tying runs in the third and the go-ahead runs in the fourth. Tewksbury had the big blow, a two-out, two-run double that put the Cardinals up, 5–3.

St. Louis scored again in the fifth, and although the Reds bullpen held the Cards after that, the Reds could not rally. Reggie Sanders homered in the sixth, but struck out with the bases loaded in the seventh.

The game was the first opener for Reds manager Davey Johnson, but he retired early after a misunderstanding with umpire Terry Tata in the fifth inning. *[Cincinnati Enquirer and Cincinnati Post]*

### 1994 OPENING DAY SCHEDULE

| APRIL 3 | NATIONAL LEAGUE |
|---|---|
| | StL vs. Cin |
| APRIL 4 | NATIONAL LEAGUE |
| NY vs. Chi | Mont vs. Hous |
| Pitts vs. SF | Phil vs. Col |
| | Atl vs. SD |
| APRIL 5 | NATIONAL LEAGUE |
| | Fla vs. LA |

### OPENING DAY TRIVIA

| | |
|---|---|
| STAR OF THE GAME | CARDINALS PITCHER BOB TEWKSBURY |
| WEATHER | 39° |
| ATTENDANCE | 32,803 |
| NOTABLE | 1ST PITCH BY NL PRES. LEONARD COLEMAN |
| RATING | ☹ |

### APRIL 3, 1994

| St. Louis | AB | R | H | BI | BB | SO | Avg. |
|---|---|---|---|---|---|---|---|
| Lankford cf | 5 | 2 | 3 | 2 | 0 | 1 | .600 |
| OSmith ss | 4 | 0 | 1 | 0 | 0 | 1 | .250 |
| Jefferies 1b | 4 | 0 | 2 | 0 | 1 | 0 | .500 |
| Zeile 3b | 5 | 1 | 1 | 0 | 0 | 1 | .200 |
| Whiten rf | 4 | 0 | 0 | 0 | 0 | 2 | .000 |
| Palacios p | 0 | 0 | 0 | 0 | 0 | 0 | --- |
| d-Perry ph | 1 | 0 | 0 | 0 | 0 | 0 | .000 |
| Perez p | 0 | 0 | 0 | 0 | 0 | 0 | --- |
| Gilkey lf | 4 | 1 | 2 | 1 | 0 | 0 | .500 |
| Alicea 2b | 2 | 1 | 0 | 2 | 2 | 0 | .000 |
| Pappas c | 3 | 1 | 1 | 0 | 1 | 0 | .333 |
| Tewksbury p | 2 | 0 | 1 | 2 | 0 | 0 | .500 |
| BJordan rf | 1 | 0 | 0 | 0 | 0 | 1 | .000 |
| Totals | 35 | 6 | 11 | 5 | 4 | 6 | |

| Cincinnati | AB | R | H | BI | BB | SO | Avg. |
|---|---|---|---|---|---|---|---|
| TFernandez 3b | 5 | 0 | 1 | 0 | 0 | 0 | .200 |
| Larkin ss | 3 | 0 | 0 | 0 | 2 | 1 | .000 |
| Morris 1b | 4 | 0 | 0 | 0 | 0 | 1 | .000 |
| Mitchell lf | 3 | 1 | 1 | 0 | 1 | 0 | .333 |
| RSanders rf | 4 | 2 | 2 | 1 | 0 | 1 | .500 |
| Kelly cf | 3 | 1 | 2 | 1 | 1 | 1 | .667 |
| Boone 2b | 4 | 0 | 1 | 0 | 0 | 1 | .250 |
| Oliver c | 2 | 0 | 1 | 1 | 0 | 0 | .333 |
| c-Howard ph | 1 | 0 | 0 | 0 | 0 | 1 | .000 |
| Dorsett c | 0 | 0 | 0 | 0 | 0 | 0 | --- |
| Rijo p | 0 | 0 | 0 | 0 | 0 | 0 | --- |
| a-LHarris ph | 1 | 0 | 0 | 0 | 0 | 0 | .000 |
| JRuffin p | 0 | 0 | 0 | 0 | 0 | 0 | --- |
| b-Branson ph | 1 | 0 | 0 | 0 | 0 | 0 | .000 |
| JBrantley p | 0 | 0 | 0 | 0 | 0 | 0 | --- |
| e-WGreene ph | 1 | 0 | 0 | 0 | 0 | 1 | .000 |
| Totals | 33 | 4 | 8 | 3 | 4 | 7 | |

| St. Louis | 102 210 000—6 11 1 |
|---|---|
| Cincinnati | 030 001 000—4 8 3 |

a-grounded out for Rijo in the 5th. b-popped out for JRuffin in the 7th. c-struck out for Oliver in the 8th. d-lined out for Palacios in the 9th. e-struck out for JBrantley in the 9th. E—Pappas (1), RSanders (1), Kelly (1), Boone (1). LOB—St. Louis 8, Cincinnati 7. 2B—Lankford (1), Tewksbury (1), Mitchell (1). HR—RSanders (1) off Tewksbury, Lankford (1) off Rijo. RBI—Lankford 2 (2), Gilkey (1), Tewksbury 2 (2), RSanders (1), Kelly (1), Oliver (1). SB—Gilkey (1), RSanders (1). CS—Alicea (1). S—OSmith, Tewksbury, Rijo. DP—St. Louis 1 (OSmith, Alicea and Jefferies).

| St. Louis | IP | H | R | ER | BB | SO | NP | ERA |
|---|---|---|---|---|---|---|---|---|
| Tewksbury W, 1-0 | 6 | 7 | 4 | 4 | 2 | 1 | 93 | 6.00 |
| Palacios | 2 | 1 | 0 | 0 | 2 | 4 | 48 | 0.00 |
| Perez S, 1 | 1 | 0 | 0 | 0 | 0 | 2 | 11 | 0.00 |
| Cincinnati | IP | H | R | ER | BB | SO | NP | ERA |
| Rijo L, 0-1 | 5 | 9 | 6 | 4 | 1 | 6 | 103 | 7.20 |
| JRuffin | 2 | 1 | 0 | 0 | 0 | 0 | 22 | 0.00 |
| JBrantley | 2 | 1 | 0 | 0 | 2 | 3 | 33 | 0.00 |

IBB—off JBrantley (Jefferies) 1. WP—Tewksbury, Palacios. PB—Oliver. Umpires—Home, Tata; First, Gregg; Second, Ripley; Third, Gorman. T—2:49. A—32,803.

# 1994: The Year of Two Openers
## Game Two: The Real Opener With Parade and Ceremonies

*The Reds and Findlay Market rolled out the Opening Day festivities for the second game of the 1994 season.*

It was the second opener in 18 hours at Riverfront Stadium, but the Monday afternoon game was the "real" inaugural as far as Reds owner Marge Schott and the fans of Cincinnati were concerned.

With Monday morning dawning bright and crisp, Schott and Reds fans shrugged off the Sunday night "opener" on ESPN like a groggy dream. All the trappings of Opening Day were on view Monday.

With 55,093 tickets sold, the game was officially a sellout, but several thousand no-shows made for plenty of empty seats at game time.

The Findlay Market parade kicked off at 11 a.m. with a record 180 entries. Parade chairman Jeff Gibbs dismissed the Sunday night game. "That was just the last exhibition game," he laughed. "It hasn't affected us at all. This is the biggest parade we've ever had."

Two elephants from the Cincinnati Zoo marched on the field prior to game time, Schott paraded her famous St. Bernard around the field, and the teams lined up on the foul lines for the traditional ceremonies. The clubs paused for a moment of silence for the late Gordy Coleman, the former Reds first baseman and longtime head of the club's speaker bureau.

The Reds responded to all the hoopla with a scintillating 10-inning triumph over the Cardinals. Left fielder Kevin Mitchell had the last hit of the game, a monstrous home run off the facing of the red seats in left field that broke a 4–4 tie and gave the Reds a 5–4 belated Opening Day win.

Mitchell had plenty of support as he went to the bat in the bottom of the 10th. Mitchell's grandmother, who was a guest of Marge Schott in her owner's box, had sent Mitchell a note in the bottom of the 10th inning urging her grandson to do well. "I'm looking down on you, so get me a good hit." Love, Gram.

Mitchell, who had been raised by his grandmother, Jose Whitfield, since he was nine, wasn't about to let her down.

The home run won the game for rookie Hector Carrasco, who made his first major league appearance as a reliever in the top of the tenth. Carrasco walked two and gave up a hit, but wriggled out of the bases-loaded situation.

The Reds took an early 4–0 lead on two-run homers by Reggie Sanders and Joe Oliver. The Cardinals fought back and tied it in the eighth, setting up the extra-inning fireworks.

Davey Johnson, experiencing his first Opening Day in Cincinnati, decided he liked the Monday opener just fine.

"I think Marge was right," said Johnson. "This is a good day for a parade, a good day for Opening Day. We'll just put an asterisk by that loss last night."

The press agreed: *The sun was shining Monday, and Reds fans were behaving as if this game against the Cardinals was really the first game. Never mind the National League Central standings with the Reds in last place with an 0–1 record. This was the one.* [**Cincinnati Enquirer and Cincinnati Post**]

| OPENING DAY TRIVIA | |
|---|---|
| STAR OF THE GAME | REDS LEFT FIELDER KEVIN MITCHELL |
| WEATHER | 57°; SUNNY |
| ATTENDANCE | 55,093 |
| NOTABLE | WALK-OFF HOME RUN |
| RATING | ⚾⚾⚾⚾⚾ |

### APRIL 4, 1994

| St. Louis | AB | R | H | BI | BB | SO | Avg. |
|---|---|---|---|---|---|---|---|
| Lankford cf | 4 | 0 | 1 | 0 | 2 | 2 | .444 |
| OSmith ss | 5 | 0 | 0 | 0 | 1 | 1 | .111 |
| Jefferies 1b | 6 | 0 | 2 | 0 | 0 | 1 | .400 |
| Zeile 3b | 4 | 1 | 1 | 0 | 1 | 0 | .222 |
| Whiten rf | 5 | 1 | 2 | 0 | 0 | 3 | .222 |
| BJordan lf | 5 | 0 | 1 | 0 | 0 | 2 | .167 |
| Murphy p | 0 | 0 | 0 | 0 | 0 | 0 | — |
| Alicea 2b | 5 | 1 | 2 | 2 | 0 | 1 | .286 |
| Pappas c | 2 | 1 | 1 | 0 | 3 | 0 | .400 |
| Cormier p | 1 | 0 | 0 | 0 | 0 | 0 | .000 |
| a-Oquendo ph | 1 | 0 | 0 | 0 | 0 | 0 | .000 |
| Habyan p | 0 | 0 | 0 | 0 | 0 | 0 | — |
| b-GPena ph | 1 | 0 | 1 | 0 | 0 | 0 | 1.000 |
| RRodriguez p | 0 | 0 | 0 | 0 | 0 | 0 | — |
| c-Perry ph | 1 | 0 | 0 | 0 | 0 | 0 | .500 |
| Sutcliffe p | 0 | 0 | 0 | 0 | 0 | 0 | — |
| Gilkey lf | 1 | 0 | 1 | 0 | 0 | 0 | .600 |
| Totals | 41 | 4 | 13 | 3 | 7 | 11 | |
| **Cincinnati** | AB | R | H | BI | BB | SO | Avg. |
| TFernandez 3b | 3 | 0 | 0 | 0 | 1 | 1 | .125 |
| Morris 1b | 5 | 0 | 2 | 0 | 0 | 0 | .222 |
| Larkin ss | 5 | 1 | 1 | 0 | 0 | 0 | .125 |
| Mitchell lf | 5 | 1 | 2 | 0 | 1 | 3 | .375 |
| RSanders rf | 4 | 1 | 2 | 2 | 0 | 0 | .500 |
| Kelly cf | 4 | 0 | 0 | 0 | 0 | 2 | .286 |
| Boone 2b | 3 | 1 | 1 | 0 | 1 | 0 | .286 |
| d-LHarris ph-2b | 1 | 0 | 0 | 0 | 0 | 0 | .000 |
| Oliver c | 3 | 1 | 2 | 1 | 0 | 0 | .333 |
| l-Walton pr | 0 | 0 | 0 | 0 | 0 | 0 | — |
| Dorsett c | 0 | 0 | 0 | 0 | 0 | 0 | — |
| Smiley p | 2 | 0 | 0 | 0 | 0 | 2 | .000 |
| Pugh p | 1 | 0 | 0 | 0 | 0 | 0 | .000 |
| McElroy p | 0 | 0 | 0 | 0 | 0 | 0 | — |
| JBrantley p | 0 | 0 | 0 | 0 | 0 | 0 | — |
| e-Howard ph | 1 | 0 | 0 | 0 | 0 | 0 | .000 |
| Carrasco p | 0 | 0 | 0 | 0 | 0 | 0 | — |
| Totals | 37 | 5 | 9 | 5 | 2 | 9 | |

```
St. Louis   000 003 010 0—4 13 1
Cincinnati  000 400 000 1—5  9 0
```

One out when winning run scored. a-popped out for Cormier in the 5th. b-singled for Habyan in the 6th. c-singled for RRodriguez in the 8th. d-fouled out for Boone in the 9th. e-flied out for JBrantley in the 9th. l-ran for Oliver in the 9th. E—Pappas (2). LOB—St. Louis 14, Cincinnati 7. 2B—Zeile (1), BJordan (1). HR—Mitchell (1) off Murphy, RSanders (2) off Cormier, Oliver (1) off Cormier. RBI—Alicea 2 (2), GPena (1), Mitchell (1), RSanders 2 (3), Oliver 2 (3). SB—Lankford (1), Larkin (1), RSanders (1). CS—Jefferies (1). DP—Cincinnati 1 (Kelly, Larkin and Morris).

| St. Louis | IP | H | R | ER | BB | SO | NP | ERA |
|---|---|---|---|---|---|---|---|---|
| Cormier | 4 | 5 | 4 | 4 | 0 | 5 | 69 | 9.00 |
| Habyan | 1 | 1 | 0 | 0 | 1 | 0 | 16 | 0.00 |
| RRodriguez | 2 | 2 | 0 | 0 | 2 | 3 | 34 | 0.00 |
| Sutcliffe | 1⅔ | 0 | 0 | 0 | 2 | 1 | 24 | 0.00 |
| Murphy L, 0-1 | ⅔ | 1 | 1 | 1 | 1 | 0 | 12 | 13.50 |
| **Cincinnati** | IP | H | R | ER | BB | SO | NP | ERA |
| Smiley | 5⅔ | 8 | 3 | 2 | 7 | 109 | | 4.76 |
| Pugh | 2 | 3 | 1 | 1 | 2 | 2 | 49 | 4.50 |
| McElroy | ⅔ | 0 | 0 | 0 | 1 | 0 | 13 | 0.00 |
| JBrantley | ⅔ | 1 | 0 | 0 | 0 | 1 | 11 | 0.00 |
| Carrasco W, 0-1 | 1 | 1 | 0 | 0 | 2 | 2 | 37 | 0.00 |

Balk—Sutcliffe. Umpires—Home, Gregg; First, Rippley; Second, Gorman; Third, Tata. T—3:47. A—55,093.

# Another Bizarre Opening Day
## 1995
### Players' Strike Delays Season; Parade Held 23 Days Before Game

*Stephanie Patton of Bridgetown heard plenty of cheers with her "Replacement Float" in the 1995 parade.*

The 1995 opener, originally scheduled for April 3, was not played until April 26, a delay of 23 days caused by the last-minute settlement of the player's strike which had begun during the 1994 season.

An agreement was reached on April 2, nullifying the owners' plans to open the season with replacement players.

With an agreement in hand, the clubs scrapped plans to open on April 3, and announced an abbreviated spring training of three weeks.

The last-minute agreement and the scuttling of the original opening date left the Findlay Market parade organizers with a difficult decision. If they held the parade as scheduled, there would be no game to follow. But the group decided to go ahead with the event.

"Too many people had invested too much time, energy and money to cancel it at the last second. We felt a responsibility to our people," explained parade chairman Kevin Luken.

The incongruity of an Opening Day parade with no Opening Day game made headlines around the country.

The parade drew only half the normal crowd, but the stalwarts prided themselves in keeping with tradition, and in thumbing their nose at Major League Baseball. The favorite entry was a 10-year-old Stephanie Patton pulling a little red wagon with a sign that proclaimed "Replacement Float."

Opening Day finally arrived on April 26. Chicago defeated Cincinnati in the opener, 7–1, the most lopsided defeat the Reds had endured on Opening Day since 1979, when they lost 11–5 to San Francisco.

The defeat was a fitting end for an opener that rang hollow in nearly every respect. Although the Reds announced a sellout of over 51,000 tickets sold, the turnstile count was only 36,062. Reds shortstop Barry Larkin noted the difference. "Normally, you've got the electricity here. Excitement in the air. The stadium is packed. That wasn't the case today," Larkin said.

Jose Rijo made his fourth consecutive Opening Day start, and he limited the Cubs to one run through the first five innings. But the Cubs pushed four more runs across in the sixth, giving Chicago starter Jim Bullinger a 5–0 lead. The lead mounted to 7–0 before Barry Larkin homered in the bottom of the eighth for the Reds only run, which went largely unnoticed because there were few fans left.

*The Reds played lousy and people were mad. They booed. They whistled. They threw garbage on the field. So many fans started wandering out in the sixth inning that you had to wonder if, during the layoff, they had forgotten how long a baseball game lasts.* [*Cincinnati Enquirer and Cincinnati Post*]

### 1995 Opening Day Schedule (All Games Delayed Until April 26)

| April 2 | National League | |
|---|---|---|
| | NY vs. Fla | |
| April 3 | National League | |
| | Chi vs. Cin | Phil vs. StL |
| | LA vs. Fla | Mont vs. Pitts |
| April 4 | National League | |
| | Atl vs. SD | Col vs. NY |
| | SF vs. Hous | |

### April 26, 1995

| CHICAGO | AB | R | H | BI | BB | SO | AVG. |
|---|---|---|---|---|---|---|---|
| Brian McRae cf | 5 | 0 | 3 | 1 | 0 | 1 | .600 |
| Rey Sanchez 2b | 4 | 1 | 1 | 0 | 0 | 0 | .250 |
| Sammy Sosa rf | 4 | 1 | 1 | 0 | 1 | 2 | .250 |
| Mark Grace 1b | 5 | 1 | 3 | 1 | 0 | 0 | .600 |
| Rick Wilkins c | 3 | 2 | 1 | 0 | 1 | 0 | .333 |
| Shawon Dunston ss | 4 | 0 | 0 | 0 | 0 | 1 | .000 |
| Steve Buechele 3b | 4 | 1 | 1 | 2 | 0 | 1 | .250 |
| Scott Bullett lf | 2 | 0 | 0 | 0 | 0 | 0 | .000 |
| Ozzie Timmons ph-lf | 0 | 1 | 0 | 1 | 2 | 0 | |
| Jim Bullinger p | 1 | 0 | 0 | 1 | 1 | 0 | .000 |
| Mike Perez p | 0 | 0 | 0 | 0 | 1 | 0 | |
| TOTALS | 32 | 7 | 10 | 6 | 6 | 5 | |
| REDS | AB | R | H | BI | BB | SO | AVG. |
| Deion Sanders cf | 4 | 0 | 1 | 0 | 0 | 0 | .250 |
| Barry Larkin ss | 3 | 1 | 2 | 1 | 1 | 0 | .667 |
| Hal Morris 1b | 3 | 0 | 0 | 0 | 1 | 1 | .000 |
| Ron Gant lf | 3 | 0 | 1 | 0 | 0 | 0 | .333 |
| Xavier Hernandez p | 0 | 0 | 0 | 0 | 0 | 0 | |
| Lenny Harris ph | 1 | 0 | 0 | 0 | 0 | 0 | .000 |
| Johnny Ruffin p | 0 | 0 | 0 | 0 | 0 | 0 | |
| Bret Boone 2b | 4 | 0 | 1 | 0 | 0 | 0 | .250 |
| Benito Santiago c | 4 | 0 | 0 | 0 | 0 | 0 | .000 |
| Reggie Sanders rf | 4 | 0 | 0 | 0 | 0 | 1 | .250 |
| Willie Greene 3b | 4 | 0 | 1 | 0 | 0 | 2 | .250 |
| Jose Rijo p | 2 | 0 | 0 | 0 | 0 | 0 | .000 |
| Thomas Howard lf | 1 | 0 | 0 | 0 | 0 | 0 | .000 |
| TOTALS | 33 | 1 | 7 | 1 | 2 | 3 | |

| | | | | | | | |
|---|---|---|---|---|---|---|---|
| CHICAGO | | | 010 004 110 | — | 7 | 10 | 0 |
| REDS | | | 000 000 010 | — | 1 | 7 | 1 |

E—Morris (1). LOB—Chicago 8, Cincinnati 7. DP—Chicago 1; Cincinnati 2. 2B—McRae (1). 3B—McRae (1). HR—Larkin (1) off MPerez. RBIs—McRae (1), Grace (1), Buechele 2 (2), Timmons (1), Bullinger (1), Larkin (1). SB—Sosa (1), DSanders (1), Larkin 2 (2). S—Sanchez, Dunston. SF—Bullinger.

| CHICAGO | IP | H | R | ER | BB | SO | NP | ERA |
|---|---|---|---|---|---|---|---|---|
| Jim Bullinger W, 1-0 | 6 | 5 | 0 | 0 | 2 | 2 | 87 | 0.00 |
| Mike Perez S, 1 | 3 | 2 | 1 | 1 | 0 | 1 | 38 | 3.00 |
| REDS | IP | H | R | ER | BB | SO | NP | ERA |
| Jose Rijo L, 0-1 | 5⅓ | 6 | 5 | 4 | 2 | 4 | 88 | 6.75 |
| Chuck McElroy | ⅔ | 1 | 0 | 0 | 1 | 0 | 12 | 0.00 |
| Xavier Hernandez | 2 | 2 | 2 | 2 | 2 | 2 | 32 | 9.00 |
| Johnny Ruffin | 1 | 0 | 0 | 0 | 1 | 1 | 18 | 0.00 |

HBP—by XHernandez (Wilkins). WP—XHernandez 2, JRuffin. PB—Wilkins. Umpires—Home, Garman; First, Randall; Second, B. Hernandez; Third, Pacheco. T—2:58. A—51,033.

### Opening Day Trivia

| Star of the Game | Chicago Pitcher Jim Bullinger |
|---|---|
| Weather | 69° |
| Attendance | 51,033 |
| Notable | Turnstile Count Was Only 36,062 |
| Rating | ☔ |

# 1996 Tragedy at Riverfront
## Umpire John McSherry Dies During First Inning of Opener

*With a stunned crowd looking on, medical personnel continue their futile efforts to revive popular umpire John McSherry.*

For only the second time in baseball history, a death occurred on the playing field during a game. Home plate umpire John McSherry collapsed just seven pitches into the 1996 opener at Riverfront Stadium.

Despite the frantic efforts of team trainers and physicians, McSherry could not be revived.

The sold-out crowd of 51,033, along with the Cincinnati and Montreal players, stood in shock and silence during the several minutes McSherry received attention on the field behind home plate. He was taken off the field and rushed to a hospital where he was pronounced dead, 54 minutes after his collapse.

The only other death on a major league playing field happened in 1920, when Cleveland shortstop Ray Chapman was hit in the head by a pitch from New York Yankee pitcher Carl Mays.

The remaining umpires told the teams they were prepared to carry on with the game. But the Reds, buoyed by an impassioned plea by Reggie Sanders, and the Expos, behind the strong leadership of manager Felipe Alou, said they would not continue. At 3:21, the Reds announced the game was postponed.

The club had not disclosed McSherry's death to the crowd, and some boos greeted the decision. Reds owner Marge Schott, who had not personally made the decision, was also surprised to hear the opener was postponed.

"I don't believe it," Schott said. "Why are they calling it? Whose decision is it? Why can't they play...?"

Schott's remarks only served to reinforce her insensitive, bullheaded image, and provoked a new wave of criticism of the embattled owner.

The day had begun with the usual ceremonies including the Findlay Market parade, which kicked off only a few hours after an early-morning snow storm dumped over an inch of snow on Cincinnati. Former Reds manager Sparky Anderson served as the grand marshal, and along with new manager Ray Knight, headlined the on-field ceremonies at Riverfront. But McSherry's death brought a sudden and tragic end to the opener, and the game was rescheduled for the next day, April 2.

Tuesday brought brighter, warmer weather, but not many people were in the mood for baseball. The official attendance was 53,136, but that was based on tickets sold for the previous day's game. In fact, the stadium was half-full. The game began not with hoopla, but with a moment of silence for McSherry. The umpires received a standing ovation when they walked onto the field.

The Reds raced off to an early lead on RBI singles by Chris Sabo and Hal Morris in the first inning. The Expos closed the gap to 2–1 in the third off Reds starter Pete Schourek. But that was the last run Schourek or the bullpen would allow. Sabo drove in two more runs, and the somber day ended in a 4–1 win for the Reds.

*[Cincinnati Enquirer and Cincinnati Post]*

### OPENING DAY TRIVIA

| | |
|---|---|
| STAR OF THE GAME | REDS THIRD BASEMAN CHRIS SABO |
| WEATHER | 56°; CLOUDY |
| ATTENDANCE | 53,136 |
| NOTABLE | UMPIRE JOHN MCSHERRY DIES ON FIELD |
| RATING | IN MEMORY OF JOHN MCSHERRY |

### 1996 OPENING DAY SCHEDULE

| APRIL 1 | NATIONAL LEAGUE |
|---|---|
| MONT VS. CIN (PP) | |
| STL VS. NY | COL VS. PHIL (PP) |
| SF VS. ATL | SD VS. CHI |
| LA VS. HOUS | PITTS VS. FLA |

### April 2, 1996

| Montreal | AB | R | H | BI | BB | SO | Avg. |
|---|---|---|---|---|---|---|---|
| Grudzielanek ss | 5 | 1 | 1 | 0 | 0 | 1 | .200 |
| Lansing 2b | 3 | 0 | 2 | 0 | 1 | 1 | .667 |
| RWhite cf | 4 | 0 | 1 | 0 | 1 | 0 | .250 |
| Alou lf | 4 | 0 | 1 | 0 | 0 | 1 | .250 |
| Segui 1b | 3 | 0 | 0 | 0 | 1 | 0 | .000 |
| Obando rf | 2 | 0 | 1 | 0 | 0 | 0 | .000 |
| Scott p | 0 | 0 | 0 | 0 | 0 | 0 | --- |
| DVeres p | 0 | 0 | 0 | 0 | 0 | 0 | --- |
| Daal p | 0 | 0 | 0 | 0 | 0 | 0 | --- |
| e-Santangelo ph | 1 | 0 | 0 | 0 | 0 | 1 | .000 |
| DFletcher c | 2 | 0 | 0 | 0 | 2 | 0 | .000 |
| Andrews 3b | 4 | 0 | 1 | 0 | 0 | 3 | .250 |
| Fassero p | 1 | 0 | 0 | 0 | 0 | 0 | .000 |
| a-Webster ph | 1 | 0 | 0 | 0 | 0 | 0 | .000 |
| Manuel p | 0 | 0 | 0 | 0 | 0 | 0 | --- |
| Dyer p | 0 | 0 | 0 | 0 | 0 | 0 | --- |
| HRodriguez rf | 2 | 0 | 1 | 0 | 0 | 0 | .500 |
| Totals | 33 | 1 | 7 | 1 | 4 | 9 | |
| Cincinnati | AB | R | H | BI | BB | SO | Avg. |
| EDavis lf | 4 | 0 | 0 | 0 | 0 | 3 | .000 |
| EOwens 2b | 3 | 0 | 1 | 0 | 0 | 0 | .333 |
| c-Branson ph-2b | 2 | 0 | 1 | 0 | 0 | 0 | .500 |
| Larkin ss | 4 | 2 | 1 | 0 | 1 | 1 | .250 |
| RSanders rf | 2 | 1 | 0 | 0 | 3 | 1 | .000 |
| Sabo 3b | 3 | 0 | 2 | 3 | 1 | 1 | .667 |
| Morris 1b | 3 | 0 | 1 | 1 | 2 | 0 | .333 |
| MKelly cf | 3 | 0 | 0 | 0 | 1 | 2 | .000 |
| JOliver c | 4 | 0 | 0 | 0 | 0 | 1 | .000 |
| Schourek p | 1 | 0 | 0 | 0 | 0 | 1 | .000 |
| b-Coleman ph | 1 | 0 | 0 | 0 | 0 | 0 | .000 |
| Pugh p | 0 | 0 | 0 | 0 | 0 | 0 | --- |
| d-LHarris ph | 1 | 1 | 1 | 0 | 0 | 0 | 1.000 |
| Moore p | 0 | 0 | 0 | 0 | 0 | 0 | --- |
| Totals | 31 | 4 | 7 | 4 | 9 | 10 | |

Montreal  001 000 000—1  7 3
Cincinnati  200 010 01—4  7 6

a-grounded out for Fassero in the 4th. b-lined out for Schourek in the 5th. c-singled for Owens in the 6th. d-doubled for Pugh in the 7th. e-struck out for Daal in the 8th. E—Grudzielanek (1), Alou (1), Andrews (1). LOB—Montreal 9, Cincinnati 14. 2B—Grudzielanek (1), Lansing (1), Larkin (1), Sabo (1), LHarris (1). RBI—RWhite (1), Sabo 3 (3), Morris (1). SB—Larkin (1), RSanders, Sabo, Morris (1). CS—EOwens. S—Schourek. DP—Cincinnati 1 (RSanders and Larkin).

| Montreal | IP | H | R | ER | BB | SO | NP | ERA |
|---|---|---|---|---|---|---|---|---|
| Fassero L, 0-1 | 4 | 4 | 2 | 2 | 4 | 4 | 77 | 4.50 |
| Manuel | ⅓ | 1 | 1 | 1 | 3 | 0 | 28 | 27.00 |
| Dyer | 1⅔ | 0 | 0 | 0 | 2 | 23 | | 0.00 |
| Scott | ⅓ | 1 | 1 | 1 | 0 | 3 | 18 | 0.00 |
| DVeres | ⅔ | 1 | 1 | 1 | 2 | 1 | 22 | 13.50 |
| Daal | ⅓ | 0 | 0 | 0 | 0 | 1 | 5 | 0.00 |
| Cincinnati | IP | H | R | ER | BB | SO | NP | ERA |
| Schourek W, 1-0 | 5 | 5 | 1 | 1 | 5 | 91 | | 1.80 |
| Pugh | 3 | 1 | 0 | 0 | 3 | 42 | | 0.00 |
| Moore S, 1 | 1 | 1 | 0 | 0 | 1 | 22 | | 0.00 |

Inherited runners-scored—Scott 2-0; Daal 3-0; Dyer 3-0. IBB—off DVeres (RSanders) 1. HBP—by DVeres (Sabo). WP—Manuel. Umpires—Home, Crawford; First, Ripoley; Second, Hallion; Third, Reiker. T—3:27. A—53,136 (52,952).

# 1997 Reds Scale Rockies
## Day Opens With Moment of Silence for McSherry

*Deion Sanders had two hits, stole two bases and scored two runs in the 1997 opener.*

### 1997 OPENING DAY SCHEDULE

| APRIL 1 | NATIONAL LEAGUE |
|---|---|
| COL VS. CIN | PHIL VS. LA |
| PITTS VS. SF | NY VS. SD |
| STL VS. MONT | LA VS. ATL |
| ATL VS. HOUS | |

Sure signs of Opening Day: Crimson water in the Tyler Davidson Fountain and elephants in the ballpark.

All the familiar elements were in place for the opening of the baseball season, and the Reds responded with an 11–4 win over the Colorado Rockies on a cool, sunny afternoon. The 11 runs tied the club's record (since 1900) for most runs on Opening Day.

The Opening Day festivities began with a moment of silence for umpire John McSherry, who collapsed and died during the 1996 opener. The club honored McSherry by naming the umpire's room at Riverfront for him.

After three years of tumult and tragedy, the 1997 opener went off as planned—except for the mound. The Ohio River flood in February swept away the dirt and clay used to rebuild the Riverfront pitching mound, an annual remodeling project completed in the days before the opener. The dirt had been been piled outside the stadium, where it was unprotected from the flood waters.

"The mound is somewhere down around Louisville," laughed the Reds new managing executive, John Allen. The ground crew labored to the last minute finding replacement soil and finishing the mound.

Neither starter took to the new hill. The Reds broke out to a quick 4–0 lead in the first inning, highlighted by a two-run homer by Willie Greene and a triple by Reggie Sanders. But Reds starter John Smiley couldn't protect the lead. The Rockies tied it, 4–4, in the fourth. But from then on, it was all Cincinnati.

The Reds went back ahead, 5–4, in the bottom of the fourth on a double by Smiley. In the sixth, the Reds batted around, scoring four more times with the aid of two Colorado errors. The Reds ran wild in the inning, stealing three bases, two by Deion Sanders, the sometimes NFL defensive back. Sanders was all about back-pedaling on the gridiron, but he motored full speed ahead on this day, earning "Star-of-the-Game" honors with two hits, two steals, two runs, an RBI and a sacrifice bunt. He put an early charge in the crowd with a lead-off double.

Reds owner Marge Schott, on baseball's suspended list for conduct unbecoming an owner, received a reprieve for the day and took an active role in the Opening Day ceremonies, which featured the annual Findlay Market parade, and a horde of animals from the Cincinnati Zoo.

*She [Schott] hugged an elephant, the governor and the 7-year-old girl who sang the national anthem. "Did you see the camels," Schott asked. "One of them tried to kiss me."*

*Schott posed for pictures with Schottzie (02) and guests, Olympic gold-medal gymnasts, Amanda Borden and Jaycie Phelps.* **[Cincinnati Enquirer and Cincinnati Post]**

### OPENING DAY TRIVIA

| STAR OF THE GAME | REDS CENTER FIELDER DEION SANDERS |
|---|---|
| WEATHER | 58°; SUNNY |
| ATTENDANCE | 54,820 |
| NOTABLE | 11 RUNS TIES REDS OPENING DAY RECORD |
| RATING | ●●●● |

### APRIL 1, 1997

| Colorado | AB | R | H | BI | BB | SO | Avg. |
|---|---|---|---|---|---|---|---|
| Young 2b | 4 | 0 | 2 | 0 | 1 | 1 | .500 |
| Burks cf-lf | 5 | 1 | 1 | 2 | 0 | 2 | .200 |
| Bichette lf | 4 | 0 | 1 | 0 | 0 | 1 | .250 |
| McCracken cf | 0 | 0 | 0 | 0 | 0 | 0 | --- |
| Walker rf | 4 | 0 | 0 | 0 | 0 | 2 | .000 |
| Galarraga 1b | 3 | 1 | 0 | 0 | 0 | 1 | .333 |
| Castilla 3b | 4 | 1 | 1 | 1 | 0 | 2 | .250 |
| Manwaring c | 3 | 0 | 1 | 0 | 0 | 1 | .333 |
| Reed p | 0 | 0 | 0 | 0 | 0 | 0 | --- |
| Burke p | 0 | 0 | 0 | 0 | 0 | 0 | --- |
| b-Vander Wal pr | 1 | 0 | 0 | 0 | 0 | 0 | .000 |
| Weiss ss | 3 | 0 | 2 | 1 | 1 | 0 | .667 |
| Ritz p | 1 | 1 | 0 | 0 | 1 | 0 | .000 |
| Dipoto p | 0 | 0 | 0 | 0 | 0 | 0 | --- |
| Reed c | 2 | 0 | 0 | 0 | 0 | 0 | .000 |
| Totals | 34 | 4 | 8 | 4 | 4 | 11 | |
| Cincinnati | AB | R | H | BI | BB | SO | Avg. |
| Sanders cf | 4 | 2 | 2 | 1 | 0 | 0 | .500 |
| Greene 3b | 4 | 2 | 2 | 1 | 1 | 1 | .500 |
| Larkin ss | 1 | 3 | 0 | 0 | 4 | 0 | .000 |
| Reese ss | 0 | 0 | 0 | 0 | 0 | 0 | --- |
| Sanders rf | 5 | 1 | 2 | 1 | 0 | 0 | .400 |
| Morris 1b | 4 | 1 | 3 | 3 | 1 | 0 | .750 |
| Sierra lf | 4 | 0 | 2 | 0 | 0 | 0 | .500 |
| Jarvis p | 1 | 0 | 0 | 0 | 0 | 0 | .000 |
| Boone 2b | 5 | 0 | 1 | 1 | 0 | 0 | .200 |
| Taubensee c | 3 | 2 | 2 | 0 | 2 | 0 | .667 |
| Smiley p | 2 | 0 | 1 | 1 | 0 | 1 | .500 |
| a-Harris pr-lf | 1 | 0 | 0 | 0 | 0 | 0 | .000 |
| Totals | 34 | 11 | 15 | 9 | 8 | 2 | |

Colorado 012 100 000—4 8 2
Cincinnati 400 104 02 —11 15 0

a-sacrificed for Smiley in the 6th. b-struck out for Burke in the 9th. E—Castilla (1), Dipoto (1). LOB—Colorado 7, Cincinnati 9. 2B—Sanders (1), Morris (1), Sierra (1), Smiley (1). 3B—Sanders (1). HR—Burks (1) off Smiley; Castilla (1)-off Smiley; Greene (1) off Ritz. RBI—Burks 2 (2), Castilla (1), Weiss (1), Sanders (1), Greene 2 (2), Sanders (1), Morris 3 (3), Boone (1), Smiley (1). SB—Young (1), Galarraga (1), Sanders 2 (2), Greene (1), Larkin 2 (2). CS—Bichette (1), Sanders (1). S—Sanders, Harris. DP—Colorado 2 (Castilla and Galarraga), (Burks and Galarraga).

| Colorado | IP | H | R | ER | BB | SO | NP | ERA |
|---|---|---|---|---|---|---|---|---|
| Ritz L, 0-1 | 5 | 8 | 5 | 5 | 4 | 2 | 90 | 9.00 |
| Dipoto | ⅔ | 5 | 4 | 4 | 2 | 0 | 31 | 54.00 |
| Reed | 1½ | 2 | 1 | 1 | 0 | 1 | 18 | .00 |
| Burke | 1 | 2 | 2 | 2 | 1 | 0 | 23 | 18.00 |
| Cincinnati | IP | H | R | ER | BB | SO | NP | ERA |
| Smiley W, 1-0 | 6 | 6 | 4 | 4 | 2 | 6 | 96 | 6.00 |
| Jarvis S, 1 | 3 | 2 | 0 | 0 | 2 | 5 | 49 | .00 |

Inherited runners-scored—Reed 2-0. IBB—off Ritz (Taubensee) 1. WP—Burke. Umpires—Home, DeMuth; First, Dreckman; Second, Darling; Third, Reliford. T—3:05. A—54820 (52,952).

# 1998
## Reese's Nightmare
### Four Errors for Reds Shortstop; Reds Lose to Padres, 10–2

*Gold Glove second baseman, Pokey Reese, had a bad day at the office in the 1998 opener.*

**1998 OPENING DAY SCHEDULE**

| MARCH 31 | NATIONAL LEAGUE | |
|---|---|---|
| SD vs. Cin | | Phil vs. NY |
| Col vs. Ariz | | Milw vs. Atl |
| SF vs. Hous | | Chi vs. Fla |
| | LA vs. StL | |
| APRIL 1 | NATIONAL LEAGUE | |
| | Pitts vs. Mont | |

The Reds lost to San Diego, 10–2; they traded their Opening Day starter on the eve of the game; they played their first opener ever in March; and the weather topped out at a summer-like 80 degrees. But all anyone remembers is four errors.

Sophomore infielder Pokey Reese, subbing for an injured Barry Larkin, made four errors in three innings, tying the modern record for all of baseball for most errors in an opening day game.

It brought out the best (?) in the writers: "HOW MANY E'S IN POKEY REESE? WELL, 4," stated *The Cincinnati Enquirer* headline writer. "REESE GOES TO PIECES," declared *The Cincinnati Post.* Reese suffered many a comparison to an employee from the Cincinnati Zoo who trailed the elephant during the pre-game ceremony and deftly caught a few droppings with ne'er an error.

Reese's nightmare began in the first inning when he threw a double-play relay ball into the dugout. In the third, Reese bobbled a grounder for his second error. Then, with runners on second and third, he mishandled Tony Gwynn's ground ball, allowing Gwynn to reach base. As Reese reached for the ball, he kicked it, allowing the runner on second to advance to third, for his third error of the inning, and fourth of the game. Blessedly, that was the last ground ball hit to Reese.

Reese's miscues helped the Padres take a 3–0 lead, and that was more than starter Kevin Brown needed. Brown pitched into the seventh, allowing only one run and five hits, while racking up seven strikeouts.

Emergency starter Mike Remlinger, a last-minute substitute for Dave Burba, who was traded 24 hours before the game (to Cleveland for Sean Casey), gave the Reds five strong innings, allowing only one earned run. But the bullpen gave up seven runs, six off rookie Ricardo Jordan in the sixth. Gwynn hit a two-run homer and Brown tripled home three more.

The day's celebration began early at Fountain Square with NBC weatherman, Al Roker, broadcasting live. His co-host on *The Today Show*, Linda Vester, a native of Milford, Ohio, threw out the first pitch.

The Findlay Market parade, as usual, preceded the game: *The parade [included] 175 groups, bands and floats and featured Cincinnati Zoo animals, the Budweiser Clydesdales pulling the Budweiser beer wagon, Miss Chiquita Banana, and the 140-year-old H. J. Heinz Co. Tally Ho wagon pulled by an eight-horse team.*

"This is what baseball is in Cincinnati," said [Reds owner Marge] Schott. "Opening Day in Cincinnati is all about the Findlay Market Parade."
**[Cincinnati Enquirer and Cincinnati Post]**

**OPENING DAY TRIVIA**

| STAR OF THE GAME | SAN DIEGO PITCHER KEVIN BROWN |
|---|---|
| WEATHER | 80°; CLOUDY |
| ATTENDANCE | 54,578 |
| NOTABLE | MOST LOPSIDED LOSS IN 39 YEARS |
| RATING | ⚾⚾ |

**MARCH 31, 1998**

| San Diego | AB | R | H | BI | BB | SO |
|---|---|---|---|---|---|---|
| QVeras 2b | 4 | 1 | 1 | 0 | 1 | 0 |
| Giovanola 2b | 0 | 0 | 0 | 0 | 0 | 0 |
| SFinley cf | 4 | 2 | 2 | 0 | 1 | 0 |
| Gwynn rf | 4 | 2 | 1 | 3 | 0 | 0 |
| Cianfrocco 1b | 1 | 0 | 0 | 0 | 0 | 1 |
| Caminiti 3b | 4 | 0 | 2 | 1 | 0 | 1 |
| Sheets pr-3b | 1 | 1 | 0 | 0 | 0 | 1 |
| GVaughn lf | 3 | 0 | 0 | 0 | 1 | 1 |
| Mouton pr-lf | 1 | 1 | 0 | 0 | 0 | 0 |
| Joyner 1b | 2 | 1 | 1 | 1 | 0 | 0 |
| MaSweeney rf | 1 | 0 | 0 | 0 | 1 | 0 |
| CHernandez c | 4 | 1 | 1 | 1 | 0 | 0 |
| Gomez ss | 4 | 0 | 0 | 0 | 0 | 0 |
| KBrown p | 4 | 0 | 3 | 3 | 0 | 0 |
| Boehringer p | 0 | 0 | 0 | 0 | 0 | 0 |
| Wengert p | 2 | 1 | 0 | 0 | 0 | 0 |
| Totals | 39 | 10 | 10 | 9 | 5 | 4 |

| Cincinnati | AB | R | H | BI | BB | SO |
|---|---|---|---|---|---|---|
| Stynes lf | 4 | 0 | 1 | 0 | 0 | 1 |
| Nunnally rf-cf | 3 | 1 | 1 | 0 | 1 | 0 |
| WGreene 3b | 3 | 0 | 0 | 0 | 1 | 1 |
| EduPerez 1b | 4 | 1 | 0 | 1 | 0 | 2 |
| RSanders cf | 2 | 0 | 1 | 0 | 2 | 0 |
| Sullivan p | 0 | 0 | 0 | 0 | 0 | 0 |
| Taubensee c | 4 | 0 | 1 | 0 | 0 | 1 |
| BBoone 2b | 4 | 0 | 1 | 1 | 0 | 1 |
| Reese ss | 2 | 0 | 0 | 0 | 0 | 0 |
| LHarris ph | 1 | 0 | 0 | 0 | 0 | 0 |
| DmJackson ss | 0 | 0 | 0 | 0 | 0 | 0 |
| Remlinger p | 1 | 0 | 0 | 0 | 0 | 0 |
| Casey ph | 1 | 0 | 0 | 0 | 0 | 1 |
| Weathers p | 0 | 0 | 0 | 0 | 0 | 0 |
| RJordan p | 0 | 0 | 0 | 0 | 0 | 0 |
| GWhite p | 0 | 0 | 0 | 0 | 0 | 0 |
| DYoung ph-rf | 2 | 0 | 0 | 0 | 0 | 0 |
| Totals | 32 | 2 | 6 | 2 | 4 | 8 |

| San Diego | 003 001 600 — 10 10 1 |
|---|---|
| Cincinnati | 000 000 110 — 2 6 4 |

E—QVeras (1), Reese 4 (4). LOB—San Diego 8, Cincinnati 7. 2B—SFinley 2 (2), KBrown (1). HR—Gwynn (1), Joyner (1). RBIs—Gwynn (1), Caminiti (1), Joyner (1), CHernandez (1), KBrown 3 (3), EduPerez (1), BBoone (1). DP—San Diego 2.

| San Diego | IP | H | R | ER | BB | SO | NP |
|---|---|---|---|---|---|---|---|
| KBrown W, 1-0 | 6⅔ | 5 | 1 | 1 | 1 | 7 | 104 |
| Boehringer | 1⅓ | 0 | 1 | 1 | 2 | 1 | 27 |
| Wengert | 1 | 1 | 0 | 0 | 1 | 0 | 20 |

| Cincinnati | IP | H | R | ER | BB | SO | NP |
|---|---|---|---|---|---|---|---|
| Remlinger L, 0-1 | 5 | 5 | 3 | 1 | 1 | 2 | 76 |
| Weathers | 1 | 1 | 1 | 1 | 0 | 0 | 17 |
| RJordan | ⅓ | 2 | 6 | 6 | 4 | 0 | 32 |
| GWhite | 1⅔ | 2 | 0 | 0 | 0 | 2 | 30 |
| Sullivan | 1 | 0 | 0 | 0 | 0 | 0 | 13 |

HBP—by Sullivan (Gomez). WP—Remlinger, GWhite. Umpires—Home, Marsh; First, Bonin; Second, Hohn; Third, Hernandez. T—2:48. A—54,578.

# 1999
# Giants Win Slugfest
## Reds Rally But Then Lose, 11–8

*Singer Loretta Lynn (left) and Marge Schott watch the flight of doves released just prior to the start of the game.*

The huge crowd basked in April sunshine. They applauded their sentimental hero, Joe Nuxhall, who was the Grand Marshal of the Findlay Market parade. They watched the Reds score six runs in the sixth inning to take a 8–6 lead.

This was a perfect Opening Day.

But the Reds bullpen collapsed, giving up five runs over the last three innings and San Francisco stole the opener, 11–8. Charlie Hayes, the Giants third baseman, had the final blow, a three-run home run into the green seats in left field in the eighth.

Brett Tomko, the Reds starter, allowed six runs in the first four innings, but the Reds, who trailed 6–2 in the sixth, mounted a furious comeback. Five of the runs came on a three-run home run by pinch-hitter Mark Sweeney, and a two-run homer by Sean Casey that put the Reds ahead. But John Hudek and Gabe White could not contain the Giants offense. Hudek gave up a tying home run to Ellis Burks in the seventh, and Hayes had the game-winner off White.

The total of 19 runs, 27 hits and five home runs made this one of the best offensive shows in Opening Day history. The 19 runs scored were the most since the 1900 opener, which featured 23 runs.

The day began with Reds owner Marge Schott kicking off the Findlay Market parade. It would be Schott's last Opening Day as owner of the Reds. Nuxhall rode in a red convertible and was warmly applauded all along the 18-block route. Several people came out of the crowd to shake his hand.

The boisterous crowd of 55,112, the eighth-largest in Opening Day history, cheered the pre-game ceremonies and the offensive fireworks: *From the entrance of the Clydesdales leading the Findlay Market parade to the singing of the national anthem by the coal miner's daughter, Loretta Lynn, to two terrific plays in right field by Dmitri Young, to the raucous reception of the Reds' six-run sixth inning, the crowd was into it.*

*People were here to have fun and spend money. The lines in front of the concession stands never let up. Beer vendors were mobbed before they even made it to the stands. The standing-room-only area on the blue level behind home plate was a dozen people deep.*

*Outside of Mr. Nuxhall and a handful of military bands and units, the last of the 140 parade entries, the Budweiser Clydesdales of St. Louis, probably received the biggest ovation from the onlookers. They held the attention of people along the route far more than the seemingly endless stream of hair-sprayed politicians and radio personalities, commercial entries, red automobiles and fire trucks.* **[Cincinnati Enquirer and Cincinnati Post]**

### OPENING DAY TRIVIA

| | |
|---|---|
| STAR OF THE GAME | GIANTS THIRD BASEMAN CHARLIE HAYES |
| WEATHER | 70°; PARTLY CLOUDY |
| ATTENDANCE | 55,112 |
| NOTABLE | 19 TOTAL RUNS MOST IN OPENER SINCE 1900 |
| RATING | ◐◐◐ |

### APRIL 5, 1999

| San Francisco | AB | R | H | BI | BB | SO | AVG |
|---|---|---|---|---|---|---|---|
| Benard cf | 5 | 1 | 1 | 0 | 0 | 3 | .200 |
| Mueller 3b | 0 | 0 | 0 | 0 | 0 | 0 | — |
| Hayes pr-3b | 4 | 2 | 2 | 3 | 0 | 0 | .500 |
| Bonds lf | 3 | 1 | 0 | 0 | 2 | 0 | .000 |
| Kent 2b | 4 | 1 | 3 | 2 | 1 | 0 | .750 |
| Snow 1b | 5 | 1 | 2 | 2 | 0 | 2 | .400 |
| Burks rf | 5 | 2 | 3 | 2 | 0 | 0 | .600 |
| Nen p | 0 | 0 | 0 | 0 | 0 | 0 | — |
| Mayne c | 5 | 0 | 1 | 0 | 0 | 1 | .200 |
| Aurilia ss | 4 | 1 | 2 | 1 | 1 | 0 | .500 |
| Gardner p | 2 | 1 | 1 | 0 | 0 | 0 | .500 |
| Tavarez p | 0 | 0 | 0 | 0 | 0 | 0 | — |
| Embree p | 0 | 0 | 0 | 0 | 0 | 0 | — |
| Santangelo ph | 0 | 1 | 0 | 0 | 1 | 0 | — |
| Johnstone p | 0 | 0 | 0 | 0 | 0 | 0 | — |
| Javier rf | 0 | 0 | 0 | 0 | 0 | 1 | — |
| **Totals** | **37** | **11** | **15** | **10** | **5** | **7** | — |
| **Cincinnati** | **AB** | **R** | **H** | **BI** | **BB** | **SO** | **AVG** |
| Cameron cf | 4 | 2 | 1 | 2 | 0 | 0 | .250 |
| Larkin ss | 5 | 1 | 1 | 1 | 0 | 0 | .200 |
| Casey 1b | 5 | 1 | 3 | 2 | 0 | 0 | .600 |
| Vaughn lf | 4 | 0 | 1 | 0 | 1 | 1 | .250 |
| Young rf | 5 | 0 | 3 | 0 | 0 | 1 | .600 |
| Taubensee c | 5 | 1 | 1 | 0 | 0 | 0 | .200 |
| Boone 3b | 4 | 1 | 0 | 0 | 0 | 0 | .000 |
| White p | 0 | 0 | 0 | 0 | 0 | 0 | — |
| Williamson p | 0 | 0 | 0 | 0 | 0 | 0 | — |
| Morris ph | 1 | 0 | 0 | 0 | 0 | 1 | .000 |
| Reese 2b | 4 | 1 | 1 | 0 | 0 | 0 | .250 |
| Tomko p | 0 | 0 | 0 | 0 | 0 | 0 | — |
| Reyes p | 1 | 0 | 0 | 0 | 0 | 1 | .000 |
| Sweeney ph | 1 | 1 | 1 | 3 | 0 | 0 | 1.000 |
| Hudek p | 0 | 0 | 0 | 0 | 0 | 0 | — |
| Lewis 3b | 1 | 0 | 0 | 0 | 0 | 0 | .000 |
| **Totals** | **40** | **8** | **12** | **8** | **1** | **4** | — |

| | | | | | |
|---|---|---|---|---|---|
| San Francisco | 300 300 230 | — | 11 | 15 | 1 |
| Cincinnati | 020 006 000 | — | 8 | 12 | 1 |

**E:** Hayes (1), Boone (1). **LOB:** San Francisco 6, Cincinnati 8. **2B:** Kent (1), Burks (1), Casey (1). **HR:** Hayes (1) off White; Burks (1) off Hudek; Casey (1) off Tavarez; Sweeney (1) off Gardner; Cameron (1) off Gardner. **RBI:** Hayes 3 (3), Kent 2 (2), Snow 2 (2), Burks 2 (2), Aurilia (1), Cameron 2 (2), Larkin (1), Casey 2 (2), Sweeney 3 (3). **SB:** Kent (1), Cameron (1). **S:** Gardner, Tomko. **DP:** Cincinnati 2 (Larkin, Reese and Casey), (Larkin, Reese and Casey).

| GIANTS | IP | H | R | ER | BB | SO | NP | ERA |
|---|---|---|---|---|---|---|---|---|
| Gardner | 5⅓ | 9 | 5 | 4 | 1 | 1 | 102 | 6.75 |
| Tavarez | ⅔ | 1 | 3 | 3 | 0 | 2 | 25 | 40.50 |
| Embree (W,1-0) | 1 | 0 | 0 | 0 | 0 | 7 | 0.00 |
| Johnstone | 1 | 0 | 0 | 0 | 0 | 0 | 9 | 0.00 |
| Nen (S,1) | 1 | 2 | 0 | 0 | 0 | 1 | 16 | 0.00 |
| **REDS** | **IP** | **H** | **R** | **ER** | **BB** | **SO** | **NP** | **ERA** |
| Tomko | 3⅓ | 8 | 6 | 6 | 3 | 1 | 81 | 14.73 |
| Reyes | 2⅓ | 1 | 0 | 0 | 0 | 3 | 27 | 0.00 |
| Hudek (L,0-1) | 1 | 3 | 3 | 3 | 1 | 0 | 29 | 27.00 |
| White | 1 | 2 | 2 | 2 | 0 | 2 | 21 | 18.00 |
| Williamson | 1 | 1 | 0 | 0 | 0 | 1 | 11 | 0.00 |

Hudek pitched to 1 batter in the 8th.
**Inherited runners-scored:** White 1-1, Reyes 3-0. **IBB:** off Tomko (Bonds) 1. **HBP:** by Tavarez (Cameron), by Tomko (Mueller). **WP:** Tavarez.
**Umpires:** Home, Crawford; First, Gregg; Second, Gorman; Third, Nauert. **T:** 3:10. **A:** 55,112 (52,953).

### 1999 OPENING DAY SCHEDULE

| APRIL 4 | NATIONAL LEAGUE | |
|---|---|---|
| COL VS. SD (IN MEXICO) | | |
| APRIL 5 | NATIONAL LEAGUE | |
| SF VS. CIN | NY VS. FLA | |
| PHIL VS. ATL | ARIZ VS. LA | |
| MILW VS. STL | MONT VS. PITTS | |
| APRIL 6 | NATIONAL LEAGUE | |
| CHI VS. HOUS | | |

# Griffey's Debut Fizzles in Drizzle
## Brewers and Reds Play 3–3 Tie

*The hometown kid, Ken Griffey, Jr., received a rousing ovation from the 2000 Opening Day crowd as he was introduced before the game.*

### 2000 Opening Day Schedule

| March 29 | National League |
|---|---|
| Chi vs. NY (in Tokyo) | |
| **April 3** | **National League** |
| Milw vs. Cin | Col vs. Atl |
| LA vs. Mont | SF vs. Fla |
| SD vs. NY | Chi vs. StL |
| Hous vs. Pitts (PP) | |
| **April 4** | **National League** |
| Hous vs. Pitts | Phil vs. Ariz |

The 2000 opener began with a thunderous ovation for Ken Griffey, Jr. and ended with a scattering of boos as the umpires called the game after a nearly three-hour rain delay.

The score stood at 3–3 in the bottom of the sixth inning. Because the game had gone the official distance, it was declared a tie and did not count in the standings. However, all statistics earned during the game were entered into the record books.

The rain wiped out what should have been one of the most memorable openers in Cincinnati history. The Findlay Market parade had a record number (200) of entries. The game had sold out in 3½ hours. The crowd of 55,596 was the largest ever in Opening Day history, and Griffey's debut, which had been compared to the coming of Babe Ruth, had been the buzz of the town for weeks after an off-season trade with Seattle returned the superstar to his hometown.

The stadium sparkled from the flares of flash cameras as Griffey trotted out of the dugout during the introduction of the starting lineup. Waves of applause rolled out of the stands and Griffey acknowledged the cheers with a doff of the cap.

His father, standing in the dugout, admitted he had a tear in his eye. His mother, however, was stuck in an elevator under the grandstand and missed the whole ceremony.

The Reds jumped out to a 3–0 lead in the first two innings, although Griffey failed to contribute, popping out in first at-bat and grounding out in the third. The crowd yearned for a home run from Junior, but the first and only long ball of the game came from the Red's Michael Tucker.

Reds starter Pete Harnisch was unable to hold the lead and the Brewers tied it in the fourth on a single by Marquis Grissom. The score remained tied until the bottom of the sixth, when the rain, which had been falling intermittently since the game began, began to fall harder. The teams headed off the field and never returned. The huge crowd dwindled away and few were left when the game was called at 5:48.

Because 5½ innings had been completed, the game was officially declared a tie. Since ties do not count in the standings, the first official game took place the next evening in very cold conditions, with the Expos winning, 5–1. Although the Reds honored all Opening Day tickets for this game, only 16,761 attended. *[Cincinnati Enquirer and Cincinnati Post]*

### Opening Day Trivia

| | |
|---|---|
| Star of the Game | Reds Center Fielder Ken Griffey, Jr. |
| Weather | 61°; Overcast; Rain |
| Attendance | 55,596 |
| Notable | Largest Opening Day Crowd Ever |
| Rating | ◐◐◐◐ |

### April 3, 2000

| Milwaukee | AB | R | H | BI | BB | SO | AVG |
|---|---|---|---|---|---|---|---|
| Grissom cf | 3 | 1 | 2 | 1 | 0 | 0 | .667 |
| Loretta ss | 3 | 0 | 0 | 1 | 0 | 1 | .000 |
| Burnitz rf | 2 | 1 | 1 | 0 | 1 | 0 | .500 |
| Jenkins lf | 3 | 0 | 1 | 0 | 0 | 0 | .333 |
| JHernandez 3b | 3 | 0 | 0 | 0 | 0 | 0 | .000 |
| KBarker 1b | 2 | 0 | 1 | 0 | 1 | 0 | .500 |
| Belliard 2b | 2 | 1 | 2 | 0 | 1 | 0 | 1.000 |
| Blanco c | 1 | 0 | 0 | 0 | 2 | 0 | .000 |
| Woodard p | 3 | 0 | 0 | 0 | 0 | 0 | .000 |
| Totals | 22 | 3 | 7 | 2 | 5 | 1 | — |
| **Cincinnati** | **AB** | **R** | **H** | **BI** | **BB** | **SO** | **AVG** |
| Reese 2b | 2 | 1 | 1 | 0 | 1 | 1 | .500 |
| Larkin ss | 3 | 1 | 2 | 1 | 0 | 0 | .667 |
| Griffey jr. cf | 2 | 0 | 0 | 0 | 0 | 0 | .000 |
| Bichette rf | 2 | 0 | 0 | 0 | 0 | 2 | .000 |
| DYoung 1b | 2 | 0 | 1 | 1 | 0 | 0 | .500 |
| Taubensee c | 2 | 0 | 0 | 0 | 0 | 0 | .000 |
| ABoone 3b | 2 | 0 | 0 | 0 | 0 | 0 | .000 |
| Tucker lf | 2 | 1 | 1 | 1 | 0 | 0 | .500 |
| Harnisch p | 1 | 0 | 0 | 0 | 0 | 0 | .000 |
| Sullivan p | 1 | 0 | 0 | 0 | 0 | 1 | .000 |
| Totals | 19 | 3 | 5 | 3 | 1 | 4 | — |

| Milwaukee | | | 002 100 _ 3 7 0 |
|---|---|---|---|
| Cincinnati | | | 210 00x _ 3 5 2 |

One out when game was called.
E: Bichette (1), Taubensee (1). LOB: Milwaukee 8; Cincinnati 2. 2B: Belliard (1), Larkin (1). HR: Tucker (1) off Woodard. RBI: Grissom (1), Loretta (1), Larkin (1), DYoung (1), Tucker (1). SB: Grissom (1).

| Milwaukee | IP | H | R | ER | BB | SO | NP | ERA |
|---|---|---|---|---|---|---|---|---|
| Woodard | 5 | 5 | 3 | 3 | 1 | 4 | 68 | 5.40 |
| **Cincinnati** | **IP** | **H** | **R** | **ER** | **BB** | **SO** | **NP** | **ERA** |
| Harnisch | 4 | 7 | 3 | 2 | 3 | 1 | 81 | 4.50 |
| Sullivan | 1⅓ | 0 | 0 | 0 | 2 | 0 | 21 | 0.00 |

Umpires: Home, Marsh; First, Hernandez; Second, Foster, Marty; Third, Kulpa.
T: 1:51. A: 55,596 (52,953).

# Reds Loss Spoils New-Look Cinergy
## 2001
### Grass, New Wall Friendly to Braves As They Whip Reds, 10–4

*Fans took in their first view of the "new" Cinergy Field on Opening Day, 2001.*

The ground crew didn't get much sleep the night before the 2001 opener. Doug Gallant, head groundskeeper at Cinergy, was up most of the night tinkering with his new grass field. The new turf had been installed in the off-season as part of the Cinergy Field renovation, triggered by the construction of Great American Ball Park, just beyond the outfield walls.

As it turned out, Gallant and his crew figured out the grass, but had trouble with the dirt. The skin portion of the infield turned hard as an executioner's heart during the opener and helped Atlanta to a 10–4 win over the Reds.

The Reds trailed by one run, 5–4, in the eighth inning, when Reds shortstop Barry Larkin made an error on a bad-hop ricochet off the infield dirt. It was a catchable ball on the old dependable Astroturf. Larkin thought the scoring decision was in error, but regardless of the ruling, the Braves immediately took advantage of the play. They tallied four times, three coming on a bases-loaded double by Quilvio Veras.

The difference in the game was the Larkin miscue and the bullpens. Neither starter was sharp; John Burkett gave up four runs in 5⅔ innings, while Reds starter Pete Harnisch allowed four runs in six innings. But the Braves bullpen shut out the Reds, while four Red relievers gave up six runs over the final three innings.

The new look at Cinergy also played a part in two other plays that turned comical. Rafael Furcal hit a home run over the left-field fence and out of the open-ended ballpark, a site not seen in Cincinnati since the days of Crosley Field. To the crowd's delight, a construction worker picked up the ball and threw it back over the fence.

In the fifth inning, Lopez lined a ball off the new "batter's eye" extension in center field. All of the 40-foot-high wall—nicknamed the "Black Monster"—was in play, but umpire Bill Miller didn't get the word. He mistakenly signalled for a home run to a rousing round of jeers from the crowd. The call flushed new manager Bob Boone out of the dugout to offer a clarification. Lopez was sent back to second.

Everybody admired the "retro" look of Cinergy (although it was minus 12,000 seats) and the big turnout for the parade: *[The day] started about 10 a.m. when an estimated 100,000 people lined the streets of Over-the-Rhine and downtown for the 82nd annual Findlay Market Parade. Dressed in costumes of the Red Stockings, baseball's first pro team, members of Historic Southwest Ohio joined the parade.*

The natural grass field was the biggest winner of the day. The view, which offered the downtown skyline, Mount Adams, the river and/or Northern Kentucky, depending on the vantage point in the stands, was also a crowd pleaser. Everything was so open, so expansive, like a real ballpark. "We actually get to see the sky," said Reds outfielder Dimitri Young. [*Cincinnati Enquirer* and *Cincinnati Post*]

### OPENING DAY TRIVIA

| | |
|---|---|
| STAR OF THE GAME | ATLANTA SHORTSTOP RAFAEL FURCAL |
| WEATHER | 57°; SUNNY |
| ATTENDANCE | 41,901 |
| NOTABLE | 1ST GAME ON GRASS IN CINCINNATI IN 31 YEARS |
| RATING | ◐◐◐◐ |

### APRIL 2, 2001

| Atlanta | AB | R | H | BI | BB | SO | Avg. |
|---|---|---|---|---|---|---|---|
| Furcal ss | 3 | 2 | 2 | 4 | 1 | 0 | .667 |
| QVeras 2b | 6 | 0 | 1 | 3 | 0 | 0 | .167 |
| AJones cf | 4 | 1 | 2 | 1 | 1 | 0 | .500 |
| CJones 3b | 4 | 0 | 1 | 0 | 1 | 0 | .250 |
| Surhoff lf | 5 | 0 | 0 | 0 | 0 | 1 | .000 |
| BJordan rf | 5 | 2 | 2 | 0 | 0 | 0 | .400 |
| JLopez c | 5 | 3 | 3 | 1 | 0 | 0 | .600 |
| Brogna 1b | 4 | 2 | 2 | 1 | 1 | 0 | .500 |
| Burkett p | 1 | 0 | 1 | 0 | 1 | 0 | 1.000 |
| MValdes p | 0 | 0 | 0 | 0 | 0 | 0 | |
| DMartinez ph | 1 | 0 | 0 | 0 | 0 | 0 | |
| KAbbott ph | 1 | 0 | 0 | 0 | 0 | 0 | .000 |
| Remlinger p | 1 | 0 | 0 | 0 | 0 | 0 | |
| Lockhart ph | 1 | 0 | 0 | 0 | 0 | 0 | .000 |
| Ligtenberg p | 0 | 0 | 0 | 0 | 0 | 0 | |
| Totals | 40 | 10 | 14 | 10 | 5 | 2 | |

| Cincinnati | AB | R | H | BI | BB | SO | Avg. |
|---|---|---|---|---|---|---|---|
| Larkin ss | 4 | 1 | 3 | 0 | 0 | 1 | .750 |
| Tucker rf | 3 | 1 | 1 | 0 | 0 | 1 | .333 |
| Griffey Jr ph | 1 | 0 | 0 | 0 | 0 | 1 | .000 |
| Sullivan p | 0 | 0 | 0 | 0 | 0 | 0 | |
| Riedling p | 0 | 0 | 0 | 0 | 0 | 0 | |
| DYoung lf | 4 | 1 | 2 | 1 | 0 | 0 | .500 |
| Casey 1b | 4 | 1 | 1 | 3 | 0 | 1 | .250 |
| Ochoa rf | 2 | 0 | 0 | 0 | 0 | 0 | |
| ABoone 3b | 4 | 0 | 1 | 0 | 0 | 1 | .250 |
| Reese 2b | 4 | 0 | 0 | 0 | 0 | 0 | .000 |
| Larue c | 3 | 0 | 0 | 0 | 1 | 0 | .000 |
| Harnisch p | 2 | 0 | 0 | 0 | 0 | 1 | .000 |
| DReyes p | 0 | 0 | 0 | 0 | 0 | 0 | |
| Williamson p | 0 | 0 | 0 | 0 | 0 | 0 | |
| WGuerrero ph | 1 | 0 | 0 | 0 | 0 | 0 | .000 |
| RMRivera cf | 1 | 0 | 0 | 0 | 0 | 0 | .000 |
| Totals | 35 | 4 | 8 | 4 | 1 | 7 | |

| | | |
|---|---|---|
| Atlanta | 001 012 141–10 14 0 | |
| Cincinnati | 000 103 000– 4 8 2 | |

E-Larkin (1), DYoung (1). LOB-Atlanta 10, Cincinnati 5. 2B-QVeras (1), BJordan (1), JLopez 2 (2), Brogna (1). HR-Furcal (1) off DReyes, Casey (1) off Burkett, AJones (1) off Harnisch, DYoung (1) off Burkett. RBIs-Furcal 4 (4), QVeras 3 (3), AJones (1), JLopez (1), Brogna (1), DYoung (1), Casey 3 (3). SF-Furcal 2

| Atlanta | IP | H | R | ER | BB | SO | NP | ERA |
|---|---|---|---|---|---|---|---|---|
| Burkett | 5⅔ | 7 | 4 | 4 | 0 | 4 | 89 | 6.35 |
| MValdes W, 1-0 | ⅓ | 0 | 0 | 0 | 0 | 0 | 3 | 0.00 |
| Remlinger | 2 | 1 | 0 | 0 | 0 | 2 | 23 | 0.00 |
| Ligtenberg | 1 | 0 | 0 | 0 | 1 | 1 | 18 | 0.00 |

| Cincinnati | IP | H | R | ER | BB | SO | NP | ERA |
|---|---|---|---|---|---|---|---|---|
| Harnisch | 6 | 6 | 4 | 3 | 2 | 0 | 74 | 4.50 |
| DReyes L, 0-1 | ⅓ | 1 | 1 | 1 | 0 | 1 | 15 | 13.50 |
| Williamson | ⅓ | 0 | 0 | 0 | 1 | 0 | 10 | 0.00 |
| Sullivan | ⅓ | 4 | 4 | 3 | 2 | 0 | 24 | 81.00 |
| Riedling | 1⅔ | 2 | 1 | 1 | 0 | 1 | 27 | 5.40 |

inherited runners-scored–MValdes 1-0, Riedling 3-0. IBB-off Sullivan (CJones) 1, off Sullivan (Furcal) 1. WP-Harnisch.

### 2001 OPENING DAY SCHEDULE

| APRIL 2 | NATIONAL LEAGUE | |
|---|---|---|
| ATL vs. CIN | | STL vs. COL |
| MONT vs. CHI | | SD vs. SF |
| PHIL vs. FLA | | MILW vs. LA |
| **APRIL 3** | **NATIONAL LEAGUE** | |
| NY vs. ATL | | PITTS vs. CIN |
| ARIZ vs. LA | | MILW vs. HOUS |

*The Chicago Cubs and the Reds line up on the foul lines for the final opener at Riverfront Stadium/Cinergy Field.*

# Reds Win Last Opener at Cinergy
## 9th-Inning Rally Beats Cubs

The final Cinergy opener came down to the final inning. With one out in the bottom of the ninth, Barry Larkin sprinted home from third base on a short fly to right field, and scored the winning run when the throw from Cubs outfielder Sammy Sosa bounced away from the catcher. Larkin's dash gave the Reds a 5–4 win in the last Opening Day at Riverfront Stadium/Cinergy Field.

The Reds finished their stay at Riverfront/Cinergy with a 20–11–1 Opening Day record.

The weather was cool, but sunny. Tens of thousands cheered the Findlay Market parade along its route from Over-the-Rhine to downtown. Cincinnati City Council canceled all of its meetings. Downtown bars and restaurants enjoyed a brisk business.

A sold-out crowd filled Cinergy. Beyond the outfield wall, the crowd could see the framework of the Great American Ball Park. Several hard-hatted construction workers donned gloves and waved Reds pennants from their perches in the girders high above the wall.

The Reds treated the fans to a quick getaway, taking a 2–0 lead on a sacrifice fly by Ken Griffey, Jr. and a single by Sean Casey. The Cubs tied the score off starter Joey Hamilton but the Reds regained the lead and took a 4–2 lead into the eighth.

But Reds right fielder Juan Encarnrcion misplayed a fly ball into a two-base error. A triple by Corey Patterson and a double by Fred McGriff tied the game, setting the scene for the dramatic ninth.

With one out, Larkin walked, Griffey singled and Casey was hit by a pitch. That brought Aaron Boone to the plate who lifted a short fly to Sosa in right field. Larkin took off for home and Sosa made a strong throw to the plate. The ball barely beat Larkin to the plate, but the throw bounced away from catcher Robert Machado and Larkin slid across safely. He was mobbed by his teammates, and the cheering crowd headed for the exits.

The day began with the Findlay Market parade, minus one scheduled entrant. A fugitive cow, which had eluded capture for 10 days after escaping from a Cincinnati stockyard, was to be one of the featured entries. But the cow, which had been adopted by artist Peter Max, became skittish and missed the parade.

The final opener at Riverfront/Cinergy brought out a gala crowd: *The atmosphere in the ballpark and on downtown's streets where the Findlay Market Opening Day Parade unfolded was as festive as it has ever been. Tens of thousands of people from all over the Tristate and beyond donned red hats, shirts and jackets, celebrating as if it were a Midwestern Mardi Gras.*

*As Reds fans filed into the stadium ticket takers carefully punched their tickets instead of the usual ripping in half so fans could keep an intact memento of Cinergy Field's final Opening Day.*
**[Cincinnati Enquirer and Cincinnati Post]**

### OPENING DAY TRIVIA

| | |
|---|---|
| STAR OF THE GAME | REDS SHORTSTOP BARRY LARKIN |
| WEATHER | 56°; SUNNY |
| ATTENDANCE | 41,913 |
| NOTABLE | 1ST OPENING DAY WIN IN 5 YEARS |
| RATING | ◐◐◐◐◐ |

### April 1, 2002

| Chicago | AB | R | H | BI | BB | SO | AVG |
|---|---|---|---|---|---|---|---|
| Deshields 2b | 4 | 0 | 1 | 1 | 1 | 2 | .250 |
| Patterson cf | 3 | 1 | 2 | 1 | 2 | 0 | .667 |
| Sosa rf | 4 | 0 | 1 | 0 | 1 | 1 | .250 |
| McGriff 1b | 5 | 0 | 1 | 1 | 0 | 1 | .200 |
| Brown lf | 5 | 1 | 1 | 0 | 0 | 0 | .200 |
| Fassero p | 0 | 0 | 0 | 0 | 0 | 0 | --- |
| Gonzalez ss | 3 | 1 | 1 | 0 | 2 | 1 | .333 |
| Hundley c | 3 | 0 | 1 | 1 | 0 | 0 | .333 |
| Farnsworth p | 0 | 0 | 0 | 0 | 0 | 0 | --- |
| Lewis lf | 1 | 0 | 1 | 0 | 0 | 0 | 1.00 |
| Stynes 3b | 4 | 0 | 0 | 0 | 1 | 0 | .000 |
| Lieber p | 2 | 0 | 1 | 0 | 0 | 1 | .500 |
| Bellhorn ph | 1 | 0 | 0 | 0 | 0 | 0 | .000 |
| Osborne p | 0 | 0 | 0 | 0 | 0 | 0 | --- |
| Machado c | 2 | 0 | 1 | 0 | 0 | 1 | .500 |
| Totals | 37 | 4 | 10 | 4 | 6 | 8 | |
| **Cincinnati** | AB | R | H | BI | BB | SO | AVG |
| Walker 2b | *4 | 2 | 3 | 1 | 0 | 0 | .750 |
| Sullivan p | 0 | 0 | 0 | 0 | 0 | 0 | --- |
| Graves p | 0 | 0 | 0 | 0 | 0 | 0 | --- |
| Guerrero ph | 1 | 0 | 0 | 0 | 0 | 0 | .000 |
| Larkin ss | 2 | 1 | 1 | 0 | 2 | 0 | .500 |
| Griffey Jr. cf | 4 | 1 | 1 | 1 | 0 | 1 | .250 |
| Casey 1b | 4 | 0 | 2 | 1 | 0 | 0 | .500 |
| Boone 3b | 4 | 0 | 0 | 1 | 0 | 1 | .000 |
| Dunn lf | 4 | 0 | 0 | 0 | 0 | 1 | .000 |
| Taylor pr-lf | 0 | 0 | 0 | 0 | 0 | 0 | --- |
| Encarnacion rf | 4 | 0 | 1 | 0 | 0 | 0 | .250 |
| Larue c | 3 | 1 | 2 | 0 | 0 | 0 | .667 |
| Hamilton p | 2 | 0 | 0 | 0 | 0 | 0 | .000 |
| Williamson p | 0 | 0 | 0 | 0 | 0 | 0 | --- |
| White p | 0 | 0 | 0 | 0 | 0 | 0 | --- |
| Clark ph | 1 | 0 | 1 | 1 | 0 | 0 | 1.00 |
| Dawkins 2b | 1 | 0 | 0 | 0 | 0 | 0 | .000 |
| Totals | 35 | 5 | 12 | 5 | 1 | 4 | |

```
Chicago      000 110 020 - 4 10 1
Cincinnati   101 001 001 - 5 12 1
```

Two outs when winning run scored.
E: Deshields (1), Encarnacion (1). LOB: Chicago 14, Cincinnati 6. 2B: McGriff (1), Brown (1), Walker 2 (2), Larue (1). 3B: Patterson (1). HR: Walker (1) off Lieber. CS: Taylor (1). SF: Griffey Jr., Boone. GIDP: McGriff. DP: Cincinnati 1 (Walker, Larkin and Casey).

| Chicago | IP | H | R | ER | BB | SO | NP | ERA |
|---|---|---|---|---|---|---|---|---|
| Lieber | 6 | 8 | 3 | 3 | 0 | 1 | 79 | 5.40 |
| Osborne | 1⅓ | 3 | 1 | 0 | 1 | 3 | 38 | 5.40 |
| Farnsworth | ⅔ | 0 | 0 | 0 | 1 | 0 | 8 | 0.00 |
| Fassero (L, 0-1) | 1⅓ | 1 | 1 | 1 | 1 | 2 | 28 | 5.40 |
| **Cincinnati** | IP | H | R | ER | BB | SO | NP | ERA |
| Hamilton | 5 | 7 | 2 | 2 | 5 | 3 | 93 | 3.60 |
| Williamson | ⅔ | 0 | 0 | 0 | 1 | 1 | 8 | 0.00 |
| White | ⅓ | 0 | 0 | 0 | 1 | 0 | 5 | 0.00 |
| Sullivan | 1⅓ | 1 | 2 | 0 | 1 | 0 | 27 | 0.00 |
| Graves (W, 1-0) | 1⅓ | 2 | 0 | 0 | 0 | 1 | 21 | 0.00 |

HBP: by Fassero (Casey), by Fassero (Larue), by Fassero (Dunn). WP: Hamilton 2. PB: Larue.
Umpires: Home, John Shulock; First, Dave Phillips; Second, Mike Everitt; Third, Doug Eddings. T: 3:23. A: 41,913 (39,800).

### 2002 OPENING DAY SCHEDULE

| APRIL 1 | NATIONAL LEAGUE | |
|---|---|---|
| CHI vs. CIN | | PHIL vs. ATL |
| PITTS vs. NY | | SD vs. ARIZ |
| | COL vs. STL | |
| APRIL 2 | NATIONAL LEAGUE | |
| SF vs. LA | | MILW vs. HOUS |
| | FLA vs. MONT | |

# Great American Ball Park Debuts
## Red-Faced Reds Lay a Big Egg at Coming-Out Party
### 2003

*Jimmy Haynes throws the first pitch at Great American Ball Park to Pittsburgh outfielder Kenny Lofton.*

On this most historic Opening Day, as the game dragged on into the late innings, with the Reds falling farther and farther behind, no doubt Reds fans hoped the sentiments of one spectator would prove true: "Twenty-five years from now, the score won't matter. All that matters is, I'll be able to say I was there."

"There" was, of course, Great American Ball Park on its inaugural day, with a full house of 42,343 Reds faithful in attendance. They toured the new park, enjoyed its lush grass field and the bleachers reminiscent of the Sun Deck at old Crosley Field. They took in the sights of the city and the Ohio River and cheered themselves hoarse during the hour-long ceremonies leading up to the first pitch.

Anything to forget the game, which the Reds lost, 10–1, to Pittsburgh. And it really wasn't that close.

Reds starter Jimmy Haynes—hardly the number-one starter the fans had expected the Reds brass to sign to open the new park—gave up six runs in the second inning, all coming on home runs: a two-run shot by Reggie Sanders, a three-run bomb by Kenny Lofton and a solo homer by Jason Kendall.

The Reds, meanwhile, could do nothing off Pittsburgh's Kris Benson. Benson pitched 6 1/3 innings, allowing three hits. By the time he departed in the seventh, the Reds trailed 9–1, and many fans had headed for the hearths on a day that had grown increasingly cold.

With the war against Iraq only a few days old, the pre-game ceremonies took on a decidedly patriotic tone. Fans found small American flag in the cupholders—courtesy of Reds owner Carl Lindner—and the stands rippled with red, white and blue as Lee Greenwood sang "God Bless the USA" and New York City's "singing policeman" Daniel Rodriguez sang the national anthem.

Former president George Bush led the cast of dignitaries. The 41st president subbed for the 43rd, his son, George W. Bush, who remained in Washington, directing the war effort. With the teams lined up on the foul lines, Bush prepared to throw out the ceremonial pitch, but there was a slight delay because there was no catcher to receive the ball. Finally, Barry Larkin grabbed a glove and took Bush's toss, "a two-seamer," said Larkin. "A good two-strike pitch."

Tom Browning served as Grand Marshal in the annual Findlay Market Parade.

*An estimated 30,000 fans—many clutching blankets and sporting parkas to combat the chilly weather—lined sidewalks as the parade snaked through Over-the-Rhine and past Fountain Square. They spotted a Pete Rose look-alike, high-stepping horses and fire engines galore [and] several floats by Cincinnati Artworks made of Louisville Slugger baseball bats.*

*Tom Browning stopped the parade shortly after it started to embrace his old boss, former Reds CEO Marge Schott.* **[Cincinnati Enquirer and Cincinnati Post]**

### 2003 Opening Day Schedule

| March 31 | National League |
|---|---|
| Pitts vs. Cin | Mont vs. Atl |
| Chi vs. NY | Phil vs. Fla |
| Milw vs. StL | LA vs Ariz |
| SF vs. SD | |
| April 1 | National League |
| Col vs. Hous | |

### Opening Day Trivia

| | |
|---|---|
| Star of the Game | Pittsburgh Starter Kris Benson |
| Weather | 53°; Partly Cloudy |
| Attendance | 42,343 |
| Notable | Kluszewski Statue Unveiled Before Game |
| Rating | ●●●●○ |

### March 31, 2003

| Pittsburgh | AB | R | H | BI | BB | SO | Avg. |
|---|---|---|---|---|---|---|---|
| Lofton cf | 4 | 2 | 2 | 3 | 1 | 0 | .500 |
| Kendall c | 5 | 1 | 1 | 1 | 0 | 0 | .200 |
| BGiles lf | 4 | 1 | 1 | 1 | 1 | 0 | .250 |
| ARamirez 3b | 5 | 1 | 2 | 0 | 0 | 2 | .400 |
| Simon 1b | 4 | 2 | 2 | 1 | 0 | 0 | .500 |
| KYoung 1b | 1 | 0 | 0 | 0 | 0 | 0 | .000 |
| RSanders rf | 5 | 1 | 3 | 2 | 0 | 2 | .600 |
| Reese 2b | 3 | 1 | 1 | 1 | 2 | 1 | .333 |
| JWilson ss | 3 | 0 | 0 | 0 | 1 | 1 | .000 |
| Tavarez p | 0 | 0 | 0 | 0 | 0 | 0 | — |
| Beimel p | 0 | 0 | 0 | 0 | 0 | 0 | — |
| Benson p | 1 | 1 | 0 | 0 | 1 | 1 | .000 |
| ANunez ss | 1 | 0 | 0 | 0 | 0 | 1 | .000 |
| **Totals** | **36** | **10** | **12** | **10** | **5** | **6** | |

| Cincinnati | AB | R | H | BI | BB | SO | Avg. |
|---|---|---|---|---|---|---|---|
| Larkin ss | 4 | 0 | 0 | 0 | 1 | 0 | .000 |
| ABoone 2b | 4 | 0 | 0 | 0 | 0 | 0 | .000 |
| Griffey Jr. cf | 4 | 0 | 1 | 0 | 0 | 1 | .250 |
| Kearns rf | 3 | 0 | 0 | 1 | 1 | 1 | .000 |
| Dunn lf | 4 | 0 | 0 | 0 | 0 | 1 | .000 |
| Casey 1b | 4 | 0 | 1 | 0 | 0 | 0 | .250 |
| Larson 3b | 4 | 0 | 0 | 0 | 0 | 0 | .000 |
| LaRue c | 3 | 0 | 0 | 0 | 1 | 1 | .000 |
| JHaynes p | 1 | 1 | 1 | 0 | 0 | 0 | 1.000 |
| a-WPena ph | 1 | 0 | 0 | 0 | 0 | 0 | .000 |
| Heredia p | 0 | 0 | 0 | 0 | 0 | 0 | — |
| Sullivan p | 0 | 0 | 0 | 0 | 0 | 0 | — |
| Riedling p | 0 | 0 | 0 | 0 | 0 | 0 | — |
| b-Taylor ph | 1 | 0 | 1 | 0 | 0 | 0 | 1.000 |
| GWhite p | 0 | 0 | 0 | 0 | 0 | 0 | — |
| Williamson p | 0 | 0 | 0 | 0 | 0 | 0 | — |
| **Totals** | **32** | **1** | **4** | **1** | **3** | **4** | |

| | | | | | | |
|---|---|---|---|---|---|---|
| Pittsburgh | 060 | 010 | 210—10 | 12 | 2 | |
| Cincinnati | 001 | 000 | 000— 1 | 4 | 0 | |

a-flied out for Haynes in the 4th. b-singled for Riedling in the 7th.
E—ARamirez (1), Reese (1). LOB—Pittsburgh 6, Cincinnati 7. 2B—BGiles (1), Simon 2 (2), Griffey Jr. (1), JHaynes (1). HR—Kendall (1) off JHaynes; Lofton (1) off JHaynes; RSanders (1) off JHaynes. RBIs—Lofton 3 (3), Kendall (1), BGiles (1), Simon (1), RSanders 2 (2), Reese 2 (2), Kearns (1). S—Benson. SF—Reese.
DP—Pittsburgh 1 (Tavarez, ANunez and KYoung); Cincinnati 1 (Kearns, Riedling, Larkin, Larson and Larkin).

| Pittsburgh | IP | H | R | ER | BB | SO | NP | ERA |
|---|---|---|---|---|---|---|---|---|
| Benson W, 1-0 | 6 1/3 | 3 | 1 | 0 | 3 | 3 | 104 | 0.00 |
| Tavarez | 1 2/3 | 0 | 0 | 0 | 0 | 1 | | 0.00 |
| Beimel | 1 | 1 | 0 | 0 | 0 | 1 | 9 | 0.00 |

| Cincinnati | IP | H | R | ER | BB | SO | NP | ERA |
|---|---|---|---|---|---|---|---|---|
| JHaynes L, 0-1 | 4 | 5 | 6 | 6 | 3 | 3 | 87 | 13.50 |
| Heredia | 1/3 | 2 | 1 | 1 | 1 | 0 | | 1427.00 |
| Sullivan | 1 2/3 | 0 | 0 | 1 | 2 | 2 | 29 | 0.00 |
| Riedling | 1 | 3 | 2 | 2 | 0 | 0 | | 1318.00 |
| GWhite | 1 | 2 | 1 | 1 | 0 | 0 | | 26 9.00 |
| Williamson | 1 | 0 | 0 | 0 | 1 | 0 | | 10 0.00 |

Inherited runners-scored—Tavarez 2-0, Sullivan 2-1. Umpires—Home, Randy Marsh; First, Larry Vanover; Second, Greg Gibson; Third, Sam Holbrook. T—3:00. A—42,343 ( , 0).

# My Cincinnati Reds Opening Day Log

### 2004 Opening Day Trivia

| | |
|---|---|
| Opponent | Chicago |
| Score | |
| Winning Pitcher | |
| Losing Pitcher | |
| Star of the Game | |
| Weather | |
| Attendance | |
| Notable | |
| Rating | |

### 2005 Opening Day Trivia

| | |
|---|---|
| Opponent | |
| Score | |
| Winning Pitcher | |
| Losing Pitcher | |
| Star of the Game | |
| Weather | |
| Attendance | |
| Notable | |
| Rating | |

### 2006 Opening Day Trivia

| | |
|---|---|
| Opponent | |
| Score | |
| Winning Pitcher | |
| Losing Pitcher | |
| Star of the Game | |
| Weather | |
| Attendance | |
| Notable | |
| Rating | |

### 2007 Opening Day Trivia

| | |
|---|---|
| Opponent | |
| Score | |
| Winning Pitcher | |
| Losing Pitcher | |
| Star of the Game | |
| Weather | |
| Attendance | |
| Notable | |
| Rating | |

### 2008 Opening Day Trivia

| | |
|---|---|
| Opponent | |
| Score | |
| Winning Pitcher | |
| Losing Pitcher | |
| Star of the Game | |
| Weather | |
| Attendance | |
| Notable | |
| Rating | |

### 2009 Opening Day Trivia

| | |
|---|---|
| Opponent | |
| Score | |
| Winning Pitcher | |
| Losing Pitcher | |
| Star of the Game | |
| Weather | |
| Attendance | |
| Notable | |
| Rating | |

# Opening Day Scrapbook

## Timeline, Records and Milestones

> "Game called at 3:30. Admission, 50¢. Children, 25¢. Gentlemen accompanied by ladies admitted to Grand Stand free."
>
> — 1880 Opening Day advertisement

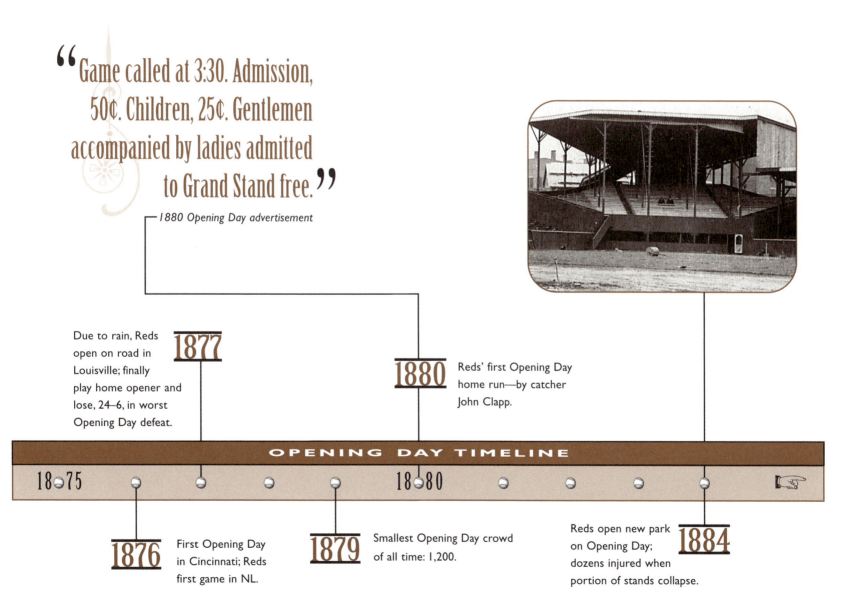

**OPENING DAY TIMELINE**

**1876** — First Opening Day in Cincinnati; Reds first game in NL.

**1877** — Due to rain, Reds open on road in Louisville; finally play home opener and lose, 24–6, in worst Opening Day defeat.

**1879** — Smallest Opening Day crowd of all time: 1,200.

**1880** — Reds' first Opening Day home run—by catcher John Clapp.

**1884** — Reds open new park on Opening Day; dozens injured when portion of stands collapse.

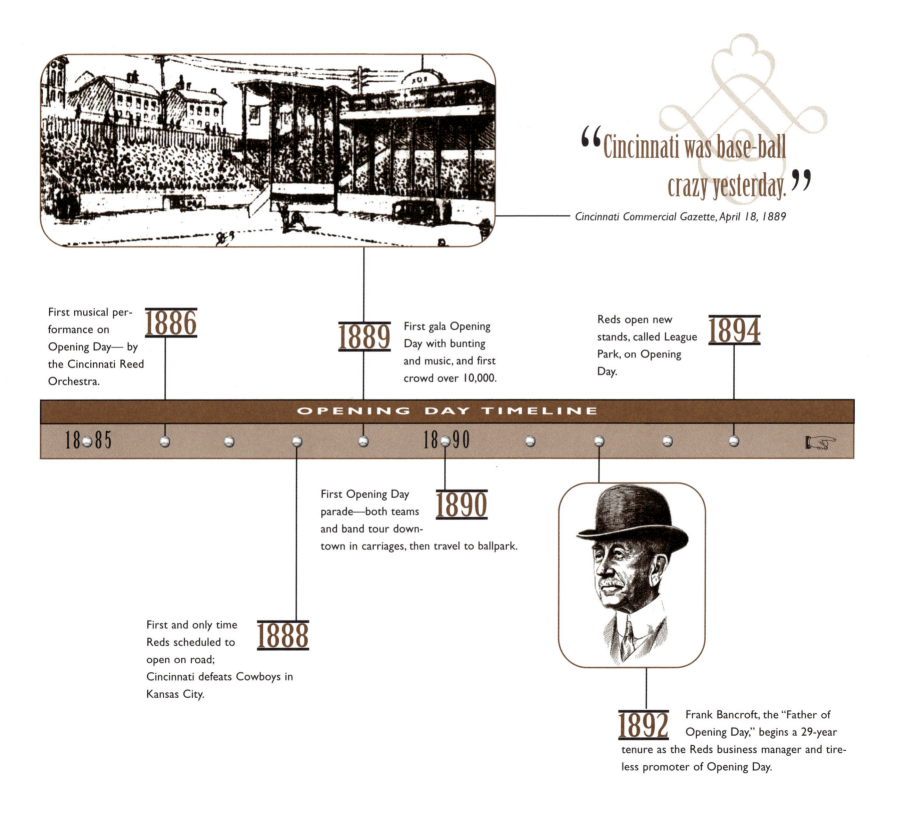

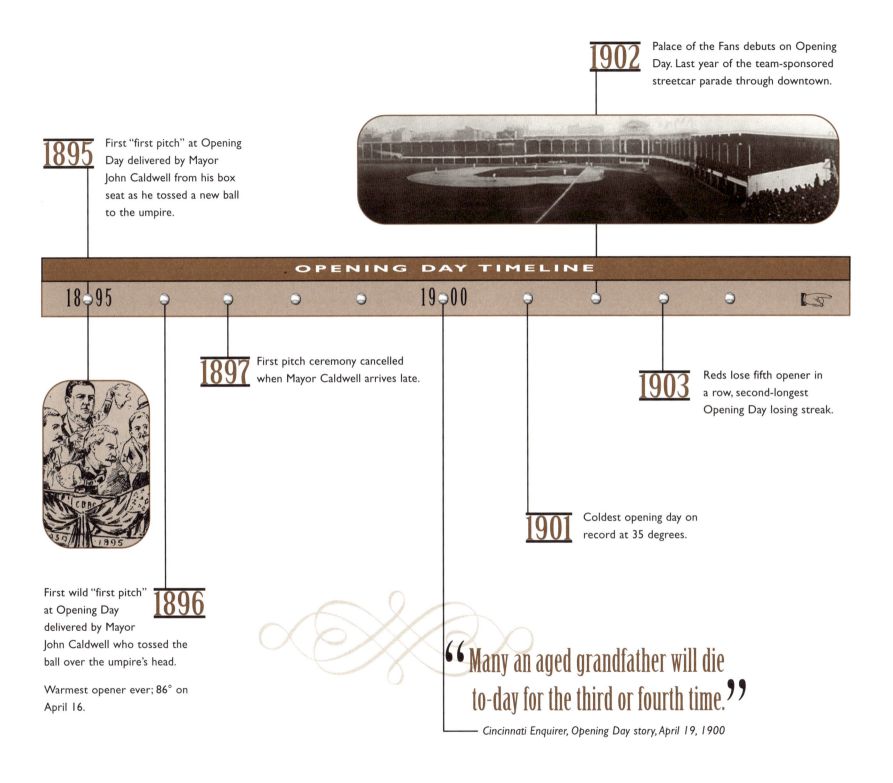

## OPENING DAY TIMELINE

**1902** — Palace of the Fans debuts on Opening Day. Last year of the team-sponsored streetcar parade through downtown.

**1895** — First "first pitch" at Opening Day delivered by Mayor John Caldwell from his box seat as he tossed a new ball to the umpire.

**1897** — First pitch ceremony cancelled when Mayor Caldwell arrives late.

**1903** — Reds lose fifth opener in a row, second-longest Opening Day losing streak.

**1901** — Coldest opening day on record at 35 degrees.

**1896** — First wild "first pitch" at Opening Day delivered by Mayor John Caldwell who tossed the ball over the umpire's head.

Warmest opener ever; 86° on April 16.

> "Many an aged grandfather will die to-day for the third or fourth time."
> — *Cincinnati Enquirer, Opening Day story, April 19, 1900*

**1905** Prior to the opener, several "rooters'" groups stage impromptu parades through downtown streets in automobiles, carriages and large horse-drawn wagons known as tallyho's, a tradition that eventually spawns the Findlay Market rooters and parade.

**1908** So many players are presented with floral bouquets before the game that one paper notes home plate resembled a "flower garden."

**1912** Redland Field opens on Opening Day, 1912; largest crowd to that time (26,336).

## OPENING DAY TIMELINE

1905   1910

> "There is not a single day in the year that is looked forward to in this city more than the opening of the baseball season."
>
> *Opening Day story, Commericial-Tribune, April 14, 1909*

**1913** First "first pitch" thrown from mound, by Mayor Henry Hunt. All previous first pitches were tossed from the stands. For the record, Hunt's toss was a ball, high and outside.

## OPENING DAY TIMELINE

**1917** — First time the "Star Spangled Banner" is played prior to the opener. Weber's military band plays the patriotic air in recognition of America's entry into WWI.

**1920** — First appearance by Findlay Market rooters on Opening Day.

John D. Rockefeller attends the opener.

**1922** — Findlay Market rooters make a presentation for the first time at home plate prior to the opener, a tradition that continues to present day. They present a huge floral horseshoe to manager Pat Moran.

Match-up of starters features two future Hall of Famers: Grover Cleveland Alexander vs. Eppa Rixey.

**1924** — First opener broadcast on radio, by WLW and WSAI. This is also the first broadcast of a Reds game at Crosley Field.

Crowd of 35,747 is largest Opening Day crowd ever at Crosley Field.

> "What's the rumpus in our nation?
> What's the cause of this sensation?
> If you listen you will note a joyful tune—
> For the very simple reason
> That another baseball season
> Will be opened up Wednesday afternoon."
>
> — *Opening Day verse, Cincinnati Commercial Tribune, April 11, 1917*

## OPENING DAY TIMELINE

**1927** — Stunt flyers entertain crowd during pre-game show with daring aerial acrobatics.

**1928** — Pitching legend Cy Young is scheduled to throw out ceremonial first pitch, but is held up in traffic and arrives late.

**1929** — Tied for fastest opener ever (with 1944) at 77 minutes.

**1930** — Reds and Pirates combine for 32 hits, the modern Cincinnati Opening Day record.

**1931** — Warmest opener on record in 20th cenutry —82° on April 14.

**1934** — Chicago's Lon Warneke loses no-hitter in bottom of ninth inning when Adam Comorosky singles with one out.

Broadcast legend Red Barber makes major league debut as Reds announcer.

> "All the schools were out yesterday afternoon, so the fatality rate among grandmothers was much less than usual."
> —*Cincinnati Enquirer, April 13, 1933*

*Larry McPhail (left of ball), Powel Crosley (right of ball) and manager Bob O'Farrell accept gifts from the Findlay Market Association prior to the 1934 opener.*

## OPENING DAY TIMELINE

**1935** — Thin layer of snow blankets Crosley Field on Opening Day morning.

Game features eight future Hall of Famers, most ever for a Cincinnati opener.

**1937** — Reds pitcher Lee Grissom marries local waitress on eve of Opening Day.

**1939** — High water invades Reds dugout on morning of Opener as nearby Millcreek reaches flood stage.

**1941** — Reds raise World Championship banner in pre-game ceremonies.

Frank McCormick becomes first and only Red to homer twice on Opening Day

> "The playing of baseball games offers a needed recreation for those at home. News and radio reports of the games are greatly desired by men in uniform in this country and abroad. We inaugurate the 1944 National League season with this in mind."
>
> *Cincinnati Baseball Club's Opening Day announcement: April 18, 1944*

**OPENING GAME TICKETS**
At STRAUS CIGAR STORE
(Sixth and Walnut) until 11 A.M.
1,500 Reserved Chairs—$1.25 including tax.

**At CROSLEY FIELD**
Box Office Open 9:30 A.M. Gates Open 11 A.M.
1,500 Reserved Chairs at $1.25, including tax.
3,000 General Admission at $1.10, including tax.
4,500 Bleacher Seats at 60c, including tax.

"**The Wild Bricklayer from Oxford dragged his aging legs around the bases and strutted in front of the stands.**"

The Cincinnati Enquirer's *description of the antics of Oxford, Ohio, native Henry Thobe who performed impromptu jigs for Opening Day fans from the 1920s to the late 1940s.*

**1951** Snow falls during first inning.

**1952** Fan locked in ballpark until late evening after cleaning crews overlook him in bathroom.

First Opening Day with four umpires.

## OPENING DAY TIMELINE

19●45 19●50

**1945** Flags at half-mast for the late President Franklin D. Roosevelt.

**1946** New compact Crosley Car, driven by inventor Powel Crosley, tours Crosley Field in pre-game ceremonies.

First televised opener. **1948**

**1954** Jim Greengrass ties a major league record with four doubles. All are ground-rule doubles, landing in the crowd seated in the outfield.

## OPENING DAY TIMELINE

**1955** — Findlay Market Parade at ballpark canceled for first time due to wet grounds.

**1956** — Dave Garroway and *The Today Show* cast broadcasts from Fountain Square on Opening Day morning.

**1959** — Last year overflow crowd sits on the field on Opening Day.

**1961** — Moment of silence observed for Powel Crosley, late owner of the Reds.

**1963** — Pete Rose makes major league debut.

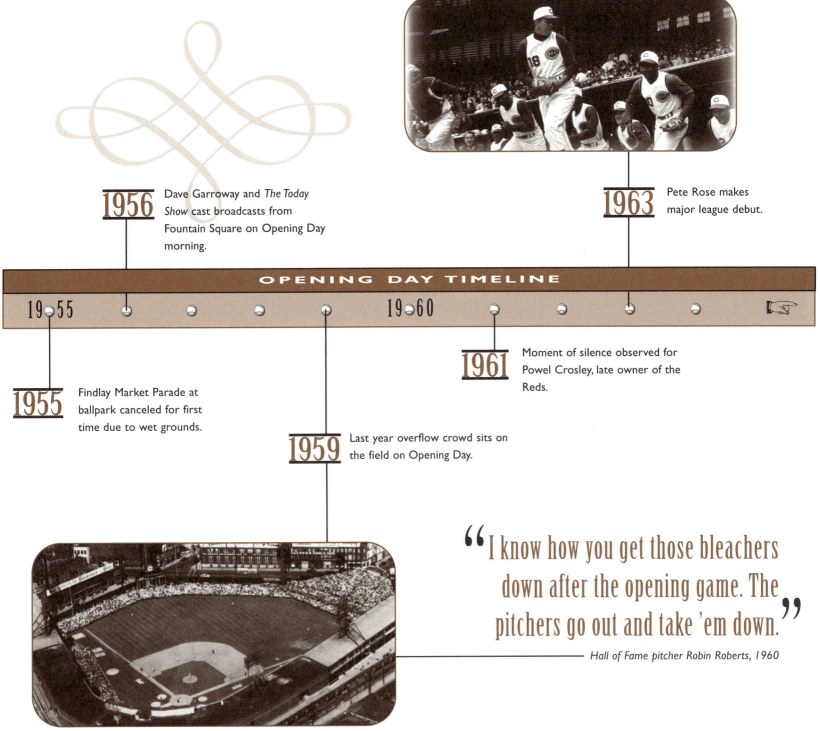

*Opening Day at Crosley Field, 1955, with overflow crowd seated in the temporary bleachers on the field.*

> "I know how you get those bleachers down after the opening game. The pitchers go out and take 'em down."
>
> — Hall of Fame pitcher Robin Roberts, 1960

**1966** First nighttime home opener after three days of rain forces Reds to open on road. The home opener is held on April 22, 11 days after it was originally scheduled.

> "As baseball spectacle, this could hardly be topped."
>
> Pat Harmon, Cincinnati Post, April 4, 1974

**1974** Greatest opening day ever, according to authors; Aaron's historic home run; Reds comeback victory; Brennaman debuts behind mike.

**1971** New Opening Day attendance record (51,702) set as Reds play first opener at Riverfront Stadium.

OPENING DAY TIMELINE

1966    1970

**1968** MLB postpones openers two days in response to Martin Luther King assassination and funeral.

**1972** Opener postponed two weeks due to players' strike.

## OPENING DAY TIMELINE

**1975** — Longest opener ever at 14 innings; Reds top Dodgers, 2–1.

**1977** — Four inches of snow blankets Riverfront turf on morning of game.

**1978** — First and only Opening Day triple play pulled off by Houston Astros.

**1981** — Match-up of starters (Tom Seaver vs. Steve Carlton) features two future Hall of Famers for only second time at a Reds opener.

**1983** — Reds fan use Opening Day to voice their disgust with Reds management after 101 losses. Over 10,000 empty outfield seats bear witness to the protest.

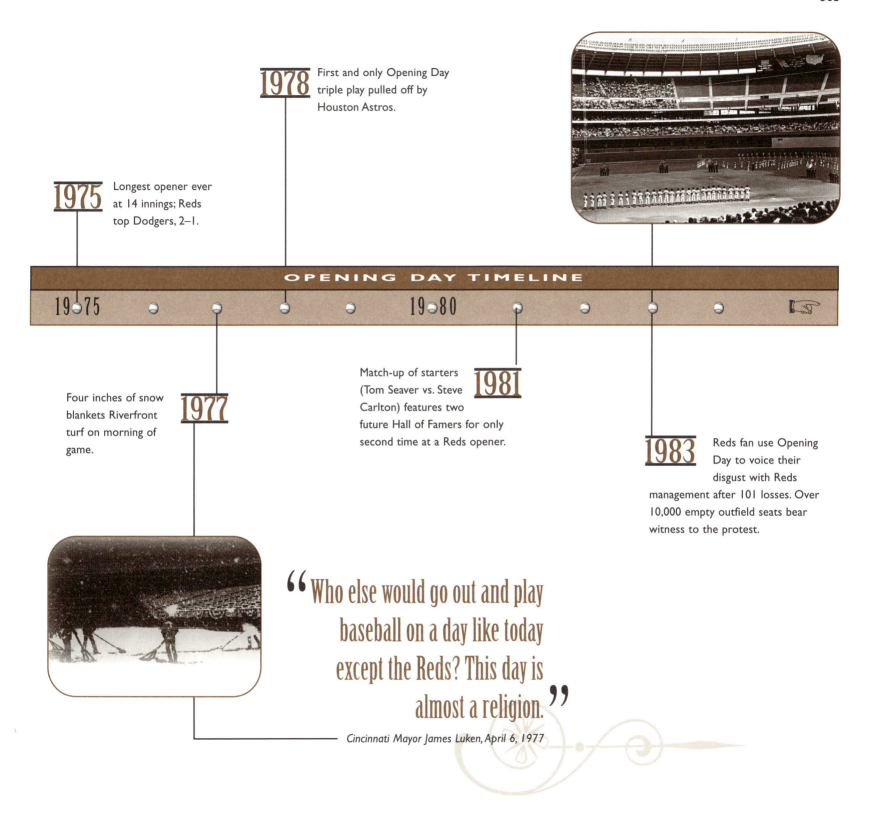

> "Who else would go out and play baseball on a day like today except the Reds? This day is almost a religion."
>
> *Cincinnati Mayor James Luken, April 6, 1977*

## 1985
Sunshine, rain, sleet and snow descend on opener.

American League sparks controversy by scheduling games to begin before Reds.

## 1990
Opener postponed one week due to labor squabbles. Reds open on road in Houston.

*In the 1990s, Marge Schott enlivened Opening Day ceremonies with her friends from the Cincinnati Zoo.*

**OPENING DAY TIMELINE**

1985 • • • • 1990 • • • • ☞

## 1994
In this year of two "openers," Reds owner and most fans boycott the Sunday night ESPN opener in favor of a traditional Monday afternoon Opening Day.

> "There is spring in the air, happy chatter on the streets and Soto on the mound. It's Opening Day in Cincinnati and, on that account, all's right with the world."

Cincinnati Enquirer *Editorial, marking Mario Soto's sixth Opening Day start in the 1980s*

> "The parade was Monday; the ushers in tuxedos were Monday; the big crowd was Monday. That's when Opening Day is, honey! Monday afternoon!"

*Former Reds Owner Marge Schott*

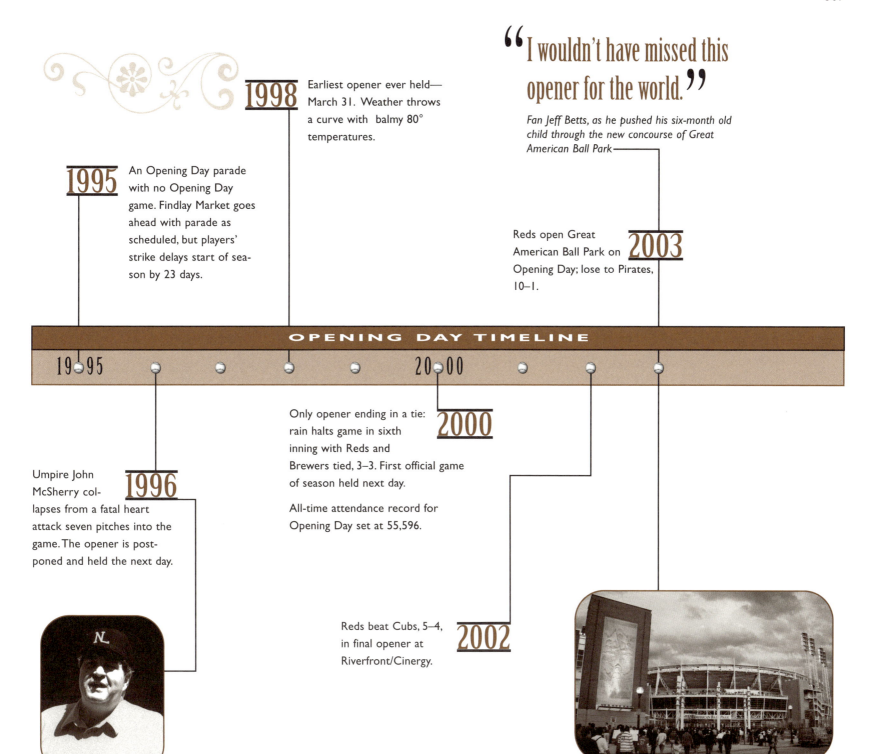

## OPENING DAY TIMELINE

**1995** — An Opening Day parade with no Opening Day game. Findlay Market goes ahead with parade as scheduled, but players' strike delays start of season by 23 days.

**1996** — Umpire John McSherry collapses from a fatal heart attack seven pitches into the game. The opener is postponed and held the next day.

**1998** — Earliest opener ever held—March 31. Weather throws a curve with balmy 80° temperatures.

**2000** — Only opener ending in a tie: rain halts game in sixth inning with Reds and Brewers tied, 3–3. First official game of season held next day.

All-time attendance record for Opening Day set at 55,596.

**2002** — Reds beat Cubs, 5–4, in final opener at Riverfront/Cinergy.

**2003** — Reds open Great American Ball Park on Opening Day; lose to Pirates, 10–1.

> "I wouldn't have missed this opener for the world."
>
> *Fan Jeff Betts, as he pushed his six-month old child through the new concourse of Great American Ball Park—*

## Only Home Openers are Counted in These Records and Milestones

## Comeback Victories

| | |
|---|---|
| 1883 vs. St. Louis | Down 5–4 in 11th, Reds Win, 6–5 |
| 1897 vs. Chicago | Down 6–4 in 9th, and 7–6 in 10th, Reds Win in 10, 8–7 |
| 1907 vs. Pittsburgh | Trailing 3–2 in 9th, Reds Win, 4–3 |
| 1924 vs. Pittsburgh | Down 5–4 in 8th, Reds Tie in 8th and Win in 9th, 6–5 |
| 1932 vs. Chicago | Down 4–1 in 9th, Reds Rally to Win, 5–4 |
| 1974 vs. Atlanta | Down 6–2 in 8th, and 6–5 in 9th, Reds Win in 11, 7–6 |
| 1981 vs. Philadelphia | Trailing 2–1 in 9th, Reds Win, 3–2 |

## Ten Worst Weather Days

| | |
|---|---|
| April 20, 1901 | 35° |
| April 16, 1887 | "Mid-30's" |
| April 16, 1935 | Light Dusting of Snow in AM—38° |
| April 8, 1985 | Snow, Rain, Sleet, Sunshine—39° |
| April 3, 1994 | Easter Sunday Night Opener—39° |
| April 15, 1952 | 40° |
| April 6, 1977 | 4 Inches of Snow on Field in AM—41° |
| April 16, 1929 / April 5, 1993 | 42° |
| April 5, 1973 | 43° |
| April 16, 1951 | Snowflakes Fall in First Inning—44° |

## Opening Day Attendance Marks

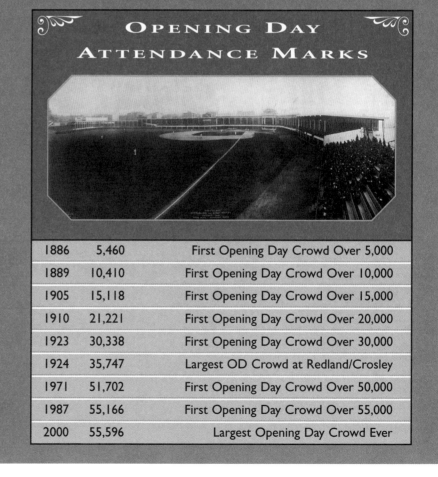

| | | |
|---|---|---|
| 1886 | 5,460 | First Opening Day Crowd Over 5,000 |
| 1889 | 10,410 | First Opening Day Crowd Over 10,000 |
| 1905 | 15,118 | First Opening Day Crowd Over 15,000 |
| 1910 | 21,221 | First Opening Day Crowd Over 20,000 |
| 1923 | 30,338 | First Opening Day Crowd Over 30,000 |
| 1924 | 35,747 | Largest OD Crowd at Redland/Crosley |
| 1971 | 51,702 | First Opening Day Crowd Over 50,000 |
| 1987 | 55,166 | First Opening Day Crowd Over 55,000 |
| 2000 | 55,596 | Largest Opening Day Crowd Ever |

## Best Pitching Performances
(Since 1900)

| Pitcher | Year | Score | |
|---|---|---|---|
| Lon Warneke (Cubs) | 1934 | 6–0 | 1-Hitter Broken up in 9th Inning; 13 Ks; 2 BB |
| Pete Schneider | 1918 | 2–0 | 1-Hitter Broken up in 4th inning; 3K; 5 BB |
| Johnny Vander Meer | 1943 | 1–0 | 11-Inning 2-Hitter; 3 Ks; 5 BB |
| Rube Benton | 1914 | 10–1 | 2-Hitter; 1 K; 6 BB |
| Deacon Phillipe (Pirates) | 1903 | 7–1 | 2 Hitter; 5 Ks; 1 BB |
| Tony Clonninger (Braves) | 1965 | 4–2 | 2-Hitter; 2 Ks; 5 BB |
| Frank Pastore | 1980 | 9–0 | 3-Hitter; 5 Ks; 0 BB |
| Fred Beebe | 1910 | 1–0 | 3 Hitter; 3 Ks; 2 BB |
| Max Surkont (Braves) | 1953 | 2–0 | 3-Hitter; 2 Ks; 0 BB |
| Ewell Blackwell | 1947 | 3–1 | 3-Hitter; 6 Ks; 6 BB |
| Jim Merritt | 1970 | 5–1 | 3-Hitter; 8 Ks; 2 BB |
| Babe Adams (Pirates) | 1911 | 14–0 | 4-Hitter; 6 Ks; 1 BB |
| Howie Camnitz (Pirates) | 1909 | 3–0 | 6-hittter; 5 Ks; 1 BB |
| Henry Wyse (Cubs) | 1944 | 3–0 | 5-Hitter; 1 K; 2 BB |
| Don Gullett | 1975 | 2–1 | 9 ⅔ Innings; 5 Hits; 4 Ks; 5 BB |
| Orval Overall (Cubs) | 1910 | 0–1 | 5-Hitter; 7 Ks; 1 BB |
| Pete Donohue | 1925 | 4–0 | 6-Hitter; 2 Ks; 0 BB |
| Mort Cooper (Cardinals) | 1943 | 0–1 | 11-Inning 6-Hitter; 4 Ks; 2 BB |
| Mario Soto | 1984 | 8–1 | 7-Hitter; 8 Ks; 1 BB |
| Tom Browning | 1991 | 6–2 | 8 ⅓ Innings; 5 Hits; 4 Ks; 1 BB |
| Jose Rijo | 1993 | 2–1 | 8 Innings; 5 Hits; 5 Ks; 0 BB |

## Victories

| Pitcher | Wins | Record |
|---|---|---|
| Mario Soto | 4 | (4-1) |
| Will White | 4 | (4-3) |
| Dolf Luque | 3 | (3-0) |
| Tony Mullane | 3 | (3-3) |
| Tom Browning | 2 | (2-0) |
| Pete Schneider | 2 | (2-0) |
| Pete Donohue | 2 | (2-1) |
| Ewell Blackwell | 2 | (2-1) |
| Jim O'Toole | 2 | (2-1) |

### Opposing Pitchers

| Pitcher | Wins | Record |
|---|---|---|
| Babe Adams (Pirates) | 2 | (2-0) |
| Waite Hoyt (Pirates) | 2 | (2-0) |
| G.C. Alexander (Chi/St. L) | 2 | (2-0) |
| Lon Warneke (Chi/St.L) | 2 | (2-0) |

## Most Strikeouts—Game
*Visiting pitcher

| Pitcher | | Year |
|---|---|---|
| Ed Morris * | 13 | 1884 |
| Lon Warneke * | 13 | 1934 |
| Gary Nolan | 12 | 1969 |
| Mario Soto | 10 | 1982 |
| Jesse Dureya | 8 | 1890 |
| Jim O'Toole | 8 | 1965 |
| Jim Merritt | 8 | 1970 |
| J.R. Richard * | 8 | 1978 |
| Steve Carlton * | 8 | 1981 |
| Mario Soto | 8 | 1984 |

## Big Offensive Days
### (Since 1900)

| | | |
|---|---|---|
| Joe Morgan | 1978 | 3 Hits, 1 HR, 1 2B, 5 RBIs, 3 runs scored, 1 SB |
| George Foster | 1980 | 3 Hits, 1 HR, 1 2B, 4 RBIs, 2 runs scored |
| Paul O'Neill | 1989 | 4 hits, 1 HR, 1 2B, 3 RBIs, 2 runs scored |
| Dain Clay | 1945 | 2 hits, 1 HR (GS), 5 RBIs, 1 run scored |
| Andy Pafko (Cubs) | 1950 | 3 hits, 2 HRs, 1 2B, 4 RBIs, 2 runs scored |
| Ripper Collins (Cubs) | 1938 | 4 hits, 1 HR, 1 2B, 2 RBIs, 3 runs scored |
| Frank McCormick | 1941 | 3 hits, 2 HRs, 2 RBIs, 2 runs scored |
| Tony Perez | 1974 | 2 hits, 1 HR, 4 RBIs, 1 run scored |
| Tony Perez | 1976 | 2 hits, 1 2B, 4 RBIs, 1 run scored |
| Eric Davis | 1987 | 3 hits, 1 HR, 2 RBIs, 3 runs scored, 2 SBs |
| Jim Greengrass | 1954 | 4 hits, 4 2Bs, 2 RBIs, 2 runs scored |
| Stan Musial (Cardinals) | 1957 | 4 hits, 2 2Bs, 2 RBIs, 1 run scored |
| Bubbles Hargrave | 1924 | 4 hits, 2 3Bs, 2 runs scored |
| Johnny Mize (Cardinals) | 1941 | 3 hits, 1 HR, 1 2B, 3 RBIs, 1 run scored |

## Openers Played
### (through 2003)

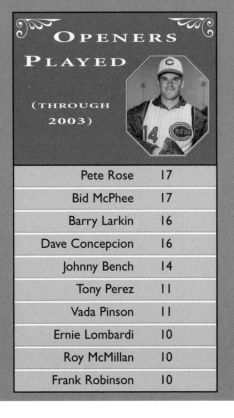

| | |
|---|---|
| Pete Rose | 17 |
| Bid McPhee | 17 |
| Barry Larkin | 16 |
| Dave Concepcion | 16 |
| Johnny Bench | 14 |
| Tony Perez | 11 |
| Vada Pinson | 11 |
| Ernie Lombardi | 10 |
| Roy McMillan | 10 |
| Frank Robinson | 10 |

## Leading Batting Averages
### (Minimum 20 ABs; through 2003)

| Hitter | Ave. | Hits/ABs |
|---|---|---|
| Ival Goodman | .419 | (13/31) |
| George Foster | .407 | (11/27) |
| Frank McCormick | .394 | (13/33) |
| Joe Morgan | .393 | (11/28) |
| Heine Groh | .375 | (9/24) |
| Grady Hatton | .375 | (12/32) |
| Dick Hoblitzell | .364 | (8/22) |
| Bid McPhee | .344 | (21/61) |
| Ernie Lombardi | .342 | (13/38) |
| Pete Rose | .338 | (22/65) |
| Barry Larkin | .325 | (21/56) |
| Gus Bell | .323 | (10/31) |
| Dave Concepcion | .313 | (20/64) |
| Billy Myers | .526 | (10/19 *) |

\* Myers finished 1 AB short of the 20-AB standard, but deserved mention.

## Home Run Leaders
(through 2003)

| Opening Day HRs | |
|---|---|
| Frank McCormick | 4 |
| Barry Larkin | 3 |
| Frank Robinson | 3 |
| Sean Casey | 2 |
| Reggie Sanders | 2 |
| Eric Davis | 2 |
| Tony Perez | 2 |
| Bobby Tolan | 2 |
| Cesar Cedeno | 2 |
| Ellis Burks | 2 |
| Mike Ivie | 2 |
| Joe Torre | 2 |
| Eddie Mathews | 2 |
| Hank Sauer | 2 |
| Enos Slaughter | 2 |
| Many Tied With | 1 |

| Grand Slams | Year | Two in One Game | Year |
|---|---|---|---|
| Bug Holliday | 1884 | Frank McCormick | 1941 |
| Dain Clay | 1945 | Andy Pafko | 1950 |
| Hank Sauer | 1952 | Eddie Mathews | 1954 |
| | | Joe Torre | 1965 |

## RBI Leaders
(through 2003)

| | |
|---|---|
| Tony Perez | 14 |
| Bug Holliday | 11 |
| Dave Concepcion | 9 |
| George Foster | 9 |
| Tommy Corcoran | 9 |
| Pete Rose | 8 |
| Frank Robinson | 8 |
| Frank McCormick | 8 |
| Barry Larkin | 7 |
| Sean Casey | 6 |
| Gus Bell | 6 |

## Offensive Highlights

| | |
|---|---|
| Most Runs by Reds (pre-1900), 18 | 1888 |
| Most Runs by Reds (post-1900), 11 | 1976, '78, '87, '97 |
| Most Hits by Both Teams (pre-1900), 44 | 1877 |
| Most Hits by Both Teams (post-1900), 32 | 1930 |
| Most Doubles by Both Teams, 13 | 1954 |
| Most Triples by Both Teams, 7 | 1912 |
| Most Home Runs by Both Teams, 5 | 1941 |
| Longest Opening Day Hit Streak, 14 Dave Concepcion | |
| Most Runs in 1 Inning by Reds, 9 | 1987 |
| Most Runs in 1 Inning by Opponent, 8 (Giants) | 1979 |

## Slowest and Fastest Openers

| | | |
|---|---|---|
| Fastest | 1:17 | 1929; 1944 |
| Last Opener Under 2 Hours | 1:56 | 1961 |
| Slowest (9 innings) | 3:27 | 1996 |
| Slowest (Extra Innings) | 3:43 | 1988 (12 innings) |

## Tragedies and Near-Tragedies

| | |
|---|---|
| 1895 | Fan Fatally Injured in Fall From Streetcar on Way to Ballpark |
| 1915 | Reds Manager Buck Herzog Nearly Chokes to Death on Gum in Dugout |
| 1923 | Boy Walking to Ballpark Accidentally Shot and Killed by Friend |
| 1941 | Fan Succumbs to Heart Attack in Stands in Third Inning |
| 1954 | Chicago's Andy Pafko Beaned by Joe Nuxhall |
| 1996 | Umpire John McSherry Dies on Field During First Inning |

## Debuts of Hall of Famers and Other Notables on Opening Day in Cincinnati

| | |
|---|---|
| 1878 | Hall of Fame Outfielder King Kelly Debuts with Reds |
| 1882 | Debut of Reds Hall of Fame Second Baseman Bid McPhee |
| 1902 | First Game for Chicago's Hall of Fame First Baseman Joe Tinker |
| 1905 | Hall of Fame Umpire Bill Klem Calls His First Game |
| 1922 | Hall of Fame Catcher Gabby Hartnett Debuts With the Cubs |
| 1927 | Pittsburgh Hall of Fame Outfielder Lloyd Waner Debuts |
| 1934 | Reds Announcer and Ford Frick Winner Red Barber Calls His 1st Game |
| 1934 | First Major League Game for Reds GM and HOF Executive, Larry MacPhail |
| 1954 | Debut of Hall of Fame Outfielder Hank Aaron With the Milwaukee Braves |
| 1956 | Debut of Reds Hall of Fame Outfielder Frank Robinson |
| 1963 | Pete Rose Debuts |
| 1970 | Debut of Reds Hall of Fame Manager Sparky Anderson |
| 1974 | First Broadcast by Reds Announcer and Frick Winner Marty Brennaman |

## Opening Day Tributes

Opening Day festivities have often included a tribute to a significant event associated with the Reds, or a national event that coincided with the start of the baseball season. A partial list includes:

| | |
|---|---|
| 1883 | Raising of the 1882 pennant |
| 1925 | Raising of 50th Anniversary NL flag |
| 1932 | Flag at half-mast for longtime club treasurer, Louis Widrig |
| 1941 | Raising of World Championship pennant |
| 1945 | Moment of silence for President Franklin D. Roosevelt |
| 1961 | Moment of silence for Reds owner Powel Crosley |
| 1965 | Plaque presented in memory of Reds manager Fred Hutchinson |
| 1981 | Moment of silence for President Ronald Reagan wounded in assassination attempt |
| 1991 | Presentation of World Series rings |
| 1996 | Moment of silence for umpire John McSherry |
| 2003 | Tribute to soldiers fighting in Iraq |

# Cincinnati Reds Opening Day Log
## (Home Openers Only)

| Date | Opponent | W-L | Score | Winning Pitcher | Losing Pitcher | Temperature | Attendance |
|---|---|---|---|---|---|---|---|
| 4/25/1876 | St Louis | W | 2–1 | Cherokee Fisher | George Bradley | NA; part cloudy | 2,000 |
| 5/14/77 * | Louisville | L | 6–24 | Jim Devlin | Bobby Matthews | 76° fair | 3,000 |
| 5/1/78 | Milwaukee | W | 6–4 | Will White | Sam Weaver | 77° clear | 2,500 |
| 5/1/79 | Troy | W | 7–5 | Will White | George Bradley | NA | 1,200 |
| 5/1/80 ∞ | Chicago | L | 3–4 | Larry Corcoran | Will White | 62° clear | 2,038 |
| 1881 | Reds Not in Professional League | | | | | | |
| 5/2/82 | Pittsburgh | L | 9–10 | Jack Leary | Will White | 55° clear | 1,500 |
| 5/1/83 | St. Louis | W | 6–5 (11) | Will White | Jumbo McGinnis | 67° clear | 3,500 |
| 5/1/84 ∞ | Columbus | L | 9–10 | Ed Morris | Will White | 80° windy | 3,200 |
| 4/20/85 * | Louisville | W | 3–1 | Will White | Phil Reccius | 75° part cloudy | 2,500 |
| 4/17/86 | Louisville | L | 1–5 | Guy Hecker | Larry McKeon | 75° part cloudy | 5,460 |
| 4/16/87 | Cleveland | W | 16–6 | Tony Mullane | George Pechiney | Mid–30s; cloudy | 2,700 |
| 5/1/88 ** | Louisville | W | 18–2 | Tony Mullane | King Ramsey | 45° cloudy | 2,200 |
| 4/17/89 | St. Louis | L | 1–5 | Silver King | Tony Mullane | 71° sunny | 10,410 |
| 4/19/90 | Chicago | L | 4–5 | Bill Hutchinson | Jesse Duryea | 50° windy | 6,000 |
| 4/22/91 | Cleveland | L | 3–6 | Cy Young | Tony Mullane | 63° damp | 4,503 |
| 4/12/92 | Pittsburgh | L | 5–7 | Mark Baldwin | Tony Mullane | 44° clear | 7,468 |
| 4/27/93 | Chicago | W | 10–1 | Tony Mullane | Wee Willie McGill | 55° sunny | 7,000 |
| 4/20/94 ◊ ∞ | Chicago | W | 10–6 | Tom Parrott | Bill Hutchinson | 50° damp | 6,285 |
| 4/18/95 | Cleveland | W | 10–8 | Frank Dwyer | Mike Sullivan | 65° clear | 13,297 |
| 4/16/96 | Pittsburgh | L | 1–9 | Pink Hawley | Billy Rhines | 86° sunny | 14,412 |
| 4/22/97 | Chicago | W | 8–7 (10) | Billy Rhines | Clark Griffith | 74° part cloudy | 11,448 |
| 4/15/98 | Cleveland | W | 3–2 | Ted Breitenstein | Cy Young | 67° sunny | 10,000 |
| 4/15/99 | Pittsburgh | L | 2–5 | Jesse Tannehill | Pink Hawley | 62° cloudy | 9,148 |
| 4/19/1900 | Chicago | L | 10–13 | Jocko Menefee | Ed Scott | 70° clear | 11,920 |
| 4/20/01 ◊ | Pittsburgh | L | 2–4 | Sam Leever | Noodles Hahn | 39° windy | 4,800 |
| 4/17/02 ∞ | Chicago | L | 1–6 | Jack Taylor | Len Swormstedt | 62° cloudy | 10,000 |
| 4/16/03 | Pittsburgh | L | 1–7 | Deacon Phillippe | Jack Harper | 51° sprinkles | 12,000 |
| 4/14/04 | Chicago | W | 3–2 | Jack Sutthoff | Jake Weimer | 48° part cloudy | 13,000 |
| 4/14/05 | Pittsburgh | L | 4–9 | Pat Flaherty | Jack Harper | 63° sunny | 15,118 |
| 4/12/06 | Chicago | L | 2–7 | Carl Lundgren | Orval Overall | 70° fair | 17,241 |
| 4/11/07 | Pittsburgh | W | 4–3 | Bob Ewing | Lefty Leifield | 45° cloudy | 10,000 |

| Date | Opponent | W-L | Score | Winning Pitcher | Losing Pitcher | Temperature | Attendance |
|---|---|---|---|---|---|---|---|
| 4/14/08 | Chicago | L | 5–6 | Orval Overall | Bill Campbell | 76° part cloudy | 19,257 |
| 4/14/09 | Pittsburgh | L | 0–3 | Howard Camnitz | Art Fromme | 50° clear | 18,000 |
| 4/14/10 | Chicago | W | 1–0 (10) | Fred Beebe | Orval Overall | 79° part cloudy | 21,221 |
| 4/12/11 | Pittsburgh | L | 0–14 | Babe Adams | Art Fromme | 64° damp | 18,000 |
| 4/11/12 ∞ | Chicago | W | 10–6 | Bert Humphries | King Cole | 75° part cloudy | 26,336 |
| 4/12/13 ◊ | Pittsburgh | L | 2–9 | Babe Adams | Art Fromme | 52° damp | 20,000 |
| 4/14/14 | Chicago | W | 10–1 | Rube Benton | Larry Cheney | 53° light rain | 15,728 |
| 4/14/15 | Pittsburgh | L | 2–9 | George McQuillan | Leon Ames | 62° crisp | 21,000 |
| 4/12/16 | Chicago | L | 1–7 | George McConnell | Fred Toney | 76° part cloudy | 24,607 |
| 4/11/17 | St Louis | W | 3–1 | Pete Schneider | Lee Meadows | 70° fair | 24,938 |
| 4/16/18 | Pittsburgh | W | 2–0 | Pete Schneider | Wilbur Cooper | 68° sunny | 19,000 |
| 4/23/19 | St Louis | W | 6–2 | Dolf Luque | Bill Sherdel | 74° part cloudy | 22,462 |
| 4/14/20 | Chicago | W | 7–3 | Dutch Ruether | Grover Alexander | 48° cloudy | 24,822 |
| 4/13/21 | Pittsburgh | W | 5–3 | Dolf Luque | Babe Adams | 70° clear | 29,963 |
| 4/12/22 | Chicago | L | 3–7 | Grover Alexander | Eppa Rixey | 52° part cloudy | 27,095 |
| 4/17/23 | St Louis | W | 3–2 (11) | Pete Donohue | Lester Sell | 52° cloudy | 30,338 |
| 4/15/24 | Pittsburgh | W | 6–5 | Tom Sheehan | Lee Meadows | 79° sunny | 35,747 |
| 4/14/25 | St Louis | W | 4–0 | Pete Donohue | Jesse Haines | 76° sunny | 31,888 |
| 4/13/26 | Chicago | W | 7-6 (10) | Jakie May | Sheriff Blake | 60° | 32,304 |
| 4/12/27 | Pittsburgh | L | 1–2 | Ray Kremer | Pete Donohue | 65° clear | 34,758 |
| 4/11/28 | Chicago | W | 5–1 | Dolf Luque | Charlie Root | 54° clear | 30,517 |
| 4/16/29 | St Louis | L | 2–5 | Grover Alexander | Red Lucas | 42° damp, windy | 24,822 |
| 4/15/30 | Pittsburgh | L | 6–7 | Steve Swetonic | Red Lucas | 80° part cloudy | 30,112 |
| 4/14/31 | St Louis | L | 3–7 | Flint Rhem | Larry Benton | 82° sunny | 29,343 |
| 4/12/32 | Chicago | W | 5–4 | Larry Benton | Guy Bush | 44° cloudy | 25,869 |
| 4/12/33 | Pittsburgh | L | 1–4 | Bill Swift | Si Johnson | 64° sunny | 25,305 |
| 4/17/34 | Chicago | L | 0–6 | Lon Warneke | Si Johnson | 67° sunny | 30,247 |
| 4/16/35 | Pittsburgh | L | 6–12 | Waite Hoyt | Tony Freitas | 38° cloudy | 27,400 |
| 4/14/36 | Pittsburgh | L | 6–8 | Waite Hoyt | Paul Derringer | 76° cloudy | 32,343 |
| 4/20/37 | St Louis | L | 0–2 (10) | Dizzy Dean | Peaches Davis | 73° part cloudy | 34,374 |
| 4/19/38 | Chicago | L | 7–8 | Charlie Root | Peaches Davis | 81° sunny | 34,148 |
| 4/17/39 | Pittsburgh | L | 5–7 | Cy Blanton | Bucky Walters | 69° sunny; shower | 30,644 |
| 4/16/40 | Chicago | W | 2–1 | Paul Derringer | Bill Lee | 69° cloudy | 34,342 |
| 4/15/41 | St Louis | L | 3–7 | Lon Warneke | Paul Derringer | 76° part cloudy | 34,940 |

| Date | Opponent | W-L | Score | Winning Pitcher | Losing Pitcher | Temperature | Attendance |
|---|---|---|---|---|---|---|---|
| 4/14/42 | Pittsburgh | L | 2–4 | Max Butcher | Bucky Walters | 72° sunny | 34,104 |
| 4/21/43 | St Louis | W | 1–0 (11) | J. Vander Meer | Mort Cooper | 48° cloudy | 27,709 |
| 4/18/44 | Chicago | L | 0–3 | Hank Wyse | Bucky Walters | 65° part cloudy | 30,154 |
| 4/17/45 | Pittsburgh | W | 7–6 (11) | Hod Lisenbee | Rip Sewell | 61° | 30,069 |
| 4/16/46 | Chicago | L | 3–4 | Ray Prim | Ed Heusser | 51° cloudy | 30,699 |
| 4/15/47 | St Louis | W | 3–1 | Ewell Blackwell | Howie Pollet | 72° sunny | 33,383 |
| 4/19/48 | Pittsburgh | W | 4–1 | Ewell Blackwell | Hal Gregg | 81° sunny | 32,147 |
| 4/19/49 | St Louis | W | 3–1 | Ken Raffensberger | Harry Brecheen | 57° | 32,118 |
| 4/18/50 | Chicago | L | 6–9 | John Schmitz | Ken Raffensberger | 72° sunny | 31,213 |
| 4/16/51 | Pittsburgh | L | 3–4 | Cliff Chambers | Ewell Blackwell | 44° cloudy | 30,441 |
| 4/15/52 | Chicago | L | 5–6 (10) | Joe Hatten | Frank Hiller | 40° cloudy | 28,517 |
| 4/13/53 | Milwaukee | L | 0–2 | Max Surkont | Bud Podbielan | 51° windy | 30,103 |
| 4/13/54 | Milwaukee | W | 9–8 | Joe Nuxhall | Chet Nichols | 81° sunny | 33,185 |
| 4/11/55 | Chicago | L | 5–7 | Sam Jones | Art Fowler | 70° part cloudy | 32,195 |
| 4/17/56 | St. Louis | L | 2–4 | Vinegar Bend Mizell | Joe Nuxhall | 48° cloudy | 32,095 |
| 4/16/57 | St. Louis | L | 4–13 | Herm Wehmeier | John Klippstein | 52° cloudy | 32,554 |
| 4/15/58 | Philadelphia | L | 4–5 | Ray Semproch | Bill Wight | 68° sunny | 33,849 |
| 4/9/59 | Pittsburgh | W | 4–1 | Bob Purkey | Ronnie Kline | 53° cloudy | 32,190 |
| 4/12/60 | Philadelphia | W | 9–4 | Brooks Lawrence | Robin Roberts | 75° sunny | 30,073 |
| 4/11/61 | Chicago | W | 7–1 | Jim O'Toole | Glen Hobbie | 56° cloudy | 28,713 |
| 4/9/62 | Philadelphia | L | 4–12 | Art Mahaffey | Joey Jay | 55° windy | 28,504 |
| 4/8/63 | Pittsburgh | W | 5–2 | Jim O'Toole | Earl Francis | 58° cloudy | 28,896 |
| 4/13/64 | Houston | L | 3–6 | Ken Johnson | Jim Maloney | 66° rain, sun | 28,110 |
| 4/12/65 | Milwaukee | L | 2–4 | Tony Cloninger | Jim O'Toole | 76° sunny, windy | 28,467 |
| 4/22/66 * ‡ | Philadelphia | L | 7–9 | Darold Knowles | Don Nottebart | 70° (night) | 10,266 |
| 4/10/67 | Los Angeles | W | 6–1 | Jim Maloney | Bob Miller | 72° cloudy | 28,422 |
| 4/10/68 ◊ | Chicago | W | 9–4 | Milt Pappas | Joe Niekro | 67° rain, sun | 28,111 |
| 4/7/69 | Los Angeles | L | 2–3 | Don Drysdale | Gary Nolan | 77° sunny | 30,111 |
| 4/6/70 | Montreal | W | 5–1 | Jim Merritt | Joe Sparma | 52° rain | 30,124 |
| 4/5/71 | Atlanta | L | 4–7 | Cecil Upshaw | Wayne Granger | 46° cloudy | 51,702 |
| 4/15/72 ◊ | Los Angeles | L | 1–3 | Don Sutton | Jack Billingham | 68° cloudy | 37,695 |
| 4/5/73 | San Francisco | L | 1–4 | Juan Marichal | Don Gullett | 42° cloudy | 51,179 |
| 4/4/74 | Atlanta | W | 7–6 (11) | Clay Carroll | Buzz Capra | 78° sunny | 52,154 |
| 4/7/75 | Los Angeles | W | 2–1 (14) | Pat Darcy | Charlie Hough | 53° sunny | 52,526 |

| Date | Opponent | W-L | Score | Winning Pitcher | Losing Pitcher | Temperature | Attendance |
|---|---|---|---|---|---|---|---|
| 4/8/76 | Houston | W | 11–5 | Gary Nolan | J.R. Richard | 56° sunny | 52,949 |
| 4/6/77 | San Diego | W | 5–3 | Woodie Fryman | Randy Jones | 38° cloudy | 51,917 |
| 4/6/78 | Houston | W | 11–9 | Pedro Borbon | J.R. Richard | 71° rain | 52,378 |
| 4/4/79 | San Francisco | L | 5–11 | Vida Blue | Tom Seaver | 47° damp | 52,115 |
| 4/9/80 | Atlanta | W | 9–0 | Frank Pastore | Phil Niekro | 56° cloudy | 51,774 |
| 4/8/81 | Philadelphia | W | 3–2 | Tom Hume | Sparky Lyle | 73° part cloudy | 51,716 |
| 4/5/82 | Chicago | L | 2–3 | Doug Bird | Mario Soto | 44° cloudy | 51,864 |
| 4/4/83 | Atlanta | W | 5–4 | Mario Soto | Steve Bedrosian | 57° sunny | 42,892 |
| 4/2/84 | New York | W | 8–1 | Mario Soto | Mike Torrez | 60° part cloudy | 46,000 |
| 4/8/85 | Montreal | W | 4–1 | Mario Soto | Steve Rogers | 39° snow, sun | 52,971 |
| 4/7/86 | Philadelphia | W | 7–4 | Mario Soto | Steve Carlton | 77° sunny | 54,960 |
| 4/6/87 | Montreal | W | 11–5 | Bill Landrum | Floyd Youmans | 47° damp | 55,166 |
| 4/4/88 | St Louis | W | 5–4 (12) | Pat Perry | Bob Forsch | 69° sunny | 55,438 |
| 4/3/89 | Los Angeles | W | 6–4 | Danny Jackson | Tim Belcher | 69° sunny | 55,385 |
| 4/17/90 *** | San Diego | W | 2–1 | Tom Browning | Andy Benes | 57° cloudy | 38,384 |
| 4/8/91 | Houston | W | 6–2 | Tom Browning | Mike Scott | 74° cloudy, rain | 55,502 |
| 4/6/92 | San Diego | L | 3–4 | Jose Melendez | Jose Rijo | 60° damp, windy | 55,356 |
| 4/5/93 | Montreal | W | 2–1 | Jose Rijo | Dennis Martinez | 45° cloudy | 55,456 |
| 4/3/94 ‡ | St Louis | L | 4–6 | Bob Tewksbury | Jose Rijo | 39° (night) | 32,803 |
| 4/26/95 ◊ | Chicago | L | 1–7 | Jim Bullinger | Jose Rijo | 69° | 51,033 |
| 4/2/96 ◊ | Montreal | W | 4–1 | Pete Schourek | Jeff Fassero | 56° cloudy | 53,136 |
| 4/1/97 | Colorado | W | 11–4 | John Smiley | Kevin Ritz | 58° sunny | 54,820 |
| 3/31/98 | San Diego | L | 2–10 | Kevin Brown | Mike Remlinger | 80° cloudy | 54,578 |
| 4/5/99 | San Francisco | L | 8–11 | Allen Embree | John Hudek | 70° part cloudy | 55,112 |
| 4/3/00 | Milwaukee | T | 3–3 (5.1) | Scott Sullivan, Steve Woodard | | 61° cloudy, rain | 55,596 |
| 4/2/01 | Atlanta | L | 4–10 | Marc Valdes | Dennys Reyes | 57° sunny | 41,901 |
| 4/1/02 | Chicago | W | 5–4 | Danny Graves | Jeff Fassero | 56° sunny | 41,913 |
| 3/31/03 ∞ | Pittsburgh | L | 1–10 | Kris Benson | Jimmy Haynes | 53° part cloudy | 42,343 |

The 2003 opener was the Reds 127th opener in organized professional baseball.

Overall record in home openers: 62–64–1  •  Record in extra-inning games: 11–2  •  Record in night openers: 0–2  •  Record in road openers: 4–1

\* Home opener; Reds opened on road due to weather (3 times: 1877, 1885, 1966)

\*\* Home opener; Reds *scheduled* to open on road (1 time: 1888)

\*\*\* Home opener; Reds opened on road after lockout of players scrambled schedule (1 time: 1990)

◊ Home opener but delayed (7 times; by rain in 1884, 1901, 1913; by Martin Luther King funeral, 1968; by labor disputes in 1972, 1995; by death of umpire John McSherry, 1996)

∞ Opening of new ballpark (6 times: 1880, 1884, 1894, 1902, 1912, 2003)

‡ Home night openers (2: 1966, 1994)

# Photographs and Illustration Credits

## Cover

Front, clockwise from top: RWP; RWP; Reds; Jon Boss
Back, clockwise from top: RWP; Enquirer; Reds

## Front Matter and Introduction

p. i, RWP; pii-iii, Jody McMillan; p. vi-viii, RWP; p. 9, Enquirer; p. 10, 11, Jim O'Toole; p. 12, (left) RWP and (right) Jim O'Toole

## Frank Bancroft

p. 13, 15, Jon Boss; p. 16, NBL; p. 18, Jon Boss; p. 19, RWP; p. 21, NBL; p. 23, CHS

## 1 Opening Day Stories

p. 26, 29, 30, John Murdough; p. 32, Bill Werber; p. 33, RWP; p. 35, CHS; p. 36, John Erardi; p. 37, Reds; p. 39, Reds; p, 40; p. 42, Enquirer; p. 43, 45, 46, 47, Reds; p. 48, 49 RWP; p. 50, 51, 53; Reds; p. 55, Enquirer; p. 56, 57, 58; Reds; p. 60, RWP; p. 61, Enquirer; p. 62, 63, 65, Reds; p. 67, RWP; p. 68, Reds; p. 69, RWP; p. 71, Enquirer; p. 72, 75, 77, 78, Reds; p. 79, 80, 81, 82, RWP; p. 83, Reds; p. 84, RWP; p. 85, Reds; p. 87, Enquirer; p. 88, 90, Reds; p. 91, 92, Enquirer; p. 93, 94, 95, 97 99; p. 100, Enquirer; p. 101, 102, 104, 105, Reds; p. 107, 108, 109, Enquirer; p. 111, Reds; p. 112, Enquirer; p. 114, Reds; p. 115, 116, Enquirer; p. 117, 118, 119, 120, 121, (right and left) Reds; 123, Enquirer; p. 125, 127, 128, Reds; p. 129, (left) Enquirer and (right) John Erardi; p. 133, 135, 136, 137, 138, 139, Reds; p. 140, RWP

## 2 History of Opening Day

p. 143, FM; p. 144, 147, 148, (top) RWP; p. 148, (bottom) Richard L. Miller Collection; p, 149, Dennis Bailey; p. 150, RWP; p. 151, DDN; p. 152, (left) Enquirer and (top) RWP; p. 153, DDN; p. 154, Reds; p. 155, RWP

## 3 Findlay Market Parade

p. 156, RWP; p. 158, Reds; p. 159, FM; p. 160, 161, Reds; p. 162, (left) Reds and (top) Miles Wolf; p. 163, (left) DDN and (right) RWP; p. 164, RWP

## 4 Year by Year at Opening Day

p. 166, 167, 168, 169, 170, 171, RWP; p. 173, CHS; p. 174, 176, 177, 178, 179, 181, 182, 183, 184, 185, 186, 187, 188, 189, 190, 191, RWP; 192, CHS; 194, 195, 196, 197, 198, RWP; p. 199, Enquirer; p. 200, RWP; p. 201, 203, Richard L. Miller Collection; p. 205, 206, 207, 208, 209, 210, 211, 212, 213, 214, 215, 216, 217, RWP; p. 218, Enquirer; p. 219, 220, 221, RWP; p. 222, Enquirer; p. 223, 224, 225, 226, 227, 228, 229, 230, 231, 232, 233, RWP; p. 234, Reds; p. 235, 236, 237, 238, 239, 240, 241, 242, 243, 244, 245, RWP; p. 246, FM; p. 247, 248, 249, 250, 251, 252, 253, 254, 255, 256, 257, 258, 259, 260, 261, 262, 263, 264, 265, 266, 267, 268, 269, 270, RWP; p. 271, Enquirer; p. 272, DDN; p. 273, RWP; p. 274, Reds; p. 275, RWP; p. 276, 277, Reds; p. 278, Enquirer; p. 279, Post; p. 280, Enquirer; p. 281, 282, 283, 284, Reds; p. 285, Enquirer; p. 286, 287, 288, 289, 290, 291, 292, Reds; p. 293, RWP

## Opening Day Scrapbook

p. 295, CHS; p. 296, RWP; p. 297, Jon Boss; p. 298, (left) Steve Wolter and (right) Dennis Bailey; p. 299, RWP; p. 300, FM; p. 301, (left and right) RWP; p. 302, (top) TSN and (bottom) RWP; p. 303, (top) Enquirer and (bottom) Richard L. Miller Collection; p. 304, (left) RWP and (right) Enquirer; p. 266, (left) RWP and (right) DDN; p. 306, 307, (left) Reds; p. 307, (right) RWP; p. 308, (left) Reds and (right) RWP; p. 309, RWP; p. 310, (top) Reds, (center) RWP, and (right), Reds; p. 311, (top left) RWP, (top right) Reds, and (bottom) Enquirer; p. 312, RWP

(Key: RWP: Road West Publishing; Enquirer: *The Cincinnati Enquirer*; Post: *The Cincinnati Post*; Reds: The Cincinnati Reds; DDN: *Dayton Daily News* Archives; CHS: Cincinnati Historical Society; NBL: National Baseball Library; TSN: *The Sporting News*; FM: Findlay Market)

# Sources and Acknowledgments

Thanks to our many friends, baseball and otherwise, for their encouragement over the past two years. Thanks to John P. Erardi, who is the inspiration for the oral histories, given his vivid memories of attending minor league games in Syracuse in the 1930s and late 1940s and watching such luminaries as Frank McCormick, Johnny Vander Meer, Hank Sauer, Jackie Robinson and Specs Toporcer, who was later immortalized in *Glory of Their Times*. Thanks to the Cincinnati Reds for their cooperation, especially Dan Stupp, Julie Hammel and Jared Rollins of the Creative Services Department.

We also extend a grateful thanks to the fans, players, club executives and others who graciously shared their stories of Opening Day; they are listed in the Table of Contents. We thank them for their significant contributions to our understanding and enjoyment of Opening Day.

Many people provided assistance in the preparation of the Frank Bancroft chapter. Special thanks to: Darryl Brock, whose guidance was invaluable; four of Banny's grandsons—Jon Bancroft Boss, for his early direction, Michael Bancroft, who provided Banny's Civil War letters and other papers, and Carter Bancroft and John Bancroft who patiently answered many questions; Terry Ingano of the Clinton (Massachusetts) Historical Society; Bill Ballou at the *Worcester Telegram and Gazette*; Karen Hart of the *Lancaster Times*; members of the Society for American Baseball Research (SABR): Dick Miller, John Richmond Husman, Dick Clark, Sammy Miller, Steve Schneider, Paul Herbert, Stuart Hodesh; Adjunct Associate Professor Edy Carro, Department of Romance Languages, University of Cincinnati, and Megan Sheehan, for their Spanish translations; Bijan Bayne and Jake Hodesh, for their knowledge of Cuban baseball and their willingness to share it; Andy Balterman, reference librarian, Public Library of Cincinnnati and Hamilton County; John Eckberg, always a great sounding board for ideas; Greg Erardi, Frank Erardi and Matt DeNinno, whose sensibilities about the great game I continue to draw upon; and to Joanne DeNinno, Nancy O'Connor and Ms. Sheehan for proofreading the manuscript.

And, as always, a warm and personal thanks to our families, especially Barb and Sallie, for their forbearance of yet another baseball project.

## General Sources

Allen, Lee. **The Cincinnati Reds**, 1948
*Cincinnati Commercial Gazette*
*Cincinnati Commercial Tribune*
*Cincinnati Enquirer*
*Cincinnati Post*
*Cincinnati Times-Star*
Cincinnati Reds Media Guides, 1967-2001
Cincinnati Reds Yearbooks, 1947-2003
Dickson, Paul. **The Dickson Baseball Dictionary**, 1989
James, Bill, John Dewan, Neil Munro and Don Zminda. **Stats All-Time Baseball Sourcebook**, 1998
Kerr, Don. **Opening Day**, 1999
Koppett, Leonard. **Koppett's Concise History of Major League Baseball**, 1998
Reach Baseball Guides, 1883–1900
Rhodes, Greg and John Erardi. **Crosley Field**, 1995
Spaulding Baseball Guides, 1876-2000
*The Sporting News*. **The Sporting News Complete Baseball Record Book**, 2000
Thorn, John, Pete Palmer and Michael Gershman. **Total Baseball** (5th and 7th Editions), 1997; 2001
Waggoner, Glen, Kathleen Moloney and Hugh Howard. **Baseball by the Rules**, 1987

## Frank Bancroft (Chapter 1) Sources

### For Banny's "Voice"

Brock, Darryl. **Havana Heat**, 2000.
Fleming, G.H. **The Unforgettable Season: The Most Exciting and Calamitous Pennant Race of All Time–1908**, 1981.
Flexner, Stuart Berg. **I Hear America Talking**, 1976.
Flexner, Stuart Berg. **Listening to America: An Illustrated History of Words & Phrases from Our Lively and Splendid Past**, 1982
Ritter, Lawrence. **The Glory of Their Times: The Story of the Early Days of Baseball Told By the Men Who Played It**, 1985.
Roth, Philip, **The Great American Novel**, 1973.
Stein, Harry. **Hoopla**, 1983.

### For Banny's Story

Books

Alexander, Charles C. **John McGraw**, 1988.
Alexander, Charles C. **Our Game: An American Baseball History**, 1991.
Baldwin, Neil. **Edison: Inventing the Century**, 1995.
Bourgeois, Anna S. **Blueswomen: Profiles of 37 Early Performers, With an Anthology of Lyrics, 1920-45**, 1996.
Charters, Samuel Barclay IV. **Jazz: New Orleans, 1885-1963, An Index to the Negro Musicians of New Orleans**, 1963.
The Cincinnati Historical Society. **The WPA Guide to Cincinnati**, 1987.
Crichton, Judy. **America 1900: The Turning Point**, 1998.
Coombs, Samm and Bob West. **Base Ball: America's National Game, 1839-1915**, 1991.
Csida, Joseph and June Bundy Csida. **American Entertainment: A Unique History of Popular Show Business**, 1978.
Curtis, Susan. **Dancing to a Black Man's Tune: A Life of Scott Joplin**, 1994.
Dabney, Wendell P. **Cincinnati's Colored Citizens**, 1926.
DeValeria, Dennis and Jeanne Burke DeValeria. **Honus Wagner**, 1996.
Eicher, David J. **The Longest Night: A Military History of the Civil War**, 2001.
Evans, Harold. **The American Century**, 1998.

Holway, John. **The Complete Book of Baseball's Negro Leagues: The Other Half of Baseball History**, 2001.

Hurley, Daniel. Cincinnati, **The Queen City**, 1982.

James, Bill. **The New Bill James Historical Baseball Abstract**, 2001.

Koehler, Lyle. **Cincinnati's Black Peoples: A Chronology and Bibliography, 1787-1982**, 1986.

Light, Jonathan Frazier. **The Cultural Encyclopedia of Baseball**, 1997.

Lomax, Michael E. **Black Baseball Entrepeneurs, 1860-1901: Operating by Any Means Necessary**, 2003.

**Nineteenth Century Stars** ("Frank Bancroft" by John Husman), by the Society for American Baseball Research, SABR, 1989.

Rhodes, Greg and John Snyder. **Redleg Journal**, 2000.

Roe, George Mortimer (ed.) **Cincinnati: The Queen City of the West**, 1895.

Rosenberg, Howard. **Cap Anson I: When Captaining a Team Meant Something: Leadership in Baseball's Early Years,** 2003.

Rucker, Mark and Peter C. Bjarkman. **Smoke: The Romance and Lore of Cuban Baseball**, 1999.

Seib, Philip. **The Player: Christy Mathewson, Baseball and The American Century**, 2003.

Sowell, Mike. **The Pitch That Killed: Carl Mays, Ray Chapman and the Pennant Race of 1920**, 1989.

Stanyan, John M. **History of the Eighth Regiment of New Hampshire Volunteers, Including Its Service As Second N.H. Cavalry**, 1998 (1892).

Trudeau, Noah Andre. **Like Men of War: Black Troops in the Civil War, 1862-65**, 1998.

Werber, Bill and Paul Rogers, III. **Memories of a Ballplayer**, 2001.

Wheeler, Lonnie and John Baskin. **The Cincinnati Game**, 1988.

## Articles

"Bannie Put In 50 Years In Baseball," *New York American*, January, 20, 1921.

"Banny, Dean of Base Ball World, is Called Out by Great Umpire," *Cincinnati Times-Star*, March 31, 1921.

"Banny's Supplication," by Groundkeeper J. Schwab, *Cincinnati Enquirer*, April 15, 1901.

"Banny's Will Leaves $25,000 To His Widow," *Cincinnati Commercial Gazette*, April 21, 1921.

"Baseball All Around the World," by Arthur Shafer, *Emslie's Weekly*, 1914.

"Baseball Notes," column by Jack Ryder, *Cincinnati Enquirer*, April 3, 1921.

"Base Ball Once More," *Worcester (Massachusetts) Daily Spy*, Dec. 30, 1879.

"Can't Get World Series Tickets; Think How She Feels," by Paul Lugananni, *Cincinnati Enquirer*, Oct. 1, 1961.

"Frank Bancroft, Baseball Dean, Dies; Aged 75, of Pneumonia," *Cincinnati Commercial Tribune*, March 31, 1921.

"Frank Bancroft, 72, Still Helping Game," by Tom Powers, *Detroit News*, 1918. (Letter of response, May 1, 1918, from F.C. Bancroft to Tom Powers.)

"Frank C. Bancroft," *Baseball Magazine*, May, 1909.

"Frank C. Bancroft," editorial, *New Bedford (Massachusetts) Evening Standard*, March 31, 1921.

"Frank C. Bancroft Dies After Long Illness; With Reds Years as Business Manager; Known to Ball Fans Throughout Country," *Cincinnati Enquirer*, March 31, 1921.

"Giants Among Men," by Frank Deford, *Sports Illustrated*, Aug. 25, 2003.

"Giants Will Honor Frank Bancroft at Polo Grounds Wednesday," by Sam Crane, publication unknown, date unknown.

"I Like Animal Acts," *Baseball Magazine*, February 14, 1914.

"Location of Old Bancroft House Will Never Be Forgotten," by Earle D. Wilson, *New Bedford (Massachusetts) Sunday Times*, July 15, 1956.

"Loyal to Reds Club and Fans; Twenty-Two Years Service; Most Famous and Popular of Business Managers," by Jack Ryder, *Cincinnati Enquirer*, 1914.

"Mighty Bancroft Struck Nothing But Gold Mines," by Bill Ballou, *The Sunday Telegram*, Oct. 13, 1985.

The New England Historical and Genealogical Register (*Thomas Bancroft and Some of His Descendants*, p. 286-87), published by the N.E. H. G. Society, Boston, Mass., July 1942.

Pension Records, Department of the Interior, Bureau of Pensions, Dec. 14, 1894, to May 20, 1921.

"Reminiscences of the Old-Timers: Two Noble Sleepers," by Fred Pfeffer, *Baseball Magazine*, August 18, 1918.

Civil War Letters of Frank Bancroft
(All letters to his father Lorey Bancroft, unless otherwise noted.)

Dec. 1, 1862, Thibadouxville, Louisiana; Nov. 4, 1863, Vermillionville, Louisiana; Nov. 5, 1863, no site given; Nov. 28, 1863, New Iberia, Louisiana; April 5, 1864, to his step-mother, Camp Pine Woods, Louisiana; July 2, 1864, Carrollton, Louisiana; Sept. 16, 1864, Camp Parapet, Louisiana; April 2, 1865, Natchez, Mississippi; April 9, 1865, Natchez, Mississippi

Other Letters

Frank C. Bancroft to Town Clerk, Lancaster, Mass., Jan. 21, 1913.

Newspapers, General

*Cincinnati Enquirer, Cincinnati Commercial Gazette, Cincinnati Commercial Tribune, Cincinnati Times-Star, Cincinnati Post*, 1892-1921, *Mobile (Alabama) Register*, March 1895.